Avinguda

17480 Roses

Rick Steves'
Marina Hotel

SPAIN

$594 281 307 $132.29

2 nights

AP 7 (or) E15 N — to C260 East

2010

BARCELONA

1. To Beach & Fòrum
2. Block of Discord
3. La Boqueria Market
4. To Casa Milà, Parc Güell & Tibidabo Amusement Park
5. Catalan Concert Hall
6. Cathedral of Barcelona
7. Chocolate Museum
8. Church of Santa Maria del Mar
9. Citadel Park
10. City History Museum
11. Columbus Monument
12. Frederic Marès Museum
13. *Golondrinas* (Cruises)
14. Liceu Opera House
15. Maritime Museum
16. To Montjuïc Sights
17. Palau Güell
18. Picasso Museum
19. Plaça de Sant Jaume
20. Plaça del Rei
21. Roman Temple
22. To Sagrada Família
23. Shoe Museum

Walks

24. Barri Gòtic Walk Start Point
25. Ramblas Ramble Start Point
26. A Short, Sweet Walk Start Point

Train Stations

27. França Station
28. To Sants Station

To Nord
Bus Station

PASSEIG DE SANT JOAN
C. D'ALÍ BEÍ
BAILÉN
C. DE VILANOVA
AV. DE ROGER DE FLOR
C. DELS ALMOGAVERS
C. DE
C. DE BUENAVENTURA MUÑOZ
NÁPLES

Arc de
Triomf Ⓜ

Arc de
Triomf

PASSEIG DE LLUÍS COMPANYS

CARRER DEL COMERÇ

PASSEIG DE PUJADES

de M. Núñez

Alt.

Pere Mitja

C. de la Sèquia

C. de M. Rec Comta
Sant Pere més Baix

Sant Pere més Alt

C. de Jaume Giralt

Carrer del Fonollar

F. CAMBÓ

C. de Colomines

Mercat
Santa
Caterina

Carrer dels Caders

LA RIBERA

C. d'en Tantarantana

C. de la Fusina

7

Museu de la
Xocolata

Museu de
Zoologia

PASSEIG DE PICASSO

Museu de
Geologia

9

PARC
DE LA
CIUTADELLA

Antica Mercat
del Born

C. de la Ribera

ZOO

CARRER DE LA PRINCESA

18

Museu
Picasso

C. de Montcada

C. de Banys Vells

C. de l'Argenteria

Carrer del Rec

Videria

27

Estacio
de França

Jaume I Ⓜ

20

10

Pl. Ángel

C. del Sots-tinent Navarro

Manresa

C. la Nau

8

Santa Maria
del Mar

Epass.

CARRER DEL DOCTOR AIGUADER

City
Hall

Carrer de Lledó

Carrer de la Ciutat

C. d'Aráulf

C. d'En Gignás

C. d'Agullers

Canvis Vells

Barceloneta

RONDA DEL LITORAL

CARRER DEL DOCTOR AIGUADER

ℹ

GÒTIC

Carrer D'Avinyo

C. d'en Carabassa

Carrer dels Codols

La Llotja

Post

C. de la Fusteria

Plaça
d'Antoni
Lopez

Barceloneta Ⓜ

CARRER DE BALBOA

CARRER DE GINEBRA

BARCELONETA

Carrer de la Maquinista

Marquet

Plata

Moll de Dipòsit

Palau
de Mar

C. de Ballard

Mercat

C. d'Andrea Dória

Carrer
La Mercé

La Mercé

Carrer Ample

C. d.

Sant Francesc

Plaça Duc
Medinaceli

Barcelona's
Head
Sculpture

MARINA

Moll de la Barceloneta

PASSEIG JOAN DE BORBÓ

Carrer de St. Charles

C. D. L'ALMIRALL CERVERA

Wax
useum

RONDA DEL LITORAL EXPRESSWAY

MOL DE BOSCH I ALSINA

PASSEIG DE COLOM

IMAX

PORT
VELL

C. del Mar

C. del Almirall Aixada

onument
a Colóm

ℹ

Old Customs
Building

"Rambla
de Mar"
Footbridge

Aquarium

Maremagnum

C. del Judici

13

Golondrinas

Moll dels Pescadors

To
Cable Car
Station

BEACH

To
Cruise Ship Terminal

To Clothing Museum

To A6 Freeway, El Escorial & Segovia

MAL

Templo de Debod

PARQUE DE LA MONTAÑA

Museo Carralbo

CALLE DE FERRAZ

Plaza de España

Calle de Manzana

Plaza de España

Calle de la Luna

CALLE DE SAN BERNARDO

Calle

de

Calle

Roqu

Calle de Irún

Paseo del Rey

Calle Cadarso

Calle Arriaza

Calle del Río

Calle de Leganitos

Calle del Fomento

Calle Estrella

GRAN

Libreros

Calle Silva San

Tudescos

Estación Príncipe Pío

C. Ilustración

SAN VICENTE

Palacio del Senado

Plaza Marina Española

SATE Police Station

Calle Torija

Plaza de Santo Domingo

Jacometrezo

Plaza del Callao

VÍA

CUESTA DE

JARDINES DE SABATINI

La Encarnación

S. Quintin

Calle de la Bola

Calle Arrieta

Calle Sto. Domingo

Santo Domingo

Callao

CAMPO DEL MORO

Palacio Real

CALLE DE BAILÉN

Plaza de Oriente

FELIPE V

Teatro Real

CARLOS II

Plaza Isabel II

Ópera

C. d. Peral

Flora

Pza. S. Martín

Plaza S. Martín

3

Calle Hileras

CALLE DE ARENAL

Calle C

4

Museo de Carruajes Reales

11

Plaza de la Amería

Requena

Plaza Ramales

Calle de los Señores

Escalinata

Independencia

Bordadores

Plaza Herradores

Mesonero

C. de

Precia

To Chapel of S. Antonio de la Florida (Goya's Tomb)

San Nicolás

Calle de Lozán

CALLE DE MAYOR

Cristóbal

Postas

Pontejos

Calle

Catedral de la Almudena

Plaza de la Villa

San Miguel Market

Plaza Mayor

Zaragoza

Esparos

Cal

i

7

PASEO CIUDAD DE PLASENCIA

CUESTA DE LA VEGA

Calle Sacramento

Concepción Jerónima

CALLE

DE

SEGOVIA

Cost. de S. Andrés

Calle del Nuncio

CALLE COLEGIADA

Romanones

Calle B. Gálinde

C. Morería

Iglesia de San Isidro

Tirso de Molina

CALLE DUQUE DE ALP

Calle Redondilla

Calle Almendro

Calle Cava Baja

Calle Cava Alta

La Latina

Calle Juanelo

Gra. S. Francisco

Calle Don Pedro

Plaza de San Francisco

Plaza de Cascorro

Encomienda

Dos Hermanas

Abades

Calle Ángel

C. Cebada

Calle Sta Ana

C. Frey

Calle Os

GRAN VÍA DE SAN FRANCISCO

Calle d. Calatrava

C. Humilladero

DE

El Rastro Flea Market

Ce. González

Calle de Rodas

Calle la Paloma

TOLEDO

Carnero

Carlos Arnices

RIBERA

DE

Martinez

Puerta de Toledo

Plaza Campillo Mundo Nuevo

Calle Mira el Sol

Calle del Casino

Glorieta de Puerta de Toledo

LOS PONTONES

PAS. DE LOS OLMOS

CALLE DE TOLEDO

RONDA

DE

CURTIDORES

C. del Gasometro

C. B. M. Lozano

To Toledo

MADRID

1 To Bullring and Airport

2 Centro de Arte Reina Sofía (*Guernica*)

3 Descalzas Royal Monastery

4 El Corte Inglés Dep't Store

5 National Archaeological Museum

6 Naval Museum

7 Plaza Mayor

8 Prado Museum

9 Retiro Park

10 Royal Botanical Garden

11 Royal Palace

12 Start of Madrid Pub Crawl

13 Start of "Welcome to Madrid" Walk

14 To Sorolla Museum, Bernabéu Stadium, Puerta de Europa & Chamartin Station

15 Thyssen-Bornemisza Museum

0		400 m
0		.25 mi

LEGEND

- Pedestrian-Friendly Area
- Popular Shopping Area
- Most direct route from Plaza Nueva to San Nicolás Viewpoint
- Landmark or Point of Interest
- *i* Tourist Information Offices
- Viewpoint
- **P** Parking

| 0 | | 200 m |
| 0 | | 200 yds |

Placeta Fatima

Calle Pino

Calle San Luis Vereda Pinchos

Calle

Pagés

PANADEROS

Plaza del Salvador

Abad

CUESTA DEL CHAPIZ

Chorrohumo Statue

San Nicolás

Great Mosque

San Agustín

CAMINO DEL SACROMONTE

SACROMONTE

Tomasas

de Trillo

Juan

de los Reyes

Santísimo

Candil

Victoria

Carnero

Zafra

DEL DARRO

PASEO DE LOS TRISTES

River

Darro

San Pedro

Bañuelo

Wall

Plaza Aljibes

Palacios Nazaries

PARTAL GARDENS

Generalife Palace

GENERALIFE GARDENS

Alcazaba

Charles V's Palace

ALHAMBRA

Cuesta de los Chinos

Theater

Justice Gate

ONE WAY →

Plaza de la Justicia

Calle

Parador de Granada San Francisco

Real

Cjón. Niño del Royo

del Aire

Peña Partida

PASEO CENTRAL

Plaza de Carros

i

Tickets

P

Entrance

GRANADA

1. Alhambra Entrance
2. Arab Baths
3. To Carthusian Monastery
4. Cathedral Entrance
5. To Center for the Interpretation of Sacromonte
6. Chorrohumo Statue
7. Corral del Carbón (Caravanserai)
8. Great Mosque
9. Moorish Baths
10. Palacios Nazaries Entrance
11. Paseo de los Tristes
12. Plaza de Bib-Rambla
13. Plaza Isabel La Católica
14. Plaza Larga
15. Plaza Nueva
16. Royal Chapel Entrance
17. San Nicolás Viewpoint

LARAÑA

To 3

Jaúregui

Azafrán

LA CALZADA

Museo Palacio de la Condesa de Lebrija

D'Cármen

Alhóndiga

CARRIÓN MEJÍA

Santiago

C. RECARDO

Amador de los Ríos

To Train Station & Airport

Cuna

Boteros

Alfalfa

Casa de Pilatos

Imperial

San Salvador

Huelva

D. PEDRO

SAN ESTEBAN

C. LUIS MONTOTO

S. Isidro

7

Francos

Pajaritos

VIRGENES

Conde

de

Ibarra

A. Quintero

A. DE MOLINA

Aire

PELAYO

I. Contreras

CAVESTANY

EMANES

G. El

Bueno

Sta. Cruz

Cruces

SAN

JOSÉ

Sta. Maria La Blanca

AV. JUAN ANTONIO

DEMETRIO DE LOS RÍOS

Angeles

Gago

Mateos

Giralda

Catedral

XIMINEZ DE ENCISO

Gral. Ríos

5 Plaza del Triunfo

BARRIO SANTA CRUZ

13 Plaza de la Santa Cruz

2 Archivo de Indias

Patio de Banderas

Alcázar

Agua

de Ribera

MENÉNDEZ

SAN BERNARDO

M. Marara

1

JARDINES DE MURILLO

Catalina

de

San Bernardo

Puerta de Jerez

ALCÁZAR GARDENS

Paseo

AV.

Av. Málaga

C. SAN FERNANDO

Plaza D. Juan de Austria

El Prado Bus Station

15

DE ROMA

14 **Universidad**

AV. DE CARLOS V

Palacio de S. Telmo

Palos de la Frontera

AV. DEL CID

Portugal Pavilion

PASEO DE LAS DELICIAS

La Rabida

Peró

AV. DE MARÍA LUISA

AV. DE PORTUGAL

AV. DE LA BORBOLLA

MARÍA LUISA PARK

Av. Isabel la Católica

Plaza de España

12

To Jerez & Arcos

AV. DE MARÍA LUISA

Avda. Roguez Caso

Av. Las Cruizadas

CONTENTS

Spain

España

Like a grandpa bouncing a baby on his knee, Spain is a mix of old and new, modern and traditional. For the tourist, Spain means bullfights, massive cathedrals, world-class art, Muslim palaces, vibrant folk life, whitewashed villages, and bright sunshine. Yes, you'll find those things...but the country's special charm lies in its people and their unique lifestyle. Spain has a richness of history, of culture, and of people that has little to do with GDP. From the stirring *sardana* dance in Barcelona to the sizzling rat-a-tat-tat of flamenco in Sevilla, this country creates its own beat amid the heat.

Spain's diverse landscape and diverse history (a blend of Roman, Muslim, and Christian) have forged a country with a wide variety of regions, languages, and customs. If you fly over Spain, you'll see that much of the country's center is a parched, red-orange desert. But Spain's topography resembles a giant upside-down bowl, with the high, flat, dry central plateau and a coastal lip. The north is mountainous and rainy; the south is hilly and hot. Ringing it all is 2,000 miles of coastline.

Spain's geography makes it less a centralized nation than a collection of distinct regions. In the central plain sits the urban

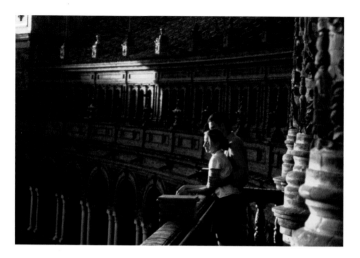

island of Madrid, a region unto itself. Just south is Toledo, a medieval showpiece and melting-pot city with Christian, Muslim, and Jewish roots. Farther south is Andalucía, a region formerly ruled by Muslims, now home to sleepy, sun-baked *pueblos blancos* (whitewashed hill towns). Spain's south coast, the Costa del Sol, is a palm tree jungle of beach resorts, casinos, time-share condos, discos, and sunburned Brits on holiday. Along the Mediterranean coast (to the east), Spain has an almost Italian vibe, and Barcelona and Catalunya keep one eye cocked toward trends sailing in from the rest of Europe. Tourism is huge here. With 40 million inhabitants, Spain entertains 50 million visitors annually.

To the north is the Basque Country, which combines spar-kling beaches, cutting-edge architecture, and proudly feisty locals. From here, gregarious modern-day pilgrims follow the Camino de Santiago westward across the parched north of Spain into mellow and lush Galicia, where moss-covered churches and tree-strewn rolling hillsides beckon. Beyond its contiguous lands, Spain clings to the last of its far-flung hold-ings: a few Mediterranean islands (including Menorca, Mal-lorca, and Ibiza), Ceuta in Morocco, and the distant Canary Islands.

"Castilian"—what we call "Spanish"—is spoken throughout the country. But Catalans (around Barcelona) speak their own Romance language, Catalan. The Galicians speak Galego. And in the far north, the Basques keep alive the ancient tongue of Euskara. A fringe group of separatist Basques (with their notorious and unpopular terrorist wing, ETA) has lobbied hard and sometimes violently for self-rule. But every region in Spain has its own dialect, customs, and (often half-hearted) separatist movement. Each region also hosts local festivals, whether parading Virgin Mary statues through the streets, running in front of a pack of furious bulls, or pelting each other with tomatoes. People think of themselves first and foremost as Basques, Catalans, Andalusians, Galicians, Leonese, and so on...and only second as Spaniards.

Spain is in Europe, but not *of* Europe—it has a unique identity and history, thanks largely to the Pyrenees Moun-

tains that physically isolate it from the rest of the Continent. For more than 700 years (711–1492), Spain's dominant culture was Muslim, not Christian. And after a brief Golden Age financed by New World gold (1500–1600), Spain retreated into three centuries of isolation (1600–1900). Spain's seclusion contributed to the creation of unusual customs—bullfights, flamenco dancing, and a national obsession with ham. Even as other countries opened up to each other in the 20th century, the fascist dictator Francisco Franco virtually sealed off Spain from the rest of Europe's democracies. But since Franco's death in 1975, Spaniards have almost swung to the opposite extreme, becoming wide open to new trends and technologies. (For more on Spanish history, see the Spain: Past & Present chapter.)

Spain Almanac

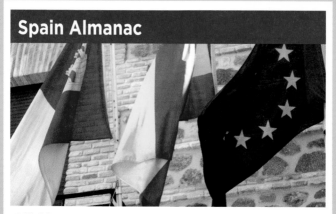

Official Name: It's officially the Reino de España (Kingdom of Spain), but locals just call it España.

Population: 40.5 million. Most speak the official national language of Castilian, but 17 percent speak Catalan, 7 percent Galego, and 2 percent Euskara (the Basque language). The country is 94 percent Roman Catholic.

Latitude and Longitude: 40°N and 4°W (similar latitude to New York City).

Area: 195,000 square miles (15 percent bigger than California). This includes the Canary and Balearic Islands, and small enclaves in Morocco. Spain's long-standing claim to Gibraltar remains a nagging dispute with Britain.

Geography: The interior of Spain is a high, flat plateau (the Meseta Central), with hot, dry summers and harsh winters. Surrounding the plateau are mountains (including the Pyrenees in the north) and 2,000 miles of coastline.

***Agua Agua* Everywhere:** A leader in hydropower and irrigation, Spain, for its size, has more man-made lakes from dams (about 1,400) than any other country. Still, the average Spaniard uses one-third less energy than the average American. Spain's 1,800 rivers are mostly small, less than 50 miles long. The 600-mile Tajo River (a.k.a. Tagus in English, or Tejo in Portuguese) runs westward from Toledo through Portugal to the Atlantic. The Guadalquivir irrigates Andalucía and makes Sevilla an oceangoing port city.

Biggest Cities: Madrid (3.2 million; at more than 2,000 feet in altitude, it's Europe's highest capital), Barcelona (1.6 million),

Valencia (810,000), and Sevilla (700,000). Spaniards are urban dwellers—only one in five lives outside a metropolitan area.

Economy: The Gross Domestic Product is $1.4 trillion (about the same as the state of New York). The GDP per capita is $33,700 (New York's is $46,600). Major moneymakers include tourism, clothes, shoes, olives, wine, oranges, machine parts, and ships. Recently it had a 17 percent unemployment rate—more than four million Spaniards were out of work.

Government: Guided symbolically by King Juan Carlos I, Spain is a parliamentary monarchy. José Luis Rodríguez Zapatero is the left-of-center prime minister. Some of the 600-plus legislators (in two houses) are elected directly, some by regional bodies or political parties. The country is divided into 19 autonomous regions (e.g., Andalucía, Catalunya, Castile–La Mancha, and Madrid).

Flag: Spain's flag has three horizontal bands of red, yellow, and red. To the left of center is the coat of arms—a shield with a crown, framed by the Pillars of Hercules that symbolically flank the Straits of Gibraltar.

Soccer: The two perennial powerhouses in *la Liga* (the League) are Real Madrid and FC Barcelona.

The Average José: The average Spaniard is 40 years old, will live to age 79, and resides in a home with one car and one TV. Almost half of Spaniards use the Internet, and 1 in 10 owns a cat. The average Spaniard has one mobile phone, 1.3 kids, and sleeps 40 minutes less every night than the typical European.

Spaniards are proud and stoic. They can be hard to get to know—but once you've made that connection, you've got a

friend for life. The Spanish people have long had a reputation as thrifty, straightforward, and unpretentious. Traditionally, their lives revolved around the Catholic Church and the family. Young adults tended to live at home until they got married—even into their late twenties. Spaniards prided themselves on their non-materialistic values, owning just one car and one TV, and living in small urban apartments instead of giant suburban houses. The notorious "machismo" culture of domineering men ruled.

But Spain's old ways have changed very quickly in the three and a half decades since Franco. While the vast majority of Spaniards are still nominally Catholic, the country is at the forefront of liberal reforms in abortion and gay marriage. Spain's extreme religiosity has been replaced by an extreme secularism. The old hierarchy of aristocrats, peasants, priests, and old ladies in black has become democratic and hang-loose. The allure of consumerism and status symbols has enticed many Spanish people to save (or borrow) for high-fashion clothes, second cars, and summer chalets, though the economic downturn has pushed materialistic dreams farther out of reach. Still, throughout its recent economic boom and bust, Spain has remained affordable for visitors.

Even as the country plunges into the 21st century, some things never change. Daily lives focus on friends and family, as they always have. Many people (especially in rural areas) still follow the siesta schedule, which emphasizes a big midday meal with the family. Spaniards tend to have a small, quick breakfast, grab a late-morning sandwich to tide them over, then gather with friends and family for the siesta. From around 1:00 to

4:00 p.m., many businesses close as people go home for lunch, to socialize, and maybe to grab a quick nap. The siesta is not so much a time to sleep as it is the opportunity for everyone to shut down their harried public life, and enjoy good food and the comfort of loved ones.

In the cool of the evening, Spain comes back to life. Whole families pour out of their apartments to stroll through the streets and greet their neighbors—a custom called the paseo. Even the biggest city feels like a rural village. People stop into bars for a drink or to watch a big soccer match on TV. They might order a bite to eat, enjoying appetizers called tapas. Around 10:00 p.m. in the heat of summer, it's finally time for a light dinner. Afterwards, even families with young children might continue their paseo or attend a concert. Spaniards are notorious night owls. Many clubs and restaurants don't even open until after midnight. Dance clubs routinely stay open until the sun rises, and young people stumble out bleary-eyed and head for work. The antidote for late nights? The next day's siesta.

Spanish food is hearty and unrefined. Remember that Spain is not Mexico—you'll find no tacos, Tabasco, or tequila. (Even things that sound Mexican can be very different—for example, a *tortilla* is an omelet.) Major meals feature meat (such as roast suckling pig) or seafood. Popular regional foods are gazpacho (cold tomato soup) and paella (seafood and meat cooked with saffron-flavored rice). Spaniards snack between meals on tapas. Most bars offer a variety of these appetizers served hot or cold. A few small plates of olives, chorizo (sausage), grilled shrimp, Russian salad, or deep-fried nuggets can add up to a multi-course meal.

The most treasured delicacy in Spain is *jamón*—cured ham that is sliced thin and served cold. Bars proudly hang pigs' legs on their walls as part of the decor. Like connoisseurs of fine wine, Spaniards debate the merits of different breeds of pigs, what part of the pig they're eating, what the pig has eaten, and the quality of curing.

Drinking is part of the Spanish meal, and part of the social ritual. Spain produces large quantities of wine, especially their spicy red Rioja, made from the *tempranillo* grape. (For more on Spanish drinks, see page 28.)

For a country its size, Spain has produced an astonishing number of talented artists with distinctive styles—from El Greco's mystical religiosity to the sober realism of Diego

Velázquez. (Madrid's Prado Museum is a veritable showcase of European Renaissance art, bought with the spoils from the New World.) Francisco Goya painted the Golden Age in decline. In the 20th century, Pablo Picasso shattered the art world, then pasted it back together by inventing Cubism. Later, he painted *Guernica,* an epic snapshot of Spain's horrific Civil War. It's one of the most powerful anti-war paintings ever created (now displayed in Madrid). Salvador Dalí created a surreal juxtaposition of old and new, while his fellow Catalan Joan Miró picked up the Surrealist baton and ran with it. Spain carries on this rich tradition today, with a thriving contemporary arts scene.

In music, Spain continues its long tradition of great guitarists—classical, flamenco, and Gipsy Kings–style "new flamenco." In dance, you'll find the fiery flamenco (from Andalucía) and the stately do-si-do of the *sardana* (from Catalunya). Contemporary film includes works by the director Pedro Almodóvar, who explores changing family and social roles as Spain moves from its conservative past to its wide-open future. And there's one contemporary Spaniard whose works will be known and appreciated for generations to come: Santiago Calatrava, an architect who designs buildings and bridges for the 21st century.

While you can see some European countries by just passing through, Spain is a destination. Learn its history and accept it on its own terms. Gain (or just fake) an appreciation for cured ham, dry sherry, and bull's-tail soup, and the Spaniards will love you for it. If you go, go all the way. Immerse yourself in Spain.

INTRODUCTION

This book will help you make the most of your trip. It breaks Spain into its top destinations—offering a balanced, comfortable mix of exciting cities and cozy towns, topped off with an exotic dollop of Morocco. It covers the predictable biggies and stirs in a healthy dose of "Back Door" intimacy. Along with seeing a bull-fight, the Prado, and flamenco, you'll greet pilgrims at Santiago de Compostela, visit a bull bar in Madrid, and buy cookies from clois-tered nuns in a sun-parched Andalusian town. I've been selective, including only the most exciting sights and experiences. Rather than listing Spain's countless whitewashed Andalusian hill towns, I recommend the top stops: Arcos de la Frontera and Ronda.

You'll get all the specifics and opinions necessary to wring the maximum value out of your limited time and money. If you plan a month or less in Spain, and you have a normal appetite for

information, this book is all you need. If you're a travel-info fiend (like me), you'll find that this book sorts through all the superlatives and provides a handy rack upon which to hang your supplemental information.

Experiencing Spain's culture, people, and natural wonders economically and hassle-free has been my goal for three decades of traveling, tour-guiding, and writing. With this book, I pass on to you the lessons I've learned, updated for 2010.

For any updates that have occurred since my recent research, see www.ricksteves.com/update, and for a valuable list of reports

INTRODUCTION

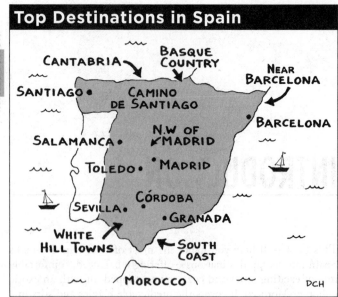

Top Destinations in Spain

CANTABRIA
BASQUE COUNTRY
NEAR BARCELONA
SANTIAGO
CAMINO DE SANTIAGO
BARCELONA
SALAMANCA
N.W OF MADRID
TOLEDO
MADRID
SEVILLA
CÓRDOBA
GRANADA
WHITE HILL TOWNS
SOUTH COAST
MOROCCO

DCH

and experiences—good and bad—from fellow travelers, check www.ricksteves.com/feedback.

The best of Spain is, of course, only my opinion. But after spending half of my adult life researching and tour-guiding in Europe, I've developed a sixth sense for what travelers enjoy.

About This Book

Rick Steves' Spain 2010 is a tour guide in your pocket. It's organized by destination. Each destination is covered as a mini-vacation on its own, filled with exciting sights and homey, affordable places to stay. In the following chapters, you'll find these sections:

Orientation includes tips on public transportation, local tour options, helpful hints, and tourist information (note that tourist information is abbreviated **TI** in this book). The "Planning Your Time" section offers a suggested schedule for how to best use your limited time.

Sights, described in detail, are rated:

▲▲▲—Don't miss;

▲▲—Try hard to see;

▲—Worthwhile if you can make it;

No rating—Worth knowing about.

Self-Guided Walks take you through interesting neighborhoods, with a personal tour guide in hand.

Sleeping describes my favorite good-value hotels, from budget deals to cushy splurges.

Eating serves up a range of options, from inexpensive eateries to fancier options, with an emphasis on quality.

Connections outlines your options for traveling to destinations by bus and train. In car-friendly regions, I've included route tips for drivers.

History and Culture gives you a quick overview of Spanish history, art, architecture, and the tradition of bullfighting.

The **appendix** is a traveler's tool kit, with telephone tips, transportation basics (on trains, buses, car rentals, driving, and flights), recommended books and films, a festival list, climate chart, handy packing checklist, hotel reservation form, Spanish survival phrases, and more.

Browse through this book, choose your favorite destinations, and link them up. Then have a *maravilloso* trip! Traveling like a temporary local, you'll get the absolute most out of every mile, minute, and euro. As you visit places I know and love, I'm happy you'll be meeting my favorite Spanish people.

Planning

This section will help you get started on planning your trip—with advice on trip costs, when to go, and what you should know before you take off.

Travel Smart

Your trip to Spain is like a complex play—easier to follow and really appreciated on second viewing. While no one does the same trip twice to gain that advantage, reading this book in its entirety before your trip accomplishes much the same thing.

This book can save you lots of time and money. But to have an "A" trip, you need to be an "A" student. While reading it, note holidays, specifics on sights, and days when sights are closed. Saturdays are virtually weekdays, with earlier closing hours. Sundays have similar pros and cons as they do for travelers in the US: Special events and weekly markets pop up, sightseeing attractions are generally open, banks and some shops are closed, public transportation options are fewer, and there's no rush hour. Rowdy evenings are rare on Sundays.

Be sure to mix intense and relaxed periods in your itinerary. To maximize rootedness, minimize one-night stands. Every trip—and every traveler—needs slack time (laundry, picnics, people-watching, and so on). Pace yourself. Assume you will return.

As you travel, take advantage of the Internet and phones to make your trip run smoothly. By going online (at Internet cafés or your hotel) and using the phone (buy a phone card or carry a mobile phone), you can get tourist information, learn the latest on

INTRODUCTION

Spain at a Glance

These attractions are listed (as in this book) roughly from north to south.

▲▲▲**Barcelona** The Catalan capital, with famous Ramblas people zone, atmospheric Gothic old town, and works by native sons Antoni Gaudí, Pablo Picasso, and Joan Miró.

▲**Near Barcelona** Top stops in Catalunya, including Salvador Dalí sights (Figueres and Cadaqués), pilgrimage to a rugged mountain retreat (Montserrat), and beach resort (Sitges).

▲**Basque Country** Feisty would-be breakaway region, anchored by the culinary capital of San Sebastián and the iconic modern Guggenheim Museum in Bilbao, with other attractions scattered through the countryside and across the border into France.

▲**The Camino de Santiago** Centuries-old pilgrimage route running across the top of Spain from France to Santiago, with stops at big cities (Pamplona, Burgos, León) and charming villages (Puente de la Reina, O Cebreiro)...and plenty of pilgrim bonding.

▲**Santiago de Compostela** Moss-covered pilgrim capital, and the top town in green Galicia.

Cantabria The rustic northern coast of Spain, featuring world-class prehistoric art (Altamira Caves) and high-mountain scenery (Picos de Europa).

▲**Salamanca** Spain's quintessential university town, with its finest main square.

▲▲**Madrid** The lively Spanish capital, boasting top-notch art treasures (Prado's collection, Picasso's *Guernica*), an unsur-

sights (special events, English tour schedule, etc.), book tickets and tours, make reservations, reconfirm hotels, research transportation connections, and keep in touch with your loved ones.

Connect with the culture. Set up your own quest for the best main square, paella, cloister, tapas bar, or whatever. Enjoy the friendliness of the Spanish people. Ask questions—most locals are eager to point you in their idea of the right direction. Slow down and be open to unexpected experiences. Keep a notepad in your pocket for organizing your thoughts. Wear your money belt, and learn the local currency and how to estimate prices in dollars. Those who expect to travel smart, do.

passed tapas scene, and urban Spain at its best.

▲**Northwest of Madrid** Sights ranging from El Escorial (imposing Inquisition palace of Spanish royalty) and the Valley of the Fallen (a stern, underground Franco-era monument to Spain's Civil War) to the pleasant towns of Segovia (with a towering Roman aqueduct) and Ávila (encircled by a medieval wall).

▲▲**Toledo** Hill-capping former capital, with a colorfully complex history, magnificent cathedral, and works by hometown boy El Greco.

▲▲▲**Granada** Grand Moorish capital, home to the magnificent Alhambra palace and still-pungent North African culture.

▲▲▲**Sevilla** Soulful, flamenco-flavored cultural capital of southern Spain.

▲**Córdoba** Home to Spain's top surviving Moorish mosque, the Mezquita.

▲**Andalucía's White Hill Towns** Classic heartland of southern Spain, famous for its windswept landscape and idyllic towns, including Arcos de la Frontera, Ronda, and Grazalema.

Spain's South Coast "Costa del Sol" beach-resort zone, featuring a few charming towns (Nerja, Tarifa, and British-flavored Gibraltar) tucked between the concrete and traffic jams.

▲**Tangier, Morocco** Newly revitalized gateway to Africa, and an easy day trip from the Costa del Sol.

Trip Costs

Five components make up your trip costs: airfare, surface transportation, room and board, sightseeing and entertainment, and shopping and miscellany.

Airfare: A basic round-trip flight from the US to Barcelona or Madrid should cost $800 to $1,600, depending on where you fly from and when you go. Smaller budget airlines provide bargain service from several European capitals to many cities in Spain (see "Cheap Flights" on page 729 for details). Always consider saving time and money in Europe by flying "open jaw" (into one city and out of another; e.g., into Barcelona and out of Santiago de

INTRODUCTION

Compostela, or Lisbon, Portugal).

Surface Transportation: For a three-week whirlwind trip of all my recommended destinations, allow $550 per person for second-class trains and buses ($750 for first-class trains). For a three-week car rental, tolls, gas, and insurance, allow $875 per person (based on two people sharing). Car rental or leases are cheapest if arranged from the US. Train passes are normally available only outside of Europe. You may save money by simply buying tickets as you go (see "Transportation" in the appendix for more details on car rental, rail trips, and bus travel).

Room and Board: You can thrive in Spain on $90 a day per person for room and board. This allows $10 for lunch, $20 for dinner, and $60 for lodging (based on two people splitting the cost of a $120 double room that includes breakfast). That's doable. If you've got more money, I've listed great ways to spend it. Students and tightwads do it on $50 a day ($25 per hostel bed, $25 for meals and snacks).

Sightseeing and Entertainment: In big cities, figure about $8–13 per major sight (Madrid's Prado, Barcelona's Picasso Museum), $4 for minor ones (climbing church towers), and about $30–45 for splurge experiences (flamenco, bullfights). An overall average of $15 a day works for most. Don't skimp here. After all, this category is the driving force behind your trip—you came to sightsee, enjoy, and experience Spain.

Shopping and Miscellany: Figure roughly $2 per coffee, beer, ice-cream cone, and postcard. Shopping can vary in cost from nearly nothing to a small fortune. Good budget travelers find that this category has little to do with assembling a trip full of lifelong and wonderful memories.

Sightseeing Priorities

Depending on the length of your trip, here are my recommended priorities:

3 days:	Madrid and Toledo
6 days, add:	Sevilla, Granada
10 days, add:	Barcelona, Andalucía (White Hill Towns)
13 days, add:	Costa del Sol, Morocco
15 days, add:	Salamanca, Segovia
17 days, add:	Santiago de Compostela
21 days, add:	Basque Region (San Sebastián and Bilbao)
25 days, add:	Camino de Santiago (by car)

This includes nearly everything on the map on page 9.

When to Go

Spring and fall offer the best combination of good weather, light crowds, long days, and plenty of tourist and cultural activities.

Major Holidays and Weekends

Popular places are even busier on weekends...and inundated on three-day weekends, when hotels, trains, and buses can get booked up before, during, and after the actual holiday. Plan ahead and reserve your accommodations and transportation (particularly for AVE trains) well in advance. Note that religious holidays are big in Spain.

In 2010, be prepared for big crowds during these holiday periods: Holy Week and Easter weekend (March 28–April 4); April Fair in Sevilla (April 20–25); the San Isidro festival in Madrid (May 15); Labor Day (May 1); Ascension (May 13); Pentecost weekend (May 22–23); Assumption weekend (Aug 14–15); Spain National Day (Oct 12); Constitution Day, followed closely by the Feast of the Immaculate Conception, plus the previous weekend (Dec 4–8); and the winter holidays (Dec 19–Jan 6). Also check the list of festivals and holidays on page 735.

Look out for local holidays that fall on a Tuesday or Thursday—the Spanish will often make it into a *puente*, meaning they'll take Monday or Friday off as well to have a four-day weekend.

July and August are the most crowded and expensive in the coastal areas, and less crowded but uncomfortably hot and dusty in the interior. Air-conditioning is worth the splurge. During these steamy months, lunch breaks can be long, especially in Andalucía.

Off-season, roughly November through March, expect sights to have shorter hours, lunchtime breaks, and fewer activities. Confirm your sightseeing plans locally, especially when traveling off-season.

While it can be brutally hot in the summer, winters can be bitter cold, and spring and fall can be surprisingly crisp. For weather specifics, see the climate chart on page 737 of the appendix.

Know Before You Go

Your trip is more likely to go smoothly if you plan ahead. Check this list of things to arrange while you're still at home.

You need a **passport**—but no visa or shots—to travel in Spain. You may be denied entry into certain European countries if your passport is due to expire within three to six months of your ticketed date of return. Get it renewed if you'll be cutting it close.

Whirlwind Three-Week Trip of Spain

Day	Plan	Sleep in
1	Arrive in Barcelona	Barcelona
2	Barcelona	Barcelona
3	Barcelona, evening train to Madrid	Madrid
4	Madrid	Madrid
5	Day trip to El Escorial/Valley of Fallen	Madrid
6	Madrid, late afternoon to Toledo	Toledo
7	Toledo, evening train to Sevilla	Sevilla
8	Sevilla	Sevilla
9	Arcos	Arcos
10	Tarifa	Tarifa
11	Day trip to Morocco	Tarifa
12	Gibraltar, on to Nerja	Nerja
13	Beach day in Nerja, evening to Granada	Granada
14	Granada	Granada
15	Travel day to Segovia	Segovia
16	Segovia, evening to Salamanca	Salamanca
17	Salamanca	Salamanca
18	Travel to Santiago	Santiago
19	Santiago	Santiago
20	Travel to San Sebastián	San Sebastián
21	San Sebastián, side-trip to Bilbao	San Sebastián

This itinerary is designed to be done by public transportation, but can be done by car with a few variations. Spain's long distances make the option of flying for at least a portion of the trip worth considering. If you rent a car, it's best for the White Hill Towns (southern Spain), El Escorial/Valley of the Fallen (northwest of Madrid), and Cantabria (northern Spain), where sparse public transportation limits the efficiency of your sightseeing. To mix car and train transportation, consider getting a Spain Rail & Drive pass.

If you're a fan of Salvador Dalí's art, or if you want to make a pilgrimage to the holy site of Montserrat, allot an extra day for Barcelona for day trips. If you want more Moorish sights, stay another day in Sevilla to make a side-trip to Córdoba (45 min on AVE high-speed train). If you're not interested in daytripping to Tangier, Morocco, you could skip Tarifa and go to Ronda instead. To allow time to explore Gibraltar, add an extra day between Tarifa (or Ronda) and Nerja. If you're exploring the Camino de Santiago by car, consider reversing the above itinerary to start in San Sebastián, and figure on adding several days to a week to your trip.

The suggested itinerary assumes you'll fly "open jaw" into Barcelona and out of San Sebastián. If you're returning to Barcelona or Madrid from San Sebastián, it's roughly an eight-hour train ride (night train possible) or a one-hour flight. Or you can cross into France and take the six-hour TGV train to Paris.

Shorter Itineraries: You can end the three-week route (described above) several days early by returning to Madrid from Salamanca and saving northern Spain for another trip. The north is less rewarding per mile and day.

Here's a two-week alternative, which could include a few car days in southern Spain near the end of your trip: Start in Barcelona (stay two days); train to Madrid (stay five days total, with two days in Madrid and three for side-trips to Toledo, El Escorial, and Segovia or Ávila); train to Granada (two days); bus to Nerja (one day, could rent car here); both Ronda and Arcos for drivers, or just Ronda by train (two days); to Sevilla (drop off car, two days); and then train to Madrid and fly home.

Where Do I Find Information On...?

Credit-Card Theft	See page 14.
Packing Light	See the packing list on page 739.
Phoning	See "Telephones" on page 712.
Language	See page 741.
Making Hotel Reservations	See page 21.
Tipping	See page 14.
Tourist Information Offices	See page 37.
Updates to This Book	See www.ricksteves.com /update

It can take up to six weeks to get or renew a passport (for more on passports, see www.travel.state.gov). Pack a photocopy of your passport in your luggage in case the original is lost or stolen.

Book your rooms well in advance if you'll be traveling during any major **holidays** (see "Major Holidays and Weekends" sidebar).

Consider **making reservations for Granada's Alhambra** before leaving home. You can reserve tickets upon arrival in Spain (ideally before you reach Granada), but I mention it here for those who like to nail things down well in advance (for more information, see page 466). You'll also need reservations if you want to visit the Salvador Dalí House near Cadaqués (see page 117).

Call your **debit- and credit-card companies** to let them know the countries you'll be visiting, so that they'll accept (and not deny) your international charges. Confirm what your daily withdrawal limit is; consider asking to have it raised so you can take out more cash at each ATM stop. Ask about international transaction fees.

If you're interested in **travel insurance**, do your homework before you buy. Compare the cost of the insurance to the likelihood of your using it and your potential loss if something goes wrong. For details on the many kinds of travel insurance, see www.ricksteves.com/plan/tips/insurance.htm.

If you're taking an **overnight train,** especially to international destinations, and you need a sleeping berth *(litera)*—and you must leave on a certain day—consider booking it in advance through a US agent (such as www.raileurope.com), even though it may cost more than buying it in Spain. All high-speed trains in Spain require a seat reservation, but it's usually possible to make arrangements in Spain just a few days ahead unless it's a holiday weekend. (For more on train travel, see "Transportation" in the appendix and www.ricksteves.com/rail.)

Since **airline carry-on restrictions** are always changing, visit the Transportation Security Administration's website (www.tsa .gov/travelers) for an up-to-date list of what you can bring on the plane with you...and what you have to check.

Practicalities

Emergency Telephone Numbers: In **Spain,** dial 091 for police help and 112 in a medical emergency. In **Morocco,** dial 19 for police. Or ask at your hotel for help. They'll know the nearest medical and emergency services.

Time: In Spain—and in this book—you'll use the 24-hour clock. It's the same through 12:00 noon, then keep going: 13:00, 14:00, and so on. For anything over 12, subtract 12 and add p.m. (14:00 is 2:00 p.m.).

Spain, like most of continental Europe, is generally six/nine hours ahead of the East/West Coasts of the US. The exceptions are the beginning and end of Daylight Saving Time: Europe "springs forward" the last Sunday in March (two weeks after most of the US), and "falls back" the last Sunday in October (one week before the US). Moroccan time can run up to two hours earlier than Spanish time. For a handy online time converter, try www .timeanddate.com/worldclock.

Business Hours: For visitors, Spain is a land of strange and frustrating schedules. Many businesses respect the afternoon siesta. When it's 100 degrees in the shade, you'll understand why.

The biggest museums stay open all day. Smaller ones often close for a siesta. Shops are generally open from 9:00 to 13:00 and from 16:00 to 20:00, longer in touristy places. Small shops are often open on Saturday only in the morning, and are closed all day Sunday. Banks are generally open Monday through Friday from 9:00 to 14:00.

Watt's Up? Europe's electrical system is different from North America's in two ways: the shape of the plug (two round prongs) and the voltage of the current (220 volts instead of 110 volts). For your North American plug to work in Europe, you'll need an adapter, sold inexpensively at travel stores in the US. As for the voltage, most newer electronics or travel appliances (such as hair dryers, laptops, and battery chargers) automatically convert the voltage—if you see a range of voltages printed on the item or its plug (such as "110–220"), it'll work in Europe. Otherwise, you can buy a converter separately in the US (about $20).

News: Americans keep in touch via the *International Herald Tribune* (published almost daily throughout Europe and online at www.iht.com). Other newsy sites are http://news.bbc.co.uk and www.europeantimes.com. Every Tuesday, the European editions of *Time* and *Newsweek* hit the stands with articles of particular interest to European travelers. Sports addicts can get their daily fix online or from *USA Today*. Many hotels have CNN and BBC television channels.

Theft Alert: Thieves target tourists throughout Spain, especially in Barcelona, Madrid, Granada, and Sevilla. While hotel rooms are generally safe, thieves break into cars, snatch purses, and pick pockets. Thieves zipping by on motorbikes grab handbags from pedestrians or even from cars in traffic (by reaching through open car windows at stoplights). A fight or commotion is created to enable pickpockets to work unnoticed. Be on guard, use a money belt, and treat any disturbance around you as a smoke screen for theft. Don't believe any "police officers" looking for counterfeit bills. Drivers should read the tips on page 727. When traveling by train, keep your luggage in sight and get a *litera* (berth in an attendant-monitored sleeping car) for safety on overnight trips.

Money

This section offers advice on getting cash, using credit and debit cards, dealing with lost or stolen cards, and tipping.

Cash from ATMs

Throughout Europe, cash machines (ATMs) are the standard way for travelers to get local currency. Travelers checks are a waste of

time (long waits at slow banks) and a waste of money in fees.

Bring plastic—credit and/or debit cards—along with several hundred dollars in hard cash as an emergency backup (in denominations of $20 bills rather than hard-to-exchange $100 bills). It's smart to bring two cards, in case one gets demagnetized or eaten by a temperamental machine. To use an ATM (called a *cajero automático*) to withdraw money from your account, you'll need a debit card (ideally with a Visa or MasterCard logo for maximum usability), plus a PIN code. Know your PIN code in numbers; there are only numbers—no letters—on European keypads.

Before you go, remember to confirm with your bank that your card will work overseas, and alert them that you'll be making withdrawals in Europe; otherwise, the bank may not approve

---

Exchange Rate

1 euro (€) = about $1.40

To convert prices in euros to dollars, add about 40 percent: €20 = about $28, €50 = about $70. Just like the dollar, one euro is broken down into 100 cents. You'll find coins ranging from €0.01 to €2, and bills ranging from €5 to €500.

Gibraltar uses pounds (£) but also takes euros; you'll get a better exchange rate using pounds (£1 = about $1.60).

For Morocco, I list prices in dirhams (the official currency; 8 dirhams = about $1), although euros and dollars are usually accepted.

---

transactions if it perceives unusual spending patterns. (Credit-card companies do the same thing—inform them of your travel plans as well.) Also ask about international fees; see "Credit and Debit Cards," below.

When using an ATM, try to take out large sums of money to reduce your per-transaction bank fees. If the machine refuses your request, try again and select a smaller amount (some cash machines limit the amount you can withdraw—don't take it personally). If that doesn't work, try a different machine.

To keep your cash safe, use a money belt—a pouch with a strap that you buckle around your waist like a belt, and wear under your clothes. Thieves target tourists. A money belt provides peace of mind, allowing you to carry lots of cash safely. Don't waste time every few days tracking down a cash machine—withdraw a week's worth of money, stuff it in your money belt, and travel!

Credit and Debit Cards

For purchases, Visa and MasterCard are more commonly accepted than American Express. Just like at home, credit or debit cards work easily at larger hotels and shops, but smaller businesses prefer payment in local currency (in small bills—break large bills at banks or larger stores). Note that many restaurants accept only cash.

Be careful: If receipts show your credit-card number, don't toss them thoughtlessly.

Fees: Credit and debit cards—whether used for purchases or ATM withdrawals—often charge additional, tacked-on "international transaction" fees of up to 3 percent plus $5 per transaction. Note that if you use a credit card for ATM transactions, it's technically a "cash advance" rather than a "withdrawal"—and subject to an additional cash-advance fee.

To avoid unpleasant surprises, call your bank or credit-card company before your trip to ask about these fees. If the fees are too high, consider getting a card just for your trip: Capital One (www .capitalone.com) and most credit unions have low-to-no international transaction fees.

If merchants offer to convert your purchase price into dollars (called dynamic currency conversion, or DCC), refuse this "service." You'll pay even more in fees for the expensive convenience of seeing your charge in dollars.

Damage Control for Lost Cards

If you lose your credit, debit, or ATM card, you can stop people from using your card by reporting the loss immediately to the respective global customer-assistance centers. Call these 24-hour US numbers collect: Visa (410/581-9994; toll-free number in Spain is 900-991-124), MasterCard (636/722-7111), and American Express (623/492-8427).

At a minimum, you'll need to know the name of the financial institution that issued you the card, along with the type of card (classic, platinum, or whatever). Providing the following information will allow for a quicker cancellation of your missing card: full card number, whether you are the primary or secondary cardholder, the cardholder's name exactly as printed on the card, billing address, home phone number, circumstances of the loss or theft, and identification verification (your birth date, your mother's maiden name, or your Social Security number—memorize this, don't carry a copy). If you are the secondary cardholder, you'll also need to provide the primary cardholder's identification-verification details. You can generally receive a temporary card within two or three business days in Europe.

If you promptly report your card lost or stolen, you typically won't be responsible for any unauthorized transactions on your account, although many banks charge a liability fee of $50.

Tipping

Tipping in Spain isn't as automatic and generous as it is in the US, but for special service, tips are appreciated, if not expected. As in the US, the proper amount depends on your resources, tipping philosophy, and the circumstances, but some general guidelines apply.

Restaurants: In most restaurants, a service charge *(servicio incluido)* is generally included in the bill, though it's customary to tip 5 percent extra for good service. If service is not included *(servicio no incluido),* tip up to 10 percent. Leave the tip on the table. It's best to tip in cash even if you pay with your credit card. Otherwise the tip may never reach your server. If you order a meal at a counter, don't tip.

Taxis: To tip the cabbie, round up. Spanish people rarely give tips in taxis, unless it's to round up to the next full euro (if the fare is €4.85, they'll give €5). If the cabbie hauls your bags and zips you to the airport to help you catch your flight, you might want to toss in a little more. But if you feel like you're being driven in circles or otherwise ripped off, skip the tip.

Special Services: It's thoughtful to tip a couple of euros to someone who shows you a special sight and who is paid in no other way. Tour guides at sights sometimes hold out their hands for tips after they give their spiel; if I've already paid for the tour, I don't tip extra, though some tourists do give a euro or two, particularly for a job well done. At hotels, porters expect a euro for each bag they carry (another reason to pack light). Leaving the maid a euro per overnight at the end of your stay is a nice touch. In general, if someone in the service industry does a super job for you, a tip of a couple of euros is appropriate...but not required.

When in doubt, ask. If you're not sure whether (or how much) to tip for a service, ask your hotelier or the tourist information office; they'll fill you in on how it's done on their turf.

Getting a VAT Refund

Wrapped into the purchase price of your Spanish souvenirs is a Value-Added Tax (VAT) of about 16 percent. If you purchase more than €90 (about $125) worth of goods at a store that participates in the VAT-refund scheme, you're entitled to get most of that tax back. Getting your refund is usually straightforward and, if you buy a substantial amount of souvenirs, well worth the hassle. If you're lucky, the merchant will subtract the tax when you make your purchase. (This is more likely to occur if the store ships the goods to your home.) Otherwise, you'll need to:

Get the paperwork. Have the merchant completely fill out the necessary refund document, *Bordereay de Vente a l'Exportation,* also called a "cheque." You'll have to present your passport at the store.

Get your stamp at the border or airport. Process your cheque(s) at your last stop in the EU (e.g., at the airport) with the customs agent who deals with VAT refunds. It's best to keep your purchases in your carry-on for viewing, but if they're too large or dangerous (such as knives) to carry on, track down the proper customs agent to inspect them before you check your bag. You're not supposed to use your purchased goods before you leave. If you show up at customs wearing your new flamenco outfit, officials might look the other way—or deny you a refund.

Collect your refund. You'll need to return your stamped document to the retailer or its representative. Many merchants work with services, such as Global Refund (www.globalrefund.com)

or Premier Tax Free (www.premiertaxfree.com), which have offices at major airports, ports, or border crossings. These services, which extract a 4 percent fee, can refund your money immediately in your currency of choice or credit your card (within two billing cycles). If the retailer handles VAT refunds directly, it's up to you to contact the merchant for your refund. You can mail the documents from home, or quicker, from your point of departure (using a stamped, addressed envelope you've prepared or one that's been provided by the merchant)—and then wait. It could take months.

Customs for American Shoppers

You are allowed to take home $800 worth of items per person duty-free, once every 30 days. The next $1,000 is taxed at a flat 3 percent. After that, you pay the individual item's duty rate. You can also bring in duty-free a liter of alcohol (slightly more than a standard-size bottle of wine; you must be at least 21), 200 cigarettes, and up to 100 non-Cuban cigars. You may take home vacuum-packed cheeses; dried herbs, spices, or mushrooms; and canned fruits or vegetables, including jams and vegetable spreads. Baked goods, candy, chocolate, oil, vinegar, mustard, and honey are OK. Fresh fruits or vegetables are not. Meats are generally not allowed, even if canned. Note that you'll need to carefully pack any bottles of wine and other liquid-containing items in your checked luggage, due to limits on liquids in carry-ons. To check customs rules and duty rates before you go, visit www.cbp.gov, and click on "Travel," then "Know Before You Go."

Sightseeing

Sightseeing can be hard work. Use these tips to make your visits to Spain's finest sights meaningful, fun, fast, and painless.

Plan Ahead

Set up an itinerary that allows you to fit in all your must-see sights. For a one-stop look at opening hours, see the "At a Glance" sidebars for the bigger cities. Most sights keep stable hours, but you can easily confirm the latest by calling the local TI.

If you'll be visiting during a holiday, find out if a particular sight will be open by phoning ahead or checking its website. And don't put off visiting a must-see sight—you never know when a place will close unexpectedly for a holiday, strike, or restoration.

When possible, visit key museums in the morning (when your energy is best) and save other activities for the afternoon. Hit the highlights first, then go back to other things if you have the stamina and time.

Depending on the sight, there are ways to avoid crowds. This book offers tips on specific sights. Try visiting the sight very early, at lunch, or very late. Evening visits (when possible) are usually peaceful with fewer crowds.

Read ahead. To get the most out of the self-guided tours and sight descriptions in this book, read them before you visit. Several cities offer sightseeing passes that are worthwhile values for serious sightseers; do the math to see if they'll save you money.

At the Sights

All sights have rules, and if you know about these in advance, they're no big deal.

Some important sights use metal detectors or conduct bag searches that will slow your entry.

At churches—which generally offer interesting art (usually free) and a cool, welcome seat—a modest dress code is encouraged and sometimes required (no bare shoulders, miniskirts, or shorts).

Most museums require you to check daypacks and coats. They'll be kept safely. If you have something you can't bear to part with, stash it in a pocket or purse. To avoid checking a small backpack, carry it (at least as you enter) under your arm like a purse. From a guard's point of view, a backpack is generally a problem while a purse is not.

Photography is often banned at major sights. Look for signs or ask. If cameras are allowed, flashes or tripods are usually not. Flashes damage oil paintings and distract others in the room. Even without a flash, a handheld camera will take a decent picture (or you can buy postcards or posters at the museum bookstore). If cameras are allowed, video cameras are, too.

Museums may have special exhibits in addition to their permanent collection. Some exhibits are included in the entry price, while others come at an extra cost. Occasionally you have to pay even if you don't want to see the exhibit.

Many sights rent audioguides, which offer dry-but-useful recorded descriptions in English (about €4). If you bring along your own pair of headphones and a Y-jack, you can sometimes share one audioguide with your travel partner and save money. Guided tours in English (usually €6 and widely ranging in quality) are most likely to be offered during peak season.

Expect changes—artwork can be on tour, on loan, out sick, or shifted at the whim of the curator. To adapt, pick up any available free floor plans as you enter. Ask the museum staff if you can't find a particular painting. Say the title or artist's name, or point to the photograph in this book, and ask, "*¿Dónde está?*" (dohn-day ay-stah; meaning, "Where is?").

Some important sights have an on-site café or cafeteria

(usually a good place to rest and have a snack or light meal). The WCs are free and generally clean.

Many sights sell postcards and guidebooks that highlight their attractions. Before you leave, scan the postcards and thumb through the biggest guidebook (or skim its index) to be sure you haven't overlooked something that you'd like to see.

Most sights stop admitting people 30–60 minutes before closing time, and some rooms close early (generally about 45 minutes before the actual closing time). Guards usher people out, so don't save the best for last.

Every sight or museum offers more than what is covered in this book. Use this information as an introduction—not the final word.

Sleeping

Spain offers some of the best accommodation values in Western Europe. Most places are government-regulated, with posted prices.

While prices are low, street noise is high (Spaniards are notorious night owls). Always ask to see your room first. Consider potential night-noise problems. Feel free to ask for another room or bargain down the price. You can request *con vista* (with a view), or *tranquilo* or *callado* (quiet). In most cases, view rooms come with street noise. You'll often sleep better and for less money in a room without a view. These days, considering the confused economy and jittery business environment, I'd email several places to see who is discounting the most. Especially off-season, you'll find prices very soft.

In the interest of smart use of your time, I favor hotels (and restaurants) handy to your sightseeing activities. Rather than list hotels scattered throughout a city, I describe my favorite couple of neighborhoods and recommend the best accommodation values in each, from $25 bunks to $330 suites.

All rooms have sinks with hot and cold water. Rooms with private bathrooms are often bigger and renovated, while the cheaper rooms without bathrooms often will be dingier and/or on the top floor. Any room without a bathroom has access to a bathroom in the corridor.

Types of Accommodations

Hotels: Don't judge hotels by their bleak and dirty entryways. Landlords, stuck with rent control, often stand firmly in the way of hardworking hoteliers who'd like to brighten up their buildings.

Any legitimate place will have a complaint book *(libro de reclamaciones)*. A request for this book will generally prompt the hotelier to solve your problem to keep you from writing a complaint.

Hotels are officially prohibited from using central heat before November 1 and after April 1 (unless it's unusually cold); prepare for cool evenings if you travel in spring and fall. Summer can be extremely hot. Consider air-conditioning, fans, and noise (since you'll want your window open), and don't be shy about asking for ice at the fancier hotels. Many rooms come with mini-refrigerators (if it's noisy at night, unplug it). Conveniently, expensive business-class hotels in big, non-resort cities often drop their prices in July and August, just when the air-conditioned comfort they offer is most important.

Most hotel rooms with air-conditioners come with control sticks (like a TV remote, sometimes requires a deposit) that generally have the same symbols and features: fan icon (click to toggle through wind power from light to gale); louver icon (choose steady air flow or waves); snowflake and sunshine icons (heat or cold, depending on season); clock ("O" setting: run X hours before turning off; "I" setting: wait X hours to start); and the temperature control (20–21 degrees Celsius is comfortable).

Historic Inns: Spain has luxurious government-sponsored, historic inns called *paradores*. These are often renovated castles, palaces, or monasteries, many with great views and stately atmospheres. While full of Old World character, they are usually run in a sterile, bureaucratic way. These are pricey (doubles $100–240, for details, bonus packages, and family deals, see www.parador.es). If you're not eligible for any deals, you'll get a better value by sleeping in what I call (and list in this book as) "poor man's *paradores*"—elegant, normal places that offer double the warmth and Old World intimacy for half the price.

Rooms in Private Homes: You'll find rooms in private homes, typically in touristy areas where locals decide to open up a spare room and make a little money on the side. These rooms are usually as private as hotel rooms, often with separate entries. Especially in resort towns, the rooms might be in small apartment-type buildings. Ask for a *cama, habitación,* or *casa particular.* They're cheap ($15–30 per bed without breakfast) and usually a good experience.

Casas Rurales: Located mainly in rural areas throughout Spain, these accommodations can be furnished rooms, whole farmhouses, villas, or sprawling ranches. Some are simple but others are luxurious, and they are mostly used by Spaniards so you'll really be going local. For many, you'll also need a car since they are in the countryside. For more information and reservations,

Sleep Code

(€1 = about $1.40, country code: 34)

To help you sort easily through these listings, I've divided the rooms into three categories based on the price for a standard double room with bath:

$$$ Higher Priced
$$ Moderately Priced
$ Lower Priced

To pack maximum information into minimum space, I use the following code to describe accommodations in this book. Prices listed are per room, not per person.

When there is a range of prices in one category, that means the price fluctuates with the season: high season (*alta*, July–Sept), shoulder season (*media*, roughly April–June and Oct), and low season (*baja*, Nov–March). The prices and seasons are posted at or near the hotel desk. In resort areas, prices go way up in high season. In Spain, some hotels include the 7 percent IVA tax in the room price; others tack it onto your bill.

S = Single room (or price for one person in a double).
D = Double or twin. Double beds are usually big enough for nonromantic couples.
T = Triple (generally a double bed with a single).
Q = Quad (usually two double beds).
b = Private bathroom with toilet and shower or tub.
s = Private shower or tub only (the toilet is down the hall).

According to this code, a couple staying at a "Db-€140" hotel would pay a total of €140 (about $195) for a double room with a private bathroom. You can assume a hotel takes credit cards unless you see "cash only" in the listing. Unless otherwise noted, hotel staff speak basic English.

If I list "Internet access," there's a public terminal in the lobby for guests to use. If I mention "Wi-Fi" or "cable Internet," you can access it in your room, but only if you have your own laptop.

---

try www.ecoturismorural.com, www.ruralalicante.es, or www.micasarural.com.

Budget Options: *Hostales* (budget hotels) and *pensiones* (guest houses) are easy to find, inexpensive, and, when chosen properly, a fun part of the Spanish cultural experience. Spain also has plenty of youth hostels and campgrounds, but considering the great bargains on other accommodations, I don't think they're worth the trouble and usually don't cover them in this book. If you're on a starvation budget or just prefer camping or hosteling, plenty of information is available in the Let's Go guidebook, through the national tourist office, and at local TIs.

Phoning
To call Spain, you'll need to know its country code: 34. To call Spain from the US or Canada, dial 011-34-local number. If calling Spain from another European country, dial 00-34-local number.

Making Reservations
Given the quality of the accommodations I've found for this book, I'd recommend that you reserve your rooms in advance, particularly if you'll be traveling during peak season. Book several weeks ahead, or as soon as you've pinned down your travel dates. Note that some national holidays jam things up and merit your making reservations far in advance (see the "Major Holidays and Weekends" sidebar earlier in this chapter). Just like at home, holidays that fall on a Monday, Tuesday, Thursday, or Friday can turn the weekend into a long holiday, so book the entire weekend well in advance.

Requesting a Reservation: To reserve, contact hotels directly by email, phone, or fax. Email is the clearest and most economical way to make a reservation. Or you can go straight to the hotel website; many have secure online reservation forms and can instantly inform you of availability and any special deals. But be sure you use the hotel's official site and not a booking agency's site—otherwise you may pay higher rates than you should. If you're phoning from the US, be mindful of time zones. Most hotels listed are accustomed to guests who speak only English.

The hotelier wants to know these key pieces of information (also included in the sample request form in the appendix and at www.ricksteves.com/reservation):
- number and type of rooms
- number of nights
- date of arrival
- date of departure
- any special needs (e.g., bathroom in the room or down the hall, twin beds vs. double bed, air-conditioning, quiet, view, ground floor, etc.)

When you request a room in writing for a certain time period, use the European style for writing dates: day/month/year. Hoteliers need to know your arrival and departure dates. For example, for a two-night stay in July, I would request "1 double room for 2 nights, arrive 16/07/10, depart 18/07/10." (Consider carefully how long you'll stay; don't just assume you can extend your reservation for extra days once you arrive.)

If you don't get a reply to your email or fax, it usually means the hotel is already fully booked (but you can try sending the message again, or call to follow up).

Confirming a Reservation: If the hotel's response tells you its room availability and rates, it's not a confirmation. You must tell them that you want that room at the given rate. Many hoteliers will request your credit-card number for a one-night deposit to hold the room. While you can email your credit-card information (I do), it's safer to share that personal info via phone call, fax, or secure online reservation form (if the hotel has one on its website).

Canceling a Reservation: If you must cancel your reservation, it's courteous to do so with as much advance notice as possible—at least three days. Simply make a quick phone call or send an email. Family-run hotels lose money if they turn away customers while holding a room for someone who doesn't show up. Understandably, some hotels bill no-shows for one night.

Some hotels have strict cancellation policies: For example, you might lose a deposit if you cancel within two weeks of your reserved stay, or you might be billed for the entire visit if you leave early. Ask about cancellation policies before you book.

If canceling via email, request confirmation that your cancellation was received to avoid being accidentally billed.

Reconfirm Your Reservation: Always call to reconfirm your room reservation a few days in advance from the road. If you'll be arriving after 17:00, let them know. Don't have the tourist office reconfirm rooms for you; they'll take a commission. On the small chance that a hotel loses track of your reservation, bring along a hard copy of their emailed or faxed confirmation.

Reserving Rooms as You Travel: For more spontaneity, you can make reservations as you travel, calling hotels a few days to a week before your visit. If you prefer the flexibility of traveling without any reservations at all, you'll have greater success snaring rooms if you arrive at your destination early in the day. When you anticipate crowds (weekends are worst), call hotels at about 9:00 on the day you plan to arrive, when the hotel clerk knows who'll be checking out and just which rooms will be available. If you encounter a language barrier, ask the fluent receptionist at your current hotel to call for you.

Eating

Spanish cuisine is hearty and served in big, inexpensive portions. You can eat well in restaurants for €15.

The Spanish eating schedule—lunch from 13:00–16:00, dinner after 21:00—frustrates many visitors. Most Spaniards eat one major meal of the day—lunch *(almuerzo)* at 14:00, when stores close, schools let out, and people gather with their friends and family for the siesta. Because most Spaniards work until 19:30, supper *(cena)* is usually served at about 21:00 or 22:00. And, since few people want a heavy meal that late, many Spaniards build a light dinner out of appetizer portions called tapas.

Don't buck this system. Generally, no self-respecting *casa de comidas* ("house of eating"—when you see this label, you can bet it's a good, traditional eatery) serves meals at American hours. If you're looking for the "non-touristy restaurant," remember that a popular spot is often filled with tourists at 20:00 and then at 22:00 the scene is entirely different—and more local.

The Spanish diet—heavy on ham, deep-fried foods (usually fried in olive oil), more ham, weird seafood, and ham again—can be brutal on Americans more accustomed to salads, fruit, and grains. There are plenty of perfectly good vegetarian and lighter options, but you'll have to take the initiative and seek them out.

Survival Tips: To get by in Spain, either adapt yourself to the Spanish schedule and cuisine, or scramble to get edible food in between. Have an early light lunch at a bar. Many Spaniards have a *bocadillo* (sandwich) at about 11:00 to bridge the gap between their coffee-and-roll breakfast and lunch at 14:00 (hence the popularity of fast-food sandwich chains such as Pans & Company). Besides *bocadillos*, bars often have slices of *tortilla española* (potato omelet) and fresh-squeezed orange juice.

Then, either have your main meal at a restaurant at 15:00, followed by a light tapas snack for dinner later; or reverse it, having a tapas meal in the afternoon, followed by a late restaurant dinner. Either way, tapas in bars are the key (see "Ordering Tapas" on the next page spread).

The secret to getting your veggies at restaurants is to order two courses, because the first course generally has a green option. Resist the cheese-and-ham appetizers and instead choose first-course menu items such as creamed vegetable soup, *parrillada de verduras* (sautéed vegetables), or *ensalada mixta* (Spaniards rarely eat only a salad, so salads tend to be small and simple—just iceberg lettuce, tomatoes, and maybe olives and tuna). Main courses such as meats or fish are usually served with only a garnish, not a side of vegetables. Fruit isn't normally served for breakfast or as a snack—it's a dessert. After-meal dessert menus usually have a fruit option.

Ordering Tapas

You can often just point to what you want, say *por favor,* and get your food, but these words will help you learn the options and fine-tune your request.

Tapas Terms

pincho	bite-size portion (not always available)
pinchito	tiny pincho
tapas	snack-size portions
ración	larger portions—half a meal, occasionally available in a smaller version called a "½ ración" *(media-ración)*
frito	fried
...a la plancha	grilled
...a la parrilla	barbecued
¿Cuánto cuesta una tapa?	How much per tapa?

Sandwich Words

bocadillo	baguette sandwich, cheap and basic, a tapa on bread
canapé	tiny open-faced sandwich
pulguitas	small closed baguette sandwich
montadito	baguette slice with the tapa "mounted" on top
flautas	sandwich made with flute-thin baguette
pepito	yet one more word for a little sandwich

Typical Tapas

aceitunas	olives
almendras	almonds
atún	tuna
bacalao	cod
banderilla	small skewer of spicy, pickled veggies— eat all at once for the real punch (it's named after the spear matadors use to spike the bull)
bombas	fried meat and potatoes ball
boquerones (en vinagre)	fresh anchovies marinated in olive oil, vinegar, and garlic
calamares fritos	fried squid rings
caracoles	snails (May–Sept)
cazón en adobo	salty, marinated dogfish
champiñones	mushrooms
croquetas de...	breaded and fried béchamel (made of flour and milk), usually with chunks of *jamón* (ham)
empanadillas	pastries stuffed with meat or seafood

ensalada rusa	potato salad with lots of mayo, peas, and carrots
espinacas (con garbanzos)	spinach (with garbanzo beans)
gambas (a la plancha, al ajillo)	shrimp (grilled, with garlic)
gazpacho	cold soup, made with tomato, bread, garlic, and olive oil
guiso	stew
mejillones	mussels
paella	rice dish with saffron, seafood, meat, and/or chicken
pan	bread
patatas bravas	fried chunks of potato with spicy tomato sauce
pescaditos fritos	assortment of fried little fish
picos	little breadsticks
pimiento (relleno)	peppers (stuffed)
pisto	mixed sautéed vegetables
pulpo	octopus
queso	cheese (or a beautiful woman)
queso manchego	sheep-milk cheese
rabas	squid tentacles
rabo de toro	bull-tail stew
revuelto de...	scrambled eggs with...
...setas	...wild mushrooms
tabla serrana	hearty plate of mountain meat and cheese
tortilla española	potato omelet
tortilla de jamón/queso	potato omelet with ham/cheese
variado fritos	typical Andalusian mix of various fried fish

Cured Meats *(Charcutería)*

jamón serrano	cured ham
jamón ibérico	best cured ham, from acorn-fed pigs
salchichón	sausage
chorizo	spicy sausage
lomo	pork tenderloin

Typical Desserts

flan de huevo	crème caramel
arroz con leche	rice pudding
helados (variados)	ice cream (various flavors)
fruta de la estación	fruit in season
queso	cheese

Breakfast

Hotel breakfasts are generally handy, optional, and pricey (€6). Start your day instead with a Spanish flair at a corner bar or at a colorful café near the town market hall (and pay just €2–3). Ask for the *desayunos* (breakfast special, usually only available until noon), which can include coffee, a roll (or sandwich), and juice for one price—much cheaper than ordering them separately. In Andalucía, get your morning protein with the *mollete con jamón y aceite,* a soft roll of bread with Spanish ham and finger-licking good olive oil (sometimes comes with cheese, too). If you like a Danish and coffee in American greasy-spoon joints, you must try the Spanish equivalent: greasy cigar-shaped fritters called *churros* (or the thicker *porras*) that you dip in warm chocolate pudding.

Here are some key words for breakfast:

café solo	shot of espresso
café con leche	espresso with hot milk
cortado	espresso with a little milk
té	tea
zumo de fruta	fruit juice
zumo de naranja (natural)	orange juice (freshly squeezed)
pan	bread
tortilla española	potato omelet (standard dish cooked fresh each morning, served in cheap slices)
sandwich (tostado)	Wonder bread (toasted)
bocadillo	baguette sandwich
...con jamón/queso/mixto	...with ham/cheese/both
...mixto con huevo	...with ham and cheese topped by an over-easy egg
croissant a la plancha	grilled croissant slathered with butter
tostada con aceite y sal (y tomate)	a standard local breakfast— toasted bread with oil and salt (sometimes comes with tomato)

Restaurants

In restaurants, don't expect "My name is Carlos and I'll be your waiter tonight" cheery service. Service is often *serio*—it's not friendly or unfriendly...just white shirt–and–bow tie proficient.

Although not fancy, Spanish cuisine comes with an endless variety of regional specialties. Two famous Spanish dishes are paella and gazpacho. Paella features saffron-flavored rice as a background for whatever the chef wants to mix in—seafood, sausage, chicken, peppers, and so on. While paella is heavy for your evening meal, jump (like everyone else in the bar) at the opportunity to snare a small plate of paella when it appears hot out of the kitchen in a tapas bar. Avoid the paella shown in pretty pictures on a separate menu—it's from the microwave. Gazpacho, an Andalusian specialty, is a chilled soup of tomatoes, bread chunks, and spices—refreshing on a hot day and commonly available in the summer. Spanish cooks love garlic and olive oil. The cheapest meal is simply a

bocadillo de jamón (sandwich of ham on French bread), sold virtually everywhere.

For a budget meal in a restaurant, try a *plato combinado* (combination plate), which usually includes portions of one or two main dishes, a vegetable, and bread for a reasonable price; or the *menú del día* (menu of the day, also known as *menú turístico*), a substantial three- to four-course meal that usually comes with a carafe of house wine.

Sometimes the distinction between a bar and a restaurant blurs. Formal restaurants have a standard à la carte menu. Most eateries have a bar with some tables in the back or outside. While tourists are often hot on tapas, these places are likely to serve *raciones* rather than tapas or restaurant entrées. Typically, couples or small groups order a few *raciones* and share the plates family-style. This can be very economical if you don't over-order.

Tapas Bars

You can eat well any time of day in tapas bars. Tapas are small portions, like appetizers, of seafood, salads, meat-filled pastries,

deep-fried tasties, and on and on—normally displayed under glass at the bar.

Tapas typically cost about €2, up to €10 for seafood. Most bars push larger portions called *raciones* (dinner plate–sized) rather than smaller tapas (saucer-sized). Ask for the smaller tapas portions or a *media-ración* (listed as ½ *ración* on a menu), though many bars simply don't serve anything smaller than a *ración*.

Eating and drinking at a bar is usually cheapest if you eat or drink at the counter *(barra)*. You may pay a little more to eat sitting at a table *(mesa)* and still more for an outdoor table *(terraza)*. Locate the price list (often posted in fine type on a wall some-where) to know the menu options and price tiers. (It's bad form to order food at the bar, then take it to a table. If you're standing and a table opens up, it's OK to move as long as you signal to the waiter; anything else you order will be charged at the higher *mesa* price.) In the right place, a quiet snack and drink on a terrace on the town square is well worth the extra charge. But the cheapest seats sometimes get the best show. Sit at the bar and study your bartender—he's an artist.

Be assertive or you'll never be served. *Por favor* (please) grabs the guy's attention. Don't worry about paying until you're ready to leave (he's keeping track of your tab). To get the bill ask: *"¿La cuenta?"* (or *la dolorosa*—meaning literally "the sadness"—always draws a confused laugh). Bars come with a formidable language barrier. A small working vocabulary is essential for tapas pro-ficiency (see "Ordering Tapas" sidebar), and will help you eat better, too.

Chasing down a particular bar for tapas nearly defeats the purpose and spirit of tapas—they are impromptu. Just drop in at any lively place. I look for the noisy spots with piles of napkins and food debris on the floor (go local and toss your trash, too), lots of locals, and the TV blaring. Popular television-viewing includes bullfights and soccer games, American sitcoms, and Spanish inter-pretations of soaps and silly game shows (you'll see Vanna Blanco). While tapas are served all day, the real action begins late—21:00 at the earliest. But for beginners, an earlier start is easier and comes with less commotion.

Get a fun, inexpensive sampler plate. Ask for *una tabla de canapés variados* to get a plate of various little open-faced sand-wiches. Or ask for a *surtido de* (an assortment of...) *charcutería* (a mixed plate of meat) or *queso* (cheese). *Un surtido de jamón y queso* means a plate of different hams and cheeses. Order bread and two glasses of red wine on the right square—and you've got a romantic (and €10) dinner for two.

Spanish Drinks

Spain is one of the world's leading producers of grapes and that means lots of excellent wine: both red *(tinto)* and white *(blanco)*. Major wine regions include Valdepeñas, Penedès (Cabernet-style wines from near Barcelona), Rioja (spicy, lighter reds from the *tempranillo* grape, from the high plains of northern Spain), and Ribera del Duero (northwest of Madrid). For a basic glass of red wine, you can order *un tinto*. But for quality wine, ask for *un crianza* (old), *un reserva* (older), or *un gran reserva* (oldest). In fact, the single most important tip for good, economic wine-drinking

How Was Your Trip?

Were your travels fun, smooth, and meaningful? If you'd like to share your tips, concerns, and discoveries, please fill out the survey at www.ricksteves.com/feedback. I value your feedback. Thanks in advance—it helps a lot.

is to ask for *un crianza*—for little or no extra money, you'll get a quality, aged wine.

Sherry, a fortified wine from the Jerez region, is a shock to the taste buds if you're expecting a sweet dessert drink. It ranges from dry *(fino)* to sweet *(dulce)*—Spaniards drink the *fino* and export the *dulce*. *Cava* is Spain's answer to champagne. Sangria (a punch of red wine mixed with fruit slices) is popular and refreshing.

Most places just have the standard local beer—a light lager—on tap. The brand is determined by regional pride, rather than quality. (For instance, Cruzcampo—which is very light so that hot, thirsty drinkers can consume more—is big in the south, while San Miguel is big in the north.) Non-alcoholic beer is quite popular and often on tap. If you say *"sin,"* which means "without," it's assumed you want a non-alcoholic beer. While *sin* comes with less than 1 percent alcohol, you can get totally alcohol-free brew by asking for "zero point zero" (0.0). To get a small draft beer, ask for a *caña* (KAHN-yah). If you'd prefer a grape juice alternative to wine, ask for *mosto*. (It comes in red and white.)

Spain's bars often serve fresh-squeezed orange juice *(zumo de naranja natural)*. For something completely different, try *horchata de chufas,* a sweet, milky beverage made from *chufa* nuts (a.k.a. earth almonds). If ordering mineral water in a restaurant, request a *botella grande de agua* (big bottle). They push the more profitable small bottles.

Here are some words to help you quench your thirst:

agua con/sin gas	water with/without bubbles
un vasito de agua	glass of tap water (the waiter may counter with "A bottle?" hoping to sell you something. Be strong and insist on tap water and you'll get it.)
una jarra de agua	pitcher of tap water
refresco	soft drink (common brands are Coca-Cola; Fanta—*limón* or *naranja;* and Schweppes—*limón* or *tónica*)
mosto	non-alcoholic grape juice served wherever wine is served

un *tinto/blanco*	small glass of house red/white wine (generally table wine)
un *crianza*	your key to a glass of aged, quality wine
chato	small glass of house wine
tinto de verano	lighter sangria (more popular with locals than sangria)
vermú	vermouth
mucho cuerpo	full-bodied
afrutado	fruity
seco	dry
dulce	sweet
cerveza	beer
caña	small glass of draft beer
sin	non-alcoholic beer
doble, tubo	tall glass of beer
¡*Salud!*	Cheers!

Traveling as a Temporary Local

We travel all the way to Europe to enjoy differences—to become temporary locals. You'll experience frustrations. Certain truths that we find "God-given" or "self-evident," such as cold beer, ice in drinks, bottomless cups of coffee, hot showers, and bigger being better, are suddenly not so true. One of the benefits of travel is the eye-opening realization that there are logical, civil, and even better alternatives. A willingness to go local ensures that you'll enjoy a full dose of Spanish hospitality.

Americans are enjoying a huge surge of popularity these days. But if there is a negative aspect to the image the Spanish have of Americans, it's that we are big, loud, aggressive, impolite, rich, and a bit naive.

While Spaniards look bemusedly at some of our Yankee excesses—and worriedly at others—they nearly always afford us individual travelers all the warmth we deserve.

Judging from all the happy feedback I receive from travelers who have used this book, it's safe to assume you'll enjoy a great, affordable vacation—with the finesse of an independent, experienced traveler.

Thanks, and *buen viaje!*

Back Door Travel Philosophy
From *Rick Steves' Europe Through the Back Door*

Travel is intensified living—maximum thrills per minute and one of the last great sources of legal adventure. Travel is freedom. It's recess, and we need it.

Experiencing the real Europe requires catching it by surprise, going casual..."Through the Back Door."

Affording travel is a matter of priorities. (Make do with the old car.) You can eat and sleep—simply, safely, and enjoyably—anywhere in Europe for $120 a day plus transportation costs. In many ways, spending more money only builds a thicker wall between you and what you traveled so far to see. Europe is a cultural carnival, and time after time, you'll find that its best acts are free and the best seats are the cheap ones.

A tight budget forces you to travel close to the ground, meeting and communicating with the people. Never sacrifice sleep, nutrition, safety, or cleanliness to save money. Simply enjoy the local-style alternatives to expensive hotels and restaurants.

Connecting with people carbonates your experience. Extroverts have more fun. If your trip is low on magic moments, kick yourself and make things happen. If you don't enjoy a place, maybe you don't know enough about it. Seek the truth. Recognize tourist traps. Give a culture the benefit of your open mind. See things as different, but not better or worse. Any culture has plenty to share.

Of course, travel, like the world, is a series of hills and valleys. Be fanatically positive and militantly optimistic. If something's not to your liking, change your liking.

Travel can make you a happier American, as well as a citizen of the world. Our Earth is home to six and a half billion equally precious people. It's humbling to travel and find that other people don't have the "American Dream"—they have their own dreams. Europeans like us, but with all due respect, they wouldn't trade passports.

Thoughtful travel engages us with the world. In tough economic times, it reminds us what is truly important. By broadening perspectives, travel teaches new ways to measure quality of life.

Globetrotting destroys ethnocentricity, helping us understand and appreciate other cultures. Rather than fear the diversity on this planet, celebrate it. Among your most prized souvenirs will be the strands of different cultures you choose to knit into your own character. The world is a cultural yarn shop, and Back Door travelers are weaving the ultimate tapestry. Join in!

BARCELONA

Barcelona is Spain's second city, and the capital of the proud and distinct region of Catalunya. With Franco's fascism now ancient history, Catalan flags wave once again. And the local language and culture are on a roll in Spain's most cosmopolitan and European corner.

Barcelona bubbles with life in its narrow Barri Gòtic alleys, along the grand boulevards, and throughout the chic, grid-planned, new part of town, called Eixample. While Barcelona had an illustrious past as a Roman colony, Visigothic capital, 14th-century maritime power, and—in more modern times—a top Mediterranean textile and manufacturing center, it's most enjoyable to throw out the history books and just drift through the city. If you're in the mood to surrender to a city's charms, let it be in Barcelona.

Planning Your Time

Located in the far northeast corner of Spain, Barcelona makes a good first or last stop for your trip. With the new AVE train, Barcelona is three hours away from Madrid. Or you could sandwich Barcelona between flights. From the US, it's as easy to fly into Barcelona as it is to land in Madrid, Lisbon, or Paris. Those who plan on renting a car at some point in their trip can cleverly start here first, fly or train to Madrid, and sightsee Madrid and Toledo, all before picking up their car—saving on several days' worth of rental fees.

On the shortest visit, Barcelona is worth one night, one day, and an evening flight or train ride out. The Ramblas is two different streets by day and by night. Stroll it from top to bottom in the evening and again the next morning, grabbing breakfast on a stool

Barcelona Overview

SEE DETAIL MAPS

1 MILE
1 KM

TIBIDABO
PARC GÜELL
AV. HOSP. MIL.
PLAÇA LESSEPS
TRAV. DE DALT
CARRER GRAN DE GRÁCIA →
GRÁCIA
SAGRADA FAMÍLIA
GRAN VIA
TO FÒRUM
TO FÒRUM
DIAGONAL
BLOCK OF DISCORD
CASA MILÀ
PASSEIG DE GRÀCIA
CITADEL PARK
OLYMPIC PORT
THE EIXAMPLE
PLAÇA DE CATALUNYA
PICASSO MUSEUM
MIRÓ PARK
OLD CITY
FRANÇA STN.
BEACH
SANTS STATION
PLAÇA D'ESPANYA
LAS RAMBLAS
BARCELONETA
MAREMAGNUM
TO MADRID
PARAL-LEL
FOUNTAINS
MIRÓ MUS.
PORT
SPANISH VILLAGE
CABLE CAR
FUNICULAR
GRAN VIA
CATALAN ART MUSEUM
OLYMPIC STADIUM
TO AIRPORT
MONTJUÏC
DCH
CRUISE SHIP TERMINAL
M E D. S E A

in a market café. Wander the Barri Gòtic (BAH-ree GOH-teek), see the cathedral, and have lunch in the Eixample (eye-SHAM-plah). The top two sights in town, Antoni Gaudí's Sagrada Família church and the Picasso Museum, are usually open until 20:00 during the summer (Picasso closed Mon). Note that if you want to tour the Catalan Concert Hall with its oh-wow Modernista interior, you'll need to reserve at least two days in advance (see page 68). The illuminated Magic Fountains on Montjuïc make a good finale for your day.

Of course, Barcelona in a day is insane. To better sample the city's ample charm, spread your visit over two or three days. With two days, you could divide-and-conquer the town geographically: one day for the Barri Gòtic (Ramblas, cathedral area, Picasso Museum); and another for the Eixample and Gaudí sights (Casa

Milà, Sagrada Família, Parc Güell). Do Montjuïc on whichever day you're not exhausted (if any).

With more time, several tempting day trips await nearby—see the Near Barcelona chapter for tips on Montserrat, Sitges, and the Salvador Dalí sights at Figueres and Cadaqués.

Orientation to Barcelona

Like Los Angeles, Barcelona is a basically flat city that sprawls out under the sun between the sea and the mountains. It's huge (1.6 million people, with about 4 million people in greater Barcelona), but travelers need only focus on four areas: the Old City, the harbor/Barceloneta, the Eixample, and Montjuïc.

A large square, Plaça de Catalunya, sits at the center of Barcelona, dividing the older and newer parts of town. Sloping downhill from the Plaça de Catalunya is the Old City, with the boulevard called the Ramblas running down to the harbor. Above Plaça de Catalunya is the modern residential area called the Eixample. The Montjuïc hill overlooks the harbor. Outside the Old City, Barcelona's sights are widely scattered. But with a map and a willingness to figure out the sleek Metro system (or a few euros for taxis), all is manageable.

Here are more details per neighborhood:

The **Old City** is where you'll probably spend most of your time. This is the compact soul of Barcelona—your strolling, shopping, and people-watching nucleus. It's a labyrinth of narrow streets that once were confined by the medieval walls. The lively pedestrian drag called the **Ramblas**—one of Europe's great people-watching streets—runs through the heart of the Old City from Plaça de Catalunya down to the harbor. The Old City is divided into thirds by the Ramblas and another major thoroughfare, Via Laietana. To the west of the Ramblas is the **Raval,** enlivened by its university and modern-art museum. The Raval is of least interest to tourists (and, in fact, some parts of it are quite seedy and should be avoided). Far better is the **Barri Gòtic** (Gothic Quarter), between the Ramblas and Via Laietana, with the cathedral as its navel. To the east of Via Laietana is the trendy **Ribera** district (a.k.a. "El Born"), centered on the Picasso Museum and the Church of Santa Maria del Mar.

The **harborfront** has been energized since the 1992 Olympics. A pedestrian bridge links the Ramblas with the modern

Cheap Tricks in Barcelona

- Arriving by train? Save time, hassle, and the cost of a Metro ride by finding out if your train stops at any of the handy downtown stations (such as Passeig de Gràcia or Plaça de Catalunya). But remember that AVE trains from Madrid stop only at the Sants Station.

- If connecting to cities elsewhere in Spain, don't overlook budget flights—which can be cheaper and faster than the train or bus (for tips, see page 729).

- For getting around the city, skip taxis and the Tourist Bus, and instead use the excellent network of Metro and buses. The T10 Card (10 rides for €7.70) makes the system super-cheap—each ride costs €0.77 instead of €1.35 for an individual ticket.

- If visiting the cathedral, go when it's free, 8:00–12:45 (until 13:45 on Sun) or 17:15–19:30; at other times, you'll pay €5 to see essentially the same thing (but note that it will cost you €2.20 to ride the elevator to the roof or to turn on the lights in the choir, both of which are included in the €5 fee). Several interesting sights around the cathedral (such as the Deacon's House and Roman Temple) are also free to enter, as well as the nearby Church of Santa Maria del Mar in La Ribera.

- One of Barcelona's most delightful Modernista sights, Antoni Gaudí's Parc Güell, is free and an enjoyable place to relax. Some expensive Gaudí sights (such as Casa Milà, Casa Batlló, and the Sagrada Família) can be just as interesting from the outside, without paying the entry fee. For a free glimpse at a Gaudí interior, visit Palau Güell (only part of the building is open during renovation, and it may begin charging admission when completed, sometime in 2011).

- Some museums have certain days and times when they don't charge admission: the Picasso and City History museums (first Sun of month and Sun afternoon), Catalan Art Museum (first Sun of month), and Frederic Marès Museum (Wed and Sun afternoon).

- When tapas-hopping, note that trendy, upscale neighborhoods—such as the Eixample and La Ribera—come with higher prices. For a cheaper and more characteristic meal, find a blue-collar neighborhood (such as Carrer de la Mercè).

Maremagnum shopping/aquarium complex. On the peninsula across the harbor is **Barceloneta,** a traditional fishing neighborhood that's home to some good seafood restaurants and a string of sandy beaches. Beyond Barceloneta, a man-made beach, several miles long, leads east to a new commercial and convention district called the **Fòrum.**

North of the Old City, beyond the bustling hub of Plaça de Catalunya, is the elegant **Eixample** district—its grid plan softened by cut-off corners. Much of Barcelona's Modernista architecture is found here. To the north is the **Gràcia** district, and beyond that, Antoni Gaudí's **Parc Güell.**

The large hill overlooking the city to the southwest is **Montjuïc,** home to a variety of attractions including some excellent museums (Catalan Art, Joan Miró) and the Olympic Stadium.

Apart from your geographical orientation, you'll need to orient yourself linguistically to a language distinct from Spanish. While Spanish ("Castilian") is widely spoken, the native tongue in this region is Catalan—nearly as different from Spanish as Italian (see the sidebar on page 44).

Tourist Information

Barcelona's TI has several branches. The main one is at **Plaça de Catalunya** (daily 9:00–21:00, under the main square near recommended hotels—look for red sign, tel. 932-853-832). Other convenient branches include at the top of the **Ramblas** (daily 9:00–21:00, at #115); **Plaça de Sant Jaume,** just south of the cathedral (Mon–Fri 9:00–20:00, Sat 10:00–20:00, Sun 10:00–14:00); **Plaça d'Espanya** (daily July–Sept 10:00–20:00, Oct–June 10:00–16:00); the **airport** (daily 9:00–21:00, offices in both terminals A and B); **Sants train station** (Mon–Fri 8:00–20:00, Sat–Sun 8:00–14:00, near track 6); **Nord bus station** (daily July–Sept 9:00–21:00, Oct–June 9:00–15:00); and more. Throughout the summer, young red-jacketed tourist-info helpers appear in the most touristy parts of town. The central information number for all TIs is 932-853-834 (www.barcelonaturisme.cat).

At any TI, pick up the free city map (can be hard to read—consider springing for a better one for €1), the small Metro map, and the free quarterly *See Barcelona* guide (practical information on museum hours, restaurants, transportation, history, festivals, and so on). The monthly *Barcelona Metropolitan* magazine and quarterly *What's On Barcelona* (both free and in English) have timely and substantial coverage of topics and events. The TI is a handy place to buy tickets for the Tourist Bus (described later, under "Getting Around Barcelona"). Some TIs (at Plaça de Catalunya, Plaça de Sant Jaume, and the airport) also provide a room-booking service.

The main TI, at Plaça de Catalunya, offers guided walks

(described later, under "Tours"). Its Modernisme desk gives out a handy route map showing all the Modernista buildings and offers a sightseeing discount package (€12 for a great guidebook and 20 percent discounts to many Modernisme sites—worthwhile if going beyond my big three; for €18 you'll also get a guidebook to Modernista bars and restaurants).

The **all-Catalunya TI** works fine for the entire region and even Madrid (Mon–Sat 10:00–19:00, Sun 10:00–14:00, on Plaça de Joan Carlos I, at the intersection of Diagonal and Passeig de Gràcia, Passeig de Gràcia 107, tel. 932-388-091).

Articket Card: This ticket includes admission to seven art museums and their temporary exhibits, including the recommended Picasso Museum, Casa Milà, Catalan Art Museum, and Fundació Joan Miró (€20, valid for six months, sold at TIs and participating museums, www.articketbcn.org). If you're planning to go to three or more of the museums, this time-saver pays for itself. To skip the ticket-buying line at a museum, show your Articket Card (to the ticket-taker, at the info desk, or at the group entrance), and you'll get your entrance ticket pronto.

Barcelona Card: This card covers public transportation (buses, Metro, Montjuïc funicular, and *golondrina* harbor tour) and includes free admission to minor sights and discounts on major sights (€26/2 days, €31.50/3 days, €36/4 days, €42/5 days, sold at TIs and El Corte Inglés department store).

Arrival in Barcelona

By Train: Virtually all trains end up at Barcelona's Sants train station (described below). But be aware that many trains also pass through other stations en route, such as **França Station** (between the Ribera and Barceloneta neighborhoods), or the downtown **Passeig de Gràcia** or **Plaça de Catalunya** stations (which are also Metro stops—and very close to most of my recommended hotels). Figure out which stations your train stops at, and get off at the one most convenient to your hotel. (AVE trains from Madrid go only to Sants Station.)

Sants Station is vast and sprawling, but manageable. In the large lobby area under the upper tracks, you'll find a TI, ATMs, a world of handy shops and eateries, and a classy, quiet Sala Euromed lounge for travelers with first-class reservations (TV, free drinks, study tables, and coffee bar). Sants is the only Barcelona station with luggage storage (small bag-€3/ day, big bag-€4.50/day, must go through security check, daily 5:30–23:00, follow signs to *consigna*, at far end of hallway from tracks 13–14).

There's also a long wall of ticket windows. Figure out which is right for you before you wait in line (all are labeled in English). Generally, the first stretch (on the left, windows 1–8) is for local trains, such as to Sitges; the next group (windows 9–21) handles advance tickets for long-distance trains; farther to the right are information windows (22–26)—go here first if you're not sure which window you want; and those at the right end (windows 27–31) sell tickets for long-distance trains leaving today. Attendants are often standing by to help you find the right line. If you know what you want, there are also automated train-ticket vending machines.

To get into downtown Barcelona from Sants Station, simply follow signs for the Metro. The L3 (green) line—described later, under "Getting Around Barcelona"—zips you directly to a number of useful points in town, including all of my recommended hotels. You can also save time by taking the *cercanías* local trains to Plaça de Catalunya, just five minutes away. Lines C1, C3, C4, or C7, departing from track 8, all take you there. Or when a train is pulling in, look at the red letter board listing the stops—Plaça de Catalunya is the first stop on the list. You can purchase tickets (€1.35) at touch-screen machines near the tracks or use your T10 card (explained later, under "Getting Around Barcelona").

If departing from the downtown **Passeig de Gràcia Station,** where three Metro lines converge with the rail line, you might find the underground tunnels confusing. You can't access the RENFE Station directly from some of the entrances. Use the northern entrances to this station (rather than the southern "Consell de Cent" entrance, which is closest to Plaça de Catalunya).

By Plane: Barcelona's **El Prat de Llobregat Airport,** eight miles southwest of town, has three terminals: A, B, and C. The bigger terminals A and B each have a post office, pharmacy, left-luggage office, plenty of good cafeterias in the gate areas, and ATMs (avoid the gimmicky machines before the baggage carousels; instead, use the bank-affiliated ATMs at the far-left end of the arrivals hall as you face the street). Airport info tel. 902-404-704.

You have two options for getting downtown cheaply and quickly: The **Aerobus** (#A1) stops immediately outside the arrivals lobby of all three terminals and in about 30 minutes takes you to downtown, where it makes several stops, including Plaça d'Espanya, Plaça de Catalunya (near many of my recommended hotels), and Passeig de Gràcia (near more hotels; every 6 min, from airport 6:00–1:00 in the morning, from downtown 5:30–24:15, buy €4.25 ticket from machine or from driver, tel. 934-156-020). The line to board the bus can be very long, but—thanks to the high frequency of buses—it moves fast.

The second option is the RENFE **train,** which involves more walking. Head down the long orange-roofed overpass between terminals A and B to reach the station (line 2, 2/hr at about :08 and :38 past the hour, 20 min to Sants Station, 25 min to Passeig de Gràcia Station—near Plaça de Catalunya and many recommended hotels, 30 min to França Station; €2.70 or covered by T10 Card, which you can purchase at automated machines at the airport train station).

A **taxi** between the airport and downtown costs about €25.

Some budget airlines, including Ryanair, use **Girona–Costa Brava Airport,** located 60 miles north of Barcelona near Girona. Sagalés buses link to Barcelona (departures timed to meet flights, 70 min, €12, tel. 935-931-300 or 902-361-550, www.sagales.com). You can also go to Girona via a Sagalés bus (hourly, 25 min, €2.85) or a taxi (€20), then catch a train to Barcelona (at least hourly, 70 min, €7). A taxi between the Girona airport and Barcelona costs at least €120. Airport info tel. 972-186-600.

By Car: Barcelona's parking fees are outrageously expensive (the one behind La Boquería market charges upwards of €25/day). You won't need a car in Barcelona because the taxis and public transportation are so good.

By Cruise Ship: If you're arriving by boat, it's about a five-minute ride (almost a mile) from the dock to the bottom of the Ramblas. The blue port-run Lanzadera bus takes you to the Columbus Monument at the bottom of the Ramblas, near the Metro Drassanes stop (€3 round-trip, €2 one-way, buses leave every 20–30 min when cruise ships arrive, tel. 932-986-000). From there you can walk or Metro to your destination. You can also taxi from the port into the center (about €15 to Plaça de Catalunya).

Helpful Hints

Theft Alert: You're more likely to be pickpocketed here—especially on the Ramblas—than about anywhere else in Europe. Most of the crime is nonviolent, but muggings do occur. Leave valuables in your hotel and wear a money belt.

Street scams are easy to avoid if you recognize them. Most common is the too-friendly local who tries to engage you in conversation by asking for the time, talking sports, asking whether you speak English, and so on. Beware of thieves posing as lost tourists who ask for your help. A typical street gambling scam is the pea-and-carrot game, a variation on the shell game. The people winning are all ringers, and you can be sure that you'll lose if you play. Also beware of groups of women aggressively selling carnations, people offering to clean off a stain from your shirt, and people picking things up in front of you on escalators. If you stop for any commotion or show on the Ramblas, put your hands in your pockets before someone else does. Assume any scuffle is simply a distraction by a team of thieves. Crooks are inventive, so keep your guard up. Don't be intimidated...just be smart.

Some areas feel seedy and can be unsafe after dark; I'd avoid the southern part of the Barri Gòtic (basically the two or three blocks directly south and east of Plaça Reial—though the strip near the Carrer de la Mercè tapas bars is better), and I wouldn't venture too deep into the Raval (just west of the Ramblas). One block can separate a comfy tourist zone from the junkies and prostitutes.

US Consulate: It's at Passeig Reina Elisenda 23 (passport services Mon–Fri 9:00–13:00, closed Sat–Sun, tel. 932-802-227).

Emergency Phone Numbers: General emergencies—112, police—092, ambulance—061 or 112.

Internet Access: Navega Web has hundreds of computers for accessing the Internet and burning pictures onto a CD. It's conveniently located across from La Boquería market, downstairs in the bright Centre Comercial New Park (daily 10:00–24:00, Ramblas 88–94, tel. 933-179-193).

Pharmacy: A 24-hour pharmacy is near La Boquería market at #98 on the Ramblas.

Laundry: Several self-service launderettes are located around the Old City. **Wash 'n Dry** is on the edge of the tourist zone, near a seedy neighborhood just down the street past the Palau Güell (self-service: wash-€5/load, dry-€2/load, daily 7:00–22:00; full-service: €15/load, daily 9:00–22:00; Carrer Nou de la Rambla 19, tel. 934-121-953).

Bike Rental: Biking is a joy in Citadel Park and along the beach (suggested route described on page 71)—but it's stressful in the city center, where pedestrians and cars rule. There are plenty of bike-rental places around Citadel Park and La Ribera's Church of Santa Maria del Mar. The handy **Un Cotxe Menys** ("One Car Less"), near the Church of Santa Maria del Mar (50 yards behind the flame memorial), rents bikes and gives out maps and proposed biking routes (€5/hr, €11/4 hrs, daily 10:00–19:00, leave €150 or photo ID for deposit, Esparteria 3, tel. 932-682-105, www.bicicleta barcelona.com); they also lead bike tours (see "Tours," page 47). To rent a bike on the Barceloneta beach, consider **Biciclot** (€6/hr, €13/3 hrs, €18/24 hrs; summer Mon–Thu 10:00–15:00 & 16:00–20:00, Fri–Sun 10:00–15:00 & 16:00–21:00; off-season Sat–Sun only; on the sand 300 yards from Olympic Village towers at Passeig Maritime 33, tel. 932-219-778). Closer to downtown, **Barcelona Rent-A-Bike** is three blocks downhill from Plaça de Catalunya (€6/2 hrs, €10/4 hrs,

€15/24 hrs, daily 9:00–20:00, inside the courtyard at Carrer dels Tallers 45, tel. 933-171-970).

Getting Around Barcelona

By Public Transit: Barcelona's Metro, among Europe's best, connects just about every place you'll visit. Rides cost €1.35. Given the excellent Metro service, it's unlikely you'll take a local bus (also €1.35), although I've noted the places where the bus makes sense. The T10 Card is a great deal—€7.70 gives you 10 rides, and the card is shareable. It's good on all Metro and local bus lines as well as the RENFE train lines (including rides to the airport and train station) and the suburban FGC lines (with service to Montserrat; see Near Barcelona chapter). Full-day and multi-day passes are also available (€5.80/1 day, €10.70/2 days, €15.20/3 days, €19.50/4 days, €23.10/5 days). Automated machines at the Metro entrance have English instructions and sell all types of tickets (these can be temperamental about accepting bills, so try to have change on hand).

Pick up the free Metro map (at any TI) and study it to get familiar with the system. There

are several color-coded lines, but most useful for tourists is the **L3 (green) line;** if you're sticking to my recommended sights and neighborhoods, you'll barely have use for any other. Handy city-center stops on this line include (in order):

Sants Estació—Main train station;

Espanya—Plaça d'Espanya, with access to the lower part of Montjuïc and trains to Montserrat;

Paral·lel—Funicular to top of Montjuïc;

Drassanes—Bottom of the Ramblas, near Maritime Museum, Maremagnum mall, and the cable car up to Montjuïc;

Liceu—Middle of the Ramblas, near the heart of the Barri Gòtic and cathedral;

Plaça de Catalunya—Top of the Ramblas and main square with TI, airport bus, and lots of transportation connections;

Passeig de Gràcia—Classy Eixample street at the Block of Discord; also connection to L2 (purple) line to Sagrada Família and L4 (yellow) line—described below;

Diagonal—Gaudí's Casa Milà; and

Lesseps—Walk or catch bus #24 to Gaudí's Parc Güell.

The **L4 (yellow) line,** which crosses the L3 (green) line at Passeig de Gràcia, is also useful. Helpful stops along here include **Jaume I** (between the Barri Gòtic/cathedral and La Ribera/

Picasso Museum) and **Barceloneta** (at the south end of the Ribera, near the harbor action).

When you enter the Metro, first look for your line number and color, then follow signs to take that line in the direction you're going. Insert your ticket into the turnstile (with the arrow pointing in), then reclaim it. On board, most trains have handy Metro-line diagrams with dots that light up next to upcoming destinations. Because the lines cross each other multiple times, there can be several ways to make any one journey. (It's a good idea to keep a general map with you—especially if you're transferring or just need a map of the entire metro system.) Watch your valuables. (If I were a pickpocket, I'd set up shop along the made-for-tourists L3/green line.)

By Tourist Bus: The handy Tourist Bus (Bus Turístic) offers three multi-stop circuits in colorful double-decker buses that go topless in sunny weather. The two-hour red route covers north Barcelona (most Gaudí sights); the two-hour blue route covers south Barcelona (Barri Gòtic, Montjuïc); and the shorter, 40-minute green route covers the beaches and Fòrum. All have headphone commentary (44 stops, daily 9:00–22:00 in summer, 9:00–21:00 in winter, buses run every 5–25 min, most frequent in summer, no green route Oct–March). Ask for a brochure (includes city map) at the TI or at a pick-up point. One-day (€21) and two-day (€27) tickets, which you can buy on the bus or at the TI, offer 10–20 percent discounts on the city's major sights and walking tours, which will likely save you about the equivalent of half the cost of the Tourist Bus.

By Taxi: Barcelona is one of Europe's best taxi towns. Taxis are plentiful (there are more than 10,000) and honest (whether they like it or not—the light on top shows which tariff they're charging). They're also reasonable (€2 drop charge, €1/kilometer, these "*Tarif 2*" rates are in effect 7:00–21:00, pay higher "*Tarif 1*" rates off-hours, luggage-€1/piece, other fees posted in window). Save time by hopping a cab (figure €8 from Ramblas to Sants Station).

Tours in Barcelona

Walking Tours—The TI at Plaça de Catalunya offers great guided walks through the **Barri Gòtic** in English only (€12, daily at 10:00, 2 hours, groups limited to 35, departs from the TI, buy your ticket 15 minutes early at the TI desk—not from the guide,

"You're not in Spain, You're in Catalunya!"

This is a popular nationalistic refrain you might see on T-shirts or stickers around town. Catalunya is *not* the land of bullfighting and flamenco that many visitors envision when they think of Spain (best to wait until you're in Madrid or Sevilla for those).

The region of Catalunya—with Barcelona as its capital—has its own language, history, and culture, and the people have a proud, independent spirit. Historically, Catalunya ("Cataluña" in Spanish, sometimes spelled "Catalonia" in English) has often been at odds with the central Spanish government in Madrid. The Catalan language and culture were discouraged or even outlawed at various times in Spanish history, as Catalunya often chose the wrong side in wars and rebellions against the kings in Madrid. In the Spanish Civil War (1936–1939), Catalunya was one of the last pockets of democratic resistance against the military coup of the fascist dictator Francisco Franco, who punished the region with four decades of repression. During that time, the Catalan flag was banned—but locals vented their national spirit by flying their football team's flag instead.

Three of Barcelona's monuments are reminders of Franco-era suppression. Citadel Park (Parc de la Ciutadella) was originally a much-despised military citadel, constructed in the 18th century to keep locals in line. The Castle of Montjuïc, built for similar reasons, has been the site of numerous political executions, including hundreds during the Franco era. The Sacred Heart Church atop Tibidabo, completed under Franco, was meant to atone for the sins of Barcelonans during the Spanish Civil War—the main sin being opposition to Franco. Although rivalry between Barcelona and Madrid has calmed down in recent times, it rages any time the two cities' football clubs meet.

in summer call ahead to reserve, tel. 933-043-123, www.barcelona-turisme.com). A local guide will explain the medieval story of the city as you walk from Plaça de Catalunya through the cathedral neighborhood, finishing at City Hall on Plaça de Sant Jaume. The TI also offers a **Picasso** walk, taking you through the streets of his youth and early career and finishing in the Picasso Museum (€18, includes museum admission, Tue, Thu, Sun at 16:00, 2 hours plus museum visit). There are also **gourmet** walks (€15, Fri and Sat at 11:00, 2 hours) and **Modernisme** walks (€12, Fri and Sat June–Sept at 18:00, Oct–May at 16:00, 2 hours). All tours depart

To see real Catalan culture, look for the *sardana* dance (described on page 62) or an exhibition of *castellers*. These teams of human-castle builders come together for festivals throughout the year to build towers of flesh that can reach more than 50 feet high, topped off by the bravest member of the team—a child! The Gràcia festival in August and the Mercè festival in September are good times to catch the *castellers*.

The Catalan language is irrevocably tied to the history and spirit of the people here. Since the end of the Franco era in the mid-1970s, the language has made a huge resurgence. Now most school-age children learn Catalan first and Spanish second. Although Spanish is understood here (and the basic survival words are the same), Barcelona speaks Catalan.

Here are the essential Catalan phrases:

English	Catalan	Pronounced
Hello	*Hola*	OH-lah
Please	*Si us plau*	see oos plow
Thank you	*Gracies*	GRAH-see-es
Goodbye	*Adéu*	ah-DAY-oo
Exit	*Sortida*	sor-TEE-dah
Long live Catalunya!	*¡Visca Catalunya!*	BEE-skah kah-tah-LOON-yah

Most place names in this chapter are listed in Catalan. Here's a pronunciation guide:

Plaça de Catalunya	PLAS-sah duh cat-ah-LOON-yah
Eixample	eye-SHAM-plah
Passeig de Gràcia	PAH-sage duh grass-EE-ah
Catedral	KAH-tah-dral
Barri Gòtic	BAH-ree GOH-teek
Montjuïc	MOHN-jew-eek

from the TI at Plaça de Catalunya.

Bus Tours—The Barcelona Guide Bureau offers several sightseeing tours leaving from Plaça de Catalunya. The **Gaudí** tour visits the facades of Casa Batlló and Casa Milà, as well as Parc Güell and the Sagrada Família (€42, includes Sagrada Família admission, daily at 9:00, 3 hours). Other tours offered year-round include: the **Montjuïc** tour (€30, daily at 12:00, 3 hours), the **All Barcelona Highlights** tour (€60, daily at 9:00, 6 hours), and the **Montserrat** tour (€40, daily at 15:00, 4 hours), which offers a convenient way to get to this mountaintop monastery if you don't want to deal with

Barcelona at a Glance

▲▲▲**Ramblas** Barcelona's colorful, gritty, tourist-filled pedestrian thoroughfare. **Hours:** Always open. See page 48.

▲▲▲**Picasso Museum** Extensive collection offering insight into the brilliant Spanish artist's early years. **Hours:** Tue-Sun 10:00-20:00, closed Mon. See page 64.

▲▲▲**Sagrada Família** Gaudí's remarkable, unfinished cathedral. **Hours:** Daily April-Sept 9:00-20:00, Oct-March 9:00-18:00. See page 77.

▲▲**City History Museum** One-stop trip through town history, from Roman times to today. **Hours:** Tue-Sat April-Sept 10:00-20:00, Oct-March 10:00-14:00 & 16:00-19:00, Sun 10:00-20:00, closed Mon. See page 63.

▲▲**Catalan Concert Hall** Best Modernista interior in Barcelona. **Hours:** 50-minute English tours daily every hour 10:00-15:00, plus frequent concerts. See page 68.

▲▲**Casa Milà** Barcelona's quintessential Modernista building, the famous melting-ice-cream Gaudí creation. **Hours:** Daily March-Oct 9:00-20:00, Nov-Feb 9:00-18:30. See page 74.

▲▲**Catalan Art Museum** World-class collection of this region's art, including a substantial Romanesque collection. **Hours:** Tue-Sat 10:00-19:00, Sun 10:00-14:30, closed Mon. See page 87.

▲**Maritime Museum** Housed in an impressive medieval shipyard, it's a sailor's delight. **Hours:** Daily 10:00-19:45. See page 59.

▲**Columbus Monument** Elevator ride to the best easy view in town. **Hours:** Daily May-Oct 9:00-20:30, Nov-April 10:00-18:30. See page 59.

---

public transportation (see Near Barcelona chapter). From April through October, the bureau offers the **Gaudí Beyond the City** tour of "off-the-beaten-path masterpieces" (€30, daily at 12:30, 3 hours), the **Modernisme & World Heritage** tour (€30, Mon, Wed, Fri at 15:30, 3 hours), the **New Architecture** tour (€30, Tue, Thu, Sat at 15:30, 3 hours), and for soccer fans the **Barça** tour (€30, daily at 9:30, 3 hours), which takes you to the Camp Nou stadium. You can get detailed information and book tickets at a TI, by going online, or simply by showing up at their departure point on Plaça de Catalunya in front of the Hard Rock Café—look for the guides

▲Cathedral of Barcelona Colossal Gothic cathedral ringed by distinctive chapels. **Hours:** Daily 8:00–19:30. See page 60.

▲Sardana Dances Patriotic dance in which proud Catalans join hands in a circle. **Hours:** Every Sun at 12:00, usually also Sat at 18:00. See page 62.

▲Church of Santa Maria del Mar Catalan Gothic church in La Ribera, built by wealthy medieval shippers. **Hours:** Daily 9:00–13:30 & 16:30–20:00. See page 69.

▲Barcelona's Beach Fun-filled, man-made stretch of sand reaching from the harbor to the Fòrum. **Hours:** Always open. See page 71.

▲Block of Discord Noisy block of competing Modernista facades by Gaudí and his rivals. **Hours:** Always viewable. See page 76.

▲Palau Güell Exquisitely curvy Gaudí interior. **Hours:** Tue–Sat 10:00–14:30, closed Sun-Mon. See page 76.

▲Parc Güell Colorful park at the center of an unfinished Gaudí-designed housing project. **Hours:** Daily 10:00–20:00. See page 82.

▲Fundació Joan Miró World's best collection of works by Catalan modern artist Joan Miró. **Hours:** Tue–Sat July–Sept 10:00–20:00, Oct–June 10:00–19:00, Thu until 21:30, Sun 10:00–14:30, closed Mon. See page 86.

▲Magic Fountains Lively fountains near Plaça d'Espanya. **Hours:** almost always May–Sept Thu–Sun 21:00–23:30, no shows Mon–Wed; Oct–April Fri–Sat 19:00–21:00, no shows Sun–Thu. See page 88.

holding orange umbrellas (tel. 933-152-261, www.barcelonaguide bureau.com).

Bike Tours—Several companies run bike tours around Barcelona. **Un Cotxe Menys** ("One Car Less") organizes three-hour English-only bike tours daily at 11:00 (April–mid-Sept also Fri–Mon at 16:30). Your guide leads you from sight to sight, mostly on bike paths and through parks, with a stop-and-go commentary (€22 includes bike rental and a drink, reservations not necessary, just show up at Plaça de Sant Jaume, next to the TI, tel. 932-682-105, www.biketoursbarcelona.com, also see bike-rental listing earlier under "Helpful Hints").

Local Guides—The Barcelona Guide Bureau is a co-op with about 20 local guides who give personalized four-hour tours starting at €202 (per person price drops as group gets bigger); **Joana Wilhelm** and **Carles Picazo** are excellent (Via Laietana 54, tel. 932-682-422 or 933-107-778, www.bgb.es). **Jose Soler** is a great and fun-to-be-with local guide who enjoys tailoring a walk through his hometown to your interests (€195/half-day per group, mobile 615-059-326, www.pepitotours.com, info@pepitotours.com).

Self-Guided Walks

Most visitors to Barcelona spend much of their time in the twisty, atmospheric Old City. These two walks will give meaning to your wandering. The first begins at Barcelona's main square and leads you down the city's main drag through one of Europe's best public spaces: the Ramblas. The second walk starts at the same square, but guides you into the heart of the Barri Gòtic, to the neighborhood around Barcelona's impressive cathedral.

▲▲▲The Ramblas Ramble: From Plaça de Catalunya down the Ramblas

Barcelona's central square and main boulevard exert a powerful pull. Many visitors spend the majority of their time doing laps on the Ramblas. While the allure of the Ramblas is fading (as tacky tourist shops and fast-food joints replace its former elegance), this is still a fun people zone that offers a good introduction to the city. See it, but be sure to venture farther afield. Here's a top-to-bottom orientation walk.

Plaça de Catalunya: This vast central square divides old and new Barcelona. It's also the hub for the Metro, bus, airport shuttle, and Tourist Bus (red northern route leaves from El Corte Inglés—described below; blue southern route leaves from the west, or Ramblas, side of the square). Overlooking the square, the huge **El Corte Inglés** department store offers everything from bonsai trees to a travel agency, plus one-hour photo developing, haircuts, and cheap souvenirs (Mon–Sat

10:00–22:00, closed Sun, pick up English directory flier, supermarket in basement, ninth-floor terrace cafeteria/restaurant has great city view—take elevator from entrance nearest the TI,

From Plaça de Catalunya down the Ramblas

NOT TO SCALE-
PLAÇA DE CATALUNYA TO COLUMBUS
MONUMENT IS A 30 MIN. WALK

- Ramblas
- Ⓜ Metro Station
- Ⓑ Bus Stop

TO Block of Discord

RAMBLA DE CATALUNYA

DE GRÀCIA

PASSEIG

BLUE TOURIST BUS

FNAC DEP'T. STORE

FGC TRAIN INFO

CAFÉ ZÜRICH

PLAÇA DE CATALUNYA
Ⓜ Catalunya

EL CORTE INGLÉS DEP'T. STORE

CANALETES FOUNTAIN

Ⓜ

❶ BIRDS

SANTA ANNA

AV. PORTAL DE L'ANGEL

AEROBUS, RED TOURIST BUS + TAXIS

ACADEMY OF SCIENCE

❷

CAFÉ GRANJA VIADER

BAROQUE CHURCH ✝ ❸

CARME

CANUDA

ROMAN NECROPOLIS

CULTURAL INFO PALAU DE LA VIRREINA

Ⓜ Liceu

FLOWER

PORTAFERRISSA

PHARMACY CIGARS

LA BOQUERÍA MARKET

❹

CARDENAL

EROTIC MUSEUM

HOSP.

BOQ.

"UMBRELLA" BLDG.

BARRI XINES

S. PAU

Miró Mosaic

FERRAN

TO PLAÇA DE S. JAUME

LICEU OPERA HOUSE

Ⓜ Liceu

NOU RAMBLA

PLAÇA REIAL

❺

PALAU GÜELL

Ⓜ Drassanes

❻

L'ARC

ESCUDELLERS

HERBOLARI FERRAN

MARITIME MUSEUM

COLUMBUS MONUMENT

TO BARCELO-NETA

PASSEIG COLÓM

PICNIC SPOT

DCH

GOLONDRINAS BOATS

RAMBLA DE MAR

HARBOR

TO MAREMAGNUM

BARCELONA

tel. 933-063-800). Across the square from El Corte Inglés is **FNAC,** a French department store popular for electronics, music, and books (on west side of square—behind blue Tourist Bus stop; Mon–Sat 10:00–22:00, closed Sun).

Four great boulevards radiate from Plaça de Catalunya: the Ramblas; the fashionable Passeig de Gràcia (top shops, noisy with traffic); the cozier, but still fash-

ionable, Rambla de Catalunya (most pedestrian-friendly); and the stubby, shop-filled and delightfully traffic-free Avinguda Portal de l'Angel. Homesick Americans can even find a Hard Rock Café. Locals traditionally start or end a downtown rendez-vous at the venerable Café Zürich (at the corner near the Ramblas).

• *Cross the street from the café to...*

❶ **The Top of the Ramblas:** Begin your ramble 20 yards down at the ornate fountain (near #129). More than a Champs-Elysées, this grand boulevard takes you from rich (at the top) to rough (at the port) in a one-mile 30-minute stroll. You'll raft the river of Barcelonan life past a grand opera house, elegant cafés, retread prostitutes, brazen pickpockets, power-dressing con men, artists, street mimes, an outdoor bird market, great shopping, and people looking to charge more for a shoeshine than what you paid for the shoes.

Grab a bench and watch the scene. Open up your map and read some history into it: You're about to walk right across medi-

eval Barcelona, from Plaça de Catalunya to the harbor. Notice how the higgledy-piggledy street plan of the medieval town was contained within the old town walls—now gone, but traced by a series of roads named Ronda (meaning "to go around"). Find the Roman town, occu-pying about 10 percent of what became the medieval town—with tighter roads yet around the cathedral. The sprawling modern grid plan beyond the Ronda roads is from the 19th century. Breaks in this urban waffle show where a little

town was consumed by the growing city. The popular Passeig de Gràcia was literally the "Road to Gràcia" (once a separate town, now a characteristic Barcelona neighborhood).

Rambla means "stream" in Arabic. The Ramblas used to be a

drainage ditch along the medieval wall that once defined what's now called the Barri Gòtic (Gothic Quarter). "Ramblas" is plural, a succession of five separately named segments, but address numbers treat it as a single long street. (In fact, street signs label it as "La Rambla," singular.) Because no streets cross the Ramblas, it has a great pedestrian feel.

You're at Rambla Canaletes, named for the fountain. The black-and-gold **Fountain of Canaletes** is the starting point for celebrations and demonstrations. Legend says that a drink from the fountain ensures that you'll return to Barcelona one day. All along the Ramblas, you'll see newspaper stands (open 24 hours, selling phone cards) and ONCE booths (selling lottery tickets that support Spain's organization of the blind, a powerful advocate for the needs of people with disabilities).

Got some change? As you wander downhill, drop coins into the cans of the human statues (the money often kicks them into entertaining gear). If you take a photo, it's considered good etiquette to drop in a coin. Warning: Wherever people stop to gawk, pickpockets are at work.

• *Walk 100 yards downhill to #115 and the...*

❷ **Rambla of the Little Birds:** Traditionally, kids bring their parents here to buy pets, especially on Sundays. Apartment-

dwellers find birds, turtles, and fish easier to handle than dogs and cats. If you're walking by at night, you'll hear the sad sounds of little tweety birds locked up in their collapsed kiosks.

Along the Ramblas, buildings with balconies that have flowers are generally living spaces; balconies with air-conditioners generally indicate offices. The Academy of Science's clock (at #115) marks official Barcelona time—synchronize.

The Carrefour Express supermarket has cheap groceries (at #113, Mon–Sat 10:00–22:00, closed Sun, shorter checkout lines in back of store).

A recently discovered **Roman necropolis** is in a park across the street from the bird market, 50 yards behind the big, modern Citadines Hotel (go through the passageway at #122). Local apartment-dwellers blew the whistle on contractors, who hoped they could finish their building before anyone noticed the antiquities they had unearthed. Imagine the tomb-lined road leading into the Roman city of Barcino 2,000 years ago.

• *Another 50 yards takes you to Carrer del Carme (at #105), and a...*

❸ Baroque Church: The big Betlem church fronting the boulevard is Baroque, unusual in Barcelona. Note the Baroque-

style sloping roofline, ball-topped pinnacles, and the scrolls above the entrance. While Barcelona's Gothic age was rich (with buildings to prove it), the Baroque age hardly left a mark. (The city's importance dropped when New World discover-ies shifted lucrative trade to ports on the Atlantic.)

For a sweet treat, head down the narrow lane behind the church (going uphill parallel to the Ramblas about 30 yards) to **Café Granja Viader** (recommended in "Eating"), which has spe-cialized in baked and dairy delights since 1870. (For more sugary treats, follow "A Short, Sweet Walk"—on page 108—which begins at the intersection in front of the church.)

• *Continue down the boulevard, stroll through the Ramblas of Flowers to the Metro stop marked by the red* M *(near #96), and...*

❹ La Boquería: This lively produce market at #91 is an explo-sion of chicken legs, bags of live snails, stiff fish, delicious oranges, and sleeping dogs (Mon–Sat 8:00–

20:00, best mornings after 9:00, closed Sun). Originally outside the walls (as many medieval markets were), it expanded into the colon-naded courtyard of a now-gone monastery. Wander around—as local architect Antoni Gaudí used to—and gain inspiration. The Francesc Conserves shop sells 25 kinds of olives (straight in, near back on right, 100-gram minimum). Full legs of ham *(jamón ser-rano)* abound; *Paleta Ibérica de Bellota* hams are the best, and cost about €120 each (see "Sampling *Serrano* Ham," page 309). Beware: *Huevos del toro* are bull testicles—surprisingly inexpensive...and oh so good. Drop by a café for an *espresso con leche* or breakfast *tortilla española* (potato omelet).

For a quick bite, visit the **Pinotxo Bar** (just to the right as you enter the market, recommended in "Eating"), where animated Juan and his family are busy feeding shoppers. (Getting Juan to crack a huge smile and a thumbs-up for your camera makes a great shot... and he loves it.) The stools nearby are a fine perch for enjoying both your coffee and the people-watching. The market and lanes nearby are busy with tempting little eateries (see page 99).

• *Now turn your attention across the boulevard.*

The **Museum of Erotica** is your standard European sex museum (€9, daily 10:00–20:00, across from market at #96).

To the left, at #100, **Gimeno** sells cigars (appreciate the dying art of cigar boxes). Go ahead, do something forbidden in America but perfectly legal here...buy a Cuban (little singles for less than €1). Tobacco shops sell stamps and phone cards—and plenty of bongs and marijuana gear (the Spanish approach to pot is very casual).

Fifty yards farther, underfoot in the center of the Ramblas, find the much-trod-upon **anchor mosaic**—a reminder of the city's attachment to the sea. Created by noted abstract artist Joan Miró, it marks the midpoint of the Ramblas. (The towering Columbus Monument in the distance—hidden by trees—is at the end of this walk.)

Continue a few more steps down to the **Liceu Opera House.** From the Opera House, cross the Ramblas to Café de l'Opera for a beverage (#74). This bustling café, with Modernista decor and a historic atmosphere, boasts that it's been open since 1929, even during the Spanish Civil War.

• *Continue down the Ramblas to #46; turn left down an arcaded lane (Correr de Colom) to a square filled with palm trees.*

❺ **Plaça Reial:** This elegant Neoclassical square has a colonial (or maybe post-colonial) ambience. It comes complete with old-fashioned taverns, modern bars with patio seating, a Sunday coin and stamp market (10:00–14:00), Gaudí's first public works (the two colorful helmeted lampposts), and characters who don't need the palm trees to be shady. **Herbolari Ferran** is a fine and aromatic shop of herbs, with fun souvenirs such as top-quality saffron, or *safra* (Mon–Fri 9:30–14:00 & 16:30–20:00, closed Sat–Sun, downstairs at Plaça Reial 18—to the right as you enter the square). The small streets

stretching toward the water from the square are intriguing, but less safe.

Back on the other side of the Ramblas, **Palau Güell** offers an enjoyable look at a Gaudí interior (Carrer Nou de la Rambla 3, partly closed for renovation, see page 76). This apartment was the first of Gaudí's innovative buildings, with a parabolic front doorway that signaled his emerging nonrectangular style.

• *Continue farther downhill on the Ramblas.*

❻ **Bottom of the Ramblas:** The neighborhood on the right-hand side, Barri Xines, is the world's only Chinatown with nothing even remotely Chinese in or near it. Named for the prejudiced notion that Chinese immigrants go hand-in-hand with poverty, prostitution, and drug dealing, the neighborhood's actual inhabitants are poor Spanish, North African, and Roma (Gypsy) people. At night, the Barri Xines is frequented by prostitutes, many of them transvestites, who cater to sailors wandering up from the port. Prostitution is nothing new here. Check out the thresholds at #22 and #24 (along the left side of the Ramblas)—with holes worn in long ago by the heels of anxious ladies.

The bottom of the Ramblas is marked by the city's giant medieval shipyards (on the right, now the impressive Maritime Museum) and the Columbus Monument (both are described on page 59). And just beyond the Columbus Monument, **La Rambla del Mar** ("Rambla of the Sea") is a modern extension of the boulevard into the harbor. A popular wooden pedestrian bridge—with waves like the sea—leads to Maremagnum, a soulless Spanish mall with a cinema, huge aquarium, restaurants

(including Tapasbar Maremagnum, recommended in "Eating"), and piles of people. Late at night, it's a rollicking youth hangout. It's a worthwhile stroll.

The Barri Gòtic:
From Plaça de Catalunya to the Cathedral

Barcelona's Barri Gòtic, or Gothic Quarter, is a bustling world of shops, bars, and nightlife packed between hard-to-be-thrilled-about 14th- and 15th-century buildings. The section near the port is generally dull and seedy. But the area around the cathedral is a tangled-yet-inviting grab bag of undiscovered courtyards, grand squares, schoolyards, Art Nouveau storefronts, baby flea markets on Thursdays, musty junk shops, classy antiques shops (on Carrer de la Palla), street musicians strumming Catalan folk songs, and balconies with domestic jungles behind wrought-iron bars. Go on a cultural scavenger hunt. Write a poem. This self-guided walk gives you a structure, covering the main sights and offering an historical overview before you get lost.

• *Start on Barcelona's bustling main square.*

Plaça de Catalunya: This square is the center of the world for seven million Catalan people. The square (described earlier at the start of my Ramblas self-guided walk) is decorated with the likenesses of important Catalans. From here, walls that contained the city until the 19th century arc around in each direction to the sea. Looking at your map of Barcelona, you'll see a regimented waffle

Barcelona's Barri Gòtic

BARCELONA

design—except for the higgledy-piggledy old town corralled by these walls.

The city grew with its history. Originally a Roman town, Barcelona was ruled by the Visigoths from the fall of Rome until 714, when the Moors arrived (they were, in turn, sent packing by the French in 801—because their stay was cut so short, there are few Moorish-style buildings here). Finally, in the 10th century, the Count of Barcelona unified the region, and the idea of Catalunya came to be. The area between Plaça de Catalunya and the old Roman walls (circling the smaller ancient town, down by the cathedral) was settled by churches, each a magnet gathering a small community outside the walls (or "extra muro"). Around 1250, when these "extra muro" communities became numerous and strong enough, the king agreed to invest in a larger wall, and Barcelona expanded. This outer wall was torn down in the 1850s and replaced by a series of circular boulevards (named Rondas).

• *From Plaça de Catalunya's TI, head downhill, crossing the busy street into a broad pedestrian boulevard called...*

Avinguda Portal de l'Angel: This boulevard is named "Gate of the Angel" for the gate in the medieval wall—crowned by an angel—that once stood here. The angel kept the city safe from plagues and bid voyagers safe journey as they left the security of the city. Imagine the fascinating scene here at the Gate of the Angel, where Barcelona stopped and the wilds began.

Walking down the Avinguda Portal de l'Angel, consider an optional detour a half-block right on **Carrer de Santa Anna,** where a lane on the right leads into a courtyard facing one of those "extra muro" churches, with a fine cloister and simple, typically Romanesque facade.

Continuing down the main boulevard, you reach a fork in the road with a blue-and-yellow-tiled **fountain.** This was once a free-standing well—in the 17th century, it was the last watering stop for horses before leaving town. Take the left fork to the cathedral (past the Architects' House with its Picasso-inspired frieze).

Enter the square, where you'll stand before two bold **towers**—the remains of the old Roman wall that protected a smaller Barcino, as the city was called in ancient times. The big stones that make up the base of the towers are actually Roman. The wall stretches left of the towers, incorporated into the Deacon's House (which you'll enter from the other side later).

• *The sights from here on are located on the map on page 61. Walk around—past the modern bronze*

letters BARCINO *and the mighty facade of the cathedral (which we'll enter momentarily)—and go inside the...*

Deacon's House: Visitors are welcome inside this mansion, which today functions as the city archives (its front door faces the wall of the church). It's a good example of a Renaissance nobleman's palace. Notice how the century-old palm tree seems to be held captive by urban man. Inside you can see the Roman stones up close. Upstairs affords a good view of the cathedral's exterior—textbook Catalan Gothic (plain and practical, like this merchant community) next to textbook Romanesque (the smaller, once freestanding, more humble church adjacent on the right—which you'll visit entering from its cloister later).

• *Exit the house to the left and follow the lane. You'll emerge at the entrance to the...*

Cathedral of Barcelona (Catedral de Barcelona): This huge house of worship is worth a look. Its vast size, peaceful cloister, and many ornate chapels—each one sponsored by a local guild—are impressive. For a self-guided tour, see the "Cathedral of Barcelona" listing, later under "Sights."

• *After visiting the cathedral's cloister, exit and walk to the tiny lane ahead on the right (far side of the statue, Carrer de Montjuïc del Bisbe). This leads to the cute...*

Plaça Sant Felip Neri: This square serves as the playground of an elementary school bursting with youthful energy. The

Church of Sant Felip Neri, which Gaudí attended, is still pocked with bomb damage from the Civil War. As a stronghold of democratic, anti-Franco forces, Barcelona saw a lot of fighting. The shrapnel that damaged this church was meant for the nearby Catalan government building (Palau de la Generalitat, described below).

Study the medallions on the wall. Guilds powered the local economy, and the carved reliefs here show that this building must have housed the shoemakers. In fact, on this square you'll find a fun little Shoe Museum (described later, under "Sights").

• *Circle the block back to the cathedral's cloister and take a right, walking along Carrer del Bisbe next to the huge building (on the right), which stretches all the way to the next square.*

Palau de la Generalitat: For nearly 600 years, this place has been the home of the Catalan government. Through good times and bad, the Catalan spirit has survived, and this building has housed its capital.

• *Continue along Carrer del Bisbe to...*

Plaça de Sant Jaume (jow-mah): This stately central square of the Barri Gòtic, once the Roman forum, has been the seat of city government for 2,000 years. Today the two top governmental buildings in Catalunya face each other: the Barcelona City Hall (Ajuntament; free but only open to the public Sun 10:00–13:30) and the seat of the autonomous government of Catalunya (Palau de la Generalitat, described previously). It always flies the Catalan flag (red and yellow stripes) next to the obligatory Spanish one. From these balconies, the nation's leaders (and soccer heroes) greet the people on momentous days.

• *Take two quick left turns from the corner of Carrer Bisbe (just 10 yards away), and climb Carrer del Paridís. Follow this street as it turns right, but pause when it swings left, at the summit of...*

"Mont" Tàber: A millstone in the corner marks ancient Barcino's highest elevation, a high spot in the road called Mount Tàber. A plaque on the wall says it all: "Mont Tàber, 16.9 meters." Step into the courtyard for a peek at a surviving corner of the imposing **Roman temple** (Temple Roma d'August) that once stood here on Mont Tàber, keeping a protective watch over Barcino (free, well-explained on wall in English, daily 10:00–14:00 & 16:00–20:00).

• *Continue down Carrer del Paridís back to the cathedral, take a right, and go downhill about 100 yards to...*

Plaça del Rei: The Royal Palace sat on this "King's Square" (a block from the cathedral) until Catalunya became part of Spain in the 15th century. Then it was the headquarters of the local Inquisition. In 1493, a triumphant Christopher Columbus, accompanied by six New World natives (whom he called "Indians") and several pure-gold statues, entered the Royal Palace. King Ferdinand and Queen Isabel rose to welcome him home, and they honored him with the title "Admiral of the Oceans."

• *Your tour is over. Nearby, just off Plaça del Rei, is the City History Museum. The Frederic Marès Museum is just up the street (toward the cathedral entrance; both described later, under "Sights"). Or simply wander and enjoy Barcelona at its Gothic best.*

Sights in Barcelona

Barcelona's Old City

I've divided Barcelona's Old City sights into three neighborhoods: near the harbor, at the bottom of the Ramblas; the cathedral and nearby (Barri Gòtic); and the Picasso Museum and nearby (La Ribera).

On the Harborfront, at the Bottom of the Ramblas

▲**Maritime Museum (Museu Marítim)**—Barcelona's medieval shipyard, the best preserved in the entire Mediterranean, is now

an impressive museum covering the salty history of ships and navigation from the 13th to the 20th centuries (but museum may close, at least partially, in 2010 for major renovations). Riveting for nautical types, and interesting for anyone, its modern and beautifully presented exhibits will put you in a seafaring mood. The museum's cavernous halls evoke the 14th-century days when Catalunya was a naval and shipbuilding power, cranking out 30 huge galleys a winter. As in the US today, military and commercial ventures mixed and mingled as Catalunya built its trading empire. The excellent included audioguide tells the story and explains the various seafaring vessels displayed—including an impressively huge and richly decorated royal galley (€6.50, €7.20 combo-ticket includes Columbus Monument—ticket prices may change due to planned 2010 renovation, daily 10:00–19:45, last entry at 19:30, breezy courtyard café, Avinguda de la Drassanes, tel. 933-429-920).

▲**Columbus Monument (Monument a Colóm)**—Marking the point where the Ramblas hits the harbor, this 200-foot-tall monument built for an 1888 exposition offers an elevator-assisted view from its top. The tight four-person elevator takes you to the glassed-in observation area at the top for congested but fine views (€2.30, daily May–Oct 9:00–20:30, Nov–April 10:00–18:30). It was here in Barcelona that Ferdinand and Isabel welcomed Columbus home after his first trip to America. It's ironic that Barcelona would so honor the man whose discoveries ultimately led to its downfall as a great trading power.

Golondrinas **Cruises**—At the harbor near the foot of the Columbus Monument, tourist boats called *golondrinas* offer two different unguided tours. The shorter version goes around the harbor in 35 minutes (€6, daily on the hour 11:30–19:00, every 30 min mid-June–mid-Sept, sometimes does not run Nov–April—call ahead, tel. 934-423-106). The longer, 1.5-hour tour goes up the coast to the new Fòrum complex and back (€12.50, can disembark at Fòrum in summer only, about 7/day, daily 11:30–19:30, shorter hours in winter).

▲Cathedral of Barcelona

Most of the construction on Barcelona's vast cathedral (Catedral de Barcelona) took place in the 14th century, during the glory days of the Catalan nation. The facade was humble, so in the 19th century the proud local bourgeoisie redid it in a more ornate Neo-Gothic style.

Cost, Hours, Location: Strangely, even though the cathedral is free to enter daily 8:00–12:45 (until 13:45 on Sun) and 17:15–19:30, you must pay €5 to enter between 12:45 and 17:15 (tel. 933-151-554). The dress code is strictly enforced; don't wear tank tops, short shorts, or short skirts.

Getting There: The huge can't-miss-it cathedral is in the center of the Barri Gòtic, on Plaça de la Seu. For an interesting way to reach the cathedral from Plaça de Catalunya, and some commentary on the surrounding neighborhood, see my self-guided walk of the Barri Gòtic, described earlier.

⊃ Self-Guided Tour: Though the cathedral is Gothic and supported by buttresses, it has smooth outside walls. That's because the supporting buttresses are on the inside, providing walls for 28 richly ornamented chapels. This, along with the interior's open and spacious feeling, is characteristic of Catalan Gothic. Typical of all medieval churches, the cathedral has an "ambulatory" plan—allowing worshippers to amble around to the chapel of their choice.

While the main part of the church is fairly plain, the **chapels,** sponsored by local guilds, show great wealth. Located in the community's most high-profile space, they provided a kind of advertising to illiterate worshippers. The Native Americans that Columbus brought to town were supposedly **baptized** in the first chapel on the left.

The chapels ring a finely carved 15th-century **choir** *(coro)*. For €2.20, you can enter and get a close-up look (with the lights on) of the ornately carved stalls and the emblems representing the various Knights of the Golden Fleece who once sat here. The chairs were folded up, giving VIPs stools to lean on during the standing parts of the Mass. Each was creatively carved and—since you couldn't

Barcelona's Cathedral Neighborhood

TO PLAÇA DE CATALUNYA VIA AVINGUDA DE PORTAL L'ANGEL

NOT TO SCALE

→ ENTRY/EXIT POINT TO SIGHTS

ARCHITECTS' HOUSE

SARDANA DANCERS

BOTERS

TO RAMBLAS

LA PALLA

PLAÇA NOVA

BARCINO

AVINGUDA CATEDRAL

DEACON'S HOUSE

PLAÇA DE LA SEU

MUSEU DIOCESÀ

PLAÇA DE SANT FELIP NERI

SHOE MUSEUM

MONT. DE BISBE

IRURITA

7 **6**

CLOISTERS

GEESE

WC

5

8

SHOP

1

2 CHOIR

CATHEDRAL

3

4

COMTES

MARÈS MUSEUM

ROYAL

PALACE

PLAÇA DEL REI

FRENERIA

CITY HISTORY MUSEUM

SANT SEVER

TO RAMBLAS

DEL BISBE

CARRER

BRIDGE OVER STREET

PALAU DE LA GENERALITAT (CATALAN GOV'T.)

C. DEL PARIDÍS

"MONT" TÀBER ROMAN TEMPLE

LLIBRETERIA

PLAÇA DE SANT JAUME

CARRER DE JAUME I

TO PICASSO MUSEUM & LA RIBERA

DCH

TO RAMBLAS

1 Baptistery
2 Choir
3 High Altar & Tomb of St. Eulàlia
4 Elevator to Roof
5 St. Jordi (St. George) Statue
6 Museum
7 Chapel of Santa Lucía
8 Chapel of Santa Rita

sit on sacred things—the artists were free to enjoy some secular and naughty fun here. Study the upper tier of carvings.

The **high altar** sits upon the tomb of Barcelona's patron saint, Eulàlia. She was a 13-year-old local girl tortured 13 times by Romans for her faith before finally being crucified on an X-shaped cross. Her X symbol is carved on the pews. Climb down the stairs for a close look at her exquisite marble sarcophagus. Many of the sarcophagi in this church predate the present building.

Sardana Dances

The patriotic *sardana* dances are held at the cathedral (every Sun at 12:00, usually also Sat at 18:00). Locals of all ages seem to spontaneously appear. For some, it's a highly symbolic, politically charged action representing Catalan unity—but for most, it's just a fun chance to kick up their heels. Participants gather in circles after putting their things in the center—symbolic of community and sharing (and the ever-present risk of theft). All are welcome, even tourists cursed with two left feet.

Holding hands, dancers raise their arms—slow-motion, *Zorba the Greek*-style—as they hop and sway gracefully to the music. The band *(cobla)* consists of a long flute, tenor and soprano oboes, strange-looking brass instruments, and a tiny bongo-like drum *(tambori)*. The rest of Spain mocks this lazy circle dance, but considering what it takes for a culture to survive within another culture's country, it is a stirring display of local pride and patriotism. The event lasts between one and two hours.

You can ride the **elevator** to the roof for a view (€2.20, no charge if you paid church entry fee, Mon–Fri 10:30–18:00, Sat 10:00–12:00, closed Sun, start from chapel left of high altar).

Enter the **cloisters** (through arch, right of high altar). Once inside, look back at the arch, an impressive mix of Romanesque and Gothic. Nearby, a tiny **statue** of St. George slaying the dragon

stands in the garden. Jordi (George) is one of the patron saints of Catalunya and by far the most popular boy's name here. Cloisters are generally found in monasteries. But this church has one because it needed to accommodate more chapels—to make more money. With so many wealthy merchants in town who believed that their financial generosity would impress God and win them favor, the church needed more private chapel space. Merchants wanted to be buried close to the altar, and their tombs also spill over into the cloister. Notice on the pavement stones, as in the chapels, the symbols of the trades or guilds: scissors, shoes, bakers, and so on.

Long ago the resident **geese**—there are always 13, in memory of Eulàlia—functioned as an alarm system. Any commotion would get them honking, alerting the monk in charge. They honk to this very day.

From the statue of St. Jordi, circle to the right (past a WC hidden on the left). The skippable little €2 **museum** (far corner) is one plush room with a dozen old religious paintings. Just beyond the museum, in the corner, built into the outside wall of the cloister, is the dark, barrel-vaulted Romanesque **Chapel of Santa Lucía**, a small church that predates the cathedral. People hoping for good eyesight (Santa Lucía's specialty) leave candles outside. Farther along the cloister, the **Chapel of Santa Rita** (her forte: impossible causes) usually has the most candles.

In the Barri Gòtic, near the Cathedral

For an interesting route from Plaça de Catalunya to the cathedral neighborhood, see my self-guided walk of the Barri Gòtic, described earlier. And if you're in town on a weekend, don't miss the *sardana* dances (see sidebar on previous page).

Shoe Museum (Museu del Calçat)—Shoe-lovers enjoy this two-room shoe museum, watched over by a we-try-harder attendant. The huge shoes at the entry are designed to fit the foot of the Columbus Monument at the bottom of the Ramblas (€2.50, Tue–Sun 11:00–14:00, closed Mon, 1 block beyond outside door of cathedral cloister, behind Plaça de G. Bachs on Plaça Sant Felip Neri, tel. 933-014-533).

▲▲City History Museum (Museu d'Història de la Ciutat)—Walk through the history of the city with the help of an included audioguide. First watch the fine nine-minute introductory video in the small theater (playing alternately in Catalan, Spanish, and English)—it's worth viewing in any language. Then take an elevator down 65 feet (and 2,000 years—see the date spin back as you descend) to stroll the streets of Roman Barcelona. You'll see sewers, models of domestic life, and bits of an early-Christian church. Finally, an exhibit in the 11th-century count's palace shows you Barcelona through the Middle Ages (€6, free all day first Sun of month and other Sun from 15:00 in summer, 16:00 in winter; Tue–Sat April–Sept 10:00–20:00, Oct–March 10:00–14:00 & 16:00–19:00, Sun 10:00–20:00, closed Mon; Plaça del Rei, enter on Vageur street, tel. 932-562-122).

Frederic Marès Museum (Museu Frederic Marès)—This eclectic collection of local artist (and pack rat) Frederic Marès sprawls around a peaceful courtyard through several old Barri

Gòtic buildings. The biggest part of the collection is sculpture, hailing from ancient times to the early 20th century. But even more interesting is Marès' vast collection of items he found representative of everyday life in the 19th century—rooms upon rooms of fans, stamps, pipes, and other bric-a-brac, all lovingly displayed. There are also several sculptures by Frederic Marès himself, and temporary exhibits (€4.20, free Wed and Sun from 15:00; open Tue–Sat 10:00–19:00, Sun 10:00–20:00, closed Mon; Plaça de Sant Iu 5–6, tel. 932-563-500, www.museumares.bcn.cat). The delightfully tranquil courtyard café offers a nice break, even if you're not going to the museum.

▲▲▲Picasso Museum (Museu Picasso)

This is the best collection in the country of the work of Spaniard Pablo Picasso (1881–1973), and—since he spent his formative years

(age 14–21) in Barcelona—it's the best collection of his early works anywhere. By seeing his youthful, realistic art, you can more fully appreciate the artist's genius and better understand his later, more challenging art. The collection, with descriptions in Catalan and English (no Castilian Spanish here), is scattered through several connected Gothic palaces, six blocks from the cathedral in the Ribera district (for more on this area, see "In La Ribera, near the Picasso Museum," later).

Cost, Hours, Location: €9, free all day first Sun of month and other Sun from 15:00, open Tue–Sun 10:00–20:00, closed Mon, Montcada 15–23, ticket office at #21, Metro: Jaume I, tel. 932-563-000, www.museupicasso.bcn.cat. The ground floor has a required bag check, as well as a handy array of other services (bookshop, WC, and cafeteria).

Crowd-Beating Tips: There's almost always a line, but it moves quickly (you'll rarely wait more than an hour to get in). The busiest time is from when it opens until about 13:00 (worst on Tuesdays), as well as on free days; generally the later in the afternoon you visit, the fewer the crowds. If you have an Articket Card (see page 38), you can skip the line by going to the group entrance.

Hungry? The museum itself has a good eatery. The Textil Café, hiding in a beautiful and inviting museum courtyard across the street, is an ideal place to sip a *café con leche* or eat a light meal (€5–10 salads, couscous, and quiche fare; Tue–Sun 10:00–24:00, closed Mon, 30 yards from Picasso Museum at Montcada 12–14, tel. 932-682-598; also hosts jazz concerts Sunday nights 21:00–23:00 weather permitting—usually not in winter, stand for free or pay €5 cover to sit). And just down the street is a neighborhood favorite for tapas, El Xampanyet (recommended in "Eating").

Background: Picasso's personal secretary amassed a huge collection of his work and bequeathed it to the city. Picasso, happy to have a fine museum showing off his work in the city of his youth, added to the collection throughout his life. (Sadly, since Picasso vowed never to set foot in a fascist, Franco-ruled Spain, and died two years before Franco, the artist never saw the museum.)

⊘ Self-Guided Tour: While the rooms are sometimes rearranged, the collection (291 paintings) is always presented chronologically. With the help of thoughtful English descriptions for each stage (and blue-shirted guards who don't let you stray), it's easy to follow the evolution of Picasso's work. The room numbers—though not exact—can help you get oriented in the museum. You'll see his art evolve in these stages:

Room 1—Boy Wonder, Age 12–14: Pablo's earliest art is realistic and serious. A budding genius emerges at age 12, as Pablo moves to Barcelona and gets serious about art. Even this young, his portraits of grizzled peasants show great psychological insight and flawless technique. You'll see portraits of Pablo's first teacher, his father *(El Padre del Artista)*. Displays show his art-school work. Every time Pablo starts breaking rules, he's sent back to the standard classic style. The assignment: Sketch nude models to capture human anatomy accurately. Early self-portraits (1896, 1897) show the self-awareness of a blossoming intellect (and a kid who must have been a handful in junior high school). When Pablo was 13, his father quit painting to nurture his young prodigy. Look closely at the portrait of his mother *(Retrato de la Madre del Artista)*. Pablo, then age 15, is working on the fine details and gradients of white in her blouse and the expression in her cameo-like face. Notice the signature. Spaniards keep both parents' surnames, with the father's first, followed by the mother's: Pablo Ruiz Picasso. Pablo was closer to his mom than his dad, and eventually he kept just her name.

Room 2—Adolescence, Developing Talent: During a short trip to Málaga, Picasso dabbles in Impressionism (otherwise unknown in Spain at the time). As a 15-year-old, Pablo dutifully enters art-school competitions. His first big work—while forced to show a religious subject (*Primera Comunión,* or *First Communion*)—is more an excuse to paint his family. Notice his sister Lola's exquisitely painted veil. This piece was heavily influenced by local painters.

Room 3—Early Success: *Ciencia y Caridad (Science and Charity),* which won second prize at a fine-arts exhibition, got Picasso the chance to study in Madrid. Now Picasso conveys real feeling. The doctor (Pablo's father) represents science. The nun represents charity and religion. From her hopeless face and lifeless hand, it seems that Picasso believes nothing will save this woman from death. Pablo painted a little perspective trick: Walk back and forth across the room to see the bed stretch and shrink. Three small studies for this painting, hanging in the back of the room, show how this was an exploratory work. The frontier: light.

Picasso travels to Madrid for further study. Finding the stuffy fine-arts school in Madrid stifling, Pablo hangs out in the Prado Museum and learns by copying the masters. Notice his nearly perfect copy of Philip IV by Diego Velázquez. Having absorbed the wisdom of the ages, in 1898 Pablo visits Horta de San Juan, a rural Catalan village, and finds his artistic independence. Poor and without a love in his life, he returns to Barcelona.

Room 4—Barcelona Freedom, 1900: Art Nouveau is the rage. Upsetting his dad, Pablo quits art school and falls in with the avant-garde crowd. These bohemians congregate daily at Els Quatre Gats ("The Four Cats," slang for "a few crazy people"—a popular restaurant to this day). Further establishing his artistic freedom, he paints portraits—no longer of his family...but of his new friends. Still a teenager, Pablo puts on his first one-man show.

Rooms 5–7—Paris, 1900–1901: Nineteen-year-old Picasso arrives in Paris, a city bursting with life, light, and love. Dropping the paternal surname Ruiz, Pablo establishes his commercial brand name: "Picasso." Here, the explorer Picasso goes bohemian and befriends poets, prostitutes, and artists. He paints Impressionist landscapes like Claude Monet, cancan dancers like Toulouse-Lautrec, still lifes like Paul Cézanne, and bright-colored Fauvist works like Henri Matisse. (*La Espera*—with her bold outline and strong gaze—pops out from the Impressionistic background.) It was Cézanne's technique of "building" a figure with "cubes" of paint that inspired Picasso to soon invent Cubism.

Temporary Exhibits: As if to cleanse the museumgoer's palate before plunging into the major works, you'll now walk through some temporary exhibits.

Room 8—Blue Period, 1901–1904: The bleak Paris weather, the suicide of his best friend, and his own poverty lead Picasso to his "Blue Period." He cranks out piles of blue art just to stay housed and fed. With blue backgrounds (the coldest color) and depressing subjects, this period was revolutionary in art history. Now the artist is painting not what he sees but what he feels. The touching portrait of a mother and child, *Desamparados* (*Despair*, 1903), captures the period well. Painting misfits and street people, Picasso, like Velázquez and Toulouse-Lautrec, sees "the beauty in ugliness." Back home in Barcelona, Picasso paints his hometown at night from rooftops (*Azoteas de Barcelona*). Still blue, here we see proto-Cubism...five years before the first real Cubist painting.

Room 9—Rose Period, 1904–1907: The woman in pink *(Retrato de la Señora Canals),* painted with classic "Spanish melancholy," finally lifts Picasso out of his funk, moving him out of the blue and into a happier "Rose Period" (of which this museum has only the one painting).

Room 11—Cubism, 1907–1920: Pablo's invention in Paris of the shocking Cubist style is well-known—at least I hope so, since this museum has no true Cubist paintings. In the age of the camera, the Cubist gives just the basics (a man with a bowl of fruit) and lets you finish it.

Also in Rooms 9 and 10—Eclectic, 1920–1950: Picasso is a painter of many styles. In *Mujer con Mantilla* (Room 9), we see a little Post-Impressionistic Pointillism in a portrait that looks like a classical statue. After a trip to Rome, he paints beefy women, inspired by the three-dimensional sturdiness of ancient statues. To Spaniards, the expressionist horse symbolizes the innocent victim (Room 10). In bullfights, the horse—clad with blinders and pummeled by the bull—has nothing to do with the fight. To Picasso, the horse symbolizes the feminine, and the bull, the masculine. Picasso mixes all these styles and symbols—including this image of the horse—in his masterpiece *Guernica* (in Madrid's Centro de Arte Reina Sofía—see page 355) to show the horror and chaos of modern war.

• *From here, backtrack through rooms 8–11, and follow signs for* Ending/Collection *to Rooms 12–14.*

Rooms 12–14—Picasso and Velázquez, 1957: Notice the small print of Velázquez's *Las Meninas* (in Madrid's Prado).

Picasso, who had great respect for Velázquez, painted more than 50 interpretations of this piece that many consider the greatest painting by anyone, ever. These two Spanish geniuses were artistic equals. Picasso seems to enjoy a relationship with Velázquez. Like artistic soul mates, they spar and tease. He dissects Velázquez, and then injects playful uses of light, color, and perspective to horse around with the earlier masterpiece. In the big black-and-white canvas, the king and queen (reflected in the mirror in the back of the room) are hardly seen, while the self-portrait of the painter towers above everyone. The two women of the court on the right look like they're in a tomb—but they're wearing party shoes. In these rooms, see the fun Picasso had playing paddle-ball with Velázquez's masterpiece—filtering Velázquez's realism through the kaleidoscope of Cubism.

All his life, Picasso said, "Paintings are like windows open to the world." In Room 14, we see the French Riviera—with simple black outlines and Crayola colors, Picasso paints sun-splashed nature and the joys of the beach. He died with brush in hand, still growing. To the end, Picasso continued exploring and loving life through his art. As a child, he was taught to paint as an adult. Now, as an old man (with little kids of his own and also-childlike artist Marc Chagall for a friend), he paints like a child.

Rooms 15–16—Ceramics, 1947: As a wrap-up, walk through 41 ceramic works Picasso made during his later years.

In La Ribera, near the Picasso Museum

There's more to the Ribera neighborhood than just the Picasso Museum. While the nearby waterfront Barceloneta district was for the working-class sailors, La Ribera housed the wealthier shippers and merchants. Its streets are lined with their fine mansions—which, like the much-appreciated Church of Santa Maria del Mar, were built with shipping wealth.

La Ribera (also known as "El Born") is separated from the Barri Gòtic by Via Laietana, a four-lane highway built through the Old City in the early 1900s to alleviate growing traffic problems. From the Plaça de l'Angel (nearest Metro stop—Jaume I), cross this busy street to enter an up-and-coming zone of lively and creative restaurants and nightlife. The Carrer de l'Argenteria ("Goldsmiths Street"—streets in La Ribera are named after the workshops that used to occupy them) runs diagonally from the Plaça de l'Angel straight down to the Church of Santa Maria del Mar. The Catalan Concert Hall is to the north.

▲▲Catalan Concert Hall (Palau de la Música Catalana)— This concert hall, finished in 1908, features my favorite Modernista interior in town (by Lluís Domènech i Muntaner). Inviting arches lead you into the 2,138-seat hall. A kaleidoscopic skylight features a choir singing around the sun, while playful carvings and mosaics celebrate music and Catalan culture. You can only get in by tour, which starts with a relaxing 12-minute video (€12, 50-min tours in English run daily every hour 10:00–15:00, may have longer hours on weekends and holidays, tour times may change based on performance schedule, about 6 blocks northeast of cathedral, tel. 932-957-200, www.palaumusica.org).

The catch: You must buy your ticket in advance to get a spot on an English guided tour (tickets available up to 7 days in advance—ideally buy yours at least 2 days before, though they're sometimes available the same day or day before). You can buy the ticket in

Barcelona's La Ribera

TO CATALAN
CONCERT HALL

TO
CATHEDRAL
+ RAMBLAS

Ⓜ METRO STATION

CHOCOLATE
MUSEUM

PL. PONS
I CLERCH

PLAÇA
DE
L'ANGEL

C. DE LA BORIA

CARDERS

ASSAONADORS

BOUGER

LA PRINCESA

COTONERS

PICASSO
MUSEUM

Ⓜ Jaume I

❶ VIGATANS

BARRA DE FERRO

GRUNYI

❺

FLASSADERS

C. DEL REC

FUSINA

DEL

COMERC

❸ BROSOLI

D'EN ROSIC

MIRALLERS

❹

MOSQUES

BORN
MARKET

❷

SOMBRERERS

ABAIX.

PASSEIG DEL BORN

SANTA
MARIA
DEL MAR

CANVIS NOUS

PL. STA. MARIA

L'ESPASERIA

❻

❼

VIDRIERIA

PESCATERIA

RIBERA

AGULLERS

CANVIS VELLS

ASES

PL.
OLLES

REA PAL

SANT JOAN

POST

CONSOLAT DE MAR

MARQUÈS DE L'ARGENTERIA

LA
LLOTJA

PLAÇA
DEL
PALAU

FRANÇA
TRAIN
STN.

PLAÇA
ANTONI
LOPEZ

AVINGUDA DEL

TO
MAREMAGNUM
+ BARCELONETA

TO
Ⓜ Barceloneta

❶ Gothic Point Hostel
❷ Sagardi Rest. & Bar
❸ Taller de Tapas
❹ El Xampanyet Bar
❺ Textil Café
❻ 1714 Massacre Monument
❼ Un Cotxe Menys Bike Rental

BARCELONA

person at the concert hall box office (open daily 9:30–15:30); by phone with your credit card (tel. 902-485-475); or online via the concert hall website (www.palaumusica.org).

It might be easier to get tickets for a **concert** (300 per year, tickets for some performances as cheap as €7, see website for details).

▲**Church of Santa Maria del Mar**—This church is the proud centerpiece of La Ribera. "Del Mar" means "of the sea," and that's where the money came from. The proud shippers built this church in only 55 years, so it has a harmonious style considered pure Catalan Gothic. As you step in, notice the figures of workers carved into the big front doors. During the Spanish Civil War (1936–1939), the Church sided with the conservative forces of Franco against the people. In

retaliation, the working class took their anger out on this church, burning all of its wood furnishings and decor (carbon still blackens the ceiling). Today it's stripped down—naked in all its Gothic glory. The tree-like columns inspired Gaudí (their influence on the columns inside his Sagrada Família church is obvious). Sixteenth-century sailors left models of their ships at the foot of the altar for Mary's protection. Even today, there remains a classic old Catalan ship at Mary's feet. As within Barcelona's cathedral, here you can see the characteristic Catalan Gothic buttresses flying inwards, defining the chapels that ring the nave (free entry, daily 9:00–13:30 & 16:30–20:00).

Exit the church from the side, and you arrive at a square with a modern **monument** to a 300-year-old massacre that's still part of the Catalan consciousness. On September 11, 1714, the Bourbon king ruling from Madrid massacred Catalan patriots, who were buried in a mass grave on this square. From that day on, the king outlawed Catalan culture and its institutions (no speaking the language, no folk dances, no university, and so on). The eternal flame burns atop this monument, and 9/11 is still a sobering anniversary for the Catalans.

To the Picasso Museum: From behind the church, the Carrer de Montcada leads two blocks to the Picasso Museum (described earlier). The street's mansions—built by rich shippers centuries ago—now house galleries, shops, and even museums. The Picasso Museum itself consists of five such mansions laced together.

Passeig del Born—Just behind the church, this long square was formerly a jousting square (as its shape indicates). This is the neighborhood center and a popular springboard for exploring tapas bars, fun restaurants, and nightspots in the narrow streets all around. Wandering around here at night, you'll find piles of inviting and intriguing little restaurants (I've listed my favorites in "Eating," page 98). Enjoy a glass of wine on the square facing the church, or consider renting a bike here for a pedal down the beach promenade to the Fòrum (described on next page).

Chocolate Museum (Museu de la Xocolata)—This museum, only a couple of blocks from the Picasso Museum (and near Citadel

Park—see below), is a delight for chocolate-lovers. Operated by the local confectioners' guild, it tells the story of chocolate from Aztecs to Europeans via the port of Barcelona, where it was first unloaded and processed. But the history lesson is just an excuse to show off a series of remarkably ornate candy sculptures. These works of edible art—which change every year but often include such Spanish themes as Don Quixote or bullfighting—begin as store-window displays for Easter or Christmas. Once the holiday passes, the confectioners bring the sculptures here to be enjoyed (€4.30, Mon and Wed–Sat 10:00–19:00, Sun 10:00–15:00, closed Tue, Carrer Comerç 36, tel. 932-687-878, www.museu xocolata.com).

Near the Waterfront, East of the Old City and Harbor

Citadel Park (Parc de la Ciutadella)—Barcelona's biggest, greenest park, originally the site of a much-hated military citadel, was transformed in 1888 for a World's Fair (Universal Exhibition). The stately Triumphal Arch at the top of the park, celebrating the removal of the citadel, was built as the main entrance. Inside, you'll find wide pathways, plenty of trees and grass, a zoo, and museums of geology and zoology. Barcelona, one of Europe's most densely populated cities, suffers from a lack of real green space. This park is a haven, and especially enjoyable on weekends when it teems with happy families. Enjoy the ornamental fountain that the young Antoni Gaudí helped design, and consider a jaunt in a rental rowboat on the lake in the center of the park. Check out the tropical Umbracle greenhouse and the Hivernacle winter garden, which has a pleasant café-bar (daily 8:00–20:00, Metro: Arc de Triomf, east of França train station).

▲**Barcelona's Beach, from Barceloneta to the Fòrum**— Barcelona has created a summer tourist beach trade by building a huge stretch of beaches east from the town center. Before the

1992 Olympics, this area was an industrial wasteland nicknamed the "Catalan Manchester." Not anymore. The industrial zone was demolished and dumped into the sea, while sand was dredged out of the sea bed to make the pristine beaches locals enjoy today. The scene is great for sunbathing and for an evening paseo before dinner. It's like a resort island— complete with lounge chairs, volleyball, showers, bars, WCs, and bike paths.

Bike the Beach: For a break from the city, rent a bike (in La

Ribera or Citadel Park—for details, see "Helpful Hints," page 41) and take the following little ride: Explore Barcelona's "Central Park"—Citadel Park—filled with families enjoying a day out (described on previous page). Then roll through Barceloneta. This artificial peninsula was once the home of working-class sailors and shippers. From the Barceloneta beach, head west to the Olympic Village, where the former apartments for 13,000 visiting athletes now house permanent residents. The village's symbol, Frank Gehry's striking "fish," shines brightly in the sun. A bustling night scene keeps this stretch of harborfront busy until the wee hours. From here you'll come to a series of man-made crescent-shaped beaches, each with trendy bars and cafés. If you're careless or curious (down by Platja de la Mar Bella), you might find yourself pedaling through people working on an all-over tan. In the distance, you see the huge solar panel marking the site of the Fòrum shopping and convention center.

The Fòrum—The original 1860 vision for Barcelona's enlargement continued the boulevard called Diagonal right to the sea. They finally realized this goal nearly a century and a half later, with the opening of the Fòrum. Go here for a taste of today's Barcelona: nothing Gothic, nothing quaint, just big and modern—a mall and a convention center. In 2004, Barcelona hosted the "Forum of the Cultures," an attempt to create a world's fair that recognized not states, but peoples. Roma (Gypsies), Basques, Māoris, Native Americans, and Catalans all assembled here in a global celebration of cultural diversity, multiculturalism, peace, and sustainability.

The Fòrum also tries to be an inspiration for environmental engineering. Waste is burned to create heat. The giant solar panel creates perfectly clean and sustainable energy. The festival was a moderate success and might be repeated as a bash for this planet's "nations without states." Local government officials hoped the event—like other "expos"—would goose development...and it did. Barcelona now has a new modern part of town.

You can get out to the Fòrum by bike, bus, or taxi via the long and impressive new beach. Or the Metro zips you there in just a few minutes from the center (L4/yellow line, Fòrum Station). Once there, browse around the modern shopping zone.

The Eixample: Modernisme and Antoni Gaudí

Wide sidewalks, hardy shade trees, chic shops, and plenty of Art Nouveau fun make the Eixample a refreshing break from the Old City. Uptown Barcelona is a unique variation on the common grid-plan city. Barcelona snipped off the building corners to create light and spacious eight-sided squares at every intersection. For the best Eixample example, ramble Rambla de Catalunya (unrelated to the more famous Ramblas) and pass through Passeig de Gràcia

Modernisme

The Renaixensa (Catalan cultural revival) gave birth to Modernisme (Catalan Art Nouveau) at the end of the 19th century. Barcelona is its capital. Its Eixample neighborhood shimmers with the colorful, leafy, flowing, blooming shapes of Modernisme in doorways, entrances, facades, and ceilings.

Meaning "a taste for what is modern"—things like streetcars, electric lights, and big-wheeled bicycles—this free-flowing organic style lasted from 1888 to 1906. Breaking with tradition, artists experimented with glass, tile, iron, and brick. The structure was fully modern, using rebar and concrete, but the decoration was a clip-art collage of nature images, exotic Moorish or Chinese themes, and fanciful Gothic crosses and knights to celebrate Catalunya's medieval glory days. It's Barcelona's unique contribution to the Europe-wide Art Nouveau movement. Modernisme was a way of life as Barcelona burst into the 20th century.

Antoni Gaudí (1852–1926), Barcelona's most famous Modernista artist, was descended from four generations of metalworkers, a lineage of which he was quite proud. He incorporated ironwork into his architecture and came up with novel approaches to architectural structure and space.

Two more Modernista architects famous for their unique style are Lluís Domènech i Muntaner and Josep Puig i Cadafalch. You'll see their work on the Block of Discord.

(described later; Metro for Block of Discord: Passeig de Gràcia, or Metro for Casa Milà: Diagonal).

The 19th century was a boom time for Barcelona. By 1850, the city was busting out of its medieval walls. A new town was planned to follow a grid-like layout. The intersection of three major thoroughfares—Gran Via, Diagonal, and Meridiana—would shift the city's focus uptown.

The Eixample, or "Expansion," was a progressive plan in which everything was made accessible to everyone. Each 20-block-square district would have its own hospital and large park, each 10-block-square area would have its own market and general services, and each five-block-square grid would house its own schools and daycare centers. The hollow space found inside each "block" of apartments would form a neighborhood park.

While much of that vision never quite panned out, the

Eixample was an urban success. Rich and artsy big shots bought plots along the grid. The richest landowners built as close to the center as possible. For this reason, the best buildings are near the Passeig de Gràcia. While adhering to the height, width, and depth limitations, they built as they pleased—often in the trendy new Modernista style.

For many visitors, Modernista architecture is Barcelona's main draw. (The TI even has a special desk set aside just for Modernisme-seekers.) And one name tops them all: **Antoni Gaudí** (1852–1926). Barcelona is an architectural scrapbook of Gaudí's galloping gables and organic curves. A devoted Catalan and Catholic, he immersed himself in each project, often living on-site. At various times, he called Parc Güell, Casa Milà, and the Sagrada Família home.

First I've covered the main Gaudí attractions close to the Old City. The Sagrada Família and Parc Güell are farther afield, but worth the trip. And since many visitors do those two sights together, I've included tips on how to connect them.

Gaudí Sights near the Old City

▲▲**Casa Milà (La Pedrera)**—This Gaudí exterior laughs down on the crowds filling Passeig de Gràcia. Casa Milà, also called La Pedrera ("The Quarry"), has a much-photographed roller coaster of melting-ice-cream eaves. This is Barcelona's quintessential Modernista building and Gaudí's last major work (1906–1910) before dedicating his final years to the Sagrada Família.

You can visit three sections of Casa Milà: the apartment, attic, and rooftop (€9.50, includes good audioguide, daily March–Oct 9:00–20:00, Nov–Feb 9:00–18:30, last entry 30 min before closing, Passeig de Gràcia 92, Metro: Diagonal, tel. 902-400-973).

As you enter, choose the 1.25-hour audioguide (which offers more listening options than the 30-minute version; either one included in admission). Then head upstairs. Two elevators take you up to either the apartment or the attic. Normally you're directed to the apartment, but if you arrive late in the day, go to the attic elevator first, then climb right up to the rooftop to make sure you have enough time to enjoy Gaudí's works and the views.

The typical fourth-floor **apartment** is decorated as it might have been when the building was first occupied by middle-class urbanites (a seven-minute video explains Barcelona society at the time). Notice Gaudí's clever use of the atrium to maximize day-light in all of the apartments.

Visit Casa Milà or Casa Batlló?

These two Antoni Gaudí houses offer similar, up-close looks at Modernista architecture. Casa Batlló's rooftop (above left) is smaller, all on one level, and less impressive than the expansive rooftop at Casa Milà (above right). But the unfurnished Casa Batlló is less of a museum and better allows the architecture to speak for itself. If you're choosing one, Casa Milà is cheaper and has the superior rooftop, but Gaudí fans will find both worthwhile.

The **attic** houses a sprawling multimedia "Gaudí Space," tracing the history of the architect's career with models, photos, and videos of his work. It's all displayed under distinctive parabola-shaped arches. While evocative of Gaudí's style in themselves, the arches are formed this way partly to support the multi-level roof above. This area was also used for ventilation, helping to keep things cool in summer and warm in winter. Tenants had storage spaces and did their laundry up here.

From the attic, a stairway leads to the fanciful, undulating, jaw-dropping **rooftop,** where 30 chimneys play volleyball with the clouds.

Back at the **ground level** of Casa Milà, poke into the dreamily painted original entrance courtyard. The first floor hosts free art exhibits.

Concerts: During July, a rooftop concert series called "Pedrera by Night" features live music—jazz, flamenco, tango—a glass of *cava*, and the chance to see the rooftop illuminated (around €12, 22:00–24:00, tel. 902-400-973).

Hungry? Stop by the recommended La Bodegueta, a long block away (daily lunch special, see "Eating" on page 106).

▲Block of Discord—Four blocks from Casa Milà, you can survey a noisy block of competing late 19th-century facades. Several of Barcelona's top Modernista mansions line Passeig de Gràcia (Metro: Passeig de Gràcia). Because the structures look as though they are trying to outdo each other in creative twists, locals nicknamed the block between Consell de Cent and Arago the "Block of Discord."

First (at #43) and most famous is Gaudí's **Casa Batlló,** with skull-like balconies and a tile roof that suggests a cresting dragon's back; Gaudí based the work on the popular legend of St. Jordi (George) slaying the dragon. The house—a rival of Casa Milà (described previously)—can also be toured (€16.50, daily 9:00–20:00, may close early for special events—closings posted in advance at entrance, tel. 932-160-306, www.casabatllo.cat). You'll see the main floor (with a funky mushroom-shaped fireplace nook), the blue-and-white-ceramic-slathered atrium, the attic (more parabolic arches), and the rooftop, all with the help of a good audioguide. It's pricey, but the interior is even more fanciful and over-the-top than Casa Milà's. There's barely a straight line in the house. By the way, if you're tempted to snap photos from the middle of the street, be careful—Gaudí died under a streetcar.

Next door, at **Casa Amatller** (#41), check out architect Josep Puig i Cadafalch's creative mix of Moorish- and Gothic-inspired architecture and iron grillwork, which decorates a step-gable like those in the Netherlands. Due to renovation, scaffolding may obscure parts of the exterior, but you can still pop inside for a peek at the elaborate entrance hall.

On the corner (at #35), **Casa Lleó Morera** has a wonderful interior highlighted by the dining room's fabulous stained glass. The architect, Lluís Domènech i Muntaner, also did the Catalan Concert Hall (you'll notice similarities).

La Rita restaurant, just around the corner on Carrer Arago, serves a fine three-course lunch for a great price from 13:00 (recommended under "Eating").

▲Palau Güell—Just as the Picasso Museum reveals a young genius on the verge of a breakthrough, this early Gaudí building (completed in 1890) shows the architect taking his first tentative steps toward what would become his trademark curvy style. The parabolic-arch doorways, viewable from the outside, are the first clue that this is not a typical townhouse. In the midst of an extensive renovation, only part of the house is open to the public: the main floor and the Neo-Gothic cellar (which was used as a stable—notice the big carriage doors in the back and the rings on some of the posts used to tie up the horses). By 2011, they hope to have more of the house open...and start charging admission (free, Tue–Sat 10:00–14:30, closed Sun–Mon, a half-block off the Ramblas at Carrer Nou de la Rambla 3–5, tel. 933-173-974, www.palauguell.cat). Even if the rooftop—with its fanciful mosaic chimneys (visible from the street if you crane your neck)—is open, I'd skip it if you plan to see the more interesting one at Casa Milà (described earlier).

▲▲▲Sagrada Família (Holy Family Church)

Gaudí's most famous and persistent work is this unfinished landmark church. He worked on the Sagrada Família from 1883

until his death in 1926. Since then, construction has moved forward in fits and starts. Even today, the half-finished church is not expected to be completed for another quarter-century. (But over 30 years of visits, I've seen considerable progress.) The temple is funded exclusively by private donations and entry fees, which is another reason its completion has taken so long. Your admission helps pay for the ongoing construction.

Cost, Hours, Location: €11, daily April–Sept 9:00–20:00, Oct–March 9:00–18:00, Metro: Sagrada Família puts you right on the doorstep—exit toward *Pl de la Sagrada Família*, tel. 932-073-031, www.sagradafamilia.cat.

Crowd-Beating Tips: The ticket line can be very long (up to about 30–45 minutes at peak times). It's generally least crowded right when the church opens and worst at high noon. You can call ahead to purchase tickets with a credit card, then pick them up when you arrive (tel. 902-101-212).

Tours: The 45-minute English tours cost €4 (May–Oct daily at 11:00 and 13:00, Nov–April usually Fri–Mon only, same times). Or rent the good 70-minute audioguide (also €4).

Elevators: Two different elevators take you partway up the towers for a great view of the city and a gargoyle's-eye perspective of the loopy church. Each one costs €2.50 (pay as you board elevator). The **Passion facade elevator** takes you 215 feet up, where you can climb higher if you want; then an elevator takes you back down. The **Nativity facade elevator** is similar, but you can also cross the dizzying bridge between the towers—and you must walk all the way down. (Some people prefer the Nativity elevator despite the additional steps because it offers close views of the facade that Gaudí actually worked on.) For the climbing sections, expect the spiral stairs to be tight, hot, and congested. Lines for both elevators can be very long (up to a 2-hour wait at the busiest times); signs along the stanchions give an estimated wait time. To avoid long lines, try getting here early and going directly to the elevators. The Nativity facade elevator generally has a shorter line.

The Construction Project: There's something powerful about an opportunity to feel a community of committed people with a vision, working on a church that will not be finished in their life-time (as was standard in the Gothic age). Local craftsmen often cap off their careers by spending a couple of years on this exciting construction site. The church will trumpet its completion with 18 spires: A dozen "smaller" 330-foot spires (representing the apostles) will stand in groups of four and mark the three entry facades of the building. Four taller towers (dedicated to the four Evangelists) will surround the two tallest, central towers: a 400-foot-tall tower of Mary and the grand 550-foot Jesus tower, which will shine like a spiritual lighthouse—visible even from out at sea. A unique exterior ambulatory will circle the building, like a cloister turned inside out. If there's any building on earth I'd like to see, it's the Sagrada Família...finished.

☉ Self-Guided Tour: To get a good rundown, follow this commentary.

• *Begin by facing the western side of the church (where you'll enter).*

Passion Facade: It seems strange to begin with something that Gaudí had nothing to do with...but that's where they put the entrance. When Gaudí died in 1926, only the stubs of four spires stood above the building site. The rest of the church has been inspired by Gaudí's vision but designed and executed by others. Gaudí knew he wouldn't live to complete the church and recognized that later architects and artists would rely on their own muses for inspiration. This artistic freedom was amplified in 1936, when Civil War shell-ing burned many of Gaudí's blueprints. Judge for yourself how the recently completed and controversial Passion facade by Josep María Subirachs (b. 1927) fits with Gaudí's original formulation (which you'll see downstairs in the museum).

Subirachs' facade is full of symbolism from the Bible. The story of Christ's Passion unfolds in the shape of a Z, from bot-tom to top. Find the stylized Alpha and Omega over the door; Jesus—hanging on the cross—with an open book (the word of God) for hair; and the grid of numbers adding up to 33 (Jesus' age

Modernista Sights

Ⓑ Bus Stop   Ⓜ Metro Station

N

TORRE DE BELLESGUARD

RONDA DE DALT

GAUDÍ HOUSE & MUSEUM

PARC GÜELL

FINCA GÜELL

COL·LEGI DE LAS TERESIANES

FINCA MIRALLES

GIRONA

#24, #92 & TOURIST BUS

LESSEPS

BUS #24

TERRACE & FRONT ENTRANCE

DIAGONAL

CASA VICENS

SANTS TRAIN STN.

GRACIA

TRAV. GRACIA

FONTANA

TRAV. DALT

HOSPITAL DE LA SANTA CREU I SANT PAU (BY MUNTANER)

BLOCK OF DISCORD
• CASA BATLLÓ - BY GAUDÍ
• CASA AMATLLER BY CADAFALCH
• CASA LLEÓ MORERA BY MUNTANER

DIAGONAL Ⓜ

CASA MILA

PROVENÇA

Ⓑ #92

AV. GAUDÍ

Ⓜ

PASSEIG

PASSEIG DE GRÀCIA

ℹ Ⓑ #19 & #50

SAGRADA FAMÍLIA

GRAN VIA

CASA CALVET

PLAÇA D'ESPANYA

PARAL·LEL

PLAÇA DE CATALUNYA & Ⓑ #24

RAMBLAS

Ⓜ

CATALAN CONCERT HALL (BY MUNTANER)

MONTJUÏC

LICEU Ⓜ

BARRI GÒTIC

OLYMPIC PORT & "FISH" (BY GEHRY)

PALAU GÜELL

Ⓜ DRASS.

FRANÇA TRAIN STN.

NOT TO SCALE

DCH

HARBOR

BARCELONA

at the time of his death). The distinct face of the man below and just left of Christ is a memorial to Gaudí.

Now look high above: The figure perched on the bridge between the towers is the soul of Jesus, ascending to heaven. The colorful ceramic caps of the towers symbolize the miters (formal hats) of bishops.

Grand and impressive as this seems, keep in mind it's only the *side* entry to the church. The nine-story apartment flat to the right will be torn down to accommodate the grand front entry. The three facades—Passion, Nativity, and Glory—will chronicle Christ's life from birth to death to resurrection.

• *We'll enter the church later. For now, look right to find the...*

School: Gaudí erected this school for the children of the workers building the church. Now it houses an exhibit focusing on the architect's use of geometric forms. You'll also see a classroom and a replica of Gaudí's desk as it was the day he died, and a model for the proposed Glory facade...the next big step.

• *Leaving the school, turn right and go down the ramp under the church, into the...*

Museum: Housed in what is someday intended to be the church's crypt, the museum runs underground from the Passion facade to the Nativity facade. The first section tells the chronological story of the Sagrada Família. Look for the replicas of the pulpit and confessional that Gaudí, the micro-manager, designed for his church. As you wander through the plaster models used for the church's construction, you'll notice that they don't always match the finished product—these are ideas, not blueprints set in stone. Photos show the construction work as it was when Gaudí died in 1926 and how it's progressed over the years. See how the church's design is a fusion of nature, architecture, and religion. The columns seem light, with branches springing forth and capitals that look like palm trees.

Walking down the long passage to the other side of the church, you'll pass under a giant plaster model of the nave (you'll see the real thing soon). Find the hanging model showing how Gaudí used gravity to calculate the perfect parabolas incorporated into the church design (the mirror above this model shows how the right-side-up church is derived from this). Nearby, you'll find some original Gaudí architectural sketches in a dimly lit room and a worthwhile 20-minute movie (generally shown in English at :50 past each hour).

Then you'll peek into a busy workshop for making plaster models of the planned construction, just like what Gaudí used—he found these helpful for envisioning the final product in 3-D. The museum wraps up with an exhibit on the design and implementation of the Passion facade.

• *Climb up the ramp and hook left to see the...*

Nativity Facade (east side): This, the only part of the church essentially finished in his lifetime, shows Gaudí's original vision. (Cleverly, this facade was built and finished first to inspire financial support, which Gaudí knew would be a challenge.) Mixing Gothic-style symbolism, images from nature, and Modernista asymmetry, it is the best example of Gaudí's unmistakable cake-in-the-rain style. The sculpture shows a unique twist on the Nativity, with Jesus as a young carpenter and angels playing musical instruments.

• *From here, you have two options:*

To take the elevator up the Nativity facade (described above), go through the small door to the right of the main door. The line stretches through an area called the Rosary Cloister.

To enter the church (where you'll also find the Passion facade eleva-

tor entrance), go in the door to the left of the main entry. First you'll pass the Montserrat Cloister, with the **Gaudí and Nature** *exhibition that compares nature, waves, shells, mushrooms, the ripple of a leaf, and so on to Gaudí's work. Then you'll enter the...*

Construction Zone (the Nave): The cranking cranes, rusty forests of rebar, and scaffolding require a powerful faith, but the

Sagrada Família offers a fun look at a living, growing bigger-than-life building. Part of Gaudí's religious vision was a love for nature. He said, "Nothing is invented; it's written in nature." His columns blossom with life, and little windows let light filter in like the canopy of a rain forest, giving both privacy and an intimate connection with God. The U-shaped choir hovers above the nave, tethered halfway up the columns. A relatively recent addition—hanging out in the middle of the back wall—is a statue of Barcelona's patron saint, St. Jordi (George of dragon-slaying fame). At the far end of the nave, you'll see the line to take the elevator up the Passion facade.

Currently, the construction is focused on a few major tasks: stabilizing the existing nave (which has been rattled by vibrations from the Metro and new AVE train lines underground) and eventually adding the third, biggest entry—the Glory facade. By 2010, the roof of the central nave should be finished and the scaffolding gone so that services can be held inside the church. They're also in the process of replacing the temporary, clear windows with stained-glass ones. The final phase is the central tower (550 feet tall), which, it's estimated, will require four underground support pylons, each consisting of 8,000 tons of cement.

Gaudí lived on the site for more than a decade and is buried in a Neo-Gothic 19th-century crypt (which is where the church began). His tomb is sometimes viewable from the museum, but will likely be closed to the public in 2010 (it may reopen at some point during the year). There's a move afoot to make Gaudí a saint. Perhaps someday, his tomb will be a place of pilgrimage. Gaudí—a faithful Catholic whose medieval-style mysticism belied his Modernista architecture career—was certainly driven to greatness by his passion for God. When undertaking a lengthy project, he said, "My client"—meaning God—"is in no hurry."

Scenic Connection to Parc Güell: If your next stop is Parc Güell (see next page), and you don't want to spring for a taxi, try this route: With the Nativity facade at your back, walk to the near-left corner of the park across the street. Then cross the street to reach the diagonal Avinguda Gaudí (between the Repsol gas station and the KFC). From here, you'll follow the funky lampposts four blocks gradually uphill (about 10 min) along Avinguda Gaudí, a pleasant shaded, café-lined pedestrian street. When you reach the striking Modernista-style Hospital de la Santa Creu i Sant Pau (designed by Lluís Domènech i Muntaner), cross the street and go up one block (left) on St. Antonio Maria Claret street to catch bus #92, which will take you to the side entrance of Parc Güell.

From the Sagrada Família, you could also get to Parc Güell by taking the Metro to Lesseps, then bus #24 (described below), but that involves two changes...and less scenery.

More Bus Connections: From the Sagrada Família, bus #19 makes an easy 15-minute journey to the Old City (stops near the cathedral and La Ribera district); bus #50 goes from the Sagrada Família to Montjuïc, skipping the funicular but taking you past all the sights (see "Getting to Montjuïc," later).

▲Parc Güell

Gaudí fans enjoy the artist's magic in this colorful park. Gaudí intended this 30-acre garden to be a 60-residence housing project—a kind of gated community. As a high-income housing development, it flopped. But as a park, it's a delight, offering another peek into the eccentric genius of Gaudí. Notice the mosaic medallions that say "park" in English, reminding folks that this is modeled on an English garden.

Cost and Hours: Free, daily 10:00–20:00, tel. 932-130-488.

Getting There: From Plaça de Catalunya, the red Tourist Bus or bus #24 will leave you at the park's side entrance, or a €6 taxi will drop you off at the main entrance. From elsewhere in the city, do a Metro-plus-bus combination: Go by Metro to the Lesseps stop. To avoid the tiring uphill 20-minute walk to the park, don't follow the *Parc Güell 1300 metros* sign; instead, exit left out of the Metro station, cross the streets Princep d'Astúries and Gran de Gràcia, and catch bus #24 (on Gran de Gràcia), which takes you to the park's side entrance in less than 10 minutes. For a more scenic approach (on bus #92) from the Sagrada Família, see the previous page.

◒ Self-Guided Tour: This tour assumes you're arriving at the front/main entrance (by taxi). If you're instead arriving by bus at the side entrance, walk straight ahead through the gate to find the terrace with colorful mosaic benches, then walk down to the stairway and front entrance.

As you wander the park, imagine living here a century ago—

if this gated community had succeeded and was filled with Barcelona's wealthy.

Front Entrance: Entering the park, you walk by Gaudí's wrought-iron gas lamps (1900–1914). His dad was a blacksmith, and he always enjoyed this medium. Two gate houses made of gingerbread flank the entrance. One houses a good bookshop, while the other is home to the skippable Center for Interpretation of Parc Güell (Centre d'Interpretació), which shows Gaudí's building methods plus maps, photos, and models of the park (€2.30, daily 11:00–15:00, tel. 933-190-222); the Gaudí House and Museum, described below, is better.

Stairway and Columns: Climb the grand stairway, past the famous ceramic dragon fountain. At the top, dip into the "Hall of 100 Columns," designed to house a produce market for the neighborhood's 60 mansions. The fun columns—each different,

made from concrete and rebar, topped with colorful ceramic, and studded with broken bottles and bric-a-brac—add to the market's vitality.

As you continue up (on the left-hand staircase), look left, down the playful "pathway of columns" that supports a long arcade. Gaudí drew his inspiration from nature, and this arcade is like a surfer's perfect tube.

Terrace: Once up top, sit on a colorful bench—designed to fit your body ergonomically—and enjoy one of Barcelona's best views. Look for the Sagrada Família church in the distance. Gaudí was an engineer as well. He designed a water-catchment system by which rain hitting this plaza would flow into and through the columns from the market below, and power the park's fountains.

When considering the failure of Parc Güell as a community development, also consider that it was an idea a hundred years ahead of its time. Back then, high-society ladies didn't want to live so far from the cultural action. Today, the surrounding neighborhoods are some of the wealthiest in town, and a gated community here would be a big hit.

Gaudí House and Museum: This pink house with a steeple, standing in the middle of the park (near the side entrance), was actually Gaudí's home for 20 years, until his father died. His humble artifacts are mostly gone, but the house is now a museum

BARCELONA

with some quirky Gaudí furniture and a chance to wander through a model home used to sell the others. While small, it offers a good taste of what could have been (€4, daily April–Sept 10:00–20:00, Oct–March 10:00–18:00).

Montjuïc

Montjuïc ("Mount of the Jews"), overlooking Barcelona's hazy port, has always been a show-off. Ages ago it had an impressive fortress. In 1929, it hosted an international fair, from which most of today's sights originated. And in 1992, the Summer Olympics directed the world's attention to this pincushion of attractions once again.

I've listed these sights by altitude, from highest to lowest; if you're visiting all of them, do them in this order so that most of your walking is downhill (for selective sightseers, the Fundació Joan Miró and Catalan Art Museum are the most worthwhile). Note that if you want to visit only the Catalan Art Museum, you can just take the Metro to Plaça d'Espanya and ride the escalators up (with some stair-climbing as well) to the museum.

Getting to Montjuïc: You have several options. The simplest is to take a **taxi** directly to your destination (about €7 from downtown).

Buses from various points in the city take you up to Montjuïc, including public bus #55 (from Plaça de Catalunya, next to Caja de Madrid building), public bus #50 (from the corner of Gran Via and Passeig de Gràcia, or from the Sagrada Família), and the blue Tourist Bus.

A **funicular** takes visitors from the Paral-lel Metro stop up to Montjuïc (covered by a Metro ticket, every 10 min, 9:00–22:00). To reach the funicular, take the **Metro** to the Paral-lel stop, then follow signs for *Parc Montjuïc* and the little funicular icon—you can enter the funicular directly without using another ticket (number of minutes until next departure posted at start of entry tunnel). From the top of the funicular, turn left and walk two minutes to the Joan Miró museum, six minutes to the Olympic Stadium, or ten minutes to the Catalan Art Museum.

From the port, the most scenic way to Montjuïc is via the **cable car,** called the 1929 Transbordador Aereo (€9.50 one-way, €12.50 round-trip, 3/hr, daily 10:45–19:00, until 20:00 in June–Sept, tel. 932-252-718).

Getting Around Montjuïc: Up top, the bus marked *Parc de Montjuïc* (#PM) loops between the sights. This circular line starts at Plaça d'Espanya and goes to the Catalan Art Museum, the Joan

Montjuïc

M METRO STATION
꒐ VIEW

¼ MILE
400 METERS

GRAN VIA DE LES CORTS CATALANES

FORMER BULLRING **O**

PLAÇA D'ESPANYA **M**

AVINGUDA DE LA

VAN DER ROHE PAVILLION

MAGIC FOUNTAINS

SPANISH VILLAGE

AVINGUDA

CATALAN ART MUSEUM

CALATRAVA TOWER

OLYMPIC + SPORTS MUSEUM

M POBLE SEC

PARAL·LEL

FUNDACIÓ JOAN MIRÓ

PARAL·LEL **M**

TO OLD CITY →

CARRER NOU DE LA RAMBLA

L'ESTADI

FUNICULAR

OLYMPIC STADIUM

POOL

SARDANA SCULPTURE

CABLE CAR

GONDOLA TO PORT

MONTJUÏC CASTLE

MIRAMAR

PASSEIG JOSEP

CARNER

DCH

Miró museum, the funicular, and the Castle of Montjuïc. The blue Tourist Bus also does a circuit around the top of Montjuïc.

Castle of Montjuïc—The castle offers great city views from its fortress and, at least for now, a military museum (€3, Tue–Sun 9:30–20:00, closed Mon); plans are underway to move the museum to the town of Figueres in 2010. The seemingly endless museum houses a dull collection of guns, swords, and toy soldiers. An interesting section on the Spanish-American War of 1898 covers Spain's valiant fight against American aggression (from Spain's perspective). Unfortunately, there are no English descriptions. Those interested in Jewish history will find a fascinating collection of ninth-century Jewish tombstones.

The castle itself has a fascist past rife with repression. It was built in the 18th century by the central Spanish government to keep an eye on Barcelona and stifle citizen revolt. When Franco was in power, the castle was the site of hundreds of political executions.

Getting There: To spare yourself the hike up to the museum, and to catch some great views of the city, take the **cable car** from just above the upper station of the Montjuïc funicular (€6 one-way, €8.30 round-trip, June–Sept daily 10:00–21:00, until 19:00

April–May and Oct, until 18:00 Nov–March).

▲**Fundació Joan Miró**—Showcasing the talents of yet another Catalan artist, this museum has the best collection of Joan Miró art anywhere. You'll also see works by other Modern artists (such as *Mercury Fountain* by the American sculptor Alexander Calder). If you don't like abstract art, you'll leave here scratching your head. But those who love this place are not faking it...they understand the genius of Miró and the fun of abstract art.

As you wander, consider this: Miró believed that everything in the cosmos is linked—colors, sky, stars, love, time, music, dogs, men, women, dirt, and the void. He mixed childlike symbols of these things creatively, as a poet uses words. It's as liberating for the visual artist to be abstract as it is for the poet: Both can use metaphors rather than being confined to concrete explanations. Miró would listen to music and paint. It's interactive, free interpretation. He said, "For me, simplicity is freedom."

COPA DEL MUNDO DE FUTBOL ESPAÑA 82

Here are some tips to help you enjoy and appreciate Miró's art: first meditate on it, then read the title (for example, *The Smile of a Tear*), then meditate on it again. Repeat the process until you have an epiphany. There's no correct answer—it's pure poetry. Devotees of Miró say they fly with him and don't even need drugs. You're definitely much less likely to need drugs if you take advantage of the wonderful audioguide, well worth the €4 extra charge (€8, Tue–Sat July–Sept 10:00–20:00, Oct–June 10:00–19:00, Thu until 21:30, Sun 10:00–14:30, closed Mon, 200 yards from top of funicular, Parc de Montjuïc, tel. 934-439-470, www.bcn.fjmiro.es). The museum has a cafeteria, café, and bookshop.

Olympic and Sports Museum (Museu Olímpic i de l'Esport)—This new attraction rides the coattails of the stadium across the street (see next listing). You'll twist down a timeline-ramp that traces the history of the Olympic Games, interspersed with random exhibits about various sports. Downstairs you'll find exhibits designed to test your athleticism, a play-by-play rehash of the '92 Barcelona Olympiad, a commemoration of Spaniard Juan Antonio Samaranch (the influential president of the IOC for two decades), a sports media exhibit, and a schmaltzy movie collage. High-tech but still hokey, the museum is worth the time and money only for those nostalgic for the '92 Games (€4, Tue–Sat April–Sept 10:00–20:00, Oct–March 10:00–18:00, Sun 10:00–14:30, closed Mon, Avinguda de l'Estadi 60, tel. 932-925-379, www.fundaciobarcelonaolimpica.es).

Olympic Stadium (Estadi Olímpic)—For two weeks in the summer of 1992, the world turned its attention to this stadium (between the Catalan Art Museum and the Fundació Joan Miró at Passeig Olímpic 17). Redesigned from an earlier 1929 version, the stadium was updated, expanded, and officially named for Catalan patriot Lluís Companys i Jover. The XXV Olympiad kicked off here on July 25, when an archer dramatically lit the Olympic torch—which still stands high at the end of the stadium overlooking the city skyline—with a flaming arrow. Over the next two weeks, Barcelona played host to the thrill of victory (mostly at the hands of Magic Johnson, Michael Jordan, Larry Bird, and the rest of the US basketball "Dream Team") and the agony of defeat (i.e., the nightmares of the Dream Team's opponents). Hovering over the stadium is the memorable futuristic Calatrava Communications Tower, used to transmit Olympic highlights and lowlights around the world. Aside from the memories of the medals, Olympic Stadium offers little to see today...except when it's hosting a match for Barcelona's soccer team, RCD Espanyol.

Spanish Village (Poble Espanyol)—This tacky five-acre model village uses fake traditional architecture from all over Spain as a shell to contain gift shops. Craftspeople do their clichéd thing only in the morning (not worth your time or €8.50, www.poble-espanyol.com). After hours, it's a popular local nightspot.

▲▲Catalan Art Museum (Museu Nacional d'Art de Catalunya)—The big vision for this wonderful museum is to

showcase Catalan art from the 10th century through about 1930. Often called "the Prado of Romanesque art" (and "MNAC" for short), it holds Europe's best collection of Romanesque frescoes (€8.50, ticket valid for two days within one month, includes audioguide, free first Sun of month, open Tue–Sat 10:00–19:00, Sun 10:00–14:30, closed Mon, last entry 30 min before closing; in massive National Palace building above Magic Fountains, near Plaça d'Espanya—take escalators up; tel. 936-220-376, www.mnac.es).

As you enter, pick up a map (helpful for such a big and confusing building). The left wing is Romanesque, and the right wing is Gothic, exquisite Renaissance, and Baroque. Upstairs is more Baroque, plus modern art, photography, coins, and more.

The MNAC's rare, world-class collection of **Romanesque** art came mostly from remote Catalan village churches in the Pyrenees (saved from unscrupulous art dealers—including many Americans). The Romanesque wing features frescoes, painted wooden altar fronts, and ornate statuary. This classic Romanesque art—with flat 2-D scenes, each saint holding his symbol, and Jesus (easy to identify by the cross in his halo)—is impressively displayed on replicas of the original church ceilings and apses.

Across the way, in the **Gothic** wing, fresco murals give way to vivid 14th-century wood-panel paintings of Bible stories. A roomful of paintings (Room 34) by the Catalan master Jaume Huguet (1412–1492) deserves a look, particularly his altarpiece of Barcelona's patron saint, George.

For a break, glide under the huge dome (which once housed an ice-skating rink) over to the air-conditioned cafeteria. This was the prime ceremony room and dance hall for the 1929 International Exposition. Then, from the big ballroom, ride the glass elevator upstairs, where the **Modern** section takes you on a delightful walk from the late 1800s to about 1930. It's kind of a Catalan Musée d'Orsay, offering a big chronological clockwise circle covering Spain's Golden Age (Zurbarán, heavy religious scenes, Spanish royals with their endearing underbites), Symbolism and Modernisme (furniture complements the empty spaces you likely saw in Gaudí's buildings), Impressionists, *fin de siècle* fun, and Art Deco.

Upstairs you'll also find photography (with a bit on how photojournalism came of age covering the Spanish Civil War), seductive sofas, and the chic Oleum restaurant, with vast city views (and €20 meals).

▲**Magic Fountains (Font Màgica)**—Music, colored lights, and huge amounts of water make an artistic and coordinated splash on summer nights at Plaça d'Espanya (20-min shows start on the half-hour; almost always May–Sept Thu–Sun 21:00–23:30, no shows Mon–Wed; Oct–April Fri–Sat 19:00–21:00, no shows Sun–Thu; from the Espanya Metro station, walk toward the towering National Palace).

Away from the Center
Tibidabo—Tibidabo comes from the Latin for "to thee I shall give," the words the devil used when he was tempting Christ. It's still an enticing offer: At the top of Barcelona's highest peak, you're offered the city's oldest fun-fair (€25, erratic hours, tel. 932-117-942, www.tibidabo.es), the Neo-Gothic Sacred Heart Church,

and—if the weather and air quality are good—an almost limitless view of the city and the Mediterranean.

Getting there is part of the fun: Start by taking the L7 line from the Plaça de Catalunya Station (under Café Zürich) to the Tibidabo stop. (The red Tourist Bus stops here, too.) Then take Barcelona's only remaining tram—the Tramvía Blau—from Plaça John F. Kennedy to Plaça Dr. Andreu (€4 round-trip, 2–4/hr). From there, take the funicular to the top (€4, fare is reimbursable with paid admission, tel. 906-427-017). A special "Tibibus" runs from Plaça de Catalunya to the park every day at 10:30 (€2.60, reimbursable with paid admission).

Nightlife in Barcelona

Sightseeing After Dark

Refer to the *See Barcelona* guide (free from TI) and ask about the latest at a TI. Major sights open until 20:00 include the Picasso Museum (closed Mon), Gaudí's Sagrada Família (daily, until 18:00 Oct–March), Casa Milà (daily, until 18:30 Nov–Feb), and Parc Güell (daily). On Thursday, Montjuïc's Joan Miró museum stays open until 21:30 (otherwise open July–Sept Tue–Sat until 20:00).

Many lesser sights also stay open at least until 20:00, such as La Boquería market (Mon–Sat), Columbus Monument (May–Oct daily), City History Museum (April–Sept Tue–Sun), Church of Santa Maria del Mar (daily), Casa Batlló (daily), Parc Güell's Gaudí House and Museum (April–Sept daily), Castle of Montjuïc (Tue–Sun), and Citadel Park (daily). The Magic Fountains on Plaça d'Espanya make a splash on weekend evenings (Fri–Sat, plus Thu and Sun in summer). The Tourist Bus runs until 22:00 every day in summer.

Music and Entertainment

The weekly *Guía del Ocio,* sold at newsstands for €1 (or free in some hotel lobbies), is a Spanish-language entertainment listing (with guidelines for English-speakers inside the back cover; www.guiadelocio.com). The monthly *Barcelona Metropolitan* magazine and quarterly *What's On Barcelona* are also helpful (free from the TI). For music, consider a performance at Casa Milà ("Pedrera by Night" July concert series, see page 75), the Liceu Opera House (page 53), or the Catalan Concert Hall (page 68). There are many nightspots around Plaça Reial (such as the popular Jamboree).

Palau de la Virreina, an arts-and-culture TI, offers information on Barcelona cultural events—music, opera, and theater (daily 10:00–20:00, Ramblas 99, see map on page 49).

Sleeping in Barcelona

Book ahead. Barcelona is Spain's most expensive city. Still, it has reasonable rooms. Cheap places are more crowded in summer; fancier business-class hotels fill up in winter and offer discounts on weekends and in summer. When considering relative hotel values, in summer and on weekends you can often get modern comfort in business-class hotels for about the same price (€100) as you'll pay for ramshackle charm (and only a few minutes' walk from the Old City action). Some TI branches (including those at Plaça de Catalunya, Plaça de Sant Jaume, and the airport) offer a room-finding service, though it's cheaper to go direct. Note that prices at the Hotel Continental Barcelona and the Hotel Continental Palacete include great all-day snack-and-drink bars; several other hotels also offer free breakfasts to those who book direct with this guidebook.

Business-Class Comfort near Plaça de Catalunya

These hotels have sliding glass doors leading to plush reception areas, air-conditioning, and perfectly sterile modern bedrooms. Most are on big streets within two blocks of Barcelona's exuberant central square. As business-class hotels, they have hard-to-pin-down prices that fluctuate wildly. I've listed the average rate you'll pay. But in summer and on weekends, supply often far exceeds the demand, and many of these places cut prices to around €100—always ask for a deal.

$$$ **Hotel Catalonia Albinoni,** the best-located of all, elegantly fills a renovated old palace with wide halls, hardwood floors, and 83 rooms. It overlooks a thriving pedestrian boulevard in front and a quiet swimming-pool garden in back (Sb-€148, Db-€183, extra bed-€35, family rooms, back rooms have private little sun terraces and cost extra; great free buffet breakfast—normally €15/person—when you book direct, pay the full rate, and show this book in 2010; lower promotional rates in summer—but free breakfast not valid with discounts, non-smoking, air-con, elevator, fee for Internet access and Wi-Fi, restaurant, a block down from Plaça de Catalunya at Avinguda Portal de l'Angel 17, tel. 933-184-141, fax 933-012-631, www.hoteles-catalonia.com, albinoni.reservas @hoteles-catalonia.es).

$$$ **Hotel Catalonia Duques de Bergara** has four stars, an elegant old entryway, splashy public spaces, slick marble and hardwood floors, 150 comfortable but nothing-fancy rooms, and a garden courtyard with a pool a world away from the big-city noise (Sb-€173, Db-€213, Tb-€243, breakfast-€15, non-smoking rooms available on request, air-con, elevator, free Internet access and

---

Sleep Code

(€1 = about $1.40, country code: 34)
S = Single, **D** = Double/Twin, **T** = Triple, **Q** = Quad, **b** = bathroom,
s = shower only. Unless otherwise noted, credit cards are
accepted, English is spoken, and prices listed generally
include the 7 percent tax. Hotel breakfasts can range from
free to simple €3 spreads to €25 buffets.

To help you easily sort through these listings, I've divided
the rooms into three categories, based on the price for a
standard double room with bath (during high season):

$$$ Higher Priced—Most rooms €150 or more.
  $$ Moderately Priced—Most rooms between €100–150.
   $ Lower Priced—Most rooms €100 or less.

While many of my recommendations are on pedestrian
streets, night noise can be a problem (especially in cheap
places, which have single-pane windows). For a quiet night,
ask for "*tranquilo*" rather than "*con vista.*"

Wi-Fi, a half-block off Plaça de Catalunya at Carrer de Bergara
11, tel. 933-015-151, fax 933-173-442, www.hoteles-catalonia.com,
duques@hoteles-catalonia.es).

$$$ Nouvel Hotel, in an elegant, Victorian-style building on
a handy pedestrian street, is less business-oriented and offers more
character than the others listed here. It boasts royal lounges and
78 comfy rooms (Sb-€102, Db-€179, includes breakfast, manager
Roberto promises a 10 percent discount on these prices with this
book in 2010—you must reserve direct via email, not their website,
extra bed-€35, deposit for TV remote-€20, air-con, elevator, free
Wi-Fi, Carrer de Santa Ana 20, tel. 933-018-274, fax 933-018-370,
www.hotelnouvel.com, info@hotelnouvel.com).

$$ Hotel Reding, on a quiet street a five-minute walk west
of the Ramblas and Plaça de Catalunya action, is a slick and sleek
place renting 44 mod rooms at a good price (Db-€120—price
includes breakfast with this book in 2010, online deals, extra bed-
€38, breakfast-€14, non-smoking rooms, air-con, elevator, free
Internet access and Wi-Fi, near Metro: Universitat, Gravina 5–7,
tel. 934-121-097, fax 932-683-482, www.hotelreding.com, reding
@oh-es.com).

$$ Hotel Duc de la Victoria, with 156 rooms, is profes-
sional yet friendly, buried in the Barri Gòtic just three blocks off
the Ramblas (Db-€140, bigger "superior" rooms on a corner with
windows on 2 sides-€25 extra, breakfast-€15, non-smoking, air-
con, elevator, free Internet access-15 min/day, fee Wi-Fi, Duc 15,

Hotels near the Ramblas

Hotels Key

❶ Hotel Catalonia Albinoni
❷ Hotel Catalonia Duques de Bergara
❸ Nouvel Hotel
❹ Hotel Reding
❺ Hotel Duc de la Victoria
❻ Hotels Lleó & Atlantis
❼ Hotel Continental Barcelona
❽ Hostería Grau & Barcelona Rent-A-Bike
❾ Hotel Jardí
❿ Hostal Opera
⓫ Hotel Neri
⓬ Hotel Regencia Colón
⓭ Hostal Campi
⓮ Hostal Maldá
⓯ To Sea Point Hostel
⓰ Launderette

tel. 932-703-410, fax 934-127-747, www.nh-hotels.com, nhducdela victoria@nh-hotels.com).

$$ Hotel Lleó (YEH-oh) is well-run, with 89 big, bright, and comfortable rooms; a great breakfast room; and a generous lounge (Db-€130 but flexes way up with demand, can be cheaper in summer, extra bed-about €25, breakfast-€12, non-smoking rooms, air-con, elevator, small rooftop pool, free Internet access and Wi-Fi, 2 blocks west of Plaça de Catalunya at Carrer de Pelai 22, tel. 933-181-312, fax 934-122-657, www.hotel-lleo.es, reservas @hotel-lleo.es).

$$ Hotel Atlantis is solid, with 50 big, homey-yet-mod rooms and great prices for the location (Sb-€90, Db-€107, Tb-€125, refreshingly stable rates, breakfast-€9, non-smoking rooms, air-con, elevator, free Internet access and Wi-Fi in lobby and on first floor, older windows let in a bit more street noise than other hotels in this category—request a quieter room in back, Carrer de Pelai 20, tel. 933-189-012, fax 934-120-914, www.hotelatlantis-bcn.com, inf@hotelatlantis-bcn.com).

Hotels with "Personality" on or near the Ramblas

These recommended places are generally family-run, with ad-lib furnishings, more character, and lower prices. Only the Jardí offers a quaint square buried in the Barri Gòtic ambience—but you're definitely paying for the location.

$ Hotel Continental Barcelona, in a building overlooking the top of the Ramblas, offers an inviting lounge and classic, tiny-view balcony opportunities if you don't mind the noise. Its comfortable rooms come with double-thick mattresses, wildly clashing carpets and wallpaper, and perhaps one too many clever ideas (they're laden with microwaves, fridges, a "command center" of light switches, and Tupperware drawers). Choose between your own little Ramblas-view balcony (where you can eat your break-fast) or a quieter back room (Sb-€87, Db-€97, twin Db-€107, Db with Ramblas balcony-€117, extra bed-€30, 5 percent discount with this book in 2010, prices include breakfast, non-smoking, air-con, elevator, free Internet access and Wi-Fi, Ramblas 138, tel. 933-012-570, fax 933-027-360, www.hotelcontinental.com, barcelona@hotelcontinental.com). J. M.'s (José María) free break-fast and all-day snack-and-drink bar make this a better deal than the price suggests.

$ Hostería Grau is homey, family-run, and almost alpine. Its 25 cheery, garden-pastel rooms are a few blocks off the Ramblas in the colorful university district. The first two floors have ceilings a claustrophobic seven feet high, then things get tall again (S-€35, D-€65, Db-€90, extra bed-€15; 2-bedroom family suites: Db-€95, Tb-€130, Qb-€160; slippery prices jump during fairs and big events, air-con, free Internet access and Wi-Fi, lots of stairs with no elevator, 200 yards up Carrer dels Tallers from the Ramblas at Ramelleres 27, tel. 933-018-135, fax 933-176-825, www.hostalgrau .com, reservas@hostalgrau.com, Monica). Before booking, con-firm the hotel's strict cancellation policy—generally if canceling a room less than 48 hours in advance (or a suite less than five days in advance), you'll pay for the first night.

$ Hotel Jardí offers 40 clean, remodeled rooms on a breezy square in the Barri Gòtic. Many of the tight, plain, comfy rooms come with petite balconies (for an extra charge) and enjoy an almost Parisian ambience. It's a good deal only if you value the cute square location. Book well in advance, as this family-run place has an avid following (small basic interior Db-€79, nicer interior Db-€89, outer Db with balcony or twin with window-€95, large outer Db with balcony or square-view terrace-€106, extra bed-€12, break-fast-€6, non-smoking, air-con, elevator, some stairs, free Wi-Fi in lobby, halfway between Ramblas and cathedral at Plaça Sant Josep Oriol 1, tel. 933-015-900, fax 933-425-733, www.hoteljardi -barcelona.com, reservations@hoteljardi-barcelona.com).

$ Hostal Opera, with 70 stark rooms 20 yards off the Ramblas, is clean, institutional, and modern. The street can feel seedy at night, but it's safe, and the hotel is very secure (Sb-€49, Db-€69, no breakfast, air-con only in summer, elevator, fee for Internet access and free Wi-Fi in lobby, Carrer Sant Pau 20, tel. 933-188-201, www.operaramblas.com, info@operaramblas.com).

Deep in the Barri Gòtic

$$$ Hotel Neri is chic, posh, and sophisticated, with 22 rooms spliced into the ancient stones of the Barri Gòtic, overlooking an overlooked square (Plaça Sant Felip Neri) a block from the cathedral. It has big plasma-screen TVs, pricey modern art on the bedroom walls, and dressed-up people in its gourmet restaurant (Db-€265, suites-€360–425, generally cheaper on weekdays, breakfast-€21, air-con, elevator, free Wi-Fi, rooftop tanning deck, St. Sever 5, tel. 933-040-655, fax 933-040-337, www.hotelneri .com, info@hotelneri.com).

$$ Hotel Regencia Colón, one block in front of the cathedral square, offers 50 solid, well-priced rooms in a handy location (Db-€120, breakfast-€12, air-con, elevator, Carrer Sagristans 13–17, tel. 933-189-858, fax 933-172-822, www.hotelregenciacolon.com, info@hotelregenciacolon.com).

Humble, Cheaper Places Buried in the Old City

$ Hostal Campi is big, subdued, and ramshackle, but offers simple class. This easygoing old-school spot rents 24 rooms a few doors off the top of the Ramblas (S-€32, D-€54, Db-€62, T-€74, Tb-€84, no breakfast, non-smoking rooms, lots of stairs with no elevator, fee for Internet access, Canuda 4, tel. & fax 933-013-545, www .hostalcampi.com, reservas@hostalcampi.com, friendly Margarita and Nando).

$ Hostal Maldá rents the best cheap beds I found in the old center. With 25 rooms above a small shopping mall near the cathedral, it's a time-warp—quiet and actually charming—but does not take reservations (though you can try calling a day before). It generally remains full through the summer, but it's worth a shot (S-€15, D-€30, T-€45, cash only, lots of stairs with no elevator, 100 yards up Carrer del Pi from delightful Plaça Sant Josep Oriol, Carrer del Pi 5, tel. 933-173-002). Good-natured Aurora doesn't speak English, but Delfi, who works only half the year, does.

Hostels in the Center of Town

Barcelona has a wonderful chain of well-run and centrally located hostels (www.equity-point.com), providing €21–26 dorm beds in 4- to 14-bed coed rooms with €2 sheets and towels, free Internet access, Wi-Fi, breakfast, lockers (B.Y.O. lock, or buy one there), and plenty of opportunities to meet other backpackers. They're open 24 hours but aren't party hostels, so they enforce quiet after 23:00. There are three locations to choose from: Eixample, Barri Gòtic, or near the beach.

$ Centric Point Hostel is a huge new place renting 430 cheap beds at what must be the best address in Barcelona (bar, kitchen, Passeig de Gràcia 33, located on map on page 97, tel. 932-151-796, fax 932-461-552, www.centricpointhostel.com).

$ Gothic Point Hostel rents 150 beds a block from the Picasso Museum (roof terrace, Carrer Vigatans 5, see map on page 69, tel. 932-687-808, www.gothicpoint.com).

$ Sea Point Hostel has 70 beds on the beach nearby (Plaça del Mar 4, tel. 932-247-075, www.seapointhostel.com).

In the Eixample

For an uptown, boulevard-like neighborhood, sleep in the Eixample, a 10-minute walk from the Ramblas action (see map on page 97).

$$ Hotel Granvía, filling a palatial 1870s mansion, offers Botticelli and chandeliers in the public areas; a sprawling, peaceful sun patio; and 54 spacious, comfy rooms. Its salon is plush and royal, making the hotel an excellent value for romantics (Sb-€80, Db-€130 or €110 July–Aug, Tb-€150, these rates promised with this book in 2010 when you reserve directly by phone or email—not on their website—and mention my name, breakfast-€11, request a quiet room if street noise bothers you, non-smoking, air-con, elevator, free Internet access and Wi-Fi, Gran Via de les Corts Catalanes 642, tel. 933-181-900, fax 933-189-997, www.nnhotels .com, hgranvia@nnhotels.com, Juan works the morning shift).

$$ Hotel Continental Palacete, with 19 rooms, fills a 100-year-old chandeliered mansion. With flowery wallpaper and cheap but fancy furniture under ornately gilded stucco, it's gaudy in the city of Gaudí. But it's also friendly, clean, quiet, and well-located. Guests have unlimited access to the extravagant "cruise-inspired" fruit, veggie, and drink buffet—worth factoring into your comparison-shopping (Sb-€100, Db-€135, €35–45 more for bigger and brighter view rooms, extra bed-€55, 5 percent discount with this book in 2010, prices include breakfast, non-smoking, air-con, free Internet access and Wi-Fi, 2 blocks north of Plaça de Catalunya at corner of Carrer Diputació, Rambla de Catalunya 30, tel. 934-457-657, fax 934-450-050, www.hotelcontinental.com, palacete@hotelcontinental.com).

$ Hostal Residencia Neutral, with a classic Eixample address and 28 very basic rooms, is a family-run time warp and a fine value (tiny S-€35, Ds-€60, Db-€65, Ts-€75, Tb-€80, Qs-€80, Qb-€85, €8 continental breakfast in pleasant breakfast room, request a back room to avoid street noise, thin walls, fans, elevator, elegantly located 2 blocks north of Gran Via at Rambla de Catalunya 42, tel. 934-876-390, fax 934-876-848, hostalneutral@arrakis.es, owner Ramón, animated Lino).

$ Hotel Ginebra is minimal, clean, and quiet considering its central location. The Herrera family rents 12 rooms in a dated apartment building overlooking the main square (Db-€75 or €80 June–Aug, extra bed-€15, breakfast-€3, air-con, elevator, Rambla de Catalunya 1/3, tel. 933-171-063, www.hotelginebra.net, info @hotelginebra.net, Juan speaks English).

Hotels and Restaurants in Barcelona's Eixample

1. Hotel Granvía
2. Hotel Continental Palacete
3. Hostal Residencia Neutral
4. Hotel Ginebra
5. Somnio Hostel
6. Centric Point Hostel
7. La Rita Restaurant
8. La Bodegueta
9. Restaurante la Palmera
10. Restaurant Flauta
11. Cinc Sentits
12. El Racó
13. To Hofmann
14. "Qu Qu" Quasi Queviures
15. Ciudad Condal Cerveceria
16. La Tramoia

$ Somnio Hostel, an innovative new place run by a pair of American expats, has both dorm beds and private rooms (dorm bed-€25, S-€42, D-€77, Db-€85, air-con, elevator, Carrer de la Diputació 251, tel. 932-725-308, www.somniohostels.com, info @somniohostels.com).

Eating in Barcelona

Barcelona, the capital of Catalan cuisine—featuring seafood— offers a tremendous variety of colorful eateries, ranging from basic and filling to chic and trendy. Because of their common struggles, Catalans seem to have an affinity for Basque culture—so you'll find a lot of Basque tapas places here, too. (For more on Basque food, see page 133.) Most of my listings are lively spots with a busy tapas scene at the bar, along with restaurant tables for *raciones*. A regional specialty is *pa amb tomaquet* (pah ahm too-MAH-kaht), bread topped with a mix of crushed tomato and olive oil.

I've listed mostly practical, characteristic, colorful, and affordable restaurants. My recommendations are grouped by neighborhood—along the Ramblas; in the Barri Gòtic; in the Ribera neighborhood (best for foodies); and in the Eixample—followed by some budget options scattered throughout the city. Note that many restaurants close in August (or July), when the owners take a vacation.

Restaurants generally serve lunch from 13:00 to 16:00 and dinner from 20:00 until very late (Spaniards don't start dinner until about 21:00). It's deadly to your Barcelona experience to eat too early—if a place feels touristy, come back later and it may be a thriving local favorite. For dessert, I've suggested "A Short, Sweet Walk" (see page 108).

Along the Ramblas

Within a few steps of the Ramblas, you'll find handy lunch places, an inviting market hall, a slew of vegetarian options, and a giant tapas bar.

Lunching Simply yet Memorably near the Ramblas

While these places are enjoyable for a lunch break during your Ramblas sightseeing, many are also open for dinner. For locations, see the map on page 102.

Taverna Basca Irati serves 40 kinds of hot and cold Basque *pintxos* for €1.80 each. These are open-faced sandwiches—like sushi on bread. Muscle in through the hungry local crowd. Get an empty plate from the waiter, and then help yourself. Every few minutes, waiters prance proudly by with a platter of new, still-warm munchies. Grab one as they pass by...it's addictive. You pay on the honor system: You're charged by the number of toothpicks left on your plate when you're done. Wash it down with €2–3 glasses of Rioja (full-bodied red wine), Txakolí (sprightly Basque white wine), or *sidra* (apple wine) poured from on high to add oxygen and bring out the flavor (daily 11:00–24:00, a block off the Ramblas, behind arcade at Carrer Cardenal Casanyes 15, Metro: Liceu, tel. 933-023-084).

Restaurant Elisabets is a happy little neighborhood eatery packed with antique radios and popular with locals for its "homecooked" three-course €10 lunch special. Stop by for lunch, survey what those around you are enjoying, and order what looks best (Mon–Sat 7:30–23:00, closed Sun and Aug, lunch special served 13:00–16:00, otherwise only €3 tapas—not full meals, 2 blocks west of Ramblas on far corner of Plaça Bonsucces at Carrer Elisabets 2, tel. 933-175-826, run by Pilar).

Café Granja Viader is a quaint time-capsule place, family-run since 1870. They boast about being the first dairy business to bottle and distribute milk in Spain. This feminine-feeling place—specializing in baked and dairy delights, toasted sandwiches, and light meals—is ideal for a traditional breakfast. Or indulge your sweet tooth: Try a glass of *orxata* (or *horchata*—*chufa*-nut milk, summer only), *llet mallorquina* (Majorca-style milk with cinnamon, lemon, and sugar), *crema catalana* (crème brûlée, their specialty), or *suis* ("Swiss"—hot chocolate with a snowcap of whipped cream). *Mel y mato* is fresh cheese with honey...very Catalan (Tue–Sat 9:00–13:45 & 17:00–20:45, Mon 17:00–20:45 only, closed Sun, a block off the Ramblas behind El Carme church at Xucla 4, tel. 933-183-486).

Picnics: Shoestring tourists buy groceries at **El Corte Inglés** (Mon–Sat 10:00–22:00, closed Sun, supermarket in basement, Plaça de Catalunya) and **Carrefour Express supermarket** (Mon–Sat 10:00–22:00, closed Sun, Ramblas 113).

In and near La Boquería Market

Try eating at La Boquería market at least once (#91 on the Ramblas). Like all farmers markets in Europe, this place is ringed by colorful, good-value eateries. Lots of stalls sell fun take-away food—

especially fruit salads and fresh-squeezed fruit juices. There are several good bars around the market busy with shoppers munching at the counter (breakfast, tapas all day, coffee). The market, and most of the eateries listed here (unless noted), are open Monday through Saturday from 8:00 until 20:00 (though things get very quiet after about 16:00) and are closed on Sunday.

Pinotxo Bar is just to the right as you enter the market. It's a great spot for coffee, breakfast (spinach tortillas, or whatever's cooking with toast), or tapas. Fun-loving Juan and his family are La Boquería fixtures. Grab a stool across the way to sip your drink with people-watching views. Have a Chucho?

Kiosko Universal is popular for its great prices on wonderful fish dishes. As you enter the market from the Ramblas, it's all the way to the left in the first alley. If you see people waiting, ask who's last in line *("¿El último?")*. You'll eat immersed in the spirit of the market (€13 fixed-price lunches with different fresh-fish options from 12:00–16:00, always packed but better before 12:30, tel. 933-178-286).

Restaurant la Gardunya, at the back of the market, offers tasty meat and seafood meals made with fresh ingredients bought directly from the market (€13 fixed-price lunch includes wine and bread, €16 three-course dinner specials don't include wine, €10–20 à la carte dishes, Mon–Sat 13:00–16:00 & 20:00–24:00, closed Sun, mod seating indoors or outside watching the market action, Carrer Jerusalem 18, tel. 933-024-323).

Bar Terrace Restaurant Ra is a lively terrace immediately behind the market (at the right end of the big parking lot) with outdoor tables filled by young, trendy, happy eaters. At lunch they serve one great salad/pasta/wine meal for €11. If you feel like eating a big salad under an umbrella...this is the place (€9–15 à la carte dishes, daily 10:00–12:30 & 13:30–16:00 & 21:00–24:00, fancier menu at night, mobile 615-959-872).

Vegetarian Eateries near Plaça de Catalunya and the Ramblas

Biocenter, a Catalan soup-and-salad restaurant popular with local vegetarians, takes its cooking very seriously and feels a bit more like a real restaurant than most (€8–9.50 weekday lunch specials include soup or salad and plate of the day, €15 dinner specials, Mon–Sat 13:00–23:00, Sun 13:00–16:00, 2 blocks off the Ramblas at Pintor Fortuny 25, Metro: Catalunya, tel. 933-014-583).

Juicy Jones is a tutti-frutti vegan/vegetarian eatery with colorful graffiti decor, a hip veggie menu (served downstairs), groovy laid-back staff, and a stunning array of fresh-squeezed juices served at the bar. Pop in for a quick €3 "juice of the day." For lunch, you can get the Indian-inspired €6 *thali* plate, the €6.25 plate of the day, or an €8.50 meal including one of the two plates plus soup or salad and dessert (daily 13:00–24:00, also tapas and salads, Carrer Cardenal Casanyes 7, tel. 933-024-330). There's another location on the other side of the Ramblas (Carrer Hospital 74).

Out at Sea, at the Bottom of the Ramblas and in Barceloneta

Tapasbar Maremagnum is a big, rollicking, sports-bar kind of tapas restaurant, great for large groups. It's a fun way to end your Ramblas walk, featuring breezy harbor views and good local food with an emphasis on the sea. Go here, not for the tapas, but to make the Maremagnum scene (daily 11:00–24:00, a 10-minute stroll past the Columbus Monument straight out the dock on Moll d'Espanya, tel. 932-258-180).

La Mar Salada is a traditional seafood restaurant with a slight modern twist, located on the strip leading to the Barceloneta beach. Their à la carte menu includes seafood–and–rice dishes, fresh fish, and homemade deserts. A nice meal will run you about €30–35 per person (Wed–Mon 12:30–23:30, closed Tue, indoor and outdoor seating, Passeig Joan de Borbó 59, tel. 932-212-127).

In the Barri Gòtic

These eateries populate Barcelona's atmospheric Gothic Quarter, near the cathedral. Choose between a sit-down meal at a restaurant, or a string of very old-fashioned tapas bars.

Dining in the Barri Gòtic

Café de l'Academia is a delightful place on a pretty square tucked away in the heart of the Barri Gòtic—but patronized mainly by the neighbors. They serve "honest cuisine" from the market with Catalan roots. The candlelit, air-conditioned interior is rustic yet elegant, with soft jazz, flowers, and modern art. And if you want to eat outdoors on a convivial, mellow square...this is the place (€10–12 first courses, €12–15 second courses, fixed-price lunch for €10 at the bar or €14 at a table, Mon–Fri 13:30–16:00 & 20:30–23:30, closed Sat–Sun, near the City Hall square, off Carrer de Jaume I up Carrer Dagueria at Carrer Lledo 1, tel. 933-198-253).

Popular Chain Restaurants: Barcelona enjoys a chain of several bright, modern restaurants, all with different names. These five are a hit for their modern, artfully presented Spanish and Mediterranean cuisine, crisp ambience, and unbeatable prices. Because of their three-course €9 lunches and €16–20 dinners (both with wine), all are crowded with locals and in-the-know tourists (all open daily 13:00–15:45 & 20:30–23:30, unless otherwise noted). My favorite of the bunch is **La Crema Canela,** which feels cozier than the others and is the only one that takes reservations

BARCELONA

Barcelona's Barri Gòtic Restaurants

THE EIXAMPLE

PLAÇA UNIV.

GRAN   VIA   DE   LES

RONDA UNIVERSITAT

CARRER PELAI

BERGARA

RAMBLA DE CATALUNYA

BALMES

RONDA

PASSEIG DE GRÀCIA

CORTS   CATALANES

To BLOCK OF DISCORD & CASA MILÀ

Ramblas

M Metro Station

B Bus Stop

PLAÇA DE CATALUNYA

SANT

EL CORTE INGLÉS DEPT. STORE

PERE

VALLDON.

MACBA CONTEMP. ART MUSEUM

FGC TRAIN INFO

M Catalunya

FONTANELLA

BUS TO AIRPORT

CATALAN CONCERT HALL

ELIS.

BONSUCCES

SANTA ANNA

COMTAL

S. P. ALT

PINTOR

FORT.

XUCLA

CARME

PORTAL DE L'ANGEL

CANUDA

MONTSIO

LA RIBERA

S. P. BAIX

EL

CULTURAL INFO PALAU DE LA VIRREINA

Liceu

PORTAFER-

RISSA PL.

AV. CATEDRAL MAURÀ

RAVAL

LA BOQUERÍA MARKET

MIRO

CARD

BOQUERIA

BANYS NOUS

PALLA

NOVA

MARES MUSEUM

CATHEDRAL

TO PICASSO MUS.

SANT PAU

M Liceu

FERRAN

PLAÇA S. JAUME

PLAÇA DE L'ANGEL

PRINCESA

LICEU OPERA HOUSE

NOU RAMBLA

PLAÇA REIAL

CITY HALL

M Jaume I

PALAU GÜELL

L'ARC TEATRE

ESCUDELLERS

PL. ORWELL

CODOLS

TO S. MARIA D. MAR

MARITIME MUSEUM

M Drassanes

GIGNAS

AMPLE

MERCE

POST

CONS. MAR.

TO BARCELONETA

COLUMBUS MONUMENT

GOLONDRINAS CRUISES

CLAVE

PL. MED.

PASSEIG DE COLOM

MOLL DE BOSCH / ALSINA / LA FUSTA

HARBOR

RAMBLA DE MAR

to MAREMAGNUM

200 YARDS

200 METERS

Restaurants Key

1. Taverna Basca Irati
2. Restaurant Elisabets
3. Café Granja Viader
4. Supermarket
5. La Boquería Market Eateries
6. Biocenter Veggie Rest.
7. Juicy Jones
8. To Tapasbar Maremagnum & La Mar Salada
9. Café de l'Academia
10. La Crema Canela
11. La Fonda
12. Les Quinze Nits
13. La Dolça Herminia
14. Carrer de la Mercè Tapas Bars
15. Maoz Falafel
16. Casa Colomina
17. Granja La Pallaresa
18. Fargas Chocolate Shop

(30 yards north of Plaça Reial at Passatge de Madoz 6, tel. 933-182-744). The rest are notorious for long lines at the door—arrive 30 minutes before opening, or be prepared to wait. Like La Crema Canela, the next two are also within a block of the Plaça Reial: **La Fonda** (Carrer dels Escudellers 10, very close to a seedy stretch of street—approach it from the Ramblas rather than from Plaça Reial, tel. 933-017-515) and **Les Quinze Nits** (on Plaça Reial at #6—you'll see the line, tel. 933-173-075). The fourth place, **La Dolça Herminia,** is near the Catalan Concert Hall (2 blocks toward Ramblas from Catalan Concert Hall at Carrer de les Magdalenes 27, tel. 933-170-676). The fifth restaurant in the chain, **La Rita,** is described later under "Restaurants in the Eixample."

Tapas on Carrer de la Mercè in the Barri Gòtic

Barcelona boasts great *tascas*—colorful local tapas bars. Get small plates (for maximum sampling) by asking for "tapas," not the bigger "*raciones*." Glasses of *vino tinto* go for about €0.50. While

trendy uptown restaurants are safer, better-lit, and come with English menus and less grease, these places will stain your journal. The neighborhood's dark, the regulars are rough-edged, and you'll get a glimpse of a crusty Barcelona from before the affluence hit. Try *pimientos de padrón*—Russian roulette with peppers that are lightly fried in oil and salted...only a few are jalapeño-spicy. At the cider bars, it's traditional to order *queso de cabrales* (a traditional, very moldy bleu cheese) and spicy chorizo (sausage), ideally prepared *al diablo* ("devil-style")—soaked in wine, then flambéed at your table.

Several places serve *leche de pantera* (panther milk)—liquor mixed with milk.

From the bottom of the Ramblas (near the Columbus Monument), hike east along Carrer Clave. Then follow the small street that runs along the right side of the church (Carrer de la Mercè), stopping at the *tascas* that look fun. For a montage of edible memories, wander Carrer de la Mercè west to east and consider these spots, stopping wherever looks most inviting. I've listed ye olde dives, but there are many trendy places here as well. Most of these places close down around 23:00.

La Pulpería (at #16) has a bit less character than the others, but eases you into the scene with fried fish, octopus, and *patatas bravas,* all with Galician Ribeiro wine. Farther down at the corner (#28), **La Plata** keeps things wonderfully simple, serving extremely cheap plates of sardines (€1.70), little salads (€1.50), and small glasses of keg wine (less than €1). **Tasca el Corral** (#17) serves mountain favorites from northern Spain by the half-*ración* (see their list), such as *queso de cabrales* and chorizo *al diablo* with *sidra* (apple wine sold by the €5 bottle). **Sidrería Tasca La Socarrena** (#21) offers hard cider from Asturias in €5 bottles with *queso de cabrales* and chorizo. At the end of Carrer de la Mercè, **Cerveceria Vendimia** slings tasty clams and mussels (hearty *raciones* for €4–6 a plate—they don't do smaller portions, so order sparingly). Sit at the bar and point to what looks good. Their *pulpo* (octopus) is more expensive and is the house specialty. Carrer Ample and Carrer Gignas, the streets parallel to Carrer de la Mercè inland, have more refined bar-hopping possibilities.

In the Ribera District, near the Picasso Museum

La Ribera, the hottest neighborhood in town, sparkles with eclectic and trendy as well as subdued and classy little restaurants hidden in the small lanes surrounding the Church of Santa Maria del Mar. While I've listed a few well-established tapas bars that are great for light meals, to really dine, simply wander around for 15 minutes and pick the place that tickles your gastronomic fancy. I think those who say they know what's best in this area are kidding themselves—it's changing too fast and the choices are too personal. One thing's for sure: There are a lot of talented and hardworking restaurateurs with plenty to offer. Consider starting your evening off with a glass of fine wine at one of the *enotecas* on the square facing the Church of Santa Maria del Mar. Sit back and admire the pure Catalan Gothic architecture. My first three listings are all on the main drag, Carrer de l'Argenteria. For locations, see the map on page 69.

Sagardi offers a wonderful array of Basque goodies—tempting *pinchos* and *montaditos* at €1.80 each—along its huge bar. Ask for a plate and graze (just take whatever looks good). You can sit on the square with your plunder for €0.55 per tapa extra. Wash it down with Txakolí, a Basque white wine poured from the spout of a huge wooden barrel into a glass as you watch. When you're done, they'll count your toothpicks to tally your bill (daily 12:00–24:00, Carrer de l'Argenteria 62–64, tel. 933-199-993).

Sagardi Euskal Taberna, hiding behind the thriving Sagardi tapas bar (described above), is a mod, rustic, and minimalist woody restaurant committed to serving Basque T-bone steaks and grilled specialties with only the best ingredients. Crisp, friendly service and a big open kitchen with sizzling grills contribute to the ambience. Reservations are smart (€10–15 first courses, €20–25 second courses, plan on €45 for dinner, daily 13:00–16:00 & 20:00–24:00, Carrer de l'Argenteria 62, tel. 933-199-993).

Taller de Tapas ("Tapas Workshop") is an upscale, trendier tapas bar and restaurant that dishes up well-presented, sophisticated morsels and light meals in a medieval-stone yet mod setting. Pay 10 percent more to sit on the square. Elegant, but a bit stuffy, it's favored by local office workers who aren't into the Old World Gothic stuff. Four plates will fill a hungry diner for about €20 (daily 8:30–24:00, Carrer de l'Argenteria 51, tel. 932-688-559).

El Xampanyet, a colorful family-run bar with a fun-loving staff (Juan Carlos, his mom, and the man who may be his father), specializes in tapas and anchovies. Don't be put off by the seafood from a tin...Catalans like it this way. A *sortido* (assorted plate) of *carne* (meat) or *pescado* (fish) with *pa amb tomaquet* (bread with crushed-tomato spread) makes for a fun meal. While it's filled with tourists during the sightseeing day, this is a local favorite after dark. The scene is great but—especially during busy times—it's tough without Spanish skills. When I asked about the price, Juan Carlos said, "Who cares? The ATM is just across the street." Plan on spending €20 for a meal with wine (same price at bar or table, Tue–Sat 12:00–16:00 & 19:00–23:30, Sun 12:00–16:00 only, closed Mon, a half-block beyond the Picasso Museum at Montcada 22, tel. 933-197-003).

In the Eixample

The people-packed boulevards of the Eixample (Passeig de Gràcia and Rambla de Catalunya) are lined with appetizing eateries featuring breezy outdoor seating. Choose between a real restaurant or an upscale tapas bar. For locations, see the map on page 97.

Restaurants in the Eixample

La Rita is a fresh and dressy little restaurant serving Catalan cuisine near the Block of Discord. Their lunches (three courses with wine for €8, Mon–Fri 13:00–15:45) and dinners (€15, à la carte, daily 20:30–23:30) are a great value. Like most of its sister restaurants—described under "Dining in the Barri Gòtic," earlier—it takes no reservations and its prices attract long lines, so arrive just before the doors open...or wait (a block from Metro: Passeig de Gràcia, near corner of Carrer de Pau Claris and Carrer Arago at Arago 279, tel. 934-872-376).

La Bodegueta is an unbelievably atmospheric below-street-level bodega serving hearty wines, homemade vermouth, *anchoas* (anchovies), tapas, and *flautas*—sandwiches made with flute-thin baguettes. Its daily €11.50 lunch special of three courses with wine is served 13:00–16:00. A long block from Gaudí's Casa Milà, this makes a fine sightseeing break (Mon–Sat 8:00–24:00, Sun 19:00–24:00, at intersection with Provenza, Rambla de Catalunya 100, Metro: Provença, tel. 932-154-894).

Restaurante la Palmera serves a mix of Catalan, Mediterranean, and French cuisine in an elegant yet smoky room with bottle-lined walls. The smoke keeps out the tourists. This place offers great food, service, and value—for me, a very special meal in Barcelona. They have three zones: the classic main room, a more forgettable adjacent room, and a few outdoor tables. I like the classic room. Reservations are smart (€12 plates, creative €15 six-plate *degustation* lunch, Tue–Sat 13:00–15:45 & 20:30–23:15, closed Sun–Mon, Enric Granados 57, at the corner with Mallorca, tel. 934-532-338).

Restaurant Flauta fills two floors with enthusiastic eaters (I like the ground floor best). It's fresh and modern, with a fun, no-stress menu featuring €5 small plates, creative €4 *flauta* sandwiches, and a €12.50 three-course lunch deal including a drink. Good €2.30 wines by the glass are listed on the blackboard. This is a place to order high on the menu for a fine, moderately priced meal (Mon–Sat 13:00–24:00, closed Sun, fun-loving and helpful staff recommends the fried vegetables, no reservations possible, just off Via Diputació at d'Aribau 23, tel. 933-237-038).

Cinc Sentits ("Five Senses"), with only about 30 seats, is my gourmet recommendation. It's a chic, minimal—but slightly snooty—smoke-free place where all the attention goes to the fine service and elegantly presented dishes. It's run by Catalans who lived in Canada (so there's absolutely no language barrier) and serve avant-garde cuisine inspired by Catalan traditions and ingredients. Their €46 and €65 *degustation menus* are unforgettable extravaganzas. Reservations are required (Tue–Sat 13:30–15:00 & 20:30–23:00, closed Sun–Mon, near Carrer d'Aragó at d'Aribau 58, tel. 933-239-490).

El Racó is a local favorite for "creative Mediterranean cuisine"—pasta, pizza, crêpes, and salads (about €7–9 each) in a modern, lively, cavernous-but-bright, air-conditioned setting (daily 13:00–24:00, Rambla de Catalunya 25, tel. 933-175-688).

A Bit Farther Out: **Hofmann** is a renowned cooking school with an excellent if pricey restaurant serving modern Mediterranean market cuisine. Dress up and dine in intimate rooms papered with photos of famous patrons. The four-course €40 lunches are made up of just what the students are working on that day—so there's no choice (watch the students as they cook). Dinners can easily cost twice as much (à la carte). Save room (and euros) for the incredible desserts. Reserve long in advance, because locals love this place (Mon–Fri 13:30–15:15 & 21:00–23:15, closed Sat–Sun and Aug, 4 blocks northwest of Casa Milà at La Granada del Penedès 14–16, tel. 932-187-165, www.hofmann-bcn.com).

Tapas Bars in the Eixample

Many trendy and touristic tapas bars in the Eixample offer a cheery welcome and slam out the appetizers. These three are my favorites.

Quasi Queviures ("**Qu Qu**" for short) serves upscale tapas, sandwiches, or the whole nine yards—classic food served fast from a fun menu with modern decor and a high-energy sports-bar ambience. It's bright, clean, and not too crowded. Walk through their enticing kitchen to get to the tables in back. Committed to developing a loyal following, they claim, "We fertilize our local customers with daily specialties" (€2–3 tapas, €5 dinner salads, €7 plates, prices 17 percent higher on the terrace, daily 8:00–24:00, between Gran Via and Via Diputació at Passeig de Gràcia 24, tel. 933-174-512).

Ciudad Condal Cerveceria brags that it serves the best *montaditos* (€2–3 little open-faced sandwiches) and beers in Barcelona. It's an Eixample favorite, with an elegant bar and tables plus good seating out on the Rambla de Catalunya for all that people-watching action. It's classier than Qu Qu and packed after 21:00, when you'll likely need to put your name on a list and wait. While it has no restaurant-type menu, the list of tapas and *montaditos* is easy, fun, and comes with a great variety (including daily specials). This place is a cut above your normal tapas bar, but with reasonable prices (most tapas around €4–5, daily until 24:00, facing the intersection of Gran Via and Rambla de Catalunya at Rambla de Catalunya 18, tel. 933-181-997).

La Tramoia, at the opposite corner from Ciudad Condal Cerveceria, serves piles of cheap *montaditos* and tapas at its ground-floor bar and at nice tables inside and out. If Ciudad Condal

Cerveceria is jammed up, you're more likely to find a seat here. The brasserie-style restaurant upstairs bustles with happy local eaters enjoying grilled meats (€6–10 plates), but I'd stay downstairs for the €4 tapas (open daily, also facing the intersection of Gran Via and Rambla de Catalunya at Rambla de Catalunya 15, tel. 934-123-634).

Budget Options Around Town

Sandwiches: Bright, clean, and inexpensive sandwich shops proudly hold the cultural line against the fast-food invasion hamburgerizing the rest of Europe. Catalan sandwiches are made to order with crunchy French bread. Rather than butter, locals prefer *tomaquet* (a spread of crushed tomatoes). You'll see two big local chains (Pans & Company and Bocatta) everywhere, but these serve mass-produced McBaguettes ordered from a multilingual menu. I've had better luck with hole-in-the-wall sandwich shops—virtually as numerous as the chains—where you can see exactly what you're getting.

Kebabs: Kebab places are a good, super-cheap standby. A favorite, **Maoz Falafel,** lets you create the falafel of your dreams for €4 (just off the City Hall square at Plaça de Sant Jaume 7).

A Short, Sweet Walk

Let me propose this three-stop dessert (or, since these places close well before the traditional Barcelona dinnertime, a late-afternoon snack). You'll try a refreshing glass of *orxata,* munch some *churros con chocolate,* and visit a fine *xocolateria,* all within a three-minute walk of each other in the Barri Gòtic just off the Ramblas. Start at the corner of Carrer Portaferrissa midway down the Ramblas. For the best atmosphere, begin your walk at about 18:00 (note that the last place is closed on Sun). For locations, see the map on page 102.

Orxata at Casa Colomina: Walk down Carrer Portaferrissa to #8 (on the right). Casa Colomina, founded in 1908, specializes in homemade *torrons*—a variation of nougat made with almond, honey, and sugar, brought to Spain by the Moors 1,200 years ago. Three different kinds are sold in big €12 slabs: *blando, duro,* and *yema*—soft, hard, and yolk (€2 smaller chunks also available). In the summer, the shop also sells ice cream and the refreshing *orxata* (or *horchata*—a drink made from the *chufa* nut). Order a glass and ask to see and eat a *chufa* nut (a.k.a. earth almond or tiger nut;

Mon–Sat 10:00–20:30, Sun 12:30–20:30, tel. 933-122-511).

Churros con Chocolate at **Granja La Pallaresa:** Continue down Carrer Portaferrissa, taking a right at Carrer Petritxol to this fun-loving *xocolateria*. Older, elegant ladies gather here for the Spanish equivalent of tea time—dipping their greasy *churros* into pudding-thick cups of hot chocolate (€4.10 for five *churros con chocolate*, Mon–Fri 9:00–13:00 & 16:00–21:00, Sat–Sun 9:00–13:00 & 17:00–21:00, Carrer Petritxol 11, tel. 933-022-036).

Homemade Chocolate at Fargas: For your last stop, head for the ornate Fargas chocolate shop. Continue down Carrer Petritxol to the square, hook left through the two-part square, and then left up Carrer del Pi—it's on the corner of Portaferrissa and Carrer del Pi. Since the 19th century, gentlemen with walking canes have dropped by here for their chocolate fix. Founded in 1827, this is one of the oldest and most traditional chocolate shops in Barcelona. If they're not too busy, ask to see the old chocolate mill *("¿Puedo ver el molino?")* to the right of the counter. They sell even tiny quantities (one little morsel) by the weight—don't be shy. A delicious chunk of the crumbly semi-sweet house specialty costs €0.45 (tray by the mill). The tempting bonbons in the window cost about €1 each (Mon–Fri 9:30–13:30 & 16:00–20:00, Sat 10:00–14:00 & 16:00–20:00, closed Sun, tel. 933-020-342).

Connections

From Barcelona by Train: Unless otherwise noted, all of these trains depart from the Sants Station; however, some trains also stop at other stations more convenient to the downtown tourist zone: França Station, Passeig de Gràcia, or Plaça de Catalunya. Figure out if your train stops at these stations (and board there) to save yourself the trip to Sants.

The new **AVE train to Madrid** has shaved hours off that journey, making it faster than flying (when you consider that you're zipping from downtown to downtown). The train departs almost hourly. The nonstop train is a little more expensive (€130, 3 hrs) than the slightly slower train that makes a few stops and adds about a half-hour (€110, 3.5 hrs). Regular reserved AVE tickets can be pre-purchased at www.renfe.es and picked up at the station. If you have a railpass, you'll pay only a reservation fee of €25 for first class, which includes a meal (€15 second class, buy at any train station in Spain). Passholders can't reserve online through RENFE but can make the reservation at www.raileurope.com for delivery before leaving the US ($17 in second class, $40 in first class).

By Train to: Sitges (4/hr, 35–40 min, €2.80), **Montserrat** (departs from Plaça d'Espanya, hourly, 1.5 hrs, €14.60 round-trip, includes cable car or rack train to monastery—see details on page

123), **Figueres** (hourly, 1.5–2 hrs, €18.60 round-trip), **Sevilla** (3/day—one fast, 6 hrs, €133; one slow, 12 hrs, €60; and one night train, 10 hrs, €90), **Granada** (1/day Wed, Fri, and Sun only, 11.5 hrs, €60; also 1 night train/day, 12 hrs, €60), **Salamanca** (8/day, 6–7.5 hrs, change in Madrid from Atocha Station to Chamartín Station via Metro; 1 direct/day, 11.25 hrs), **San Sebastián** (2/day, 6–8.5 hrs, €40–60), **Málaga** (3/day—one fast, 5.5 hrs, €135; one slow, 13 hrs, €60; and one night train, 13 hrs, €62), **Lisbon** (no direct trains, head to Madrid and then catch night train to Lisbon, 17 hrs, about €100), **Nice** (1/day via Montpelier, about €100; cheaper connections possible with multiple changes including Cerbère), **Avignon** (5/day, fewer on weekends, 6–9 hrs, about €40, or about €65 for change in Montpellier), **Paris** (3/day, 9 hrs, 1–2 changes; 1 night train/day, 12 hrs, about €200, or €50 with railpass, reservation mandatory). Train info: tel. 902-240-202, www.renfe.es.

By Bus to: Madrid (14/day, 8 hrs, €28—a fraction of the AVE train price, departs from Nord bus station at Metro: Arc de Triomf on line 1, bus info tel. 902-260-606, Alsa bus company tel. 902-422-242), **Salamanca** (2/day, 11 hrs, Alsa buses), **Cadaqués** (2/day, 2.75 hrs, €21.15). Sarfa buses serve all the **coastal resorts** (tel. 902-302-025, www.sarfa.com). For bus schedules, see www.barcelonanord.com.

By Plane: Check the reasonable flights from Barcelona to Sevilla or Madrid. Vueling is Iberia's most popular discount airline (e.g., Barcelona–Madrid flights as low as €30 if booked in advance, tel. 902-333-933, www.vueling.com). Iberia (tel. 902-400-500, www.iberia.com) and Air Europa (tel. 902-401-501 or 932-983-907, www.aireuropa.com) offer €80 flights to Madrid. Also, for flights to other parts of Europe, consider British Airways (tel. 902-111-333, www.britishairways.com), easyJet (tel. 902-299-992, www.easyjet.com), and Ryanair (www.ryanair.com). Most use Barcelona's **El Prat de Llobregat Airport** (tel. 902-404-704), but Ryanair uses an airport 60 miles away called **Girona-Costa Brava** (tel. 972-186-600). Information on both airports can be found on the official Spanish airport website, www.aena.es.

For details on getting between either airport and downtown Barcelona, see "Arrival in Barcelona—By Plane," page 39.

NEAR BARCELONA

Figueres • Cadaqués • Sitges • Montserrat

Four fine sights are day-trip temptations from Barcelona.

Fans of Surrealism can combine a fantasy in Dalí-land by stopping at the Dalí Theater-Museum in Figueres (about two hours from Barcelona) and spending a day or two in the classy but sleepy port-town getaway of Cadaqués (pictured above, an hour from Figueres). Note that the Salvador Dalí House in Cadaqués requires reservations to visit (specifics covered later in this chapter). For the consummate day at the beach, head 45 minutes south to the charming and free-spirited resort town, Sitges. Pilgrims with hiking boots head an hour into the mountains for the most sacred spot in Catalunya: Montserrat.

Figueres

The town of Figueres (feeg-YEHR-ehs)—conveniently connected by train to Barcelona—is of sightseeing interest only for its Salvador Dalí Theater-Museum. In fact, the entire town seems Dalí-dominated.

Getting to Figueres: Figueres is an easy day trip from Barcelona, or a handy stopover en route to France (trains between Barcelona and France stop in Figueres). Trains to Figueres from Barcelona depart from Sants Station or from the RENFE Station at Metro: Passeig de Gràcia (hourly, 1.5–2 hrs, €18.60 round-trip). For bus connections to Cadaqués, see page 117.

Arrival in Figueres: From the train station, simply follow

Near Barcelona

FRANCE

SPAIN

TO COLLIOURE & PERPIGNAN

CERBÈRE
PORTBOU
PORT LLIGAT
FIGUERES
CADAQUÉS
ROSES
PÚBOL
GIRONA-COSTA BRAVA
GIRONA
MACANET
TOSSA
MANRESA
MONISTROL DE MONT.
BLANES
CREMALLERA RACK RAILWAY
MONT.-AERI
MONT-SERRAT
CABLE CAR
COSTA

RAIL
BUS

VILA-FRANCA
TO MADRID
SITGES
EL PRAT DE LLOBREGAT AIRPORT
BARCELONA

COSTA DAURADA

DCH

50 MILES
50 KM

Museu Dalí signs (and the crowds) for the 15-minute walk to the museum.

Sights in Figueres

▲▲▲Dalí Theater-Museum (Teatre-Museu Dalí)

This is *the* essential Dalí sight—and, if you like Dalí, one of Europe's most enjoyable museums, period. Inaugurated in 1974, the museum is a work of art in itself. Ever the entertainer and

promoter, Dalí personally conceptualized, designed, decorated, and painted it to showcase his life's work. The museum fills a former theater and is the artist's mausoleum (his tomb is in the crypt below center stage). It's also a kind of mausoleum to Dalí's creative spirit.

Dalí had his first public art

showing at age 14 here in this building when it was a theater, and he was baptized in the church just across the street. The place was sentimental to him. After the theater was destroyed in the Spanish Civil War, Dalí struck a deal with the mayor: Dalí would rebuild the theater as a museum to his works, Figueres would be put on the sightseeing map...and the money's been flowing in ever since.

Even the building's exterior—painted pink, studded with golden loaves of bread, and topped with monumental eggs and a geodesic dome—exudes Dalí's outrageous public persona.

Cost, Hours, Information: €11; July–Sept daily 9:00–20:00; June daily 9:30–18:00; Oct and March–May Tue–Sun 9:30–18:00, closed Mon; Nov–Feb Tue–Sun 10:30–18:00, closed Mon; last entry 45 minutes before closing, tel. 972-677-500, www.salvador -dali.org. The free bag check has your belongings waiting for you at the exit.

Coin-Op Tip: Much of Dalí's art is movable and coin-operated—bring a few €0.20 and €0.50 coins.

Visiting the Museum: The museum has two parts—the theater-mausoleum and the "Dalí's Jewels" exhibit in an adjacent building. There's no logical order for a visit (that would be un-Surrealistic). And, naturally, there's no audioguide. Dalí said there are two kinds of visitors: those who don't need a description, and those who aren't worth a description.

❷ Self-Guided Tour: At the risk of offending Dalí, I've written this loose commentary to attach some meaning to your visit.

Stepping into the **theater** (with its audience of statues), face the stage—and Dalí's unmarked crypt. You know how you can never get a cab when it's raining? Pop a coin into Dalí's personal 1941 Cadillac, and it rains inside the car. Look above, atop the tire tower: That's the boat enjoyed by Dalí and his soul mate, Gala—his emotional life preserver, who kept him from going overboard. When she died, so did he (for his last seven years). Blue tears made of condoms drip below the boat.

Up on the **stage,** squint at the big digital Abraham Lincoln, and president #16 comes into focus. Approach the painting to find that Abe's facial cheeks are Gala's butt cheeks. Under the painting, a door leads to the **Treasures Room,** with the greatest collection of actual Dalí original oil paintings in the museum. (Many of those you see on the walls are prints.) You'll see Cubist visions of Cadaqués and dreamy portraits of Gala. Crutches—a recurring Dalí theme—represent Gala, who kept him supported whenever a meltdown threatened.

The famous **Homage to Mae West room** is a tribute to the sultry seductress. Dalí loved her attitude. Saying things like, "Why marry and make one man unhappy, when you can stay single and make so many so happy?" Mae West was to conventional

Salvador Dalí
(1904–1989)

When Salvador Dalí was asked, "Are you on drugs?" he replied, "I am the drug...take me."

Labeled by various critics as sick, greedy, paranoid, arrogant, and a clown, Dalí produced some of the most thought-provoking and trailblazing art of the 20th century. His erotic, violent, disjointed imagery continues to disturb and intrigue today.

Born in Figueres to a well-off family, Dalí showed talent early. He was expelled from Madrid's prestigious art school—twice—but formed longtime friendships with the playwright Federico García Lorca and filmmaker Luis Buñuel.

After a breakthrough art exhibit in Barcelona in 1925, Dalí moved to Paris. He hobnobbed with fellow Spaniards Pablo Picasso and Joan Miró, along with a group of artists exploring Sigmund Freud's theory that we all have a hidden part of our mind, the unconscious "id," that surfaces when we dream. Dalí became the best-known spokesman for this group of Surrealists, channeling his id to create photorealistic dream images (melting watches, burning giraffes) set in bizarre dreamscapes.

His life changed forever in 1929, when he met an older, married Russian woman named Gala who would become his wife, muse, model, manager, and emotional compass. Dalí's popular-

morality what Dalí was to conventional art. Climb to the vantage point where the sofa lips, fireplace nostrils, painting eyes, and drapery hair come together to make the face of Mae West.

Dalí's art can be playful, but also disturbing. He was passionate about the dark side of things, but with Gala for balance, he managed never to go off the deep end. Unlike Pablo Casals (the Catalan cellist) and Pablo Picasso (another local artist), Dalí didn't go into exile under Franco's dictatorship. Pragmatically, he accepted both Franco and the Church, and was supported by the dictator. Apart from the occasional *sardana* dance (see page 62), you won't find a hint of politics in Dalí's art.

ity spread to the US, where he (and Gala) weathered the WWII years.

In his prime, Dalí's work became less Surrealist and more classical, influenced by past masters of painted realism (Velázquez, Raphael, Ingres) and by his own study of history, science, and religion. He produced large-scale paintings of historical events (e.g., Columbus discovering America, the Last Supper) that were collages of realistic scenes floating in a surrealistic landscape, peppered with thought-provoking symbols.

Dalí—an extremely capable technician—mastered many media, including film. *An Andalusian Dog* (*Un Chien Andalou*, 1929, with Luis Buñuel) was a cutting-edge montage of disturbing, eyeball-slicing images. For Alfred Hitchcock, he designed the big-eye backdrop for the dream sequence of *Spellbound* (1945). He made jewels for the rich and clothes for Coco Chanel, wrote a novel and an autobiography, and pioneered what would come to be called "installations." He also helped develop "performance art" by showing up at an opening in a diver's suit or by playing the role he projected to the media—a super-confident, waxed-mustached artistic genius.

In later years, Dalí's over-the-top public image contrasted with his ever-growing illness, depression, and isolation. He endured the scandal of a dealer overselling "limited editions" of his work. When Gala died in 1982, Dalí retreated to his hometown, living his last days in the Torre Galatea of the Theater-Museum complex, where he died of heart failure.

Dalí's legacy as an artist includes his self-marketing persona, his exceptional ability to draw, his provocative pairing of symbols, and his sheer creative drive.

Wander around. You can spend hours here, wondering, is it real or not real? Am I crazy, or is it you? Beethoven is painted with squid ink applied by a shoe on a stormy night. Jesus is made with candle smoke and an eraser. It's fun to see the Dalí-ization of art classics. Dalí, like so many modern artists, was inspired by the masters—especially Velázquez.

The former theater's **smoking lounge** is a highlight, displaying portraits of Gala and Dalí (with a big eye, big ear, and a dark side) bookending a Roman candle of creativity. The fascinating ceiling painting shows the feet of Gala and Dalí as they bridge earth and the heavens. Dalí's drawers are wide open and empty, indicating that he gave everything to his art.

Leaving the theater, keep your ticket and pop into the adjacent **"Dalí's Jewels"** exhibit. It shows sketches and paintings of jewelry Dalí designed, and the actual pieces jewelers made from those surreal visions: a mouth full of pearly whites, a golden finger corset, a fountain of diamonds, and the breathing heart. Explore the ambiguous perception worked into the big painting titled *Apotheosis of the Dollar.*

Cadaqués

Since the late 1800s, Cadaqués (kah-dah-KEHS) has served as a haven for intellectuals and artists alike. The fishing village's craggy coastline, sun-drenched colors, and laid-back lifestyle inspired Fauvists such as Henri Matisse and Surrealists such as René Magritte, Marcel Duchamp, and Federico García Lorca. Even Picasso, drawn to this enchanting coastal haunt, painted some of his Cubist works here.

Salvador Dalí, raised in nearby Figueres, brought international fame to this sleepy Catalan port in the 1920s. As a kid, Dalí spent summers here in the family cabin, where he was inspired by the rocky landscape that would later be the backdrop for many Surrealist canvases. In 1929, he met his future wife, Gala, in Cadaqués. Together, they converted a fisherman's home in nearby Port Lligat into their semi-permanent residence, dividing their time between New York, Paris, and Cadaqués. And it was here that Dalí did his best work.

In spite of its fame, Cadaqués is mellow and feels off the beaten path. If you want a peaceful beach-town escape near Barcelona, this is a good place. From the moment you descend into the town, taking in whitewashed buildings and deep blue waters, you'll be struck by the port's tranquility and beauty. Join the locals playing chess or cards at the cavernous Casino Coffee House (harborfront, with games and Internet access). Have a glass of *vino tinto* or *cremat* (a traditional rum-and-coffee drink served flambé-style) at one of the seaside cafés. Savor the lapping waves, brilliant sun, and gentle breeze. And, for sightseeing, the reason to come to Cadaqués is the Salvador Dalí House, a 20-minute walk from the town center at Port Lligat.

Tourist Information: The TI is at Carrer Cotxe 2 (July–Sept Mon–Sat 9:00–21:00, Sun 10:00–13:00, shorter hours off-season plus closed for lunch, tel. 972-258-315).

Getting to Cadaqués

Reaching Cadaqués is very tough without a car. There are no trains and only a few buses a day.

By Car: It's a twisty drive from Figueres (figure 45–60 min). In Cadaqués, drivers should park in the big lot just above the city—don't try to park near the harborfront. To reach the Salvador Dalí House, follow signs near Cadaqués to Port Lligat (easy parking).

By Bus: Cadaqués is connected by Sarfa buses to **Figueres** (3/day, 60 min, €4.75) and to **Barcelona** (2/day, more in July–Aug, 2.75 hrs, €21.15). Bus info: Barcelona tel. 902-302-025, Cadaqués tel. 972-258-713, Figueres tel. 972-674-298, www.sarfa.com. (Note that it's generally more expensive to dial 902 numbers.)

Sights near Cadaqués

In Port Lligat

▲▲▲Salvador Dalí House (Casa Museu Salvador Dalí)— Once Dalí's home, this house gives fans a chance to explore his

labyrinthine compound. This is the best artist's house I've toured in Europe. It shows how a home can really reflect the creative spirit of an artistic genius and his muse. The ambience both inside and out is perfect for a Surrealist hanging out with his creative playmate. The bay is ringed by sleepy islands. Fishing boats are jumbled on the beach. After the fishermen painted their boats, Dalí asked them to clean their brushes on his door—creating an abstract work of art he adored (which you'll see as you line up to get your ticket).

The interior is left almost precisely as it was in 1982, when Gala died and Dalí moved out. See Dalí's studio (the clever easel cranks up and down to allow the artist to paint while seated, as he did eight hours a day); the bohemian-yet-divine living room (complete with a mirror to reflect the sunrise onto their bed each morning); the phallic-shaped swimming pool, which was the scene of orgiastic parties; and the painter's study (with his favorite mustaches all lined up). Like Dalí's art, his home is offbeat, provocative, and fun.

Cost and Hours: €10; mid-June–mid-Sept daily 9:30–21:00; mid-March–mid-June and mid-Sept–early Jan Tue–Sun 10:30–18:00, closed Mon; closed early Jan–mid-March. Last tour departs 50 minutes before closing.

Touring the House: Reservations are mandatory—call or go online in advance to book a time (tel. 972-251-015, www.salvador-dali.org). Only 8–10 people are allowed in (no large groups) every 10 minutes. In summer, book a week in advance. You must arrive 30 minutes early to pick up your ticket, or they'll sell it. Once inside, there are five sections, each with a guard who gives you a brief explanation in English, and then turns you loose for a few minutes. The entire visit takes 50 minutes. Before your tour, enjoy the 15-minute video that plays in the waiting lounge (with walls covered in Dalí media coverage) just across the lane from the house.

Getting There: Parking is free nearby. There are no buses or taxis. The house is a 20-minute, one-mile walk over the hill from Cadaqués to Port Lligat. (The path, which cuts across the isthmus, is much shorter than the road.)

Sleeping in Cadaqués

$$ Hotel Llané Petit, with 37 spacious rooms (half with view balconies), is a small resort-like hotel with its own little beach, a 10-minute walk south of the town center (Db-€150 mid-July–Aug, €120 in shoulder season, €90 in winter, €10 more for seaview rooms, air-con, elevator, Dr. Bartomeus 37, tel. 972-251-020, fax 972-258-778, www.llanepetit.com, info@llanepetit.com). Book direct with this guidebook to get a free €12 breakfast (not valid on weekends and mid-July–Aug).

$ Hotel Nou Estrelles is a big concrete exercise in efficient, economic comfort. Facing the bus stop a few blocks from the waterfront, this family-run hotel offers 15 rooms at a great value (Db-€82 in high season, €68 in shoulder season, €55 in winter, extra bed-€10, breakfast-€7, air-con, elevator, Carrer Sant Vicens, tel. 972-259-100, www.hotelnouestrelles.com, nouestrelles@yahoo .es, Emma).

$ Hostal Marina is a cheap, low-energy place, with 27 rooms and a great location a block from the harborfront main square (D-€40, Db-€50, balcony rooms-€10 extra, cheaper off-season, no breakfast, no elevator, no English, Riera 3, tel. 972-159-091).

Sleep Code

(€1 = about $1.40, country code: 34)
S = Single, **D** = Double/Twin, **T** = Triple, **Q** = Quad, **b** = bathroom, **s** = shower only. Unless otherwise noted, credit cards are accepted and English is spoken.

To help you easily sort through these listings, I've divided the rooms into two categories, based on the price for a standard double room with bath (during high season):

$$ Higher Priced—Most rooms €85 or more.
$ Lower Priced—Most rooms less than €85.

Eating in Cadaqués

Plenty of eateries are along the beach. A lane called Carrer Miguel Rosset (across from Hotel La Residencia) also has several places worth considering. At **Casa Anita** you'll sit with others around a big table and enjoy house specialties such as *calamares a la plancha* (grilled squid) and homemade *helado* (ice cream). Finish your meal with a glass of sweet Muscatel (closed Mon, Calle Miquel Rosset 16, tel. 972-258-471, Juan and family).

Sitges

Sitges (SEE-juhz) is one of Catalunya's most popular resort towns. Because the town beautifully mingles sea and light, it's long been an artists' colony. Here you can still feel the soul of the Modernistas... in the architecture, the museums, the salty sea breeze, and the relaxed rhythm of life.

Today's Sitges is a world-renowned vacation destination among the gay community. Despite its jet-set status, the Old Town has managed to retain its charm. With a much slower pulse than Barcelona, Sitges is an enjoyable break from the big city.

Getting to Sitges: Southbound trains depart Barcelona from Sants Station (take train on the green line toward Sant Vincenç de Calders, 4/hr, 35–40 min, €2.80 each way). Closer to Barcelona's city center, you can catch this same train at the Passeig de Gràcia RENFE Station.

Orientation to Sitges

Tourist Information

The **main TI** is a couple of blocks northwest of the train station (mid-June–mid-Sept Mon–Sat 9:00–20:00, closed Sun; mid-Sept–mid-June Mon–Fri 9:00–14:00 & 16:00–18:30, closed Sat–Sun; Sínia Morera 1).

Convenient branch kiosks are in front of the **train station** (mid-June–mid-Sept daily 9:00–13:00 & 17:00–21:00, closed off-season) and down at the start of the **beach promenade** (mid-June–mid-Sept Mon–Sat 10:00–14:00 & 16:00–20:00, Sun 10:00–14:00; mid-Sept–mid-June Sun–Thu 10:00–14:00, Fri–Sat 10:00–14:00 & 16:00–19:00).

Sitges' TIs share the same phone number (tel. 902-103-428) and website (www.sitgestur.com). At any TI, pick up the good map (with info on sights on the back) and brochures for any museums that interest you. The TI can also help you find a room.

Arrival in Sitges

From the train station, exit straight ahead (past a TI kiosk—open in summer) and walk down Carrer Francesc Gumà. When it dead-ends, continue right onto Carrer de Jesús, which takes you to the town's tiny main square, Plaça del Cap de la Villa. (Keep an eye out for directional signs.) From here, turn right down Carrer Major ("Main Street"), which leads you past the old market hall (now an art gallery) and the town hall, to a beautiful terrace next to the main church. From here, you can poke into the Old Town or take the grand staircase down to the beach promenade.

Sights in Sitges

Sitges basically has two attractions: Its tight-and-tiny Old Town (with a few good museums) and its long, luxurious beaches.

Old Town—Take time to explore the old town's narrow streets. They're crammed with cafés, boutiques, and all the resort staples.

The focal point, on the waterfront, is the 17th-century Baroque-style **Sant Bartomeu i Santa Tecla Church.** The terrace in front of the church will help you get the lay of the land.

As an art town, Sitges has seen its share of creative people—some of whom have left their mark in the form of appealing museums. Walking along the water behind the church, you'll find two of the town's three museums. The **Museu Maricel** displays the eclectic artwork of a local collector, including some Modernista works. The museum also shows off works by local Sitges artists, and a collection of maritime-themed works. The **Museu Cau Ferrat** bills itself as a "temple of art," as collected by local intellectual Santiago Rusiñol. In addition to paintings and drawings, you'll find ironwork, glass, and ceramics. Also on this square, you'll see **Palau Maricel**—a sumptuous old mansion that's sometimes open to the public for concerts in the summer (ask at TI).

The third museum, **Museu Romàntic**—offering a look at 19th-century bourgeois lifestyles in an elegant mansion—is a few blocks up (one block west of main square: Head out of the square on the main pedestrian street, then take the first right turn, to

Sant Gaudenci 1). Inside, amidst gilded hallways, you'll find a collection of more than 400 dolls (€3.50/museum or €6.50 combo-ticket for all three, same hours for all three museums: July–Sept Tue–Sat 9:30–14:00 & 16:00–19:00, Sun 10:00–15:00; Oct–June Tue–Sat 9:30–14:00 & 15:30–18:30, Sun 10:00–15:00; closed Mon year-round).

Beaches—Nine beaches, separated by breakwaters, extend about a mile southward from town. Stroll down the seaside promenade, which stretches from the town to the end of the beaches. Anyone can enjoy the sun, sea, and sand; or you can rent a beach chair to relax like a pro. About halfway, the crowds thin out, and the last three beaches are more intimate and cove-like. Along the way, restaurants and *chiringuitos* (beachfront bars) serve tapas, paella, and drinks.

If you walk all the way to the end, you can continue inland to enjoy the nicely landscaped **Terramar Gardens** (Jardins de Terramar; free, daily mid-June–mid-Sept 10:30–20:30, mid-Sept–mid-June 9:00–19:00).

Sleeping in Sitges

Because it's an in-demand resort town, hotel values are not much better here than in Barcelona (especially in summer). But if you prefer a swanky beach town to a big city, consider these options. Note that this is a party town, so expect some noise after hours (request a quiet room). I've listed peak-season prices (roughly mid-July–mid-Aug); these drop substantially off-season. The first one is on the beach, while the other two are old villas with colorful tile floors a few blocks into town.

$$ Hotel Celimar, with 26 small but modern rooms, occupies a classic Modernista building facing the beach (Db-€150, €20 extra for sea view, average price off-season-€100, check website for latest prices, air-con, free Wi-Fi, elevator, Paseo de la Ribera 20, tel. 938-110-170, fax 938-110-403, www.hotelcelimar.com, info @hotelcelimar.com).

$$ Hotel Romàntic is family-run, old-fashioned-elegant, and quirky. Its 78 rooms (including some in the annex, Hotel de la Renaixença) are nothing special, but the whole place feels classic and classy—especially the plush lounge and bar (S-€70, Sb-€85, D-€100, Db-€115, €10 extra for balcony, includes breakfast, no air-con or elevator, free Wi-Fi, Sant Isidre 33, tel. 938-948-375, fax 938-114-129, www.hotelromantic.com, romantic@hotelromantic .com).

$$ El Xalet (as in "Chalet") is of a similar vintage, with a little less style and lower prices. They have 11 rooms in the main hotel and another 12 in their annex, Hotel Noucentista, up the street—both in fine old Modernista buildings (Db-€100, €25 extra for suite, includes breakfast, air-con, free Wi-Fi, Carrer Illa de Cuba 35, tel. 938-110-070, fax 938-945-579, www.elxalet.com, info@elxalet.com).

Montserrat

Montserrat—the "serrated mountain"—rockets dramatically up from the valley floor northwest of Barcelona. With its unique rock formations, a dramatic mountaintop monastery (also called Montserrat), and spiritual connection with the Catalan people and their struggles, it's a popular day trip. This has been Catalunya's most important pilgrimage site for a thousand years. Hymns explain how the mountain was carved by little angels with golden saws. Geologists blame nature at work.

Once upon a time, there was no mountain. A river flowed here, laying down silt that hardened into sedimentary layers of hard rock. Ten million years ago, the continents shifted, and the land around the rock massif sank, exposing this series of peaks that reach upwards to 4,000 feet. Over time, erosion pocked the face with caves and cut vertical grooves near the top, creating the famous serrated look.

The monastery is nestled in the jagged peaks at 2,400 feet, but it seems higher because of the way the rocky massif rises out of nowhere. The air is certainly fresher than in Barcelona. In a quick day trip, you can view the mountain from its base, ride a funicular up to the top of the world, tour the basilica and museum, touch a Black Virgin's orb, hike down to a sacred cave, and listen to Gregorian chants by the world's oldest boys' choir.

Montserrat's monastery is Benedictine, and its 30 monks carry on its spiritual tradition. Since 1025, the slogan *"ora et labora"* ("prayer and work") has pretty much summed up life for a monk here.

The Benedictines welcome visitors—both pilgrims and tourists—and offer this travel tip: Please remember that the most important part of your Montserrat visit is not enjoying the architecture, but rather discovering the religious, cultural, historical, social, and environmental values that together symbolically express the life of the Catalan people.

Tickets to Montserrat

Various combo-tickets cover your journey to Montserrat, as well as some of the sights you'll visit there. All begin with the train from Barcelona's Plaça d'Espanya, and include either the cable car or rack railway—you'll have to specify one or the other when you buy the ticket (same price for either option). You can't go one way and come back the other, unless you pay extra (about €5) for the leg that's not included in your ticket.

The basic option is to buy a **train ticket** to Montserrat (€14.60 round-trip, includes the cable car or rack railway to monastery, Eurailpass not valid, tel. 932-051-515, www.fgc .es). Note that if you buy this ticket in Barcelona, then decide at Montserrat that you want to use the funiculars, you can buy a €7.75 ticket covering both funiculars at the TI or at either funicular.

If you plan to do some sightseeing once at Montserrat, it makes sense to spend a little more on one of two combo-tickets from the train company: The €22.50 **Trans Montserrat** ticket includes your Metro ride in Barcelona to the train station, the train trip, the cable car or rack railway, unlimited trips on the two funiculars at Montserrat, and entrance to the audiovisual presentation. The €36.95 **Tot Montserrat** ticket includes all of this, plus the good Museum of Montserrat and a self-service lunch.

If you plan to do it all, you'll save at least €5 with either of these combo-tickets. You can buy any of these tickets from the automated machines at Barcelona's Plaça d'Espanya Station (tourist officials are standing by in the morning to help you figure it out). But buying the ticket at the station doesn't let you use your included Metro ride *to* the station. Instead, buy the ticket in advance at the Plaça de Catalunya TI in Barcelona, or at the uncrowded FGC La Molina office next to Plaça de Catalunya (Mon–Fri 10:00–14:00 & 16:30–20:30, Sat 10:00–14:00, closed Sun, see map on page 49 for location, Pelai 17–39 Triangle, tel. 933-664-553, helpful Anna).

Getting to Montserrat

Barcelona is connected to the valley below Montserrat by a convenient train; from there, a cable car or rack railway (your choice) takes you up to the mountaintop. Both options are similar in cost and take about the same amount of time (hourly trains, 1.5 hrs each way from downtown Barcelona to the monastery). For ticket options, see the "Tickets to Montserrat" sidebar. Driving or taking the bus round out your options.

Train Plus Cable Car or Rack Railway

By Train: Trains leave hourly from Barcelona's Plaça d'Espanya to

Montserrat. Take the Metro to Espanya, then follow signs showing a picture of a train to the FGC (Ferrocarrils de la Generalitat de Catalunya) underground station. Once there, look for train line R5 (direction: Manresa, departures at :36 past each hour).

You'll ride about an hour on the train. As you reach the base of the mountain, you have two options: Get out at Montserrat-Aeri for the cable car, or continue another few minutes to the next stop—Monistrol de Montserrat (or simply "Monistrol de M.")—for the rack railway. (You'll have to make this decision when you buy your ticket in Barcelona—see "Tickets to Montserrat" sidebar.)

By Cable Car, at the Montserrat-Aeri Stop: Departing the train, follow signs to the cable-car station (€5.40 one-way, €8.50 round-trip, covered by your train or combo-ticket, 4/hr, 5-min trip, daily March–Oct 9:40–14:00 & 14:35–19:00, Nov–Feb 10:10–14:00 & 14:35–17:45—note the lunch break). Because the cable car is smaller than the train, don't linger or you might have to wait for the next car. On the way back down, cable cars depart from the monastery at :40 past the hour to make the Barcelona-bound trains leaving at :48 past the hour. In summer, the last efficient departure is at 18:40 (off-season at 17:40). Although there's a later cable-car departure from the monastery (at 19:00, or 17:45 off-season), it entails almost an hour-long wait for the next Barcelona-bound train.

By Rack Railway (Cremallera), at the Monistrol de Montserrat Stop: From this stop, you can catch the Cremallera rack railway up to the monastery (€5.05 one-way, €8 round-trip, cheaper off-season, covered by your train or combo-ticket, hourly, 20-min trip, www.cremallerad-montserrat.com). On the return trip, this train departs the monastery at :15 past the hour (:22 past the hour on winter weekdays), allowing you to catch the Barcelona-bound train leaving Monistrol de Montserrat at :44 past the hour. The last convenient connection back to Barcelona leaves the monastery at 18:15 (or 20:15 in July–Aug). Confirm the schedule when you arrive, as specific times tend to change year to year. Note that there is one intermediate stop on this line (Monistrol-Vila, at a large parking garage), but—going in either direction—you want to stay on until the end of the line.

Cable Car or Rack Train? For the sake of scenery and fun, I enjoy the little German-built cable car more than the rack railway. Departures are more frequent (4/hr rather than hourly on the railway), but because the cable car is small, you might have to wait a while to get on. Paying the extra €5 to do both (explained in "Tickets to Montserrat" sidebar) isn't worthwhile.

By Car or Bus

By Car: Once drivers get out of Barcelona (Road #82, then C-55), it's a short 30-minute drive to the base of the mountain, then a 10-minute series of switchbacks to the actual site (where you can find parking for €5/day). It may be easier to park your car down below and ride the cable car up.

By Bus: One bus per day connects downtown Barcelona directly to the monastery at Montserrat (departs from Viriat Street near Barcelona's Sants Station daily at 9:15, returns from the monastery to Barcelona at 18:00 June–Sept or at 17:00 Oct–May, €4.85 one-way, one-hour trip depending on traffic). However, since the other options are scenic, fun, and relatively easy, the only reason to take this bus is to avoid transfers.

Orientation to Montserrat

When you arrive at the base of the mountain, look up the rock face to find the cable-car line, the monastery near the top, and the tiny building midway up (marking the Sacred Cave).

However you make your way up to the Montserrat monastery, it's easy to get oriented once you arrive at the top. Everything is within a few minutes' walk of your entry point. All of the transit options converge at the big train station, including the rack railway and cable car down to the valley. Above those are both funicular stations—one up to the ridgetop, the other down to the Sacred Cave trail. Across the street is the TI, and above that (either straight up via the stairs, or up the ramp around the left side) is the main square. To the right of the station, a long road leads along the cliff to the parking lot; a humble farmers market along here sells produce.

Crowd-Beating Tips: Arrive early or late, as tour groups mob the place midday. Crowds are less likely on weekdays and worst on Sundays.

Tourist Information

The square below the basilica houses a helpful TI, right across from the train station (daily from 9:00, closes just after last train heads down—roughly 18:15, or 20:15 in July–Aug, tel. 938-777-701, www.montserratvisita.com). Pick up the free map and get your questions answered. A good audioguide, available only at the TI, describes the general site and basilica, and also covers the Museum of Montserrat (€5, includes book). If you're a hiker, buy a hiking

The History of Montserrat

The first hermit monks built huts at Montserrat around A.D. 900. By 1025, a monastery was founded. The Montserrat Escolania, or Choir School, soon followed, and is considered to be the oldest music school in Europe (they still perform—see "Choir Concert" on page 129).

Legend has it that in medieval times, some shepherd children saw lights and heard songs coming from the mountain. They traced the sounds to a cave (now called the Sacred Cave, or Santa Cova), where they found the Black Virgin statue (La Moreneta), making the monastery a pilgrim magnet.

In 1811, Napoleon's invading French troops destroyed Montserrat's buildings, though the Black Virgin, hidden away by monks, survived. Then, in the 1830s, the Spanish royalty—tired of dealing with pesky religious orders—dissolved the monasteries and convents.

But in the 1850s, the monks returned as part of Catalunya's (and Europe's) renewed Romantic appreciation for all things medieval and nationalistic. (Montserrat's revival coincided with other traditions born out of rejuvenated Catalan pride: the much-loved Football Club Barcelona, Barcelona's Palace of Catalan Music, and even the birth of local sparkling wine, *cava*.) Montserrat's basilica and monastery were reconstructed and became, once more, the strongly beating spiritual and cultural heart of the Catalan people.

Then came Franco, who wanted a monolithic Spain. To him, Montserrat represented Catalan rebelliousness. During Franco's rule, the *sardana* dance was still illegally performed here (but with a different name), and literature was published in the outlawed Catalan language. In 1970, 300 intellectuals demonstrating for more respect for human rights in Spain were locked up in the monastery for several days by Franco's police.

But now Franco is history. The 1990s brought another phase of rebuilding (after a forest fire and rain damage), and the Montserrat community is thriving once again, unafraid to display its pride for the Catalan people, culture, and faith.

brochure here. Trails offer spectacular views (on clear days) to the Mediterranean and even (on clearer days) to the Pyrenees.

The audiovisual center (upstairs from the TI) provides some cultural and historical perspective. The lame interactive exhibition—nowhere near as exciting as the mountains and basilica outside—includes computer touch-screens and a short 20-minute video in English. Learn about the mountain's history, and get a glimpse into the daily lives of the monastery's resident monks (€2, covered by Trans Montserrat and Tot Montserrat combo-tickets, same hours as TI).

Self-Guided Spin-Tour

From the monastery's main square, Plaça de Santa Maria, face the main facade and take this spin tour, moving from right to left: Like a good pilgrim, face Mary, the centerpiece of the facade. Below her to the left is St. Benedict, the sixth-century monk who established the rules that came to govern Montserrat's monastery. St. George, the symbol of Catalunya, is on the right (amid victims of Spain's Civil War).

Five arches line the base of the church. The one on the far right leads pilgrims to the high point of any visit, the Black Virgin (a.k.a. La Moreneta). The center arch leads into the basilica, and the arch second from left directs you to a small votive chapel filled with articles representing prayer requests or thanks.

Left of the basilica, the delicate arches mark the old monks' cloister. Below that are four trees planted by the monks, hoping to harvest only their symbolism (palm = martyrdom, cypress = eternal life, olive = peace, and laurel = victory). Next to the trees are a public library and peaceful reading room. The big archway is the private entrance to the monastery. Then comes the modern hotel and, below that, the modern, white museum. Other buildings provide cells for pilgrims. The Sant Joan funicular lifts hikers up to the trailhead (you can see the tiny building at the top). From there, you can take a number of fine hikes (described later in this section). Another funicular station descends to the Sacred Cave. And, finally, five arches separate statues of founders of the great religious orders. Step over to the arches for a commanding view (on a clear day) of the Llobregat River, meandering all the way to the Mediterranean.

Sights in Montserrat

Basilica—Although there's been a church here since the 11th century, the present structure was built in the 1850s, and the facade only dates from 1968. The decor is Neo-Romanesque, so popular with the Romantic artists of the late 19th century. The basilica itself is ringed with interesting chapels, but the focus is on the Black Virgin sitting high above the main altar.

Montserrat's top attraction is **La Moreneta,** the small wood statue of the Black Virgin, discovered in the Sacred Cave in the 12th century. Legend says she was carved by St. Luke (the Gospel writer and supposed artist), brought to Spain by St. Peter, hidden away in the cave during the Moorish invasions, and miraculously discovered by shepherd children. (Carbon dating says she's 800 years old.) While George is the patron saint of Catalunya, La Moreneta is its patroness, having been crowned as such by the pope in 1881. "Moreneta" is usually translated as "black" in

English, but the Spanish name actually means "tanned." The statue was originally lighter, but darkened over the centuries from candle smoke, humidity, and the natural aging of its original varnish. Pilgrims shuffle down a long and ornate passage leading alongside the church for their few moments alone with the virgin (free, daily 8:00–10:30 & 12:00–18:30, plus 19:30–20:15 in summer, www .abadiamontserrat.net). The church itself has longer hours and daily services (Mass at 11:00, vespers at 18:45).

Join the line of pilgrims (along the right side of the church). Though Mary is behind a protective glass case, the royal orb she cradles in her hands is exposed. Pilgrims touch Mary's orb with one hand and hold their other hand up to show that they accept Jesus. Newlyweds in particular seek Mary's blessing.

Immediately after La Moreneta, turn right into the delightful Neo-Romanesque prayer chapel, where worshippers sit behind the Virgin and continue to pray. The ceiling, painted in the Modernista style in 1898 by Joan Llimona, shows Jesus and Mary high in heaven. The trail connecting Catalunya with heaven seems to lead through these serrated mountains. The figures depicted lower are people symbolizing Catalan history and culture.

You'll leave by walking along the Ave Maria Path (along the outside of the church), which thoughtfully integrates nature and the basilica. Thousands of colorful votive candles are all busy helping the devout with their prayers. Before you leave the inner courtyard and head out into the main square, pop into the humble little room with the many votive offerings. This is where people leave personal belongings (wedding dresses, baby's baptism outfits, wax replicas of body parts in need of healing, and so on) as part of a prayer request or as a thanks for divine intercession.

Museum of Montserrat—The bright, shiny, and cool collection of paintings and artifacts was mostly donated by devout Catalan Catholics. While it's nothing really earth-shaking, you'll enjoy an air-conditioned wander past lots of antiquities and fine artwork. Head upstairs first to see some lesser-known works by the likes of Picasso, El Greco, Caravaggio, Monet, Renoir, Pissarro, Degas, John Singer Sargent, and some local Modernista artists. One gallery shows how artists have depicted the Black Virgin of Montserrat over the centuries in many different styles. There's even a small Egyptian section, with a sarcophagus and mummy. Down on the main floor, you'll see ecclesiastical gear, a good icon collection, and more paintings, including—at the very end—a Dalí painting, some Picasso sketches and prints, and a Miró (€6.50, covered by Tot Montserrat combo-ticket; July–Aug daily 10:00–19:00; Sept–June Mon–Fri 10:00–17:45, Sat–Sun 10:00–18:45; tel. 938-777-745).

Sant Joan Funicular—This funicular climbs 820 feet above the monastery in five minutes (€4.35 one-way, €6.90 round-trip,

covered by Trans Montserrat and Tot Montserrat combo-tickets, goes every 20 min, more often with demand). At the top of the funicular, you are at the starting point of a 20-minute walk that takes you to the Sant Joan Chapel (follow sign for *Ermita de St. Joan*). Other hikes also begin at the trailhead by the funicular (get details from TI before you ascend; basic map with suggested hikes posted by upper funicular station). For a quick and easy chance to get out into nature, simply ride up and follow the most popular hike, a 45-minute mostly downhill loop through mountain scenery back to the monastery. To take this route, go left from the funicular station; the trail—marked *Monestir de Montserrat*—will first go up to a rocky crest before heading downhill.

Sacred Cave (Santa Cova)—The Moreneta was originally discovered in the Sacred Cave (or Sacred Grotto), a 40-minute hike down from the monastery (then another 50 minutes back up). The path (c. 1900) was designed by devoted and patriotic Modernista architects, including Gaudí and Josep Puig i Cadafalch. It's lined with Modernista statues depicting scenes from the life of Christ. While the original Black Virgin statue is now in the basilica, a replica sits in the cave. A three-minute funicular ride cuts 20 minutes off the hike (€1.75 one-way, €2.80 round-trip, covered by Trans Montserrat and Tot Montserrat combo-tickets, goes every 20 min, more often with demand).

If you're here late in the afternoon, check the funicular schedule before you head into the Sacred Cave to make sure you don't miss the final ride down. Missing the last ride could mean catching a train back to Barcelona later than you had planned.

Choir Concert—Montserrat's Escolania, or Choir School, has been training voices for centuries. Fifty young boys, who live and study in the monastery itself, make up the choir, which performs daily except Saturday (Mon–Fri at 13:00, Sun–Thu at 18:45, and Sun also at 12:00, choir on vacation late June–late Aug). The boys sing for only 10 minutes, the basilica is jam-packed, and it's likely you'll see almost nothing. Also note that if you attend the evening performance, you'll miss the last funicular down the mountain.

Sleeping in Montserrat

An overnight here gets you monastic peace and a total break from the modern crowds. There are ample rustic cells for pilgrim visitors, but tourists might prefer this place:

$$ Hotel Abat Cisneros, a three-star hotel with 82 rooms and all the comforts, is low-key and appropriate for a sanctuary (Sb-€38–61, Db-€65–101, price depends on season, includes breakfast, half- and full-board available, elevator, fee for Internet access and free Wi-Fi, tel. 938-777-701, fax 938-777-724, www .abadiamontserrat.cat, reserves@larsa-montserrat.cat).

Eating in Montserrat

Montserrat is designed to feed hordes of pilgrims and tourists. You'll find a cafeteria along the main street (across from the train station) and more eateries (including a grocery store and bar with simple sandwiches) where the road curves on its way up to the basilica. Or pack a picnic from Barcelona.

BASQUE COUNTRY

Euskal Herria

Straddling two nations on the Atlantic Coast—stretching about 100 miles from Bilbao, Spain, north to Bayonne, France—lies the ancient, free-spirited land of the Basques. The Basque Country is famous for its sunny beaches and scintillating modern architecture...and for its feisty, industrious natives.

It's also simply beautiful: Bright, white chalet-style homes with deep-red and green shutters scatter across lush, rolling hills, the Pyrenees Mountains soar high above the Atlantic, and surfers and sardines share the waves.

Insulated from mainstream Europe for centuries, the plucky Basques have just wanted to be left alone for more than 7,000 years. An easily crossed border separates the French *Pays Basque* from the Spanish *País Vasco,* allowing you to sample both sides from a single base (in Spain, I prefer fun-loving San Sebastián; in France, I hang my hat in cozy St. Jean-de-Luz).

Much unites the Spanish and French Basque regions: They share a cuisine, Union Jack–style flag (green, red, and white), and common language (Euskara), spoken by about a half-million people. (Virtually everyone also speaks Spanish or French.) And both have been integrated by their respective nations, sometimes forcibly. The French Revolution quelled French Basque ideas of independence; 130 years later, Spain's Generalísimo Francisco Franco attempted to tame his own separatist-minded Basques.

But over the last generation, things have started looking up. The long-suppressed Euskara language is enjoying a resurgence. And, as the European Union celebrates ethnic regions rather than nations, the Spanish and French Basques are feeling more united. This heavily industrialized region is enjoying a striking 21st-century renaissance. In Spain, the dazzling new architecture of the Guggenheim Bilbao modern-art museum and the glittering resort of San Sebastián are drawing enthusiastic crowds. And in France, long-ignored cities such as Bayonne and the surfing mecca of Biarritz are being revitalized. At the same time, traditional small towns—like Spain's Lekeitio and Hondarribia, and France's St. Jean-de-Luz and nearby mountain villages—are also thriving, making the entire region colorful, fun, welcoming...and unmistakably Basque.

Planning Your Time

One day is enough for a quick sample of the Basque Country, but two or three days lets you breathe deep and hold it in. Where you go depends on your interests: Spain or France? Cities (such as Bilbao and Bayonne) or resorts (such as St. Jean-de-Luz and San Sebastián)?

If you want to slow down and focus on Spain, spend one day relaxing in San Sebastián and the second side-tripping to Bilbao (and Guernica if you have a car).

Better yet, take this easy opportunity to dip into France. Sleep in one country, then side-trip into the other, devoting one day to Spain (San Sebastián and maybe Bilbao), and a second day to France (St. Jean-de-Luz and Bayonne).

Wherever you go, most of your sightseeing will be cultural, scenic, and culinary; in the Basque Country, museum-going takes a backseat to relaxing.

Getting Around the Basque Country

The tourist's Basque Country—from Bilbao to Bayonne—stays close to the coastline. Fortunately, everything is connected by good roads and public transportation.

By Bus and Train: From San Sebastián, the bus is the best way to reach Bilbao (and from there, Guernica). To go between San Sebastián and France, a train—with a transfer in Hendaye—is your best bet (2/hr, takes 1 hour between San Sebastián and St. Jean-de-Luz; faster but less frequent by bus: Mon–Sat 2/day direct, 45 min). Once in France, the three main towns (St. Jean-de-Luz, Bayonne, Biarritz) are connected by bus (trains also zip between St. Jean-de-Luz and Bayonne). Even if you rent a car, I'd do these three towns by public transit. Specific connections are explained in each section.

Note that a few out-of-the-way areas—Spain's Lekeitio and Bay of Biscay, France's Basque villages of the interior—are impractical by public transportation...but worth the trouble by car.

By Car: San Sebastián, Bilbao, St. Jean-de-Luz, and Bayonne

Basque Country

are connected by a convenient expressway, called A-8 in Spain and A-63 in France (rough timings: Bilbao to San Sebastián, 1.25 hours; San Sebastián to St. Jean-de-Luz, 45 min; St. Jean-de-Luz to Bayonne, 30 min).

Language Warning: For the headers throughout this chapter, I've listed place names using the Spanish or French spelling first and the Euskara spelling second. In the text, I use the spelling that prevails locally. While most people refer to towns by their Spanish or French names, road signs list places in the national language and in Euskara. The Spanish or French version is sometimes scratched out by independence-minded locals, so you might have to navigate by Euskara names.

Also note that in terms of linguistic priority (e.g., museum information), Euskara comes first, Spanish and French second, and English a distant fourth...and it often doesn't make the cut.

Cuisine Scene in the Basque Country

Mixing influences from the mountains, sea, Spain, and France, Basque food is reason enough to visit the region. The local cuisine—dominated by seafood, tomatoes, and red peppers—offers some spicy dishes, unusual in most of Europe. While you'll find similar specialties throughout the Basque lands, Spain is still Spain and France is still France. Here are some dishes you're most likely to find in each area.

Who Are the Basques?

To call the Basques "mysterious" is an understatement. Before most European nations had ever set sail, Basque whalers competed with the Vikings for control of the sea. During the Industrial Revolution and lean Franco years, Basque steel kept the Spanish economy alive. In the last few decades, the separatist army ETA has given the Basque people an unwarranted reputation for violence. And through it all, the Basques have spoken a unique language that to outsiders sounds like gibberish or a secret code.

So, just who are the Basques? Even for Basques, that's a difficult question. According to traditional stereotypes, Basques are thought of as having long noses, heavy eyebrows, floppy ears, stout bodies, and a penchant for wearing berets. But widespread Spanish and French immigration has made it difficult to know who actually has Basque ethnic roots. (In fact, some of the Basques' greatest patriots have had no Basque blood.) And so today, anyone who speaks the Basque language, Euskara, is considered a "Basque."

Euskara, related to no other surviving tongue, has been used since Neolithic times—making it, very likely, the oldest European language that's still spoken. With its seemingly impossible-to-pronounce words filled with k's, tx's, and z's (rest rooms are *gizonak* for men and *emakumeak* for women), Euskara makes speaking French suddenly seem easy. (Some tips: *tx* is pronounced "ch," while *tz* is pronounced "ts." Other key words: *kalea* is "street," and *ostatua* is a cheap hotel.) Kept alive as a symbol of Basque cultural identity, Euskara is typically learned proudly as a second or third language. Many locals can switch effortlessly from Euskara to Spanish or French. Basques wave their language like a flag—look for Euskara street signs, menus, and signs in shops.

The Basque economy has historically been shaped by three factors: the sea, agriculture, and iron deposits.

Basque sailors were some of the first and finest in Europe, as they built ever-better boats to venture farther and farther into the Atlantic in search of whales. (These long journeys were made possible by the invention of *bacalao*—dried, salted cod that could last for months to sustain whalers.) By the year 1000, Basque sailors were chasing whales a thousand miles from home, in the Norwegian fjords. Despite lack of physical evidence, many historians surmise that the Basques must have sailed to the Americas before Christopher Columbus.

When the "Spanish" era of exploration began, Basques continued to play a key role, as sailors and shipbuilders. Columbus'

Santa María was likely Basque-built, and his crew included many Basques. History books teach that Ferdinand Magellan was the first to circumnavigate the globe, with the footnote that he was killed partway around. Who took over the ship for the rest of the journey, completing the circle? The Basque sailor Juan Sebastián de Elcano. And a pair of well-traveled Catholic priests, known for their far-reaching missionary trips that led to founding the Jesuit order, were also Basques: St. Ignatius of Loyola and St. Francis Xavier.

Later, the Industrial Age swept Europe, gaining a foothold in Iberia when the Basques began using their rich iron deposits to make steel. Pioneering Basque industrialists set the tempo as they dragged Spain into the modern world. Cities such as Bilbao were heavily industrialized, sparking an influx of workers from around Spain (which gradually diluted Basque blood in the Basque Country).

The independence-minded Basques are notorious for their stubbornness. In truth, as a culturally and linguistically unique island surrounded by bigger and stronger nations, the Basques have learned to compromise. Historically Basques have remained on good terms with outsiders, so long as their traditional laws, the *Fueros*, were respected. While outdated, the *Fueros* continue to symbolize a self-governance that the Basques hold dear. It is only when foreign law has been placed above the *Fueros*—as many of today's Basques feel Spanish law is—that the people become agitated.

In recent years, most news of the Basques—especially in Spain—has been made by the terrorist organization ETA. (ETA stands for the Euskara phrase Euskadi Ta Askatasuna, or "Basque Country and Freedom"; *eta* also means "and" in Euskara.) ETA has been blamed for more than 800 deaths since 1968. The violence ebbs and flows, but ETA tends to focus on political targets, and their activities go largely unnoticed by tourists. While many people in the Basque Country would like a greater degree of autonomy from Madrid, only a tiny minority of the population supports ETA and the vast majority rejects violence.

Throughout the Basque Country, in Spain and in France, the Basque spirit remains strong (and Basque nationalists with websites prefer the more generic .com to .es).

This is only a first glimpse into the important, quirky, and fascinating Basque people. To better understand the Basques, there's no better book than Mark Kurlansky's *The Basque History of the World*—essential pre-trip reading for historians.

Spanish Basque Cuisine: Hopping from bar to bar sampling *pintxos*—the local term for tapas—is a highlight of any trip (for details, see sidebar on page 154). Local brews include *sidra* (hard apple cider) and *txakoli* (cha-koh-LEE, a local light, sparkling white wine—often theatrically poured from high above the glass for aeration).

French Basque Cuisine: The red peppers (called *piments*) hanging from homes in small villages end up in *piperade,* a dish that combines peppers, tomatoes, garlic, ham, and eggs. Look for anything "Basque-style" (*basquaise*)—cooked with tomato, eggplant, red pepper, and garlic. Don't leave without trying *ttoro* (tchoo-roh), a seafood stew that is the Basque Country's answer to bouillabaisse and cioppino. *Marmitako* is a hearty tuna stew. Local cheeses come from Pyrenean sheep's milk *(pur brebis),* and the local ham *(jambon de Bayonne)* is famous throughout France. After dinner, try a shot of *izarra* (herbal-flavored brandy). To satisfy your sweet tooth, look for *gâteau basque,* a local tart filled with cream or crème with cherries from Bayonne. Hard apple cider is the locally made beverage, but the region's wine, Irouleguy, isn't worth its price.

Spanish Basque Country (El País Vasco)

Four of the seven Basque territories lie within Spain. Many consider Spanish Basque culture to be feistier and more colorful than the relatively integrated French Basques—you'll hear more Euskara spoken here than in France.

For 40 years, the figure of Generalísimo Franco loomed large over the Spanish Basques. Franco depended upon Basque industry to keep the floundering Spanish economy afloat. But even as he exploited the Basques economically, he so effectively blunted Basque culture that the language was primarily Spanish by default. Franco kicked off his regime by offering up the historic Basque town of Guernica as target practice to his ally Hitler's air force. The notorious result—the wholesale slaughter of innocent civilians—was immortalized by Pablo Picasso's mural *Guernica.*

But Franco is long gone, and today's Basques are looking to the future. The iron deposits have been depleted, prompting the Basques to re-imagine their rusting cities for the 21st century. True to form, they're rising to the challenge. Perhaps the best example is Bilbao, whose iconic Guggenheim Museum—built on the former site of an industrial wasteland—is the centerpiece of a bold new skyline.

San Sebastián is the heart of the tourist's *País Vasco,* with its sparkling beach picturesquely framed by looming green mountains and a charming Old Town with gourmet *pintxos* (tapas) spilling out of every bar. On-the-rise Bilbao is worth a look for its landmark Guggenheim and its atmospheric Old Town. For small-town fun, drop by the fishing village of Lekeitio (near Bilbao). And for history, Guernica has some intriguing museums.

This chapter focuses on Basque destinations on or near the ocean. Some inland Basque towns and cities—including Pamplona—are covered in the Camino de Santiago chapter.

San Sebastián / Donostia

Shimmering above the breathtaking Concha Bay, elegant and prosperous San Sebastián (Donostia in Euskara) has a favored location

with golden beaches, capped by twin peaks at either end, and a cute little island in the center. A delightful beachfront promenade runs the length of the bay, with an intriguing Old Town at one end and a smart shopping district in the center. It has 180,000 residents and almost that many tour-

ists in high season (July–Sept). With a romantic setting, a soaring statue of Christ gazing over the city, and a late-night lively Old Town, San Sebastián has a Rio de Janeiro aura. While the actual "sightseeing" isn't much, the scenic city itself provides a pleasant introduction to Spain's Basque Country. And as a culinary capital of Spain, it dishes up some of the top tapas anywhere.

In 1845, Queen Isabel II's doctor recommended she treat her skin problems by bathing here in the sea. (For modesty's sake, she would go inside a giant cabana that could be wheeled into the surf—allowing her to swim far from prying eyes, never having to set foot on the beach.) Her visit mobilized Spain's aristocracy, and soon the city was on the map as a seaside resort. By the turn of the 20th century, San Sebastián was the toast of the belle époque, and a leading resort for Europe's beautiful people. Before World War I, Queen María Cristina summered here and held court in her Miramar Palace overlooking the crescent beach (the turreted, red-brick building partway around the bay). Hotels, casinos, and theaters flourished. Even Franco enjoyed 35 summers in a place he was sure to call San Sebastián, not Donostia.

Planning Your Time

San Sebastián's sights can be exhausted in a few hours, but it's a great place to be on vacation for a full, lazy day (or longer). Stroll the two-mile-long promenade and scout the place you'll grab to work on a tan. The promenade leads to a funicular that lifts you to the Monte Igueldo viewpoint. After exploring the Old Town and port, walk up to the hill of Monte Urgull. If you have more time, enjoy the delightful aquarium. Modern art–lovers can venture to the Chillida-Leku Museum on the outskirts. A key ingredient of any visit to San Sebastián is enjoying tapas in the Old Town bars.

Orientation to San Sebastián

The San Sebastián that we're interested in surrounds Concha Bay (Bahía de la Concha). It can be divided into three areas: Playa de la Concha (best beaches), the shopping district (called Centro), and the skinny streets of the grid-planned Old Town (called Parte Vieja, to the north of the shopping district). Centro, just east of Playa de la Concha, has beautiful turn-of-the-20th-century architecture, but no real sights. A busy drag called Alameda del Boulevard (or just "Boulevard") stands where the city wall once ran, and separates the Centro from the Old Town.)

It's all bookended by mini-mountains: Monte Urgull to the north and east, Monte Igueldo to the south and west. The river (Río Urumea) divides central San Sebastián from the district called Gros (which—contrary to its name—is actually quite nice, with a lively night scene and surfing beach).

Tourist Information

San Sebastián's TI, conveniently located right on the Boulevard, has information on city and regional sights, as well as bus and train schedules. Pick up the free map and the *Holiday Guide* booklet, which has English descriptions of the three walking tours—the Old Town/Monte Urgull walk is best (July–Sept daily 8:30–20:00; Oct–June Mon–Thu 9:00–13:30 & 15:30–19:00, Fri–Sat 9:30–19:00, Sun 10:00–14:00; Boulevard 8, tel. 943-481-166, www.sansebastianturismo.com).

Arrival in San Sebastián

By Train: The town has two train stations (neither has luggage storage). If you're coming on a regional Topo train from Hendaye/

Hendaia on the French border, get off at the **EuskoTren Station** (end of the line, called Amara). It's a level 15-minute walk to the center: Exit the station and walk across the long plaza, then veer left and walk eight blocks down Calle Easo (toward the statue of Christ hovering on the hill) to the beach. The Old Town will be ahead on your right, with Playa de la Concha to your left. To speed things up, catch bus #21, #26, or #28 along Calle Easo and take it to the Boulevard stop, near the TI at the bottom of the Old Town.

If you're arriving by train from elsewhere in Spain (or from France after transferring in Irún), you'll get off at the main **RENFE Station.** It's just across the river from the Centro shopping district. There are no convenient buses from the station—to get to the Old Town and most recommended hotels, catch a taxi (stand out front, €5.40 to downtown). Or just walk—cross the fancy dragon-decorated María Cristina Bridge, turn right onto the busy avenue called Paseo de los Fueros, and follow the Urumea River until the last bridge.

By Bus: A few buses—such as those from Hondarribia and the airport—can let you off at pretty Plaza de Gipuzkoa (first stop after crossing the river, in Centro shopping area, one block from the Boulevard, TI, and Old Town). But most buses—including those from Bilbao—take you instead to San Sebastián's makeshift "bus station" (dubbed Amara) at a big roundabout called Plaza Pío XII. It's basically a parking lot with a few bus shelters and a TI kiosk. At the end of the lot nearest the big roundabout, you'll see directional signs pointing you toward the town center (about a 30-minute walk). To save time and energy, walk one block in that direction to catch local bus #21, #26, or #28 to the Boulevard stop, near the TI at the start of the Old Town.

By Plane: San Sebastián Airport is beautifully situated along the harbor in the nearby town of Hondarribia, 12 miles east of the city (just across the bay from France). An easy bus (#I-2) connects the airport to San Sebastián's Plaza de Gipuzkoa, just a block south of the Boulevard and TI (€2, about 3/hr, 25 min, runs daily 7:45–20:20). A taxi into town costs about €30. For flight information, call 943-668-500.

If you arrive at Bilbao Airport, go out front and take the Pesa bus directly to San Sebastián (€15, pay driver, runs hourly, 1 hr, drops off at Plaza Pío XII, www.pesa.net).

By Car: Take the Amara freeway exit, follow *centro ciudad* signs into the city center, and park in a pay lot (many are well-signed). If you're picking up or returning a rental car, the "Big Autorental"—which includes Hertz (Zubieta 5, tel. 943-461-084) and Avis (Triunfo 2, tel. 943-461-527)—is near Hotel Niza along the beach, and Europcar is at the RENFE train station (tel. 943-322-304).

Helpful Hints

Internet Access: A half-dozen Internet cafés are well-advertised throughout the Old Town, most offering fast access for about €2 per hour. And these days, government-subsidized Wi-Fi access is available just about everywhere (including at most hotels).

Bookstore: Elkar, an advocate of Basque culture and literature, has two branches side-by-side in the Old Town. One focuses on Basque literature and the other has a wide selection of guidebooks, maps, and books in English (Mon–Sat 10:00–14:00 & 16:00–20:00, closed Sun, Calle Fermín Calbetón 30, tel. 943-420-080).

Laundry: Wash & Dry is in the Gros neighborhood, across the river (self-service daily 8:00–22:00, drop-off service Mon–Fri 9:30–13:00 & 16:00–20:00, Iparragirre 6, tel. 943-293-150).

Bike Rental: Rare for Spain, the city has some great bike lanes and is a good place to enjoy on two wheels. Try **Bici Rent Donosti** (also rents scooters, Avenida de Zurriola 22, 3 blocks across river from TI, mobile 655-724-458) or **Bicicletas Alai** (behind Amara bus station, Avenida de Madrid 24, tel. 943-470-001).

Marijuana: While Spain is famously liberal about marijuana laws, the Basque Country is even more so. Walking around San Sebastián, you'll see "grow shops" sporting the famous green leaf (shopkeepers are helpful if you have questions). While the sale of marijuana is still illegal, the consumption of marijuana is decriminalized and people are allowed to grow enough for their personal use at home. With the town's mesmerizing aquarium and delightfully lit bars filled with enticing munchies, it just makes sense here.

Getting Around San Sebastián

By Bus: Along the Boulevard at the bottom edge of the Old Town, you'll find a line of public buses ready to take you anywhere in town; give any driver your destination, and he'll tell you the number of the bus to catch (€1.20, pay driver).

Some handy bus routes: #21, #26, and #28 connect the Amara bus and EuskoTren Stations to the TI (get off at the Boulevard stop); #16 begins at the Boulevard/TI stop, goes along Playa de la Concha and through residential areas, and eventually arrives at the base of the Monte Igueldo funicular. The TI has a bus-route map (or see www.ctss.es).

By Taxi: Taxis start at €5.40, which covers most rides in the center. You can't hail a taxi on the street—you must call one (tel. 943-404-040 or 943-464-646) or find a taxi stand (most convenient along the Boulevard).

Tours in San Sebastián

Walking Tours—The TI runs English-language **walking tours** of the Old Town (Parte Vieja), Monte Urgull, and Centro (€6, 1.5 hours, July–Aug daily at 10:00, Sept–June weekends only at 11:00, confirm schedule with TI). The TI also rents **audioguides** (€10/2 hrs).

Local Guides—Itsaso Petrikorena is good (mobile 647-973-231, betitsaso@yahoo.es). Gabriella Ranelli, an American who's lived in San Sebastián for 20 years, specializes in culinary tours. She can take you on a sightseeing spin around the Old Town, along with a walk through the market and best *pintxo* bars (€135/half-day, €180/day, more for driving into the countryside, mobile 609-467-381, www.tenedortours.com, info@tenedortours.com). Gabriella also organizes cooking classes, where you shop at the market, then join a local chef to cook up some tasty *pintxos* of your own (€115 per person for a small group).

Tours on Wheels—Two tour options on wheels (following a similar route around the bay) are available, but most travelers won't find them necessary in this walkable city: The **"txu-txu"** tourist train (€4.50, daily 11:00–19:00, runs later in summer, 40-min round-trip, tel. 943-422-973); and the **Donosti Tours** hop-on, hop-off bus tour (follows two different routes—one along the bay and the other around the city; €12/route, or €14 for both, about 1 hour each, ticket good for 24 hours, leaves from Victoria Eugenia theater on the Boulevard, tel. 696-429-847).

Sights in San Sebastián

▲▲Old Town (Parte Vieja)

Huddled in the shadow of its once-protective Monte Urgull, the Old Town is where San Sebastián was born about 1,000 years ago. Because the town burned down in 1813 (as Spain, Portugal, and England fought the French to get Napoleon's brother off the Spanish throne), the architecture you see is generally Neoclassical and uniform. Still, the grid plan of streets hides heavy Baroque and Gothic churches, surprise plazas, and fun little shops, including venerable pastry stores, rugged produce markets, Basque-independence souvenir shops, and seafood-to-go delis. The highlight of the Old Town is its array of incredibly lively tapas bars—though here, these snacks are called *pintxos* (PEEN-chohs; see "Eating in San Sebastián"). To see the fishing industry in action, wander out to the port (described later).

While the struggle for Basque independence is currently in a relatively calm stage with most people opposing violent ETA tactics, there are still underlying tensions between Spain and

BASQUE COUNTRY

San Sebastián

□ = SEE OLD TOWN DETAIL MAP

P PARKING

☀ VIEW

1 Hotel Arrizul & Pensión Kursaal
2 Hotel Niza
3 Pensión Bellas Artes
4 Pensión Añorga
5 Miramar Palace
6 La Perla Spa & Café de la Concha
7 Launderette

DCH

the Basque people. In the middle of the Old Town, Calle Juan de Bilbao is the political-action street. Here you'll find people more sympathetic to the struggle (while for others, it's a street to avoid). Pop into Bar Herria (marked by the Basque flag at #14) to see political art, posters, fliers for independence activities, and photos of (violent) political prisoners above the bar. While prisoners are generally incarcerated near their families in Spain, these were spread all over the country, angering loved ones and creating a controversy. Speaking Basque is encouraged in this bar; taking photos is not.

Flagpoles mark "private eating clubs" throughout the Old Town (otherwise unmarked). Basque society is matrilineal and very female-oriented. A husband brings home his paycheck and hands it directly to his wife, who controls the house's purse strings (and everything else). Basque men felt they needed a place where they could congregate and play "king of the castle," so they formed these clubs where members could reserve a table and cook for their friends. While the clubs used to be exclusively male, women are now allowed as invited guests...but never in the kitchen, which remains the men's domain.

▲**Plaza de la Constitución**—The Old Town's main square is where bullfights used to be held. Notice the seat numbering on the

balconies: Even if you owned an apartment here, the city retained rights to the balconies, which it could sell as box seats. (Residents could peek over the paying customers' shoulders.) Above the clock, notice the seal of San Sebastián: A merchant ship with sails billowing in the wind. The city was granted trading rights by the crown—a reminder of the Basque Country's importance in Spanish seafaring. Inviting café tables spill into the square from all corners.

Museum of San Telmo—This museum, closed for renovation, will reopen in a few years as the Basque museum of anthropology. Rooms arranged around the peaceful cloister of a former Dominican monastery will hold artifacts telling the history of this region, dating back to ancient Roman times (Plaza Zuloaga 1, tel. 943-481-580).

▲**Bretxa Public Market (Mercado de la Bretxa)**—Wandering through the public market is a fun way to get in touch with San Sebastián and with Basque culture. Although the big, white market building facing the Boulevard has been converted into a modern shopping mall, the farmers produce market thrives here (lined up along the left side of the building), as well as the fish and

BASQUE COUNTRY

meat market (behind it and underground). To get to the fish and meat market, walk past the produce vendors (look under the eaves of the modern building to see what the farmers are selling), and find a big glass cube in the square, where an escalator will take you down into the market (Mon–Fri 8:00–14:00 & 17:00–20:00, Sat 8:00–14:00, closed Sun, Plaza de Sarriegi).

At the bottom of the escalator, notice the **fish stall** on the left (marked *J. Ma. Mujika*). In the case, you'll see different cuts of *bacalao* (cod). Entire books have been written about the importance of cod to the evolution of seafaring in Europe. The fish could be preserved in salt to feed sailors on ever-longer trips into the North Atlantic, allowing them to venture beyond the continental shelf (where they could catch fresh fish). Cod was also popular among Catholic landlubbers on Fridays. Today cod remains a Basque staple. People still buy the salted version, which must be soaked for 48 hours (and the water changed three times) to become edible. If you're in a rush, you can buy de-salted cod...but at a cost in flavor. Stroll behind this stall to explore the fresh fish market— often with the catch of the day set up in cute little scenes.

Take the escalator up, and cross the busy street to the **Aitor Lasa** cheese shop (Mon–Fri 8:30–14:00 & 17:15–20:00, Sat 8:30–14:30, closed Sun, Aldamar 12, tel. 943-430-354). Pass the fragrant piles of mushrooms at the entrance and head back to the display case, showing off the Basque specialty of *idiazábal*—raw sheep's milk cheese. Notice the wide variety, which depends on the specific region it came from, whether it's smoked or cured, and for how long it's been cured *(curación)*. If you're planning a picnic, this is a very local (and expensive) ingredient. The owners are evangelical about the magic of combining the local cheese with walnuts and *casero* (homemade) apple jam.

The Port

At the west end of the Old Town, protected by Monte Urgull, is the port. Take the passage through the wall at the appropriately named Calle Puerto, and jog right along the level, portside promenade, Paseo del Muelle. You'll pass fishing boats unloading the catch of the day (with hungry locals looking on), salty sailors' pubs, and fishermen mending nets. Also along this strip are the skip-

pable Naval Museum and the entertaining aquarium. The trails to the top of Monte Urgull are just above this scene, near Santa María Church (or climb up the stairs next to the aquarium).

Cruises—Small boats cruise from the Old Town's port to the island in the bay (Isla Santa Clara), where you can hike the trails and have lunch at the lone café, or pack a picnic before setting sail (cheap ferry departs June–Sept only, on the hour from 12:00–13:00 & 16:00–20:00). The good ship *City of San Sebastián* gives one-hour tours of the bay for €8.

Naval Museum (Museo Naval)—This museum's two floors of exhibits describe the seafaring city's history, revealing the intimate link between the Basque culture and the sea (€1.20, free on Thu, borrow English description at entry, Tue–Sat 10:00–13:30 & 16:00–19:30, Sun 11:00–14:00, closed Mon, Paseo del Muelle 24, tel. 943-430-051).

▲▲**Aquarium**—San Sebastián's aquarium is surprisingly good. Exhibits are thoughtfully described in English and include a history of the sea, a collection of naval vessels, and models showing various drift-netting techniques. You'll see a petting tank filled with nervous fish; a huge whale skeleton; a trippy illuminated, slowly tumbling tank of jellyfish; and a mesmerizing 45-foot-long tunnel that lets you look up into a wet world of floppy rays, menacing sharks, and local fish. The local section ends with a tank of shark fetuses safely incubating away from hungry predators. The new tropical wing causes local kids to holler "Nemo!" (€12, €6 for kids under 13; Mon–Fri 10:00–14:00 & 15:00–19:00, Sat–Sun 10:00–14:00 & 16:00–20:00; at the end of Paseo del Muelle, tel. 943-440-099, www.aquariumss.com).

▲**Monte Urgull**—The once-mighty castle (Castillo de la Mota) atop the hill deterred most attackers, allowing the city to prosper in the Middle Ages. The free museum within the castle, featuring San Sebastián history, is mildly interesting. The best views from the hill are not from the statue of Christ, but from the ramparts on the left side (as you face the hill), just above the port's aquarium. **Café El Polvorín,** nestled in the park, is a free-spirited place with salads, sandwiches, and good sangria.

A walkway allows you to stroll the mountain's entire perimeter near sea level. This route is continuous from Hotel Parma to the aquarium, and offers an enjoyable after-dinner wander. You can also walk a bit higher up over the port (along the white railing)—called the *paseo de las curas,* or "priest's path," where the clergy could stroll unburdened by the rabble in the streets below. These paths are technically open only from sunrise to sunset (daily May–Sept 8:00–21:00, Oct–April 8:00–19:00), but you can often access them later.

The Beach and Beyond

▲▲**La Concha Beach and Promenade**—The shell-shaped Playa de la Concha, the pride of San Sebastián, has one of Europe's loveliest stretches of sand. Lined with a two-mile-long promenade, it allows even backpackers to feel aristocratic. Although it's pretty empty off-season, in summer, sunbathers pack its shores. But year-round, it's surprisingly devoid of eateries and money-grubbing businesses. There are free showers, and *cabinas* provide lockers, showers, and shade for a fee. For a century, the lovingly painted wrought-iron balustrade that stretches the length of the promenade has been a symbol of the city; it shows up on everything from jewelry to headboards. It's shaded by tamarisk trees, with branches carefully pruned into knotty bulbs each winter that burst into leafy shade-giving canopies in the summer—another symbol of the city. **Café de la Concha**, while serving mediocre food, is reasonably priced, and you can't beat the location of its terrace overlooking the beach (weekday lunch special–€13).

The Miramar palace and park, which divides the crescent beach in the middle, was where Queen María Cristina held court when she summered here. Her royal changing rooms are used today as inviting cafés, restaurants, and a fancy spa.

La Perla Spa—The spa overlooking the beach attracts a less royal crowd today and appeals mostly to visitors interested in sampling "the curative properties of the sea." You can enjoy its Talasso Fitness Circuit, featuring a hydrotherapy pool, relaxation pool, panoramic Jacuzzi, cold-water pools, seawater steam sauna, dry sauna, and a relaxation area (€24 for 2-hour fitness circuit, €30 for 3-hour circuit, daily 8:00–22:00, €3 caps and €1 rental towels, bring or buy a swimsuit, on the beach at the center of the crescent, Paseo de la Concha, tel. 943-458-856, www.la-perla.net).

Monte Igueldo—For commanding city views (if you ignore the tacky amusements on top), ride the funicular up Monte Igueldo, a mirror image of Monte Urgull. The views over San Sebastián, along the coast, and into the distant green mountains are sensational day or night. The entrance to the funicular is on the road behind the tennis club on the far western end of Playa de Ondarreta, which extends from Playa de la Concha to the west (funicular–€2.50 round-trip; July–mid-Sept daily 10:00–22:00;

April–June and mid-Sept–Oct daily 11:00–20:00; Nov–March Mon–Tue and Thu–Fri 11:00–18:00, Sat–Sun 11:00–20:00, closed Wed). If you drive to the top, you'll pay €2 to enter. The #16 bus takes you from the Old Town to the base of the funicular in about 10 minutes.

In Gros

Gros and Zurriola Beach—The district of Gros, just east across the river from the Old Town, offers a distinct Californian vibe. Literally a dump a few years ago, today it has a surfing scene on Zurriola Beach (popular with students and German tourists), a futuristic conference center (described next), and (in the works for 2013) a new promenade that will arc over the water and under Monte Ulía.

▲Kursaal Conference Center and Kubo Gallery—These two Lego-like boxes (just east and across the river from the Old Town, in Gros) mark the spot of what was once a grand casino, torn down by Franco to discourage gambling. Many locals wanted to rebuild it as it once was, in a similar style to the turn-of-the-20th-century buildings in the Centro. But, in an effort to keep up with the postmodern trends in Bilbao, city leaders opted instead for Rafael Moneo's striking contemporary design. The complex is supposed to resemble the angular rocks that make up the town's breakwater. The Kursaal houses a theater, conference facilities, some gift shops and travel agencies, a restaurant, and the Kubo Gallery. The gallery offers temporary exhibits promoting contemporary Basque artists (free, daily 11:30–13:30 & 17:00–21:00). Each exhibit is complemented by a 10-minute video that plays continuously in the gallery theater.

Near San Sebastián: Chillida-Leku Museum

Eduardo Chillida (1924–2002), a popular Basque sculptor, is the focus of this enjoyable museum on the outskirts of town. Chillida

worked rough, heavy materials (such as iron and marble) into huge but delicate-seeming abstract sculptures. You might not have heard of Chillida, but you've likely seen his big, blocky works, which decorate cities around Spain and throughout Europe. In San Sebastián, among the rocks at the west end of the beachfront promenade, you'll find one of Chillida's most famous works: the "wind combs" *(peine del viento)*.

The museum has three parts: The entry area shows a 45-minute film loop of the artist at work; the grounds—with beautiful grassy rolling hills and trees—display his larger works, mostly of iron or rose marble; and a 16th-century farmhouse—which the artist renovated expressly for this purpose—shows off some of his smaller works (of bronze, felt, clay, alabaster, and so on).

As you explore, notice the way Chillida began with imposing chunks of media, then carved passages into them to allow light and air to penetrate an otherwise impenetrable block. This has the unexpected effect of making big, clumsy things seem light and graceful. Most of his works are carved from a single piece. The artist believed that works should be unique and evolve organically—he'd contemplate the medium and listen to what it had to say before carving it up. As you stroll the grounds surveying the works, imagine both the intense pressure and the delicate touch required to persuade these materials to become art.

Because it takes some effort to get here, the museum is best for people who know Chillida and appreciate his work. Art-lovers in the region to visit the Guggenheim might find this to be the perfect complement.

Cost and Hours: €8.50, good €4 audioguide; July–Aug Mon–Sat 10:30–20:00, Sun 10:30–15:00; Sept–June Wed–Mon 10:30–15:00, closed Tue; Barrio Jáuregui 66, Hernani, tel. 943-336-006, www.museochillidaleku.com.

Getting There: It's on the edge of San Sebastián, about a €10 taxi ride from the Old Town. You can also take bus #G-2 from near the Perla Spa along the beach or from Calle Okendo near the Boulevard (direction: Hernani, €1.25, 2/hr, departs on the hour and half-hour).

Sleeping in San Sebastián

Rates in San Sebastián fluctuate with the season. When you see a range of prices in these listings, the top end is for summer (roughly July–Sept), and the low end is for the shoulder season (May–June and Oct); outside of these times, you'll pay even less. Since breakfast is often not included, I've recommended some good options elsewhere in town (see "Eating in San Sebastián").

In or Near the Old Town

$$$ **Hotel Parma** is a business-class place with 27 fine rooms and family-run attention to detail and service. It stands stately and quiet on the edge of the Old Town, away from the bar-scene noise, and overlooks the river and a surfing beach (Sb-€63–86, windowless interior Db-€93–130, view Db-€113–144, breakfast-€9, air-con, modern lounge, free Wi-Fi, Paseo de Salamanca 10, tel. 943-428-893, fax 943-424-082, www.hotelparma.com, hotelparma@hotelparma.com; Iñaki, Pino, and Ana).

> # Sleep Code
>
> **(€1 = about $1.40, country code: 34)**
> **S** = Single, **D** = Double/Twin, **T** = Triple, **Q** = Quad, **b** = bathroom,
> **s** = shower only. You can assume these places accept credit
> cards and English is spoken unless otherwise noted. Breakfast
> is generally not included (unless noted). This code applies
> to this chapter's listings in both Spain and France. The word
> *ostatua* (which you'll see throughout the Basque Country)
> means "pension."
>
> To help you sort easily through these listings, I've divided
> the rooms into three categories based on the price for a
> standard double room with bath in peak season:
>
> **$$$ Higher Priced**—Most rooms €90 or more.
> **$$ Moderately Priced**—Most rooms between €60-90.
> **$ Lower Priced**—Most rooms €60 or less.

$$ Pensión Edorta ("Edward"), deep in the Old Town, elegantly mixes wood, brick, and color into 12 modern, stylish rooms (D-€40–60, Db-€60–80, extra bed-€20–25, elevator, Calle Puerto 15, tel. 943-423-773, fax 943-433-570, www.pensionedorta .com, info@pensionedorta.com, Javier).

$ Pensión Amaiur is a flowery place with long, skinny halls and great-value rooms within the Old Town. Kind Virginia gives the justifiably popular *pensión* a homey warmth. Her 13 color-ful, cozy rooms share seven bathrooms (S-€28–42, quiet interior D-€38–50, exterior D-€45–60, T-€60–80, Q-€75–95, family room, kitchen facilities, free Wi-Fi, next to Santa María Church at Calle 31 de Agosto 44, tel. 943-429-654, www.pensionamaiur .com, amaiur@telefonica.net).

Across the River, in Gros

The pleasant Gros district—San Sebastián's "uptown"—is marked by the super-modern, blocky Kursaal conference center. The nearby Zurriola Beach is popular with surfers. These hotels are less than a five-minute walk from the Old Town. See the map on page 142.

$$$ Hotel Arrizul is bright and fresh, with mod and mini-malist decor in each of its 12 rooms (Sb-€65–88, Db-€99–133, breakfast-€6, air-con, elevator, free Wi-Fi, Peña y Goñi 1, tel. 943-322-804, fax 943-326-701, www.arrizulhotel.com, info@arrizul hotel.com).

$$ Pensión Kursaal has 10 basic but colorful rooms (Db-€63–82, family room, elevator, pay Internet access, free Wi-Fi, Peña y Goñi 2, tel. 943-292-666, fax 943-297-536, www.pension esconencanto.com, kursaal@pensionesconencanto.com).

On the Beach

$$$ Hotel Niza, set in the middle of Playa de la Concha, is often booked well in advance. Half of its 40 rooms (some with balconies) overlook the bay. From its chandeliered and plush lounge, a classic elevator takes you to its comfortable, pastel rooms with wedding-cake molding (tiny interior Sb–€58–64, Db–€123–140, view rooms cost the same—requests with reservation considered... but no promises, extra bed–€22, only streetside rooms have air-con, fans on request, great buffet breakfast–€11, free Internet access and Wi-Fi, parking–€15/day—must reserve in advance, Zubieta 56, see map on page 142 for location, tel. 943-426-663, fax 943-441-251, www.hotelniza.com, niza@hotelniza.com). The breakfast room has a sea view and doubles as a bar with light snacks throughout the day (Bar Biarritz, daily 7:30–24:00). The cheap and cheery Italian restaurant downstairs, called La Pasta Gansa, serves good pizzas, pastas, and salads (closed Tue).

Between the Beach and EuskoTren Station

See the map on page 142 for locations.

$$ Pensión Bellas Artes, while farther from the Old Town than my other listings, is worth the 15-minute walk. Lively Leire, who lived in New York and runs her *pensión* with pride, rents 10 small, well-appointed, tidy rooms with thoughtful extra touches like fresh flowers in each room and a loaner laptop. Leire and her charming mother love to give their guests sightseeing and dining tips (Sb–€47–59, Db–€77–84, extra bed–€24, no breakfast, non-smoking, elevator, free Internet access and Wi-Fi, near EuskoTren Station at Urbieta 64, tel. 943-474-905, fax 943-463-111, www.pension-bellasartes.com, info@pension-bellasartes.com).

$$ Pensión Añorga, a simple, well-run place with no public spaces, rents 15 rooms a couple of blocks off the beach in the modern part of town (S–€26–30, Db–€42–72—€42 off-season weekdays, €52 off-season weekends, €52 May–June, €72 July–Sept, prices soft off-season, Wi-Fi, Calle Easo 12, first floor, tel. 943-467-945, www.pensionanorga.es, contacto@pensionanorga.es, Josefina and Margarita).

Eating in San Sebastián

Basque food is regarded as some of the best in Spain...and San Sebastián is the culinary capital of the Basque Country. What the city lacks in museums and sights, it more than makes up for in food. (For tips on Basque cuisine, see page 133.) San Sebastián is proud of its many Michelin-rated fine-dining establishments. But these require a big commitment of time and money. Most casual visitors will prefer to hop from pub to pub through the Old Town, following the crowds between Basque-font signs. I've listed a couple of solid traditional restaurants, but for the best value and memories, I'd order top-end dishes with top-end wine in top-end bars.

Pintxo Bar-Hopping

San Sebastián's Old Town provides the ideal backdrop for tapas-hopping; just wander the streets and straddle up to the bar in the liveliest spot. Calle Fermín Calbetón has about the best concentra-
tion of bars; the streets San Jerónimo and 31 de Agosto are also good. Before you choose, study the "Tapas Cheat Sheet" sidebar.

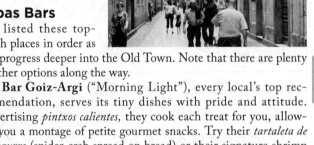

Tapas Bars

I've listed these top-
notch places in order as you progress deeper into the Old Town. Note that there are plenty of other options along the way.

Bar Goiz-Argi ("Morning Light"), every local's top rec-
ommendation, serves its tiny dishes with pride and attitude. Advertising *pintxos calientes,* they cook each treat for you, allow-
ing you a montage of petite gourmet snacks. Try their *tartaleta de txangurro* (spider-crab spread on bread) or their signature shrimp kebab. A good selection of open wine bottles are clearly priced and displayed on the shelf (great prices, no chairs, congregate at bar, closed Mon–Tue, Calle Fermín Calbetón 4).

Bar Borda-Berri (loosely "Mountain Hut"), a couple doors down, features a more low-key ambience and top-quality €3 *pintxos.* There are only a few items at the bar; check out the chalk-
board menu for today's options, order, and they'll cook it fresh. The specialty here is melt-in-your-mouth beef cheeks *(carrillera de tenera)* in a red-wine sauce, risotto with wild mushrooms, and foie gras (grilled goose liver) with apple jelly, which is even bet-
ter paired with a glass of their best red wine (closed Mon, Calle Fermín Calbetón 12).

Bar Txepetxa is *the* place for anchovies. A plastic circle dis-
playing a variety of *antxoas* tapas makes choosing your anchovy treat easy. These fish are fresh—not cured and salted like those most Americans hate (€2.10/*pintxo,* Calle Pescaderia 5).

Bar Tamboril is a traditional (but non-smoking) place right on the main square favored for its seafood, mushrooms (*txampis tamboril*), and anchovy tempura along with its good prices. Their list of hot *pintxos* (grab the little English menu on the bar) makes you want to break the one-tapa-per-stop rule (Calle Pescaderia 2).

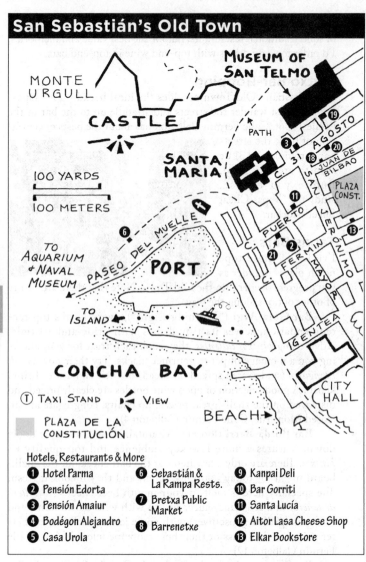

San Sebastián's Old Town

MONTE URGULL

CASTLE

MUSEUM OF SAN TELMO

PATH

SANTA MARIA

100 YARDS

100 METERS

TO AQUARIUM & NAVAL MUSEUM

PASEO DEL MUELLE

PORT

TO ISLAND

CONCHA BAY

⊤ TAXI STAND

VIEW

BEACH→

PLAZA DE LA CONSTITUCIÓN

CITY HALL

C. 31 AGOSTO

C. SAN JERÓNIMO

JUAN DE BILBAO

PLAZA CONST.

PUERTO

C. SAN FERMIN

MAYOR

IGENTEA

Hotels, Restaurants & More

1. Hotel Parma
2. Pensión Edorta
3. Pensión Amaiur
4. Bodégon Alejandro
5. Casa Urola
6. Sebastián & La Rampa Rests.
7. Bretxa Public Market
8. Barrenetxe
9. Kanpai Deli
10. Bar Gorriti
11. Santa Lucía
12. Aitor Lasa Cheese Shop
13. Elkar Bookstore

Bar Herria, which flies the Basque flag above its door, is on a street avoided by many locals opposed to the violent tactics of the ETA. I'd just get a drink here, and ponder the art, notices, and propaganda of the independence movement. Photos of political prisoners (with contact information—note they're scattered all over Spain) hang in a thought-provoking line above the bar (Calle Juan de Bilbao 14).

CALLE ALDAMAR

PASEO SALAMANCA

URUMEA

TO
GROS,
ZURRIOLA BEACH
& KURSAAL
CONFERENCE
CENTER

INIGO

SAN

NARRAR

ARR.

BETÓN

CAL.

ESCALATOR DOWN
TO PUBLIC MKT.

BRETXA
MARKET

SAN JUAN

REINA
REGENTE

ZURRIOLA

RIVER

PASEO REP. ARGENTINA

EMBELTRÁN

ALAMEDA DEL

ALAMEDA

VERGARA

BLVD.

OKENDO

BEN.

N

HERNANI

GARIBA

PEÑA.

ELCANO

GIPUZKOA
PLAZA

ANDIA

CAMINO

DCH

TO
RENFE
TRAIN
STN.

BASQUE COUNTRY

Tapas Bars
- ⑭ Bar Goiz-Argi
- ⑮ Bar Borda-Berri
- ⑯ Bar Txepetxa
- ⑰ Bar Tamboril
- ⑱ Bar Herria
- ⑲ La Cuchara de San Telmo
- ⑳ A Fuego Negro
- ㉑ Cervecerias La Mejillonera

La Cuchara de San Telmo, with cooks taught by a big-name Basque chef, is a cramped place that devotes as much space to its thriving kitchen as its bar. It has nothing precooked and set on the bar—you order your mini-gourmet plates with a spirit of adventure from the constantly changing blackboard. Their foie gras with apple jelly is rightfully famous (€3 *pintxos,* closed Mon, tucked away on a lonely alley called Santa Corda behind Museum of San Telmo at 31 de Agosto #28).

Do the Txikiteo Tango—
Tapas Cheat Sheet

Txikiteo (chih-kee-TAY-oh) is the Basque word for hopping from bar to bar, enjoying characteristically small sandwiches and tiny snacks (*pintxos*, PEEN-chohs) and glasses of wine. Local competition drives small bars to lay out the most appealing array of

pintxos. The selection is amazing, but the key to eating well here is going for the *pintxos calientes*—the hot tapas advertised on blackboards and cooked to order. Tapas are best, freshest, and accompanied by the most vibrant crowd from 12:00 to 14:00 and from 20:00 to 22:30. Watch what's being served—the locals know each bar's specialty. No matter how much you like a place, just order one dish; you want to be mobile.

Later in the evening, bars get more crowded and challenging for tourists. To get service amid the din, speak loudly and direct (little sweet voices get ignored), with no extra words. Expect to share everything. Double-dipping is encouraged. It's rude to put a dirty napkin on the table; it belongs on the floor.

If you can't get the bartender's attention to serve you a particular *pintxo*, don't be shy—just grab it and a napkin, and munch away. You pay when you leave; just keep a mental note of the tapas you've eaten. There's a code of honor. Everyone is part of the extended Basque family.

If you want a meal instead of *pintxos*, some bars—even ones that look only like bars from the street—have attached dining rooms, usually in the back.

Pintxos

antxoas	anchovies (not the cured, heavily salted kind you always hated)
bocadillos	baguette sandwiches
bacalao	cod (served lots of ways)
txampis (chahm-pees)	mushrooms
gambas	shrimp
patatas bravas	crisp potato cubes served with a spicy sauce
tortilla	big round omelet pie served by the slice (many varieties)

txangurro (chang-GOO-roh)	spider crab, a delicacy, often mixed with onions, tomatoes, and wine, served hot or made into a spread to put on bread

Descriptions

brocheta	anything on a stick
calientes	served hot and cooked to order (listed on chalkboard, not already on the bar)
cazuelas	hot meal-size servings (like *raciones* in Spanish)

Drinks

caña (KAHN-yah)	draft beer
mosto	non-alcoholic grape juice that comes in red or white (for when you've had enough beer and wine)
Rioja	a better wine
sidra	cider that's a bit more alcoholic than beer
sin (seen)	non-alcoholic beer (literally means "without")
tinto	red house wine (will generally get you rotgut)
txakoli (chah-koh-lee)	fresh white wine, poured from high to "break against the glass" and aerate it to add sparkle. Good with seafood, and therefore fits the local cuisine well.
un crianza	a glass of nicely aged wine. It's smart to ask for this instead of "*un tinto*" to get better quality for nearly the same price.
vaso de agua	glass of tap water (they'll ask you "bottled?" and you say no)
zurito (tthhoo-ree-toh)	small beer

Paying the Bill

Zenbat da?	"How much?"
Me cobras?	"What's the damage?" (a fun way to say "The bill, please")

BASQUE COUNTRY

A Fuego Negro is cool and upscale compared to the others, with a hip, slicker vibe and a blackboard menu of *pintxos* and drinks (there's an English translation sheet). They have a knack for mixing gourmet pretentiousness with whimsy here; enjoy their serious and extensive wine selection (closed Mon, 31 de Agosto #31). An inviting little section in the back makes this a sit-down dining opportunity.

Cervecerias La Mejillonera is famous among students for its big cheap beers, *patatas bravas*, and mussels ("*tigres*" is the spicy favorite). A long, skinny stainless-steel bar and lots of photos make ordering easy—this is the only place in town where you pay when served (Puerto 15, tel. 943-428-465).

Restaurants

Bodégon Alejandro is a good spot for modern Basque cuisine in a dark and traditional setting (3-course fixed-price meal-€35, from 13:00 and 20:30, closed Sun–Mon, and on Tue except in Aug, in Old Town on Calle Fermín Calbetón 4, tel. 943-427-158).

Casa Urola, a block away, is a fine option for a traditional, sit-down Basque meal (more expensive, €16–22 entrées, €41 tasting menu, from 13:00 and 20:00, closed Wed and Sun, reservations smart, Calle Fermín Calbetón 20, tel. 943-423-424).

Seafood along the Port: For seafood with a salty sailor's view, check out the half-dozen hardworking, local-feeling restaurants that line the harbor on the way to the aquarium. Along here, locals like **Sebastián** (more traditional, closed Tue) and **La Rampa** (more upscale, closed Tue and Wed).

Picnics and Takeout

A picnic on the beach or atop Monte Urgull is a tempting option. You can assemble a bang-up spread at the **Bretxa Public Market** at Plaza de Sarriegi (described on page 143).

Upscale **Barrenetxe** has an amazing array of breads, prepared foods, and some of the best desserts in town. In business since 1699, their somewhat formal service is justified (closed Sun, Plaza de Guipúzcoa 9, tel. 943-424-482).

Kanpai, a high-quality deli serving Basque and international cuisine, is run by Davíd and his mother. Step up to the display case and get something "to go" for an easy and tasty picnic. Davíd offers a fun tasting from his newfangled wine machine (€3 for 4 tastes, daily 10:00–15:00 & 17:00–21:00, San Lorenzo 4, tel. 943-423-884).

Breakfast

If your hotel doesn't provide breakfast—or even if it does—consider one of these places. The first is a traditional stand-up bar, while the second is a greasy spoon.

Bar Gorriti, delightfully local, is packed with market workers and shoppers starting their day. You'll stand at the bar and choose a hot-off-the-grill *francesca jamon* omelet (fluffy mini-omelet sandwich topped with a slice of ham) and other goodies (€2 each). This and a cup of coffee makes for a very Basque breakfast (daily, breakfast served 8:00–10:00, facing the side of the big white market building at San Juan 3, tel. 943-428-353). By the time you get there for breakfast, many market workers will be taking their mid-morning break.

Santa Lucía, a 1950s-style diner, is ideal for a cheap Old Town breakfast or *churros* break (*churros* are like deep-fried, sweet French fries that can be dipped in pudding-like hot chocolate). Photos of two dozen different breakfasts decorate the walls, and plates of fresh *churros* keep patrons happy. Grease is liberally applied to the grill...from a squeeze bottle (daily 8:30–21:30, Calle Puerto 6, tel. 943-425-019).

Connections

By Train

San Sebastián has two train stations: RENFE and EuskoTren (described in "Arrival in San Sebastián," page 138). The station you use depends on your destination.

RENFE Station: This station handles long-distance destinations within Spain (most of which require reservations). Connections include **Irún** (12/day, 25 min), **Hendaye,** France (7/day, 30 min), **Madrid** (3/day, 5–6 hrs), **Burgos** (4/day, 3 hrs), **León** (1/day, 5 hrs), **Pamplona** (3/day, 2 hrs), **Salamanca** (1/day, 6 hrs), **Vitoria** (5/day, 1.75 hrs), **Barcelona** (2/day, one fast—6 hrs on new Alvia train; one slow—8.5 hrs), and **Santiago de Compostela** (1/day, 11 hrs, final destination A Coruña).

EuskoTren Station: If you're going into France, take the regional Topo train (which leaves from the EuskoTren Station) over the French border into **Hendaye** (2/hr, 45 min, departs EuskoTren Station at :15 and :45 after the hour 6:15–21:45). From Hendaye, connect to France's SNCF network (www.sncf.com), where connections include **Paris** (4/day direct, 5.5–6 hrs, or 8.5-hr night train, reservations required). Unfortunately, San Sebastián's EuskoTren Station doesn't have information on Paris-bound trains from Hendaye. Don't buy the Spanish ticket too far in advance—EuskoTren tickets to Hendaye must be used within two hours of purchase (or else they expire).

Also leaving from San Sebastián's EuskoTren Station are slow regional trains to destinations in Spain's Basque region, including **Bilbao** (hourly, €10.50 round-trip ticket saves €2, 2.5 hrs—the bus is faster; EuskoTren info: tel. 902-543-210, www.euskotren.es). Although the train ride from San Sebastián to Bilbao takes twice as long as the bus, it passes through more interesting countryside. The Basque Country shows off its trademark green and gray: lush green vegetation and gray clouds. It's an odd mix of heavy industrial factories, small homegrown veggie gardens, streams, and every kind of livestock you can imagine.

By Bus

San Sebastián's "bus station," called Amara for the neighborhood, is a congregation of bus parking spots next to the big Hotel Amara Plaza, at the roundabout called Plaza Pío XII (on the river, four blocks south of EuskoTren Station). Some schedules are posted at various stops, but confirm departure times and buy your tickets in advance at any of the bus companies with offices on either side of the block north of the station area (toward downtown, along Avenida de Sancho el Sabio and Paseo de Vízcaya). The Pesa office, which serves St. Jean-de-Luz and Bilbao, is located on the same side as the station, at Avenida de Sancho el Sabio 33 (tel. 902-101-210, www.pesa.net). The Alsa office—which serves Madrid, Burgos, and León, and has baggage storage—is at Paseo de Vízcaya 16 (tel. 902-422-242, www.alsa.es).

From San Sebastián, buses go to **Bilbao** (get ticket from Pesa office, 2/hr, hourly on weekends, 6:30–22:00, 1.25 hrs, €9, departs from Amara; morning buses fill with tourists, commuters, and students, so consider buying your ticket the day before; once in Bilbao, buses leave you at Termibús stop with easy subway connections to the Guggenheim modern-art museum); **Bilbao Airport** (a Pesa bus goes directly to the airport from San Sebastián's Plaza Pío XII, €15, pay driver, hourly, 1 hr), **Pamplona** (La Roncalesa office, 8/day, 1 hr, €7), **León** (Alsa office, 1/day, 6 hrs, €28), **Madrid** (Alsa office, 8/day, 6 hrs direct, otherwise 7 hrs, €30–42; same bus stops at **Burgos**), and **Barcelona** (Vibasa office, 2/day and 1 at night, 7.5 hrs, €27).

To visit **Hondarribia** (described on page 175), you can catch bus #I-2 much closer to the center at Plaza Gipuzkoa (1 block south of TI; about 3/hr, 30 min, €2, same bus goes to airport en route to Hondarribia).

Buses to French Basque Country: A bus goes from San Sebastián's Amara bus station to **St. Jean-de-Luz** (Mon–Sat only, 2/day at 9:00 and 14:30, none on Sun, 45 min, €4 each way, get ticket from Pesa office, only 1/week off-season), then continues directly to **Biarritz** (1.25 hrs from San Sebastián) and **Bayonne** (1.5 hrs from San Sebastián, tel. 902-101-210, www.pesa.net).

Between San Sebastián and Bilbao: The Bay of Biscay

Between the two Spanish Basque cities of San Sebastián and Bilbao is a beautiful countryside of rolling green hills and a scenic, jagged coastline that looks almost Celtic. Aside from a scenic joyride, this area merits a visit for the cute fishing and resort town of Lekeitio.

Route Tips for Drivers

San Sebastián and Bilbao are connected in about an hour and a quarter by the A-8 expressway (€8 toll). While speedy and scenic, this route is nothing compared to some of the free, but slower, back roads connecting the two towns.

If side-tripping from San Sebastián to Bilbao, you can drive directly there on A-8 in the morning. But coming home to San Sebastián, consider this more scenic route: Take A-8 until the turn-off for Guernica, then head up into the hills on BI-635. After visiting Guernica, follow signs along the very twisty road to Lekeitio (about 40 min). Leave Lekeitio on the road just above the beach; after crossing the bridge, take the left fork and follow BI-3428 to Ondarroa (with a striking modern bridge and nice views back into the steep town), Mutriku, and Deba to hug the coastline east to San Sebastián. There's a fine photo-op pull-out as you climb along the coast just after Deba. Soon after, you'll have two opportunities to get on the A-8 (blue signs) for a quicker approach to San Sebastián; but if you've enjoyed the scenery so far, stick with the coastal road (white signs, N-634) through Zumaia and Getaria, rejoining the expressway at Zarautz.

Lequeitio / Lekeitio

A small fishing port with an idyllic harbor and a fine beach, Lekeitio (leh-KAY-tee-oh) is just over an hour by bus from Bilbao and an easy stop for drivers. It's protected from the Bay of Biscay by a sand spit that leads to the lush and rugged little San Nicolás Island. Hake boats fly their Basque flags and proud Basque locals black out the Spanish translations on street signs.

Lekeitio is a teeming resort during July and August (when its population of 7,000 triples as big-city Basque folks move into their vacation condos). Isolated from the modern rat race by its location down a long, windy little road, it's a backwater fishing village the rest of the year.

While sights are humble here, the 15th-century St. Mary's Parish Church is a good example of Basque Gothic, with an impressive altarpiece (Mon–Sat 8:00–12:00 & 17:00–19:30, closed Sun). The town's back lanes are reminiscent of old days when fishing was the only industry. Fisherwomen sell their husbands' catches each morning from about 10:30 along the port. The golden crescent beach is as inviting as the

sandbar, which—at low tide—challenges you to join the seagulls out on San Nicolás Island.

Getting There: Buses connect Lekeitio with **Bilbao** (hourly, 1.25 hrs; same bus stops at **Guernica,** 40 min) and **San Sebastián** (4/day Mon–Fri, 2/day Sat–Sun, 1.25 hrs). But this stop is most logical for those with a car. Drivers can park most easily in the lot near the bus station. Exit the station left, walk along the road, then take the first right (down the steep, cobbled street) to reach the harbor. There is no luggage storage in town.

Tourist Information: The TI faces the fish market next to the harbor (July–Aug daily 10:00–14:00 & 16:00–20:00; Sept–June Tue–Sat 10:30–13:30 & 16:00–19:00, Sun 10:00–14:00, closed Mon; tel. 946-844-017).

Sleeping: **$$ Emperatriz Zita Hotel** is the obvious best bet for your beach-town break. It's named for Empress Zita (who lived here in exile after her Habsburg family lost World War I and was booted from Vienna). Zita's mansion burned down, but this 1930s rebuild still has a belle époque aristocratic charm, solid classy furniture in 42 spacious rooms, real hardwood floors, and an elegant spa in the basement. Located on the beach a few steps from the harbor, with handy free parking and a view restaurant, it's a fine value (Sb-€62–72, Db-€76–92, Db suite-€108–120, views—ask for *vistas del mar*—are worth the extra €6, high prices are for mid-June–mid-Sept and Fri–Sat all year, extra bed-€25, breakfast-€10, elevator, free Wi-Fi, Santa Elena Etorbidea, tel. 946-842-655, fax 946-243-500, www.aisiahoteles.com, lekeitio@aisiahoteles.com). The hotel also has a thermal seawater pool, Jacuzzi, and full-service spa (all available at reasonable prices).

Eating: Although it's sleepy in the off-season, the harbor promenade is made-to-order in summer for a slow meal or a tapas crawl. **Restaurante Zapirain,** hiding in the narrow streets a few blocks up from the harbor, is a local favorite for fancy seafood. This cozy white-tablecloth eatery fills one small room with 10 tables of happy eaters (€15 starters, €20 main dishes, closed Tue, Igualdegi 3, tel. 946-840-255).

Guernica / Gernika

The workaday market town of Guernica (GEHR-nee-kah) is near and dear to Basques and pacifists alike. This is the site of the Gernikako Arbola (oak tree of Gernika), which marked the assembly point where the regional Basque leaders, the Lords of Bizkaia, met through the ages to assert their people's freedom. Long the symbolic heart of Basque separatism, it was also a natural target for Franco (and his ally Hitler) in the Spanish Civil War—resulting in an infamous bombing raid that left the town in ruins (see "The Bombing of Guernica"), as immortalized by Picasso in his epic work *Guernica.*

Today's Guernica, rebuilt after being bombed flat in 1937 and nothing special at first glance, holds some of the Basque Country's more compelling museums. And Basque bigwigs have reclaimed the town as a meeting point—they still elect their figurehead leader on that same ancient site under the oak tree.

Orientation to Guernica

Guernica is small (about 15,000 inhabitants) and compact, focused on its large market hall (Monday market 9:00–14:00).

Tourist Information: The TI is in the town center (Mon–Sat 10:00–14:00 & 16:00–19:00—no lunch break in summer, Sun 10:00–14:00, Artekalea 8, tel. 946-255-892, www.gernika-lumo .net). Pick up the free, good town map. If you'll be visiting both the Peace Museum and the Basque Country Museum, buy the €5.25 combo-ticket here.

Arrival in Guernica: Drivers will find a handy parking lot near the train tracks at the end of town. Buses drop off along the main road skirting the town center. No matter where you enter, the TI is well-signed (look for yellow *i* signs)—head there first to get your bearings.

BASQUE COUNTRY

Sights in Guernica

I've arranged Guernica's sights in the order of a handy sightseeing loop from the TI.

• *Exit the TI to the left, cross the street, and walk up the left side of the square, where you'll find the...*

▲**Gernika Peace Museum**—Because of the brutality of the Guernica bombing, and the powerful Picasso painting that documented the atrocities of war, the name "Guernica" has become synonymous with pacifism. This thoughtfully presented exhibit has taken a great tragedy of 20th-century history and turned it into a compelling cry for peace in our time. Borrow the English translations at the entry, request an English showing of the movie upstairs, and head up through the two-floor exhibit. The first floor begins by considering different ways of defining "peace." You'll then enter an apartment and hear Begoña describe her typical Guernica life in the 1930s...until the bombs dropped (a mirror effect shows you the devastating aftermath). You'll exit into an exhibit about the town's history, with a special emphasis on the bombing. Finally, a 10-minute movie shows grainy footage of the destruction, and ends with a collage of peaceful reconciliations in recent history—in Ireland, South Africa, Guatemala, Australia, and Berlin. On the second floor, Picasso's famous painting is superimposed on three transparent panels to highlight different themes. The exhibit concludes with a survey of the recent history of conflicts in the Basque Country (€4; July–Aug Tue–Sat 10:00–20:00, Sun 10:00–15:00, closed Mon; Sept–June Tue–Sat 10:00–14:00 & 16:00–19:00, Sun 10:00–14:00, closed Mon; Foru Plaza 1, tel. 946-270-213, www.peacemuseumguernica.org).

• *Continue uphill to the big church. At the road above the church, you can turn right and walk a block and a half to find an underwhelming tile replica of* **Picasso's** **Guernica** *(left-hand side of the street). Or you can head left to find the next two attractions.*

▲**Basque Country Museum (Euskal Herria Museoa)**—This well-presented, newly renovated exhibit offers a good overview of Basque culture and history. Start in the ground-floor theater and see the overview video (request English). Follow the suggested route and climb chronologically up through Basque history, with the necessary help of an included audioguide. You'll find exhibits about traditional Basque architecture and landscape, and a region-by-region rundown of the Basque Country's seven territories. One interesting map shows Basque emigration over the centuries—including to the US. The top floor is the most engaging, highlighting Basque culture: sports, dances, cuisine, myths and legends, music, and language, plus a wraparound movie featuring images of a proud people living the Basque lifestyle (€3, includes audioguide,

The Bombing of Guernica

During the Spanish Civil War, Guernica was the site of one of history's most reviled wartime acts.

Monday, April 26, 1937, was market day, when the town was filled with farmers and peasants from the countryside selling their wares. At about four-forty in the afternoon, a German warplane appeared ominously on the horizon, and proceeded to bomb bridges and roads surrounding the town. Soon after, more planes arrived. Three hours of relentless saturation bombing followed, as the German and Italian air forces pummeled the city with incendiary firebombs. People running through the streets or along the green hillsides were strafed with machine-gun fire. As the sun fell low in the sky and the planes finally left, hundreds—or possibly thousands—had been killed, and many more wounded. (Because Guernica was filled with refugees from other besieged towns, nobody is sure how many perished.)

Hearing word of the attack in Paris, Pablo Picasso—who had been commissioned to paint a mural for the 1937 world's fair—was devastated at the news of what had gone on in Guernica. Inspired, he painted what many consider the greatest antiwar work of art, ever. (For more on this great painting, now displayed in Madrid, see page 356.)

Why did the bombings happen? Reportedly, Adolf Hitler wanted an opportunity to try out his new saturation-bombing attack strategy. Francisco Franco, who was fed up with the independence-minded Basques, offered up their historic capital as a candidate for the experiment.

There's no doubt that Guernica, a gateway to Bilbao, was strategically located. But historians believe most of the targets here were far from strategic. Why attack so mercilessly, during the daytime, on market day, when innocent casualties would be maximized? Like the famous silent scream of Picasso's *Guernica* mother, this question haunts pacifists everywhere to this day.

Tue–Sat 10:00–14:00 & 16:00–19:00, Sun 11:00–15:00, closed Mon, Allendesalazar 5, tel. 946-255-451).

▲▲**Gernika Assembly House and Oak Tree**—In the Middle Ages, the meeting point for the Basque general assembly was under the old oak tree on the gentle hillside above Guernica. The tradition continues today, as the tree stands at the center of a modest but interesting complex celebrating Basque culture and self-government (free, daily 10:00–14:00 & 16:00–18:00, until 19:00 in summer, on Allendesalazar, tel. 946-251-138).

As you enter the grounds, you'll see an **old trunk** in the small colonnade dating from the 1700s. Basque traditions have lived much, much longer than a single tree's life span. When one dies, it's replaced with a new one. This is the oldest surviving trunk.

The exhibit has four parts: A stained-glass window room, the oak-tree courtyard, the assembly chamber, and a basement theater (request the 10-minute video in English that extols the virtues and beauties of the Basque Country).

Inside the first building, find the impressive **stained-glass window room.** The computer video here gives a good six-minute

overview of the exhibit (plays in English when you click). The gorgeous stained-glass ceiling is rife with Basque symbolism. The elderly leader stands under the oak holding a book with the "Old Law" *(Lege Zarra),* which are the laws by which the Basques lived for centuries. Below him are groups representing the three traditional career groups of this industrious people: sailors and fishermen; miners and steelworkers; and farmers. Behind them all is a classic Basque landscape: on the left is the sea, and on the right are rolling green hills dotted with red-and-white homes.

Out back, a tribune surrounds the fateful **oak tree.** This little fella is from 2005, planted here when the earlier one "finished out its life cycle" after standing here for nearly a century and a half. This tree is a descendant of that one, and (supposedly) of all the trees here since ancient times. This location is where Basque leaders have met in solidarity across the centuries. In the Middle Ages, after Basque lands became part of Castile, Castilian kings came here to pledge respect to the old Basque laws. When Basque independence came under fire in the 19th century, patriots rallied by singing a song about this tree ("Ancient and holy symbol / Let thy fruit fall worldwide / While we gaze in adoration / Upon thee, our blessed tree"). After the 1937 bombing, in which this tree's predecessor was miraculously unscathed, hundreds of survivors sought refuge under its branches. Today, although official representatives in the Spanish government are elected at the polls, the Basques choose their figurehead leader, the Lehendakari ("First One"), in this same spot.

Step back inside and enter the **assembly chamber**—like a mini-parliament for the region of Bizkaia ("Vízcaya" in Spanish, "Biscay" in English; one of the seven Basque territories). Notice the holy water and the altar—a sign that there's no separation of church and state in Basque politics. The paintings show the Lords of Bizkaia swearing allegiance to the Old Law.

Connections

Guernica is well-connected to **Bilbao** (hourly to Bilbao's Atxuri Station, 40 min; also 4 buses/hr, 40 min) and to **Lekeitio** (hourly buses, 40 min). Connections are sparser on weekends. The easiest way to connect to San Sebastián is via Bilbao, though you can also get there on the slow Topo train (transfer in Lemoa).

Bilbao / Bilbo

In recent years, Bilbao (bil-BOW, rhymes with "cow") has seen a transformation like no other Spanish city. Entire sectors of the industrial city's long-depressed port have been cleared away to allow construction of a new opera house, convention center, and the stunning Guggenheim Museum.

Bilbao feels at once like a city of the grim industrial past...and of an exciting new future. It mingles beautiful but crumbling old buildings; eyesore high-rise apartment blocks; brand-new super-modern additions to the skyline (such as the Guggenheim); and, scattered in the lush green hillsides all around the horizon, typical whitewashed Basque homes with red roofs. Bilbao enjoys a vitality and well-worn charm befitting its status as a regional capital of culture and industry.

Planning Your Time

For most visitors, the Guggenheim is the main draw (and many could spend the entire day there). But with a little more time, it's also worth hopping on a tram to explore the atmospheric Old Town (Casco Viejo). Don't bother coming to Bilbao on Monday, when virtually all its museums—including the almighty Guggenheim—are closed (except in July–Aug).

Orientation to Bilbao

When you're in the center, Bilbao feels smaller than its population of 500,000. The city, nestled amidst green hillsides, hugs the

Bilbao River as it curves through town. The Guggenheim is more or less centrally located near the top of that curve; the bus station is to the west; the Old Town (Casco Viejo) and train stations are to the east; and a super-convenient and fun-to-ride green tram called the EuskoTran ties it all together.

Tourist Information

Bilbao's handiest TI is next to the Guggenheim (July–Aug daily 10:00–19:00; Sept–June Tue–Sat 11:00–18:00, Sun 11:00–15:00, closed Mon; Avenida Abandoibarra 2, tel. 944-710-301, www .bilbao.net). There are also branches at the airport and at Arriaga Theater near the Old Town. Pick up a city map and the bimonthly *Bilbao Guide*. If you're interested in something beyond the Guggenheim, ask about walking tours and grab the Bilbao museums brochure (describing museums dedicated to everything from bullfighting and seafaring to sports and Holy Week processionals).

Arrival in Bilbao

Most travelers—whether arriving by train, bus, or car—will want to go straight to the Guggenheim. Thanks to a perfectly planned tram system (EuskoTran), this couldn't be easier. From any point of entry, simply buy a €1.20 single-ride ticket at a user-friendly green machine (€3.30 for an all-day pass), hop on a green-and-gray tram, enjoy the Muzak, and head for the Guggenheim stop (there's only one line so you can't get lost, trams come every 10–15 min, www.euskotran.es). When you buy your ticket, validate it immediately at the machine (follow the red arrow), since you can't do it once onboard. If you get lost, ask: *"¿Dónde está el museo Guggenheim?"* (DOHN-day ay-STAH el moo-SAY-oh "Guggenheim"). Note that the only luggage storage in town is at the Termibús Station (not at either train station).

By Train: Bilbao's **RENFE Station** (serving most of Spain) is on the river in central Bilbao. The train station is on top of a small shopping mall. To reach the tram to the Guggenheim, descend into the stores. Leave from the exit marked *Hurtado de Amézaga,* and go right to find the BBK bank. Enter, find the *Automatikoa* door on the right, and buy your ticket at the green machine marked *Abando* (the machine is mixed in with a bunch of ATMs). Leave the bank and continue right around the corner. Validate your ticket at the machines at the tram stop before boarding the tram marked *Basurto.*

Trains coming from San Sebastián arrive at the riverside **Atxuri Station,** southeast of the museum. From here, the tram (direction: Basurto) follows the river to the Guggenheim stop.

By Bus: Buses stop at the **Termibús Station** on the western edge of downtown, about a mile southwest of the museum. The station has luggage lockers and a left-luggage desk (€2/bag). The tram (San Mamés Station) is on the road just below the station—look

Bilbao

ET TRAM

M METRO STATION

P PARKING

1 Gran Hotel Domine Bilbao
2 Hotel Bilbao Jardines
3 Iturrienea Ostatua
4 Hotel Arriaga
5 La Estrella Ostatu
6 Pensión Ladero

for the steel *CTB* sign, buy and validate a ticket at the machine, and hop on the tram (direction: Atxuri) to the Guggenheim.

By Plane: Bilbao's compact, modern, user-friendly airport is about six miles north of downtown. Everything branches off the light-and-air-filled main hall, designed by prominent architect Santiago Calatrava. A handy bus (#3247) takes you directly to the center (€1.25, pay driver, 3/hr, 20-min trip, makes three stops downtown—the first one is closest to the Guggenheim—before ending at the Termibús Station). To find the bus, turn right out of the terminal. A taxi into town costs about €20. To get to San Sebastián, you can take a direct bus from Bilbao Airport (€15, pay driver, runs hourly, 1 hour, drops off at Plaza Pío XII, www.pesa.net). A taxi directly to San Sebastián will run you €150.

By Car: A big underground car park is near the museum; if you have a car, park it here and use the tram. From the freeway, take the exit marked *Centro* (with "bulls'-eye" symbol), follow signs to *Guggenheim* (you'll see the museum), and look for the big "P" that marks the garage.

Sights in Bilbao

▲▲▲Guggenheim Bilbao

While the collection of art in this museum is no better than that in Europe's other great modern-art museums, the build-

ing itself—designed by Frank Gehry and opened in 1997— is the reason why so many travelers happily splice Bilbao into their itineraries.

Cost, Hours, Location: €13, includes excellent audioguide; July–Aug daily 10:00–20:00; Sept–June Tue–Sun 10:00–20:00, closed Mon; same-day re-entry allowed—get bracelet on your way out; café—see "Eating," later in this section, no photos inside, tram stop: Guggenheim, Metro stop: Moyua, Avenida Abandoibarra 2, tel. 944-359-080, www.guggenheim-bilbao.es. For guided tours in English, call 944-359-090 for a schedule.

Background: Frank Gehry's groundbreaking triumph offers a fascinating look at 21st-century architecture. Using cutting-edge technologies, unusual materials, and daring forms, he created a piece of sculpture that smoothly integrates with its environment and serves as the perfect stage for some of today's best art. Clad in limestone and titanium, the building connects the city with its river. Gehry meshed many visions. To him, the building's multiple forms jostle like a loose crate of bottles. The building is inspired by a silvery fish...and also evokes wind-filled sails heading out to sea. Gehry keeps returning to his fish motif, reminding visitors that, as a boy, he was inspired by carp...even taking them into the bathtub with him.

❸ **Self-Guided Tour:** The audioguide will lead you room-by-room through the collection, but this information will get you started.

Guarding the main entrance is artist Jeff Koons' 42-foot-tall **West Highland Terrier.** Its 60,000 plants and flowers, which blossom in concert, grow through steel mesh. A joyful structure, it brings viewers back to their childhood...perhaps evoking human-kind's relationship to God...or maybe it's just another notorious Koons hoax. One thing is clear: It answers to "Puppy." Although the sculpture was originally intended to be temporary, the people of Bilbao fell in love with Puppy—so they bought it.

Descend to the **main entrance.** After buying your ticket, be sure to pick up the free exhibit audioguide. Also pick up the English brochure explaining the architecture and museum layout (at the information desk) and the monthly bulletin detailing the art currently on display.

After presenting your ticket, enter the **atrium.** This acts as the heart of the building, pumping visitors from various rooms on three levels out and back, always returning to this central area before moving on to the next. The architect invites you to caress the sensual curves of the walls. There are virtually no straight lines (except the floor). Notice the sheets of glass that make up the elevator shaft—overlapping each other like a fish's scales. The various glass and limestone panels are each unique, designed by a computer and shaped by a robot...as will likely be standard in constructing the great buildings of the future.

From the atrium, step out onto the riverside **terrace.** The "water garden" lets the river symbolically lap at the base of the building. This pool is home to two unusual sculptures (which appear occasionally throughout the day): a five-part "fire fountain" (notice the squares in the pool to the right) and a "fog sculpture" that billows up from below.

Still out on the terrace, notice the museum's commitment to public spaces: On the right, a grand **staircase** leads under a big green bridge to a tower; the effect wraps the bridge into the museum's grand scheme. The 30-foot-tall **spider,** called *Maman* ("Mommy"), is a French artist's depiction of her mother: She spins a beautiful and delicate web of life...which is used to entrap her victims. (It makes a little more sense if you understand that the artist's mother was a weaver. Or maybe not.)

Gehry designed the vast **ground floor** mainly to house

often-huge modern-art installations. Computer-controlled lighting adjusts for different exhibits. Surfaces are clean and bare, so you can focus on the art. While most of the collection comes and goes, Richard Serra's huge *Matter of Time* sculpture in the largest gallery is permanent (who would want to move those massive metal coils?). The intent is to have visitors walk among these metal walls—the "art" is experiencing this journey.

Because this museum is part of the Guggenheim "family" of museums, the **collection** perpetually rotates among the sister Guggenheim galleries in New York, Venice, and Berlin. The best approach to your visit is simply to immerse yourself in a modern-art happening, rather than to count on seeing a particular piece or a specific artist's works.

Twenty galleries occupy three floors. Use the handy touch-screens scattered throughout the museum to figure out exactly where you are and what's left to see, since the organic floor plan can be confusing.

Or, if you're not turned on by this kind of art, just rattle around the inside of the remarkable building for a while. Especially around the atrium, every angle morphs the building into a whole new experience.

You can't fully enjoy the museum's architecture without taking a circular stroll up and down each side of the river along the handsome promenade and over the two modern pedestrian bridges. (After you tour the museum, you can borrow a free "outdoor audioguide" to learn more—but it doesn't say much or take you across the river.) The building's skin—shiny, metallic, with a scale-like texture—is made of thin titanium, carefully created to give just the desired color and reflective quality. The external appearance tells you what's inside: the blocky limestone parts contain square-shaped galleries, while the titanium sections hold nonlinear spaces.

As you look out over the rest of the city, think of this: Gehry designed his building to reflect what he saw here in Bilbao. Now other architects are, in turn, creating new buildings that complement his. It's an appealing synergy for this old city.

To get to the Old Town from the Guggenheim, take the tram that leaves from the river level behind the museum, just past the kid-pleasing fountain. Hop off at the Arriaga stop, near the dripping-Baroque riverfront theater of the same name. From here, it's a short walk into the twisty Old Town.

Old Town (Casco Viejo)

Bilbao's Old Town, with tall, narrow lanes lined with thriving shops and tapas bars, is worth a stroll. Because the weather is wetter here than in many other parts of Spain (hence the green hillsides), the little balconies that climb the outside walls of buildings are glassed in, creating cozy little breakfast nooks.

Whether you want to or not, you'll eventually wind up at Old Bilbao's centerpiece, the **Santiago Cathedral,** a 14th-century Gothic church with a tranquil interior that's recently been scrubbed clean inside and out (free, €1 to dip into cloister, Mon–Sat 10:00–13:00 & 17:00–19:30, closed Sun).

Various museums (including those dedicated to diocesan art and the Holy Week processions) are in or near the Old Town, but on a quick visit only one is worth considering...

Basque Museum (Euskal Museoa)—It's fitting that Bilbao, a leading city of Spain's Basque region, would have a museum dedicated to its unique culture. Unfortunately, the almost complete lack of English leaves the exhibits, much like the Basques themselves, shrouded in mystery. Around a ground-floor cloister, you'll see old stone monuments. The first floor delves into the Basque cultural heritage, displaying ceramics, guns, looms, and other tools. Special emphasis is given to nautical artifacts from this seafaring people; Basque settlers in the American West; and the pastoral lifestyles of rural Basques. The top floor is dedicated to archaeology, with exhibits about old tools and settlements (€3, Tue–Sat 11:00–17:00, Sun 11:00–14:00, closed Mon, Miguel de Unamuno Plaza 4, tel. 944-155-423, www.euskal-museoa.org).

Sleeping in Bilbao

(€1 = about $1.40, country code: 34)
Bilbao merits an overnight stay. Even those who are only interested in the Guggenheim find that there's much more to see in this historic yet quickly changing city. Unless otherwise noted, the seven percent tax is not included in the prices listed below.

Near the Guggenheim Museum
$$$ Gran Hotel Domine Bilbao is *the* place for wealthy modern-art fans looking for a splurge close to the museum. It's right across the street from the Guggenheim, with decor (by a prominent Spanish designer) clearly inspired by Gehry's masterpiece. The hotel is gathered around an atrium with a giant "stone tree" and other artsy flourishes. Its 145 plush rooms are distinctly black, white, steel, and very postmodern (standard Db-€130, museum-view "executive" rooms for €20 more, rates can vary widely with events and demand, breakfast extra, non-smoking rooms, air-con,

BASQUE COUNTRY

Ventas Shops

Scattered between France and Spain and along the foothills of the Pyrenees, you'll see many signs for *ventas* (from the Spanish *vender*, "to sell"). Follow one of these signs to a cultural detour. Originally used as contraband outposts, *ventas* shops operate as café, bar, restaurant, grocery store, gas station, cheap boutique, and more. Most are lost in the hills and hard to find, and many still don't have signs—locals just know where they are. Today, they are legal in a borderless Europe, and they still offer inexpensive products. Customers are mostly the French Basque, who cause traffic jams on weekends driving to the border to do cheap shopping or fill the gas tank. In most *ventas*, gas is cheaper by 25 percent, cigarettes and alcohol leave by the case, and the Spanish, French, and Euskara languages mingle as locals enjoy a coffee or beer among hanging garlands of cheap hams.

---

elevator, free Internet and Wi-Fi, great museum-view breakfast terrace, Alameda Mazarredo 61, tel. 944-253-300, fax 944-253-301, www.granhoteldominebilbao.com, recepcion.domine@hoteles-silken.com).

In the Old Town

To reach the Old Town, take the tram to the Arriaga stop.

$$ Hotel Bilbao Jardines, a fresh new place buried in the Old Town, is the most hotelesque option, with 32 modern but basic rooms (Sb-€58, Db-€75, cheaper off-season, breakfast-€4.50, quieter rooms in back, air-con, elevator, free Wi-Fi, Calle Jardines 9, tel. 944-794-210, fax 944-794-211, www.hotelbilbaojardines.com, info@hotelbilbaojardines.com).

$ Iturrienea Ostatua, on a pedestrian street in the Old Town, is a tidy pension renting 21 rooms packed with brick, stone, and antiques (Sb-€50, Db-€60, twin Db-€66, Tb-€80, prices include tax, €10–15 more July–Aug, breakfast-€8, free Wi-Fi, near the river at Santa María 14, tel. 944-161-500, fax 944-158-929, www.iturrieneaostatua.com, info@iturrieneaostatua.com).

$ Hotel Arriaga offers 21 traditional but well-maintained rooms and a spirited reception (Sb-€45, Db-€54, extra bed-€11, some rooms overlook a busy street—request a quiet back room, free Wi-Fi, parking-€11, Ribera 3, tel. 944-790-001, fax 944-790-516). As you cross the bridge from the station, it's just behind the big theater of the same name.

$ La Estrella Ostatu has 26 simple but neat rooms up a twisty staircase near the Basque Museum (Sb-€35, Db-€60 in summer, cheaper off-season, breakfast-€3–4, María Muñoz 6, tel. 944-164-

066, fax 944-150-731, www.laestrellaostatu.com, laestrellabilbao @yahoo.es, just enough English spoken).

$ Pensión Ladero, renting ramshackle but cheap rooms, is a fine budget option in the Old Town. They don't accept reservations, so call upon arrival to check availability (S-€24, D-€36, T-€53, Q-€63, up 4 flights of stairs; 7 rooms up a very tight spiral staircase share 1 bathroom, while 11 rooms use the other 3 bathrooms on the main floor; cash only, Lotería 1, tel. 944-150-932, www .pensionladero.es). You'll find the *pensión* just before the cathedral at the center of the Old Town. This is a better value than the more prominent Pensión Roquefer across the street.

Eating in Bilbao

Near the Guggenheim Museum

The easiest choice is the good cafeteria in the museum itself (upper level, separate entry above museum entry; Tue–Sun 9:00–21:00, closed Mon, €15 lunch deal offered 13:00–15:15). The streets in front of the museum have a handful of both sit-down and carry-out eateries (cafés, pizzerias, sandwich shops) to choose from.

In the Old Town

Bilbao has a thriving restaurant and tapas-bar scene. For pointers on Basque food, see page 133. You'll find plenty of options on the lanes near the cathedral. Most restaurants around the Old Town advertise a fixed-price lunch for around €10.

The street **El Perro** is tops for the tasty little tapas called *pintxos* (PEEN-chohs). **Xukela Bar** is my favorite, with its inviting atmosphere, good wines, and an addictive array of €1.50 tapas spread along its bar. If it's not busy, you can assemble a plate of tapas and sit at one of the cozy restaurant tables (El Perro 2, tel. 944-159-772). On **Calle Santa María,** three bars—Gatz, Santa María, and Kasko—are worth considering.

El Perro street is also good for sit-down restaurants. Browse the menus and interiors and choose your favorite. Well-regarded options include three places virtually next door to each other: Egiluz (€10 meals); Río-Oja (€8 specialties, focus on shareable traditional dishes called *kazuelitas*); and Rotterdam (€10–15 meals). Eateries also abound on **Jardines** street, including the popular Breton (meals and *pintxos*, at #11, closed Mon).

Connections

From Bilbao by Bus to: San Sebastián (2/hr, hourly on weekends, 6:00–22:30, 1.25 hrs, arrives at San Sebastián's Amara Station), **Guernica** (4/hr, 40 min), **Lekeitio** (hourly, 1.25 hrs), **Pamplona**

It Happened at Hendaye

If taking the train between the Spanish and French Basque regions, you'll change trains at the nondescript little Hendaye Station. While it seems innocent enough, this was a site of a fateful meeting between two of Europe's most notorious 20th-century dictators.

In the days before World War II, Adolf Hitler and Francisco Franco maintained a diplomatic relationship. But after the fall of France, they decided to meet secretly in Hendaye to size each other up. On October 23, 1940, Hitler traveled through Nazi-occupied France, then waited impatiently on the platform for Franco's delayed train. The over-eager Franco hoped the Führer would invite him to join in a military alliance with Germany (and ultimately share in the expected war spoils).

According to reports of the meeting, Franco was greedy, boastful, and misguided, leading Hitler to dismiss him as a buffoon. Franco later spun the situation by claiming that he had cleverly avoided being pulled into World War II. In fact, his own incompetence is what saved Spain. Had Franco made a better impression on Hitler here at Hendaye, it's possible that Spain would have entered the war...which could have changed the course of Spanish, German, and European history.

(6/day, 2 hrs), **Burgos** (4–5/day, 2 hrs), **Santander** (hourly, 90 min, transfer there to bus to **Santillana del Mar** or **Comillas**—see Cantabria chapter). These buses depart from Bilbao's Termibús Station.

By RENFE Train to: Madrid (2/day, 6 hrs), **Barcelona** (2/day, 6.5–9 hrs), **Burgos** (5/day, 3 hrs), **Salamanca** (1/day, 5 hrs), **León** (1/day, 5 hrs), **Santiago de Compostela** (1/day direct, 11 hrs). Remember, these trains leave from the RENFE Station, across the river from the Old Town. Note that in a few years, a planned new train line will connect Bilbao to other cities in a snap (30 min to San Sebastián, 2.25 hrs to Madrid, 5.5 hrs to Paris)—but it's still slow trains for now.

By EuskoTren to: San Sebastián (hourly, long and scenic 2.5-hour trip to San Sebastián's EuskoTren Station, €6, www.euskotren.es), **Guernica** (hourly, 40 min). These trains depart from Bilbao's Atxuri Station, just beyond the Old Town.

Between San Sebastián and St. Jean-de-Luz: Hondarribia

Just 45 minutes apart by car, San Sebastián and St. Jean-de-Luz bridge the Spanish and French Basque regions. Between them you'll find the functional towns of Irún (Spain), Hendaye (France), and the delightful hill town of Hondarribia, which is worth a visit if you have time to spare.

Fuenterrabía / Hondarribia

For a taste of small-town *País Vasco*, dip into this enchanting, seldom-visited town (more commonly known by its Euskara name rather than the Spanish version, Fuenterrabía). Much smaller

and easier to manage than San Sebastián, and also closer to France (across the picturesque Bay of Txingudi from Hendaye), Hondarribia allows travelers a stress-free opportunity to enjoy Basque culture. While it's easy to think of this as a border town (between France and Spain), culturally it's in the middle of the Basque Country.

The town comes in two parts: the lower port town and the historic, balcony-lined streets of the hilly and walled upper town. The upper town, which feels quite manicured, is a delightful place to poke around if you have time. The main square is fronted by Charles V's austere, oddly squat castle (now a parador inn—see below). You can follow the TI's self-guided tour of the Old Town (English brochure available) or just lose yourself within the walls to explore the plazas.

In the modern lower town, straight shopping streets serve a local clientele, and a pleasant walkway takes strollers along the beach.

Arrival in Hondarribia: Drivers can use the metered parking by the port (marked with blue lines, prepay for parking at machine). Buses into town stop near the TI.

Tourist Information: The TI is located where the lower town and the upper town meet, two blocks up from the port on Jabier Ugarte 6 (July–Sept daily 10:00–14:00 & 15:00–19:00; Oct–June Mon–Fri 9:00–13:30 & 16:00–18:30, Sat–Sun 10:00–14:00; tel. 943-645-458).

Sleeping: Accommodations are pricey here, but it's a nice small-town alternative to San Sebastián. **$$$ Parador El Emperador,** with 36 rooms housed in a former imperial fortress, is the town's splurge (Sb-€165, Db-€205, elevator, free Wi-Fi, Plaza de Armas 14, tel. 943-645-500, fax 943-642-153, www .parador.es, hondarribia@parador.es). Tourists are allowed to have sangria in the *muy* cool bar, though the terraces are for guests only. **$$$ Hotel San Nikolas,** facing the parador from across the square, offers a more affordable alternative, with 18 nicely appointed rooms (many with views) above a smoky local café (Sb-€70–90, Db-€90–100, higher price is for mid-July–mid-Sept, can be even cheaper Mon–Thu outside of summer, breakfast not included, elevator, free Wi-Fi, Plaza de Armas 6, tel. 943-644-278, fax 943-646-217, www.hotelsannikolas.com, info @hotelsannikolas.com).

Connections

From Hondarribia by Bus to: San Sebastián (about 3/hr, 30 min on express bus, departs from near TI—same bus also stops at airport; or twice as long on local public bus), **Hendaye** on the French border (2/hr, 20 min, June–Sept only). A bus stop in Hondarribia is across from the post office, one block below the TI.

By Boat to: Hendaye (4/hr in summer, 2/hr off-season, 10 min, runs about 11:00–19:00 or until dark).

French Basque Country (Le Pays Basque)

Compared to their Spanish cousins across the border, the French Basques seem French first and Basque second. You'll see less Euskara writing here. But these destinations have their own special spice, mingling Basque and French influences with beautiful rolling countryside and gorgeous beaches. If you've been traveling in Spain, consider visiting (or even sleeping in) France for a change of pace. Your taste buds will enjoy the side-trip.

My favorite home base here is the central, comfy, and manageable resort village of St. Jean-de-Luz. It's a stone's throw to Bayonne (with its big-city bustle and fine Basque museum) and the snazzy beach town of Biarritz. A drive inland rewards you with a panoply of adorable French Basque villages. And St. Jean-de-Luz is a relaxing place to "come home" to, with its mellow ambience, fine strolling atmosphere, and good restaurants.

St. Jean-de-Luz / Donibane Lohizune

St. Jean-de-Luz (san zhahn-duh-looz) sits happily off the beaten path, cradled between its small port and gentle bay. The days when whaling, cod fishing, and pirating made it wealthy are long gone, as tourism has become the economic mainstay. Pastry shops serve Basque specialties, and store windows proudly display berets (a Basque symbol). Pedestrians lick ice cream and stroll traffic-free streets, while soft, sandy beaches tempt travelers to toss their itineraries into the bay. The knobby little mountain, La Rhune, towers above the festive scene. Locals joke that if it's clear enough to see La Rhune's peak, it's going to rain, but if you can't see it, it's raining already.

The town has precious little of sightseeing importance. But it's a fine base for exploring the Basque Country, and a relaxing beach and port town that provides the most enjoyable dose of Basque culture in France. In July and August, the town fills with French tourists from the north—especially the first two weeks of August, when it's practically impossible to find a room without a reservation made long in advance.

Orientation to St. Jean-de-Luz

St. Jean-de-Luz's old city lies between the train tracks, the Nivelle River, and the Atlantic. The main traffic-free street, rue Gambetta, channels walkers through the center, halfway between the train tracks and the ocean. The small town of Ciboure, across the river, holds nothing of interest.

The only sight worth entering in St. Jean-de-Luz is the church where Louis XIV and Marie-Thérèse tied the royal knot (Eglise St. Jean-Baptiste, described below). St. Jean-de-Luz is best appreciated along its pedestrian streets, lively squares, and golden, sandy beaches. The park at the far eastern end of the beachfront promenade at Pointe Ste. Barbe makes a good walking destination, with views and walking trails.

Tourist Information

The helpful TI is next to the big market hall, along the busy boulevard Victor Hugo (July–Aug Mon–Sat 9:00–19:30, Sun 10:00–13:00 & 15:00–19:00; Sept–June Mon–Sat 9:00–12:30 & 14:00–19:00, Sun 10:00–13:00—except Jan–March, when it's closed Sun; 20 boulevard Victor Hugo, tel. 05 59 26 03 16, www .saint-jean-de-luz.com or www.terreetcotebasques.com).

Dipping into France

If you're heading from Spain to France, you don't have to worry about border stops or currency changes (both countries use the euro). But here are a few other practicalities:

Phones: France's telephone country code is 33. Remember that Spanish phone cards and stamps will not work in France. If you have a cell phone with a Spanish SIM card, it may work here—but at a much higher rate per minute (although texting is cheap).

Hours: France typically does not use the same "siesta" system as Spain, so shops don't close for a mid-afternoon break. The French eat dinner closer to the European mainstream time (around 19:00–21:00)—much earlier than Spaniards do.

Restaurant Tips: In France, if you ask for the *menu* (muh-noo), you won't get a list of dishes; you'll get a fixed-price meal. *Menus*, which include three or four courses, are generally a good value if you're hungry: You'll get your choice of soup, appetizer, or salad; your choice from three or four main-course options with vegetables; plus a cheese course and/or a choice of desserts. Service is included (*service compris* or *prix net*), but wine and other drinks are generally extra.

French Survival Phrases: While some French Basques speak Euskara, most speak French in everyday life. You'll find these phrases useful:

Good day.	*Bonjour.*	bohn-zhoor
Mrs. / Ma'am	*Madame*	mah-dahm
Mr. / Sir	*Monsieur*	muhs-yur
Please?	*S'il vous plaît?*	see voo play
Thank you.	*Merci.*	mehr-see
You're welcome.	*De rien.*	duh ree-ahn
Excuse me.	*Pardon.*	par-dohn
Yes. / No.	*Oui. / Non.*	wee / nohn
Okay.	*D'accord.*	dah-kor
Cheers!	*Santé!*	sahn-tay
Goodbye.	*Au revoir.*	oh vwahr
women / men	*dames / hommes*	dahm / ohm
one / two / three	*un / deux / trois*	uhn / duh / twah
Do you speak English?	*Parlez-vous anglais?*	par-lay voo ahn-glay

Arrival in St. Jean-de-Luz

By Train or Bus: From the station, the pedestrian underpass leads toward the TI and the center of Old Town (just a few blocks away—see map).

By Car: Follow signs for *Centre-Ville*, then *Gare* and *Office de Tourisme*. The Old Town is not car-friendly. There's free parking behind the train station or pay to park in the big new underground garage near the TI (€13/day). Hotels or the TI can advise you.

By Plane: The nearest airport is in Biarritz, 10 miles to the northeast. The tiny airport is easy to navigate, with a useful TI desk (airport tel. 05 59 43 83 83, www.biarritz.aeroport.fr). To reach St. Jean-de-Luz, you can take a public bus (€3, 7/day, 30 min, tel. 05 59 26 06 99 for schedule) or a 20-minute taxi ride (about €30).

Helpful Hints

Market Days: Tuesday and Friday mornings (and summer Saturdays), the farmers' stands spill through the streets from Les Halles covered market on boulevard Victor Hugo, and seem to give everyone a rustic whiff of "life is good."

Supermarkets: A **Petit Casino** grocery is across from the market hall, next to the TI (8:30–13:00 & 15:30–19:30).

Internet Access: Run by friendly Irish expats Margaret and Peter, **Internet World** is best (July–Aug Mon–Sat 9:00–24:00, Sun 10:00–18:00; Sept–June Mon–Sat 10:00–18:00, closed Sun; 7 rue Tourasse, tel. 05 59 26 86 92).

Laundry: Laverie du Port at 5 place du Maréchal Foch (full-service for €12/load available Mon–Fri 9:30–12:30 & 14:30–19:00, Sat 9:30–13:00, closed Sun; cheaper self-service available daily 7:00–21:00).

Car Rental: Avis, at the train station, is handiest (Mon–Sat 8:00–12:00 & 14:00–18:00, closed Sun, tel. 05 59 26 76 66, fax 05 55 26 19 42).

Self-Guided Walk

Welcome to St. Jean-de-Luz

To get a feel for the town, take this hour-long self-guided stroll. You'll start at the port and make your way to the historic church.

Port: Begin at the little working port (at place des Corsaires, just beyond the parking lot). Pleasure craft are in the next port over. While fishing boats used to catch lots of whales and anchovies, now they take in sardines and tuna, and take out tourists on joyrides (two boats advertise mini-Atlantic cruises and fishing excursions, summer only, no guides, €9/45 min, €15/2 hours). Anchovies, once a big part of the fishing business, were being overfished into extinction so have been protected by the EU for the last few years.

St. Jean-de-Luz feels cute and nonthreatening now, but in the 17th century it was home to the Basque Corsairs. With the French government's blessing, these pirates who worked the sea—and enriched the town—moored here.

• *After you walk the length of the port, on your right is the tree-lined...*

Place Louis XIV: The town's main square, named for the king who was married here, is a hub of action that serves as the town's communal living room. During the summer, the bandstand features traditional Basque folk music and dancing at 21:00 (almost nightly July–Aug, otherwise Sun and Wed). Facing the square is the City Hall (Herriko Etchea) and the "House of Louis XIV" (in which he lived for 40 festive days in 1660). A visit to this house is worthwhile only if you like period furniture (€5, open April–mid-Oct, visits by 40-min guided tour only, 2–4/day, in French with English handouts, closed Tue and mid-Oct–March—when the privately owned mansion is occupied by the same family who've had it for over three centuries, tel. 05 59 26 27 58). The king's visit is memorialized by a small black equestrian statue at the entrance of the City Hall (a miniature of the huge one that marks the center of the Versailles courtyard). The plane trees, with truncated branches looking like fists, are cut back in the winter so in the summer they come back with thick shady foliage.

• *Opposite the port on the far side of the square is...*

Rue de la République: From place Louis XIV, this historic lane leads to the beach. Once the home of fishermen, today it's lined with mostly edible temptations. Facing the square, the shop **Macarons Adam** still bakes (according to the family recipe) the macaroons Louis XIV enjoyed during his visit. You can try one (€1), or sample a less historic but just as tasty *gâteau basque,* a baked tart with a cream or cherry filling (€1.70). Farther down rue de la République, you'll find the **Pierre Oteiza** shop, stacked with rustic Basque cheeses and meats from mountain villages (with a few samples generally out for the tasting). You'll likely eat on this lane tonight. **Kaiku,** the town's top restaurant, fills the oldest building in St. Jean-de-Luz (with its characteristic stone lookout tower), dating from the 1500s. This was the only building on the street to survive a vicious 1558 Spanish attack. Each end of the street is flanked by cannon, which may be from Basque pirate ships. At the upper end of the street, notice the photo of fisherwomen with baskets on their heads, who would literally run to Bayonne to sell their fresh fish.

• *Continue to the...*

Beach: A high embankment protects the town from storm waters, but generally the Grande Plage—which is lovingly groomed daily—is the peaceful haunt of sun-seekers and happy children. Walk the elevated promenade (to the right). Various

St. Jean-de-Luz

1. Hôtel de la Plage
2. Hôtel Les Almadies
3. Hôtel Colbert
4. Hôtel Ohartzia
5. Hôtel Le Petit Trianon
6. La Ruelle &
   Le Kaiku Rests.
7. Chez Maya Petit
   Grill Basque
8. Zoko Moko
9. Muscade Tarterie
10. Maison Paries
11. Launderette
12. Internet Café
13. Grocery
14. Les Halles Market

BASQUE COUNTRY

DCH

Pelota

In keeping with their seafaring, shipbuilding, and metalworking heritage, Basque sports are often feats of strength: Who can lift the heaviest stone? Who can row the fastest and farthest?

But the most important Basque sport of all is *pelota*—similar to what you might know as jai alai. Players in white pants and red scarves or shirts use a long, hook-shaped wicker basket (called a *txistera* in Euskara) to whip a ball (smaller and far bouncier than a baseball) back and forth off walls at more than 150 miles per hour. This men's-only game can be played with a wall at one or both ends of the court. Most matches are not professional, but betting on them is common. It can also be played without a racket—this slow-motion handball version is used as a starter game for kids.

It seems that every small Basque town has two things: a church and a *pelota* court (called *frontón*). While some *frontóns* are simple and in poor repair, others are freshly painted as a gleaming sign of local pride.

The TI in St. Jean-de-Luz sells tickets and has a schedule of matches throughout the area; you're more likely to find a match in summer (21:00, almost daily July–mid-Sept, afternoon matches sometimes on Sat–Sun). Matches are held throughout the year (except for winter) in the villages (ask for details at TI). The professional *cesta punta* matches on Tuesdays and Fridays often come with Basque folkloric half-time shows.

tableaux tell history in French. Storms (including a particularly disastrous one in 1749) routinely knocked down buildings. Repeated flooding around 1800 drove the population down by two-thirds. Finally, in 1854, Napoleon III—who had visited here and appreciated the town—began building the three breakwaters you see today. After decades spent piling 8,000 fifty-ton blocks, by 1895 the town was protected. To develop their tourist trade, they built a casino and a fine hotel, and even organized a special getaway train from Paris. During those days there were as many visitors as residents (3,000).

• *Stroll past the late Art Deco–style La Pergola, which houses a casino and the Hélianthal spa center (entrance around back) and overlooks the beach. Anyone in a white robe strolling the beach is from the spa. Beyond La Pergola is the Neo-Romantic Grand Hôtel (c. 1900), with an inviting terrace for a coffee break. From here, dive back into town until you reach the bustling...*

Rue Gambetta: Turn right and circle back to your starting point, following the town's lively pedestrian shopping street. You'll notice many stores selling the renowned *linge Basque*—cotton linens such as tablecloths, napkins, and dishcloths, in the characteristic Basque red, white, and green.

• *Just before place Louis XIV, you'll see the town's main church.*

Eglise St. Jean-Baptiste: The marriage of Louis XIV and Marie-Thérèse put St. Jean-de-Luz on the map, and this church is where it all took place. The ultimate in political marriages, the knot tied between Louis XIV and Marie-Thérèse in 1660 also cinched a reconciliation deal between Europe's two most powerful countries. The king of Spain, Philip IV—who lived in El Escorial Palace—gave his daughter in marriage to the king of France, who lived in Versailles. This marriage united Europe's two largest palaces, which helped end a hundred years of hostility and forged an alliance that enabled both to focus attention on other matters (like England). Little St. Jean-de-Luz was selected for its 15 minutes of fame because it was roughly halfway between Madrid and Paris, and virtually on the France–Spain border. The wedding cleared out both Versailles and El Escorial palaces, as anyone who was anyone attended this glamorous event.

The church, centered on the pedestrian street rue Gambetta, seems modest enough from the exterior...but step inside (daily

8:00–12:00 & 14:00–18:00). The local expertise was in shipbuilding, so the ceiling resembles the hull of a ship turned upside down. The dark wood balconies running along the nave segregated the men from the women and children (men went upstairs until the 1960s, as they still do in nearby villages) and were typical of Basque churches. The number of levels depended on the importance of the church, and this church, with three levels, is the largest Basque church in France.

The three-foot-long paddle-wheel ship hanging in the center was a gift from Napoleon III's wife, Eugènie. It's a model of an ill-fated ship that had almost sunk just offshore when she was on it. The 1670 Baroque altar feels Franco-Spanish and features 20 French saints. Locals of this proud and rich town call it the finest in the Basque Country. The box across from the pulpit was reserved for leading citizens who were expected to be seen in church and set a good example. Today the mayor and city council members sit here on festival Sundays. The place has great acoustics, and the 17th-century organ is still used for concerts (€10, mostly in summer, ask for schedule and buy tickets at TI).

As you leave the church, turn left to find the bricked-up doorway—the church's original entrance. According to a quaint but untrue legend, it was sealed after the royal marriage (shown on the wall to the right in a photo of a painting) to symbolize a permanent closing of the door on troubles between France and Spain.

Sleeping in St. Jean-de-Luz

(€1 = about $1.40, country code: 33, * = French hotel rating system, 0–4 stars)

Hotels are a good value here. The higher prices are for peak season (generally July–Sept). In winter, some prices drop below those I've listed. Most hoteliers speak English. Breakfast costs extra, except at my first listing. Those wanting to eat and sleep for less will do slightly better just over the border, in San Sebastián.

$$$ Hôtel de la Plage*** has the best location, right on the ocean. Its 22 rooms, 16 with ocean views, have a lively yellow-and-blue modern nautical decor (Db-€88–118, ocean view Db-€128–168, prices fluctuate with demand, family rooms, includes breakfast, air-con, elevator, free Wi-Fi with this book, garage-€12, 33 rue Garat, tel. 05 59 51 03 44, fax 05 59 51 03 48, www.hoteldelaplage.com, reservation@hoteldelaplage.com, run by friendly Pierre, Yannik, and Frederic).

$$$ Hôtel Les Almadies***, on the main pedestrian street, is a bright boutique hotel with seven flawless rooms, comfy public spaces with clever modern touches, a pleasant breakfast room and lounge, an inviting sun deck, and a caring owner (Db-€80–130, higher prices are for rooms with tubs, buffet breakfast-€12, free Wi-Fi, parking-€10, 58 rue Gambetta, tel. 05 59 85 34 48, fax 05 59 26 12 42, www.hotel-les-almadies.com, hotel.lesalmadies @wanadoo.fr, Monsieur and Madame Hargous will charm you with their Franglish).

$$$ Hôtel Colbert***, a Best Western, has 34 modern, tastefully appointed rooms across the street from the train station (Sb-€75–119, Db-€80–128, €10 extra for slightly bigger "superior" rooms, breakfast-€13, air-con, elevator, free Wi-Fi, 3 boulevard du Commandant Passicot, tel. 05 59 26 31 99, fax 05 59 51 05 61, www .hotelcolbertsaintjeandeluz.com, contact@hotelcolbertsaintjeande luz.com).

$$ Hôtel Ohartzia** ("Souvenir"), one block off the beach, is comfortable, clean, peaceful, and characteristic, with the most charming facade I've seen. It comes with 17 simple but well-cared-for rooms, generous and homey public spaces, and a delightful garden. The higher prices are for the four rooms with tubs (mid-July–Sept Db-€79–89, April–mid-July Db-€68–72, Oct–March Db-€68–72, extra bed-€15, 28 rue Garat, tel. 05 59 26 00 06, fax 05 59 26 74 75, www.hotel-ohartzia.com, hotel.ohartzia @wanadoo.fr). Their desk is technically open only 8:00–21:00, but owners Madame and Monsieur Audibert (who speak little English) live in the building; their son Benoît speaks English well.

$$ Hôtel Le Petit Trianon**, on a major street a couple of blocks above the Old Town's charm, is simple and traditional, with 26 decent rooms and an accommodating staff (July–Sept Db-€77; mid-March–June and Oct–mid-Nov Db-€65; even less off-season, air-con, free Wi-Fi, garage-€10, 56 boulevard Victor Hugo, tel. 05 59 26 11 90, fax 05 59 26 14 10, www.hotel-lepetittrianon.com, lepetittrianon@wanadoo.fr). To get a room over the quieter courtyard, ask for *côté cours* (coat-ay coor).

Eating in St. Jean-de-Luz

St. Jean-de-Luz restaurants are known for offering good-value, high-quality cuisine. You can find a wide variety of eateries in the old center. For forgettable food with unforgettable views, choose from several places overlooking the beach. Most places serve from 12:15 to 14:00, and from 19:15 on. Remember, in France *menu* means a fixed-price, multi-course meal.

The traffic-free rue de la République, which runs from place Louis XIV to the ocean promenade, is lined with hardworking restaurants (two of which are recommended below). Places are empty at 19:30, but packed at 20:30. Making a reservation, especially on weekends or in summer, is wise. Consider a fun night of bar-hopping for dinner in San Sebastián instead (an hour away in Spain, described on page 137).

La Ruelle serves good, traditionally Basque cuisine—mostly seafood—in a convivial dining room packed with tables, happy eaters, and kitschy Basque decor. André and his playful staff obviously enjoy their work, which gives this popular spot a relaxed and fun ambience. They offer a free sangria to diners with this book. Portions are huge; their €18 *ttoro* (seafood stew) easily feeds two—splitting is okay if you order two starters (€18–23 *menus*, closed Tue–Wed Oct–May, 19 rue de la République, tel. 05 59 26 37 80).

Le Kaiku is *the* gastronomic experience in town. They serve modern, creatively presented cuisine, and specialize in wild seafood (rather than farmed). This dressy place is the most romantic in town, but manages not to be stuffy (*menus* for €32, try €50 "Trust Serge" extravaganza, closed Tue–Wed, 17 rue de la République, tel. 05 59 26 13 20, Serge and Julie). For the best experience, talk with Serge about what you like best and your price limits—he would love to dazzle you with his €50 menu.

Chez Maya Petit Grill Basque serves hearty traditional Basque cuisine. Their €17 *ttoro* was a highlight of my day. They have €21 and €30 *menus*, but à la carte is more interesting. If you stick around in warm weather, you'll see the clever overhead fan system kick into action (closed Wed, 2 rue St. Jacques, tel. 05 59 26 80 76).

Zoko Moko offers Mediterranean nouveau cuisine, with small portions on big plates. Get an *amuse-bouche* (an appetizer chosen by the chef) and a *mignardise* (a fun bite-sized dessert) with each main plate ordered (€22 *plats*, Rue Mazarin 6, tel. 05 59 08 01 23, owner Charles).

Fast and Cheap: Consider the take-away crêpe stands on rue Gambetta. For a sit-down salad or a tart—either sweet or savory—consider **Muscade Tarterie** (€7–10 per slice, closed Mon, 20 rue Garat, tel. 05 59 26 96 73). **Maison Paries** is a favorite for its traditional sweets. Locals like their fine chocolates, *tartes*, macaroons, fudge (*kanougas*), and *touron* (marzipan)—brought by Jews who stopped here just over the border in 1492 after being expelled from Spain (9 rue Gambetta, tel. 05 59 26 01 46).

Connections

The train station in St. Jean-de-Luz is called St. Jean-de-Luz-Ciboure. Its clever departure board displays lights next to any trains leaving that day. Buses leave from the green building across the street. There is reduced bus and rail service on Sundays and off-season.

From St. Jean-de-Luz by Train to: Bayonne (hourly, 25 min), **St. Jean-Pied-de-Port** (4/day, 6/day in summer, 1.5 hrs, transfer in Bayonne), **Paris** (4 direct TGV connections per day, 5 hrs), **Bordeaux** (11/day, 2 hrs), **Sarlat** (4/day, 4 hrs, transfer in Bordeaux), **Carcassonne** (5/day, 6 hrs, transfers likely in Bayonne and Toulouse).

By Train to San Sebastián: First, take the 10-minute train to the French border town of Hendaye (Gare SNCF stop, about 10/day). Or get to Hendaye by bus (3/day, 35 min); check the schedule to see which leaves first.

Leave the Hendaye Station to the right, and look for the light-blue EuskoTren building, where you'll catch the commuter train into San Sebastián (2/hour, generally at :03 and :33 after the hour 7:00–22:00, 30-min trip—faster but less frequent by bus). This milk-run train is known as the Topo ("Mole") train, since it goes underground part of the time.

By Bus: Buses leave across the street from the train station. A

Spanish bus runs to **San Sebastián** (Mon–Sat only, 2/day direct, 45 min, only 1/week off-season, info in Spain tel. 902-101-210). Local bus #26 connects St. Jean-de-Luz either to **Bayonne** or **Biarritz** almost hourly. Confusingly, this one bus can run two different routes (one to Bayonne, the other to Biarritz Centre, 40 min to either one)—check the destination carefully. Another bus connects St. Jean-de-Luz to **Sare** (Mon–Fri 4/day, Sat 1/day, none Sun, 30 min).

By Taxi to: San Sebastián will cost you about €75 for up to four people, but it's convenient (tel. 05 59 26 10 11 or tel. 06 25 76 97 69).

By Excursion Bus: The TI has information and sells tickets for popular day-trip excursions, including **Guggenheim Bilbao** (€35 round-trip, includes €13 museum admission, Wed only, departs 9:30 from bus terminal next to train station, returns 19:30). Other day trips are available (Ainhoa, Espelette, St. Jean-Pied-de-Port, and San Sebastián).

Route Tips for Drivers

A one-day side-trip to both Bayonne and Biarritz is easy from St. Jean-de-Luz. These three towns form a sort of triangle (depending on traffic, each one is less than a 30-minute drive from the other). Hop on the autoroute to Bayonne, sightsee there, then take the N-10 road into Biarritz. Leaving Biarritz, continue along the coastal N-10. In Bidart, watch (on the right) for the town's proud *frontón* (*pelota* court). Consider peeling off to go into the village center of Guéthary, with another *frontón*. If you're up for a walk on the beach, cross the little bridge in Guéthary, park by the train station, and hike down to the walkway along the surfing beach (lined with cafés and eateries). When you're ready to move on, you're a very short drive from St. Jean-de-Luz.

Bayonne / Baiona

To feel the urban pulse of French Basque Country, visit Bayonne—modestly but honestly nicknamed "your anchor in the Basque Country" by its tourist board. With frequent, fast connections with

St. Jean-de-Luz (25 min by train, 40 min by bus), Bayonne makes an easy half-day side-trip.

Come here to browse through Bayonne's atmospheric and well-worn yet lively Old Town, and to admire its impressive Museum of Basque Culture. Known for establishing Europe's first whaling industry and for inventing the bayonet, Bayonne is more famous today for its ham *(jambon de Bayonne)* and chocolate.

Get lost in Bayonne's Old Town. In pretty Grand Bayonne, tall, slender buildings, decorated in Basque fashion with green-and-red shutters, climb above cobbled streets. Make sure to stroll the streets around the cathedral and along the banks of the smaller Nive River, where you'll find the market (Les Halles).

Orientation to Bayonne

Bayonne's two rivers, the grand Adour and the petite Nive, divide the city into three parts: St. Esprit, with the train station; and the more interesting Grand Bayonne and Petit Bayonne, which together make up the Old Town.

Tourist Information

The TI is in a modern parking lot a block off the mighty Adour River, on the northeastern edge of Grand Bayonne. They have very little in English other than a map and a town brochure (Mon–Fri 9:00–18:30, Sat 10:00–18:00, closed Sun except 10:00–13:00 in July–Aug, place des Basques, tel. 08 20 42 64 64).

Arrival in Bayonne

By Train: The TI and Grand Bayonne are a 10-minute walk from the train station: Walk straight out of the station, cross the traffic circle, and then cross the imposing bridge (pont St. Esprit). Once past the big Adour River, continue across a smaller bridge (pont Mayou), which spans the smaller Nive River. Stop on pont Mayou to orient yourself: You just left Petit Bayonne (left side of Nive River). Ahead of you is Grand Bayonne (spires of cathedral straight ahead, TI a few blocks to the right). The Museum of Basque Culture is in Petit Bayonne, facing the next bridge up the Nive River.

By Car and Bus: The handiest parking is also where buses arrive in Bayonne: next to the TI at the modern parking lot on the edge of Grand Bayonne. To reach the town center from here, first walk with the busy road on your left to the big park. Then turn right and walk with the park on your left-hand side. After a few blocks, you'll see atmospheric streets leading up to the cathedral on your right; if you continue straight, you'll reach the bridge over the Nive River called pont Mayou (described above).

To reach this parking lot, **drivers** take the *Bayonne Sud* exit from the autoroute, then follow green *Bayonne Centre* signs, then white *Centre-Ville* signs (with an *i* for tourist information). You'll see the lot on your right. In high season, when this lot can be full, use one of the lots just outside the center (follow signs to *Glain* or *Porte d'Espagne* as you arrive in town), then catch the little orange *navette* (shuttle bus) to get into the center (free, find route maps posted at stops in town, every 7 min, Mon–Sat 7:30–19:30, closed Sun).

Sights in Bayonne

▲**Museum of Basque Culture (Musée Basque)**—This museum (in Petit Bayonne, facing the Nive River at pont Marengo) explains French Basque culture from cradle to grave—in French, Euskara, and Spanish. The only English you'll read is "do not touch" (unless you buy their informative English booklet for €5). Artifacts and videos take you into traditional Basque villages and sit you in the front row of time-honored festivals—letting you envision this otherwise hard-to-experience culture (€5.50, July–Aug daily 10:00–18:30, also open and free Wed evenings 18:30–20:30; Sept–June Tue–Sun 10:00–18:30, closed Mon; last entry one hour before closing, 37 quai des Corsaires, tel. 05 59 59 08 98, www.musee-basque.com).

On the ground floor, you'll begin by walking through some 16th-century gravestones, then see a display of carts and tools used in rural life. Look for the *laiak*—distinctive forked hoes used to work the ground. At the end of this section, you'll watch a grainy film on Basque rural lifestyles.

The next floor up begins by explaining that the house *(etxea)* is the building-block of Basque society. More than just a building, it's a social institution—Basques are named for their house, not vice versa. You'll see models and paintings of Basque houses, then domestic items, a giant door, kitchen equipment, and furniture (including a clever combination bench-table, near the fireplace). After an exhibit on Basque clothing, you'll move into the nautical life, with models, paintings, and actual boats. The little door leads to a model of the port of Bayonne in 1805, back when it was a strategic walled city.

Upstairs, you'll learn that the religious life of the Basques was strongly influenced by the Camino de Santiago pilgrim trail, which passes through their territory. One somber room explains Basque funeral traditions. The section on social life includes a video of Basque dances (typically accompanied by flute and drums). These are improvised, but according to a clearly outlined structure—not unlike a square dance. The prominence given to the sport of *pelota* (see sidebar on page 182) indicates its importance to these people. One dimly lit room shows off several types of baskets *(chistera),* gloves, and balls used for the game, and videos show how these items are made. The museum wraps up with a brief lesson on the region's history from the 16th to the 20th centuries, including exhibits on the large Jewish population here (who had fled from a hostile Spain) and the renaissance of Basque culture in the 19th century.

Cathédrale Ste. Marie—Bankrolled by the whaling community, this cathedral sits dead-center in Grand Bayonne and is worth a peek (free, Mon–Sat 10:00–11:45 & 15:00–17:45, Sun 15:30–18:00). Find the unique keystones on the ceiling along the nave, then circle behind the church to find the peaceful 13th-century cloisters (free, daily 9:00–12:30 & 14:00–17:00, until 18:00 mid-May–mid-Sept).

Sweets Shops—With no more whales to catch, Bayonne turned to producing mouthwatering chocolates and marzipan; look for shops on the arcaded rue du Port Neuf (running between the cathedral and the Adour River).

Ramparts—The ramparts around Grand Bayonne are open for walking and great for picnicking (access from park at far end of TI parking lot). However, the ramparts do not allow access to either of Bayonne's castles—both are closed to the public.

Eating in Bayonne

Le Bayonnais, next door to the Museum of Basque Culture, serves traditional Basque specialties à la carte. Sit in the blue-tiled interior or out along the river (€17 lunch *menu,* closed Sun–Mon, quai des Corsaires 38, tel. 05 59 25 61 19).

La Cidrerie Txotx (pronounced "choch") has a Spanish-bodega ambience under a chorus line of hams. Or you can sit outside, along the river just past the market hall (€7–10 Basque tapas or €12–16 *plats,* daily, 49 quai Jauréguiberry, tel. 05 59 59 16 80).

A la Bolée serves up €6–9 sweet and savory crêpes in a cozy atmosphere along the side of the cathedral (daily, 10 place Pasteur, tel. 05 59 59 18 75).

If the weather is good, consider gathering a **picnic** from the pedestrian streets and head for the park around the ramparts below the *jardin botanique* (benches galore).

Connections

From Bayonne, you can reach **St. Jean-de-Luz** by bus (#26, almost hourly, 40 min) or by train (hourly, 25 min). To **Biarritz**, the bus is best (take the unfortunately named "STAB" bus #1 to reach Biarritz Centre, departs every 10 min, takes 20 min). There's also a train from Bayonne up to **St. Jean-Pied-du-Port** (4/day, 6/day in summer, 1 hr). Bus #23 takes you to the inland Basque villages of **Espelette** and **Ainhoa** (4/day Mon–Fri only, none Sat–Sun, 25 min to Espelette, 35 min to Ainhoa).

Biarritz / Biarritz

A glitzy resort town steeped in the belle époque, Biarritz (BEE-ah-ritz) is where the French Basques put on the ritz. In the 19th

century, this simple whaling harbor became, almost overnight, a high-class aristocrat-magnet dubbed the "beach of kings." While St. Jean-de-Luz and Bayonne are more fully French and more fully Basque, the made-for-international-tourists, jet-set scene of Biarritz is not without its charms. Perched over a popular surfing beach, anchored by grand hotels and casinos, hemmed in by jagged and picturesque rocky islets at either end, and watched over by a lighthouse on a distant promontory, Biarritz is a striking beach resort. However, for sightseers with limited time, it's likely more trouble than it's worth.

Orientation to Biarritz

Biarritz feels much bigger than its population of 30,000. The town sprawls, but virtually everything we're interested in lines up along the waterfront: the beach, promenade, hotel and shopping zone, and TI.

Arrival in Biarritz
By Car: Drivers follow signs for *Centre-Ville*, then carefully track signs for specific parking garages. The most central garages are called *Grande Plage, Casino, Bellevue,* and *St. Eugénie* (closest to the water). Signs in front of each one tell you if it's full *(complet),* in which case, move on to the next one.

    By Bus: Buses stop at "Biarritz Centre," a parking lot next to the TI (STAB buses to/from Bayonne stop along the side of the lot, while buses to/from St. Jean-de-Luz stop at the end of the lot). If you're taking a bus, be aware that some stop at the outskirts of town—only take one to "Centre."

    Don't bother taking the **train** to or from Biarritz, as the station is about two miles from the tourist area (buses #2 and #9 connect the train station to the city center).

    There is no baggage storage in Biarritz.

Tourist Information

The TI is in a little pink castle two blocks up from the beach (just above the beach and casino, hiding behind the City Hall/*hôtel de ville*—look for signs). Pick up the free map and get details on any sightseeing that interests you (July–Aug daily 9:00–19:00; Sept–June Mon–Fri 9:00–18:00, Sat–Sun 10:00–17:00; Square d'Ixelles, tel. 05 59 22 37 10, www.biarritz.fr).

Sights in Biarritz

There's little of "sightseeing" value in Biarritz. The TI can fill you in on the town's four museums (Marine Museum—described below; Chocolate Planet and Museum—intriguing, but a long walk from the center; Oriental Art Museum—large and diverse collection of art from across Asia; and Biarritz Historical Museum—really?).

Your time is best spent strolling along the various levels that climb up from the sea. From the TI, you can do a loop: First head west on the lively **pedestrian streets** that occupy the plateau above the water, which are lined with restaurants, cafés, and high-class, resorty "window-licking." (Place Georges Clemenceau is the grassy "main square" of this area.)

Work your way out to the point with the **Marine Museum** (Musée de la Mer). The most convenient of Biarritz's attractions, this pricey Art Deco museum-aquarium wins the "best rainy-day option" award, with a tank of seals and a chance to get face-to-teeth with live sharks (€8, around 9:30–18:00, daily April–Oct, closed Mon Nov–March, tel. 05 59 22 33 34, www.museede lamer.com).

Whether or not you're visiting the museum, it's worth hiking down to the entrance, then wandering out on the walkways that connect the big offshore rocks. These lead to the so-called **Virgin Rock** (Rocher de la Vierge), topped by a statue of Mary. Spot any surfers?

From here, stick along the water as you head back toward the TI. After a bit of up and down over the rocks, don't miss the trail down to **Fishermen's Wharf** (Port des Pêcheurs), a little pocket of salty authenticity that clings like barnacles to the cliff below the hotels. The remnants of an aborted construction project from the town's glory days, this little fishing settlement of humble houses and rugged jetties seems to faintly echo the Basque culture that thrived here before the glitz hit. Many of the houses have been taken over by the tourist trade (gift shops and restaurants).

Continuing along the water (and briefly back up to street level), make your way back to the town's centerpiece, the **big beach** (Grande Plage). Dominating this inviting stretch of sand is the Art Deco casino, and the TI is just above that. If you haven't yet taken the time on your vacation to splash, wade, or stroll on the beach...now's your chance.

Connections

Biarritz is connected by bus #26 to **St. Jean-de-Luz** (nearly hourly, 40 min). Buses run by the company called "STAB" take you to **Bayonne** (#1, departs every 10 min, takes 20 min).

Villages in the French Basque Country

Traditional villages among the green hills, with buildings colored like the Basque flag, offer the best glimpse at Basque culture. Cheese, hard cider, and *pelota* players are the primary products of these villages, which attract few foreigners but many French summer visitors. Most of these villages have welcomed pilgrims bound for Santiago de Compostela since the Middle Ages. Today's hikers trek between local villages or head into the Pyrenees. The most appealing villages lie in the foothills of the Pyrenees, spared from beach-scene development.

Use St. Jean-de-Luz as your base to visit the Basque sights described below. For information on another French Basque village a bit farther away—St. Jean-Pied-de-Port (Donibane Garazi)—see page 201. You can reach some of these places by public transportation, but the hassle outweighs the rewards.

Do a circuit of these towns in the order they're listed here (and, with time, also add St. Jean-Pied-de-Port at the end). Assuming you're driving, I've included route instructions as well.

• *From St. Jean-de-Luz, follow signs for* Ascain, *then* Sare. *On the road toward Sare, you'll pass the station for the train up to...*

La Rhune / Larrun

Between the villages of Ascain and Sare, near the border with Spain, a small cogwheel train takes tourists to the top of La Rhune, the region's highest peak (2,969 feet). You'll putt-putt up the hillside for 30 minutes in an open-air train car to reach panoramic views of land and sea (€14 round-trip for adults, €8 for kids, runs mid-March–mid-Nov, departures weather-dependent—so the trip is worthless if it's not clear, departures every 35 min when busiest in July–Aug, tel. 05 59 54 20 26, www.rhune.com).

• *Continue along the same road to...*

BASQUE COUNTRY

Sare / Sara

Sare, which sits at the base of the towering mountain La Rhune, is among the most picturesque villages—and the most touristed. It's easily reached from St. Jean-de-Luz by bus or car. The small TI is on the main square (Mon–Fri 9:30–12:30 & 14:00–18:00, Sat 9:30–12:30, closed Sun, tel. 05 59 54 20 14). Nearby is a cluster of hotels and the town church (which has an impressive interior, with arches over the altar and Basque-style balconies lining the nave). At the far end of the square is the town's humble *frontón*.

• *Leaving Sare, first follow signs for St. Pée, then watch for the turnoff to...*

Ainhoa / Ainhoa

Ainhoa is a colorful, tidy, picturesque one-street town that sees fewer tourists (which is a good thing). Its chunks of fortified walls and gates mingle with red-and-white, half-timbered buildings. The 14th-century church—with a beautiful golden *retable* (screen behind the altar)—and the *frontón* (*pelota* court) share center stage.

Ainhoa is also a popular starting point for hikes into the hills. For a spectacular village-and-valleys view, drive five minutes (or walk 90 sweaty minutes) up the steep dirt road to the Chapelle de Notre-Dame d'Aranazau ("d'Aubepine" in French). Start in the parking lot directly across the main street from the church, then head straight uphill. Follow signs for *oratoire*, then count the giant white crosses to the top.

• *As you leave Ainhoa, you'll have to backtrack the way you came in to find the road to...*

Espelette / Ezpeleta

Espelette won't let you forget that it's the capital of the region's AOC red peppers *(piments d'Espelette)*, with strands of them dangling like good-luck charms from many houses and storefronts. After strolling the charming cobbled center, wander downhill at the end of town to find the town church and the well-restored château and medieval tower, which now houses the town hall, an exhibition, and the TI (Mon–Fri 8:30–12:30 & 14:00–18:00, Sat 9:30–12:30, closed Sun, tel. 05 59 93 95 02).

Sleeping and Eating: For a good regional meal, consider the **$$ Hôtel Euzkadi** restaurant, with a *muy* Spanish ambience (€25–32 *menus,* daily 12:30–14:00 & 19:30–21:00, closed Mon–Sun off-season, 285 Karrika Nagusia, tel. 05 59 93 91 88). The hotel has 27 rooms with modern touches and a swimming pool (Sb-€41–43, Db-€52–65, air-con, elevator, free Wi-Fi, www.hotel-restaurant -euzkadi.com).

• *From Espelette, if you have time, you can simply follow signs to* St. Jean-Pied-de-Port *(covered in next chapter).*

BASQUE COUNTRY

THE CAMINO DE SANTIAGO

*St. Jean-Pied-de-Port • Pamplona • Burgos •
León • O Cebreiro • Lugo*

The Camino de Santiago—the "Way of St. James"—is Europe's ultimate pilgrimage route. Since the Middle Ages, humble pilgrims have trod hundreds of miles across the north of Spain to pay homage to the remains of St. James in his namesake city, Santiago de Compostela. After several lonely centuries, today the route has been rediscovered, and more and more pilgrims are traveling—by foot, bike, and horse—along this ancient pathway.

While dedicating a month of your life to walk the Camino is admirable, you might not have that kind of time. But with a car (or public transportation), any traveler can use the Camino as a sightseeing spine—a string of worthwhile cities, towns, and countryside sights—and an opportunity to periodically "play pilgrim."

Begin in the French foothills of the Pyrenees, in the Basque village of St. Jean-Pied-de-Port. Twist up and over rugged Roncesvalles Pass into Spain, and on to Pamplona—the delightful, Basque-flavored capital of Navarre, famous for its Running of the Bulls. From here, head west through the fertile hills of Navarre to the vineyards of La Rioja, then across the endless wheat fields and rough, arid plains of northern Castile to Burgos and León, with their beautiful dueling Gothic cathedrals—one a riot of architectural styles, the other gracefully simple but packed with stained glass.

As the path crosses into Galicia near the time-passed stony mountain village of O Cebreiro, the terrain changes, becoming lush and green. This last leg of the journey, in Galicia, is the most popular: Pilgrims pass simple farms, stone churches, moss-covered homes with slate roofs, apple orchards, flocks of sheep, dense

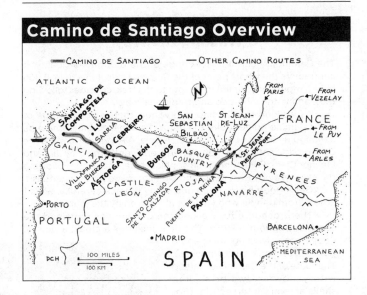

Camino de Santiago Overview

forests of oak, sweet chestnut, and eucalyptus...and plenty of other pilgrims. Just before Santiago, the ancient walled Roman city of Lugo is a worthwhile detour for car travelers.

Whether undertaken for spiritual edification or sightseeing pleasure, the Camino de Santiago ties together some of Spain's most appealing landscape, history, architecture, and people.

Getting Around the Camino de Santiago

By Car: This chapter is geared for car pilgrims who want to trace the Camino and linger at the highlights. Italicized directions marked by a bullet point are designed for drivers (with specific route tips, road numbers, and directional signs). To supplement these instructions, it's essential to get a good road map (most TIs can give you a free map covering just their province, or you can buy a better one by Michelin or Mapa Total for about €6). Driving the full Camino nonstop would take about 12 hours. Assuming you're taking the most direct (expressway/*autovía*) route, figure these estimated times for specific legs of the Camino by car (these times don't take into account stops or detours, such as the La Rioja Wine Loop):

- St. Jean-Pied-de-Port to Pamplona—1.5 hours
- Pamplona to Burgos—3.5 hours
- Burgos to León—2 hours
- León to Astorga—1 hour
- Astorga to O Cebreiro—1.5 hours
- O Cebreiro to Lugo—1 hour
- Lugo to Santiago—1.5 hours

Walking the Way

The Camino by car? Purists cringe at the thought—arguably, it contradicts the whole point of the Camino to do it in a rush. If you have a month of your life to devote to the trek, consider following the Camino the intended and traditional way.

As walking the Camino is in vogue, there's no shortage of good Camino guidebooks and maps. Try *Walking the Camino de Santiago* by Bethan Davies and Ben Cole, *A Pilgrim's Guide to the Camino de Santiago* by John Brierly, or *Buen Camino* by Jim and Eleanor Clem. For a more philosophical take, check out *Following the Milky Way* by Elyn Aviva and *On Pilgrimage* by Jennifer Lash.

Get a good book. Read and study it. Pack carefully. Solicit advice from people who've done it. Then enjoy the journey.

The procedure for walking the Camino has remained the same throughout history. The gear includes a cloak; a pointy, floppy hat; a walking stick; and a gourd (for drinking from wells). The route of the Camino is marked with yellow arrows or scallop shells at every intersection. (For more on the significance of these items, and others, see "The Symbols of Santiago," on page 206.)

Early in the journey, pilgrims buy their "credential" *(credencial)*—a sort of passport, which they get stamped and dated at churches and lodgings along the way. (They can also show it to stay at cheap *refugios* and to get a reduced pilgrim's rate at many museums and churches en route.) At the end, they present their stamped credential in Santiago and receive a special certificate called a *compostela*. Only those who meet the two principal criteria qualify: You must do the pilgrimage for "spiritual" reasons; and you must walk at least the last 100 kilometers (about 62 miles, roughly from Sarria) or ride your bike or horse the last 200 kilometers (124 miles) into Santiago.

Doing the entire French Road from the border to Santiago takes about four to six weeks on foot (averaging 12–15 miles per day, with an occasional rest day—32 days is a typical Camino). Bikers can do it in about two weeks. Many of the trails, originally dirt paths, are now being paved. The journey itself is a type of hut-hopping: At regular intervals along the route (about every 5–10 miles), pilgrims can get a bunk for the night at humble little hostels called *albergues* (ahl-BEHR-gehs), *refugios* (reh-FOO-hee-ohs), or *hospitales* (oh-spee-TAH-lehs). Some of these are run by the government (€5–10 per bunk, closer to €3 in

Galicia, even if they're "free" a donation is requested; no reservations
taken—first-come, first-served, with
priority given to credential-holding
pilgrims arriving on foot). Others are
privately run (typically a bit more
expensive—€10-20—and sometimes
take reservations). A wide variety of
other accommodations are available
for those who prefer more comfort,
ranging from simple *hostales* to grand
hotels and *paradores* (I've listed my
favorites in this chapter).

What began as a religious trek to
atone for one's sins has evolved into
a journey undertaken by anyone—spiritual or secular—who just
wants some time to think. While some pilgrims do the trip for
"fun," those who take it seriously caution that it's one of the most
wrenching things you can do. After a few weeks on the Camino,
many pilgrims begin to develop a telltale limp...you'll notice it
getting more pronounced as you move west. (There's a reason
old pilgrim hostels are sometimes called "hospitals.")

But there are worse things than blisters and sore muscles.
The Camino can take a psychological toll on pilgrims. Trudging
step after step across endless plains toward an ever-receding
horizon, you're forced to introspection. Religious or not, you
can't help but come to terms with your regrets, demons, "sins,"
or anything else that's on your conscience.

This process of self-reflection is symbolized by picking up
a small stone somewhere early on the Camino, then depositing
it at the Iron Cross near the end of the trek—releasing yourself
from whatever's been weighing you down. The absolution of
sins that awaited medieval pilgrims isn't so different from the
"find myself" motives of today's iPhone-toting tourists. Whether
you're pardoned by the Church, or simply unburdened of what's
been nagging you, it's liberating all the same.

On a lighter note, a wonderful pilgrim camaraderie per-
colates along the length of the Camino, as a United Nations of
vagabonds—young and old—swap stories and tips. Driving, on
foot, or on bike, you'll keep crossing paths with the same pilgrims
again and again...the guy who checked in before you at the hotel
last night is at the cathedral with you the next morning. Along
the way, the standard greeting (like a Jacobean "Happy Travels")
is *"Buen Camino!"*

No matter how you get to Santiago, you'll share in the jubila-
tion pilgrims have felt through the ages when—four miles out of
town—the spires of the cathedral come into view.

Many freeways are marked *Autovía Camino de Santiago* to keep you on track. But be warned that *Camino de Santiago* directional signs in small towns can be misleading, since they're sometimes intended for foot pilgrims, not drivers—navigate by town names and road numbers instead.

By Public Transportation: Most of the Camino route can be done by bus and/or train. However, it can be difficult, or even impossible, to reach some of the out-of-the-way stops between the big cities (such as O Cebreiro), and there's no good, direct link from St. Jean-Pied-de-Port to Pamplona. Where feasible, I've listed train and bus connections for each of the main stops.

The Old-Fashioned Way: If you're walking or biking the entire Camino, don't rely exclusively on my coverage in this chapter (which describes the major towns and cities, but ignores so much more). Equip yourself with a good day-by-day guidebook with details on each leg, and get good advice about what to pack. For starters, see the "Walking the Way" sidebar in this chapter.

Planning Your Time

Drivers begin in Basque Country (San Sebastián in Spain or St. Jean-de-Luz in France), where you can pick up your rental car. If you're in a hurry or don't plan to visit France, you can skip St. Jean-Pied-de-Port and connect easily to Pamplona from Spain's Basque Country.

Day 1: Drive through the French Basque villages (see previous chapter) to St. Jean-Pied-de-Port, then over Roncesvalles Pass to Pamplona. Sleep in Pamplona.

Day 2: Explore Pamplona, then drive westward to Burgos (stopping en route at Puente de la Reina, and detouring for the La Rioja Wine Loop if you have time and a healthy interest in wine). Sleep in Burgos.

Day 3: Sightsee Burgos this morning, then drive to León and dip into the cathedral there. Sleep in León—or, if you're tired of big cities, continue an hour farther to sleep in Astorga.

Day 4: Continue westward to Galicia, stopping at O Cebreiro and Lugo before arriving at Santiago de Compostela.

Orientation to the Camino

The term "Camino de Santiago" actually refers to several different routes, beginning in different parts of Spain, France, Portugal, and beyond. All (like this chapter) travel from east to west. The most popular has always been the so-called "French Road" (Camino Francés), which covers nearly 500 miles across northern Spain from the French border to Santiago—and that's the route described here. We'll begin in the French Basque town of St. Jean-Pied-de-Port, cross over the Pyrenees at Roncesvalles, then pass through three northern Spanish cities (Pamplona, Burgos, León), before climbing into green Galicia, ending at Santiago de Compostela.

Tourist Information: Pilgrims will find no shortage of helpful resources along the way. In addition to TIs in each town (listed in this chapter), you'll also find "Pilgrim Friend" associations and other offices (often attached to an *albergue* or *refugio*) that offer kind advice to the weary traveler.

Holy Year: The Compostela Holy Year *(Ano Xacobeo)* is celebrated in years when the Feast of St. James (July 25) falls on a Sunday—which includes 2010. Expect traffic on the trails to double, and the pilgrim atmosphere to be even more festive. The buzz is that even the pope will pay a visit in 2010.

Tours: Iberian Adventures runs guided and self-guided walking tours in English for individuals and small groups along the Camino de Santiago and in the La Rioja wine region. Company owner Jeremy Dack highlights each area's natural environment, history, culture, cuisine, and wine, and emphasizes environmental awareness and respect for local customs (mobile 620-939-116, www .iberianadventures.com, info@iberianadventures.com). Jeremy also leads hiking tours of Spain's major mountain ranges.

St. Jean-Pied-de-Port

Just five miles from the Spanish border, the walled town of St. Jean-Pied-de-Port (sahn zhahn-pee-duh-por) is the most popu-

lar village in all the French Basque countryside (you may also see it labeled as Donibane Garazi, its Basque name). Traditionally, St. Jean-Pied-de-Port has been the final stopover in France for Santiago-bound pilgrims, who gathered here to cross the Pyrenees together and con-

tinue their march through Spain. The scallop shell of "St. Jacques" (French for "James") is etched on walls throughout the town.

Visitors to this town are equal parts pilgrims and French tourists. Gift shops sell a strange combination of pilgrim gear (such as quick-drying shirts and shorts) and Basque souvenirs. This place is packed in the summer (so come early or late).

Orientation to St. Jean-Pied-de-Port

Tourist Information

The TI, on the main road along the outside of the walled Old Town, can give you a town map (hours vary, generally July–Aug Mon–Sat 9:00–19:00, Sun 10:00–12:00; Sept–June Mon–Sat 9:00–12:00 & 14:00–18:00, Sun 10:00–12:00; maybe less in winter; tel. 08 10 75 36 71). For Camino information, you'll do better at the Pilgrim Friends Office (described below).

Arrival in St. Jean-Pied-de-Port

Parking is ample and well-signed from the main road. If arriving by **train,** exit the station to the left, then follow the busy road at the traffic circle toward the city wall.

Sights in St. Jean-Pied-de-Port

There's little in the way of sightseeing here, other than pilgrim-spotting. But St. Jean-Pied-de-Port feels like the perfect "Welcome to the Camino" springboard for the upcoming journey. Many modern pilgrims begin their Camino in this traditional spot because of its easy train connection to Bayonne, and because—as its name implies ("St. John at the Foot of the Pass")—it offers a very challenging but rewarding first leg: up, over, and into Spain.

Cross the old bridge over the Nive River (the same one that winds up in Bayonne) to the **Notre-Dame Gate,** which was once a drawbridge. Then head up the main walking drag, **rue de la Citadelle.** With its rosy-pink buildings and ancient dates above its doorways, this lane simply feels old. Notice lots of signs for *chambres* (rooms) and *refuges*—humble, hostel-like pilgrim bunkhouses.

Partway up, on the left at #39, look for the **Pilgrim Friends Office** (Les Amis du Chemin de Saint-Jacques, daily 7:30–12:00 & 13:30–20:30 & 21:30–22:30, tel. 05 59 37 05 09). This is where pilgrims check in before their long journey to Santiago; 32,000 pilgrims started out here last year (compared to just 4,000 a decade ago). For €2, a pilgrim can buy the official credential *(credenciel)* that she'll get stamped at each

Best Stages for a Short Walk

The Camino de Santiago is divided into stages of about 12–15 miles apiece (approximately one day's walk). Even if you're doing most of the Camino by car, consider taking an extra day or two to walk one of these recommended stages (to get back to your car, catch a bus—TIs have schedules—or, where buses aren't an option, take a taxi). These stages are scattered throughout the Camino, and listed from east to west.

Roncesvalles to Zubiri (21.5 km/13.5 miles)—This is the first stage in Spain, after the arduous trek over the Pyrenees. It's mostly (though not entirely) downhill, through rolling hills and meadows, amidst sheep and charming villages.

Puente de la Reina to Estella (19 km/12 miles)—Here the Camino becomes a bit more level and arid. This leg begins in an appealing pilgrim town, then passes through gentle farm fields and along a three-and-a-half-mile stretch of Roman road (from Cirauqui to Lorca).

Pieros to Villafranca del Bierzo (7.5 km/5 miles)—For this stretch, the Camino ascends through the hilly El Bierzo region, en route to Galicia. The last bit of this leg takes you through vineyards and vegetable patches into Villafranca, entering town at the Romanesque church of Santiago.

Ambasmestas to O Cebreiro (13.2 km/8.2 miles)—If you're not intimidated by a steep uphill hike, this leg is a gorgeous introduction to Galicia—culminating at the perfect little hilltop village.

Sarria to Portomarin (21.5 km/13.5 miles)—Because it's about 100 kilometers (62 miles) from Santiago (the minimum to qualify for a *compostela* certificate), Sarria is a popular starting point for short-haul pilgrims. From here, you can make it to Santiago in less than a week. The terrain: pretty Galicia.

THE CAMINO DE SANTIAGO

stop between here and Santiago to prove she walked the whole way and earn her *compostela* certificate. Pilgrims also receive a warm welcome, lots of advice, and help finding a bunk (the well-traveled staff swears that no pilgrim ever goes without a bed in St. Jean-Pied-de-Port).

A few more steps up, you'll pass the skippable €3 Bishop's Prison (Prison des Evêques, on the left). Continue on up to the **citadel,** dating from the mid-17th century—when this was a highly strategic location, keeping an eye on the easiest road over the Pyrenees between Spain and France. While not open to the public (as it houses a school), the grounds around this stout fortress offer sweeping views over the French Basque countryside.

Sleep Code

(€1 = about $1.40, France country code: 33, Spain country code: 34)
S = Single, **D** = Double/Twin, **T** = Triple, **Q** = Quad, **b** = bathroom, **s** = shower only, * = French hotel rating system (0–4 stars). Unless otherwise noted, credit cards are accepted and English is spoken. Breakfast is generally not included.

To help you easily sort through these listings, I've divided the rooms into three categories, based on the price for a standard double room with bath during high season (breakfast and 7 percent IVA tax not included):

$$$ Higher Priced—Most rooms €95 or more.
  $$ Moderately Priced—Most rooms between €55–95.
    $ Lower Priced—Most rooms €55 or less.

Sleeping in St. Jean-Pied-de-port

Lots of humble pilgrim dwellings line the main drag, rue de la Citadelle. If you're looking for a bit more comfort, consider these options.

$$ Hotel Ramuntcho** is the only real hotel option in the Old Town, located partway up rue de la Citadelle. Its 16 rooms above a restaurant are straightforward but modern (Sb-€64–74, Db-€70–79, 1 rue de France, tel. 05 59 37 03 91, fax 05 59 37 35 17, http://perso.wanadoo.fr/hotel.ramuntcho, hotel.ramuntcho @wanadoo.fr).

$$ Itzalpea, a café and teahouse, rents five rooms along the main road just outside the Old Town (Db-€60–76 depending on size, includes breakfast, air-con, 5 place du Trinquet, tel. 05 59 37 03 66, fax 05 59 37 33 18, www.maisondhotes-itzalpea.com, itzalpea@wanadoo.fr).

$ Chambres Chez l'Habitant has five old-fashioned, pilgrim-perfect rooms along the main drag. Welcoming Maria and Jean Pierre speak limited English, but their daughter can help translate (€20 per person in D, Db, Q, or Qb, includes breakfast, 15 rue de la Citadelle, tel. 05 59 37 05 83).

Connections

A scenic train conveniently links St. Jean-Pied-de-Port to **Bayonne** (4/day, 6/day in summer, 1 hr), and from there to **St. Jean-de-Luz** (about 30 min beyond Bayonne). It's about a 1.25-hour drive from St. Jean-de-Luz. Unfortunately, there are no buses from St. Jean-Pied-de-Port to **Pamplona;** to connect them by public transport, you'll have to go back to Bayonne, then to San Sebastián, then catch a bus or train to Pamplona from there.

Between St. Jean-Pied-de-Port and Pamplona

The first stretch of the Camino, crossing the Pyrenees from France into Spain, is among the most dramatic. While there's little in the way of civilization, it's a memorable start for the journey.

• *From St. Jean-Pied-de-Port, follow road signs to* Arnéguy *on road D-933. (But be warned that the road signs for the Camino de Santiago take a much more roundabout high-mountain, one-lane road instead of the direct road to the border.)*

Crossing the Pyrenees: Roncesvalles (Roncevaux / Orreaga)

As you go over the stone bridge in the village of **Arnéguy,** you're also passing from France to Spain. For centuries, this bridge was the site of a delicate dance between nervous smugglers and border guards. Today you'll barely notice you've crossed a border.

The road meanders through a valley before twisting up to the pass called **Puerto de Ibañeta** (also known as the Roncesvalles Pass). This scrubby high-mountain pass is one of the Basque Country's most historic spots. The most accessible gateway through the Pyrenees between France and Spain, this pass has been the site of several epic battles. According to a popular medieval legend, Charlemagne's nephew Roland was killed fighting here. Vengeful Basque tribes, seeking retribution for Charlemagne's sacking of Pamplona, followed the army as it began its return to France—and felled the mighty Roland along this very road. Several centuries later, Napoleon used the same road to invade Spain.

Coming down from the pass, you reach **Roncesvalles / Orreaga** ("Valley of Pines"), which gave this area its name. This jumble of buildings surrounding a monastery is sort of a pilgrim depot, where travelers can pause to catch their collective breath after clearing the first arduous leg of the Camino. The big building

on the right is a simple *refugio,* filled with bunk beds. In the afternoon, you might see pilgrims washing their clothes at the spigots in front, then hanging them to dry amidst the cows and knobby trees out back. The big church (on the left) has a tourable cloister and museum

The Symbols of Santiago

The pilgrim route leading to Santiago de Compostela—and the city itself—are rife with symbolism. Here are a few of the key items you'll see along the way.

- **St. James:** The Camino's namesake is also its single biggest symbol. St. James can be depicted three ways: as a pilgrim, as an apostle, and as a Crusader (slaughtering Moors). For more, see "The Three Santiagos," on page 268.
- **The Scallop Shell** *(Vieira):* Figuratively, the various routes from Europe to Santiago come together like the lines of a scallop shell. And literally, scallops are abundant on the Galician coast. Though medieval pilgrims only carried shells with them on the return home—to prove they'd been here, and to scoop water from wells—today's pilgrims also carry them on the way *to* Santiago. The yellow sideways shell that looks like a starburst marks the route for bikers.
- **The Gourd:** Gourds were used by pilgrims to drink water and wine.
- **The Yellow Arrow:** These arrows direct pilgrims at every intersection from France to Santiago.
- **The Red Cross:** This long, skinny cross with curly ends at the top and sides, and ending in a sword blade at the bottom, represents the Knights of Santiago. This 12th-century Christian military order had a dual mission: to battle Muslim invaders while providing hospice and protection to pilgrims along the Camino de Santiago.
- **The Tomb and Star:** St. James' tomb (usually depicted as a simple coffin or box), and the stars that led to its discovery, appear throughout the city of Santiago, either together or separately.

(€4). As you leave town, you pass the first sign for Santiago de Compostela...790 kilometers (490 miles) straight ahead.

From here to Pamplona, the Camino passes through some pretty rolling hills and meadows, and several appealing villages. The first after Roncesvalles, called **Auritz / Burguete,** was supposedly Hemingway's favorite place to fish for trout when he needed to recover from a Pamplona bender.

• *Around that next bend is the first big city on the Camino: Pamplona.*

Pamplona

Proud Pamplona, with stout old walls standing guard in the Pyrenees foothills, is the capital of the province of Navarre ("Navarra" in Spanish). At its peak in the Middle Ages, Navarre was a grand kingdom that controlled parts of today's Spain and France. (The current king of Spain, Juan Carlos, is a descendant of the French line of Navarre royalty.) After the French and Spanish parts split, Pamplona remained the capital of Spanish Navarre.

Today Pamplona feels at once affluent (with the sleek new infrastructure of a town on the rise), claustrophobic (with its warren of narrow lanes), and fascinating (with its odd traditions, rich history, and ties to Hemingway). Culturally, the city is a lively hodgepodge of Basque and *Navarro* (Basques call the city Iruña). Locals like to distinguish between *Vascos* (people of Basque citizenship—not them) and *Vascones* (people who identify culturally as Basques—as do many *Navarros*).

And, of course, Pamplona is best known as the host of one of Spain's (and Europe's) most famous festivals: the Running of the Bulls (held in conjunction with the Fiesta de San Fermín, July 6–14). But there's more to this town than bulls—and, in fact, visiting at other times is preferable to the crowds and 24/7 party atmosphere that seize Pamplona during the festival. Contrary to the chaotic or even backwards image that its famous festival might suggest, you'll find Pamplona welcoming, sane, and enjoyable.

Orientation to Pamplona

Pamplona has about 200,000 people. Most everything of interest is in the tight, twisting lanes of the Old Town (Casco Antiguo), centered on the main square, Plaza del Castillo. The newer Ensanche ("Expansion") neighborhood just to the south—with a sensible grid plan—holds several good hotels and the bus station.

Tourist Information

Pamplona's well-organized TI overlooks a small square called Plaza de San Francisco in the heart of the Old Town. Pick up the handy map/guide and get your questions answered (Mon–Sat 10:00–14:00 & 16:00–19:00, Sun 10:00–14:00, Eslava 1, tel. 848-420-420).

Local Guide: Francisco Glaría is a top-notch guide—and simply a delight to be with—who enjoys leading visitors through Pamplona (€140/half-day up to 4 hours, tel. 948-383-755, mobile 629-661-604, www.novotur.com, novotur@novotur.com).

Pamplona

- Running of the Bulls Route
- **P** Parking
- View

200 YARDS
200 METERS

THE CAMINO DE SANTIAGO

BUS STATION   DCH

1. Gran Hotel La Perla
2. Hostal Navarra
3. Hotel Europa & Café Niza
4. Hotel Castillo de Javier
5. Pension Arrieta
6. Bar Cervecería La Estafeta & Bodegon Sarria
7. Gaucho Bar
8. Café Roch
9. Calle San Nicolás Eateries
10. Café Iruña
11. San Ignacio Restaurante
12. Ultramarinos Beatriz Shop
13. Kukuxumusu T-Shirt Shop
14. Hemingway Bust
15. Navarre Govt. Building

Arrival in Pamplona

You can store bags at the bus station, but not at the train station.

By Bus: The sleek new user-friendly bus station is underground along the western edge of the Ensanche area, about a 10-minute walk from the Old Town sightseeing zone. On arrival, go up the escalator, cross the street, turn left, and walk a half-block, where you can turn right down the busy Conde Oliveto street. Along this street, you're near several of my recommended accommodations; or you can walk two blocks to the big traffic circle called Plaza Príncipe de Viana. From here, turn left up Avenida de San Ignacio to reach the Old Town.

By Train: The RENFE Station is farther from the center, across the river to the northwest. It's easiest to hop on public bus #9 (every 12–20 min), which drops you at the big Plaza Príncipe de Viana traffic circle south of the Old Town (described above).

By Car: Everything is well-marked: Simply follow the bull's-eyes to the center of town, where individual hotels are clearly sign-posted. There's also handy parking right at Plaza del Castillo.

By Plane: The Pamplona Airport is located about four miles outside the city (tel. 902-404-704, www.aena.es). Bus #21 connects the airport to downtown (hourly, €1).

Self-Guided Walk

The Walking of the Tourists

Even if you're not in town for the famous San Fermín festival, you can still get a good flavor of the town by following in the foot- and hoof-steps of its participants. This walk takes you through the town center along the same route of the famous Running of the Bulls.

• *Begin in front of the...*

City Hall (Ayuntamiento): When Pamplona was just starting out, many Camino pilgrims who had been "just passing through"

decided to stick around. They helped to build the city you're enjoying today, but tended to cling to their own regional groups, which squabbled periodically. So in 1423, the King of Navarre (Charles III) tore down the internal walls and built a City Hall here to unite the community. This version (late Baroque, from the 18th century) is highly symbolic: Hercules demonstrates the city's strength, while the horn-blower trumpets Pamplona's greatness.

The festival of San Fermín begins and ends on the balcony of this building (with the flags). When the bulls start running, they

Camino de Santiago: Eastern Half

come in this direction from the street to the left of the City Hall. Look for the line of metal squares in the pavement, used to secure barricades for the run. There are four rows, creating two barriers on each side. The inner space is for press and emergency medical care, while spectators line up along the outer barrier. This first stretch is uphill, allowing the bulls to use their strong hind legs to pick up serious momentum.

• *Follow the route of the bulls two blocks down Mercaderes street (next to Alexander Jewelry). Turn right onto...*

La Estafeta Street: At this turn, the bulls—who are now going downhill—begin to lose their balance, often sliding into the barricade. (Note that if you want to side-trip to the cathedral—described under "Sights in Pamplona"—it's dead ahead, three

CAMINO DE SANTIAGO
EXPRESSWAYS
OTHER ROADS
AIRPORTS (NOT ALL SHOWN)

blocks up the skinny lane called Curia from this corner.)

Once the bulls regain their footing, they charge up the middle of La Estafeta. Notice how narrow this street is: No room for barricades... no escape for *mozos*.

On days that the bulls aren't running, La Estafeta is one of the most appealing streets in Pamplona. It's home to some of the best tapas bars in town (see "Eating in Pamplona"). Because the Old Town was walled right up until 1923, space in here was at a premium—making houses tall and streets narrow.

Partway down the first block on the right, look for the hole-in-the-wall **Ultramarinos Beatriz** shop (at #22)—makers of the best treats in Pamplona (Mon–Fri 9:00–14:00 & 16:30–20:00, Sat 9:00–14:00, closed Sun, tel. 948-220-618). Anything with

The Running of the Bulls: Fiesta de San Fermín

"A San Fermín pedimos, por ser nuestro patrón,
nos guíe en el encierro, dándonos su bendición."
"We ask San Fermín, because he is our Patron, to guide us
through the Running of the Bulls, giving us his blessing."
—Song sung before the run

For nine days each July, a million visitors pack into Pamplona
to watch a gang of reckless, sangria-fueled adventurers thrust
themselves into the path of an oncoming herd of furious bulls.
Locals call it *El Encierro* (literally, "the enclosing"—as in, taking
the beasts to be enclosed in the bullring)...but everyone else
knows it as the "Running of the Bulls."

The festival begins at City Hall on noon on July 6, with
various events filling the next nine days and nights. Originally
celebrated as the feast of San Fermín—who is still honored by a
religious procession through town on July 7—it has since evolved
into a full slate of live music, fireworks, general revelry, and an
excuse for debauchery. After dark, the town erupts into a rollicking party scene. To beat the heat, participants chug refreshing
sangria or *kalimotxo* (*calimocho* in Spanish)—half red wine, half
cola. The town can't accommodate so many guests, so some
visitors day-trip in from elsewhere (such as San Sebastián), and
many young tourists simply pass out in city parks overnight
(public showers are on Calle Hilarión Eslava in the Old Town).

The Running of the Bulls takes place each morning of the
festival and is broad-
cast nationwide on live
TV. The bulls' photos
appear in the local paper
beforehand, allowing
runners to size up their
opponents. If you're
here to watch, stake
your claim at a vantage
point along the outer
barrier by 6:30 or 7:00 in the morning. Don't try to stand along
the inner barrier—reserved for press and medical personnel—or
you'll be evicted when the action begins.

Before the run starts, runners sing a song to San Fermín
(see lyrics above) three times to ask for divine guidance. Soon
the bulls will be released from their pen near Cuesta Santo
Domingo. From here, they'll stampede a half-mile through the
town center...with thrill-seekers called *mozos* (and female *mozas*)
running in front of the herd, trying to avoid a hoof or horn in the
rear end.

Mozos traditionally wear white with strips of red tied around their necks and waists, and carry a newspaper to cover the bull's eyes when they're ready to jump out of the way. Two legends explain the red-and-white uniform: One says it's to honor San Fermín, a saint (white) who was martyred (red); the other says that the runners dress like butchers, who began this tradition. (The bulls are color-blind, so they don't care.)

At 8:00, six bulls are set loose. The beginning of the run is marked by two firecrackers—one for the first bull to leave the pen, and another for the last bull. The animals charge down the street, while the *mozos* try to run in front of them for as long as possible before diving out of the way. The bulls are kept on course by fencing off side-streets (with openings just big enough for *mozos* to escape). Shop windows and doors are boarded up.

A bull becomes most dangerous when separated from the herd. For this reason, a few steer—who are calmer, slower, have bigger horns, and wear a bell—are released with the bulls, and a few more trot behind them to absorb angry stragglers and clear the streets. (There's no greater embarrassment in this *machismo* culture than to think you've run with a bull...only to realize later that you actually ran with a steer.)

The bulls' destination: the bullring...where they'll be ceremonially slaughtered as the day's entertainment. (For more on bull-fighting, see page 708 in the appendix.)

If you're considering running with the bulls yourself, it's essential to equip yourself with specific safety information not contained in this book. Locals suggest a few guidelines: First, understand that these are very dangerous animals, and running with them is entirely at your own risk. Be as sober as possible, and wear good shoes to protect your feet from broken glass and from being stepped on by bulls and people. (Runners wearing sandals might be ejected by police.) You're not allowed to carry a backpack, as its motion could distract the bulls. If you fall, never stand up—it's better to be trampled by six bulls than to be gored by one. Ideally, try to get an experienced *mozo* to guide you on your first run.

Cruel as this all seems to the bulls—who scramble for footing on the uneven cobblestones as they rush toward their doom in the bullring—the human participants don't come out unscathed. Each year, dozens of people are gored, trampled, or otherwise injured. Over the last century, 15 runners have been killed at the event. But far more people have died from overconsumption of alcohol.

The festival ends at midnight on July 14 when the townspeople congregate in front of the City Hall, light candles, and sing their sad song, "Pobre de Mí": "Poor me, the Fiesta de San Fermín has ended."

chocolate is good, but the mini-croissants are sensational. They come in two types: *garrotes de chocolate,* filled with milk chocolate; or *cabello de angel,* filled with sweet fibers (€3 for a box of six). So simple...but oh so good.

Halfway down the street, notice the alley on the right leading to the main square (we'll circle back to the square later). Farther down, near the very end of La Estafeta (on the right, at #76), look for the shop called **Kukuxumusu**—Euskara for "the kiss of a flea." These whimsical, locally designed cartoon T-shirts are a local favorite. The giant digital clock outside the shop counts down to the next Running of the Bulls.

• *La Estafeta eventually leads you right to Pamplona's...*

Bullring: At the end of the run, the bulls charge down the ramp and through the red door. The bullring is used only nine days each summer (during the festival). The original arena from 1923 was expanded in the 1960s (see the extension at the top), doubling its capacity and halving its architectural charm. Bullfights start at 18:00, and tickets are expensive. But the price plummets if you buy tickets from scalpers after the first or second bull. The audience at most bullfights is silent, but Pamplona's spectators are notorious for their raucous behavior. They're known to intentionally spill things on tourists just to get a reaction...if you respond with a laugh and a positive attitude, they'll respect you and you'll have the time of your life.

Look for the big bust of **Ernest Hemingway,** celebrated by Pamplona as if he were a native son. Hemingway came here for the first time during the 1923 Running of the Bulls. Inspired by the spectacle and the gore, he later wrote about the event in his bullfighting classic *The Sun Also Rises.* He said that he enjoyed seeing two wild animals running together: one on two legs, and the other on four. This literary giant put Pamplona and its humble, obscure bullfighting festival on the world map; visitors come from far and wide even today, searching for adventure in Hemingway's Pamplona. He came to his last Running of the Bulls in 1959 and reportedly regretted the attention his writing had brought to what had been a simple local festival. But the people of Pamplona appreciate "Papa" as one of their own. At the beginning of the annual festival, young people tie a red neckerchief around this statue so Hemingway can be properly outfitted for the occasion.

• *Walk 20 yards along the right side of the bullring, then cross the busy street and walk a block into the pedestrian zone to the life-size...*

Running of the Bulls Monument (Monumento al Encierro): This new statue (from 2007, pictured on page 212) shows six bulls, two steer, and 10 runners in action. Find the self-portrait of the sculptor (bald, lying down, and about to be gored). The statue has quickly become a local favorite, but is not without controversy: There are 10 *mozos* but no *mozas*—where are the female runners?

• *From here, you can turn right and walk two blocks up the street to the main square...*

Plaza del Castillo: While not as grand as Spain's top squares, there's something particularly cozy and livable about Pamplona's.

It's dominated by the Navarre government building (sort of like a state capitol). Several Hemingway sights surround this square. The Hotel Perla in the corner was his favorite place to stay. It recently underwent a head-to-toe five-star renovation, but they kept Hemingway's room exactly as he liked it, right down to the furniture he used while writing...and two balconies overlooking the bull action on Estafeta street (see listing in "Sleeping in Pamplona"). He also was known to frequent Bar Txoko at the top of the square (as well as pretty much every other bar in town) and the venerable Café Iruña at the bottom of the square. Café Iruña actually has a separate "Hemingway Corner" room, with a life-size statue of "Papa" to pose with (see listing in "Eating in Pamplona").

• *You've survived the run. Now enjoy the rest of Pamplona's sights.*

Sights in Pamplona

▲Cathedral (Catedral)

The Camino de Santiago is lined with great cathedrals, but—frankly—Pamplona's is an also-ran. Still, the cathedral does have some unique sights and a fine museum that are worth a visit.

Cost and Hours: €4.40, Mon–Fri 10:00–14:00 & 16:00–19:00 (no lunch break mid-July–mid-Sept), Sat 10:00–14:00, closed Sun, tel. 948-212-594.

❍ Self-Guided Tour: The cathedral—a Gothic core wrapped in a Neoclassical shell—is a bit drab from the outside. But the inside is more appealing. Head up the street to the right, follow signs for *entrada a museo*, buy your ticket, go inside, and turn right into the **museum.** The highlight here is the fascinating collection of old Mary sculptures from local village churches. Since they're displayed chronologically, you can actually watch artistic styles evolve. The earliest ones, from the 12th century, show a very stiff, uncaring Mary—she's not touching, or even looking at, the Baby Jesus, who's perched stiffly on her lap like a ventriloquist's dummy. But as women gained more power in the 13th century, we see Mary loosen up and morph into a good mother—smiling, playfully holding the orb (representing perfection), and finally (gasp!) touching her baby with her hands. In the 14th century, Mary boldly stands up and even cradles Jesus. And by the 17th century, she's looking like a real mother.

The museum is displayed in the former refectory (dining hall) of the monks. Find the small, attached room where you can peer up inside the five gigantic chimneys. Exiting the museum, notice the fountain at the corner of the cloister—used to wash up at mealtime.

Continue around the cloister and find the side entrance into the cathedral. Above the door, see the depiction of the Dormition (eternal sleep, rather than death) of Mary...with Jesus up above, returning the favor of her evolving maternity by cradling her soul like a baby as she's welcomed into heaven.

The cathedral interior is Gothic. In the **choir,** look for the statue nicknamed "Mary of the Adopted Child." The Baby Jesus was stolen from this statue in the 16th century and replaced with a different version...which looks nothing like his mother. (The mother, dating from the 13th century, is the only treasure surviving from the previous church that stood on this spot.)

The prominent **tomb** dominating the middle of the nave holds Charles III (the king of Navarre who united the disparate groups of Pamplona) and his wife. The blue fleur-de-lis pattern is a reminder that the kings of Navarre once controlled a large swath of France. Notice that Charles' face is realistic, indicating that it was sculpted while he was still alive, while his wife's face is idealized—done after she died. Around the base of the tomb, monks from various orders mourn the couple's death.

In the back-left corner chapel, find the Renaissance **crucifix**—shockingly realistic for a no-name artist of the time (compare it to the more typical one in the next chapel over). The accuracy of Christ's musculature leads some to speculate that the artist had a model. (When you drive a nail through a foot, toes splay as you see here...but rarely see on other crucifixes of the time.) It's said that if the dangling lock of hair touches Jesus' chest, the world will end.

Corner of the White Horse Ramparts View: Leaving the cathedral, circle the church, passing the front facade again, around to the tree-lined square. Continue to the small viewpoint overlooking the ramparts. This is your best chance to see part of Pamplona's imposing **city walls**—designed to defend against potential invaders from the Pyrenees, still 80 percent intact, and now an inviting parkland. Belly up to the overlook, with views across the city's suburban sprawl. Beyond those hills on the horizon to the left are San Sebastián and the Bay of Biscay. Camino pilgrims enter town through the gate below and on the left. This area is popular with people who are in town for the Running of the Bulls but didn't make hotel reservations. Sadly, it's not unusual for people to fall asleep on top of the wall...then roll off to their deaths.

Other Churches

As a prominent town on a pilgrim route, Pamplona has its share of other interesting churches. These two are worth a quick visit. They're both on the Camino trail through town; to reach them, simply head west along Calle Mayor from the City Hall Square (where the self-guided walk began).

Church of San Saturnino—The most important pilgrim church in Pamplona, this is an architectural combination: 15th-century Gothic, 18th-century Baroque in front. Duck inside (free, daily 9:15–12:30 & 18:00–20:00). This is where pilgrims can get their credential stamped (someone's usually on duty in the pews). At the end across from where you enter, you'll see an altar with the Holy Virgin of the Camino. As you continue your journey, you'll notice that most churches along the Camino are dedicated to Mary. According to legend, when St. James himself came on a missionary trip through northern Spain, he suffered a crisis of faith around Zaragoza (not far from here). But, inspired by the Virgin, he managed to complete his journey to Galicia. Pilgrims following in his footsteps find similar inspiration from Mary today.

Church of San Lorenzo—Though San Fermín is a big name in town, he doesn't have a church of his own. But you will find him

in a giant side-chapel of this church, overlooking the ring road at the edge of the Old Town (free, Mon–Fri 8:15–12:00 & 18:30–20:00, Sat–Sun 8:15–12:00 & 18:00–20:00). Enter the church and turn right down the transept to find the statue of **San Fermín,** dressed in red and wearing a gold miter (tall hat). Pamplona was founded by the Roman Emperor Pompey (hence the name) in the second century B.C. Later, a Roman general here became the first in the empire to allow Christians to worship openly. The general's son—Fermín—even preached the word himself...until he was martyred. Fermín has been the patron saint here ever since. Just below the statue's Adam's apple, squint to see a reliquary holding Fermín's actual finger. The statue—gussied up in an even more over-the-top miter and staff—is paraded around on Fermín's feast day, July 7, which was the origin of today's bull festival. This chapel is the most popular place in town for weddings.

Sleeping in Pamplona

(€1 = about $1.40, country code: 34)

Because Pamplona is a business-oriented town, prices go up during the week; on weekends (Fri–Sun), you can usually score a discount. When I've listed a range, you can assume the high prices are for weekdays (Mon–Thu). All prices go way, way up for the San Fermín festival, when you must book as far in advance as possible.

$$$ Gran Hotel La Perla is the town's undisputed top splurge. Hemingway's favorite hotel, sitting right on the main square, has recently undergone a top-to-bottom five-star renovation. Its 44 rooms offer luxury at Pamplona's best address (standard Db-€240, bigger and fancier rooms-€280–450, breakfast-€25, air-con, elevator, Plaza del Castillo 1, tel. 948-223-000, fax 948-222-234, www.granhotellaperla.com, informacion@granhotellaperla.com). Well-heeled lit-lovers can drop €470 for a night in the Hemingway room, still furnished as it was when "Papa" stayed there (with a brand-new bathroom grafted on the front).

$$ Hostal Navarra is the best value in Pamplona, with 15 modern, well-maintained, clean rooms. Near the bus station, but an easy walk from the Old Town, it's well-run by Miguel (Sb-€45, Db-€60, includes tax, breakfast-€7, non-smoking, free Wi-Fi, Calle Tudela 9, tel. 948-225-164, fax 948-223-426, www.hostalnavarra.com, info@hostalnavarra.com).

$$ Hotel Europa, a few blocks off the square, offers 21 rooms with reasonable prices for its high class and ideal location (Sb-€69–78, Db-€75–92, breakfast-€9.50, non-smoking rooms, air-con, elevator, free Wi-Fi, Calle Espoz y Mina 11, tel. 948-221-800, fax 948-229-235, www.hreuropa.com, europa@hreuropa.com). The ground-floor restaurant is a well-regarded splurge.

$$ Hotel Castillo de Javier, right on the bustling San Nicolás bar street (request a quieter back room), rents 19 simple, new-feeling rooms (Sb-€45, Db-€62, includes tax, breakfast-€4.30, air-con, elevator, free cable Internet, Calle San Nicolás 50–52, tel. 948-203-040, fax 948-203-041, www.hotelcastillodejavier.com, info@hotelcastillodejavier.com). This is a step up from the several cheap *hostales* that line the same street.

$ Pension Arrieta is an old-fashioned budget option renting 12 basic rooms in two buildings in the new part of town. Carmen and Maximo don't speak English, but their daughter does (D-€45, Db-€55, a few euros more July–Sept, Calle de Emilio Arrieta 27, tel. 948-228-459).

Eating in Pamplona

All of these eateries are within a couple minutes' walk of each other and the tapas bars make a wonderful little pub crawl.

Tapas Crawl

Tapas on Calle de la Estafeta: The best concentration of trendy tapas bars is on and near the skinny drag called La Estafeta. My favorites here are **Bar Cervecería La Estafeta** (daily, at #54, tel. 948-222-157) and **Bodegon Sarria** (great bull photos, English menu, dining room to enjoy Navarre dishes, at #52, tel. 948-227-713).

Gaucho Bar is a proud little place—runner-up in the last local tapas contest—serving gourmet tapas cooked to order for €2.50–3 each. You could sit down and enjoy three tapas, and have an excellent meal (daily, just a few steps off the main square at Calle Espoz y Mina 7, tel. 948-225-073, no English).

Café Niza is a mod place with whimsical nouvelle-cuisine *pinchos* (€2–3), where the day's special tapas are featured on little plush red couches on the bar (if eaters get a comfy place to sit, why not the food?). Huge windows behind the bar show the chef busy at work. His "Pork Porky" was recently the region's *pincho* champion (study the menu, prices same at tables and bar, a block from Gaucho Bar, across street from Hotel Europa at Calle del Duque de Ahumada 2, tel. 948-220-055).

Café Roch is a time-warp with a line of delightful tapas (€1.60 each). Their most popular are the stuffed pepper and the fried Roquefort (find #35 on Plaza del Castillo—it's a block away at Calle de las Comedias 6, tel. 948-222-390).

Tapas on Calle San Nicolás: The narrow and slightly seedy Calle San Nicolás has more than its share of hole-in-the-wall tapas joints, with an older, more traditional clientele, and greasier, more straightforward tapas.

Restaurants

Café Iruña, which clings to its venerable past and its connection to Hemingway (who loved the place), serves up drinks out on the main square and food in the delightful old 1888 interior. While the food is mediocre, the ambience is great. Find the little "Hemingway's Corner" (El Rincón de Hemingway) side-eatery in back, where the bearded one is still hanging out at the bar. Enjoy black-and-white photos of Ernesto, young and old, in Pamplona (€13 fixed-price meal for lunch and dinner, pricier €21 Sat dinner deal, open daily, Plaza del Castillo 44, tel. 948-222-064).

San Ignacio Restaurante is a good choice for a real restaurant, with a classy upstairs dining room serving local fare (€10–15 starters, €15–20 main dishes, fixed-price meal-€15 on weekdays or €40 on weekends, open daily for lunch 13:00–15:30, Thu–Sat also dinner from 21:00, facing the back of the Navarre government building at Avenida San Ignacio 4, tel. 948-221-874).

Connections

Note that the bus station is closer to the Old Town than the train station, and most connections are faster by bus anyway.

From Pamplona by Bus to: Burgos (3/day, 2.5 hrs), **San Sebastián** (8/day, 1 hr), **Bilbao** (6/day, 2 hrs), **Madrid** (6/day, 5 hrs). For bus schedules, see www.autobusesdenavarra.com, tel. 948-203-566.

By Train to: Burgos (1/day, 2 hrs), **San Sebastián** (3/day, 2 hrs), **León** (1/day, 4 hrs), **Madrid** (4/day direct, 3 hrs).

From Pamplona to Burgos

The stretch of the Camino between Pamplona and Burgos is particularly appealing, with several tempting stopovers. As you finish your descent from the rugged Pyrenees, you enter the flatter, more cultivated landscape that typifies the long middle stretch of the Camino (basically from here to Galicia). The two best stops along here are the small town of Puente de la Reina (with an iconic old bridge and fun pilgrim vibes) and a potential detour for wine-lovers through La Rioja wine country.

• *Begin by taking the A-12 expressway west from Pamplona (toward Logroño). Consider stopping in Puente de la Reina, as it's a very easy detour—the exit (Puente de la Reina norte) is well-marked from the expressway.*

Puente de la Reina / Gares

The Camino de Santiago's two French routes converge in this cozy sun-baked village, just one walking stage (about 12 miles) west of Pamplona. Named for a graceful 11th-century stone bridge at its center, the village retains a pilgrim's vibe (**TI** right by the bridge, Tue–Sat 10:00–13:00 & 16:00–19:00, Sun 11:00–14:00, closed Mon, tel. 948-340-845). All the sights here fall on a straight axis: church, main street, and bridge. Parking the car and wandering around here gives "car hikers" a whiff of Camino magic.

As you enter the town, watch (on the left) for the **Church of the Crucifixion** (Iglesia del Crucifijo), with a stork's nest on the steeple. The Knights Templar, who came to protect pilgrims from the Moors, likely founded this church in the 12th century. Inside you'll find a distinctive Y-shaped crucifix that shows a Christ who's dead, yet still in pain (by a German craftsman—a reminder of the rich influx of pan-European culture the Camino enjoyed). It was likely carried by German pilgrims all the way across Europe to this spot. Across the street is a pilgrims' *refugio,* offering bunks and credential stamps to Camino walkers.

The straight, wide Calle Mayor connects the church and *refugio* with the bridge. Classic Camino towns feature main drags like this one. They were born as a collection of services flanking the path. Pilgrims needed to eat, sleep, pray, and deal with health problems. The more stone a house showed off (rather than brick), the wealthier the owner. You'll see modern flooring being stripped away to reveal now-trendy river-pebble cobbles inside.

The main street leads directly to the most interesting sight in town (and its namesake), the **"Bridge of the Queen"** (which you'll see on the right as you drive across the modern bridge near the end

of town). With a graceful six-arch Romanesque design that peaks in the middle, the bridge represents life: You can't quite see where you're going until you get there. The extra holes were designed to let high water through, so that water pressure wouldn't push the stone construction over—clever 11th-century engineering. Pilgrims enjoy congregating on the riverbank under the arches of this bridge—a great place for a stretch-your-legs stop. Ponder this scene: the bridge, pilgrims, the flowing river, happy birdsong...it's timeless.

• *From here, hop immediately back on the A-12 expressway (toward Estella) to speed along. As you pass by Estella/Lizarra (home to the imposing Romanesque Palace of the Kings of Navarre), you'll gradually begin to notice that you're entering wine country—with scrubby vegetation, red soil, and hill towns dotting the landscape. Take exit 44, direction: Ayegui, and follow signs to* Irache Monastery.

Even if you're on the expressway, it's worth another quick detour (again well-signed, just beyond Estella) to the fun...

Irache Monastery and Wine Fountain (Monasterio de Irache)

This monastery, sitting amidst vineyards, has a unique custom of offering free wine to pilgrims. From the parking lot near the monastery, walk down following signs for *fuente de vino* to find a faucet that dispenses free wine (daily 8:00–20:00; also one for water).

La Rioja Wine Loop

Serious wine-lovers enjoy detouring off the Camino at Logroño to visit the wine village of Laguardia, tour some unique wineries, and sample Rioja wine.

For many lovers of Spanish wines, it just doesn't get better than Rioja (ree-OH-ha). Rioja wine is a D.O.C. product, meaning that by definition it can only be produced in La Rioja region. Protected from the elements by the Cantabrian Mountains to the north (which you'll see from Laguardia), vineyards have thrived in the valley of the Ebro River since Roman times. Rioja wines (which can be red, white, or rosé) grow in a variety of soil types dominated by red clay and limestone. The reds, made primarily from the *tempranillo* grape (Spain's "noble grape"), are medium- to full-bodied in the Bordeaux style and characterized by aging in oak barrels—infusing them with overtones of vanilla. With their balance of tannins and fruitiness, red Riojas go well with grilled meats and strong cheeses, such as an aged manchego. You'll see four types of Rioja wines, depending on how long they've been aged (from shortest to longest, and cheapest to most expensive): simply Rioja (or sometimes *cosecha*, "harvest"), Rioja Crianza, Rioja Reserva, and Rioja Gran Reserva.

Be warned that the Rioja region is not well set up for impromptu visitors. All wine-tasting experiences prefer reservations, and most require them. You can't just go tasting on the fly as you can elsewhere in Europe. If you're serious about your Rioja, set up here for a day or two, do some homework (www.laguardia-alava.com is helpful), and reserve at the wineries of your choice. Although Laguardia is connected by bus to Pamplona (via Logroño), most of the experience here lies in the countryside—workable only by car.

• *From Logroño, follow A-124 northwest (toward Vitoria, through more and more scenic vineyards, with a picturesque mountain ridge as a backdrop) to Laguardia, and park just outside the town wall.*

Laguardia is the scenic center of La Rioja wine-tasting country. This walled town—literally "The Guard," for its position watching out for potential invaders coming in from the mountains—is perched on a promontory with fine views of the surrounding region. There's not much in the way of sightseeing, but poke around a bit. Under your feet are more than 200 wine cellars (*bodegas*) where Rioja quietly ages. Only two in town are open for visitors: **El Fabulista** (€6 tasting, tel. 945-621-192) and **Carlos San Pedro** (€3.50 tasting, tel. 605-033-043); for both, you can try just dropping in, but it's better to call ahead. Laguardia's **TI**

can give you information on wine-tastings in town and nearby, but—again—they'll warn you that most wineries require reservations (TI open Mon–Fri 10:00–14:00 & 16:00–19:00, Sat 10:00–14:00 & 17:00–19:00, Sun 10:45–14:00, Plaza San Juan, tel. 945-600-845, www.laguardia-alava.com).

The countryside around Laguardia is blanketed with vineyards. For those just passing through, three wine-related attractions are worth considering. All are within a few minutes' drive of Laguardia. Note that Ysios and Marqués de Riscal are architectural gems worth dropping by to see even if you couldn't care less about the wine:

Villa Lucía is a sort of wine museum about La Rioja's favorite product, as well as its traditional architecture. As with everything around here, it's wise to call ahead if you want to join a tour (various programs for €6–14, Tue–Sun 10:00–14:00 & 17:00–20:00, closed Mon, on the right as you reach the edge of town, tel. 945-600-032, www.villa-lucia.com).

Ysios is a modern winery with an undulating silver roof designed by the bold and prolific Spanish architect Santiago Calatrava. Wine-lovers enjoy the tours of the cellar, in which countless casks age under the wavy ceiling (€5, includes one taste; Mon–Fri at 11:00, 13:00, and 16:00; Sat–Sun at 11:00 and 13:00; one hour, call first to ensure a space, tel. 945-600-640, www.bodegasysios.com). But even from the outside, it's a worthwhile photo op for anyone (just a three-minute drive behind Laguardia, toward the mountains—behind the town, look for *Ysios* signs; you'll see the building from far off).

• *From the Laguardia area, follow signs south to Elciego (on A-3210) to reach...*

Marqués de Riscal, in the village of Elciego, was one of the pioneer winemakers of the Rioja wine industry. Its new winery features a distinctive hotel designed by Frank Gehry (of Bilbao Guggenheim fame). The wine cellar is tourable (€10, 1/day in English, closed Mon, call first, tel. 945-180-888, www.marques deriscal.com). The hotel (Db-€400–1,000), with its colorful, wavy design, is striking in such a humble village.

• *Just to the northwest is the midsized town of Haro, offering even more tasting opportunities. But if you're ready to move along, you can head south from Elciego toward Cenicero. In Cenicero, you can rejoin the AP-68 expressway, or continue down (following signs for Nájera) to highway N-120 to join the Camino road into Burgos.*

The Spanish poem on the sign explains, "To drink without abusing, we invite you happily; but to be able to take it along, you must pay for the wine." In other words, pilgrims are allowed to drink as much wine as they like...provided they don't take any with them. (While the wine is free, you'll likely end up buying a little glass from the machine, essentially paying €1 for a glass of bad wine.) Note the webcam—if you have your cell phone on you, text friends to look for you at www.irache.com. Hi, Mom!

• *Continuing south, you can choose your route: To save time, zip on the A-12 expressway right to Logroño. But for a scenic and only slightly slower meander through some cute villages (El Busto, Sansol) and larger towns (Los Arcos and Viana), take the expressway only as far as Los Arcos, then follow N-111 from there. Either way, you'll end up at...*

Logroño and La Rioja

Just before the skippable big city of Logroño, you'll cross the Ebro River. Today, as in centuries past, this river marks the end of the Basque territory (and Navarre) and the beginning of the rest of Spain. With 150,000 residents, Logroño is the largest city of La Rioja. Renowned for its robust wines, the Rioja region has historically served as a buffer between the Basques and the powerful forces to the south and east (the Moors or the Castilian Spaniards).

• *Again, choose your route from here. If you have time, and a healthy interest in wine (and vineyard scenery), detour off the Camino by heading north on A-124 to the village of Laguardia, rejoining the expressway (and the Camino) later. For this option, see the "La Rioja Wine Loop" sidebar on the previous page spread. Otherwise, stick on the expressway to Santo Domingo de la Calzada.*

Note that west of Logroño, the expressway does a big jog to the north (AP-68, then AP-1). You'll save miles (though not necessarily time) and stick closer to the Camino if instead you take the N-120 highway from here to Burgos. Along the way is...

Santo Domingo de la Calzada

This Rioja town has a fine cathedral, oodles of historic buildings, tranquil squares, and all the trappings of a pilgrim zone (seashells in the pavement, *refugios*, vending machines, and launderettes). You'll see images of a rooster and a hen everywhere in town, thanks to a colorful local legend: A chaste pilgrim refused to be seduced by the amorous daughter of an innkeeper. For revenge, she hid a silver cup in his bed and accused him of theft. The judge, eager to hang the lad, proclaimed that the pilgrim was as dead as the roasted rooster and hen the judge was about to eat. The charred birds suddenly stood up and began to crow, saving the pilgrim from certain death.

Most of the attractions cluster in the shadow of the cathedral tower on Plaza del Santo. You can visit the **cathedral** (€3.50, Mon–Sat 9:30–13:30 & 16:00–18:30, closed Sun) or have a drink at the bar in the very atmospheric atrium lounge of the fancy **parador** hotel, just across the square (Db-€149, tel. 941-340-300). The **TI** is just up Calle Mayor (daily 10:00–14:00 & 16:00–20:00, at #70, tel. 941-341-230).

• *Soon after Santo Domingo de la Calzada, you pass into the region of...*

Castile and León (Castilla y León)

Welcome to Spain's largest "state" (about the size of Indiana). If you've always wanted to see the famous plains of Spain...this is it. This vast, arid high-altitude Meseta Central ("Inner Plateau") stretches to hilly, rainy Galicia in the northwest and all the way past Madrid to the south coast. Those walking the entire Camino find this flat, dry stretch to be either the best part (getting away from it all with a pensive stroll) or the worst part (boring and potentially blistering-hot).

• *The next big city on the Camino is just around the bend: Burgos.*

Burgos

Burgos (BOOR-gohs) is a pedestrian-friendly city lined up along its pretty river. Apart from its epic history and urban bustle, Burgos has one major claim to touristic fame: its glorious Gothic-style cathedral, packed to the gills with centuries' worth of elaborate decorations.

Like so many towns in the north of Spain, the burg of Burgos was founded during the Reconquista to hold on to land that had been won back from the Moors. Its position on the Camino de Santiago, and the flourishing trade in wool (sent to the Low Countries to become Flemish tapestries), helped it to

THE CAMINO DE SANTIAGO

Burgos

200 YARDS
200 METERS

1 Mesón del Cid
2 Hotel Cabildo
3 El Hotel Jacobeo
4 Pensión Peña
5 Calle Sombrerería Eateries
6 Casa Pancho
7 Casa Ojeda

Ⓑ Bus Stop

thrive. Beginning in 1230, it became the capital of the kingdom of Castile for half a millennium (having usurped the title from León). The town's favorite son is the great 11th-century Spanish hero El Cid (Spaniards say "el theeth"), who valiantly fought against the Moors. The 20th century saw the town decline, even as it briefly became the capital of Franco's forces during the Civil War. Later the dictator industrialized Burgos to even out the playing field (Catalunya and the Basque Country—on the political and geographical fringes of Spain—had previously been the centers of industry).

Today's Burgos feels workaday, but with a hint of elegance, as stately plane trees line up along the riverside promenade. And watching over everything is that grand cathedral.

Orientation to Burgos

With about 175,000 inhabitants, Burgos is bisected by the Arlanzón River. The Old Town is centered on the huge cathedral. The city center is mostly pedestrianized and very manageable.

Tourist Information

Burgos' TI is on the square along the side of the cathedral (just across from the side entrance). Pick up the free map and information brochure (daily 10:00–14:00 & 16:30–19:30, July–Aug daily 10:00–20:00, Plaza del Rey San Fernando, tel. 947-288-874, www.aytoburgos.es).

Arrival in Burgos

By Bus: The bus station is just across the river from the cathedral. Exit the station to the left, then turn right at the busy street and cross the bridge (you'll see the spires).

By Train: Burgos' Rosa de Lima Station is a long 40-minute walk from town, and the bus service into town isn't much of a help to tourists (bus #25 to Plaza España, then a 15-min walk to cathedral, 2/hr, no buses Sat–Sun). Unless you're poor or a pilgrim, catch a taxi for €6.

By Car: It's easy and well-signed. Simply follow signs to the city center *(centro ciudad)*, then look for a pay garage when you see the cathedral spires.

Sights in Burgos

▲▲Cathedral (Catedral)

Burgos is rightfully famous for its showpiece Gothic cathedral. With its soaring, frilly spires and an interior that's been augmented across the centuries, Burgos' cathedral is an impressive sight.

Unfortunately, the church's cultural and spiritual significance is badly presented; what precious English information it provides is stilted and boring. Fortunately, you're holding a self-guided tour in your hands.

Cost and Hours: €5, or €2.50 for pilgrims; mid-March–Oct daily 9:30–19:30; Nov–mid-March daily 10:00–19:00; last entry one hour before closing, free lockers, www.catedralde burgos.es. The self-guided tour below covers the basics. The €3.50 audioguide offers little of interest.

❍ Self-Guided Tour: Begin by facing the **main facade** of the grand church, which was built over the course of a century. You

can read the building's history into its architecture: It was started by French architects in the 13th century, who used a simple, graceful style similar to the famous Notre-Dame (mentally erase the tops of the spires and you'll see that famous Parisian cathedral). In the 14th century, German cathedral-builders took over, adding the flamboyant fringe to the tops of the towers (similar to the cathedral in Köln, Germany).

The entrance on this side is open only for worshippers, who have access to two chapels at the back of the cathedral (where hourly Mass takes place). Tourists head around the right side of the church to buy tickets and enter. As you walk there, you'll realize that this "front door" facade is only one small part of the vast complex—more spires and frills lie beyond.

Buy your ticket and enter through the side door. After you show your ticket, you'll turn left and do a clockwise spin around the church, stopping at many of the 18 **chapels.** These chapels were added over many centuries, in different styles, and decorated in creative ways by a wide range of benefactors. (To aid with navigation for certain stops, I've listed the numbers that are posted for audioguide users.) The first few chapels are just a warm-up: the Chapel of St. John of Sahagún (#6) features a Baroque relic altar and some frescoes (unusual in this church), while the Chapel of the Presentation (#8) features a painting by an Italian Renaissance master, Il Piombo.

At the back of the church, the barriers separate the worship area from the tourist zone. But look high up, just to the right of the rose window, to see the church mascot: The **"Fly-Catcher" clock** (El Papamoscas), which rings out every quarter-hour. Above the clock is a whimsical statue of its German maker, whose mouth opens and closes when the bell rings at the top of each hour. (The tourists who congregate here and crane their necks to gape up at the show seem to be imitating the clock-maker.)

Continue to the next chapel, dedicated to **St. Anne** (Santa Ana, #12). Here you'll find a spectacular Gothic altar, showing the family tree of Jesus springing out of a reclining Jesse. (The sculptor included his self-portrait as one of the evangelists—find the bespectacled guy, the second from left in the bottom row.) Facing the altar is a Flemish tapestry and some original 15th-century vestments.

You've now circled back around to the transept. On your left are the sumptuous **Golden Stairs** (#13, designed by a Flemish

Renaissance master who had studied under Michelangelo). On the right, you can enter the choir area. Step into the very center of the choir—also the very center of the cathedral—and place yourself directly under the sumptuous Plateresque-style dome, then look up and spin. Look back down again to see the **tomb of El Cid** (Rodericus Didaci Campidoctor) and his wife (#15). (El Cid's well-traveled remains were interred in Valencia, then in various points in Burgos, before being brought here in the early 20th century.)

Take a look at the **main altar**, with a fine statue of Mary slathered in silver. Also poke around the carved wooden **choir**, with a giant 16th-century songbook for Gregorian chants and two organs (used only for special occasions).

Directly behind the main altar, enter the cathedral's best chapel, the **Chapel of the High Constable** (#22). Because it has its

own altar, two side naves, and a choir and organ (in the back), it's been called "the cathedral within the cathedral." A high constable is a knight who won a crown in battle for his king or queen— the highest of VIPs in the Middle Ages. And yet, this chapel shows the influence not of a powerful man, but of a powerful woman. It was commissioned by the high constable's wife (who's entombed with him at the center of the chapel). She wanted the chapel decorations to demonstrate equality of the sexes (a

bold statement in the late 15th century). Notice that most of the decorations on "his" side (left) are male-oriented, including the two brutes holding the coat of arms up above, and the figures on the side altar. But "her" decorations (right) are more feminine—

damsels holding the coat of arms, and mostly women decorating the side altar. The yin and yang of the sexes is even suggested by the black-and-white flooring. Also notice a pair of fine paintings here (unrelated to the sexual politics): on "his" side, a beautiful Flemish depiction of a woman in a red dress (likely from the school of Hans Memling); and on "her" side, Mary Magdalene, by a favorite pupil of Leonardo da Vinci's (who probably put his own touches on the work, as well).

Continuing around, you'll enter the **cloister** (#24), walking past the beautifully carved main sacristy (#23). The tour route takes you counterclockwise around this cloister, to a few more chapels and museum exhibits: The Corpus Christi Chapel (#26) features stairs up to the library (closed to the public) and access to the chapter house (#27), where the monks would meet. The next chapel (Santa Catalina's Chapel, #28) displays a remarkable 10th-century Bible. In the same case is a copy of El Cid's pre-nup. (To protect his assets, he found a clever legal loophole to transfer ownership of all he had to his wife.) Around the top of this room are dozens of paintings depicting centuries' worth of bishops.

Continuing to the **Chapel of St. John the Baptist and St. James** (#29), you find the cathedral's museum collection, including ecclesiastical items (such as some exquisitely detailed crosses and chalices), an emotive statue of Christ being whipped, and an altar depicting St. James the Moor-Slayer (see page 265).

Finally you'll head downstairs to the **lower cloister** (#33). At the foot of the stairs is a schmaltzy portrait of El Cid, and beyond that is a model of the original Romanesque church (with the current, Gothic footprint around it for comparison). You'll also spot a large model of the entire cathedral complex...to get your bearings on all that you've just seen from the inside.

Now go in peace.

Other Sights

On a short visit, the cathedral is all that's worth seeing in Burgos. But if you're killing time here, a few other attractions might be worth a look.

Plaza Mayor and Promenade—Burgos' main square, a long block from the cathedral, is urban-feeling and strangely uninviting, with long marble benches. The stone building with two clock towers is the town hall; if you walk under here, you'll emerge at the city's delightful riverside promenade. Lined with knobby plane trees and outdoor cafés, it has an almost Provençal ambience. Going left along the promenade takes you to **Plaza del Mío Cid,** with an equestrian statue celebrating Burgos' favorite son, "My El Cid." Going right along the promenade leads you to the impressive **St. Mary's Gate,** one of six surviving entrances of this stout-walled city's original 12 gates (built in the 13th century, decorated in 16th-century Renaissance style). Look up at the gate, and in a deep, strong voice, declare: "Burgos." Passing through this gate takes you directly to the cathedral.

▲**Huelgas Monastery**—In addition to its grand cathedral, Burgos has a pair of impressive monasteries. The Cistercian monastery of

Huelgas is the easiest to reach (though still a bit of a walk from the cathedral). Entrance is by one-hour tour only, and English tours are very rare (€5, free on Wed, open Tue–Sat 10:00–13:00 & 15:45–17:30, Sun 10:30–14:00, closed Mon, tours depart about every 20 min, try asking your guide for some English info, tel. 947-201-630). Inside you'll see a "pantheon" of royal tombs, a Gothic cloister with Mudejar details, a chapter house with 13th-century stained glass, and a Romanesque cloister. The highlight is a statue of St. James with an arm that could be moved to symbolically "knight" the king by placing a sword on his shoulders (since only a "saint"—or statue of a saint—was worthy of knighting royalty). Finally you'll tour a museum of rare surviving clothes from common people (not just religious vestments) from the 13th and 14th centuries.

Getting There: It's about a 20-minute walk west of the city center, or you can take bus #5, #7, or #35 (catch the bus across the bridge from the cathedral).

The other monastery, **Cartuja de Miraflores,** is farther out of town (details at TI); seeing both Huelgas and Miraflores is redundant unless you adore monasteries.

Museums—Burgos has a few other museums that might be worth a look. On the hill behind the cathedral, the **Centro de Arte** is a contemporary art museum with temporary exhibits (free, Tue–Sat 11:30–14:00 & 17:00–21:00, Sun 11:00–14:30, closed Mon, tel. 947-256-550). And just across the river, near the bus station, is the **Museo de Burgos,** which celebrates the cultural heritage of

Burgos province. Its five floors of painting and sculpture and two floors of archaeological exhibits ring the gorgeous courtyard of a fine old 1540 convent. The somewhat hard-to-appreciate museum hopes to display the sword of El Cid in the near future (€1.20, €1 audioguide; July–Sept Tue–Sat 10:00–14:00 & 17:00–20:00, Sun 10:00–14:00; Oct–June Tue–Sat 10:00–14:00 & 16:00–19:00, Sun 10:00–14:00; closed Mon, Calle Miranda 13, tel. 947-265-875).

Near Burgos: Santo Domingo de Silos

The unassuming village of Santo Domingo de Silos—about 40 miles (an hour's drive) south of Burgos—has a fine Benedictine monastery that's become a quirky footnote in popular music. The monastery's monks are famous for their melodic Gregorian chants, which were recorded and released as the hugely popular album *Chant* in 1994. (It went on to sell six million copies.) Although the monks don't perform concerts, some of their daily services—which are free and open to the public—include chanting. The lengthy vespers *(visperas)* service is entirely chanted (daily at 19:00, 2.5 hours); there's also some chanting at the shorter Eucharist service (Mon–Fri at 9:00, Sat–Sun at 12:00). You can tour the cloister and museum (€3, open to the public Tue–Sat 10:00–13:00 & 16:30–18:00, Sun 16:30–18:00 only, closed Mon). Call to confirm before making the trip (tel. 947-390-049, www .abadiadesilos.es).

Sleeping in Burgos

(€1 = about $1.40, country code: 34)
When I've listed a price range, it fluctuates with demand; the top rates are for summer (June–Sept).

$$ Mesón del Cid enjoys Burgos' best location, gazing across a quiet square at the cathedral's front facade (full-frontal cathedral views are worth the extra €15). The 55 rooms in two buildings come with classy tile floors and old-fashioned furniture (Sb-€60–70, Db-€70–90, includes tax, breakfast-€11, air-con, elevator, free Internet access and Wi-Fi, Plaza de Santa María 8, tel. 947-208-715, fax 947-269-460, www.mesondelcid.es, mesondelcid @mesondelcid.es).

$$ Hotel Cabildo offers modern class for reasonable prices. Its lobby and 57 rooms are slick and stylish (Sb-€60–65, Db-€65–80, air-con, elevator, non-smoking rooms, free cable Internet, request quiet room, Avenida del Cid 2, tel. 947-257-840, fax 947-204-320, www.hotelcabildo.com, cabildo@hotelcabildo.com).

$$ El Hotel Jacobeo is a cheaper option, with 14 modern rooms along a lively pedestrian street (Sb-€35–40, Db-€50–60, breakfast-€4.50, free Wi-Fi, all rooms face the back—so it's quiet,

Calle de San Juan 24, tel. 947-260-102, fax 947-260-100, www
.hoteljacobeo.com, hoteljacobeo@hoteljacobeo.com).

$ Pensión Peña is Burgos' best budget option. Lively Loli,
who speaks no English, rents eight simple but well-maintained
rooms (sharing three bathrooms) in an old apartment building.
Loli takes no advance reservations, but you can call in the morning
to see if she has a room (S-€21–22, D-€27–28, La Puebla 18, tel.
947-206-323, mobile 639-067-089).

Eating in Burgos

Several good eateries are on Calle Sombrerería: **Bar Gaona Jardin,**
at #29, has a leafy interior and cooks up nice, hot tapas. **Estrella de
Galicia,** with a modern, bright ambience, offers a preview of the
cuisine you'll enjoy in Santiago—Galician food, wine, and beer
(€10 meal offered weekdays, €5–6 *raciones*, €10–15 main dishes,
daily, alongside church at Calle de la Paloma 35, tel. 947-276-902).
Across the street, **Cervecería Morito** offers a more chaotic local
ambience—one tight room with tables and a bar, or pay a little more
to eat at the terrace across the road (€3 sandwiches, €5–7 *raciones,*
handy photo menu, daily, Calle Sombrerería 27, tel. 947-267-555).

Casa Pancho is a long, inviting bar where hardworking José,
Angel, and Begona churn out fresh-cooked tapas. Two or three
tapas off of their *Carta de los Pinchos* can make a fine meal (the
menu's photos of dishes are described in English). Their specialty is
cojonuda (quail egg, blood sausage, and green pepper on bread—all
for €1). You're welcome to take a table for about 10 percent extra—
still a great value (daily, Calle San Lorenzo 13, tel. 947-203-405).
A couple more good tapas bars are within steps of here.

Casa Ojeda is a venerable institution that's a reliable choice
for a real restaurant meal. Specializing in Burgos cuisine, they offer
seating at the bar downstairs (tapas, €6 half-*raciones*, €13 combo-
plate) or in the upstairs dining room (pricier meals: €10 starters,
€20–25 mains). Relax and enjoy the subdued, rapidly aging ambience (closed Sun, Calle Vitoria 5, tel. 947-171-256).

Connections

From Burgos by Bus to: Pamplona (3/day, 2.5 hrs), **León** (4/day,
3 hrs, Alsa), **Bilbao** (4/day, 2 hrs, Continental), **Santiago de
Compostela** (1/day, 8 hrs, Alsa), **San Sebastián** (6/day, 3 hrs),
Salamanca (2/day, 3–4 hrs, Alsa), **Madrid** (9/day, 3 hrs, Continental). Keep in mind that Sunday connections are very sparse.

By Train to: Pamplona (1/day, 2 hrs), **León** (3/day, 2 hrs),
Bilbao (4/day, 3 hrs), **San Sebastián** (4/day, 3 hrs), **Salamanca**
(2–3/day, 3 hrs), **Madrid** (7/day, 5 hrs).

La Historia del Camino

The first person to undertake the Camino de Santiago was... Santiago himself. After the death of Christ, the apostles scattered to the corners of the earth to spread the Word of God. Supposedly, St. James went on a missionary trip from the Holy Land all the way to the northwest corner of Spain, which, at that point, really was the end of the world. (For more on St. James, see the sidebar on page 265.)

According to legend, St. James' remains were discovered in 813 in the town that would soon bear his name. This put Santiago de Compostela on the map, as one of three places—along with Rome and Jerusalem—where remains of apostles are known to be buried. In 951, Godescalco, the Bishop of Le Puy in France, walked to Santiago de Compostela to pay homage to the relics. As other pilgrims followed his example, the Camino de Santiago informally emerged. Then, in the 12th century, Pope Callistus II decreed that any person who walked to Santiago in a Holy Year, confessed their sins, and took communion at the cathedral would be forgiven. This opportunity for a cheap indulgence made the Camino de Santiago one of the most important pilgrimages in the world.

It's probably no coincidence that St. James' remains were "discovered" and promoted just as the Reconquista was in full swing. The pope's decree helped to consolidate the Christians' hold over lands retaken from the Moors. Pilgrims were ideal candidates to repopulate and defend northern Spain. Many of those who made the journey to Santiago stuck around somewhere along the route (often because of privileges granted them by local rulers who needed help rebuilding). It became a self-sustaining little circle: Pilgrims came along the Camino, saw great sights, and decided to stay...to build even greater sights for the next pilgrims to enjoy.

The Christian monarchy designated an old Roman commercial road from France across northern Iberia as the "official" route, and soon churches, monasteries, hostels, hospitals, blacksmiths, and other pilgrims' services began to pop up. Religious-military orders such as the Knights of Santiago and the Knights Templar protected the route from bandits and fought alongside Christian armies against the Moorish resurgence, allowing the evolving Catholic state to gather strength in the safe haven created by the Camino.

In the Middle Ages, pilgrims came to Santiago from all over Europe—mostly from France, but also from Portugal, Italy, Britain, the Netherlands, Germany, Scandinavia, and Eastern Europe. Many prominent figures embarked on the journey, including St. Francis of Assisi, Dutch painter Jan van Eyck, and the Wife of Bath in Chaucer's *Canterbury Tales*.

This steady flow of pilgrims from around Europe inevitably resulted in a rich exchange of knowledge, art, and architecture. Even today, you'll find magnificent cathedrals along the Camino in cities such as Burgos and León, which incorporated and improved on the latest in cathedral design from France at that time.

By 1130, the trek was so popular that it prompted a French monk named Aimery Picaud to pen (likely with the help of some ghost-writers) a chronicle of his journey, including tips on where to eat, where to stay, the best way to get from place to place, and how to pack light and use a money belt. This *Codex Calixtinus* (Latin for "Camino Through the Back Door") was the world's first guidebook—the great-great-granddaddy of the one you're holding right now.

In the age of Columbus, the Renaissance, and the Reformation, interest in the Camino dropped way off. When the Moors were finally defeated in 1492, the significance of Reconquista icon, St. James, fell by the wayside. The discovery of the New World in the same year led both the Church and the monarchy to turn their attention across the Atlantic, and the pilgrimage began to wane. That was followed by a century of religious wars pitting Catholics against Protestants, which also distracted potential pilgrims. Feeling threatened by the pirate Francis Drake (not considered "sir" in Spain), the church hid the remains of St. James—so thoroughly that they were actually lost for generations. Meanwhile, the rise of humanism during the Renaissance diminished the mystique of the pilgrimage. For the next centuries, and as recently as a few decades ago, only a few hardy souls still followed the route.

Then, in the late 1960s, a handful of parish priests along the Camino began working to recover the route, establishing associations of "friends of the Camino" that would eventually agree on a path and mark it. In 1982, and again in 1989, Pope John Paul II visited Santiago de Compostela, reminding the world of the town's historic significance. In 1987, the European Union designated the Camino as Europe's first Cultural Itinerary. And after the success of the 1992 Expo in Sevilla, the Galician government decided to pour funds into reviving the tradition for the Holy Year in 1993. They made Santiago a high-profile destination and shelled out big pesetas for concerts by stars including the Rolling Stones, Bruce Springsteen, and Julio Iglesias (whose father was born in Galicia).

The plan worked, and now—aided by European Union funding—the route has enjoyed a huge renaissance of interest, with 100,000 pilgrims each year trekking to Santiago. Even Shirley MacLaine has made the journey (her book *The Camino: A Journey of the Spirit* is popular among pilgrims). Cyclists and horse riders are now joining hikers on the journey, and these days it's "in" to follow the seashells to Santiago.

From Burgos to León

While there are some worthwhile stops between Burgos and León, this is a good place to put some serious miles under your belt: Follow signs for the A-231 expressway and zip between the cities in less than two hours. Sticking with the true Camino—a confusing spaghetti of roads without a single, straight highway to keep you on track—takes you through a poorer, very humble countryside with few sights. Some travelers enjoy dipping into towns along here such as **Castrojeriz, Frómista,** and **Carrión de los Condes,** but on a tight itinerary, your time is better spent in Burgos or León.

León

With a delightfully compact Old Town (surrounded by ugly sprawl), León (lay-OWN) has an enjoyable small-town atmosphere. But most importantly, it has a pair of sights that serve as a textbook for medieval European art styles: Romanesque (the San Isidoro Monastery, with astonishingly well-preserved frescoes) and Gothic (the cathedral, with the best stained glass outside of France).

León means "lion" in Spanish—but in this case, the name derives from Rome's seventh legion, which was stationed here. Founded as a Roman camp at the confluence of two rivers in A.D. 68, León gradually grew prosperous because of the gold trade that passed through here (mined in the Las Médulas hillsides to the west). Later, as the Moors were pushed ever southward, the capital of the Reconquista moved from Ovideo to here in 910, and for three centuries, León was the capital of a vast kingdom (until it was supplanted by Burgos). Today's León has relatively little industry, but is the capital of one of Spain's biggest provinces, making it an administrative and business center. It's also a major university town, with some 15,000 students who provide it with an enjoyable vitality.

Orientation to León

The big city of León, with 140,000 people (200,000 in the metro area), sits along the Bernesga River. On a short visit, tourists can ignore everything outside the rectangular Old Town, which is set a few blocks up from the river.

Tourist Information

León's TI is on the square facing the cathedral (July–Sept daily 9:00–20:00; Oct–June Mon–Fri 9:00–14:00 & 17:00–20:00,

León

① La Posada Regia
② NH Plaza Mayor
③ Hostal Albany
④ Hostal Boccalino
⑤ Hostal San Martín
⑥ Plaza San Martín Tapas Bars

THE CAMINO DE SANTIAGO

Sat–Sun 10:00–14:00 & 17:00–20:00; Plaza de la Regla 3–4, tel. 987-237-082).

Local Guide: Blanca Lobete is an excellent teacher who energetically shares León's architectural gems with travelers (3-hour tour–€88, mobile 669-276-335, guiaslegio@hotmail.com).

Arrival in León

By Train or Bus: The train and bus stations are along the river, about a 15-minute walk from the town center. To reach the Old Town from the stations, cross the big bridge and walk straight up Avenida Ordoño II. You'll hit the turreted Gaudí building, marking the start of the Old Town. From here, the San Isidoro Museum is to the left, and the cathedral is straight ahead (up Calle Ancha).

By Car: Compared to the other cities in this chapter, León is not well-signed. Do your best to follow directions to the city center *(centro ciudad)*; once there, you can park in a very convenient underground parking garage at Plaza Santo Domingo (€16/day), right at the start of the Old Town (and within a three-minute walk of all my recommended accommodations). Nearby, Plaza Mayor also has a parking garage.

THE CAMINO DE SANTIAGO

Sights in León

León's two most worthwhile sights complement each other perfectly: the remarkable Romanesque frescoes at San Isidoro, and the gorgeous stained glass of the cathedral. While you can do these in either order, to appreciate the architectural progression it makes sense to do San Isidoro first. (If you're rushed and have time for only one, make it the cathedral.)

▲▲San Isidoro Museum (Museo de San Isidoro)

San Isidoro is an 11th-century Romanesque church that's been gradually added on to over the centuries. The church itself is free and always open to worshippers. But the attached museum is the real attraction. Inside you'll see a library, cloister, chapter house, and a "pantheon" of royal tombs featuring some of the most exquisite Romanesque frescoes in Spain.

Cost and Hours: €4; July–Aug Mon–Sat 9:00–20:00, Sun 9:00–14:00; Sept–June Mon–Sat 10:00–13:30 & 16:00–18:30, Sun 10:00–13:30; Plaza San Isidoro 4, tel. 987-876-161.

❍ Self-Guided Tour: Buy your ticket and go directly into the **Royal Pantheon** (Pantéon Real). This area, now enclosed in the middle of the complex, was once the portico in front of the west door of the church. In 2002, historians discovered the tombs of several medieval kings and queens (which are now held in the stone tombs). But who's buried here pales in comparison to the beautiful, vivid frescoes on the vaulting above them. Created in the late 11th and early 12th centuries, these frescoes have never been repainted—they're incredibly well-preserved. While most Romanesque frescoes have been moved to museums, this is a rare opportunity to see some *in situ* (where they were originally intended).

Follow along as the frescos trace the life of Christ (counter-clockwise starting on the wall in the front right corner). In the scene of the Annunciation, you'll notice a sense of motion (Mary's billowing clothes) that's unusual for typically stiff and un-lifelike Romanesque art. Above that, on the ceiling in the corner, an angel appears to shepherds dressed in traditional 11th-century Leonese clothing. There's even a Leonese mastiff dog, lapping at his master's milk (while he's distracted by the angel).

In the next ceiling section (closer to the entry), Roman soldiers carry out the gruesome slaughter of the innocents. Then it's time for the Last Supper (center of the ceiling). As you take in the bold colors, notice that only 11 of the Apostles have halos...all but Judas (under the table). At the corner, find the black rooster *(gallus)*, a symbol of Jesus, who harkened the dawn of a new day for God's people. But in the next section, we see the rooster used as a different symbol—as Peter denies Christ three times before the cock crows. Also see Jesus' arrest, Simon helping Jesus carry the cross, and Pontius Pilate washing his hands of the whole business. Finally (on wall, left of main altar) we see Jesus nailed to the cross.

The final panel, in the middle of the room, is the most artistically and thematically impressive: Jesus returning triumphant to judge the living and the dead. He's depicted here as Pantocrator ("all-powerful"). Over his shoulders are the symbols for alpha and omega, and he's surrounded by the four evangelists, depicted—according to the prophecy of Ezekiel—as animals: angel, bull, eagle, and lion. The most interesting detail is the calendar running along the archway near Jesus' right hand. The 12 medallions—one for each month (labeled in Latin)—are symbolized by people's activities during that month. In January, the man closes one door (or year) while he opens the next. He proceeds to warm himself by the fire (February), prune (March), plant his crops (April), harvest (July), forage (September), slaughter the fattened pig (October), and bless his bread by the fire at Christmas (December). The message: Jesus is present for this entire cycle of life.

There's more to the museum. Continue into the **cloister,** where you'll find a small room with a giant 12th-century rooster weathervane that used to top the nearby tower (now replaced by a replica)—a symbol of the city.

You can also climb the tight spiral staircase (near where you came in) to the evocative old **library** (with a giant Mozarabic

Bible from 960—you can page through a facsimile in the gift shop) and the **chapter house,** displaying a glittering assortment of Romanesque reliquary chests.

Our tour is over. But for a peek at a remaining section of León's **Roman walls,** turn right out of the museum, then head right down the street.

• *For the most interesting approach to the cathedral, walk south from the San Isidoro Museum (and the surviving chunk of wall) along the busy street called Ramón y Cajal. At the roundabout (Plaza Santo Domingo), turn left. You're at the start of...*

Calle Ancha and the Old Town

This "Wide Street," which cuts through the heart of the Old Town, was widened in the mid-19th century to create an appropriate pathway to the cathedral. It was lined with grand mansions of local wealthy people who wanted to live close to God. It's only been pedestrianized for the last decade, creating a much-enjoyed people zone.

At the start of Calle Ancha, the turreted medieval-looking building is the **Casa de Botines**—one of few works by Antoni Gaudí outside of Catalunya (another is the Bishop's Palace in Astorga, described later in this chapter). Now the Casa de Botines is a bank and generally not open to visitors

unless there's a special exhibition. Gaudí preferred to use local materials, such as the slate roof (typical in León province). The rough stone exterior is intended to hang on to falling snow to create an atmospheric effect. Over the door is St. George, the patron saint of Gaudí's native Catalunya. Notice the architect himself on the bench across the square, appreciating his work.

As you walk up Calle Ancha toward the cathedral, the neighborhood to the left is called **Barrio del Cid** (for a supposed former resident). The area to the right is known as the **Barrio Húmedo,** or "Wet Quarter," for all the bars that speckle its streets (see "Eating in León"). Deep in the Barrio Húmedo is the appealing main square, or **Plaza Mayor,** overshadowed by the cathedral a few blocks down Calle Ancha.

▲▲Cathedral (Catedral)

León's 13th-century Gothic cathedral is filled with some of the finest stained glass in all of Europe.

Cost and Hours: Free, Mon–Sat 8:30–13:30 & 16:00–19:00 (until 20:00 June–Aug), Sun 8:30–13:30 & 17:00–19:00.

◐ Self-Guided Tour: Take a look at the **facade.** If you've just seen Burgos' cathedral, León's—while impressive—might seem a

letdown. Reserve judgment until you get inside. León's cathedral was actually built in response to the one in Burgos, to keep León on the map after Burgos wrested capital status from León in 1230. But, while Burgos' was built over two centuries, this cathedral took only about 50 years to complete. The focus was on creating a simple, purely Gothic cathedral to showcase its grand stained-glass windows. The three porticos (doorways with pointed arches) are textbook Gothic. Notice the gap between the two towers and the main facade, which allows even more light to reach those windows. This also gives the cathedral a feeling of lightness. The one exception to the pure-Gothic construction: Notice the tower on the right is a bit taller—it was capped in the 15th century with a frilly spire to keep up with what was going on in Burgos.

Now approach the **main door,** above which is a carving of the Last Judgment. Above Mary, St. Michael weighs souls to determine who is going to party with the musicians of heaven (left; his scale bar is missing) or burn with the cauldrons and demons of hell (right). If you look carefully, you'll see that all of those kicking back in heaven are members of the clergy or royalty. This subtle message made the Camino de Santiago even more appealing to pilgrims: If you weren't a priest or an aristocrat, completing the Camino was your only ticket to eternal bliss.

Before entering, ponder the crucial role that **light** plays in this house of holy glass. Like all cathedrals, the main door faces the west, and the altar (at the far end) faces east—toward Jerusalem. But that also means that the sun rises behind the altar (where Jesus symbolically resides) and sets at the Last Judgment. This theme is continued again and again inside.

Speaking of which, go on in and let your eyes adjust to the light. Notice how the purely Gothic structure—extremely high, with columns and pointed arches to direct your gaze ever heavenward—really allows the stained glass to take center stage. Of all this glass (the second-most glass in any European cathedral, after Chartres in France), 70 percent is original, from the 13th to the 16th centuries.

Imagine how the light in here changes, like living inside a kaleidoscope, as the sun moves across the sky each day. Notice that the colors differ thematically in various parts of the cathedral. Above the main door, the rose window (dedicated, like the cathedral itself, to St. Mary, with 12 angels playing instruments around her) is the most colorful, as it receives the most light at the end of the day. Turning to face the front altar, notice that the glass on the left (north) side of the church, which gets less light, symbolizes darkness and obscurity—blue dominates this side. The glass on the right (south) side of the church, which is bathed in light much of the day, symbolizes brightness and has a greater variety of colors.

Now trace the layers of Gothic cathedral construction from the bottom up, as the building (like your eyes) stretches ever higher, closer to God. The lowest level is the stone foundation (with pointed archways embedded in the walls), symbolic of the mineral world. The first windows show flowers, trees, and animals—the natural world. At the top of each nature window are three medallions showing the human world: common people doing their thing—both vices and virtues.

Above this first row of windows, notice the stone gallery (used for window maintenance). It's very rare to even have windows in this section of a cathedral (in this case, replicas of coats-of-arms of nobles who funded the cathedral's construction). The tall windows at the very top show biblical characters. On the left (north) side—the "darkness" side, before Christ—is the Old Testament; on the right (south) side—the "light" side, after Christ—is the New Testament. The two sides meet at the rose window (above the main altar) of Jesus—who is illuminated by the rising sun each morning, enlightening the entire cathedral.

If you notice **scaffolding**, it's part of a painstaking restoration of the cathedral's windows. Each piece of glass is being carefully removed from its old iron frame and reset in a brass frame. If there's scaffolding up under the main rose window, you may be able to climb up to see the work, and the window, up close (€2, entrance outside—around the left side as you face the main facade, tours every 30 min, Spanish only, closed Sun–Mon).

Peek into the carved wooden **choir** at the center of the nave (closed to visitors). The curved wooden part over the top of the chair is a "sounding board" *(tornavóz),* helping voices to carry. The giant glass door replaced a solid wooden one in the early 20th century—opening up the church even more to God's light.

Head for the **transept.** Unfortunately, this part of the cathedral almost didn't survive a well-intended but botched Baroque-era reconstruction. A heavy dome placed over the transept proved too heavy for the four graceful main pillars, causing a significant chunk of the church to collapse. The transept's blue (north) rose window, featuring Christ, survives from the 13th century, while the red (south) one, with Mary, is from the 19th century.

Circling back behind the altar, you'll find a chapel with the **"White Virgin,"** the original 13th-century statue (whose face was painted white) from the front facade of the church. Note the differences between the 16th-century stained glass above the Virgin (with one large, multi-paneled scene) and the 13th- and 14th-century glass in the flanking chapels (with one scene per panel—and even tinier bits of glass).

From the left transept, you can pay €1 to enter the **cloister** (same hours as cathedral except closed Sat afternoon and all day Sun). Here you'll see some giant discarded Baroque elements (such as turret-tops) that were added to the facade in the 16th century, and later removed because they cluttered up the architectural harmony. The cloister also offers a good view of the flying buttresses that made the stained glass structurally possible. By removing the weight from the walls and transferring it to these buttresses, medieval engineers could build higher and make larger and larger windows.

Sleeping in León

(€1 = about $1.40, country code: 34)

All of these listings are inside the Old Town. If there's a range, you can assume that the high end is for summer.

$$$ La Posada Regia is a smart little hotel with 36 rooms in two buildings just off the main walking street. The old-fashioned, pleasant decor is a combination of wood beams and patches of stone (Sb-€55–65, Db-€90–120, includes breakfast, Regidores 9–11, tel. 987-213-173, fax 987-213-031, www.regialeon.com, posada@regia leon.com).

$$$ NH Plaza Mayor is the Old Town splurge, with 51 rooms right on Plaza Mayor (some with views for no extra charge—request one). Part of a classy chain, this place offers modern four-star comfort at reasonable prices (Sb-€80–100, Db-€90–120, breakfast-€12, non-smoking rooms, air-con, elevator, pay Wi-Fi, Plaza Mayor 15, tel. 987-344-357, fax 987-215-596, www.nh-hotels .com, nhplazamayor@nh-hotels.com).

$$ Hostal Albany offers 19 very mod rooms at a good price, just a few steps off the main walking street and cathedral square (Sb-€38–49, Db-€54–65, includes tax, breakfast-€3.50, air-con, elevator, free cable Internet, Calle La Paloma 13, tel. 987-264-600, www.albanyleon.com, info@albanyleon.com).

$$ Hostal Boccalino, spacious and practical, rents 35 good rooms at a good price on a stately square facing the monastery (Sb-€47, Db-€67, Tb-€88, free Wi-Fi and drinks from cooler, Plaza de

San Isidoro 9, tel. 987-220-017, boccalino_3@hotmail.com).

$ Hostal San Martín is a fine budget option, with 12 rooms overlooking a small square in the Old Town (S-€20, Db-€40, Tb-€52, includes tax, free Wi-Fi, request quiet room in back, Plaza Torres de Omaña 1, tel. 987-875-187, fax 987-875-249, www .sanmartinhostales.com, sanmartinhostal@hotmail.com).

Eating in León

León is one of few Spanish cities whose bars still honor the old tradition of giving a free (if modest) tapa to anyone buying a drink. Your best bet for finding eats in León is to stroll the **Barrio Húmedo** area, south of Calle Ancha. This zone is packed with restaurants and bars offering good food and ambience.

Plaza San Martín Pub Crawl: In the "wet quarter," locals head for Plaza San Martín to eat and drink. Survey the many little bars on or near the square, noting how locals know each bar's specialty and generally stick to that specialty when ordering. Consider these joints: **La Bicha** is a dirty little hole-in-the-wall where Paco works hard maintaining his reputation for making León's best *morcilla* (made of tripe—like haggis without the skin). He'll fry up a plateful and serve it with some buttered toast and a nice *crianza* wine (plate big enough for four, €6). **El Llar** is famous for its potatoes (free with a drink). Of the two sauces, I'd get the cheese (tapas in bar, restaurant upstairs serves €5–10 starters and €12–15 main dishes). **Bar Rebote** serves six different croquettes—one free with each drink. **Mesón el Tizón** fills one tight room with a bar in front and seating in back—order hot *raciones* from its chalkboard menu.

Connections

From León by Bus to: Astorga (hourly, 50 min), **Burgos** (4/day, 3 hrs), **Santiago de Compostela** (6/day, 7 hrs), **Madrid** (10/day, 4 hrs). Note that all buses are run by Alsa.

By Train to: Burgos (3/day, 2 hrs), **Pamplona** (1/day, 4 hrs), **Santiago de Compostela** (1/day, 6 hrs), **Madrid** (11/day, 4 hrs).

From León to Galicia

This is arguably the most diverse stretch of the Camino. It begins in the flatness of the Meseta Central around León. Then, around Astorga, the landscape gradually becomes more varied and lush, as the Camino approaches the mountainous El Bierzo region (the northwest fringe of Castile and León). Before you know it, you're in the very Celtic-feeling terrain of Galicia.

• *Begin by making your way west, to Astorga. You can stay on the*

N-120 highway, or pay a €4 toll to zip there more quickly on the AP-71 expressway.

Astorga

Astorga (ah-STOR-gah) sits at the intersection of two ancient roads: the Camino and a north–south trade route from Sevilla to the north coast. When León was a humble Roman camp, "Asturica" was the provincial capital. But today, the fortunes are reversed, as welcoming, laid-back, sleepy Astorga (with about 15,000 people)—just big enough to have some interesting sight-seeing and good hotels and restaurants—is a nice small-town alternative to the big city of León. The main attraction here is the memorable Bishop's Palace by Antoni Gaudí.

Tourist Information: Astorga's TI shares a square with the Bishop's Palace and cathedral (daily in summer 10:00–13:30 & 16:00–19:00, closed Sun–Mon off-season, Plaza Eduardo de Castro 5, tel. 987-618-222).

Arrival in Astorga: The **bus** station is just outside the Old Town, behind the Bishop's Palace. **Drivers** follow signs for *centro ciudad* and *centro urbano*, drive through the middle of town, and park in front of the TI and cathedral (to park in a blue-painted spot, prepay at the meter and put the ticket on your dashboard).

Sights: The striking **Bishop's Palace** (Palacio Episcopal), rated ▲, is a fanciful Gothic-style castle. It's one of the few build-

ings that Catalan architect Antonio Gaudí built outside his native land. Inside you'll see Gaudí's genius in the bishop's fine rooms, decorated with frescoed tapestries. The palace hosts a museum that describes the Camino and the history of Astorga, and provides a safe place for some of the region's fine medieval church art. You'll see a 17th-century statue of Pilgrim James, a few historical Camino documents, ecclesiastical gear, and a gallery of contemporary Spanish art from the surrounding region. Not as good as it should be, with little posted information (and none in English), the museum is worthwhile mostly for a chance to see a very medieval Gaudí interior (€2.50, €4 combo-ticket with cathedral museum—see below; late-March–late-Sept Tue–Sat 10:00–14:00 & 16:00–20:00, Sun 10:00–14:00, closed Mon; off-season Tue–Sat 11:00–14:00 & 16:00–18:00, Sun 11:00–14:00, closed Mon; tel. 987-616-882).

Next to (and upstaged by) the palace is Astorga's light-filled Gothic **cathedral,** with a marvelously carved choir. It's free to enter in the morning (9:00–11:00), but after 11:00 you can get in

Camino de Santiago: Western Half

only by paying for the attached museum, which shows off a treasury collection of paintings, altarpieces, and vestments (€2.50, €4 combo-ticket with Bishop's Palace, daily April–Sept 10:00–14:00 & 16:00–20:00, Oct–March 11:00–14:00 & 16:00–18:00). Rounding out Astorga's attractions are a chocolate museum and a Roman museum.

Sleeping in Astorga: If you prefer to sleep in a small town, Astorga is a good alternative to the big city of León (though values here are no better than in the city).

$$ Hotel Gaudí has 35 woody rooms over a restaurant across from the cathedral; some have views of the Bishop's Palace (Sb-€48–50, Db-€72–78, breakfast-€7, air-con in most rooms, elevator, free Wi-Fi, Plaza Eduardo de Castro 6, tel. 987-615-654, fax

987-615-040, www.hotelgaudiastorga.com, reservas@hotelgaudi astorga.com).

$$ Astur Hotel Plaza, which feels more business-class, has 37 rooms right on the main square. Choose between a room overlooking the square—with a clock tower that clangs every 15 minutes—or a quieter back room (Sb-€47–52, Db-€66–76, breakfast-€7, air-con, Wi-Fi, Plaza de España 2–3, tel. 987-618-900, fax 987-618-949, www.asturplaza.com, asturplaza@asturplaza.com).

Eating: **Restaurante Las Termas,** a couple of blocks from the cathedral right along the Camino, is well-regarded for its food—especially the traditional stew, *cocido maragato* (€10–16 main dishes, open for lunch only, closed Mon, Calle Santiago 1, tel. 987-602-212). **Hotel Gaudí,** listed above, has an atmospheric bar with tapas and *raciones,* and a restaurant with €13–16 fixed-price meals and €10–20 main dishes (open daily).

Transportation Connections: Astorga is well-connected by bus to **León** (hourly, 50 min), **Ponferrada** (hourly, 1 hr), **Villafranca del Bierzo** (4/day, 2 hrs), and **Lugo** (5/day, 3 hrs).

• *After Astorga, you can either zip up to Galicia on the A-6 expressway (toward Ponferrada), or stick with the Camino a bit farther south on much slower regional roads (LE-142). These two routes converge again at the small city of Ponferrada. Soon after, A-6 climbs up into the hills and to the town of Villafranca del Bierzo (described below).*

If you're sticking with the Camino, you'll be near the...

Iron Cross (Cruz de Ferro)

Near the top of Mount Irago is an iron cross atop a tall wooden pole, set in a huge pile of stones built up over the years by pilgrims unloading their "sins" brought from home (or picked up en route). It's a major landmark for Camino pilgrims, but difficult to reach for drivers (figure an hour's hike off the main road). From the cross, it's a 30-minute walk to the nearly ruined stone village of Foncebadón.

Villafranca del Bierzo

Villafranca is the capital of the westernmost part of León, El Bierzo, which is trying to build a good reputation for its wine and culinary specialties. Dubbed "Little Compostela" for its array of historical buildings, this town is set in an attractive hilly terrain strewn with grapevines, cherry trees, and vegetable patches. While hardly thrilling, Villafranca del Bierzo is worth a quick stop for its pilgrim ambience (TI tel. 987-540-028).

Church of St. James' Gate of Forgiveness—To play pilgrim, hike from the main square up to the town's stout 14th-century castle (not open to the public). Then follow signs to the Romanesque 12th-century Church of St. James (Santiago). The church has a "gate of forgiveness" *(puerta de pardon,* on the side facing the town). Thanks to a 16th-century papal ruling, if a pilgrim had come this far, fell ill, and couldn't continue over the rugged terrain to Santiago, he or she was pardoned anyway. (Handy loophole.)

Villafranca *Albergue*—Next to the church is a funky pilgrims' dorm with oodles of pilgrims bonding. It was built on the site of a medieval clinic that cared for those who needed to take advantage of the *puerta de pardon* (at the time, the clinic here was the only source of medical aid for 300 miles). Today this 80-bed volunteer-run *albergue* provides €5 bunks to 10,000 pilgrims a year. If you'd like to learn about the system (or buy a scallop shell), stop in. They welcome curious non-pilgrims, albeit with the motto, "The tourist demands, the pilgrim thanks."

• *Just after Villafranca del Bierzo on the A-6 expressway, you cross into the final region on the Camino: Galicia.*

Galicia

In its final stretch, the Camino leaves the broad expanse of the Meseta Central and climbs steeply into Galicia (gah-LEE-thee-ah). Green and hilly, Galicia shatters visitors' preconceptions about Spain. There's something vaguely Irish about Galicia—and it's not just the mossy stonework and green, rolling hills. The region actually shares a strain of Celtic heritage with its cousins across the Cantabrian Sea. People here are friendly, and if you listen hard enough, you might just hear the sound of bagpipes.

• *Shortly after entering Galicia, take the freeway exit for Pedrafita do Cebreiro. From Pedrafita, a well-maintained mountain road (LU-633) twists its way up to the classic Galician pilgrim village of O Cebreiro.*

O Cebreiro

An impossibly quaint hobbit hamlet perched on a ridge high above nothing, O Cebreiro (oh theh-BRAY-roh) whispers,

"Welcome to Galicia." This rustic village evokes an uncomplicated, almost prehistoric past, when people lived very close to nature, in stone igloos with thatched roofs. With sweeping views across the verdant but harsh Galician landscape, O Cebreiro is constantly pummeled by some of the fiercest weather in Spain. And it's all within a five-minute drive of the freeway.

Wander around. Enjoy the remoteness. O Cebreiro smells like wood fires, manure, and pilgrim B.O. Get a snack or drink at a bar, or browse through a gift shop. A few simple townspeople (who jabber at each other in Galego—see page 255—and cock their heads quizzically when asked about newfangled inventions like email) share the town with weary pilgrims on an adrenaline high after finally reaching Galicia. The local dogs, who've known each other their whole lives, still bark at each other territorially from across the street, completely ignoring the backpackers who regularly trudge through town.

Sights in O Cebreiro

▲**Pallozas**—From Celtic times 1,500 years ago, right up until the 1960s, the villagers of O Cebreiro lived in humble round stone huts with peaked thatched roofs, called *pallozas*. One of the nine surviving *pallozas* has been turned into a loosely run museum, where an attendant is paid by the government to welcome visitors and answer questions (free, Wed–Sun 11:00–14:00 & 15:00–18:00, closed Mon–Tue; if a door of a round hut is open, poke inside). Here visitors can learn about the lifestyle of the people who lived in *pallozas* until not so long ago. Entering a *palloza*, you'll find the only "private" room in the house, belonging to the parents. Beyond that is a living area around a humble fire. (Notice there's no chimney—smoke lets itself out through the thatch.) Ponder the ancient furniture. Surrounding the fire are clever benches (which were also used, by the kids, as very hard beds) with pull-down counters so they could double as a table at mealtime. The big beam with the chain could be swung over the fire for cooking. Looking up, you'll see the remains of a wooden ceiling that prevented sparks from igniting the thatch. The giant black-metal spirals suspended from the ceiling were used to smoke chorizo (sausage)—very efficient. Attached to this living area is a miniature "barn." Animals lived on the lower level, while people slept on the upper level (which has been removed, but you can still see on the wall where the floor was once supported)—kept warm by all that livestock body heat. About a dozen people (and their animals) lived in one small hut. But thanks to the ideal insulation provided by the thatch, and the warmth from the fire and animals, it was toasty even through the difficult winter.

▲**Royal St. Mary's Church (Santa María la Real)**—All roads lead to the village church. Founded in the year 836—not long after the remains of St. James were found in Santiago—this pre-Romanesque building is supposedly the oldest church on the entire French Road of the Camino. The interior is surprisingly spacious, but very simple (free, daily 9:00–21:00). Notice the sunken floor: The building is actually embedded into the ground for added protection against winter storms. The desk inside stamps pilgrims' credentials and sells votive candles. (I don't think there's anything wrong with giving your guidebook an O Cebreiro stamp—I did.) The baptistery, in a tiny side room near the entrance, is separate from the main part of the church, as dictated by ancient tradition. It has a giant and very rough font used for immersion baptisms. In the chapel to the right of the main altar is a much-revered 12th-century golden chalice and reliquary, which holds items relating to a popular local miracle: A peasant from a nearby village braved a fierce winter snowstorm to come to this church for the Eucharist. The priest scoffed at his devotion, only to find that the host and wine had physically turned into the body and blood of Christ, staining the linens beneath them, which are now in the silver box.

Eating and Sleeping in O Cebreiro

(€1 = about $1.40, country code: 34)
The only businesses in town are a half-dozen very humble pub/restaurants, which feed pilgrims and other visitors hearty Galician cuisine in a smoky atmosphere. You'll see signs offering a stick-to-your-ribs €9 "pilgrim menu." Many of these places also rent a few rooms upstairs. Be warned that these rooms are very rustic, English can be tricky, and reservations are only by phone. Try **$ Hospedería San Giraldo de Aurillac** (Db-€50, 17 rooms in 3 buildings, tel. 982-367-182); **$ Casa Carolo** (D-€33, Db-€45, tel. 982-367-168); or **$ Mesón Antón** (D/Db-€38, tel. 982-151-336). The *albergue,* which is open only to pilgrims, is perched on a hill at the edge of town and charges €3 per bed.

Connections

• *From O Cebreiro, you've got another route decision to make.*
   To stick with the Camino, you'll continue on LU-633, along twisty roads, toward Santiago. Along the way, you'll pass through some interesting larger towns: **Sarria,** *which is just over 100 kilometers (62 miles) from Santiago, is a popular place to begin a truncated pilgrimage (since you need to walk at least that far to earn your* compostela *certificate).* **Portomarín** *is a relatively new town, built only after the River Miño was flooded to create a reservoir in the 1950s. The stout and blocky late-Romanesque Church of San Juan was moved to a new site, stone by stone—and if you look closely enough, you can see how the stones were numbered to keep track of where they fit.*

THE CAMINO DE SANTIAGO

I prefer the faster expressway route (backtrack to A-6, which you'll take north, following signs for A Coruña), which offers the opportunity to dip into an appealing walled city, Lugo.

Lugo

While not technically on the French Road of the Camino de Santiago, the midsized city of Lugo (pop. 90,000) warrants a detour for car travelers. Boasting what are arguably the best-preserved Roman walls in Spain—a mile and a third long, completely encircling the town, draped with moss, and receding into the misty horizon—Lugo offers an ideal place for an evocative stroll. Lugo feels like a poor man's Santiago, with a patina of poverty and atmospherically crumbling buildings. Evocative chimneys thrust up through rickety old slate roofs. And yet, there's something proud and welcoming about the town. Aside from the walls, Lugo has a cathedral and gregarious Galician charm, making it a fine place to spend some time.

Orientation to Lugo

Tourist Information

The TI is a few steps up a pedestrian street off the main square, Plaza Maior—look for the yellow signs (July–Aug Mon–Sat 10:00–14:00 & 16:00–20:00, Sept–June until 19:00, closed Sun year-round, Rúa Conde Pallares 2, tel. 982-231-361).

Arrival in Lugo

The **bus** station is just outside the town walls; once inside the Old Town, the main square and TI are a block away. The **train** station is two blocks east of the town walls. **Drivers** follow signs to *centro ciudad* and *centro urbano*. Once you enter the town walls, parking garages are signed.

Sights in Lugo

The town's **Roman walls** *(murallas Romanas)* are free and always open, providing a kind of circular park where locals and visitors can stroll at rooftop level. You can access the walls at various points around town (you'll find stairs near most of the gates where traffic enters the Old Town), and it takes about 45 minutes to walk the entire way around. With less time, the most interesting stretch is along the west side of town: Walk up the ramp behind the cathedral and turn right, watching behind you for tingly views of the walls and cathedral spires.

Lugo's **cathedral** is vast, dark, and dusty, with a glittering silver altarpiece (free, daily 8:00–20:30, €2 to enter cloister). While it's a fine cathedral, it pales in comparison to Santiago's. Lugo also has a provincial museum and a Roman museum.

Sleeping in Lugo

(€1 = about $1.40, country code: 34)
Sleeping in Lugo is worth considering to break the long journey to Santiago from Cantabria or León. Budget *hostales* cluster just southeast of the town walls (near the bus station). The following two hotels are the only ones inside the Old Town.

$$$ Pazo Orban e Sangro is the town splurge, renting 12 rooms with hardwood floors, flat-screen TVs, and luxurious furnishings. It's just inside the town walls near the cathedral (Db-€100–120, includes breakfast, air-con, elevator, free cable Internet, Travesía do Miño, tel. 982-240-217, fax 982-245-645, www.pazodeorban.es, info@pazodeorban.es).

$$ Hotel Méndez Núñez, right in the heart of the Old Town, has a classy old lobby, a medieval-feeling lounge, and 70 rooms with worn furniture but new bathrooms (Sb-€50, Db-€60, breakfast-€6, air-con, elevator, free Internet access and Wi-Fi, Calle Reina 1, tel. 982-230-711, fax 982-229-738, www.hotelmendeznunez.com, hotel@hotelmendeznunez.com).

Connections

Lugo is connected by bus to **Santiago de Compostela** (7/day, 2 hrs, run by Empresa Freire), **Astorga** (5/day, 2.5 hrs, run by Alsa), and **León** (2/day, 4 hrs, run by Alsa).

• *After Lugo, the end is in sight. You have one final route decision to make: The fastest way (about 1.5 hrs to Santiago) is to stick with the A-6 expressway north to A Coruña, then pay €5 to take the AP-9 tollway back south to Santiago. But if you'd like to rejoin the Camino for the last stretch—following in the footsteps (or tire treads) of a millennium of pilgrims—follow signs from Lugo toward Ourense (on N-540/N-640, about 20–30 min longer than expressway option). In Guntín, split off on N-547 and head for Santiago de Compostela.*

However you arrive, see the next chapter and enjoy one of Europe's great pilgrim cities.

Buen Camino!

SANTIAGO DE COMPOSTELA

The best destination in the northwestern province of Galicia, Santiago de Compostela might well be the most magical city in Spain. This place has long had a powerful and mysterious draw on travelers—as more than a thousand years' worth of pilgrims have trod the desolate trail across the north of Spain just to peer up at the facade of its glorious cathedral.

But there's more to this city than pilgrims and the remains of St. James. Contrary to what you've heard, the rain in Spain does *not* fall mainly on the plain—it falls in Galicia. This "Atlantic Northwest" of Spain is like the Pacific Northwest of the United States: hilly, lush terrain that enjoys far more precipitation than the interior, plus dramatic coastal scenery, delicious seafood, fine local wines, and an easy-going ambience. The Spanish interior might be arid, but the northwest requires rain gear. Even the tourists here have a grungy vibe: Packs of happy hippie pilgrims seek to find themselves while hiking the ancient Camino de Santiago from France (described in the previous chapter). Santiago has a generally festive atmosphere, as travelers from every corner of the globe celebrate the end of a long journey. It's a sturdy city that, in its day, was one of Europe's most important religious centers, built of granite turned mossy green by the notorious weather.

Planning Your Time

Santiago's biggest downside is its location: Except by air, it's a very long trip from any other notable stop in Spain. But if you decide to visit, you—like a millennium's worth of pilgrims before you—will find it's worth the trek. You can get a good feel for Santiago in a day, but a second day relaxing on the squares makes the long trip

Galego

Like Catalunya and the Basque Country, Galicia has its own distinctive language. Galego (called *gallego* in Spanish, and sometimes called "Galician" in English) is a mix between Spanish and Portuguese. Historically, Galego was closer to Portuguese. But Queen Isabel imported the Spanish language to the region in the 15th century, and ever since, the language has gradually come to sound more and more like Spanish. In an attempt at national unity, Franco banned Galego in the mid-20th century (along with Catalan and the Basque language, Euskara). During these trying times, Galicians spoke Spanish in public—and Galego at home. Since the end of the Franco era, Galego is a proud part of this region's cultural heritage. Street signs and sight names are posted in Galego, and I've followed suit in this chapter.

If you don't speak Spanish, you'll hardly notice a difference. Most apparent is the change in articles: *el* and *la* become *o* and *a*—so the big Galician city La Coruña is known as "A Coruña" around here. You'll also see a lot more *x*'s, which are pronounced "sh" (such as "Xacobeo," shah-koh-BAY-oh, the local word for St. James' pilgrimage route). The Spanish greeting *buenos días* becomes *bos días* in Galego. The familiar *plaza* becomes *praza*. And if you want to impress a local, say *graciñas* (grah-THEEN-yahs)—a super-polite thank you.

here more worthwhile.

The city has one real sight: the cathedral, with its fine museum and the surrounding squares. The rest of your visit is for munching seafood, pilgrim-watching, and browsing the stony streets. The highlight of a visit just may be hanging out on the cathedral square at about 10:00 to welcome pilgrims completing their long journey.

Orientation to Santiago

Santiago is built on hilly terrain, with lots of ups and downs. The tourist's Santiago is small: You can walk across the historic center, or Zona Monumental, in about 15 minutes. There you'll find the city's centerpiece— the awe-inspiring cathedral—as well as several other churches, a maze of pretty squares, a smattering of small museums, a bustling restaurant scene, and all of my recommended hotels.

The historic center is circled by a

Cheap Tricks in Santiago de Compostela

- As a pilgrim mecca, Santiago's accommodations, eateries, and sights are geared for low-budget travelers. It's an affordable place to visit. Hotel values are excellent here.
- Santiago's top sight—its cathedral—is free to enter. Attend a pilgrim Mass (also free), especially if the giant *botafumiero* incense burner will be swinging.
- Virtually all of the city's other attractions—including the Museum of Pilgrimages, Galicia Dixital, the Museum of the Galician People, the Galician Contemporary Art Museum, and the market—are also free.

busy street that marks the former location of the town wall (easy to see on a map). Outside of that is the commercial city center, which is a modern, urban district called Céntrico. A 10-minute walk through Céntrico takes you to the train station.

Tourist Information

On Rúa do Vilar in the town center there are two separate information offices: one for the region and pilgrims, and the other for visitors to the city.

The city TI is at Rúa do Vilar 63 (daily June–Sept 9:00–21:00, Oct–May 9:00–14:00 & 16:00–19:00, tel. 981-555-129, www.santiagoturismo.com). It runs walking tours and rents MP3-player audioguides (see "Tours," later). Ask the TI what's going on when you're in town, and grab a free copy of the monthly *Culturall*.

The office for the region of Galicia and for pilgrims shares a location at Rúa do Vilar 30 (Mon–Fri 10:00–20:00, Sat 11:00–14:00 & 17:00–19:00, Sun 11:00–14:00, tel. 981-584-081, www.turgalicia.es).

Arrival in Santiago de Compostela

Note that there's luggage storage at the bus station (and downtown, at Mundonet—see "Helpful Hints," next page)—but not at the train station.

By Train: Santiago's train station is on the southern edge of the modern Céntrico district. You'll find ATMs, a cafeteria, and a helpful train information office. Computer screens show upcoming departures. To reach the center of town, leave the station and walk up the grand granite staircase, jog right, cross the busy Avenida de Lugo, and walk uphill for 10 minutes on Rúa do Hórreo to Praza de Galicia. A taxi to your hotel will cost about €5.

By Bus: The bus station is about a 15-minute, mostly uphill walk northeast of the cathedral. Exit the station straight ahead (on Rúa de Ánxel Casal) and go to the roundabout called Praza da Paz. Turn left here onto Rúa da Pastoriza, which will bring you into town. To avoid the hike, I'd rather hop on local bus #5 (€1) and take it to the Praza de Galicia, a few steps from the historical center.

By Plane: Santiago's small airport (airport code: SCQ) is about six miles from the city center. A bus connects the airport to the bus station, then to Rúa do Doutor Teixeiro, a long block beyond Praza de Galicia at the south end of the historical center (€2, runs at least hourly, 20–30-min trip). A taxi into town costs about €18.

By Car: There are only two freeway off-ramps to the city. The north exit #67 is best for the airport and the old center.

Helpful Hints

Closed Days: Many museums (except church-related ones) are closed on Monday. The colorful produce market is closed on Sunday, slow on Monday, and busiest on Thursday and Saturday mornings.

Church Hours: The cathedral and other major churches in Santiago are open 9:00–21:00 without a siesta, while minor ones have limited visiting hours. There are special Masses for pilgrims daily at noon in the cathedral. The big Masses on Sunday are at 10:00 and noon.

Holy Year 2010: On years that the Feast of St. James (July 25) falls on a Sunday, it's a special Compostela Holy Year (*Ano Xacobeo* in Galego)—with 25 percent more pilgrims than usual coming to Santiago, more special services in the cathedral, and hotel prices jacked up with the heightened demand. The next one is not for another decade.

Festivals: Late July is the main party time in Santiago, when the city hosts a world music festival and impromptu concerts all over town, and the royal family (or their representative) attends Mass in Santiago (with fireworks on July 24 and 31). The second-most important musical event in town—with several days of free concerts—occurs around Ascension (May 13 in 2010).

Internet Access: You'll see signs around the historic center. The handiest and best-equipped is **Cyber Nova 50** (Mon–Fri 9:00–24:00, Sat–Sun 10:00–23:00; faxing, phones, printing, and other services; Rúa Nova 50, tel. 981-575-188). Nearby is **Mundonet** (daily 10:00–23:00, also offers baggage storage and disc-burning, just above the other end of Rúa Nova at Rúa de Xelmírez 19). If you have a laptop, many cafés in town

Santiago de Compostela

1. Praza do Obradoiro
2. Praza da Inmaculada
3. Praza Quintana
4. Praza das Praterías
5. Praza de Cervantes
6. Regional & Pilgrim Info Center
7. Office for Pilgrims
8. Internet Cafés (2)
9. To Launderette
10. Folk Music Clubhouse

offer free Wi-Fi with a purchase (look for window signs).

Laundry: You'll find a self-service *lavandería* called **Axiña** a 15-minute walk from the historic center (€5.30/load self-service, €6.60 for full service, Mon–Fri 8:30–13:00 & 16:00–20:30, Sat 8:30–13:30, closed Sun and in Aug, Rúa de Ramón Cabanillas 1, tel. 981-591-323).

Shopping: Jet, the black gemstone (called *azabache* in Spanish) similar to onyx, is believed to keep away evil spirits—and to bring in tourist euros. Along with jet, the silver trade has long been important in Santiago...and continues to be a popular item for tourists. Although the Galicians are a superstitious people and have beliefs about good and bad witches, the made-in-Taiwan witches you see in souvenir shops around the city are a recent innovation. Maybe the best souvenir is a simple seashell, like the ones pilgrims carry with them along the Camino.

Best Views: There are beautiful views back toward the cathedral from the Alameda park. From the cathedral, follow Rúa do Franco to the end. Swing right into the park and continue up Paseo de Santa Susana to the viewpoint *(mirador)* along Paseo da Ferradura. There is another excellent view from the very top of the park (clearly marked on TI maps).

Tours in Santiago

The TI offers a two-hour English-language **walking tour** that covers the cathedral and the surrounding plazas (€10, April–Oct Tue and Sun at 17:00, get details at the city TI). Ask about the TI's other tours, including gastronomy tours, nighttime tours, and more. Or you can rent an **MP3-player audioguide** at the city TI, and follow the suggested three-hour route (€12/24-hour rental). Either tour is better than taking the silly **tourist train,** which only does a circuit around the outskirts of the old city (€5, 45 min, meet in front of the cathedral in the Praza do Obradoiro).

It's easy to visit the cathedral and nearby sights on your own with the information in this book. But if you have the extra cash, you could hire a **local guide** (for 3.5 hours: €80 Mon–Fri, €90 Sat–Sun). Patricia Furelos (mobile 630-781-795, patriciaguia @latinmail.com) and Manuel Ruzo (mobile 639-888-064, manuel @artnaturagalicia.com) are equally good, or contact the Association of Professional Guides of Galicia (tel. 981-569-890, fax 981-553-329, guiasgalicia@ctv.es).

Sights in Santiago

▲▲The Cathedral

Santiago's cathedral isn't the biggest in Spain, nor is it the most impressive. Yet it's certainly the most mystical, exerting a spiritual magnetism that attracts people from all walks of life and from all corners of the globe. (To more fully appreciate the pilgrim experience, before visiting the cathedral read the first part of the Camino de Santiago chapter.)

Exploring one of the most important churches in Christendom, you'll do some time travel, putting yourselves in the well-worn shoes of the millions of pilgrims who have trekked many miles to this powerful place.

• *Begin facing the cathedral's main facade, in the big square called...*

Praza do Obradoiro

Find the pavement stone with the scallop shell right in the middle of this square. For more than a thousand years, this spot has been

where millions of tired pilgrims have taken a deep breath and thought to themselves: "I made it!" To maximize your chance of seeing pilgrims, be here at about 10:00—the last stop on the Camino de Santiago is two miles away, and pilgrims try to get to the cathedral in time for the 12:00 Mass. It's great fun to chat with pilgrims who've just completed their journey. They seem to be very centered and content with the experience, and tuned in to the important things in life...like taking time to talk with others. You'll likely see pilgrims arrive separately who met previously along the way, and then leave together, having reunited at the grand finale. Every time I visit, I find myself taking photos for people and agreeing to email copies to them. Even if you're shy, it's a fun and easy way to meet pilgrims by offering to capture their personal triumphs.

• *Before heading into the cathedral, take a spin around the square (start facing the cathedral).*

To your left is the **Hospital of the Catholic Monarchs** (Hostal dos Reis Católicos). Isabel and Ferdinand came to Santiago in 1501 to give thanks for successfully forcing the Moors out of Granada. When they arrived, they found many sick pilgrims at the square. (Numerous pilgrims came to Santiago to ask for help in overcoming an illness, and the long walk here often only made their condition worse.) Isabel and Ferdinand decided to build this hospital to give pilgrims a place to recover on arrival (you'll see their coats of arms flanking the intricately carved entryway). It was free, and remained a working hospital until 1952 (many locals were actually born

here)—when it was converted into a fancy parador and restaurant (see "Sleeping" and "Eating" sections). The modern white windows with the old granite facade might seem jarring—but this contrast is very common in Galicia, maximizing the brightness provided by any sunny spells in this notoriously rainy region.

Another 90 degrees to the left is the Neoclassical **City Hall** (Concello). Notice the equestrian statue up top. That's St. James, riding in from heaven to help the Spaniards defeat the Moors. All over town, Santiago's namesake and symbol—a Christian evangelist on a horse, killing Muslims with his sword—is out doing his bloody thing. See any police on the square? There's a reason for their presence. In its medieval day, Santiago's cathedral was one of the top three pilgrimage sites in the Christian world (after Jerusalem and Rome). It remains important today, and with St. James taking such joy in butchering Muslims, it is considered a high-profile target for Islamic fundamentalists.

Completing the square (90 more degrees to the left) is the original **University** building (its rectory faces the square, the tower behind with the flags marks the original building—now the library). Santiago has Spain's third-oldest university, with more than 30,000 students (medicine and law are especially popular).

You'll likely see Spanish school groups on the square, field-tripping from all over the country. Teachers love to use this spot for an architecture lesson, since it features four different architectural styles (starting with the cathedral and spinning left): 18th-century Baroque; 16th-century Plateresque; 18th-century Neoclassical; and medieval Romanesque (the door of the rectory).

• *Now take a look at the...*

Cathedral Facade

Twelve hundred years ago, a monk followed a field of stars (probably the Milky Way) to the little Galician village of San Fiz de Solovio and discovered what appeared to be the long-lost tomb of

St. James. On July 25, 813, the local bishop declared that St. James' remains had been found. They set to building a church here and named the place Santiago (St. James) de Compostela (*campo de estrellas,* or "field of stars," for the celestial bodies that guided the monk).

For the last 12 centuries, the cathedral you see today has gradually been added on to the original simple chapel. By the 11th century, the church was overwhelmed by the crowds. Construction of a larger cathedral began in 1075, and the work took 150 years. (The granite workers who built it set up shop on this very square—still called Praza do Obradoiro, literally, "Workers' Square.") Much of the design is attributed to a palace artist named Maestro Mateo, whom you'll meet a little later.

The exterior of the cathedral you see today is *not* the one that medieval pilgrims saw (though the interior is much the same). In the mid-18th century, Santiago's bishop—all fired up from a trip to Baroque-slathered Rome, and wanting to improve the original, now-deteriorating facade—decided to spruce up the building with a new Baroque exterior. He also replaced the simple stonework in the interior with gaudy gold.

Study the facade. Atop the middle steeple is St. James (dressed like the pilgrim he was). Beneath him is his tomb, marked by a star—one of the many symbols you'll see all over the place (see "The Symbols of Santiago" in the Camino de Santiago chapter). On either side of the tomb are Theodorus and Athanasius, James' disciples who brought his body to Santiago. On the side pillars are, to the left, James' father Zebedee, and to the right, his mother Salomé.

Don't you wish you had a miniature replica of this beautiful facade to carry around with you? Actually, you probably do. Check your pocket for a copper-colored euro coin worth €0.01, €0.02, or €0.05. There it is! Of all the churches in Spain, they chose this one as their representative in euro-land. It's even more important when you consider the significance of the images depicted on Spain's other euro coinage: a portrait of the author of *Don Quixote,* Miguel de Cervantes, Spain's greatest contributor to world literature; and the current king, Juan Carlos I. Sevilla and Toledo may have bigger cathedrals, but Santiago has the symbolism to propel its church into this powerful triumvirate.

The cathedral also houses a museum with three parts; as you face this facade, the door to the main museum is to the right, the entry to the crypt is dead ahead (under the staircase), and the door on the left leads to an empty palace and the cathedral rooftop (both described later in this chapter).

• *Now, head up the stairs and enter the cathedral (daily 9:00–21:00; if a service is going on, the front entrance is usually closed—enter around either side about hundred yards to the left or the right). Once inside, go to the rear of the nave and look up at the Portico of Glory (currently covered in scaffolding).*

Portico of Glory

Take a step back in time (remember, this used to be the main facade of the cathedral—sculpted in about 1180 by Maestro Mateo). Imagine you're a medieval pilgrim, and you've just walked 500 miles from the Frankish lands to reach this cathedral. You're here to request the help of St. James in recovering from an illness or to give thanks for a success. Maybe you've come to honor the wish of a dying relative or to be forgiven for your sins. Whatever the reason, you came here on foot.

You can't read, but you can tell from the carved images that this magnificent door represents the Glory of God. Old Testament prophets on the left announce Christ's coming. New Testament apostles on the right spread his message. Jesus reigns directly above, approachable to the humble Christian pilgrim via St. James with his staff.

Theologically, pilgrims are coming not for St. James, but to get to Christ via St. James. While most of the statuary is covered with scaffolding until at least 2011, look for Jesus, front and center, surrounded by Matthew, Mark, Luke, and John. Beside them are angels carrying tools for the Crucifixion—the cross, the crown of thorns, the spear, and a jug of vinegar. Arching above them are 24 musicians playing celestial music—each one with a different medieval instrument. Below St. James is a column with the Tree of Jesse—showing the genealogy of Jesus with Mary near the top, and above her, the Holy Trinity: Father, Son, and a dove representing the Holy Spirit.

As a pilgrim, you would walk to the column in the middle of the entryway (now ringed by a railing to keep crowds from gathering here). Squint down the nave to the end, and you'll see the stone statue of St. James that marks his tomb. Trembling with excitement at the culmination of your long journey, you'd place your hand into the well-worn finger holes on the column (see five grooves at about chest level) and bow your head, giving thanks to St. James for safe passage. Then you'd go around to the other side of the post and, at knee level, see Maestro Mateo, who carved this fine facade. What a smart guy! Kneel and tap your head against his three times—to help improve your intelligence (a ritual among university students here.) Such a high-profile self-portrait of an artist in the 12th century was unprecedented. In Santiago, he was something like the Leonardo of his day.

• *Now wander down the...*

Nave

Look up, noticing the barrel vault and the heavy, dark Romanesque design of the church. (The original freestanding church had about 80 glorious alabaster windows. They are now mostly bricked up due to a complex of buildings built around the church.) Up near the top, notice the gallery. This is where sweaty, smelly pilgrims slept.

• *Continue up the nave until you reach the high altar, where you'll see a thick rope hanging from a pulley system high in the dome, which is sometimes attached to the...*

Botafumeiro

This huge silver-plated incense burner (120 pounds and about the size of a small child) is suspended from the ceiling during special

Masses (occurring about 25 times a year; ask at the TI if one is scheduled during your visit) or when a pilgrim pays about €250 to see it in action. As 2010 is a Holy Year, it will swing nearly daily at the end of each pilgrims' Mass at 12:00. Supposedly the custom of swinging this giant incense dispenser began in order to counteract the stench of the pilgrims. After communion, eight men (called *tiraboleiros*) pull on the rope, and this huge contraption swings in a wide arc up and down the transept, spewing sweet-smelling smoke. If you're here to see it, the most impressive view is sitting or standing on either side of the main altar. From this position, the *botafumeiro* seems to whiz directly over your head. When not in use, the *botafumeiro* and a replica are kept on display in the cathedral library (see "Cathedral Museum," later in this chapter).

• *Stand in the center of the nave, in front of the...*

Altar

The big gold altar has all three representations of St. James in one place (see "The Three Santiagos" later in this chapter): up top, on a white horse, is James the *Matamoros*—Moor-Slayer; below that (just under the canopy) is pilgrim James; and below that is the original stone Apostle James by Maestro Mateo—still pointing down to his tomb after all these centuries.

St. James

Santiago is Spanish for "St. James." James and his brother John, sons of Zebedee and Salomé, were well-off fishermen on the Sea of Galilee. One fateful day, a charismatic visionary came and said to them, "Come with me, and I will make you fishers of men." They threw down their nets and became apostles.

Along with Peter, James and John were supposedly Jesus' favorites—he called them the "sons of thunder." Some historians even think Jesus and James might have been related. (This close relationship makes James an even more appealing object of worship.)

After Jesus' death, the apostles spread out and brought his message to other lands. St. James spent a decade as a missionary bringing Christianity to the farthest reaches of the known world—which, back then, was northwest Spain. The legend goes that as soon as he returned home to the Holy Land in A.D. 44, James was beheaded by Herod Agrippa. Before his body and head could be thrown to the lions—as was the custom in those days—they were rescued by two of his disciples, Theodorus and Athanasius.

These two brought his body back to Spain in a small boat and entombed it in the hills of Galicia—hiding it carefully so it would not be found by the Roman authorities. There it lay hidden for almost eight centuries. In 813, a monk—supposedly directed by the stars—discovered the tomb, and the local bishop proudly exclaimed that St. James was in Galicia. Santiago de Compostela was born.

But is this the *real* story? Historians figure the "discovery" of the remains of St. James in Spain provided a necessary way to rally Europe against the Moors, who had invaded Spain and were threatening to continue into Europe. The "marketing" of St. James was further bolstered by his miraculous appearance, on horseback and wielding a sword, to fight for the Christian army in the pivotal battle of Clavijo during the Reconquista. With St. James *Matamoros* ("the Moor-Slayer") in Iberia, all of Europe was inspired to rise up and push the Muslims back into Africa...which they finally did in 1492. James eventually became Spain's patron saint, and for centuries Spanish armies rode into battle with the cry *"Santiago y cierra España!"* ("St. James and strike for Spain!").

Sure, the whole thing was likely a propaganda hoax to get a local populace to support a war. But yesterday's and today's pilgrims may not care whether the body of St. James actually lies in this church. The pilgrimage to Santiago is a spiritual quest powered through the ages by faith.

The dome over the altar was added in the 16th century to bring some light into this dark Romanesque church.

On the columns up and down the nave and transept, notice the symbols carved into the granite. These are the markings of the masons who made the columns—to keep track of how many they'd be paid for.

• *Following the pilgrims' route, go down the ambulatory on the left side of the altar—passing where the* botafumeiro *rope is moored to the pillar—and walk down the little stairway (see the green light, on your right) to the level of the earlier, 10th-century church and the...*

Tomb of St. James

There he is, in the little silver chest, marked by a star—Santiago. Pilgrims kneel in front of the tomb and make their request or say their thanks.

• *Continue through the little passage, up the stairs, turn left and wander around the ambulatory, noticing the various chapels (built by noblemen who wanted to be buried close to St. James). At the very back of the church (behind the altar) is the greenish...*

Holy Door—Open in 2010

This special door is open only during Holy Years, when pilgrims use it to access the tomb and statue of the apostle. The current door, sculpted by a local artist for the 2004 Holy Year, shows six scenes from the life of St. James: the conversion moment when Jesus invited those Galilean fishermen to become "fishers of men"; Jesus with the 12 apostles (James is identified by his scallop shell); James doing his "fishing" in Spain; his return to Jerusalem in A.D. 44 to be beheaded; the ship taking his body back to Spain; and the discovery of James' body by a local monk in 813. At the bottom, the little snail is the symbol of the pilgrim...slow and steady, with everything on its back.

Hug St. James

There's one more pilgrim ritual to complete. Find the little door near the exit from the tomb (perhaps with a line of pilgrims—10 yards away, by another green light, closed 13:30–16:00 and after 20:00). Climb the stairs under the huge babies, find Maestro Mateo's stone statue of St. James—gilded and caked with precious gems. Embrace him from behind and enjoy a saint's-eye view of the cathedral...under the vigilant eye of a cathedral watchman, there to ensure the unholy temptation to pry loose a jewel doesn't overcome you.

• *Congratulations, pilgrim! You have completed the Camino de Santiago. Now go in peace.*

▲▲**Cathedral Museum (Museo da Catedral) and Crypt**—The cathedral's museum shows off some interesting pieces from the fine treasury collection and artifacts from the cathedral's history. It's laid out chronologically from bottom to top. There's virtually no English inside, so pick up the included English guide booklet as you enter (€5, or €3 for pilgrims; June–Sept Mon–Sat 10:00–14:00 & 16:00–20:00, Sun 10:00–14:00; Oct–May Mon–Sat 10:00–13:30 & 16:00–18:30, Sun 10:00–13:30; tel. 981-569-327, www .catedraldesantiago.es).

On the ground floor, you'll find the remaining pieces of Maestro Mateo's original stone choir (stone seats for priests; these seats filled the center of the nave in the 12th century), pieced together as part of a new replica. Nearby, look for a miniature model of the choir. Notice the expressive faces Mateo carved into the granite. While working in the Romanesque style, he was well ahead of his time artistically. Consider the value culturally of a place in Europe where people from all corners came together, shared, and then dispersed. Consider also that this was the first architectural style named not for a particular empire or ethnic group, and that it covered all of Europe: Romanesque. In some ways, the concept of Europe as a civilization was being born when Santiago was in its 12th-century heyday. You'll also see fragments of Roman settlements, dating from before the tomb of St. James was discovered here.

On the first floor, find two statues of a pregnant Mary. While this theme is unusual in most of Europe, it's common in Galicia.

The coin collection shows off examples of money that pilgrims brought with them from all over Europe (see the displayed map). The dirham coin in the center case is dated 387. Muhammad became a prophet in 612; therefore, this is from the year 997 on the Christian calendar. The map on the wall illustrates the various pilgrimage routes. The original route was along the coast. Today's route (parallel but farther south) was established after that area was taken from the Muslims to help consolidate Christian control. To answer the common question, "Why the shell?" notice how trails from all across Europe converge, eventually coming together (like the lines on the scallop shell) at Santiago.

On the second floor, you'll enter the cloister. The tombs lining the cloister floor hold the remains of priests from the cathedral.

The Three Santiagos

You'll see three different depictions of St. James in the cathedral and throughout the city:

1. Apostle James: James dressed in typical apostle robes, often indiscernible from the other apostles (sometimes with a pilgrim's stick or shell).

2. Pilgrim James: James wearing some or all of the traditional garb of the Camino de Santiago pilgrim: a brown cloak, floppy hat, walking stick, shell, gourd, and sandals. Among pilgrims, he's the one carrying a book.

3. Crusader James, the Moor-Slayer: Centuries after his death, the Spaniards called on St. James for aid in various battles against the Moors. According to legend, St. James appeared from the heavens on a white horse and massacred Muslim foes. Locals don't particularly care for this depiction—especially these days, when the rising tide of Islamic fundamentalists could justifiably find it provocative.

In the courtyard, you'll see a fountain (which once stood in front of the cathedral and was used by pilgrims to cleanse themselves) and the original church bells (replaced with new models in 1989). As you walk left (clockwise) around the cloister, the first door leads to the Royal Chapel, with a beautiful-smelling cedar altar that houses dozens and dozens of relics. The centerpiece (eye level) holds the remains (likely the skull) of St. James the Lesser (the *other* Apostle James). Look up to find St. James riding heroically out of the woodwork to rally all Europe to reconquer the Iberian Peninsula. This altarpiece was restored after a fire around 1900.

Cross the hall to the treasury. Look for the wood altar, carved in England (c. 1420), depicting the tale of St. James—including his beheading, and his body being taken back to Galicia. The fancy solid-gold monstrance is used for carrying the communion host around the cathedral on Corpus Christi (the wafer sits in the little round window in the middle). Pilgrims hugged this jeweled, silver cape of St. James for 300 years until it was finally replaced in 2004 by the one above the altar, which pilgrims hug today.

• *Return to the cloister and back through the door you entered to the library.*

The library is where they store old books, a funky rack for reading those huge tomes ("turn pages" by spinning the rack), and the *botafumeiro* (gigantic incense burner). There's always a replica here offering a close-up look. The next room shows how tapestries could warm a stone palace. Notice the painted ceilings. To prove that they're carved out of granite, one patch is left unpainted to expose the stone.

Pass back through the library and go up one more floor. If the doors are open, enjoy views from a fine balcony overlooking Praza do Obradoiro. Then walk through several rooms of tapestries.

The first room is from designs by Rubens. The two middle rooms show idealistic 18th-century peasant life—wives helping their men to be less moronic (but there's still a man peeing in the corner). Don't miss the intimate 18th-century Madonna and Child statue in the glass case. The nursing *Virgen de la Leche* looks out at us as she feeds her son. The last room has a tapestry, based on a design by Goya, with exacting details of life in around 1790.

After visiting the museum, drop into the **crypt** (same ticket, under main stairs into cathedral) and see some serious medieval engineering. Since the church was built on a too-small hill, the crypt was made to support the part of the nave that hung over the hillside. The Romanesque vaulting and carved decoration is more Maestro Mateo mastery. Look at the medieval musical instruments—models of the impressively realistic ones featured in Mateo's heavenly Portico of Glory.

Gelmírez Palace (Pazo de Xelmírez)—Though the rooms of this now-empty medieval home (the traditional residence of the archbishop) are stark and stony, the attraction here is the opportunity to walk on the rooftop of the cathedral. The experience offers little more than a fine view and a chance to burn your clothes at the cross—a once-common practice for pilgrims. You can visit the palace and rooftop only with a one-hour tour, which is usually in Spanish; try dropping by or calling ahead to see if an English tour is scheduled, and to reserve a spot (€10, or €8 if you bought a ticket to the Cathedral Museum, tours depart hourly 10:00–14:00 & 16:00–20:00, tel. 981-552-985, www.archicompostela.org).

Cathedral Squares

There is a square on each side of the cathedral. You've already visited Praza do Obradoiro, in the front. Here are the other three, working clockwise (to reach the first one, go up the passage—which street musicians appreciate for its acoustics—to the left as you're facing the main cathedral facade).

Praza da Inmaculada—This was the way most medieval pilgrims using the French Road actually approached the cathedral. Across the square is **St. Martin's Monastery** (Mosteiro de San Martiño Pinario), one of two monasteries that sprang up around the church to care for pilgrims. Today, it houses a museum of ecclesiastical artifacts and special exhibits. To the left of the monastery's main door is a fun multimedia exhibit called "Galicia Dixital" (see description later in this chapter).

Walk to the corner of the square with the arcade, and go to the post with the sign for Rúa da Acibechería (next to the garbage can, under the streetlight). If you look to the roof of the cathedral, between the big dome and the tall tower, you can make out a small green cross. This is where the clothes of medieval pilgrims were burned when they finally arrived at Santiago. This ritual was created for hygienic reasons in an age of frightful diseases...and filthy pilgrims.

• *Continue along the arcade and around the corner, and you'll enter...*

Praza Quintana—The door of the cathedral facing this square is the Holy Door, only opened during Holy Years. There's St. James, flanked by the disciples who brought his body back to Galicia. Below them are more Biblical characters, perhaps the 12 apostles and 12 prophets. Tip: Old Testament prophets hold scrolls. New Testament apostles hold books.

Across the square from the cathedral stands the imposing **St. Pelayo Monastery** (Mosteiro San Paio). The windows of its cells (now used by Benedictine sisters—notice the bars and privacy screens) face the cathedral. The church at the north end of this monastery is worth a peek. It has a frilly Baroque altar and a statue with a typical Galician theme: a pregnant Mary (to the left as you face main altar). The nuns sing at the evening vespers following the 19:30 Mass (Mon–Sat). Just off this sanctuary is the entrance to the monastery's **Sacred Art Museum** (Museo de Arte Sacra), with a small but interesting collection (€1.50, Mon–Sat 10:30–14:00 & 16:00–19:00, closed Sun). The nuns of St. Pelayo make Galicia's famous *tarta de Santiago*—almond cake with a cross of Santiago in powdered sugar dusted on top. To buy one, exit the church to the right, head up the stairs, and walk around behind the monastery to find the entrance on Rúa de San Paio de Antealtares. Once inside, go to the small window on the left (generally open Mon–Sat 9:00–14:00 & 15:00–19:00; they only sell entire cakes—a big one for €10 and a very big one for €18).

• *Continue around to the...*

Praza das Praterías—This "Silversmiths' Square" is where Santiago's silver workers used to have their shops (and some still do). Overlooking the square is a tall **tower.** Imagine the fortified cathedral complex before the decorative Baroque frills were added; it looked more like a hulking fortress for fending off invading enemies from Normans to Moors to English pirates.

The **fountain** features a woman sitting on St. James' tomb, holding aloft a star—a typical city symbol. The mansion facing the cathedral is actually a collection of buildings with a thin-yet-effective Galician Baroque facade built to give the square architectural harmony. Its centerpiece even copies the fountain's star.

Beyond the fountain, a few steps down Rúa do Vilar (on the left) is the **Office for Pilgrims.** While tourists aren't really welcome in here, this is where pilgrims stop to pick up their *compostela*, the certificate that documents their successful *camino*. (The adjacent gift shop displays a copy of one in its window.)

More Sights

▲▲Market (Praza de Abastos)—This wonderful market, housed in Old World stone buildings, offers a fine opportunity to

do some serious people-watching (Mon–Sat 8:00–14:00, closed Sun). Monday's the least interesting day, since the fishermen don't go out on Sunday. It's busiest and best on Thursday and Saturday, when villagers from the countryside come to sell things.

The market was built in the 1920s (to consolidate Santiago's many small markets) in a style perfectly compatible with the medieval wonder that surrounds it. Today it offers an opportunity to get up close and personal with some still-twitching seafood. Keep an eye out for the specialties you'll want to try later—octopus, shrimp, crabs, lobsters, and expensive-as-gold *percebes* (barnacles; see sidebar in "Eating in Santiago"). You'll also see the local *chorizo* (spicy sausage).

Grelos are a local type of turnip greens with a thick stalk and long, narrow leaves—grown only here, and often used in the *caldo galego* soup. The little green *pimientos de padrón* (in season June–Oct) look like jalapeños, but lack the kick...sometimes.

In the cheese cases, you'll see what look like huge yellow Hershey's Kisses...or breasts. This cheese is called *tetilla* (breasts). According to local legend, artists at the cathedral sculpted a woman very curvaceously and the locals loved it. The bishop made them redo the statue with less sexy lines, so the locals got even by making their cheese look like breasts. Through the centuries since, Santiago has been full of tasty reminders of a woman's physical beauty.

▲Museum of Pilgrimages (Museo das Peregrinacións)—This museum examines various aspects of the pilgrimage phenomenon. You'll see a map of pilgrimage sites around the world, and then learn more about the pilgrimage that brings people to Santiago. There are models of earlier versions of the cathedral, explanations of the differing depictions of St. James throughout history (apostle, pilgrim, and Crusader), and coverage of the various routes to Santiago and stories of some prominent pilgrims. This well-presented place lends historical context to all of those backpackers you see in the streets. While exhibits are not described in English, the thorough info sheets available throughout the museum are well worth reading (usually free, sometimes €2.40, Tue–Fri 10:00–20:00, Sat 10:30–13:30 & 17:00–20:00, Sun 10:30–13:30, closed Mon, Rúa de San Miguel 4—but they plan to move to Praza das Praterías in 2011, tel. 981-581-558, www.mdperegrinacions.com).

Galicia Dixital—Housed in the St. Martin's Monastery, this futuristic, kid-friendly exhibit uses various kinds of technology to explore Galicia and Santiago in virtual reality. You'll visit several exhibits, accompanied by a Spanish-speaking guide. First you'll take a 3-D surround-sound tour of the squares around the cathedral. Then you go on *A Vertixe*—which means "the vertigo," as you'll soon learn. A motion-simulator 3-D "roller-coaster" ride zips you around the top of the cathedral, then underground. You can don a *casco virtual* ("virtual helmet") and wander through the cathedral. Other 3-D movies include a submarine trip through Galicia's waterways for a look at sealife, and an animated tour of the cathedral with a strange little pilgrim creature. While enjoyable, you can't shake the feeling that you could step outside and see most of this stuff in person (free, Mon–Sat 10:30–14:00 & 16:00–20:30, closed Sun; must go on one-hour guided visits, which leave about every 30 min; last visits begin at 13:00 and 19:30, tel. 981-554-048).

Museum of the Galician People (Museo do Pobo Galego)—This museum gives insights into rural Galician life. As you tour this collection, remember that if you side-trip a few miles into the countryside, you'll find traditional lifestyles thriving even today.

Beautifully displayed around an 18th-century cloister, the museum springs from a unique triple staircase, which provided privacy to various hierarchies of the monks who lived here, depending on which stairway you climbed. The collection shows off boat-building and fishing techniques, farming implements and simple horse-drawn carts, tools of trade and handicrafts (including carpentry, pottery, looms, and baskets), traditional costumes, and a collection of musical instruments, with an emphasis on the bagpipes *(gaitas)*. If the farm tools seem old-fashioned, there's a reason: Old inheritance laws mean that plots are increasingly smaller, so modern farming machinery is impractical—keeping traditional equipment alive. There's virtually no English, except for a helpful €1.50 guidebook (free entry, Tue–Sat 10:00–14:00 & 16:00–20:00, Sun 11:00–14:00, closed Mon, at northeast edge of historical center in monastery of San Domingos de Bonaval, just beyond Porta do Camiño, tel. 981-583-620, www.museodopobo.es). Behind the museum is a plush and peaceful park—once crowded with tombstones.

Next door, in the striking modern building, is the **Galician Contemporary Art Museum** (Centro Galego de Arte Contemporánea), with continually rotating exhibits—mostly by local artists (free, Tue–Sun 11:00–20:00, closed Mon, tel. 981-546-619, www.cgac.org).

City of Culture of Galicia (Cidade da Cultura de Galicia)—This super-modern cultural complex is being built on a hillside near Santiago de Compostela. Based on an incredibly ambitious conceptual design that's proving far more costly to implement than expected, the project is intended to put Santiago on the map as a 21st-century city (similar to Bilbao's Guggenheim). These days the complex is becoming something of a white elephant, as delays and an ever-inflating price tag are giving local residents a taste of builders' remorse. Even if it does get finished, locals don't know what it will contain...except megalomania (www.cidadedacultura.es).

Entertainment in Santiago

Street Music—You'll likely hear bagpipes (*gaitas*) being played in the streets of Santiago. Nobody knows for certain how this unlikely instrument caught on in Galicia, but the tradition has supposedly been passed down since the Celts lived here. (Bagpipes seem to be unique to Celts like the Scottish and Irish but nearly all ethnic groups have had bagpipes in their past. If anything, the Celts just endured their sound more willingly.) Some singers use bagpipes, too, including Milladoiro (a group popular with Galicians in their 40s and 50s) and Carlos Nuñez (trendy with younger people today). Caped university students, called *tunas*, can be seen singing traditional songs (without bagpipes) around town every night during the summer.

Galician Folk-Music Concerts—While the summertime is lively with folk-music concerts (ask for details at the TI), the rest of the year is not. One good bet is to drop by a practice session of the troupe called Cantigas e Agarimos (meets Wed and Fri at 21:30 for an hour, maybe at Rúa da Algalia de Arriba 11 or possibly playing at a nearby location—confirm schedule at TI, tel. 981-581-257). Since 1921, this group has shared the traditional Galician culture with visitors in performances throughout the year.

Sleep Code

(€1 = about $1.40, country code: 34)
S = Single, **D** = Double/Twin, **T** = Triple, **Q** = Quad, **b** = bathroom, **s** = shower only. Unless otherwise noted, credit cards are accepted, English is spoken, and breakfast generally costs extra.

    To help you easily sort through these listings, I've divided the rooms into three categories, based on the price for a standard double room with bath:

  $$$ **Higher Priced**—Most rooms €85 or more.
   $$ **Moderately Priced**—Most rooms between €50–85.
    $ **Lower Priced**—Most rooms €50 or less.

Sleeping in Santiago

To cater to all those pilgrims, Santiago has a glut of cheap, basic accommodations. There aren't many affordable big hotels in town for tour groups, so they tend to stay along the Rías Baixas (fjord-like estuaries) about an hour to the south, where beds are cheap. That means many of Santiago's visitors are day-trippers, arriving at about 10:30 and leaving in the afternoon. After dark, it's just you, the locals, the pilgrims, and St. James. High season is roughly Easter through September; most places charge more during this time. The trickiest dates to book are Easter Sunday weekend and the Feast of St. James (July 24–25)—so if you plan to be in town around these times, reserve your rooms well ahead. When I list a range of prices, it represents low season to high season. Any single prices listed are an average (midseason). The *hostales* speak enough English to make a reservation by phone (though sometimes not much more).

    $$$ Altaïr Hotel is owned by the Liñares family (see later Costa Vella listing), but caters to a different clientele. Located in a renovated three-story residence, its 11 spacious rooms and mod decor can best be described as "rustic minimalist." Exposed stone walls and open beams mixed with a sleek design provide a unique yet surprisingly affordable experience (Sb-€70–80, Db-€90–110, superior Db-€110–130, extra bed-€20, breakfast free with this book in 2010, free Wi-Fi, request a non-smoking room, affordable laundry service for guests, Rúa dos Loureiros 12, tel. & fax 981-554-712, www.altairhotel.net, info@altairhotel.net).

    $$$ Hostal dos Reis Católicos (Hospital of the Catholic Monarchs) was founded by the Catholic Monarchs at the beginning of the 16th century to care for pilgrims arriving from the Camino. It was converted into an upscale parador 50 years ago.

Santiago Hotels and Restaurants

1. Altaïr Hotel
2. Hostal dos Reis Católicos, Dos Reis & Enaxebre Rest.
3. Hotel Virxe da Cerca
4. Hotel Residencia Costa Vella, Pension Girasol & Café Costa Vella
5. Hotel Arias Nunes
6. Hotel San Clemente
7. Hotel Pombal
8. Hostal Suso
9. Hospedaje Ramos
10. Hostal Residencia Giadás
11. Casa Marcelo Restaurante
12. El Mercadito Restaurante
13. O Gato Negro
14. A Curtidoría Restaurante
15. O Beiro Vinoteca
16. Restaurante Casa Manolo
17. O Dezaseis Restaurante
18. Cotolay Bar Restaurante
19. La Bodeguilla de San Roque
20. Triángulo das Verduras Vegetarian Rest.
21. Café Casino

This grand building has 137 rooms surrounding a series of four courtyards packed with Santiago history. It has the best address in Santiago...and prices to match (standard Db-€265 including tax and breakfast, Praza do Obradoiro 1, tel. 981-582-200, fax 981-563-094, santiago@parador.es). This place still remembers its roots, offering a free breakfast to pilgrims who've hiked the Camino (the first 10 to arrive each day—usually around 8:00).

$$$ Hotel Virxe da Cerca is on the edge of the historical center, across the street from the market. Its standard rooms are in a modern building, but some of its "superior" and all of its "special" historic rooms—with classy old stone and hardwoods—are in a restored 18th-century Jesuit residence. While the modern rooms feel particularly impersonal, all 43 rooms surround a lush garden oasis (standard Db-€85–105, superior Db-€10 extra, bigger "special" Db-€20 extra, breakfast-€10, beautiful glassed-in breakfast room overlooks garden, elevator, free Internet access and Wi-Fi, Rúa da Virxe da Cerca 27, tel. 981-569-350, fax 981-586-925, www.pousadasdecompostela.com, vdacerca@pousadasdecompostela.com).

$$ Hotel Residencia Costa Vella is my favorite spot in Santiago, with 14 comfortable rooms combining classic charm and modern comforts. The glassed-in breakfast room and lounge terrace overlook a peaceful garden, with lovely views of a nearby church and monastery and into the countryside beyond. They deserve a feature in *Better Stones and Tiles* magazine (Sb-€55, standard Db-€75, Db with balcony-€90, breakfast-€6, 10 percent discount in winter, free Wi-Fi, affordable laundry service for guests, parking-€10/day, Rúa da Porta da Pena 17, tel. 981-569-530, fax 981-569-531, www.costavella.com, hotelcostavella@costavella.com, friendly José, Roberto, and wonderful staff).

$$ Hotel Airas Nunes, Hotel San Clemente, and **Hotel Pombal** are affiliated with Hotel Virxe da Cerca. They're uniformly good, stress-free, and professional-feeling, all located in restored old buildings with classy touches. All three hotels charge €6 for breakfast and €20 for extra beds, and share the same contact info (tel. 981-569-350, www.pousadasdecompostela.com, info@pousadasdecompostela.com). Hotel Airas Nunes is deep in the old center a few blocks in front of the cathedral (10 rooms, Db-€70–95, Rúa do Vilar 17, reception tel. 981-554-706). Hotel San Clemente is just outside the historical center (Db-€70–95, Rúa de San Clemente 28, reception tel. 981-569-260). Hotel Pombal is a slight step up from the other two in terms of quality and price. Situated in Alameda Park, many of its rooms offer great views of the cathedral (Db-€80–95, €10 more for views, Rúa do Pombal 12, reception tel. 981-552-645).

$ Hostal Suso, run by the four Quintela brothers, is a great value offering 10 inexpensive, new-feeling rooms around an airy atrium over a cheery—if smoky—little bar in the heart of Santiago (Sb-€20, Db-€40–45, breakfast-€3–5, Rúa do Vilar 65, tel. 981-586-611, hostalsuso@gmail.com).

$ Hospedaje Ramos rents 10 big, tasteful, clean rooms right in the center. It has lots of stairs, which is a blessing since they take you farther away from the night noise (Sb-€23, Db-€36, includes tax, no breakfast, Rúa da Raiña 18, tel. 981-581-859, Louis speaks a few words of English).

$ Hostal Residencia Giadás, tucked away just beyond the market, faces a tidy little square as if it owns it. The eight rooms, some with slanted floors, are simple but charming (Sb-€28–32, Db-€45–49, Tb-€60–66, elevator, next to Porta do Camiño at Praza do Matadoiro 2, tel. 981-587-071, lolagiadas@gmail.com, delightful Lola and the Giadás family).

$ Pension Girasol rents 12 decent rooms above a cheery cafeteria for a good price in a great neighborhood (S-€20–22, Sb-€35–40, D-€36–40, Db-€45–50, Porta da Pena 4, tel. 981-566-287, www.hgirasol.com, girasol@hgirasol.com).

Eating in Santiago

Strolling through the streets of Santiago is like visiting a well-stocked aquarium: Windows proudly display every form of edible

sealife, including giant toothy fish, scallops and clams of every shape and size, monstrous shrimp, and—most importantly—octopus. The fertile fjords of the Galician coast are just 20 miles away, and the region's many fishing villages keep the capital city swimming in seafood. As the seafood is so fresh, the focus here is on purity rather than sauces. The seafood is served simple—generally just steamed or grilled, and seasoned only with a little olive oil, onions, peppers, and paprika.

Tasting octopus *(pulpo)* is obligatory in Galicia; it's most often prepared *a la gallega* (also called *pulpo a feira*): After the octopus is beaten to tenderize it, then boiled in a copper pot, its tentacles are snipped into bite-size pieces with scissors. It's topped with virgin olive oil, coarse sea salt, and a mixture of sweet and spicy paprika, then served on a round wooden plate. Eat it with toothpicks, never a fork. It's usually accompanied by large hunks of country bread to sop up the olive oil, and washed down by local red *mencia* or white *ribeiro* wine, often served in little saucer-like ceramic cups (*cunca*).

Not a fan of seafood? You can slurp the *caldo galego*, a traditional broth that originally came from the leftover stock used to prepare an elaborate Sunday feast (cabbage or *grelos*, potatoes, and so on—not too exciting, but providing comfort on a rainy day). Starting in July, look for *pimientos de padrón*—miniature green peppers sautéed in olive oil with a heavy dose of rock salt.

Restaurants generally serve lunch from 13:00 to 16:00 and dinner from 20:00 until very late (Spaniards don't start dinner until about 21:00). It's frustrating to try to eat before the locals do. If you find a restaurant serving before 13:00 or 21:00, you'll be all alone with a few sorry-looking tourists. Early-bird eaters should know that ordering a drink at any bar will generally get you a free tapa—Santiago is one of the few places in Spain that still honors this tradition.

For a quick meal on the go, grab a traditional meat pie, or *empanada*, which comes *de carne* (with pork), *de bonito* or *de atún* (tuna), *de bacalao* (salted cod), *de zamburiñas* (tiny scallops), *de berberechos* (cockles)—and these days, even *de pulpo* (octopus).

And for dessert: Locals enjoy *queixo con mel* (cheese with honey) at the end of a meal. In the tourist zones, bakeries push samples of *tarta de Santiago*, the local almond cake. Historically, the cake was cooked by sisters in Santiago's convents.

Gourmet Dining, Modern Cuisine

Casa Marcelo, Santiago's elite gourmet restaurant, earned a Michelin star for its international cuisine. If you want to dine elegantly and have the money, this dressy 11-table is the place. For €60 (plus wine) you get a fixed-price meal featuring the chef's seasonal specials. The kitchen is in plain view, so you'll get caught up in the excitement of cooking (lunch Tue–Sat, dinner Thu–Sat, closed Sun–Mon, reservations required—usually days in advance, down the steep lane below the cathedral, at Rúa das Hortas 1, tel. 981-558-580).

El Mercadito Restaurante is a classy but trendy eight-table establishment with a following among locals. It seems that Chef Gonzalo Rei is going for a Michelin star with his well-presented and creative contemporary cuisine. He serves only an eight-course, €45 tasting menu (closed Sun–Tue, hike below the cathedral, past Casa Marcelo to Rúa das Galeras 18, tel. 981-574-239).

Restaurant Row in the Old Center: Rúa do Franco

Since hungry pilgrims first filled the city in the Middle Ages, Rúa do Franco (named not for the dictator but for the first French pilgrims) has been lined with eateries and bars. Today this street, which leads away from the cathedral, remains lively with foreign visitors—both tourists and pilgrims. There are plenty of seafood places, a few time-warp dives, and several lively bars with little €1.50 *montaditos* (sandwiches) for the grabbing. I'd stroll it once to see what appeals, and then go back to eat. **O Gato Negro,** a smoky, no-frills seafood tapas bar stuck in the past and filled with loyal locals, is worth seeking out. It's one of the last places to serve *ribeiro* wine in a ceramic cup (near Rúa do Franco at Rúa da Raiña).

Memorable Eating in the Old Center

A Curtidoría Restaurante ("The Tannery") is a modern, spacious, and romantic place in the old town, rare for its open feeling. While the food is nothing exceptional, the setting is enjoyable and it's a solid value (lunch special menu, paella and fish, €15–20 per plate, Rúa da Conga 2, tel. 981-554-342).

O Beiro Vinoteca, designed to show off the fine wines of Galicia and Spain, serves by the glass from a huge menu and complements its wine with simple, appropriate *raciones*. Run by Pepe Beiro, it's much classier than your average tapas bar. The tasting action is on the ground floor while the tables for dining are upstairs. If you drop in for just a glass of wine, you'll get a free tapa (closed Sun, half a block from cathedral at Rúa da Raiña 3, tel. 981-581-370).

Hostal dos Reis Católicos, the fancy old hospital sharing the square with the cathedral, has two fine restaurants. The main restaurant, **Dos Reis,** fills a former stable with a dramatic stone vault. It offers international dishes—often with live piano and nearly dead guests. A typical parador restaurant, it comes with stiff tuxedoed service, white tablecloths, and not a hint of fun (daily, tel. 981-582-200). Surprisingly, a few steps away is a wonderful alternative; **Enxebre** has a livelier easygoing-tavern vibe, good traditional Galician food, and reasonable prices (€5–14 dishes, daily, tel. 981-050-527).

Restaurante Casa Manolo serves only one thing: an €8.50 fixed-price meal. It's where students on a tight budget go for a classy meal out. This smart little family-run eatery combines sleek contemporary design, decent Galician and Spanish food, and excellent prices. The service is rushed (which is a good thing if you're in a hurry), but the value is unbeatable (for €8.50 you get two generous courses, water, bread, and dessert; arrive when they open or plan on waiting; Mon–Sat lunch 13:00–16:00, dinner 20:00–23:30, Sun lunch only, at the bottom of Praza de Cervantes, tel. 981-582-950).

SANTIAGO DE COMPOSTELA

Percebes = Barnacles

Local barnacles, called *percebes,* are a delicacy. Since they grow only on rocks that see a lot of dangerous waves, it takes specialists—a team of two gatherers— to harvest them; one with a rope tied to his waist, the other spotting him from above. Because of the danger, barnacles are really expensive. You'll see them stacked in the windows of seafood bars that charge about €7 per 100 grams ($40 a pound). Check the price carefully and confirm it clearly. There are variations that can cost many times that already expensive figure. Two beers and a small 100-gram plate to split make a wonderful snack. Just twist, rip, and bite—it's a bit like munching the necks off of butter clams. I ask for toasted bread on the side.

For the freshest *percebes* at half the price—and twice the experience—buy them from any fisherwoman at the market. Let Ramon or Maria at Churro-Mania boil them for you right there in their market café. They'll boil up any seafood you buy in the market (it takes just a few minutes), charging €3 per person for table service, plus 10 percent of your market bill; you must bring the receipt for whatever they're cooking up for you (Mon–Sat 11:00–14:00, closed Sun, aisle 5 in the market, mobile 616-911-228).

Budget Values Away from the Tourist Center

O Dezaseis ("The Sixteen") is every local's favorite (and mine too). As soon as you walk down into its sprawling, high-energy vaulted dining room, you know this is the best place in town. In-the-know locals are dining under stone walls, heavy beams, and modern art while enjoying friendly service. You can choose from meat and fish plates (€11–14), but simply ordering one *ración* per person (€4–11) and splitting their hearty mixed salad for some veggies makes a fine and inexpensive meal. They do octopus just right here and have good wines at good prices (closed Sun, reservations smart, Rúa de San Pedro 16, tel. 981-564-880).

Cotolay Bar Restaurante and two adjacent bar-restaurants are a hit with locals for drinks with free tapas. They are good budget bets for a meal of *raciones* without the tourists (€5–9 *raciones*, closed Sun, Rúa de San Clemente, tel. 981-573-014).

La Bodeguilla de San Roque offers a good selection of *raciones* and wines in a relaxed neighborhood atmosphere. If the upstairs restaurant is full, have a drink at the bar to pass the time

SANTIAGO DE COMPOSTELA

(€5–8 *raciones*, Rúa da San Roque 13, tel. 981-564-379).

Triángulo das Verduras Vegetarian Restaurant is a homey place providing a healthy break from all the ham and tapas and a chance to hang out with a different local crowd (closed Tue, €8 plates and salads, Praza das Peñas 2, tel. 981-576-212).

Cafés

Café Costa Vella, actually the breakfast room and garden of a highly recommended hotel (see earlier listing), is a little Eden tucked just beyond the tourist zone. The café welcomes non-guests for coffee and a relaxing break in a poetic time-warp garden with leafy views (great €3 toasted sandwiches, plus a wide array of drinks, daily 8:00–23:00, Rúa da Porta da Pena 17, tel. 981-569-530).

Café Casino, a former private club, is a tired taste of turn-of-the-20th-century elegance with occasional live piano music. Local tour guides recommend this café to their timid British groups, who wouldn't touch an octopus with a 10-foot pole. While they have sandwiches and salads, I would just consider this an elegant coffee or tea stop (Rúa do Vilar 35).

Connections

From Santiago de Compostela by Train to: Madrid (2/day, 8–9.5 hrs, overnight train departs at 22:35, arrives in Madrid Chamartín at 7:45), **Salamanca** (take train to Zamora—2/day, 5 hrs—then transfer to hourly bus for 1-hr ride to Salamanca), **León** (1/day direct, 6 hrs), **Bilbao** (1/day direct, 11 hrs), **San Sebastián** (1/day direct, 11 hrs), **Santander** (1/day, 13 hrs, transfer in Palencia), **Lugo** (3/day, 3–4 hrs, requires transfer in A Coruña—bus is better), **Porto,** Portugal (2/day via Vigo, 3.25 hrs). Train info: tel. 902-240-202, www.renfe.es.

By Bus to: Lugo (7/day, 2 hrs), **Madrid** (5/day, 8 hrs, includes night bus 21:30–6:30, arrives at Estación Sur), **Salamanca** (2/day, 1 with a transfer in Vigo, 7 hrs), **Astorga** (5/day, 5 hrs), **León** (5/day, 7 hrs), **Burgos** (1 night bus/day, 23:15–6:15), **Bilbao** (3/day, 2 continue to **San Sebastián,** includes 2 night buses, 9.5–12 hrs to Bilbao, 1.5 hrs more to San Sebastián), **Porto,** Portugal (2/day, 4 hrs). Bus info: tel. 981-542-416. All long-distance destinations are served by the Alsa bus company (tel. 902-422-242, www.alsa.es).

CANTABRIA

If you're connecting the Basque Country and Galicia (Santiago de Compostela) along the coast, you'll go through the provinces of Cantabria and Asturias. Both are interesting, but Cantabria (kahn-TAH-bree-ah) has a few villages and sights that are especially worth a visit. The quaint town of Santillana del Mar makes a fine home base for visiting the prehistoric Altamira Caves replica. Comillas is a pleasant beach town.

The dramatic peaks of the Picos de Europa and their rolling foothills define this region, giving it a more rugged feel than the "Northern Riviera" ambience of the Basque region. A drive through the Cantabrian countryside is rewarded with endless glimpses of charming stone homes. Though it's largely undiscovered by Americans, Cantabria is heavily touristed by Europeans in July and August, when it can get very crowded.

Planning Your Time

Cantabria doesn't rank high on the list of sightseeing priorities in Spain. Don't go out of your way to get here. However, if you're passing through, there are some charming diversions along the way. A night or two in this region breaks up the long drive from Bilbao to Santiago (figure over seven hours straight through).

Assuming you're coming from San Sebastián, this is a good plan:

Day 1: Leave San Sebastián early for the Guggenheim in Bilbao (trip takes about an hour by expressway, longer along the coast). After seeing the museum, continue on to explore (and sleep in) Santillana del Mar or Comillas. If you arrive early enough,

Cantabria

PICOS DE EUROPA

ATLANTIC OCEAN

SANTANDER

To PLYMOUTH, ENGLAND

LAREDO

N-634

To BILBAO & SAN SEBASTIÁN

A-8

SANTILLANA DEL MAR

COMILLAS

ALTAMIRA CAVES

C A N T A B R I A

N-623

To BURGOS & MADRID

A-67

SAN VICENTE

UNQUERA

A-8

N-621

PANES

POTES

N-611

To PALENCIA

RIBA-DESELLA

LLANES

COVA-DONGA

C-6312

PUENTE PONCEBOS

FUENTE DÉ

POR-TILLA

CARES GORGE

CAÍN

RIAÑO

ASTURIAS

GIJÓN

A-8

N-634 CANGAS DE ONIS

N-625

To OVIEDO & SANTIAGO

To LEÓN

20 MILES
30 KM

DCH

CANTABRIA

you might have time to see the Altamira Caves (near Santillana) tonight.

Day 2: Troglodytes will want to visit the Altamira Caves replica right when it opens (9:30). Hikers and high-mountain fans will make a beeline for Fuente Dé in the Picos de Europa. If you get an early start on either of these attractions, you can still make it to Santiago de Compostela by the end of a very long day (figure six hours from this region to Santiago). It's saner to sleep a second night in this area, in which case it's possible (though rushed) to do both the caves and the mountains on Day 2.

Getting Around Cantabria

This region is best by car; public transportation is complicated, and the payoffs are not so great. Unless they have a special interest in prehistoric art, non-drivers will want to skip Cantabria.

By Car: Drivers enjoy Cantabria. The A-8 expressway runs roughly along the coast from San Sebastián to Gijón, where it becomes an express two-lane highway the rest of the way to A Coruña in Galicia. To reach Santillana del Mar and Comillas, follow signs to *A-67* (a jog off the expressway toward Santander), then take the exit for CA-131 (signed for *Santillana del Mar*). This highway takes you through Santillana, Comillas, and San Vicente de la Barquera. After San Vicente, in Unquera, CA-131 intersects with N-621, which leads south through La Hermida Gorge into the Picos de Europa (follow signs for *Potes*). If you want to go directly to the Picos, there's an exit for N-621 directly off the A-8 expressway.

By Bus: Without a car, you'll rely on the bus from the port city of Santander—Cantabria's capital and transportation hub. Buses run from Santander to Santillana del Mar, Comillas, and San Vicente de la Barquera (5–7/day each way, about 35 min from Santander to Santillana, then 15 min to Comillas, then 15 more min to San Vicente, tel. 942-720-822, www.santandereabus.com).

A different bus goes from Santander to Potes in the Picos de Europa (2–3/day, 2.25 hours, tel. 942-880-611). There's also a bus from León to Potes, but only in summer (1/day, 3 hours).

By Train: Santander, the region's public transportation hub, is connected by train with **Madrid** (3/day, 4.5–5 hours, Chamartín Station), **Bilbao** (3/day, 3 hours on FEVE), and **Santiago de Compostela** (1/day, 13 hrs, transfer in Palencia). A scenic train line called the FEVE runs from Bilbao to Santander and to Ovideo, but it's not particularly helpful for visiting the destinations in this chapter (www.feve.es).

Santillana del Mar

Every guidebook imparts the same two tidbits about Santillana del Mar: One is that it's known as the "town of three lies," as it's nei-

ther holy *(santi)*, nor flat *(llana)*, nor on the ocean *(del Mar)*. The other is that the existentialist philosopher Jean-Paul Sartre once called it the "prettiest village in Spain."

The town is worth the fuss. Santillana is a proud little stone village, with charming time-warp qualities that have (barely) survived the stampede of multinational tour groups here to visit the nearby Altamira Caves. Despite it all, the town is what Spaniards would call *preciosa*.

Santillana is three cobbled streets and a collection of squares, climbing up over mild hills from where the village meets the main road. While Santillana has several sights that cater to the tourist throngs (including a much-promoted zoo), the only sight that makes a visit worthwhile—aside from the town itself—is the cave paintings of Altamira in the nearby countryside (see "Altamira Caves," on page 286).

Tourist Information: The modern TI is right at the entrance to the town (daily July–mid-Sept 9:00–21:00, off-season 9:30–13:30 & 16:00–19:00, Jesús Otero 20, tel. 942-818-251). Only residents (and guests of hotels that offer parking) are allowed to drive in the center—leave your car in the big lot by the TI (pay in-season, free off-season).

Sleeping in Santillana

Santillana makes a good home base for visiting the region and the caves. My listings are right in town; you'll find the first three places on Santillana's main square, Plaza Ramón Pelayo. The fourth is farther up, just around the corner (to the right) from the big Collegiate Church.

$$$ Paradores: Two swanky, arrogant *paradores* hold court on the main square—**Parador de Santillana** (Sb-€137, Db-€144–173 depending on amenities, breakfast-€17, Plaza Ramón Pelayo 11, tel. 942-818-000, fax 942-818-391, santillana@parador.es) and **Parador de Santillana Gil Blas** (Sb-€127, Db-€159–278 depending on amenities, breakfast-€16, same address, tel. 942-028-028, fax 942-818-391, santillanagb@parador.es).

CANTABRIA

Sleep Code

(€1 = about $1.40, country code: 34)
S = Single, **D** = Double/Twin, **T** = Triple, **Q** = Quad, **b** = bathroom, **s** = shower only. Unless otherwise noted, English is spoken, credit cards are accepted, and tax is not included. Prices vary with season (highest July–Aug and Holy Week). I've listed shoulder- and peak-season rates.

To help you sort easily through these listings, I've divided the rooms into three categories based on the price for a standard double room with bath:

$$$ Higher Priced—Most rooms €110 or more.
$$ Moderately Priced—Most rooms between €70–110.
$ Lower Priced—Most rooms €70 or less.

$$ Hotel Altamira offers 32 well-priced rooms in an atmospheric 16th-century palace on the main square (Sb-€50–55, standard Db-€72–84, big Db with sitting room a worthwhile splurge at €82–100, 20 percent more in Aug and Holy Week, cheaper Nov–March, extra bed-€20, breakfast-€5.50, Calle Cantón 1, tel. 942-818-025, fax 942-840-136, www.hotelaltamira.com, info @hotelaltamira.com).

$ Hospedaje Octavio is a fine budget option with 11 comfortable wood-beamed rooms (Db-€30–40 depending on season, cheaper for bathroom on the hall, Plaza Las Arenas 4, tel. & fax 942-818-199, pensioncasaoctavio@gmail.com, Octavio and Milagros don't speak English but their sons do).

Altamira Caves

Not far from Santillana del Mar is a replica of a cave containing some of the best examples of prehistoric art anywhere. In 1879, the young daughter of a local archaeologist discovered several 14,000-year-old paintings in a limestone cave. By the 1960s and 1970s, it became a tremendously popular tourist destination. All of the visitors got to be too much for the delicate paintings, and the cave was closed in 1979. But now a replica cave and museum have opened near the original site, allowing visitors to once again experience these pieces of prehistoric artwork, in something approximating their original setting.

Cost, Hours, Location: €3, free Sat from 14:30 and Sun; May–Oct Tue–Sat 9:30–20:00, can be open even later some nights in summer, Sun 9:30–15:00, closed Mon; Nov–April Tue–Sat 9:30–18:00, Sun 9:30–15:00, closed Mon; last tour departs 30 min before closing (tel. 942-818-815, http://museodealtamira.mcu .es). The caves are on a ridge in the countryside a little over a mile southwest of Santillana del Mar. There's no public transportation to the site. To get from Santillana del Mar to the caves, it's either a 30-minute walk or a taxi ride (mobile 608-483-441). Bolder travelers hitch a ride with a friendly tour bus.

Visiting the Caves: While you can't actually visit the original caves, prehistoric-art fans will still find Altamira worth the trip. Your visit has two parts: First, there's a fine museum with good English descriptions, featuring models and reproductions of the cave dwellers who made these drawings (and their clothes, tools, and remains). Videos and illuminated pictures help bring these people to life. The second part is a 30-minute guided tour of the highly detailed replica cave. Unfortunately, English-speakers get no respect at Altamira: Posted information in English is measly, and tours in English are rare. If your guide speaks English, ask if he or she will translate the highlights for you. Otherwise, follow along with my self-guided tour, below.

Note that if all you're really interested in is the art itself, other replicas are on display in the National Archaeological Museum in Madrid (just the paintings, not the cave experience); see page 360. Remember—what you'll see at Altamira are replicas, too.

Reservations: Only 240 people are allowed to enter the replica caves each hour (20 people/tour, tours leave every 5 min—or when enough people gather, never more than a 30-min wait). This means that in the busy summer season, spaces fill up fast. In July and August and on free Sundays, they recommend getting to the museum when it opens (9:30) to claim your tour appointment.

Better yet, make an advance reservation (no extra charge) through the bank Santander Centro Hispano—drop by a branch, or even easier, call them (tel. 902-242-424, wait through recording and ask for English-speaker). You can also make a reservation (for Tue–Sat) online using a credit card; go to http://museodealtamira .mcu.es and look for the link to the bank (in Spanish only). Request a specific date and time (one-hour window) for your tour. At the caves, pass any wait time by exploring the museum.

Self-Guided Tour

You'll begin the tour by watching a four-minute film about the various inhabitants of the cave, the discovery of the paintings in 1879, and the era of over-visitation. Then the guide leads you into the first part of the cave, where you're on your own for English information. The English descriptions that the guide eagerly points out are marginally helpful. So here's what your guide is talking about:

In the Cave

Remember that this isn't the actual cave. It's a painstaking replica (called *Neocueva*, or "Neo-cave"), achieved with special computers, so that the cave art can still be enjoyed without endangering the actual paintings. The Neo-cave also simulates the original cave's temperature, sounds, and humidity.

About 14,000 years ago, hunters, gatherers, and fishermen lived in these caves. They huddled around a fire, protected from the elements. They liked the location because of its proximity to the ocean and a river.

Excavation Site

This area displays tools used by modern scientists to dig up relics from various periods. We're talking about the Upper Paleolithic era—the time of Cro-Magnon cave people, with big hands and high foreheads. The Upper Paleolithic is divided into three periods, and this cave was inhabited, on two separate occasions, during two of those periods: the Solutrean (about 18,500 years ago) and the Magdalenian (14,000 years ago). You'll see that there are three layers to the excavation: On the bottom are artifacts from Solutrean cavemen (hunting tools and chips of flint); above that is mostly clay, with the remains of a cave bear you'll see in a few minutes; and the top layer holds hearths and tools from the Magdalenian period.

As you continue on to the next stop, you'll pass the bones of a cave bear that once lived in Altamira. Nearby, look for his paw prints.

Artists' Workshop

See the tools used by the prehistoric artists, as well as a video showing how the paintings were created. The most dramatic paintings—all the red buffaloes—were made with reddish ochre dissolved in water, outlined in black charcoal. Marrow-burning stone lamps provided light. Many of the images were engraved into the surface of the cave (using flint) before being painted. The reproductions in this Neo-cave were done using the same techniques.

Art!

Finally we reach the paintings themselves. While most tourists gasp, some hum the *Flintstones* theme.

This part of the cave has various names, including the "Great

Hall," the "Polychrome Room," or even "the Sistine Chapel of Prehistoric Art." The ledge with the lights shows the floor level of the original cave. This didn't give the cavemen much room to paint, making their creations even more remarkable. Among the fauna in this room are 16 bison, a couple of running boars, some horses, and a giant deer—plus a few handprints and several mysterious symbols.

Unfortunately, the posted English information ends here. These are some of the things to look for (as your guide is pointing them out to the ooh-ing and ahh-ing Spaniards in your group):

Bumps and Cracks: Notice that the artists incorporated the ceiling's many topographical features into their creations (see the bison with the large, swollen back, or the one with the big head).

Overlap: Some paintings actually overlap onto each other. These were painted during two different eras. (The most impressive batch—including all those bison—is thought to be by the same artist.)

Detail: While a few paintings are incomplete, others are finished. Check out the bison with the highly detailed hooves and beard.

The "Old Horse": The horse with its back against the wall is probably among the oldest in the cave.

The "Great Deer": The biggest painting of all (over seven feet across) is the deer with the little black bison under his chin. Notice it's not quite in proportion; due to the tight quarters, the artist couldn't take a step back to survey his work.

Symbols: The strange hieroglyphic-like symbols scattered around the cave, called tectiforms, are difficult to interpret. Scientists have found very similar symbols in caves that were far apart, and wondered if they were some sort of primitive written language (for example, an outline of a horse with a particular symbol might explain how to set traps for hunting).

Behavior: The artists captured not only the form, but also the behavior of the animals they depicted. Notice the lowing bison; the curled-up bison; the bison turning its head; and the running boars (with the extra legs).

What's amazing about these paintings is simply that they were made by Cro-Magnon cave people. And yet, the artists had an amazing grasp of delicate composition, depicting these animals with such true-to-life simplicity. Some of them are mere outlines, a couple of curvy lines—masterful abstraction that could make Picasso jealous.

So why did they make these paintings? Nobody knows for sure. General agreement is that it's not simply for decoration, and that it must have served some religious or shamanistic purpose.

CANTABRIA

Final Cave

The most impressive paintings were discovered in a single room (whose replica you just visited). However, beyond that room, the cave extended another several hundred feet, though that area was not reproduced. As you leave this replica cave, you'll see a few more replicas—mostly carvings—that came from other parts of the original cave. Most of them are those mysterious symbols, but at the very end you'll also see three masks carved into the rock.

And with that, your cave visit is over. Yabba dabba doo!

Comillas

Just 15 minutes beyond Santillana del Mar, perched on a hill overlooking the Atlantic, you'll find quirky Comillas. Comillas

presides over a sandy beach, but feels more like a hill town, with twisty lanes clambering up away from the sea. Comillas is not as undeniably charming as Santillana—it would do well to go traffic-free, as its neighbor has. But it makes for a fine home base if you prefer beach access and a more lived-in feel to touristy quaintness.

Most notably, Comillas also enjoys a surprising abundance of striking Modernista architecture. Three buildings line up along a ridge at the west end of town (just beyond the town center and parking lot, over the big park). Antoni Gaudí, Barcelona's favorite son, designed a villa here called El Capricho—now a restaurant (see below). Next door is the pointy spire of a 17th-century church, and at the end of the row is the Palace of Sobrellano, by Gaudí's mentor Joan Martorell, which hints at early Barcelona-style Modernisme. Peering back at these buildings from a parallel ridge is the huge Pontifical University building, decorated by yet another early-20th-century Catalan architect, Lluís Domènech i Muntaner. These Modernista masterpieces are compliments of Don Antonio López y López, who left Spain to find fortune in America. He returned to Barcelona (where he acquired a taste for Gaudí and company) and eventually became the Marquis of Comillas.

The beachside road below is lined with tacky tourist hotels, but the town center, up on the hill, is much more pleasant—with an odd jumble of squares surrounding the big Parochial Church.

CANTABRIA

Tourist Information: The westernmost square, Plaza Joaquín de Piélagos, is where you'll find the TI (unpredictable hours, posted as July–Aug daily 9:00–21:00; Sept–June Mon–Sat 10:30–13:30 & 16:30–19:30, Sun 10:30–13:30, but often closed; Calle Aldea 6, tel. 942-720-768).

Sleeping in Comillas

($1 = about €1.40, country code: 34)
Both of these listings are in the town center, south of the big Parochial Church, near the long, skinny restaurant-lined Plaza de Primo de Rivera (also known as "El Corro"). The first hotel is the big red building a block off the south end of the square; the other is a few blocks above the square, on the uphill street with the blue-trimmed railing.

$$ Hotel Marina de Campíos offers 20 modern, colorful rooms, each one named for a different opera (standard Db-€70–110, "junior" Db-€95–130, "senior" Db-€140–160, higher prices are for mid-July–Aug, includes breakfast and tax, hotel closed mid-Dec–mid-Jan, elevator, Calle General Piélagos 14, tel. 942-722-754, fax 942-722-749, www.marinadecampios.com, reservas @marinadecampios.com).

$ Pasaje San Jorge, with 11 basic but comfortable rooms in a 100-year-old house, hovers just over the town center (Db-€60–65, or €70 July–Aug and Holy Week, cheaper off-season, includes breakfast and tax, Calle Carlos Díaz de la Campa 16, tel. & fax 942-720-915, www.pasajesanjorge.com, pasajesanjorge@pasajesan jorge.com).

Eating in Comillas

El Capricho is a surprising piece of Antoni Gaudí architecture hiding on a ridge above Comillas' center. The sunflower-dappled exterior alludes to Gaudí's plan for the building: His "sunflower design" attempted to maximize exposure to sunshine by arranging rooms so that they would get sun during the part of the day that they were most used. Today, the building is an exclusive-feeling restaurant serving traditional Spanish cuisine. Look around the back for the sculpture of the architect admiring his work. Don't even try to get inside if you're not eating here. Reservations are smart, especially in season (€20–30 entrées, Mon–Sat 13:00–16:00 & 21:00–23:30, Sun 13:00–16:00 only; shorter hours in winter—lunch ends at 15:30 and dinner at 23:00, also closed Mon; tel. 942-720-365). There are two roads to this hard-to-find restaurant; both are at the west end of town, and both are sometimes closed. Ask locally for directions.

Near Comillas: San Vicente de la Barquera

As you continue west from Comillas, the road becomes bumpy and follows the coast, soon crossing a wide bay over a long, dramatic bridge to San Vicente de la Barquera. This salty seaside resort overlooks a boat-filled harbor, with glimpses of the dramatic Picos de Europa in the distance.

Picos de Europa

The Picos de Europa—comprising one of Spain's most popular national parks—are a relatively small stretch of cut-glass mountain peaks (the steepest in Spain, some taller than 8,500 feet) just 15 miles inland from the ocean. These dramatic mountains are home to goats, brown bears, eagles, vultures, wallcreepers (rare birds), and happy hikers. Outdoorsy types could spend days exploring this dramatic patch of Spain, which is packed with visitors in the summer. For our purposes, we'll focus on the two most important excursions: taking the Fuente Dé funicular up to a mountaintop, and hiking the yawning chasm of the Cares Gorge.

Orientation

The Picos de Europa are a patch of mountains covering an area of about 25 miles by 25 miles. They're located where three of Spain's regions converge: Cantabria, Asturias, and León. (Frustratingly, each region's tourist office pretends that the parts of the park in the other regions don't exist—so it's very hard to get information, say, about Asturias' Cares Gorge in Potes, Cantabria.) In addition to three regions, the park contains three different limestone massifs, or large masses of rock, separated by rivers.

As you venture into the Picos de Europa, pick up a good map; the green 1:80,000-scale map that you'll see is handy, featuring roads, trails, and topographical features. Serious hikers will want a guidebook (I like the Sunflower guide, published by a British company—www.sunflowerbooks.co.uk). These resources, along with a wide variety of other maps and books, are available locally.

I'll focus on the Cantabrian part of the Picos, which contains the region's most accessible and enjoyable bits: the scenic drive through La Hermida Gorge, the charming mountain town of Potes, and the sky-high views from the top of the Fuente Dé cable car. This part of the Picos is doable as a long day trip from Santillana del Mar or Comillas (but is easier if you stay in Potes). The next best activity (in León and Asturias, not Cantabria) is the Cares Gorge

hike—deeper in the park and requiring another full day.

Getting Around the Picos de Europa

The Picos de Europa are best with a car. If you don't have wheels, skip it, because bus connections are sparse, time-consuming, and frustrating (see "Getting Around Cantabria," page 284).

The A-8 expressway squeezes between the Picos and the north coast of Spain; roads branch into and around the Picos, but beware: Many of them traverse high-mountain passes—often on bad roads—and can take longer to drive through than you expect. *Puerto* means "pass" (slow going) and *desfiladero* means "gorge" (quicker but often still twisty).

Assuming you're most interested in Potes and Fuente Dé, you'll focus on the east part of the park, approaching from the A-8 expressway (or from Santillana del Mar and Comillas). You'll go through Unquera and catch N-621 into the park (follow signs for *Potes*). Wind your way through La Hermida Gorge (Desfiladero de la Hermida) en route to Potes.

The Cares Gorge can be approached from either the south (the village of Caín, deep in the mountains beyond Potes) or the north (Puente Poncebos, with easier access).

If you're really serious about tackling the region, and want to do both Fuente Dé and the Cares Gorge, the most sensible plan is this: On Day 1, drive from Comillas/Santillana del Mar to Potes and do the Fuente Dé cable car and hike (sleep in Potes); on Day 2, day-trip to the Cares Gorge hike via Caín (sleep in Potes); and on Day 3, move on to your next destination.

Sights in the Picos de Europa

I've arranged these sights as you'll come to them if you approach from the northeast (that is, from the expressway, Santillana del Mar, or Comillas).

Potes—This quaint mountain village, at the intersection of four valleys, is the hub of Cantabria's Picos de Europa tourist facilities. It's got an impressive old convent and a picturesque stone bridge spanning the Río Deva. It's a good place to buy maps and books. Check in at the **TI** with any travel questions (unpredictable hours, but generally July–Sept daily 10:00–14:00 & 16:00–19:00; less off-season—often closed Sun and Mon afternoons and all day Tue; Plaza de las Serna s/n, tel. 942-730-787).

Sleeping in Potes: **$ Casa Cayo** has 17 cozy rooms and a fine restaurant that overlooks the river (Sb-€35, Db-€50, Tb-€65, but these rates could go up due to major renovations, tax included but breakfast extra, closed Christmas–Feb, Calle Cántabra 6, tel. 942-730-150, fax 942-730-119, www.casacayo.com, informacion @casacayo.com).

▲▲**Fuente Dé Cable Car (Teleférico Fuente Dé)**—Perhaps the single most thrilling activity in Picos de Europa is to take the cable car at Fuente Dé. The longest single-span cable car in Europe zips you up 2,600 feet in just four ear-popping minutes, but in summer, you may have to wait more than two hours to take it. Once at the top (altitude 6,000 feet), you're rewarded with a breathtaking panorama of the Picos de Europa. The huge, pointy Matterhorn-like peak on your right is Peña Remoña (7,350 feet). The cable-car station on top has WCs, a cafeteria (commanding views, miserable food), and a gift shop (limited hiking guides— equip yourself before you ascend).

Once you're up there, those with enough time and strong knees should consider hiking back down. From the cable-car station at the top, follow the yellow-and-white signs to *Espinama*, always bearing to the right. You'll hike gradually uphill (gain about 300 feet), then down (3,500 feet) the back side of the mountain, with totally different views than the cable-car ride up: green, rolling hills instead of sharp, white peaks. Once in Espinama, you'll continue down along the main road back to the parking lot at the base of the cable car (signs to *Fuente Dé*). Figure about four hours total (nine miles) from the top back to the bottom. Note that the trails are covered by snow into April, and sometimes even May; ask at the ranger station near Potes about conditions before you hike (see "Information," on next page).

Cost, Hours, Location: €14 round-trip, €8 one-way (if you're hiking down), every 30 minutes (or with demand), daily in summer 9:00–20:00, in winter 10:00–18:00, closed Jan unless weather is unseasonably good. When it's busy, there are constant departures. Note that this is a very popular destination in summer, and you may have to wait in long lines both to ascend and to descend (up to 2.5 hours in early Aug, 1 hour in late July; quieter in June, early July, and Sept—if you're concerned, call ahead to find out how long the wait is before you make the 14-mile drive from Potes). The road dead-ends at Fuente Dé, so you'll have to backtrack to return to Potes. If you're relying on public transportation, you can take the bus from Potes to Fuente Dé (2/day)—but it runs only in summer.

Information: Cable car tel. 942-736-610. The Picos de Europa National Park runs a helpful information kiosk in the parking lot during peak season (July–Aug), with handouts and advice on hikes (including the one described above). Even better, stop at the bigger National Park office on the way to Fuente Dé from Potes; about a mile after you leave Potes, look on the right for the green *Picos de Europa* signs (daily in summer 9:00–20:00, in winter 9:00–18:00, tel. 942-730-555).

▲**Cares Gorge (Garganta del Cares)**—This impressive gorge hike—surrounded on both sides by sheer cliff walls, with a long-distance drop running parallel to (and sometimes under) the trail—is ideal for hardy hikers. The trail was built in the 1940s to maintain the hydroelectric canal that runs through the mountains, but today it has become an extremely popular summer-hiking destination. The trail follows the Río Cares seven miles between the towns of Caín (in the south) and Camarmeña (near Puente Poncebos, in the north). Along the way, you'll cross harrowing bridges and take trails burrowed into the rock face. Because it's deeper in the mountains and requires a good six hours (13 miles round-trip, with some ups and downs), it's best left to those who are really up for a hike and not simply passing through the Picos. Visitors who just want a glimpse will hike only partway in before heading back.

Getting There: To reach Caín from Potes, you'll drive on rough, twisty roads (N-621) over the stunning Puerto de San Gloria pass (5,250 feet, watched over by a sweet bronze deer), into a green, moss-covered gorge. Just past the village of Portilla de la Reina, turn right (following signs for *Santa Marina de Valdeón*) to reach Caín. Note that this is a very long day trip from Potes, and almost brutal if home-basing in Comillas or Santillana del Mar.

The approach to the gorge from the north (Puente Poncebos) is easier, but won't take you near Potes and Fuente Dé. You can reach Puente Poncebos via AS-114 to Las Arenas, then follow the Cares River on AS-264 to Puente Poncebos.

CANTABRIA

SALAMANCA

This sunny sandstone city boasts Spain's grandest plaza, its oldest university, and a fascinating history, all swaddled in a strolling, college-town ambience. Salamanca—a youthful and untouristy Toledo—is a series of monuments and clusters of cloisters. The many students help keep prices down. Take a paseo with the local crowd down Calle de Rúa Mayor and through Plaza Mayor. The young people congregate until late in the night, chanting and cheering, talking and singing. When I asked a local woman why young men all alone on Plaza Mayor suddenly break into song, she said, "Doesn't it happen where you live?"

Planning Your Time

Salamanca, with its art, university, and atmospheric Plaza Mayor, is worth a day and a night, but it is stuck out in the boonies. It's feasible as a side-trip from Madrid (it's 2.5 hours one-way from Madrid by car, bus, or train), even with a stop in Ávila on the way. If you're bound for Santiago de Compostela or Portugal, Salamanca is a natural stop.

Orientation

Tourist Information

The main TI is on **Plaza Mayor** (summer: Mon–Fri 9:00–14:00 & 16:30–20:00, Sat 10:00–20:00, Sun 10:00–14:00; winter: Mon–Sat until 18:30, Sun until 14:00; Plaza Mayor 19, tel. 923-218-342). Pick

Salamanca

TO BULLRING

FRANCIA

BUS STATION

TO MAIN TRAIN STATION (½ MILE)

AV. DE CHAMPAGNAT

AV. DE VILLACOBOS

AV. F.VILLALOBOS

CAMPO SAN FRAN.

DR.T.VILLA

AV. DE MIRAT

PLAZA DE ESPAÑA

Le Mans

Camp.

ZAMORA

TORO

ESTACIÓN

ALAMEDILLA PARQUE

❸

POST

PLAZA MAYOR

PLAZA DE LAS AUGUSTINAS

RAMON

PRIOR

PL. SANTA EULALIA

AZAFRANAL

❷

VISTA

CANALEJA

❶

TO

❹

CASA DE LOS CONCHES ✝ ℹ

S. ANT.

UNIVERSITY

ℹ

MAYOR

MKT.

BUS TO TRAIN STN.

CATHEDRALS
OLD (SMALLER) + NEW

ANTIGUA

PLAZA ANAYA

CALLE SAN PABLO

SAN JUSTO

GRAN VIA

PASEO

SAN VICENTE

RIBERA D. PUENTE

LAS DUEÑAS

SAN ESTEBAN

CASA LIS

PASEO RECTOR ESPERABÉ

RIO

PUENTE ROMANO

ART NOUVEAU MUSEUM

PARQUE FLUVIAL

TO E-3 CIUDAD RODRIGO + COIMBRA (PORTUGAL)

PUENTE NUEVO

PRINCIPE ASTURIAS

TORMES

🔭 VIEW

P PARKING

☐ SEE DETAIL MAP

400 YARDS

400 METERS

DCH

TO N-501 + SEGOVIA

❶ Le Petit Hotel

❷ Rest. La Fonda Casa de Comidas del Arcediano

❸ Carrefour Express Supermarket

❹ To Salamanca Alamedilla Train Station

up the free map, city brochure, and current list of museum hours.

Another TI at **Casa de Las Conchas** on Calle de Rúa Mayor serves the region and province, as well as the city (July–mid-Sept daily 9:00–20:00; mid-Sept–June Mon–Sat 9:30–14:00 & 16:00–19:00, Sun 9:30–17:00; tel. 923-268-571). Summertime-only TIs spring up at the train and bus stations.

The TI website (www.salamanca.es) is a good source of practical information, including a printable city-center map *(Plano de la ciudad)* and directions on how to arrive from various points in

Spain. Unfortunately, Salamanca offers relatively little in the way of organized tourism for the English-speaking visitor.

Arrival in Salamanca

From either Salamanca's train or bus station to Plaza Mayor, it's a 25-minute walk, an easy bus ride (€0.85, pay driver), or a €5 trip by taxi. The train station has no lockers; day-trippers can store bags at the bus station (*consignas*; €2, at bay level facing main building on your left).

By Train: Salamanca has two train stations: the main train station and (a bit closer to the town center) the Salamanca Alamedilla train station. To walk from the main train station into the center, exit left and walk down to the ring road, cross it at Plaza de España, then angle slightly left up Calle Azafranal. Alternatively, from the main station you can take bus #1, which lets you off at Plaza del Mercado (the market), next to Plaza Mayor. Some trains continue on to the Salamanca Alamedilla train station, which is closer to town: Walk down Avenida Alamedilla past a park to Plaza de España, then to Calle Azafranal. Note that you cannot depart from or buy tickets at the Alamedilla Station.

By Bus: To walk into the center, exit right and walk down Avenida Filiberto Villalobos; take a left on the ring road and the first right on Ramón y Cajal, head through Plaza de las Augustinas, and continue on Calle Prior to reach Plaza Mayor. Or take bus #4 (exit station right, catch bus on same side of the street as the station) to the city center; the closest stop is on Gran Vía, about two blocks east of Plaza Mayor (ask the driver or a fellow passenger, "*¿Para Plaza Mayor?*").

By Car: Drivers will find a handy underground parking lot at Plaza Santa Eulalia (€11.50/day, open 24 hours daily). Two other convenient lots are Parking Plaza del Campillo and Parking Lemans (€13.50/day).

Helpful Hints

Book Ahead for September: A religious festival fills up hotels and increases room prices.

Internet Access: Cyberplace Internet is at Plaza Mayor 10 (Mon–Fri 11:00–23:00, Sat–Sun 16:00–23:00, first floor, tel. 923-264-281). **Navega Internet Center,** nearby, has several computers and a call center, and sells phone cards (Mon–Sat 11:00–24:00, Sun 16:00–24:00, between Plaza del Mercado and Gran Vía at Obispo Jarrín 14, tel. 923-215-447). Perhaps your most efficient Internet access is at the laundry (see below).

Laundry: It's a five-minute walk from Plaza Mayor to the self-service launderette, which also has five Internet terminals

(€6.50/load for wash and dry, €2/hr for Internet access, Mon–Fri 10:00–14:00 & 16:00–20:00, Sat 10:00–14:00, closed Sun and Aug 15–30; Pasaje Azafranal 18, located in passageway a half-block north of Plaza Santa Eulalia; tel. 923-260-216, helpful Juan Carlos).

Travel Agency: Viajes Salamanca books flights, trains, and some buses, including buses to Coimbra, Portugal (Calle Prior 11, tel. 923-211-414).

Local Guide: Ines Criado Velasco, a good English-speaking guide, is happy to tailor a town walk to your interests (€80/2 hrs—a special rate for readers of this book in 2010, €95/3–5 hrs, €150/day, for groups of 1–30, tel. 923-207-414, mobile 609-557-528, inescriado@yahoo.es).

Tourist Tram: The small tram you might see waiting at the New Cathedral does 20-minute loops through town with Spanish narration (€3.80, daily 10:00–14:00 & 16:00–20:00, departs every 30 min from cathedral, mobile 649-625-703).

Sights in Salamanca

▲▲**Plaza Mayor**—Built from 1729 to 1755, this ultimate Spanish plaza is a fine place to nurse a cup of coffee (try the venerable Art Nouveau–style Café Novelty) and watch the world go by.

The town hall, with the clock, grandly overlooks the square. The Arco del Toro (built into the eastern wall) leads to the covered market. While most European squares honor a king or saint, this golden-toned square—ringed by famous Castilians—is for

all the people. The square niches above the colonnade surrounding the plaza depict writers (Miguel de Cervantes), heroes and conquistadors (Christopher Columbus and Hernán Cortés), as well as numerous kings and dictators (Francisco Franco).

Plaza Mayor has long been Salamanca's community living room. The most important place in town, it seems to be continually hosting some kind of party. Imagine the excitement of the days (until 1893) when bullfights were held in the square. Now old-timers gather here each day, remembering an earlier time when the girls would promenade clockwise around the colonnade while the boys cruised counterclockwise, looking for the perfect *queso* (cheese), as they'd call a cute dish. Perhaps the best time of all for people-watching is Sunday after Mass (13:00–15:00), when the grandmothers gather here in their Sunday best.

Cheap Tricks in Salamanca

- Drinks ordered at a bar usually come with a free *pincho*, a taste of one of the larger portions of tapas. Sometimes you can even choose between several options. You can have a light meal for the price of three drinks while standing or sitting at the bar. Try the Cervantes Bar.
- Remember that you can linger at any bar, café, or restaurant as long as you like. Have a two-hour coffee in one of the Plaza Mayor cafés, or simply plop yourself down in the middle of the square and watch the paseo without spending a *céntimo*.
- Free sights include the New Cathedral and the Museum of the University. The University is free on Monday morning, and the Old Cathedral tower is free on Tuesday from 10:00 to 12:00.
- Readers with PDAs or smartphones running Windows Mobile can download a free detailed guide to Salamanca at www.salamanca.es (click on the "for your PDA" link).

▲▲**Cathedrals, Old and New**—These cool-on-a-hot-day cathedrals share buttresses, and are both richly ornamented. You get to the old through the new. Before entering the New Cathedral, check out its ornate front door (west portal on Rúa Mayor). The **facade** is decorated Plateresque, with masonry so intricate it looks like silverwork *(plata)*. It's Spain's version of Flamboyant Gothic. At the side door (around the corner to the left as you face the main entrance), look for the astronaut added by a capricious restorer in 1993. This caused an outrage in town, but now locals shrug their shoulders and say, "He's the person closest to God." I'll give you a chance to find him on your own. Otherwise, look at the end of this listing for help.

The **"New" Cathedral** was built from 1513 to 1733 and is a spacious, towering mix of Gothic, Renaissance, and Baroque. Fancy stone trim is everywhere, and the dome decoration is particularly wonderful. Occasionally the music is live, not recorded. The *coro*, or choir, blocks up half of the church (normal for Spanish Gothic), but its wood carving is sumptuous; look up to see the recently restored, elaborate organ (free; daily April–Sept 9:00–20:00, sometimes closed 14:00–16:00; Oct–March 9:00–13:00 & 16:00–18:00).

The entrance to the **Old Cathedral** (12th-century Roman-esque) is near the rear of the new one (€4.50, free English leaflet; daily April–Sept 10:00–19:30, sometimes closed 13:30–16:00; Oct–March 10:00–12:30 & 16:00–17:30; if you attend Mass in the Old Cathedral, entry is free, but the cloister isn't). Sit in a front pew to study the altarpiece's 53 scenes from the lives of Mary and Jesus (by the Italian Florentino, 1445) surrounding a precious 12th-century statue of the Virgin of the Valley. High above, notice the dramatic Last Judgment fresco of Jesus sending condemned souls into the literal jaws of hell.

Head into the **cloister** (off the right transept) and explore the chapels, notable for their unusual tombs, ornate altarpieces, and ceilings with leering faces. If you speak Spanish, press the button on the wall at the entrance of each chapel to hear a description. In the Capilla de Santa Barbara (second on the left as you enter), you can sit like students did for their tests. During these final exams, a stern circle of professors formed around the student at the tomb of the Salamanca bishop, who founded the University of Salamanca around 1230. (The university originated with a group of teacher-priests who met in this room.)

As you continue through the cloister, you'll see the chapter-house *(salas capitulares)*, contained in three rooms on your left, with a gallery of 15th-century Castilian paintings. Next is the Capilla de Santa Catalina, with two rows of spooky saint statues and two original gargoyles from the cathedral, in the form of a seahorse and a frog. The Capilla de Anaya, farthest from the cloister entrance, has a gorgeously carved 16th-century alabaster tomb (with the dog and lion at its foot making peace—or negotiating who gets to eat the worried-looking rabbit) and a wooden 16th-century Mudejar organ. (Mudejar is the Romanesque-Islamic Moorish design style made in Spain after the Christian conquest.)

For a fantastic view of the upper floors and terraces of both cathedrals, and a look at the inside passages with small exhibits about the cathedrals' history and architecture, visit the **tower** (marked *Jerónimos*). It was sealed after Lisbon's 1755 earthquake to create structural support and reopened in 2002. You may be able to reach the tower from inside the Old Cathedral (this entrance is open sporadically); if not, exit the cathedral to the left to find a separate entrance around the corner (free Tue 10:00–12:00, otherwise €3.50, daily 10:00–20:00, Jan–Feb until 18:00, last entry 45 min before closing).

Finally, go find that astronaut: He's just a little guy, about the size of a Ken-does-Mars doll, entwined in the stone trim to the left of the door, roughly 10 feet up. If you like that, check out the dragon (an arm's length below). Historians debate whether he's eating an ice-cream cone or singing karaoke.

▲▲**University**—The University of Salamanca, the oldest in Spain (est. 1230), was one of Europe's leading centers of learning for 400 years. Columbus came here for travel tips. Today, while no longer so prestigious, it's laden with history and popular with Americans, who enjoy its excellent summer program. The old lecture halls around the cloister, where many of Spain's

Golden Age heroes studied, are open to the public (€4, free Mon mornings, Mon–Fri 9:30–13:30 & 16:00–19:30, Sat until 19:00, Sun 10:00–13:30, last entry 30 min before closing, enter from Calle Libreros, tel. 923-294-400, ext. 1150).

The ornately decorated grand **entrance** of the university is a great example of Spain's Plateresque style. The people studying the facade aren't art fans. They're trying to find a tiny frog on a skull that students looked to for good luck.

But forget the frog. Follow the facade's symbolic meaning. It was made in three sections by Charles V. The bottom celebrates the Catholic Monarchs. Ferdinand and Isabel saw that the university had no buildings befitting its prestige, and they granted the money for this building. The Greek script says something like "From the monarchs, this university. From the university, this tribute as a thanks."

The immodest middle section celebrates the grandson of Ferdinand and Isabel, Charles V. He appears with his queen, as well as the Habsburg double-headed eagle and the complex coat of arms of the mighty Habsburg Empire. Since this is a Renaissance structure, it features Greek and Roman figures in the shells. And, as a statement of educational independence from medieval Church control, the top shows the pope flanked by Hercules and Venus.

After paying admission, you get a free English-language leaflet full of details; to follow it, go left (clockwise around the courtyard) upon entering.

In the **Hall of Fray Luis de León,** the narrow wooden-beam tables and benches—whittled down by centuries of studious doodling—are originals. Professors spoke from the Church-threatening *cátedra,* or pulpit. It was here that freethinking brother Luis de León returned, after the Inquisition jailed and tortured him for five years for challenging the Church's control of the word of God by translating part of the Bible into Castilian. He started his first post-imprisonment lecture with, "As we were saying..." Such courageous men of truth believed the forces of the Inquisition were not even worth acknowledging.

The altarpiece in the chapel on the opposite side of the court-yard depicts professors swearing to Mary's virginity. (How did they know?) Climb upstairs for a peek into the oldest library in Spain. Outside the library, look into the courtyard at the American sequoia, brought here 150 years ago and standing all alone. Notice also the big nests in the bell tower. Storks stop here from February through August on their annual journey from Morocco to north-ern Europe. There are hundreds of such stork nests in Salamanca.

As you leave the university, you'll see the statue of Fray Luis de León. Behind him, to your left, is the entrance to a peaceful courtyard. Within the courtyard is the Museum of the University, notable for Gallego's fanciful 15th-century *Sky of Salamanca* (free, Tue–Sat 10:00–14:00 & 16:00–20:00, Sun 10:00–14:00, closed Mon, no photos allowed).

Can't forget about the frog? It's on the right pillar of the facade, nearly halfway up, on the leftmost of three skulls.

▲Art Nouveau Museum (Museo Art Nouveau y Art Deco)— Located in the Casa Lis, this museum—with its beautifully dis-played collection of stained glass, vases, furniture, jewelry, cancan statuettes, and toy dolls—is a refreshing change of pace. Nowhere else in Spain will you enjoy an Art Nouveau collection in a build-ing from the same era. Find the stunning sculptures of Josephine Baker and Carmen Miranda, along with lots of pieces by René Lalique. The museum is a donation of a private collection. The English brochure contains a translation of the Spanish text posted in each room of the collection (€3, mid-Oct–March Tue–Fri 11:00–14:00 & 16:00–19:00, Sat–Sun 11:00–20:00; April–mid-Oct Tue–Fri 11:00–14:00 & 17:00–21:00, Sat–Sun 11:00–21:00; closed Mon, strictly no photos—required camera check at ticket counter, between the cathedrals and the river at Calle Gibraltar 14, tel. 923-121-425, www.museocasalis.org).

Church of San Esteban—Dedicated to St. Stephen (Esteban) the martyr, this complex contains a recently restored cloister, tombs, museum, sacristy, and church. The visitors' entrance is to the right of the church entrance, which is closed except during services.

Before you enter, notice the Plateresque facade and its bas-relief of the stoning of St. Stephen. The crucifixion above is by Italian Renaissance artist Benvenuto Cellini.

After buying your ticket, walk around the cloister to the opposite corner, where signs indicate ways to the church *(iglesia)*, sacristy *(sacristía)*, choir *(coro)*, and museum *(museo)*. Head to the church first. Once inside, follow the free English pamphlet. The nave is overwhelmed by a 100-foot, 4,000-piece wood altarpiece by José Benito Churriguera (1665–1725) that replaced the original Gothic one in 1693. You'll see St. Dominic on the left, St. Francis on the right, and a grand monstrance holding the Communion wafers in the middle, all below a painting of St. Stephen being stoned. This is a textbook example of the intricately detailed Churrigueresque style that influenced many South American mission buildings. Quietly ponder the dusty, gold-plated cottage cheese, as tourists shake their heads and say "too much" in their mother tongue.

Upstairs, step into the balcony choir loft for a fine overview of the nave. The staircase itself is architecturally unique, built without any interior support; the staircase is still standing, but you'll notice that when you walk, you definitely lean inward. The big spinnable book holder in the middle of the room held giant music books—large enough for all to chant from in an age when there weren't enough books for everyone.

The museum next door has temperature-controlled glass cases that preserve illustrated 14th- to 16th-century Bibles and choir books. Notice also how the curved ivory Filipino saints all look like they're carved out of an elephant's tusk. And don't miss the fascinating "chocolate box reliquaries" on the wall from 1580. Survey whose bones are collected between all the inlaid ivory and precious woods (€3, Mon–Tue 16:00–20:00, Wed–Sat 10:00–14:00 & 16:00–20:00, Sun 10:00–14:00, closes at 19:00 Tue–Sat in winter, last entry 45 min before closing, tel. 923-215-000).

Convento de las Dueñas—Located next door to the Church of San Esteban, the much simpler *convento* is a joy. It consists of a double-decker cloister with a small museum of religious art. Check out the stone meanies exuberantly decorating the capitals on the cloister's upper deck (€2, Mon–Sat in summer 10:30–12:45 & 16:30–18:45, in winter 11:00–12:45 & 16:30–17:30, closed Sun, no English info). The nuns sell sweets daily except Sunday (€4.50 for a small box of their specialty, *amarguillos*—almonds, egg whites, and sugar; no assortments possible even though their display box raises hopes).

Roman Bridge—Historians enjoy the low-slung Roman Bridge (Puente Romano), much of it original, spanning the Río Tormes. The *ibérico* (ancient pre-Roman) faceless bull blindly guards the entrance to the bridge; you'll find this symbol of Salamanca on every city coat of arms in town.

▲*Tuna* **Music**—Traditionally, Salamanca's poorer students earned money to fund their education by singing in the streets. This 15th- to 18th-century tradition survives today, as musical groups of students (representing the various faculties)—dressed in the traditional black capes and leggings—sing and strum mandolins and guitars. They serenade the public in the bars on and around Plaza Mayor. The name *tuna,* which has nothing to do with fish, refers to a vagabond student lifestyle, and later was applied to the music these students sing. They're out only on summer weeknights (singing for tips from 22:00 until after midnight), because they make more serious money performing for weddings on weekends.

Sleeping in Salamanca

Salamanca, a student town, has plenty of good eating and sleeping values. All but one of my listings (Le Petit Hotel) are on or within a three-minute walk of Plaza Mayor. Directions are given from Plaza Mayor, assuming you are facing the building with the clock (e.g., 3 o'clock is 90 degrees to your right as you face the clock). The city is noisy on the weekends, so if you're a light sleeper, ask for an interior room.

$$$ Petit Palace Las Torres, on Plaza Mayor, is a remodeled chain hotel with 53 modern, spacious rooms (several with see-through bathroom doors), and all the amenities (Sb-€60–150, Db-€60–170, Tb-€90–220, lower prices are for non-view rooms and weekdays, higher prices are for Plaza Mayor views and weekends, 30 percent more during religious festival in Sept, breakfast-€8, air-con, elevator, free Wi-Fi and Internet access in lobby, a few free loaner bikes, pay parking at nearby Lemans lot, exit Plaza Mayor at 11 o'clock to find hotel entry just off square at Calle Concejo 4, tel. 923-212-100, fax 923-212-101, www.hthotels.com, tor@hthotels.com).

$$$ Hotel Torre del Clavero has little character, but its 26 rooms are clean and contemporary. It's conveniently located between Plaza Mayor and the Church of San Esteban, across the

---

Sleep Code

(€1 = about $1.40, country code: 34)
S = Single, **D** = Double/Twin, **T** = Triple, **Q** = Quad, **b** = bathroom, **s** = shower only. Unless otherwise noted, credit cards are accepted, English is spoken, and the IVA tax (7 percent) and breakfast are not included.

To help you easily sort through these listings, I've divided the rooms into three categories, based on the price for a standard double room with bath during high season:

  $$$ Higher Priced—Most rooms €70 or more.
    $$ Moderately Priced—Most rooms between €40-70.
      $ Lower Priced—Most rooms €40 or less.

Central Salamanca

Buildings Around Plaza Mayor

(B) **Bus Stop**

1. Petit Palace Las Torres
2. Hotel Torre del Clavero
3. Hotel Room Mate Vega
4. Hostal Plaza Mayor
5. To Le Petit Hotel & Rest. La Fonda Casa de Comidas del Arcediano
6. Hostería Casa Vallejo
7. Hostal Los Angeles & Internet Café
8. Hostal Las Vegas Centro
9. Restaurante Chez Victor
10. Café Real
11. Cervantes Bar Restaurant
12. Café Novelty
13. Mesón de las Conchas
14. Restaurante Isidro & Restaurante Comercio
15. Launderette & Internet Access
16. Internet Café

SALAMANCA

street from the Clavero tower. Its private garage is a plus for drivers (Sb-€45–72, Db-€80–125, higher rates are for weekends and holidays, extra bed-€25, breakfast-€7.50, parking-€11/day; from Casa de las Conchas on Calle de Rúa Mayor, go three blocks south on Calle de Jesús to Calle del Consuelo 21, or from Gran Vía turn onto Calle de las Varillas then left onto Calle del Consuelo; tel. 923-280-410, fax 923-217-708, www.hoteltorredelclavero.com, info@hoteltorredelclavero.com).

$$$ Hotel Room Mate Vega, across the street from the covered market, has mod wannabe-hip business-class rooms in a good location (Sb-€65, Db-€80, Tb-€110, more on weekends and holidays, includes breakfast, air-con, elevator, free Wi-Fi and Internet access, parking-€9/day, 2 blocks off Plaza Mayor, across from covered market, exit Plaza Mayor at 3 o'clock, Plaza del Mercado 16, tel. 923-272-250, fax 923-270-932, www.room-matehotels.com, vega@room-matehotels.com).

$$ Hostal Plaza Mayor, with 19 finely decorated but small rooms, has a good location a block southwest of Plaza Mayor (Sb-€30–36, Db-€50–60, Tb-€75–90, air-con, most rooms served by elevator, attached restaurant, exit Plaza Mayor at 7 o'clock, Plaza del Corrillo 20, tel. 923-262-020, fax 923-217-548, www.hostal plazamayor.es, hostalplazamayor@hotmail.com).

$$ Le Petit Hotel, while away from the characteristic core, faces a peaceful park and a church, two blocks east of Gran Vía. It rents 23 spotless and homey yet modern rooms. The rooms with views of the church are brightest, and the fourth floor has been recently renovated—request *vista de iglesia* and *cuarta planta* (Sb-€36, Db-€49, Tb-€59, Qb-€69, breakfast-€4, cash only, air-con, elevator, desk staffed but phone not answered after 22:30, about six blocks east of Plaza Mayor at Ronda Sancti Spiritus 39; exit Plaza Mayor at 3 o'clock and continue east, turn left on Gran Vía, right on Sancti Spiritus at Banco Simeon, and left after the church; tel. 923-600-773, www.lepetithotel.net, reserve by simply calling and leaving your name and time of arrival no more than 15 days in advance, Hortensia doesn't speak English).

$$ Hostería Casa Vallejo is family-run and welcoming, with 12 rustic and renovated rooms a block away from Plaza Mayor. The attached tapas bar/restaurant is a tasty deal (Sb-€30–38, Db-€45–80, €12 each for third and fourth person, breakfast-€3, air-con, elevator, San Juan de la Cruz 3, tel. 923-280-421, fax 923-213-112, www.hosteriacasavallejo.com, info@hosteriacasavallejo .com, Amparo).

$$ Hostal Los Angeles rents 15 simple but cared-for rooms, four of which overlook the square. Stand on the balcony and inhale the essence of Spain. View rooms are popular and more expensive—when you reserve, request *"Con vista, por favor"*

(S-€15–30, Sb-€25–40, D-€30–38, Db-€35–55, T-€65, Tb-€75, Q-€85, includes tax, breakfast on plaza-€5, Plaza Mayor 10, about 3 o'clock, tel. & fax 923-218-166, www.pensionlosangeles.com, info@pensionlosangeles.com, Orlando).

$ **Hostal Las Vegas Centro** is clean, bright, quiet, and cheap, with 17 cozy rooms (Sb-€24, Db-€36–40, Tb-€55, Qb-€75; 2 blocks off Plaza Mayor, exit the square about 7 o'clock, toward cathedral at Meléndez 13, first floor; tel. & fax 923-218-749, www.lasvegascentro.net, reservas@lasvegascentro.es).

Eating in Salamanca

Local specialties include *serrano* ham, which is in just about everything (see "Sampling *Serrano* Ham" sidebar), roast suckling pig (called *tostón* around here), and *sopa de ajo*, the local garlic soup. *Patatas meneadas* (potatoes with Spanish paprika and bacon) is a simple but tasty local tapa. If you always wanted seconds at Communion, buy a bag of the local specialty called *obleas*—flat wafers similar to giant Communion hosts.

Restaurants generally serve lunch from 13:00 to 16:00 and dinner from 20:00 until very late (Spaniards don't start dinner until about 21:00).

Dining Well

Restaurante Chez Victor is the result of the marriage of a Castilian chef (Victor) and a French food-lover (Margarite). This family-run place, elegantly decorated with a feminine French touch and bouquets on the tables, serves modern and creative Franco/Castilian fare—perhaps your best €35–40 meal in town (Tue–Sat 14:00–15:30 & 21:00–23:30, Sun 14:00–15:30; closed Sun eve and Mon; also closed Easter week, Aug, and Christmas; air-con, Espoz y Mina 26, tel. 923-213-123).

La Fonda Casa de Comidas del Arcediano is a dark, woody place with solid, traditional cuisine that caters to locals. You'll happily spend about €22 for three courses (Tue–Sun 13:30–16:00 & 21:00–24:00, closed Mon, smoky, reserve on weekends, 15 yards down the arcade from corner of Gran Vía and Cuesta de Sancti Spiritus at La Reja 2, tel. 923-215-712).

On Plaza Mayor and Rúa Mayor

Here you can enjoy a meal sitting on the finest square in Spain and savor some of Europe's best people-watching. The bars, with little tables spilling onto the square, serve *raciones* and €2 glasses of wine. A *ración de la casa* (house specialty of hams, sausages, and cheese), a *ración* of *patatas bravas* (chunks of potatoes with a slightly spicy tomato sauce), and two glasses of wine makes a nice dinner for two

Sampling *Serrano* Ham

Jamón serrano is cured in the *sierras* (mountains) of Spain. While there are many variations of this cured ham from dif-

ferent regions of Spain, Spanish people have a special appreciation for *jamón ibérico,* made with the back legs of black pigs fed mainly on acorns. Originating in Spain, these black pigs are fatter and happier (slaughtered much later than regular pigs). Spaniards treasure memories of grandpa thinly carving a *jamón,* supported in a *jamonero* (ham-holder), during Christmas, just as we savor the tur-

key-carving at Thanksgiving. To sample this delicacy without the high price tag you'll find in bars and restaurants, go to the local market, ask for 100 grams (*cien gramos de jamón ibérico extra;* about €70/kilo, so your portion will run about €7), and enjoy it as a picnic with red wine and bread.

for about €25—one of the best eating values in all of Europe. For dessert, stroll with an ice-cream cone from Café Novelty.

Café Real serves bar snacks in a tapas style (daily 8:00–24:00, tel. 923-210-556).

Cervantes Bar is more of a restaurant, with a wide selection of meals, €8 salads, and sandwiches. They also have an indoor section with tables that overlook Plaza Mayor from one floor up; it's a popular student hangout. Don't forget to ask for your *pincho,* a snack that comes with your drink, if you're standing at the bar (daily 10:00–24:00, tel. 923-217-213).

Café Novelty is Plaza Mayor's Art Nouveau café. It dates from 1905—and has some customers who look like they've been there since it opened. It's filled with character and literary memories. The metal sculpture depicts a famous local writer, Torrente Ballester (daily 8:00–24:00, tel. 923-214-956). Their ice cream sweetens a stroll around the plaza.

Mesón de las Conchas, on the main pedestrian drag to the cathedral, attracts a mix of locals and tourists. They offer good prices for tapas and meals—but, as is common here, they bump up tapa prices for outdoor seating (daily, bar 8:00–24:00, restaurant 12:30–16:00 & 20:00–24:00, Calle de Rúa Mayor 16, tel. 923-212-167).

Eating Simply, but Well

There are plenty of good, inexpensive restaurants between Plaza Mayor and Gran Vía, and as you leave Plaza Mayor toward Calle de Rúa Mayor. The tapas places along and around Calle de Rúa Mayor are abundant and often overrun with students.

Restaurante Isidro is a thriving local (and guidebook) favorite—a straightforward, hardworking eatery run by Alberto—offering a good assortment of fish and specialty meat dishes (€10 fixed-price meal, also à la carte €15–25 dinners, Tue–Sat 13:00–16:00 & 20:00–24:00, Sun 13:00–16:00, closed Mon, big portions, good roasts, quick and friendly service, Pozo Amarillo 19, about a block north of covered market near Plaza Mayor, tel. 923-262-848).

Restaurante Comercio, next door and also run by Alberto, offers the same quality food and prices as Isidro in a more contemporary setting. If Isidro is closed, pop over to Comercio to eat just as well.

The **Pans & Company** sandwich chain is always fast and affordable, with a branch on Calle Prior across from Burger King and another on Calle de Rúa Mayor (both open daily 10:30–24:00).

Picnics: The covered *mercado* (market) on Plaza Mercado has fresh fruits and veggies (Mon–Sat 8:00–14:30, closed Sun, on east side of Plaza Mayor). A small El Arbol grocery, three blocks east of Plaza Mayor at Iscar Peyra 13, has just the basics (Mon–Sat 9:30–21:30, closed Sun). For variety, the big Carrefour Express supermarket is your best bet, but it's a six-block walk north of Plaza Mayor on Toro (Mon–Sat 9:30–21:30, closed Sun, across from Plaza San Juan de Sahagún and its church).

Connections

From Salamanca by Train to: Madrid (7/day, 2.5 hrs, Chamartín Station, some are commuter trains with limited luggage space), **Ávila** (6/day, 1 hr), **Barcelona** (8/day, 6–7.5 hrs, change in Madrid from Chamartín Station to Atocha Station via Metro; 1 direct/day, 11.25 hrs), **Santiago** (first take hourly bus for 1-hr ride to Zamora, then transfer to train—2/day, 5 hrs to Santiago), **Burgos** (2–3/day, 2.5 hrs), **Lisbon,** Portugal (1/day, 7 hrs, departs Salamanca Station at about 4:50 in the morning, no kidding; catch a taxi to the train station, taxi-€4–5, ask your hotel to arrange taxi in advance). Train info: tel. 902-240-202, www.renfe.es.

By Bus to: Madrid (€20 one-way, hourly express, 2.5 hrs, arrives at Madrid's Mendez Álvaro Station, Auto-Res buses, www.auto-res.net), **Segovia** (2/day, 3 hrs; transfer in Labajos, could make a brief stop in Ávila en route, Auto-Res or La Sepulvedana buses, consider reserving a seat for the Salamanca–Labajos leg in advance), **Ávila** (4/day, 2/day on weekends, 1.5 hrs, Auto-Res buses), **Ciudad Rodrigo** (nearly hourly, 1 hr, El Pilar buses),

Salamanca Area

Santiago (2/day, 1 with a transfer in Vigo, 7 hrs), **Barcelona** (2/day, 11 hrs, Alsa buses), **Burgos** (2/day, 3–4 hrs, Alsa buses), **Coimbra,** Portugal (1/day, departs at 12:30, 5 hrs, one-way-€34, round-trip-€58; same bus continues to **Lisbon** in 8.25 hrs, one-way-€44, round-trip-€76; Alsa buses, tel. 902-422-242, www.alsa .es). Bus info: tel. 923-236-717 or 902-020-052 (Auto-Res).

Ciudad Rodrigo

Ciudad Rodrigo is worth a visit only if you're driving from Salamanca to Coimbra, Portugal (although buses connect Salamanca and Ciudad Rodrigo with surprising efficiency in about an hour).

This rough-and-tumble old town of 16,000 people caps a hill overlooking the Río Agueda. Spend an hour wandering among the Renaissance mansions that line its streets and exploring its cathedral and Plaza Mayor. Have lunch or a snack at **El Sanatorio** (Plaza Mayor 14, tel. 923-460-024). The tapas are cheap, the crowd is local, and the walls are a Ciudad Rodrigo scrapbook, including some bullfighting that makes the Three Stooges look demure.

Ciudad Rodrigo's cathedral—pockmarked with scars from Napoleonic cannon balls—has some entertaining carvings in the choir and some pretty racy work in its cloisters. Who says, "When you've seen one Gothic church, you've seen 'em all"?

The **TI** is two blocks from Ciudad Rodrigo's Plaza Mayor,

just inside the old wall near the cathedral (Mon–Fri 9:00–14:00 & 17:00–19:00, Sat–Sun 10:00–14:00 & 17:00–20:00, Plaza Ameyuelas 5, tel. 923-460-561). They can recommend a good hotel, such as Hotel Conde Rodrigo (34 rooms, Sb-€75, Db-€80, extra bed-€18, air-con, elevator, Plaza San Salvador 9, tel. 923-461-408, www.conderodrigo.com, info@conderodrigo.com).

MADRID

Today's Madrid is upbeat and vibrant, still enjoying a post-Franco renaissance. You'll feel it. Even the living-statue street performers have a twinkle in their eyes.

Madrid is the hub of Spain. This modern capital—Europe's highest, at more than 2,000 feet—has a population of 3.2 million. Like its people, the city is relatively young. In 1561, when Spain ruled the world's most powerful empire, King Philip II decided to move his capital from Toledo to Madrid. One hundred years ago, Madrid had only 400,000 people—so the majority of today's Madrid is modern sprawl surrounding an intact, easy-to-navigate historic core.

To support their bid to host the 2012 Olympics, Madrid began some massive city-improvement building projects. Although they lost, the construction continues as if they won. Politicians who back these projects have been rewarded both financially (locals claim some corrupt officials are getting kickbacks) and politically—residents love to see all the new squares, pedestrian streets, beltway tunnels, parks, and Metro stations popping up. As the city eyes another Olympics bid for 2016, construction won't let up soon.

Madrid's ambitious improvement plans include the creation of a wonderful new pedestrian street crossing the city from the Prado to the Royal Palace. Strolling Calle de las Huertas from Plaza Mayor to the Prado (and the newly pedestrianized Calle del Arenal), you see how the investment is turning ramshackle zones into trendy ones. A new macro-Metro station near Puerta del Sol—to accommodate a new, super-efficient commuter line connecting the two train stations and the main square—is due to be finished in 2010.

By installing posts to keep cars off sidewalks, making the streets safer after dark, and restoring old buildings, Madrid is working hard to make itself more livable...and fun to visit.

Tourists are the real winners. Dive headlong into the grandeur and intimate charm of Madrid. The lavish Royal Palace, with its gilded rooms and frescoed ceilings, rivals Versailles. The Prado has Europe's top collection of paintings. The city's huge Retiro Park invites you to take a shady siesta and hopscotch through a mosaic of lovers, families, skateboarders, pets walking their masters, and expert bench-sitters. Save time for Madrid's elegant shops and people-friendly pedestrian zones. On Sundays, cheer for the bull at a bullfight or bargain like mad at a mega-size flea market. Lively Madrid has enough street-singing, bar-hopping, and people-watching vitality to give any visitor a boost of youth.

Planning Your Time

Divide your time between Madrid's top three attractions: the Royal Palace (worth a half-day), the Prado Museum (also worth a half-day), and its bar-hopping contemporary scene. On a Sunday, consider allotting extra time for the flea market (year-round) and/or a bullfight (some Sundays Easter–mid-Oct, especially during San Isidro festival mid-May).

Madrid is worth two days and three nights on even the fastest trip. I'd spend them this way:

Day 1: Take a brisk 20-minute good-morning-Madrid walk from Puerta del Sol to the Prado (from Puerta del Sol, walk three blocks south to Plaza del Ángel, then take the pedestrianized Calle de las Huertas). Spend the rest of the morning at the Prado, then take an afternoon siesta in Retiro Park, or tackle modern art at the Centro de Arte Reina Sofía (Picasso's *Guernica*) and/or the Thyssen-Bornemisza Museum. Ride bus #27 from the Prado out through Madrid's modern section for a dose of the non-touristy, no-nonsense big city. Have dinner at 20:00, with tapas around Plaza Santa Ana.

Day 2: Follow my "Welcome to Madrid" self-guided walk (see page 328), tour the Royal Palace, and have lunch at Café Oriente or near Plaza Mayor. Your afternoon is free for other sights, shopping, or a side-trip to El Escorial (closed Mon; see next chapter). Be out at the magic hour—before sunset—when beautifully lit people fill Madrid.

Note that many top sights are closed on Monday, including the Prado, Thyssen-Bornemisza Museum, and El Escorial; sights remaining open on Monday include the Royal Palace (open daily) and Centro de Arte Reina Sofía (closed Tue). For good day-trip possibilities from Madrid, see the next two chapters (Northwest of Madrid and Toledo).

Orientation to Madrid

Puerta del Sol marks the center of Madrid. No major sight is more than a 20-minute walk or a €4 taxi ride from this central square. The Royal Palace (to the west) and the Prado Museum and Retiro Park (to the east) frame Madrid's historic center. This zone can be covered on foot. Southwest of Puerta del Sol is a 17th-century district with the slow-down-and-smell-the-cobbles Plaza Mayor and memories of preindustrial Spain. North of Puerta del Sol runs Calle de Gran Vía, and between the two are lively pedestrian shopping streets. Gran Vía, bubbling with shops and cinemas, leads to the modern Plaza de España. From the Prado, the Paseo de la Castellana is a straight boulevard cutting north through the modern town to the "gateway to Europe" towers. Between Puerta del Sol and the Atocha train station stretches the colorful, up-and-coming multiethnic Lavapiés district (see the "The Lavapiés District Tapas Crawl," page 384).

Tourist Information

Madrid's many TIs share a phone number (tel. 915-881-636) and website (www.esmadrid.com).

The best TI is on **Plaza Mayor** (daily 9:30–20:30, air-con, limited free Internet access). It's centrally located and innovative, offering several €4 English guided walks a day (described later in "Tours in Madrid") and a free downloadable MP3 self-guided tour. They also provide the SATE police service to aid foreigners who've run into trouble.

Madrid's other TIs have the same hours (Mon–Sat 8:00–20:00, Sun 9:00–14:00): near the **Prado Museum** (Duque de Medinaceli 2, behind Palace Hotel); **Chamartín train station** (near track 20); **Atocha train station** (in AVE side); and **airport** (Terminal 1 and Terminal 4). Small info kiosks are in **Plaza de Callao** and in **Plaza de Cibeles** (daily 9:30–20:00).

At any TI, pick up a map, the handy *Traveler's Tips* booklet, the *Es Madrid* English-language monthly, and confirm your sightseeing plans. The TI's free *Public Transport* map is very well-designed to meet travelers' needs and has the most detailed map of the center. Get this and use it. TIs have the latest on bullfights and *zarzuela* (light Spanish opera). Only the most hyperactive travelers could save money buying the **Madrid Card,** which covers 40 museums and the Madrid Vision bus tour (€45/24 hrs, €58/48 hrs, €72/72 hrs).

For entertainment listings, the TI's printed material is not very good. Pick up the Spanish-language weekly entertainment guide *Guía del Ocio* (€1, sold at newsstands) or check their complete website: www.guiadelocio.com. It lists daily live music (*"Conciertos"*), museums (*"Museos"*—with the latest times and special exhibits), restaurants (an exhaustive listing), kids' activities (*"Los Niños"*), TV schedules, and movies (*"V.O."* means original version, *"V.O. en inglés sub"* means a movie is played in English with Spanish subtitles rather than dubbed).

If you're heading to other destinations in Spain, stop by the Plaza Mayor office, which often has free maps and brochures (in English). Since many small-town TIs keep erratic hours and run out of these pamphlets, get what you can in Madrid. You can also get schedules for buses and some trains, allowing you to avoid unnecessary trips to the various stations. The TI's free and amazingly informative *Mapa de Comunicaciones España* is a road map of Spain that lists all the tourist offices and highway SOS numbers. (If they're out, ask for the route map sponsored by the Paradores hotel chain, the camping map, or the golf map.)

For tips on sightseeing, hotels, and more, visit www.madrid man.com, run with passion by American Scott Martin.

Arrival in Madrid

By Train

Madrid's two train stations, Chamartín and Atocha, are both on Metro lines with easy access to downtown Madrid. (For Atocha Station, use the "Atocha RENFE" Metro stop; the stop named simply "Atocha" is farther from the station.) Chamartín handles most international trains and the AVE train to Segovia. Atocha generally covers southern Spain, as well as the AVE trains to Barcelona, Córdoba, Sevilla, and Toledo. Both stations offer long-distance trains *(largo recorrido)* as well as smaller local trains *(regionales* and *cercanías)* to nearby destinations.

Buying Tickets: You can buy tickets at the stations, at a travel agency, or online. (For all the details, see "Buying Train Tickets" on page 720 in the appendix.) Convenient travel agencies for buying tickets in Madrid include the El Corte Inglés Travel Agency at Atocha (Mon–Fri 7:00–22:00, Sat–Sun only for urgent arrangements, on ground floor of AVE side at the far end) and the El Corte Inglés department store at Puerta del Sol (see "Helpful Hints," page 320).

Traveling Between Chamartín and Atocha Stations: To travel between the two stations, you can take the Metro (line 1, 30–40 min, €1, see "Getting Around Madrid" on page 323), but the *cercanías* trains are faster (6/hr, 12 min, €1.15, free with rail-pass or any train ticket to Madrid—show it at ticket window in the middle of the turnstiles, departs from Atocha's track 2 and generally Chamartín's track 1, 3, 8, or 9—but check the *Salidas Inmediatas* board to be sure). A faster Atocha–Sol–Chamartín *cercanías* line is supposed to be completed in 2010.

Chamartín Station

The TI is opposite track 19. The impressively large information, tickets, and customer-service office is at track 11. You can relax in the Sala VIP Club if you have a first-class railpass and first-class seat or sleeper reservations (between tracks 13 and 14, cooler of free drinks). Luggage storage *(consignas)* is across the street, opposite track 17. The station's Metro stop is also called Chamartín (not "Pinar de Chamartín").

Atocha Station

The station is split in two: an AVE side (mostly long-distance trains) and a *cercanías* side (mostly local trains to the suburbs or *cercanías* and the Metro for connecting into downtown). These two parts are connected by a corridor of shops. Each side of the station has separate schedules and customer-service offices. The TI, which is in the AVE side, offers tourist info, but no train info (Mon–Sat 9:00–20:00, Sun 9:00–14:00, tel. 915-284-630).

MADRID

Greater Madrid

CHAMARTÍN TRAIN STATION ✚ ℹ️

Ⓜ️ Chamartín

M-30 FREEWAY

PLAZA DE CASTILLA

← **BERNABÉU STADIUM**

Santiago Bernabéu

N

1 MILE

1 KM

MURILLO

CASTELLANO

BRAVO

TO EL ESCORIAL & SEGOVIA

TO BARAJAS AIRPORT, BARCELONA & ➍

A-2

FERNANDEZ

J. COSTA

A-6

ARCO VICTORIA

SAN BERNARDO

AMÉRICA

SOROLLA MUSEUM

Ventas

Ⓜ️ **VENTAS BULLRING** ●

Moncloa Ⓜ️

➌

PRINCESA

Ⓜ️ Iglesia

RECOLETOS

PLAZA COLÓN

ALCALÁ

CASA DE CAMPO

➋

PLAZA ESPAÑA

Norte Ⓜ️

MALA-SAÑA

GRAN VÍA

Sol Ⓜ️

RETIRO PARK

PRÍNCIPE PÍO TRAIN & BUS STATIONS

Royal Palace

★ **SOL**

ℹ️

PRADO

MANZANARES

CALLE TOLEDO

✚ **PLAZA MAYOR**

Atocha RENFE Ⓜ️

ATOCHA TRAIN STN.

MENDEZ ALVARO

MEDITERRANEO

A-3

CABEZA

✚ ℹ️

Ⓜ️

➊

Palos de la Frontera

DCH

TO ➎ & TOLEDO VIA N-401

➊ Estación Sur de Autobuses

➋ Príncipe Pío Station (Sepulvedana Buses)

➌ Intercambiador de Moncloa

➍ To Intercambiador de Avenida de América

➎ To Plaza Elíptica Station

▭ = **HISTORIC CITY CENTER** SEE DETAIL MAPS

Ⓜ️ METRO STATION - NOT ALL SHOWN

→ BUS #27 SELF-GUIDED TOUR

There are three ticket offices at Atocha: The *cercanías* side has a small office for local trains and a big office for major trains (such as AVE). The AVE side has a pleasant, airy ticket office that also sells tickets for AVE and other long-distance trains (there are two lines: "Advance Sale" or "Selling Out Today"). If the line at one office is long, check the other offices. Grab a number from a machine to get your turn in line. For major destinations (such as Barcelona, San Sebastián, or Córdoba), you can use your credit card to avoid the lines—look for the ATM-like touch-screen machines to the right of the entrance.

Atocha's **AVE side,** which is in the towering old-station building, is remarkable for the lush, tropical garden filling its grand hall. It has the slick AVE trains, other fast trains (Grandes Líneas), a pharmacy (daily 8:00–22:00, facing garden), and the wicker-elegant Samarkanda—both an affordable cafeteria (daily 13:00–20:00) and a pricey restaurant (daily from 21:00, tel. 915-309-746). Luggage storage *(consigna)* is below Samarkanda (daily 6:00–22:20). In the departure lounge on the upper floor, TV monitors announce track numbers. For information, try the *Información* counter (daily 6:30–22:30), next to Centro Servicios AVE (which handles only AVE changes and problems). The *Atención al Cliente* office deals with problems on Grandes Líneas (daily 6:30–23:30). Also on the AVE side is the Club AVE/Sala VIP, a lounge reserved solely for AVE business-class travelers and for first-class ticket-holders or Eurailers with a first-class reservation (upstairs, past the security check on right; free drinks, newspapers, showers, and info service).

On the *cercanías* **side** of Atocha Station, you'll find the local *cercanías* trains, *regionales* trains, some eastbound faster trains, and the "Atocha RENFE" Metro stop. The *Atención al Cliente* office in the *cercanías* section has information only on trains to destinations near Madrid.

Terrorism Memorial: The terrorist bombings of March 11, 2004, took place in Atocha and on local lines going into and out of the station. Security is understandably tight here. A moving memorial is in the *cercanías* part of the station near the Atocha RENFE Metro stop. Walk inside and under the cylinder to read the thousands of condolence messages in many languages (daily 10:00–20:00). Its 36-foot cylindrical glass memorial towers are visible from outside on the street.

By Bus

Madrid has several bus stations: Príncipe Pío (for Segovia, Metro: Príncipe Pío); Estación Sur Autobuses (for Ávila and Granada, Metro: Méndez Álvaro); Plaza Elíptica (for Toledo, Metro: Plaza Elíptica); Estación Intercambiador (for El Escorial, Metro: Moncloa); and Intercambiador de Avenida de América (for Pamplona and Burgos, Metro: Avenida de América). For details, see "Connections" at the end of this chapter.

By Plane

For information on Madrid's Barajas Airport, see the end of this chapter.

Helpful Hints

Theft Alert: Be wary of pickpockets, anywhere, anytime. Areas of particular risk are Puerta del Sol (the central square), El Rastro (the flea market), Gran Vía (the paseo zone: Plaza del Callao to Plaza de España), the Ópera Metro station (or anywhere on the Metro), bus #27, the airport, and any crowded streets. Be alert to the people around you: Someone wearing a heavy jacket in the summer is likely a pickpocket. Lately, Romanian teenagers dress like American teens and work the areas around the three big art museums; being under 18, they can't be arrested by the police. Assume a fight or any commotion is a scam to distract people about to become victims of a pickpocket. Wear your money belt. The small streets north of Gran Vía are particularly dangerous, even before nightfall. Muggings occur, but are rare. For help, see the next listing.

Tourist Emergency Aid: SATE is a centrally located police office offering emergency aid to victims of theft. Help ranges from canceling stolen credit cards to assistance in reporting a crime (daily 9:00–22:00, near Plaza de Santo Domingo at Calle Leganitos 19, 24-hr tel. 902-102-112, English spoken once you get connected to a person). The Plaza Mayor TI is a kind of SATE branch.

Prostitution: Diverse by European standards, Madrid is spilling over with immigrants from South America, North Africa, and Eastern Europe. Many young women come here, fall on hard times, and end up on the streets. While it's illegal to make money from someone else selling sex (i.e., pimping), prostitutes over 18 can solicit legally (€30, FYI). Calle de la Montera (leading from Puerta del Sol to Plaza Red de San Luis) is lined with what looks like a bunch of high-school girls skipping out of school for a cigarette break. Again, don't stray north of Gran Vía around Calle de la Luna and

Heart of Madrid

M METRO STATION PEDESTRIAN ZONES

200 YARDS
200 METERS

TO PLAZA DE ESPAÑA

MALASAÑA

SAN BERN.

GRAN VÍA

LEGANITOS

GATE POLICE

TORIJA

PLAZA SANTO DOMINGO **M** S. Dom. **M** Callao GRAN VÍA McD.

Gran Vía

PLAZA CALLAO

RED LIGHTS

TO PLAZA CIBELES

DESCALZAS ROYAL MONASTERY

PLAZA CARMEN

CARMEN

PRECIADOS

MONTERA

CAJA MADRID

TO ROYAL PALACE

EL CORTE INGLES DEPT. STORE

ARENAL

ALCALÁ

Sevilla **M**

TO THYSSEN & PRADO MUSEUMS

PUERTA DEL SOL
Sol **M**

"TÍO PEPE" SIGN

SEVILLA

MAYOR

McD. KILO ZERO SAN JERÓNIMO

CORREO

CARRETAS

CADIZ

POZO

MINA

CRUZ VICTORIA

NUÑEZ

PRINCIPE

ECHEGARAY

V. DE LA VEGA

POSTAS

ESPART.

ZARAGOZA

BOLSA

ESPOZ Y

PLAZA SANTA ANA

PRADO

PLAZA MAYOR

CAVA SAN MIG.

SAN MIGUEL MKT.

CUCHILLEROS

TOLEDO

PLAZA SANTA CRUZ

PLAZA JACINTO BENAVENTE

CINE IDEAL

PLAZA ANGEL

PLAZA ANGEL

DR. CORT.

ATOCHA

HUERTAS

TO PRADO

Anton Martin **M**

TO EL RASTRO FLEA MARKET (SUNDAYS)

LAVAPIÉS

TO ATOCHA STN. & REINA SOFÍA MUSEUM

DCH

Plaza Santa María Soledad—while the streets may look inviting...this area is a meat-eating flower.

Embassies: The US Embassy is at Serrano 75 (tel. 915-872-200); the Canadian Embassy is at Nuñez de Balboa 35 (tel. 914-233-250).

One-Stop Shopping: The dominant department store is **El Corte Inglés,** which takes up several huge buildings in the commercial pedestrian zone just off Puerta del Sol (Mon–Sat 10:00–22:00, Sun 11:00–21:00, navigate with the help of the info desk near the door of the main building—the tallest building with the biggest sign, Preciados 3, tel. 913-798-000). They give out fine, free Madrid maps. In the main building, you'll find two handy travel agencies (see listing at end of this section), a post office, a modern cafeteria (seventh floor), and a supermarket with a fancy "Club del Gourmet" section in the basement. Across the street is its Librería branch—a huge bookstore. The second building fronting Puerta del Sol contains six floors of music, computers, home electronics, and SIM cards for mobile phones, with a box office on the top floor selling tickets to whatever's on in town. Locals figure you'll find anything you need at El Corte Inglés. Salespeople wear flag pins indicating which languages they can speak.

Internet Access: There are plenty of centrally located places to check your email. Any *locutorio* call center should have a few computers and is generally the cheapest. Near Plaza Santa Ana (and great if you're waiting for the tapas-crawl action to heat up), **La Bolsa de Minutos** has plenty of fast terminals (daily 9:30–24:00, Calle Espoz y Mina 17, tel. 915-322-622). **BBIG** has more than 100 terminals, is non-smoking, and seats casual Internet surfers apart from noisy, intense gamers (daily 9:30–24:00, at the corner of Puerta del Sol and the street that connects it to Plaza Mayor, at Mayor 1—on the second floor above Sol Park casino, tel. 915-312-364). Both places have disc-burning services and a helpful staff.

Phone Cards: You can buy cheap international phone cards at some newsstands, at Internet cafés, or at the easy-to-find *locutorio* call centers (but these are generally uncomfortable places to sit and talk). When choosing a phone card, remember that toll-free numbers start with 900, whereas 901 and 902 numbers can be expensive. Ask your hotel if they charge for the 900 number before making calls.

Bookstores: For books in English, try **FNAC Callao** (Calle Preciados 28, tel. 915-956-100), **Casa del Libro** (English on ground floor in back, Gran Vía 29, tel. 915-212-219), and **El Corte Inglés** (guidebooks and some fiction, in its Librería branch kitty-corner from main store, fronting Puerta del Sol—see "One-Stop Shopping," on previous page).

Laundry: Onda Blu will wash, dry, and fold your laundry (€5 self-service, €8 full-service, daily 9:30–22:00, León 3, east of Plaza Santa Ana, tel. 913-695-071, Ana). **Express Laundry Service** is a tiny shop that offers full-service laundry (€7 to wash and dry a big load, generally same-day service, Mon–Sat 9:30–20:30, closed Sun, between Puerto del Sol and Plaza Santa Ana at Calle Espoz y Mina 22, mobile 679-060-239).

Travel Agencies: The grand department store **El Corte Inglés** has two travel agencies (air and rail tickets, but not reservations for railpass-holders, €2 fee, on first and seventh floors, Mon–Sat 10:00–22:00, Sun 11:00–21:00, just off Puerta del Sol, tel. 913-798-000).

Madrid Metro

Pinar de Chamartín **(BLUE) 1**

Chamartín RENFE

Plaza de Castilla

Cuatro Caminas **(RED) 2**

La Elipa **(RED) 2**

Moncloa **(YELLOW) 3**

BULL RING

Ventas

BUS #27

Iglesia

Tribunal

Plaza de España

Callao

Gran Vía

Sevilla

Banco de España

Retiro

S. Domingo

Ópera

Sol

PRADO

ROYAL PALACE

PLAZA MAYOR

Tirso de Molina

Lavapiés

Antón Martín

Embajadores

REINA SOFÍA

Atocha

Atocha RENFE

NOT ALL LINES + STATIONS ARE SHOWN

──── METRO LINE **1 BLUE**
──── METRO LINE **2 RED**
──── METRO LINE **3 YELLOW**
- - - - BUS #27
· · · · · #M1 ELECTRIC BUS
+++++ RAIL (LONG DISTANCE)
+—+—+ RAIL (CERCANÍAS COMMUTER LINE)

Villaverde Alto **3 (YELLOW)**

Valdecarros **1 (BLUE)**

DCH

NOT TO SCALE

Getting Around Madrid

If you want to use Madrid's excellent public transit, my two best tips are these: Pick up and study the fine *Public Transit* map/flier (available at TIs), and take full advantage of the cheap 10-ride Metrobus ticket deal (see below).

By Metro: The city's broad streets can be hot and exhausting. A subway trip of even a stop or two saves time and energy. Madrid's Metro is simple, speedy, and cheap (€1/ride within zone A—which covers most of the city, but not trains out to the airport;

runs 6:00–1:30 in the morning, www.metromadrid.es or www
.ctm-madrid.es). The 10-ride Metrobus ticket can be shared by several travelers and works on both the Metro and buses (€7.40—or
€0.74 per ride, sold at kiosks, tobacco shops, and in Metro). Insert
your Metrobus ticket in the turnstile (it usually shows how many
rides remain on it), then retrieve it as you pass through. Stations
offer free system maps (see basic map of three main lines on previous page). Navigate by Metro stops (shown on city maps). To
transfer, follow signs to the next Metro line (numbered and color-
coded). The names of the end stops are used to indicate directions.
Green *salida* signs point to the exit. Using neighborhood maps and
street signs to exit smartly saves lots of walking. And watch out for
thieves.

By Bus: City buses, while not as easy as the Metro, can be
useful (€1 tickets sold on bus, or €7.40 for a 10-ride Metrobus
ticket—see above; bus maps at TI or info booth on Puerta del
Sol, poster-size maps are usually posted at bus stops, buses run
6:00–24:00, much less frequent *Buho* buses run all night).

By Taxi: Madrid's 15,000 taxis are reasonably priced and easy
to hail. Foursomes travel as cheaply by taxi as by Metro. A ride
from the Royal Palace to the Prado costs about €4. After the €2
drop charge, the per-kilometer rate depends on the time: *Tarifa
1* (€1/kilometer) should be charged Mon–Sat 6:00–22:00; *Tarifa
2* (€1.10/kilometer) is valid after 22:00 and on Sundays and holidays. If your cabbie uses anything rather than *Tarifa 1* on weekdays
(shown as an isolated "1" on the meter), you're being cheated. Rates
can be higher if you go outside Madrid. Other legitimate charges
include the €5.50 supplement for the airport, the €3 supplement for
train or bus stations, and €13.50 per hour for waiting. Make sure
the meter is turned on as soon as you get into the cab so the driver
can't tack anything onto the official rate. If the driver starts adding
up "extras," look for the sticker detailing all legitimate surcharges
(which should be on the passenger window).

Tours in Madrid

Discover Madrid—The Plaza Mayor TI organizes a daily schedule of cheap, interesting guided walks. Tours last about 90 minutes,
are in English only, cost €4, and depart daily—generally from the
Plaza Mayor TI at 10:00, 12:00, and 16:00. Groups are often very
small, so you almost feel like you have a private guide. Just buy
your ticket at the TI a few minutes before departure.

Madrid Vision Hop-On, Hop-Off Bus Tours—Madrid Vision
offers two different hop-on, hop-off circuits of the city: historic
and modern. Buy a ticket from the driver (€17/1 day, €21/2 days)
and you can hop from sight to sight and route to route as you like,

listening to a recorded English commentary along the way. Each route has about 15 stops and takes about 90 minutes, with buses departing every 10 or 20 minutes. The two routes intersect at the south side of Puerta del Sol and in front of Starbucks across from the Prado (daily 9:30–24:00 in summer, 10:00–19:00 in winter, tel. 917-791-888, www.madridvision.es).

LeTango Tours—Carlos Galvin, a Spaniard who speaks flawless English (and has led tours for my groups since 1998), and his wife from Seattle, Jennifer, offer private tours in Madrid and other parts of Spain. Carlos mixes a market walk in the historic center with a culinary-and-tapas crawl to get close to the Madrileños, their culture, and their food. His walk gives a fine three-hour orientation and introduction to the fascinating and tasty culture of Madrid, plus travel tips (€95 per person, 10 percent cash discount, includes tastes in the market and light tapas at the end, minimum 2 people, alcohol-free and gourmet versions available, family-friendly, price goes down with more people). They also offer city, regional, and all-Spain tours and Madrid apartment rentals (about €170/night for 4 people) as explained on their website (tel. 913-694-752, mobile 661-752-458, www.letango.com, info@letango.com).

Local Guides—**Frederico and Cristina** are licensed guides who lead city walks through the pedestrian streets of the historic core of Madrid. Fred, Cris, and their team offer an all-ages tour of the big museums, including the Royal Palace, the Prado, and the Reina Sofía, as well as a tapas tour. Or, if you're looking to get outside Madrid, consider their guided tour to surrounding towns using public transit (per-tour costs: Mon–Fri €160, Sat–Sun €190, 10 percent Rick Steves discount, admissions and tapas not included, 3–5 hours, tel. 913-102-974, mobile 649-936-222, www.spainfred .com, spainfred@gmail.com).

Inés Muñiz Martin is a good guide for Madrid and the region (€140 for up to 4 hours, €170 on weekends and holidays, these rates include discount for Rick Steves readers, mobile 629-147-370, www.immguidedtours.com, info@immguidedtours.com).

Susana Jarabo, with a master's in art history, is another excellent independent guide (mobile 667-027-722, susanjarabo@yahoo .com).

Hernán Amaya Satt directs a group of licensed guides who take individuals around Madrid by foot or by car on 18 personalized tours (rates vary according to tour and number of people, 20 percent discount off official rates for Rick Steves readers, mobile 680-450-231, www.madrid-museum-tours.org, info@madrid -museum-tours.org).

Stephen Drake-Jones, a British expat, gives walks of historic old Madrid almost daily. A historian with a passion for the Duke

Madrid at a Glance

▲▲▲**Prado Museum** One of the world's great museums, loaded with masterpieces by Diego Velázquez, Francisco de Goya, El Greco, Hieronymus Bosch, Albrecht Dürer, and more. **Hours:** Tue–Sun 9:00–20:00, closed Mon. See page 342.

▲▲▲**Royal Palace** Spain's sumptuous, lavishly furnished national palace. **Hours:** April–Sept Mon–Sat 9:00–19:00, Sun 9:00–16:00; Oct–March Mon–Sat 9:30–18:00, Sun 9:00–15:00. See page 336.

▲▲▲**Centro de Arte Reina Sofía** Modern-art museum featuring Picasso's epic masterpiece *Guernica.* **Hours:** Mon and Wed–Sat 10:00–21:00, Sun 10:00–14:30, closed Tue. See page 355.

▲▲**Puerta del Sol** Madrid's lively central square. **Hours:** Always bustling. See page 328.

▲▲**Thyssen-Bornemisza Museum** A great complement to the Prado, with lesser-known yet still impressive works and an especially good Impressionist collection. **Hours:** Tue–Sun 10:00–19:00, closed Mon. See page 354.

▲▲**Bullfight** Spain's controversial pastime. **Hours:** Scattered Sundays and holidays March–mid-Oct, plus almost daily May–early June. See page 363.

▲**Zarzuela** Madrid's delightful light opera. **Hours:** Evenings. See page 365.

▲**Plaza Mayor** Historic cobbled square. **Hours:** Always open. See page 332.

▲**Retiro Park** Festive green escape from the city, with rental rowboats and great people-watching. **Hours:** Closes at dusk. See page 358.

▲**National Archaeological Museum** Traces the history of Iberia through artifacts, plus a replica of the Altamira Caves. **Hours:** Tue–Sat 9:30–20:00, Sun 9:30–15:00, closed Mon. See page 360.

▲**Clothing Museum** A clothes look at the 18th–21st centuries. **Hours:** Tue–Sat 9:30–19:00, Sun 10:00–15:00, closed Mon. See page 360.

▲**Chapel of San Antonio de la Florida** Church with Goya's tomb, plus frescoes by the artist. **Hours:** Tue–Fri 9:30–20:00, Sat–Sun 10:00–14:00, closed Mon. See page 360.

▲**El Rastro** Europe's biggest flea market. **Hours:** Sun 9:00–15:00, best before 11:00. See page 364.

▲**Royal Botanical Garden** A relaxing museum of plants, with specimens from around the world. **Hours:** Daily 10:00–21:00, until 18:00 in winter. See page 359.

▲**Naval Museum** Seafaring history of a country famous for its Armada. **Hours:** Tue–Sun 10:00–14:00, closed Mon and Aug. See page 359.

CaixaForum Impressive exhibit hall with free world-class art exhibits. **Hours:** Daily 10:00–20:00. See page 359.

Descalzas Royal Monastery Working monastery with fine art and tapestries. **Hours:** Tue–Thu and Sat 10:30–12:30 & 16:00–17:30, Fri 10:30–12:30, Sun 11:00–13:30, closed Mon. See page 359.

Sorolla Museum Spanish painter Joaquín Sorrolla's former home and studio. **Hours:** Tue–Sat 9:30–20:00, Sun 10:00–15:00, closed Mon. See page 360.

Municipal Museum Chronicles Madrid's history via paintings, models, and a movie (closed through 2011).

Royal Tapestry Factory Traditional tapestries woven on site. **Hours:** Mon–Fri 10:00–14:00, closed Sat–Sun and Aug. See page 361.

Temple de Debod Actual ancient Egyptian temple relocated to Madrid. **Hours:** April–Sept Tue–Fri 10:00–14:00 & 18:00–20:00, Sat–Sun 10:00–14:00, closed Mon; Oct–March Tue–Fri 9:45–13:45 & 16:15–18:15, Sat–Sun 10:00–14:00, closed Mon. See page 361.

of Wellington (the general who stopped Napoleon), Stephen founded Madrid's Wellington Society and has been its chairman for over 30 years. For €35, you become a member and get a two-hour tour with a drink and tapas stop (morning or afternoon). His €50 VIP evening tour lasts three hours and includes three stops for drinks and tapas. Eccentric Stephen sorts out Madrid's Habsburg and Bourbon history. He likes his wine—if that's a problem, skip the tour. He also does day trips in the countryside (from €275 per couple; mobile 609-143-203, www.wellsoc.org, chairman@wellsoc.org).

Big-Bus City Sightseeing Tours—Julia Travel offers standard guided bus tours departing from Plaza de España 7 (office open Mon–Fri 8:00–19:00, Sat–Sun 8:00–15:00, tel. 915-599-605). Their city tours include a three-hour Madrid tour with a live guide in two or three languages (€20, one stop for a drink at Hard Rock Café, one shopping stop, no museum visits, daily at 15:00, no reservation required—just show up 15 min before departure). Julia Travel also runs tours to destinations near Madrid. The Valley of the Fallen and El Escorial tour is particularly efficient, given the lousy bus connections for this route (€47, 5 hours, makes the day trip easy—blitzing both sights with a commentary en route and no time-stealing shopping stops, Tue–Sun at 9:00, none Mon). Three trips include Toledo: one of the city itself (€39/5 hours, daily at 9:00 and 15:00, or €52/8 hours, daily at 9:15), one of Madrid and Toledo together (€52, half-day in Toledo plus panoramic 3-hour Madrid tour, daily at 9:00), and a marathon tour of El Escorial, Valley of the Fallen, and Toledo (€95, full day, Tue–Sun at 9:00, none Mon). Note that only the Toledo-only full-day tours include the cathedral. The half-day Toledo and combo-tours skip this town's one must-see sight...but not the long shopping stops, because the shops give kickbacks to the guides.

Self-Guided Walk

Welcome to Madrid:
From the Puerta del Sol to the Royal Palace
Connect the sights with the following commentary. Allow an hour for this half-mile walk. Begin at Madrid's central square, Puerta del Sol (Metro: Sol).

▲▲Puerta del Sol
The bustling Puerta del Sol is named for a long-gone medieval gate with the sun carved onto it. It's a hub for the Metro, buses, political demonstrations, and pickpockets.
• *Stand by the statue of King Charles III and survey the square.*

From Puerta del Sol to the Royal Palace

1. Puerta del Sol
2. Governor's Office
3. Salon La Mallorquina Pastry Shop
4. Calle de Postas
5. Plaza Mayor
6. Torre del Oro Bar Andalú
7. Mercado de San Miguel
8. Mesones (Cave Bars)
9. Convent Pastries
10. City Hall
11. Real-Estate Office
12. Cathedral of Almudena
13. Royal Palace

M Metro Station
Pedestrian Zones
Walking Tour Route

Because of his enlightened urban policies, King Charles III (who ruled until 1788) is affectionately called "the best mayor of Madrid." He decorated the city squares with fine fountains, got those meddlesome Jesuits out of city government, established the public school system, mandated underground sewers, made the Retiro a public park rather than a royal retreat, and generally cleaned up Madrid.

Look behind the king. The statue of the bear pawing the berry bush and the *madroño* trees in the big planter boxes are symbols of the city. Bears used to live in the royal hunting grounds outside Madrid. And the *madroño* trees produce a berry that makes the traditional *madroño* liqueur.

The king faces a red-and-white building with a bell tower. This was Madrid's first post office, founded by Charles III in the 1760s. Today, it's the county governor's office, though it's notorious for having been Francisco Franco's police headquarters. An amazing number of those detained and interrogated by the Franco police "tried to escape" by jumping out the windows to their deaths. Notice the hats of the civil guardsmen at the entry. It's said the hats have square backs, cleverly designed so that the men can lean against the wall while enjoying a cigarette.

Appreciate the harmonious architecture of the buildings that circle the square. Crowds fill the square on New Year's Eve as the rest of Madrid watches the action on TV. As Spain's "Big Ben" atop the governor's office chimes 12 times, Madrileños eat one grape for each ring to bring good luck through each of the next 12 months.

• *Cross the square, walking to the governor's office.*

Look at the curb directly in front of the entrance to the **governor's office.** The scuffed-up marker is "kilometer zero," the very center of Spain (with its six main highways indicated). Near the entrance are two plaques expressing thanks from the regional government to its citizens for assisting in times of dire need. To the left of the entrance, a plaque on the wall honors those who helped during the terrorist bombings of March 11, 2004.

A similar plaque on the right marks the spot where the war against Napoleon started in 1808. Napoleon wanted his brother to be king of Spain. Trying to finagle this, he brought nearly the entire Spanish royal family to France for negotiations. An anxious crowd gathered outside this building awaiting word of the fate of their royals. This was just after the French Revolution, and there was a general nervousness between France and Spain. When the people of Madrid heard that Napoleon had appointed his own brother as the new king of Spain, they gathered angrily in the streets. The French guard simply massacred the mob. Painter Francisco de Goya, who worked just up the street, observed the event and captured the tragedy in his paintings *Second of May, 1808* and *Third of May, 1808,* now in the Prado (for more on Goya, see page 345).

From Puerta del Sol to Plaza Mayor

On the corner of Calle Mayor and Puerta del Sol (downhill end of Puerta del Sol, across from McDonald's) is the busy *confitería*

Salon La Mallorquina (daily 9:00–21:15, closed mid-July–Aug). Go inside for a tempting peek at racks with goodies hot out of the oven. Enjoy observing the churning energy at the bar lined with locals popping in for a fast coffee and a sweet treat. The shop is famous for its cream-filled *Napolitana* pastry (€1). Or sample Madrid's answer to doughnuts, *rosquillas* (*tontas* means "silly"—plain, and *listas* means "all dressed up and ready to go"—with icing, €0.50 each). The room upstairs is more genteel.

From inside the shop, look back toward the entrance and notice the tile above the door with the 18th-century view of Puerta del Sol. Compare this with today's view out the door. This was before the square was widened, when a church stood where the *Tío Pepe* sign stands today. The French used this church to detain local patriots awaiting execution. (The venerable *Tío Pepe* sign, advertising a famous sherry for more than 100 years, was Madrid's first billboard, and today it's the only such ad allowed on the square.)

• *Cross busy Calle Mayor, round McDonald's, and veer up the pedestrian alley called* **Calle de Postas.**

The street sign shows the post coach heading for that famous first post office. Medieval street signs included pictures so the illiterate could "read" them. Fifty yards up the street, at Calle San Cristóbal, is Pans & Company, a popular Catalan sandwich chain. While Spaniards consider American fast food unhealthy—both culturally and physically—the local fast-food chains seem to be more politically and nutritionally correct.

• *From here, hike up Calle San Cristóbal.*

Within two blocks, you'll pass the local feminist bookshop (Librería Mujeres) and reach a small square. At the square, notice the big brick 17th-century Ministry of Foreign Affairs building (with the pointed spire)—originally a jail for aristocratic prisoners, since even the black sheep of fine families were given special treatment.

• *Turn right, and walk down Calle de Zaragoza under the arcade into the...*

▲Plaza Mayor

This square, built in 1619, is a vast cobbled traffic-free chunk of 17th-century Spain. Each side of the square is uniform, as if a grand palace were turned inside-out. The statue is of Philip III, who ordered the square's construction. Before the statue stood here, this site served as the city's theater/multimedia center of the 17th century. Upon this stage, much Spanish history has been played out: bullfights, fires, royal pageantry, and events of the gruesome Inquisition. Reliefs serving as seatbacks under the lampposts tell the story. During the Inquisition, many were tried here—suspected heretics, Protestants, Jews, tour guides without a local license, and Muslims whose "conversion" to Christianity was dubious. The guilty were paraded around the square before their execution, wearing billboards listing their many sins (bleachers were built for bigger audiences, while the wealthy rented balconies). Some were slowly strangled as they held a crucifix, hearing the reassuring words of a priest as this life was squeezed out of them with a garrote. Others were burned.

The square is painted a democratic shade of burgundy—the result of a citywide vote. Since Franco's death in 1975, there's been a passion for voting here. Three different colors were painted as samples on the walls of this square, and the city voted for its favorite.

A stamp-and-coin market bustles here on Sundays from 10:00 to 14:00; on any day, it's a colorful and affordable place to enjoy a cup of coffee. Throughout Spain, lesser *plazas mayores* provide peaceful pools in the river of Spanish life. The TI (daily 9:30–20:30, wonderfully air-conditioned and with free but limited Internet access) is under the building on the north side of the square, the Casa de la Panadería, decorated with painted figures (it once housed the Bakers'

Guild). The TI is also a meeting point for cheap daily walking tours—consider dropping by to reserve a spot (see "Tours in Madrid," earlier).

• *For some interesting, if gruesome, bullfighting lore, drop by the...*

Torre del Oro Bar Andalú

This bar is a good spot for a drink to finish off your Plaza Mayor visit (northwest corner of square, to the left of the Bakers' Guild). The bar has *Andalú* (Andalusian) ambience and an entertaining staff. Warning: They push expensive tapas on tourists. But buying a beer is safe and painless—just order a *caña* (small beer, shouldn't cost more than €2.50). The price list posted outside the door makes your costs perfectly clear (*mostrador* indicates the price at the bar).

The interior of the Torre del Oro bar is a temple to bullfighting, festooned with gory decor. Notice the breathtaking action captured in the many photographs. Look under the stuffed head of Barbero the bull. At eye level, you'll see a *puntilla*, the knife used to put a bull out of his misery at the arena. This was the knife used to kill Barbero. The plaque explains: weight, birth date, owner, date of death, which matador killed him, and the location. Just to the left of Barbero, there's a photo of Franco with a very famous bullfighter. This is Manuel Benítez Pérez—better known as El Cordobés, the Elvis of bullfighters and a working-class hero. At the top of the stairs to the WC, find the photo of El Cordobés and Robert Kennedy—looking like brothers. At the end of the bar in a glass case is the "suit of lights" the great El Cordobés wore in his ill-fated 1967 fight. With Franco in attendance, El Cordobés went on and on, long after he could have ended the fight, until finally the bull gored him. El Cordobés survived; the bull didn't. Find another photo of Franco with El Cordobés at the far end, to the left of Segador the bull. Under the bull (to the left, over the counter) is a photo of El Cordobés' illegitimate son kissing a bull. Disowned by El Cordobés senior, yet still using his dad's famous name after a court battle, the new El Cordobés is one of this generation's top fighters.

Consider taking a break at one of their sidewalk tables (or at any café/bar terrace facing Madrid's finest square). Cafetería Margerit (nearby) occupies the sunniest corner of the square and is a good place to enjoy a coffee with the view. The scene is easily worth the extra euro you'll pay for the drink.

Strolling from Plaza Mayor to the Royal Palace

Leave Plaza Mayor on Calle Ciudad Rodrigo (to your right as you exit the bull bar). You'll pass a series of fine turn-of-the-20th-century storefronts and sandwich joints, such as Casa Rúa, famous for their cheap *bocadillos de calamares*—fried squid rings on a roll.

From the archway, you'll see the covered **Mercado de San Miguel** (ornate iron posts, on left). This historic market has morphed into a gourmet food mall.

Before passing the market hall, look left down the street called Cava de San Miguel. If you like sangria and singing, come back after 22:00 and visit one of the *mesones* that line the street. These cave-like bars stretch way back and get packed with locals out on tacky dates who—emboldened by sangria, the setting, and Spain—might suddenly just start singing. It's a lowbrow, electric-keyboard, karaoke-type ambience, best on Friday and Saturday nights. There's a reason for these underground vaults—Plaza Mayor was built on a slope and they are part of a structural system that braces the leveled plaza.

• *On the opposite (downhill) side of the market, follow the pedestrian lane left. At the first corner, turn right and cross the small plaza to the modern brick* **convent**.

Notice the proud coat of arms over the convent's main entry. In Spain, the most prestigious thing a noble family could do was build and maintain a convent. To harvest all the goodwill created in your community, you'd want your family's insignia right there for all to see.

The door on the right says *venta de dulces* (sweets for sale). To buy goodies from the cloistered nuns, buzz the *monjas* button, then wait patiently for the sister to respond over the intercom. Say *"dulces"* (DOOL-thays), and she'll let you in (Mon–Sat 9:30–13:00 & 16:00–18:30, closed Sun). When the lock buzzes, push open the door and follow the sign to *torno*, the lazy Susan that lets the sisters sell their baked goods without being seen (smallest quantity: half, or *medio*, kilo—around €8). Of the many choices listed (all good), *galletas* (shortbread cookies) are the least expensive. The *pastas de almendra* (almond cookies) are a treat.

• *Follow Calle del Codo (where those in need of bits of armor shopped— see the street sign) uphill around the convent to Plaza de la Villa, the square where the* **City Hall** *is located.*
Stop at the gate before entering the square to notice (on your left) what's considered the oldest door in town on Madrid's oldest building—made of flint and inhabited since 1480.

Imagine how Philip II took this city by surprise when he decided to move the capital of Europe's largest empire—in the 17th century, even bigger than ancient Rome—from Toledo to humble Madrid. With no great edifices to administer their empire, the Habsburgs went on a building spree. But since their empire was drained of its riches by prolonged religious wars, they built Madrid with brick instead of more expensive and elegant granite.

The statue in the garden is of Don Alvaro de Bazán—mastermind of the Christian victory over the Turkish Ottomans at the naval battle of Lepanto in 1571. This pivotal battle, fought off the coast of Greece, slowed the Turkish threat to Christian Europe. This square was the heart of medieval Madrid, though little remains of the 14th-century town.

From here, busy Calle Mayor leads downhill for a couple more blocks to the Royal Palace. Halfway down (on the left), at #75, a **real-estate office** *(inmobiliaria)* advertises apartments for rent (apartments or condos, priced by the month—are in the hundreds or low thousands of euros) and condos for sale (with six-digit prices). To roughly convert square meters to square feet, multiply by 10. Notice how, for large items, locals still think in terms of *pesetas* ("pts"), the Spanish currency before euros took over in 2002.

A few steps farther down, on a tiny square opposite the recommended Casa Ciriaco restaurant (at #84—see page 380), a statue memorializes the 1906 anarchist bombing. The target was the royal couple as they paraded by on their wedding day. While the crowd was throwing flowers, an anarchist (what terrorists used to be called) threw a bouquet lashed to a bomb from a balcony of #84, which was a hotel at the time. He missed the royal newly-weds, but killed 23 people. Gory photos of the event hang inside the restaurant (to the right of the entrance).

• *Continue down Calle Mayor. Within a couple of blocks, you'll come to a busy street, Calle de Bailén.*

Across the busy street is Madrid's **Cathedral of Almudena** (built 1883–1993). While it faces the Royal Palace, you'll enter on the side from Calle de Bailén. Before entering (€1 donation requested), notice the central door featuring a relief of the cathedral's 1993 consecration with Pope John Paul II, King Juan Carlos, Queen Sofía, and Princess María Mercedes (the king's mom, in a wheelchair). While the exterior is a contemporary mix, the interior is Neo-Gothic, with a refreshingly modern and colorful ceiling, glittering 5,000-pipe organ, and a fine 15th-century painted altarpiece—striking in the otherwise modern interior. The historic highlight is the 12th-century coffin (empty, painted leather on wood, in a chapel behind the altar) of Madrid's patron saint, Isidro. A humble peasant, Isidro loved the handicapped and performed miracles. Forty years after he died, this coffin was opened and his body was found miraculously preserved, which convinced the pope to canonize him as the patron saint of Madrid and of farmers, with May 15 as his feast day.

Next to the cathedral is the **Royal Palace.** Visit the palace

Cheap Tricks in Madrid

- Instead of expensive city tour buses, take bus #27 on a €1 sightseeing joyride past some major Madrid landmarks. Catch the bus in front of the Royal Botanical Garden on the Paseo del Prado and ride it to the Plaza Castilla (the end of the line). This ride is described later in this chapter, under "Experiences in Madrid."
- Some major sights are free to enter at certain times (for example, the Prado is free Tue–Sat 18:00–20:00 and Sun 17:00–20:00, while the Centro de Arte Reina Sofía is free Sat afternoon after 14:30 and all day Sun). These Madrid sights are always free: CaixaForum, Naval Museum, Chapel of San Antonio de la Florida, Bullfighting Museum, Caja Madrid, and the Temple de Debod.
- The Plaza Mayor TI organizes cheap 90-minute English-language guided walks. Called Discover Madrid, they have different themes, run several times a day, and cost only €4.
- The Plaza Mayor TI has limited free Internet access.

now, using my self-guided tour (see below).

• *When you're finished, you may want to...*

Return to Puerta del Sol

With your back to the palace, face the equestrian statue of Philip IV and (beyond the statue) the Neoclassical **Royal Theater** (Teatro Real, rebuilt in 1997). On your left, the once-impressive **Madrid Tower** skyscraper marks the Plaza de España. Walk behind the Royal Theater (on the right, passing Café de Oriente—a favorite with theater-goers) to another square, where you'll find the Ópera Metro stop and the wonderfully pedestrianized Calle del Arenal, which leads back to Puerta del Sol.

Sights in Madrid

▲▲▲Royal Palace (Palacio Real)

Europe's third-greatest palace (after Versailles and Vienna's Schönbrunn), with arguably the most sumptuous original interior, is packed with tourists and royal antiques.

After a fortress burned down on this site in the 18th century, King Philip V commissioned this huge palace as a replacement. Though he ruled Spain for 40 years, Philip V was very French. (The grandson of Louis XIV, he was born in Versailles and preferred speaking French.) He ordered this palace to be built as his own Versailles (although his wife's Italian origin had a tremendous impact on the style). It's big—more than 2,000 rooms, with tons of luxurious tapestries, a king's ransom of chandeliers, priceless porcelain, and bronze decor covered in gold leaf. While these days the royal family lives in a mansion a few miles away, this place still functions as a royal palace, and is used for formal state receptions, royal weddings, and tourists' daydreams.

The lions you'll see throughout were symbols of power. The Bourbon kings considered previous royalty not up to European par, and this palace—along with their establishment of a Spanish porcelain works and tapestry works—was their effort to raise the bar.

Cost and Hours: €8 without a tour, €10 with a 60-min tour (explained below); April–Sept Mon–Sat 9:00–19:00, Sun 9:00–16:00; Oct–March Mon–Sat 9:30–18:00, Sun 9:00–15:00; last entry one hour before closing. The palace can close if needed for a royal function; you can call a day ahead to check (tel. 914-548-800).

Crowd-Beating Tips: The palace is most crowded on Wednesdays, when it's free for locals. To minimize lines, either arrive early, or go late any day except Wednesday.

Getting There: To get to the palace from Puerta del Sol, walk down the pedestrianized Calle del Arenal. If arriving by Metro, get off at the Ópera stop.

Services: At the palace, there are free lockers and a WC just past the ticket booth. Upstairs, you'll find a fine air-conditioned cafeteria (with salad bar) and a more serious bookstore.

Touring the Palace: A simple one-floor, 24-room one-way circuit is open to the public. You can wander on your own or join an English-language tour (check time of next tour and decide as you buy your ticket; the English-language tours depart sporadically, not worth a long wait). The tour guides, like the museum guidebook, show a passion for meaningless data. The €2.30 audioguides are much more interesting, and they complement what I describe below. If you enjoy sightseeing cheek-to-cheek, crank up the volume and share the audioguide with your companion. The armory and the pharmacy (included in your ticket) are in the courtyard. Photography is not allowed.

➋ **Self-Guided Tour:** If you tour the palace on your own, here are a few details beyond what you'll find on the little English descriptions posted in each room.

1. The Palace Lobby: In the old days, horse-drawn carriages would drop you off here. Today, limos for gala events do the same thing. Look for a sign that divides the visitors waiting for a tour from those going in alone. The modern black bust in the corner is of the current, very popular constitutional monarch—King Juan Carlos I. He's a "peoples' king," credited with bringing democracy to Spain after Franco.

2. The Grand Stairs: Fancy carpets are rolled down (notice the little metal bar-holding hooks) for formal occasions. At the top of the first landing, the blue-and-red coat of arms represents Juan Carlos. While Franco chose him to be his successor, J. C. knew Spain was ripe for democracy. Rather than become "Juan the Brief" (as some were nicknaming him), he turned real power over to the parliament. You'll see his (figure) head on the back of the Spanish €1 and €2 coins. At the top of the stairs (before entering first room, right of door) is a white marble bust of J. C.'s great-great-g-g-g-great-grandfather

Philip V, who began the Bourbon dynasty in Spain in 1700 and had this palace built.

3. Guard Room: The palace guards used to hang out in this relatively simple room. Notice the fine clocks. Charles IV, a great collector, amassed more than 700. The 150 clocks displayed in this palace are all in working order. Look up, and see the first ceiling fresco in a series by the great Venetian painter Giambattista (or G. B.) Tiepolo (also see "Throne Room," below). Most of what you see in the palace dates from the 18th century. But the carpet in this room was made in 1991 (see the corner folded over). While modern, it's made the traditional way—by hand in Madrid's royal tapestry factory.

4. Hall of Columns: Originally a ballroom and dining room, today this space is used for formal ceremonies. (For example, this is where Spain formally joined the European Union in 1985—see plaque on far wall.) The tapestries (like most you'll see in the palace) are 17th-century Belgian, from designs by Raphael. The central theme in the ceiling fresco is Apollo driving the chariot of the sun, while Bacchus enjoys wine, women, and song with a convivial gang. This is a reminder that the mark of a good king is to drive the chariot of state as smartly as Apollo, while providing an environment where the people can enjoy life to the fullest.

5. Throne Room: Red velvet walls, lions, and frescoes of Spanish scenes symbolize the monarchy in this Rococo riot. The 12 mirrors, impressive in their day, each represent a different month. The chandeliers (silver and crystal from Murano near Venice) are the best in the house. While the room is decorated in the 18th-century style, the throne dates only from 1977. In Spain, a new one is built for each king or queen (with a gilded portrait on the back). This is where the king's guests salute Juan Carlos before dinner. He receives them relatively informally...standing at floor level, rather than seated up on the throne. The coat of arms above the throne shows the complexity of the Bourbon empire across Europe—which, in the 18th century, included Tirol, Sicily, Burgundy, the Netherlands, and more.

The ceiling fresco (1764) is the last great work by Italian master G. B. Tiepolo, who died in Madrid in 1770. This painting celebrates the days of the vast Spanish empire—upon which the sun also never set. Find the Native American (hint: follow the rainbow to the macho red-caped conquistador who motions to someone he conquered).

The next several rooms were the living quarters of King Charles III (ruled 1759–1788). After his lunch room (with the round sofa in the center), you come to the...

6. Antechamber: The four paintings are of King Charles IV (looking a bit like a dim-witted George Washington) and his wife, María Luisa (who wore the pants in the palace)—all originals by Francisco de Goya. To meet the demand for his work, he made copies of these (which you'll see in the Prado). The clock—showing Cronus, god of time, in porcelain, bronze, and mahogany—sits on a music box. The gilded decor you see throughout the palace is bronze with gold leaf. Velázquez's famous painting *Las Meninas* (which you'll marvel at in the Prado) originally hung in this room.

7. Gasparini Room: This was meant to be Charles III's bedroom, but wasn't finished when he died. Instead, with its painted stucco ceiling and inlaid Spanish marble floor, it was the royal dressing room. It's a triumph of the Rococo style, with exotic motifs that were in vogue during that period. The Asian influence, also trendy at the time, is clear in the corners of the ornate ceiling. During restoration in 1992, the silk wallpaper was replaced with the original embroidery. Note the fine micro-mosaic table—a typical royal or aristocratic souvenir from any visit to Rome in the mid-1800s. For a divine monarch, dressing was a public affair. The court bigwigs would assemble here as the king, standing on a platform—notice the height of the mirrors—would pull on his leotards and toy with his wig.

In the next room, the silk wallpaper is new (*J.C.S.* indicates King Juan Carlos and Queen Sofía).

• *Pass through the silk room to reach...*

8. Charles III Bedroom: This room is dedicated to Charles III, known as one of the enlightened monarchs, who died here in his bed in 1788. His grandson, Ferdinand VII, commissioned the fresco on the ceiling, showing thanks to God for the birth of the first male grandson (that would be Ferdy himself) to continue the dynasty. Decorated in 19th-century Neoclassical style, the chandelier is in the shape of the fleur-de-lis (symbol of the Bourbon family) capped with a Spanish crown. The thick walls separating each room hide service corridors for servants, who scurried about generally unseen.

9. Porcelain Room: The several hundred plates that line this room were disassembled for safety during the Spanish Civil War. (Find the little screws in the greenery that hide the seams.)

The Neoclassical Yellow Room was a study for Charles III. Notice the fine chandelier, with properly cut crystal that shows all the colors of the rainbow.

10. Gala Dining Room: Up to 12 times a year, the king entertains as many as 144 guests at this bowling lane–size table, which can be extended to the length of the room. Find the two royal chairs. (Hint: With the modesty necessary for 21st-century monarchs, they are only a tad higher than the rest.) The parquet floor was the preferred dancing surface when balls were held in this fabulous room. Note the vases from China and the fresco depicting Christopher Columbus with exotic souvenirs and new, red-skinned friends. Imagine the lighting when the 15 chandeliers (and their 900 bulbs) are fired up.

11. Cinema Room (Sala de Monedas y Medallas): In the early 20th century, the royal family enjoyed "Sunday afternoons at the movies" here. Today, this room stores glass cases filled with coins and medals. The table used to be set up with lavish bouquets of flowers and fruits, which ended up in the dining room as centerpieces, effectively making it impossible for guests to talk across the table.

12. Silver Room: This collection of silver tableware dates from the 19th century. The older royal silver was melted down by Napoleon's brother to help fund wars of the Napoleonic age. If you look carefully, you can see quirky royal necessities, including a baby's silver rattle.

13. China Rooms: Several collections of china from different kings (some actually from China, others from royal workshops in Europe such as Sèvres and Meissen) are displayed in this room. This room illustrates how any self-respecting royal family in Europe would have had its own porcelain works (the technique was a royal secret).

• *Exit to the hallway and notice the interior courtyard you've been circling one room at a time. You can see how the royal family lived in the spacious middle floor while staff was upstairs, and the kitchens, garage, and storerooms were on the ground level. Between statues of the giants of Spanish royal history (Isabel and Ferdinand), you'll enter the...*

14. Royal Chapel: This chapel (likely closed for restoration in 2010) is used for private concerts and funerals. The royal coffin sits here before making the sad trip to El Escorial to join the rest of Spain's past royalty (see next chapter).

15. Queen's Boudoir: This room was for the ladies.

16. Stradivarius Room: The queen likes classical music. When you perform for her, do it with these precious 350-year-old violins. Of all of the instruments Antonius Stradivarius made, only 300 survive. This is the only matching quartet: two violins, a viola, and a cello.

17. Billiards and Smoking Rooms: The billiards room (with its English men's-club paneling) and the adjacent smoking room were for men only. The porcelain and silk of the smoking room imitates a Chinese opium den, which, in its day, was furnished only with pillows.

18. Queen's Tearoom: Small and intimate, the Neoclassical Wedgwood-like decoration stands out.

19. Fine Woods Room: Fine 18th- and 19th-century French inlaid-wood pieces decorate this room.

Exit the palace down the same grand stairway you climbed 24 rooms ago. Cross the big courtyard, heading to the far right corner to the...

20. Armory: Here you'll find the armor and swords of Ferdinand (husband of Isabel), Charles V (ruler of Spain at its peak of power), and Philip II (Charles' son, who watched Spain start its long slide downward).

Just inside the entry, you'll see the oldest piece in the collection: the shield of Boabdil, the last Moorish king who surrendered Granada in 1492. This main room is dominated by the armor of Charles V and Philip II—who dominated Europe in the 16th century. At the far end you'll meet Charles V on horseback. The mannequin of the king wears the same armor and assumes the same pose made famous by Titian's painting.

The tapestry above the armor warmed the walls of the otherwise stark palace that predated this one. Tapestries traveled ahead of royals to decorate their living space. They made many palaces "fit for a king" back when the only way to effectively govern was to be on the road a lot.

Circle the big room clockwise. The long wall on the left displays the armor of Charles V. The opposite wall showcases the armor and weapons of Philip II. Philip, who impoverished Spain with his wars against the Protestants, anticipated that debt collectors would ransack his estate after his death and specifically protected his fine collection of armor.

Downstairs is more armor, a mixed collection mostly from the 17th century. Notice the life-saving breastplates dimpled with bullet dents before you leave (to right of exit door).

Climb the steps from the armory exit to the viewpoint. This

vast palace backyard, today a city park, was the king's hunting ground.

21. Pharmacy: The royal pharmacy is opposite the armory, near the entry. Wander through six rooms stacked with jars and jugs of herbal cures, past exotic beakers, and under portraits of royal doctors with good English descriptions explaining 18th- and 19th-century medicine.

The upstairs, above the exit, has an air-conditioned cafeteria and a bookstore, which has a good variety of books on Spanish history. As you leave the palace, walk around the corner to the left, along the palace exterior, to the grand yet people-friendly Plaza de Oriente (with my recommended lunch spot, Café de Oriente; wonderful €13 lunch special, Mon-Fri 13:00-16:00). Throughout Europe, energetic governments are turning formerly car-congested wastelands into public spaces like this. Madrid's last mayor was nicknamed "The Mole" for all the digging he did. Where's all the traffic? Under your feet.

Madrid's Museum Neighborhood

Three great museums, all within a 10-minute walk of each other, cluster in east Madrid: El Prado (Europe's top collection of paintings), the Thyssen-Bornemisza Museum (a baron's collection of European art, from the old masters to the moderns), and the Centro de Arte Reina Sofía (modern art, including Picasso's famous *Guernica*).

If visiting all three museums, save a few euros by buying the *Paseo del Arte* **combo-ticket** (€14.40, buy at any of the three museums, good for a year). Note that it's free to enter the Prado Tuesday–Saturday 18:00–20:00, and Sunday 17:00–20:00, and the Reina Sofía Saturday 14:30–21:00 and Sunday 10:00–14:30 (both are free anytime for those under 18). The Prado and Thyssen-Bornemisza are closed Monday, and the Reina Sofía is closed Tuesday.

▲▲▲Prado Museum

With more than 3,000 canvases, including entire rooms of masterpieces by superstar painters, the Prado (PRAH-doh) is overwhelming. But if you use the free English floor plan (pick up as you enter) and follow my self-guided tour (see below), you'll be impressed. The Prado is *the* place to enjoy the great Spanish painter Francisco de Goya, and it's also the home of Diego Velázquez's *Las Meninas*, considered by many to be the world's finest painting, period. In addition to Spanish works,

Madrid's Museum Neighborhood

- ▬ PEDESTRIAN ZONES
- ← BLDG. ENTRANCES
- Ⓜ METRO STATION
- Ⓑ BUS #27 STOPS

Map labels: TO SOROLLA MUSEUM, TO BULLRING + AIRPORT, PUERTA DE ALCALÁ, Retiro Ⓜ, PLAZA DE CIBELES, PLAZA DE CIBELES, Banco de España Ⓜ, ALCALÁ, NAVAL MUSEUM, TO LAKE, ZARZUELA THEATER, THYSSEN MUSEUM, CALLE MONTALBAN, C. JUAN DE MENA, CALLE MAURA, RETIRO, TO PUERTA DEL SOL, CONGRESO DE LOS DIPUTADOS, CASON DE BUEN RETIRO, SAN JERONIMOS, PLAZA SANTA ANA, CERVANTES, PRADO MUSEUM, PARK, TO PLAZA MAYOR, HUERTAS, PLAZA PLATERIA MARTINEZ, Antón Martín, ROYAL BOTANICAL GARDEN, CAIXAFORUM, 200 YARDS, 200 METERS, TO Lavapiés Ⓜ, CUESTA MOYANO, PASEO DEL DUQUE, REINA SOFÍA MUSEUM, Ⓜ Atocha, Atocha RENFE, ATOCHA RENFE STATION

- ❶ Hotel Lope de Vega
- ❷ Hostales Gonzalo & Cervantes
- ❸ Taberna de Dolores
- ❹ VIPS Café (under Palace Hotel)
- ❺ Viva la Vida Organic Market & Vegetarian Buffet

DCH

you'll find paintings by Italian and Flemish masters, including Hieronymus Bosch's delightful *Garden of Delights* altarpiece.

Cost and Hours: €6, free Tue–Sat 18:00–20:00 and Sun 17:00–20:00, and free anytime to anyone under 18. Open Tue–Sun 9:00–20:00, closed Mon, last entry 30 min before closing.

Location: It's at the Paseo del Prado. The Banco de España (line 2) and Atocha Metro (line 1) stops are each a five-minute walk from the museum.

The Prado Expansion: The first extension, inaugurated in

2007, was partially constructed in the cloister of the 17th-century San Jerónimos church. This spacious addition houses a sculpture gallery and temporary exhibits, as well as a café and gift shop. The adjacent army museum is moving to Toledo, which will open up space for sculpture and decorative arts.

Crowd-Beating Tips: Lunchtime (14:00–16:00) and week-days are generally less crowded. It's always packed when free and on weekends; it's worth paying the entry price on other days to have your space. Free tickets are issued only after 18:00.

Entrances: You can buy your ticket at the Goya entrance. From the ticket office, go around the corner to the left and into the big service-filled Jerónimos entrance. (The Murillo entrance, the one across from the Royal Botanical Garden, is for advance book-ings such as school groups.) Pick up a detailed map and consider renting an audioguide.

Tours: Take a tour, rent the €3 audioguide, buy a guidebook, or use my self-guided commentary (next). Given the ever-chang-ing locations of paintings (making my self-guided tour tough to follow), the audioguide (with 120 paintings described) is a good investment, allowing you to wander. When you see a painting of interest, simply punch in the number and enjoy the description. You can return the audioguide at any of the exits. And, if you're on a tight budget, remember that two can crank up the volume, listen cheek-to-cheek, and share one machine.

Services and Information: Your bags will be scanned (just like at the airport) before you leave them at the free and manda-tory baggage storage (no water bottles, food, backpacks, or large umbrellas allowed inside). A cafeteria is in the extension area near the Jerónimos entrance. Tel. 913-302-800, http://museoprado .mcu.es.

Photography: Not allowed.

⊖ Self-Guided Tour: Thanks to Gene Openshaw for writing the following tour.

New World gold funded the Prado, the greatest painting museum in the world. You'll see world-class Italian Renaissance art (especially Titian), Northern art (Bosch, Rubens, Dürer), and Spanish art (El Greco, Velázquez, and Goya). This huge museum is not laid out chronologically, so this tour will not be chronologi-cal. Instead, we'll hit the highlights with a minimum of walking. Make sure to have a map (free, available at entry). If you can't find a particular painting, ask a guard.

• *Start at the Room of the Muses (Sala de los Muses), the center of the*

Prado Museum Overview

NOTE: NUMBERS INDICATE ROOM NUMBERS

SECOND FLOOR

GOYA 85, 89, 90–94

EL GRECO 9a, 10a

TITIAN + RUBENS 7a, 8a, 9, 11

VELÁZQUEZ 12, 14–16, 18

COUNTER-REFORMATION 18a, 28

GOYA ENTRANCE UPPER

ROTUNDA

STAIRS

GOYA 16b, 19–21, 29, 32, 34–39

FIRST FLOOR

LOBBY: CAFÉ, GIFT SHOP + INFO BOOTHS

JERÓNIMOS ENTRANCE

MURILLO ENTRANCE (GROUPS)

NORTHERN ART

MEDIEVAL 56a, 56b

ITALIAN RENAISSANCE

GOYA 66, 67

GOYA ENTRANCE LOWER

ROTUNDA

STAIRS

VELÁZQUEZ ENTRANCE

GROUND FLOOR

building. Go upstairs to the main gallery, filled with Golden Age Spanish art. Go right past the Spanish masters. At the far end of the hall, find Murillo, Rooms 28 and 29.

Bartolomeo Murillo's *Immaculate Conception (La Inmaculada "de El Escorial")* puts a human face on the abstract Catholic doctrine that Mary was conceived and born free of original sin. Floating in a cloud of Ivory Soap purity, this "immaculate" virgin radiates youth and wholesome goodness. (You'll find Murillo and his style described in the Sevilla chapter, page 520.)

• At the far end of the gallery, go into the round Room 32 where you'll see many royal portraits by Goya.

Francisco de Goya (1746–1828): Follow this complex man through the stages of his life—from dutiful court painter, to political rebel and scandal-maker, to the disillusioned genius of his "dark paintings."

The Family of Charles IV (La Familia de Carlos IV) is all decked out in their Sunday best for this group portrait. Goya himself stands to the far left, painting the court (a tribute to Velázquez in *Las Meninas*)...and revealing the shallow people beneath the royal trappings. King Charles, with his ridiculous hairpiece and goofy smile, was a vacuous, henpecked husband. His domi-

neering queen upstages him, arrogantly stretching her swanlike neck. The other adults, with their bland faces, are bug-eyed with stupidity.

• *Find the staircase or elevator behind* The Family of Charles IV *and head up to the second floor.*

Rooms 90–94 display canvases that were Goya's designs to make tapestries for nobles' palaces. The scenes make it clear that, while revolution was brewing in America and France, Spain's lords and ladies played—picnicking, dancing, flying kites, playing paddleball and Blind Man's Bluff, or just relaxing in the sun—the well-known *The Parasol (El Quitasol)* is in Room 85.

• *Return down the stairs to the first floor, Room 36.*

Rumors flew that Goya was fooling around with the vivacious Duchess of Alba, and he may have painted her in a scandalous

pose. You'll find two similar paintings, the *Nude Maja (La Maja Desnuda)* and *Clothed Maja (La Maja Vestida)*. A *maja* was the name for a trendy, working-class girl. Whether she's a duchess or a *maja*, Goya had painted a naked lady. And

that was enough to risk incurring the wrath of the Inquisition. The *Nude* stretches in a Titian-esque pose to display her charms, the pale body highlighted by cool green sheets. According to a believable legend, the two paintings were displayed in a double frame, with the *Clothed Maja* sliding over the front to hide the *Nude* from Inquisitive minds.

• *Go back by the stairs still on the first floor, Room 39.*

Goya became a political liberal, a champion of democracy. He was crushed when France's hero of the Revolution, Napoleon, morphed into a tyrant and invaded Spain. On the *Second of May, 1808,* Madrid's citizens were protesting the occupation in Puerta del Sol, when the French sent in their dreaded Egyptian mercenaries. They plow through the dense tangle of Madrileños, who have nowhere to run. The next day, the *Third of May, 1808,* the French rounded up ringleaders and executed them. The colorless firing squad—a faceless machine of death—mows them down, and they fall in bloody, tangled heaps. Goya throws a harsh prison-yard floodlight on the main victim, who spreads his arms Christ-like to ask, "Why?"

Politically, Goya was split—he was a Spaniard but he knew France was leading Europe into the modern age. His art, while political, has no Spanish or French flags. It's a universal comment on the horror of war. Many consider Goya the last classical and first modern painter...the first painter with a social conscience.

• *To find the "dark paintings," silently flagellate yourself, then go downstairs to Rooms 66 and 67.*

The Colossus shows the destitution following the war with France. This was the world as Goya saw it. Depressed and deaf from syphilis, he retired to his small home and smeared the walls with his "dark paintings"...dark in color and in mood. From this point until his death, Goya would paint his nightmares...literally. The style is considered Romantic—emphasizing emotion over beauty—but it foreshadows 20th-century Surrealism with its bizarre imagery and Expressionism, thick brushstrokes and cynical outlook.

Stepping into Room 67 you are surrounded by art from Goya's dark period. He painted what he felt with a radical technique not burdened with reality—a century before his time. And he painted without being paid for it. This room contains, I believe, the first rare art done without a commission.

Dark forces convened continually in Goya's dining room, where *The Witches' Sabbath (El Aquelarre)* hung. The witches, who look like skeletons, swirl in a frenzy around a dark, Satanic goat in monk's clothing who presides over the obscene rituals. The main witch exudes wild-eyed adoration and lust, while a noble lady (right of center) folds her hands primly in her lap ("I thought this was a Tupperware party!"). Or, perhaps it's a pep rally for her execution, maybe inspired by the excited frenzy that accompanied Plaza Mayor executions. Nobody knows for sure.

In the *Battle to the Death (Duelo a Garrotazos),* two giants stand face to face, buried up to their knees, and flail at each other with clubs. It's a standoff between superpowers in the never-ending cycle of war—a vision of a tough time when people on the streets would kill for a piece of bread.

In *Saturn Devouring One of His Sons (Saturno)*, we see Saturn—fearful that his sons would overthrow him as king of the Roman gods—eating one of them. Saturn, also known as Cronus (Time), may symbolize how time devours us all. (Either way, the painting brings new meaning to the term "child's portion.")

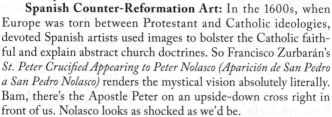

The Dog (El Perro) is, according to some, the hinge between classic art and modern art. The dog, so full of feeling and sadness, is being swallowed by quicksand...much as, to Goya, the modern age was overtaking a more classical era.

• *Go back upstairs into Room 18a.*

Spanish Counter-Reformation Art: In the 1600s, when Europe was torn between Protestant and Catholic ideologies, devoted Spanish artists used images to bolster the Catholic faithful and explain abstract church doctrines. So Francisco Zurbarán's *St. Peter Crucified Appearing to Peter Nolasco (Aparición de San Pedro a San Pedro Nolasco)* renders the mystical vision absolutely literally. Bam, there's the Apostle Peter on an upside-down cross right in front of us. Nolasco looks as shocked as we'd be.

• *Velázquez can be found in Rooms 18 and 16–14, with a grand finale in large lozenge-shaped Room 12.*

Diego Velázquez (1599–1660): Velázquez (vel-LAHTH-keth) was the photojournalist of court painters, capturing the Spanish king and his court with a blend of formal portrait and candid snapshot.

Prince Balthazar Carlos on Horseback (El Príncipe Baltasar Carlos, a Caballo) is exactly the kind of portrait Velázquez was called on to produce. The prince prances like a Roman emperor—only this "emperor" is just a cute little five-year-old acting oh so serious. Get up close and notice that his remarkably detailed costume is nothing but a few messy splotches of pink and gold paint—the proto-Impressionism Velázquez helped pioneer.

The Surrender of Breda (La Rendición de Breda) is a piece of artistic journalism, chronicling Spain's victory over the Dutch. The defeated Dutchman starts to kneel, but the Spaniard stops him—no need to rub salt in the wound. Twenty-five lances silhouetted against the sky reinforce the optimistic calm-after-the-battle mood.

Velázquez's boss, King Philip IV, had an affair, got caught, and repented by commissioning the *Crucifixion (Cristo Crucificado)*.

Christ hangs his head, humbly accepting his punishment, while Philip is left to stare at the slowly dripping blood, contemplating how long Christ had to suffer to atone for Philip's sins.

Velázquez's *The Maids of Honor (Las Meninas)* is a peek at nannies caring for Princess Margarita and, at the same time, a behind-the-scenes look at Velázquez at work. One hot summer day in 1656, Velázquez (at left, with paintbrush and Dalí moustache) stands at his easel and stares out at the people he's painting—the king and queen. They would have been standing about where we are, and we see only their reflection in the mirror at the back of the room. Their daughter (blonde hair, in center) watches her parents being painted, joined by her servants *(meninas)*, dwarfs, and the family dog. Also, at that very moment, a man happens to pass by the doorway at back and pauses to look in.

This frozen moment is lit by the window on the right, splitting the room into bright and shaded planes that recede into the distance. The main characters look right at us, making us part of

the scene, seemingly able to walk around, behind, and among the characters.

If you stand in the center of the room, the 3-D effect is most striking. This is art come to life. Now look around and see how Velázquez enjoyed capturing light—and capturing the moment.

Velázquez's *The Drinkers (Los Borrachos)* is a cell-phone snapshot in a blue-collar bar, with a couple of peasants mugging for a photo-op with a Greek god—Bacchus, the god of wine. This was an early work, before he got his court-painter gig. A personal homage to the hardworking farmers enjoying the fruit of their labor, it shows how Velázquez had a heart for real people and believed they deserved portraits, too.

• *To find works by Titian, you will need to visit several rooms (Room 11, 7a, 8a). Start in Room 11.*

Titian (c. 1490–1576): Titian painted portraits of Spain's two Golden Age kings—both staunch Catholics—who amassed this racy collection. *Charles V on Horseback (El Emperador Carlos V en la Batalla de Muhlberg,* Room 11) rears on his horse, raises his lance, and rides out to crush an army of Lutherans. Charles, having inherited many kingdoms and baronies through his family connections, was the world's most powerful man in the 1500s.

• *Sitting amid the Titian collection (in Room 9) are works by Rubens, described below. But for now, we'll continue with Titian in Room 8a.*

Danae and the Shower of Gold (Danae Recibiendo la Lluvia de Oro), from Greek mythology, shows the princess opening her legs to receive Zeus, the lecherous king of the gods, who descends as a shower of gold. Danae is helpless with rapture, while her servant tries to catch the holy spurt with a towel.

In contrast, Charles V's son, *Philip II (Felipe II),* looks pale, suspicious, and lonely—a scholarly and complex figure. He built the austere, monastic palace at El Escorial, but also indulged himself with Titian's bevy of Renaissance Playmates—a sampling of which is here in the Prado.

• *Now backtrack to Room 9 to see more flesh.*

Peter Paul Rubens (1577–1640): A native of Flanders, Rubens painted Baroque-style art meant to play on the emotions, titillate the senses, and carry you away. *Diana and Her Nymphs Discovered by a Satyr (Diana y sus Ninfas Sorprendidas por Sátiros)* ripples from left to right with a wave of figures, as the nymphs flee from the half-human sex predators. But Diana, queen of the hunt, turns to bravely face the satyrs with her spear. All of Rubens' trademarks are here—sex, violence, action, emotion, bright colors, fleshy bodies—with the wind-machine set on 10.

Rubens' *The Three Graces (Las Tres Gracias)* celebrate cellulite. Their ample, glowing bodies intertwine as they exchange meaningful glances. The Grace at left is Rubens' young second wife, who shows up fairly regularly in his paintings.

• *El Greco's works are nearby, in Rooms 9a and 10a.*

El Greco (1541–1614): El Greco was born in Greece (his name is Spanish for "The Greek"), trained in Venice, then settled in Toledo—60 miles from Madrid. His paintings are like Byzantine icons drenched in Venetian color and fused in the fires of Spanish mysticism. (For more on El Greco, see page 439 and visit Toledo.)

In *Christ Carrying the Cross (Cristo Abrazado a la Cruz),* Jesus accepts his fate, trudging toward death with blood running down his neck. He hugs the cross and directs his gaze along the crossbar. His upturned eyes (sparkling with a streak of white paint) lock onto his next stop—heaven.

The Adoration of the Shepherds (La Adoración de los Pastores), originally painted for El Greco's own burial chapel in Toledo, has the artist's typical two-tiered composition—heaven above, earth below. The long, skinny shepherds are stretched unnaturally in between, flickering like flames toward heaven.

The Nobleman with His Hand on His Chest (El Caballero de la Mano al Pecho) is an elegant and somewhat arrogant man whose hand has the middle fingers touching—El Greco's trademark way of expressing elegance (or was it the 16th-century symbol for "Live long and prosper"?). The signature is on the right in faint Greek letters—"Doménikos Theotokópoulos," El Greco's real name.

• *Say hello one more time to* Las Meninas *on the way to the stairs and elevator off Room 14. Then go down to the ground floor.*

Italian Renaissance: During its Golden Age (the 1500s), Spain may have been Europe's richest country, but Italy was still the most cultured. Spain's kings loved how Italian Renaissance artists captured a three-dimensional world on a two-dimensional canvas, bringing Bible scenes to life and celebrating real people and their emotions.

Raphael's *Christ Falls on the Way to Calvary (Caída en el Camino del Calvario)* is a study in contrasts. Below the crossbar, Christ and the women swirl in agonized passion. Above, bored soldiers mill about on the bleak hill where Jesus will die.

In the *Death of the Virgin (El Tránsito de la Virgen)*, Mantegna masters Renaissance 3-D. The apostles mourn in a crowded room, while the floor tiles recede into the distance, creating the subconscious effect of carrying Mary's soul out the window into the serene distance.

Fra Angelico's *The Annunciation (La Anunciación)* is half medieval piety, half Renaissance realism. In the crude Garden

of Eden scene (on the left), a scrawny, sinful First Couple hovers unrealistically above the foliage, awaiting eviction. The angel's Annunciation to Mary (right side) is more Renaissance, both with its upbeat message (that Jesus will be born to redeem sinners like Adam and Eve) and in the budding photorealism, set beneath 3-D arches. (Still, aren't the receding bars of the porch's ceiling a bit off? Painting three dimensions wasn't that easy.)

• *Go to Room 50.*

Here you'll find Spain's medieval roots. This art features nothing but saints and Bible scenes—appropriate for a country whose extreme religious devotion was forged in seven centuries of bloody war against Muslims.

• *Backtrack to Room 49, take a left through 57b, then through 57, turn left into 58 to see...*

Northern Art: *The Descent from the Cross (El Descendimiento de la Cruz)* is a masterpiece by Flemish painter Roger van der Weyden, showing the psychological character of real people in a contemporary (1435) scene to portray this Biblical event. The Flemish were masters of detail, as you can see in the cloth, jewels, faces, and even tears. The creative composition suggests that, in losing her son, Mary suffered along with Jesus. As the Netherlands was then a part of the Spanish empire, this painting ended up in Madrid.

• *Next, go from Room 58a to 56a to see Bosch's* Garden of Earthly Delights.

Hieronymous Bosch (c. 1450–1516), in his cryptic triptych *The Garden of Earthly Delights (El Jardín de las Delicias)*, relates the message that the pleasures of life are fleeting, so we'd better avoid them or we'll wind up in hell. The large altarpiece has so many interesting small figures that it helps to "frame off" small sections to catch the details. Here's the big picture: In the central panel, men on horseback ride round and round, searching for but never reaching the elusive Fountain of Youth. Others frolic in earth's "Garden," oblivious to where they came from (paradise, left panel) and where they may end up (hell, right panel). On the left, innocent Adam and Eve get married, with God himself performing the ceremony. The right panel is hell, a burning wasteland where genetic-mutant demons torture sinners. Everyone gets their just desserts, like the glutton who is eaten and re-eaten eternally. In the center, hell is literally frozen over. A creature with a broken eggshell body, tree-trunk legs, and a witch's cap stares out—it's the face of Bosch himself. Many other fascinating *El Boscos* are in this room.

On the opposite wall, Pieter Bruegel (BROY-gull) the Elder's work chronicles the 16th century's violent Catholic-Protestant wars in *The Triumph of Death (El Triunfo de la Muerte)*. The painting is one big, chaotic battle, featuring skeletons attacking helpless mortals. Bruegel's message is simple and morbid: No one can escape death.

• *Find Dürer's work nearby, in Room 55b.*

Albrecht Dürer's *Self-Portrait (Autorretrato)* is possibly the first true self-portrait. The artist, age 26, is dolled up in a fancy Italian hat and permed hair. He'd recently returned from Italy and wanted to impress his fellow Germans with his sophistication. But Dürer wasn't simply vain. He'd grown accustomed, as an artist in Renaissance Italy, to being treated like a prince. Note Dürer's signature, the pyramid-shaped "A. D." (D inside the A) on the windowsill.

Dürer's *Adam and Eve* (two separate panels) are the first full-size nudes in Northern European art. Like Greek statues, they pose in their separate niches, with three-dimensional, anatomically correct bodies. This was a bold humanist proclamation that the body is good, man is good, and the things of the world are good.

• *The Prado is also good, but our tour is over. Exit through Room 55 and continue through the red-painted walls to the bright and open space of the Prado extension, where you'll find the café, exhibit halls of the San Jerónimos cloister, and the Jerónimos exit.*

▲▲Thyssen-Bornemisza Museum

Locals call this stunning museum simply the Thyssen (TEE-sun). It displays the impressive collection that Baron Thyssen (a wealthy German married to a former Miss Spain) sold to Spain for $350 million. The museum offers a unique chance to enjoy the sweep of all art history—including a good sampling of the "isms" of the 20th century—in one collection. It's basically minor works by major artists and major works by minor artists. (Major works by major artists are in the Prado.) But art-lovers appreciate how the good baron's art complements the Prado's collection by filling in where the Prado is weak—such as Impressionism, which is the Thyssen's forte.

Cost and Hours: €6 (up to €5 more for optional special exhibits); children under 12 free, Tue–Sun 10:00–19:00, closed Mon, last entry 30 min before closing.

Location: The museum is kitty-corner from the Prado at Paseo del Prado 8 in Palacio de Villahermosa (Metro: Banco de España).

Services and Information: Free baggage storage, €4 audioguide, café, shop, no photos, tel. 914-203-944, www.museo thyssen.org.

Touring the Museum: After purchasing your ticket, continue down the wide main hall past larger-than-life paintings of King Juan Carlos and Queen Sofía, and then paintings of the baron (who died in 2002) and his art-collecting baroness, Carmen. At the info desk, pick up two museum maps (one for numbered rooms, another for lettered rooms): Each floor is divided into two separate areas: the permanent collection (blue-numbered rooms) and additions from the baroness since the 1980s (red-lettered rooms). Most visitors stick to the permanent collection.

Ascend to the top floor and work your way down, taking a delightful walk through art history. Visit the rooms on each floor in numerical order, from Primitive Italian (Room 1) to Surrealism and Pop Art (Room 48).

Temporary exhibits at the Thyssen often parallel those at the free **Caja Madrid** exhibit hall (Tue–Sat 10:00–20:00, closed Mon, tel. 913-792-050, www.fundacioncajamadrid.es), across from the Descalzas Royal Monastery on Plaza San Martín.

Afterwards, if you're heading to Centro de Arte Reina Sofía and you're tired, hail a cab at the gate to zip straight there.

▲▲▲Centro de Arte Reina Sofía

Perhaps Europe's most enjoyable modern art museum, the Reina Sofía shows off an exceptional collection of 20th-century art in

what was Madrid's first public hospital (notice the iron-barred windows—facing the court-yard—for the mentally ill ward).

The new curator, who has a passion for cinema, has paired paintings with films from each decade throughout the museum. This provides a fascinating insight into the social context that inspired the art of Spain's tumultuous 20th century. Make a point to understand why a particular film was chosen, in order to gain an insight into Spain's 20th-century scars.

Cost and Hours: €6, free Sat afternoon after 14:30 (less crowded after 15:00) and all day Sun, always free to those under 18 and over 65. Even if admission is free when you visit, grab a ticket anyway. The museum is open Mon and Wed–Sat 10:00–21:00, Sun 10:00–14:30, closed Tue.

Location: It's across from the Atocha Metro station at Santa Isabel 52. In the Metro station, follow signs for Reina Sofía. At the opening into a square, look for the exterior glass elevators. There are two entrances: the old entrance (leads to permanent collection first; on Calle Sánchez Bustillo, on a big square close to the Metro stop) and the new entrance (mostly for tour groups).

Services and Information: Good brochure, no tours in English, hardworking €4 audioguide, no photos, free baggage storage. The *librería* just outside the new addition has a larger selection of Picasso and Surrealist reproductions than the main gift shop at the entrance. Tel. 914-675-062, www.museoreinasofia.es.

Touring the Museum: The permanent collection is on the second and fourth floors; temporary exhibits are on the first and third floors. Ride the fancy glass elevator to the second floor and follow the room numbers for art chronologically displayed from 1900 to 1940. The fourth floor continues the collection, from 1940 to 1980.

Picasso's *Guernica*: The museum is most famous for Pablo Picasso's *Guernica* (second floor, Room 7), an epic painting showing the horror of modern war. Notice the two rooms of studies Picasso did for *Guernica*, filled with iron-nail tears and screaming mouths. *Guernica* was displayed at the Museum of Modern Art in New York City until Franco's death, and now it reigns as Spain's national piece of art (see the sidebar on the next page spread).

Guernica

Perhaps the single most impressive piece of art in Spain is Pablo Picasso's *Guernica*. The monumental canvas—one of Europe's must-see sights—is not only a piece of art but a piece of history, capturing the horror of modern war in a modern style.

Pablo Picasso (1881–1973), a Spaniard, was in Paris in 1937, preparing an exhibition of paintings for the city's world's fair. Meanwhile, a bloody Civil War was being fought in his own country. The legally elected democratic government was being challenged by traditionalist right-wing forces under Francisco Franco. Franco would eventually win and rule the country with an iron fist for three decades.

On April 27, 1937, Guernica—a proud Basque market town in northern Spain—was the target of the world's first saturation-bombing raid on civilians. Franco gave permission to his fascist ally, Hitler, to use the town as a guinea pig to try out Germany's new air force. The raid leveled the town, causing destruction that was unheard-of at the time (though by 1944 it would be commonplace). For more on the town of Guernica and the bombing, see page 163.

News of the bombing reached Picasso in Paris. He scrapped earlier plans and immediately set to work sketching scenes of the destruction as he imagined it. In a matter of weeks, he put these bomb-shattered shards together into a large mural (286 square feet). For the first time, the world could see the destructive force of the rising fascist movement—a prelude to World War II.

The bombs are falling, shattering the quiet village. A woman looks up at the sky (far right), horses scream (center), and a man falls from a horse and dies, while a wounded woman drags herself through the streets. She tries to escape, but her leg is too thick, dragging her down, like trying to run from something in a nightmare. On the left, a bull—a symbol of Spain—ponders it all, watching over a mother and her dead baby...a modern *pietà*. A woman in the center sticks her head out to see what's going on. The whole scene is lit from above by the stark light of a bare bulb. Picasso's painting threw a light on the brutality of Hitler and Franco, and suddenly the whole world was watching.

Picasso's abstract, Cubist style reinforces the message. It's as if he'd picked up the shattered shards and pasted them onto a canvas. The black and white tones are as gritty as the black-and-white newspaper photos that reported the bombing. The drab colors create a depressing, almost nauseating mood.

Picasso chose images with universal symbolism, making the work a commentary on all wars. Picasso himself said that the central horse, with the spear in its back, symbolizes humanity succumbing to brute force. The fallen rider's arm is severed and his sword is broken, more symbols of defeat. The bull, normally a proud symbol of strength and independence, is impotent and frightened. Near the bull, the dove of peace can do nothing but cry.

The bombing of Guernica—like the entire Spanish Civil War (1936-1939)—was an exercise in brutality. As one side captured a town, it might systematically round up every man, old and young—including priests—line them up, and shoot them in revenge for atrocities by the other side.

Thousands of people attended the Paris fair, and *Guernica* caused an immediate sensation. They could see the horror of modern war technology, the vain struggle of the Spanish Republicans, and the cold indifference of the fascist war machine. After the Paris exhibition, *Guernica* was exiled to America until Franco's death. Picasso also vowed never to return to Spain while Franco ruled. (Franco outlived him.)

With each passing year, the canvas seemed more and more prophetic—honoring not just the hundreds or thousands that died in Guernica, but also the 600,000 victims of Spain's bitter Civil War, and the 80 million worldwide that perished in World War II. Picasso put a human face on what we now call "collateral damage."

After pondering the destruction of war, visit the room farthest back from the painting (confusingly, also numbered 7) to see photos of Picasso creating this masterpiece.

The film in the room directly opposite *Guernica* is *España 1936*, produced by the Madrid government (Spain's "last red city") late in the war, with a fierce anti-Franco perspective. Of course, Franco won. The theater about 90 feet to the right of *Guernica* shows a 1971 satirical documentary that uses clips from post-civil war propaganda films praising Franco. It's called *Songs After a War* (*Canciones para después de una Guerra)* and couldn't be shown in Spain until after Franco's death.

Don't miss the model of the Spanish Pavilion at the 1937 Paris Expo. Picasso was readying to paint something light and "typically Spanish," such as flamenco and matadors, for the Expo. But the bombing of Guernica jolted him into the realization that "the real Spain" was a country torn by civil war. The pavilion was a vessel for anti-Franco propaganda and its centerpiece was *Guernica*.

After a 44-year exile in New York, *Guernica* finally came home to Spain on September 11, 1981.

Salvador Dalí: The museum houses an easy-to-enjoy collection by other modern artists, including more of Picasso and a mind-bending room of works by Salvador Dalí. The early Dalí is in Room 3; the signature Dalí works are in Room 12. *The Great Masturbator* is exhausting psychologically, depicting in its surrealism a lonely, highly sexual genius, in love with his muse, Gala, while she is still married to a French poet. Check out the propaganda movie produced by the Spanish Republic (pre-Franco) that shows the sad state of its people.

Room 10 is a treat for movie and Surrealism buffs: Two circa-1930 films—*The Andalusian Dog* and *The Golden Age*—by director Luis Buñuel, who had help from friends Dalí and the poet Federico García Lorca, play continuously. Lorca and Dalí were members of "The Generation of '27," a group of nonconformist creative Spanish bohemians who had a huge influence culturally and artistically on their era.

Near the Prado

▲Retiro Park (Parque del Buen Retiro)—Once the private domain of royalty, this majestic park has been a favorite of Madrid's commoners since Charles III decided to share it with his subjects in the late 18th century. Siesta in this 300-acre green-and-breezy escape from the city. At midday on Saturday and Sunday, the area around the lake becomes a street carnival, with jugglers, puppeteers, and lots of local color. These peaceful gardens offer great picnicking and people-watching. From the Retiro Metro stop, walk to the big lake (El Estanque), where you can cheaply rent a rowboat. Past the lake, a grand boulevard of statues leads to the Prado.

▲**Royal Botanical Garden (Real Jardín Botánico)**—After your Prado visit, you can take a lush and fragrant break in this sculpted park. Wander among trees from around the world. The flier in English explains that this is actually more than a park—it's a museum of plants (€2, daily 10:00–21:00, until 18:00 in winter, entry opposite Prado's Murillo/south entry, Plaza de Murillo 2).

▲**Naval Museum (Museo Naval)**—This museum tells the story of Spain's navy, from the Armada to today, in a plush and fascinating-to-boat-lovers exhibit. Given Spain's importance in maritime history, there's quite a story to tell (free, no English anywhere, Tue–Sun 10:00–14:00, closed Mon and Aug, a block north of the Prado across boulevard from Thyssen-Bornemisza Museum, Paseo del Prado 5, tel. 915-239-884, www.museonavalmadrid .com). Because this is a military facility, you'll need to show your passport to get in.

CaixaForum—Across the street from the Prado and Royal Botanical Garden, you'll find this impressive exhibit hall with sleek architecture and an outdoor hanging garden—a bushy wall festooned with greens designed by a French landscape artist. The forum, funded by La Caixa Bank, features world-class art exhibits—generally 20th-century art, well-described in English and changing three times a year. Ride the elevator to the top, where you'll find a chic café with €12 lunch specials and sperm-like lamps swarming down from the ceiling, and explore your way down (free, daily 10:00–20:00, Paseo del Prado 36, tel. 913-307-300, www.obrasocial.lacaixa.es).

Elsewhere in Madrid

Descalzas Royal Monastery (Monasterio de las Descalzas Reales)—Madrid's most visit-worthy monastery was founded in the 16th century by Philip II's sister, Joan of Habsburg (known to Spaniards as Juana, and to Austrians as Joanna). She's buried here. The monastery's chapels are decorated with fine art, Rubens-designed tapestries, and the heirlooms of the wealthy women who joined the order (the nuns were required to give a dowry). Because this is still a working Franciscan monastery, tourists can visit only when the nuns vacate the cloister, and the number of daily visitors is limited. The scheduled tours often sell out—come in the morning to buy your ticket, even if you want an afternoon tour (€5, visits guided in Spanish or English depending on demand, Tue–Thu and Sat 10:30–12:30 & 16:00–17:30, Fri 10:30–12:30, Sun 11:00–13:30, closed Mon, Plaza de las Descalzas Reales 3, near the Ópera Metro stop and just a short walk from Puerta del Sol, tel. 914-548-800). The free **Caja Madrid** exhibit hall is across the street from the monastery (Tue–Sat 10:00–20:00, closed Mon).

▲National Archaeological Museum (Museo Arqueológico Nacional)—This fine museum gives you a chronological walk through the story of Iberia on one convenient floor. With a rich collection of artifacts (but a maddening refusal to describe anything in English), it shows off the wonders of each age: Celtic pre-Roman, Roman, a fine and rare Visigothic section, Moorish, Romanesque, and beyond (always free; open Tue–Sat 9:30–20:00, Sun 9:30–15:00, closed Mon; Calle Serrano 13, Metro: Serrano or Colón, tel. 915-777-912). Outside, underground in the museum's garden, is an underwhelming replica artwork from northern Spain's Altamira Caves (big on bison), giving you a faded peek at the skill of the cave artists who created the originals 14,000 years ago. For more on the real Altamira Caves, see page 286 in the Cantabria chapter.

Sorolla Museum (Museo Sorolla)—Joaquín Sorrolla (1863–1923) is known for his portraits, landscapes, and use of light. It's a relaxing experience to stroll through the rooms of his former house and studio, especially to see the lazy beach scenes of his hometown Valencia. Take a break after your visit to reflect in the small garden in front of his house (€3, free on Sun, open Tue–Sat 9:30–20:00, Sun 10:00–15:00, closed Mon, General Martínez Campos 37, Metro: Iglesia, tel. 913-101-584, http://museosorolla.mcu.es).

Municipal Museum (Museo Municipal)—Follow the history of Madrid in old paintings and models (but no English). As you enter, notice Pedro de Ribera's fine Baroque door featuring "St. James the Moor-Slayer" (described on page 265). The museum is closed for a major renovation through 2011 (Calle Fuencarral 78, Metro: Tribunal or Bilbao, tel. 917-011-863).

▲Clothing Museum (Museo del Traje)—This museum shows the history of clothing from the 18th century until today. In a cool and air-conditioned chronological sweep, the museum's one floor of exhibits includes regional ethnic costumes, a look at how bullfighting and the French influenced styles, accessories through the ages, and Spanish flappers. The only downside of this marvelous modern museum is that it's a long way from anything else of interest (€3, free Sat 14:30–19:00 and all day Sun, open Tue–Sat 9:30–19:00, Sun 10:00–15:00, closed Mon, last entry 30 min before closing, Avenida Juan Herrera 2; Metro: Moncloa and a longish walk, bus #46, or taxi; tel. 915-497-150).

▲Chapel of San Antonio de la Florida—In this simple little Neoclassical chapel from the 1790s, Francisco de Goya's tomb stares up at a splendid cupola filled with his own proto-Impressionist frescoes. He frescoed this using the same unique technique that he used for his "dark paintings." Use the mirrors to enjoy the drama and energy he infused into this marvelously restored masterpiece (free, Tue–Fri 9:30–20:00, Sat–Sun 10:00–14:00, closed Mon, Glorieta de San Antonio de la Florida, tel. 915-420-722). This chapel is a five-minute walk down Paseo de San Antonio de la Florida from Metro: Príncipe Pío (and its bus station, serving Segovia).

Royal Tapestry Factory (Real Fábrica de Tapices)—Have a look at traditional tapestry-making (€3.50, by tour only, on the half-hour, Mon–Fri 10:00–14:00, closed Sat–Sun and Aug, some English tours, Calle Fuenterrabia 2, Metro: Menendez Pelayo, take Gutenberg exit, tel. 914-340-550). You can actually order a tailor-made tapestry (starting at $10,000).

Temple de Debod—In 1968, Egypt gave Spain its own ancient temple. It was a gift of the Egyptian government, which was grateful for Franco's help in rescuing monuments that had been threatened by the rising Nile waters above the Aswan Dam. Consequently, Madrid is the only place I can think of in Europe where you can actually wander through an intact original Egyptian temple—complete with fine carved reliefs from 200 B.C. (free; April–Sept Tue–Fri 10:00–14:00 & 18:00–20:00, Sat–Sun 10:00–14:00, closed Mon; Oct–March Tue–Fri 9:45–13:45 & 16:15–18:15, Sat–Sun 10:00–14:00, closed Mon, in Parque de Montaña, north of the Royal Palace). Set in a romantic park that locals love for its great city views (especially at sunset), the temple—as well as its art—is well-described. Popular as the view may be, the uninspiring "grand Madrid view" only causes me to wonder why anyone would build a city here.

Experiences in Madrid

▲▲**Self-Guided Bus Tour: Paseo de la Castellana**—Tourists risk leaving Madrid without ever seeing the modern "Manhattan" side of town. But it's easy to do. From the Prado Museum, bus #27 makes the trip straight north along Paseo del Prado and then Paseo de la Castellana, through the no-nonsense skyscraper part of this city of more than three million. The line ends at what's called Puerta de Europa (Gate of Europe), twin office towers that are designed to lean at a 15-degree angle. This trip is simple and cheap (€1, buses run every 10 min, sit on the right if possible, beware of pickpockets). You just joyride for 30 minutes to the last stop, get out when everyone else does, ogle the skyscrapers, and catch the Metro for a 20-minute ride back to the city's center. At twilight, when fountains and facades are floodlit, the ride is particularly enjoyable.

Bus #27 rumbles from Atocha Station past the Royal Botanical Garden (opposite McDonald's) and the Velázquez entrance to the Prado (if you're starting from here, catch the bus from the museum side to head north).

Look out for these landmarks: the Prado Museum (right); a square with a fountain of Neptune (left); an obelisk and war memorial to those who have died for Spain (right, with the stock market behind it); the Naval Museum (right); Plaza de Cibeles with the fancy post office (right, now used as City Hall; other huge buildings such as the Bank of Spain line the square); and then the National Library (right).

When you come to a square with a statue of Columbus, it marks the end of the historic town and the beginning of the modern city. At this point the boulevard changes its name. It used to be named for Franco; now it's named for the people he no longer rules—*la Castellana* (Castilians). Next comes the American Embassy (hard to see behind its fortified wall, right) and Franco's ministries (left, typical fascist architecture, c. 1940s, some still used). Continuing up the boulevard, look left to see the Picasso Tower (which looks like one of New York's former World Trade Center towers, because both buildings were designed by the same architect), the huge Bernabéu soccer stadium (right, home of Real Madrid, Europe's most successful soccer team, see page 364), and the Ministry of Defense (left).

Your trip ends at Plaza de Castilla, where you can't miss the avant-garde Puerta de Europa, consisting of twin leaning office towers, one with the big green logo of the Bank of Madrid. In the distance, you can see three of the tallest buildings in Spain. The plaza sports a futuristic obelisk by contemporary Spanish architect Santiago Calatrava.

It's the end of the line for the bus and for you. There is an easy, direct return to Puerta del Sol via the Metro, or cross the street and ride bus #27 along the same route back to the Prado or Atocha Station.

▲**Electric Minibus Joyride Through Lavapiés**—For a relaxing ride through the characteristic old center of Madrid, hop little electric minibus #M1 (€1, 5/hr, 20-min trip, 8:00–20:00). These are designed mostly for local seniors who could use a lift (offer your seat if there's a senior standing). Catch the minibus at the Sevilla Metro stop and simply ride it to the end (Metro: Embajadores). Enjoy this gritty slice of workaday Madrid—both people and architecture—as you roll slowly through Plaza Santa Ana, down a bit of the pedestrianized Calle de las Huertas, past newly gentrified Tirso de Molina (with junkies now replaced by a family-friendly flower market), through Plaza de Lavapiés and a barrio of African and Bangladeshi immigrants until you get to Embajadores. From there you can catch the next #M1 minibus (which returns to the Sevilla Metro stop along a different route) or descend into the subway system.

▲▲**Bullfight**—Madrid's Plaza de Toros hosts Spain's top bull-fights on some Sundays and holidays from March through mid-October, and nearly every day during the San Isidro festival (May through early June—often sold out long in advance). Fights start between 17:00 and 21:00 (early in spring and fall, late in summer). The bullring is at the Ventas Metro stop (a 15-min Metro ride from Puerta del Sol, tel. 913-562-200, www.las-ventas.com). For info on the "art" of bullfighting, see page 708.

Bullfight tickets range from €5 to €150. There are no bad seats at the Plaza de Toros; paying more gets you in the shade and/or closer to the gore. (The action often intentionally occurs in the shade to reward the expensive-ticket holders.) To be close to the bullring, choose areas 8, 9, or 10; for shade: 1, 2, 9, or 10; for shade/sun: 3 or 8; for the sun and cheapest seats: 4, 5, 6, or 7. Note these key words: *corrida*—a real fight with professionals; *novillada*—rookie matadors and younger bulls. Getting tickets through your hotel or a booking office is convenient, but they add 20 percent or more and don't sell the cheap seats. There are two booking offices; call both before you buy: at Plaza del Carmen 1 (Mon–Sat 9:30–13:00 & 16:30–19:00, Sun 9:30–13:30, tel. 915-319-131, or buy online at www.bullfightticketsmadrid.com; run by English-speaking José, who also sells soccer tickets) and at Calle Victoria 3 (Mon–Fri 10:00–14:00 & 17:00–19:00, Sat–Sun 10:00–14:00, tel. 915-211-213). To save money, you can stand in the ticket line at the bullring. Except for important bullfights—or during the San Isidro festival—there are generally plenty of seats available. About a thousand tickets are held back to be sold in the five days leading up to a fight, including the day of the fight. Scalpers hang out before the popular fights at the Calle Victoria booking office. Beware: Those buying scalped tickets are breaking the law and can lose the ticket with no recourse.

For a dose of the experience, you can buy a cheap ticket and just stay to see a couple of bullfights. Each fight takes about 20 minutes, and the event consists of six bulls over two hours. Or, to keep your distance but get a sense of the ritual and gore, tour the bull bar on Plaza Mayor (described earlier as part of the city walk).

Madrid's **Bullfighting Museum** (Museo Taurino) is not as good as Sevilla's or Ronda's (free, Tue–Fri 9:30–14:30, Sun 10:00–13:00, closed Sat and Mon and early on fight days, at the back of bullring, tel. 917-251-857).

"Football" and Bernabéu Stadium—Madrid, like most of Europe, is enthusiastic about soccer (which they call *fútbol*). The Real Madrid team plays to a spirited local crowd Saturdays and Sundays from September through May (tickets from €50—sold at bullfight box offices listed above). One of the most popular sightseeing activities among European visitors to Madrid is touring the 80,000-seat stadium. The €15 tour includes the box seats, dressing rooms, technical zone, playing field, trophy room, and a big panoramic stadium view (daily 10:00–19:00, Metro: Santiago Bernabéu, www.realmadrid.com, tel. 913-984-300).

Shopping in Madrid

Shoppers focus on the colorful pedestrian area between Gran Vía and Puerta del Sol. The giant Spanish department store El Corte Inglés, a block off Puerta del Sol, is a handy place to pick up just about anything you need (Mon–Sat 10:00–22:00, Sun 11:00–21:00, see page 321).

El Rastro: Europe's biggest flea market, rated ▲, is a field day for shoppers, people-watchers, and thieves (Sundays only, 9:00–15:00, best before 11:00). Thousands of stalls titillate more than a million browsers with mostly new junk. Locals have lamented the tackiness of El Rastro lately—you'll find cheap underwear and bootleg CDs, but no real treasures. Start at the Plaza Mayor, with its stamp- and coin-collectors market (see below),

and head south or take the Metro to Tirso de Molina. Walk downhill, finishing at the Puerta de Toledo Metro stop. El Rastro offers a fascinating chance to see gangs of young thieves overwhelming and ripping off naive tourists with no police anywhere in sight. Seriously: Don't even bring a wallet. The pickpocket action is brutal, and tourists are targeted.

While the flea market can be a downer, Europe's biggest stamp and coin market, thriving simultaneously on Plaza Mayor, is a genteel delight. Watch the old-timers paging lovingly through each other's albums, looking for win-win trades.

Fans: Casa de Diego sells *abanicos* (fans), *mantones* (typical Spanish shawls), *castañuelas* (castanets), *peinetas* (hair combs), and umbrellas. Even if you're not in the market, it's fun to watch the women flip open their final fan choices before buying (Mon–Sat 9:30–20:00, closed Sun, Puerta del Sol 12, tel. 915-226-643).

Classical Guitars: Guitar-lovers know that the world's finest classical guitars are made in Spain. Several of the top workshops, within an easy walk of Puerta del Sol, offer inviting little showrooms with a peek at their craft and an opportunity to strum the final product. Consider the workshops of José Romero (Calle de Espoz y Mina 30, tel. 915-214-218) and José Ramirez (Calle de la Paz 8, tel. 915-314-229). Union Musical is a popular guitar shop off Puerta del Sol (Carrera de San Jerónimo 26, tel. 914-293-877). If you're shopping, be prepared to spend €1,000.

Nightlife in Madrid

Those into clubbing may have to wait until after midnight for the most popular places to even open, much less start hopping. Spain has a reputation for partying very late, not ending until offices open in the morning. If you're people-watching early in the morning, it's actually hard to know who is finishing their day and who's just starting it. Even if you're not a party animal after midnight, make a point to be out with the happy masses, luxuriating in the cool evening air between 22:00 and midnight. The scene is absolutely unforgettable.

▲▲▲**Paseo**—Just walking the streets of Madrid seems to be the way the Madrileños spend their evenings. Even past midnight on a hot summer night, entire families with little kids are strolling, enjoying tiny beers and tapas in a series of bars, licking ice cream, and greeting their neighbors. A good area to wander is along Gran Vía (from about Metro: Callao to Plaza de España). Or start at Puerta del Sol, and explore in the direction of Plaza Santa Ana. The newly pedestrianized Calle de las Huertas is also understandably popular with strollers.

▲**Zarzuela**—For a delightful look at Spanish light opera that even English-speakers can enjoy, try zarzuela. Guitar-strumming Napoleons in red capes; buxom women with masks, fans, and castanets; Spanish-speaking pharaohs; melodramatic spotlights; and aficionados clapping and singing along from the cheap seats, where the acoustics are best—this is zarzuela...the people's opera. Originating in Madrid, zarzuela is known for its satiric humor and surprisingly good music. You can buy tickets at Theater Zarzuela, which alternates between zarzuela, ballet, and opera throughout the year (€16–40, box office open 12:00–18:00 for advance tickets or until showtime for that day, Jovellanos 4, near the Prado, Metro: Sevilla or Banco de España, tel. 915-245-400, http://teatrodela zarzuela.mcu.es; to purchase online, go to the theater section of www.servicaixa.com and choose the English version). The TI's monthly guide has a special zarzuela listing.

▲▲**Flamenco**—Although Sevilla is the capital of flamenco, Madrid has three easy and affordable options. And on summer evenings, Madrid puts on live flamenco events in the Royal Palace gardens (ask TI for details).

Taberna Casa Patas attracts big-name flamenco artists. You'll quickly understand why this intimate (30 tables, 120 seats) and smoky venue is named "House of Feet." Since this is for locals as well as tour groups, the flamenco is contemporary and may be jazzier than your notion—it depends on who's performing (€31, Mon–Thu at 22:30, Fri–Sat at 21:00 and 24:00, closed Sun, 75–90 min, price includes cover and first drink, reservations smart, no flash cameras, Cañizares 10, tel. 913-690-496, www.casapatas .com). Its restaurant is a logical spot for dinner before the show (€30 dinners, Mon–Sat from 20:00). Or, since it's three blocks south of the recommended Plaza Santa Ana tapas bars, this could be your post-tapas-crawl entertainment.

Las Carboneras, more downscale, is an easygoing, folksy little place a few steps from Plaza Mayor with a nightly hour-long flamenco show (€33 includes an entry and a drink, €61 gets you a table up front with dinner and unlimited cheap drinks if you reserve ahead, manager Enrique promises a €5 per person discount if you book direct and show this book in 2010, Mon–Thu at 22:30 and often at 20:30, Fri–Sat at 20:30 and 23:00, closed Sun, reservations recommended, Plaza del Conde de Miranda 1, tel. 915-428-677). While Las Carboneras lacks the pretense of Casa Patas, Casa Patas has better-quality artists and a riveting seriousness. Considering that Las Carboneras raised its prices to essentially match Casa Patas, the "House of Feet" is the better value.

Las Tablas Flamenco offers a less expensive nightly show respecting the traditional art of flamenco. You'll sit in a plain room with a mix of tourists and locals in a modern, nondescript office block just over the freeway from Plaza de España (€24 with drink, reasonable drink prices, Sun–Thu 22:30, Fri–Sat 20:00 & 22:00, 75-min show, corner of Calle de Ferraz and Cuesta de San Vicente, tel. 915-420-520, www.lastablasmadrid.com).

Regardless of what your hotel receptionist may want to sell you, other flamenco places—such as Arco de Cuchilleros (Calle de los Cuchilleros 7), Café de Chinitas (Calle Torija 7, just off Plaza Mayor), Corral de la Morería (Calle de Morería 17), and Torres Bermejas (off Gran Vía)—are filled with tourists and pushy waiters.

Mesones—These long, skinny cave-like bars, famous for customers drinking and singing late into the night, line the lane called Cava de San Miguel, just west of Plaza Mayor. If you were to toss lowbrow locals, Spanish karaoke, electric keyboards, crass tourists, cheap sangria, and greasy calamari into a late-night blender and turn it on, this is what you'd get. It's generally lively only on Friday and Saturday.

Late-Night and Jazz Bars—If you're just picking up speed at midnight, and looking for a place filled with old tiles and a Gen-X crowd, power into **Bar Viva Madrid** (daily 13:00–3:00 in the morning, downhill from Plaza Santa Ana on Calle Manuel Fernández y González, tel. 914-293-640). The same street has other late-night bars filled with music. Or hike on over to **Chocolatería San Ginés** (described on page 384) for a dessert of *churros con chocolate*.

For live jazz, **Café Central** is the old town favorite. Since 1982, it's been known as the place where rising stars get their start (€14, 22:00 nightly, cheap drinks, great scene, Plaza del Angel 10, tel. 913-694-143, www.cafecentralmadrid.com).

Movies—During Franco's days, movies were always dubbed into Spanish. As a result, movies in Spain remain about the most often dubbed in Europe. Dubbing was encouraged by Franco's xenophobia and the need to censor popular entertainment during his rule. When dubbing a movie, you can change the meaning and almost no one knows. To see a movie with its original soundtrack, look for "*V.O.*" (meaning "original version"). Cine Ideal, with nine screens, is a good place for the latest films in *V.O.* (€7.50, 5-min walk south of Puerta del Sol at Calle del Dr. Cortezo 6, tel. 913-692-518 for info). For extensive listings, see the *Guía del Ocio* entertainment guide (€1 at newsstands, www.guiadelocio.com) or a local newspaper.

Sleeping in Madrid

Madrid has plenty of centrally located budget hotels and *pensiónes*. Most of the accommodations I've listed are within a few minutes' walk of Puerta del Sol.

You'll have no trouble finding a sleepable double for €40, a good double for €80, and a modern, air-conditioned double with

Sleep Code

(€1 = about $1.40, country code: 34)
S = Single, **D** = Double/Twin, **T** = Triple, **Q** = Quad, **b** = bathroom, **s** = shower only. Unless otherwise noted, credit cards are accepted, English is spoken, and breakfast is *not* included.

To help you easily sort through these listings, I've divided the rooms into three categories, based on the price for a standard double room with bath during high season:

$$$ **Higher Priced**—Most rooms €100 or more.
$$ **Moderately Priced**—Most rooms between €70-100.
$ **Lower Priced**—Most rooms €70 or less.

all the comforts for €110. Prices vary throughout the year at bigger hotels, but remain about the same for the smaller hotels and *hostales*. It's almost always easy to find a place. Anticipate full hotels only during May (the San Isidro festival, celebrating Madrid's patron saint with bullfights and zarzuelas—especially around his feast day on May 15) and September (when conventions can clog the city). During the hot months of July and August, prices can be soft—always ask for a discount.

Given the current financial downturn, big hotels are coming up empty and are desperately discounting, which is taking lots of business away from smaller hotels that are already inexpensive. To get the best price, email big business-class hotels and let them bid for your business.

With all of Madrid's street noise, I'd request the highest floor possible. Also, twin-bedded rooms are generally a bit larger than double-bedded rooms for the same price. During slow times, drop-ins can often score a room in business-class hotels for just a few euros more than the budget hotels (which don't have prices that fluctuate as wildly with demand).

Fancier Places in the Pedestrian Zone Between Puerta del Sol and Gran Vía

These business-class hotels are good values for those wanting to spend a little more. Their formal prices may be inflated, but most offer weekend and summer discounts when it's slow. Again, if you're interested in staying at a business-class hotel, email around for the best price. Drivers pay about €24 a day in garages. Use Metro: Sol for all but Hotel Opera (Metro: Ópera).

$$$ Hotel Liabeny rents 220 plush, spacious, business-class rooms offering all the comforts (Sb-€110, Db-€125, Tb-€176, 10 percent cheaper mid-July–Aug and Fri–Sat, breakfast-€16, air-con, sauna, gym, off Plaza del Carmen at Salud 3, tel. 915-319-000, fax 915-327-421, www.liabeny.es, info@liabeny.es).

$$$ Hotel Preciados, a four-star business hotel, has 73 fine, sleek, and modern rooms as well as elegant lounges. It's well-located and reasonably priced for the luxury it provides (Db-€125–160, prices are often soft, checking Web specials in advance or dropping in will likely snag a room for around €100, breakfast-€15, just off Plaza de Santo Domingo at Calle Preciados 37, tel. 914-544-400, fax 914-544-401, www.preciadoshotel.com, preciadoshotel @preciadoshotel.com).

$$$ Hotel Carlos V is a Best Western with 67 sharp high-ceilinged rooms, elegant breakfast, and a pleasant lounge (Sb-€95, standard Db-€115, Tb-€135, tax not included, breakfast-€9, air-con, non-smoking floors, elevator, Wi-Fi, Maestro Victoria 5,

MADRID

Madrid's Center— Hotels and Restaurants

Ⓜ Metro Station

▭ Pedestrian Zones

200 YARDS

200 METERS

DCH

For eateries near Plaza Mayor and Plaza Santa Ana, please see those maps.

❶ Hotel Liabeny

❷ Hotel Preciados

❸ Hotel Carlos V

❹ Petit Palace Posada del Peine

❺ Hotel Europa & Cafeteria

❻ To Hotel Opera

❼ Hotel Plaza Mayor

❽ Hostales Acapulco & Triana; Pension Arcos

❾ Hostal Aliste

❿ Hostales Res. Luis XV, Jerez & Metropol

⓫ Ateneo Hotel

⓬ Hostales Mayrit & Ivor

⓭ Hostal Santa Cruz

⓮ Restaurante Puerto Rico

⓯ El Corte Inglés Cafeteria

⓰ Casa Labra Taberna Rest.

⓱ La Gloria de Montera Rest. & Fresc Co Buffet

⓲ Artemisia II Veggie Rest.

⓳ Artemisia I Veggie Rest.

⓴ Rodilla; Pans & Co.

㉑ Chocolaterías Valor

㉒ Chocolatería San Ginés

㉓ Launderette

㉔ Internet Cafés (2)

tel. 915-314-100, fax 915-313-761, www.hotelcarlosv.com, recepcion @hotelcarlosv.com).

$$$ Petit Palace Posada del Peine feels like part of a big modern chain (which it is), but fills its well-located old building with fresh, efficient character. Behind the ornate and sparkling Old World facade is a comfortable and modern business-class hotel with 67 rooms just a block from Plaza Mayor (Db-€100–160 depending on demand, tax not included, breakfast-€9, air-con, Calle Postas 17, tel. 915-238-151, fax 915-232-993, www.hthoteles .com, pos@hthoteles.com).

$$ Hotel Europa, with sleek marble, red carpet runners along the halls, happy Muzak charm, and an attentive staff, is a tremendous value. It rents 103 squeaky-clean rooms, many with balconies overlooking the pedestrian zone or an inner courtyard. They are honest and offer a straight price (Sb-€74, Db-€92, Db with view-€110, Tb-€130, Qb-€155, Quint/b-€175, tax not included, breakfast extra, air-con, elevator, free Internet access, Calle del Carmen 4, tel. 915-212-900, fax 915-214-696, www.hoteleuropa.net, info @hoteleuropa.net, run by Antonio and Fernando Garaban and their helpful and jovial staff, Javi and Jim). The convenient Europa cafeteria-restaurant next door is a lively and convivial scene—fun for breakfast (see page 382 in "Eating").

$$ Hotel Ópera, a serious and contemporary hotel with 79 classy rooms, is located just off Plaza Isabel II, a four-block walk from Puerta del Sol toward the Royal Palace (Db-€75–95 but prices spike wildly with demand, includes breakfast, air-con, elevator, free Internet access, ask for a higher floor—there are nine—to avoid street noise, Cuesta de Santo Domingo 2, Metro: Ópera, tel. 915-412-800, fax 915-416-923, www.hotelopera.com, reservas @hotelopera.com). Hotel Ópera's cafeteria is understandably popular. Consider their "singing dinners"—great operetta music with a delightful dinner—offered nightly at 22:00 (around €65, reservations smart, call 915-426-382 or reserve at hotel).

$$ Hotel Plaza Mayor, with 34 solidly outfitted rooms, is tastefully decorated and beautifully situated a block off Plaza Mayor (Sb-€65, Db-€85, superior Db-€95, Tb-€115, director Leo offers travelers who book direct with this book a free breakfast in 2010, air-con, elevator, Wi-Fi, Calle Atocha 2, tel. 913-600-606, fax 913-600-610, www.h-plazamayor.com, info@h-plaza mayor.com).

Cheaper Bets near Puerta del Sol and Gran Vía

These three are all in the same building at Calle de la Salud 13, overlooking Plaza del Carmen—a little square with a sleepy, almost Parisian ambience.

$ Hostal Acapulco rents 16 bright rooms with air-conditioning and all the big hotel gear. The neighborhood is quiet enough that it's smart to request a room with a balcony (Sb-€49–54, Db-€59–64, Tb-€77–80, elevator, free Internet access and Wi-Fi, fourth floor, tel. 915-311-945, fax 915-322-329, hostal_acapulco @yahoo.es, Ana and Marco).

$ Hostal Triana, also a fine deal, is bigger—with 40 rooms— and offers a little less charm for a little less money (Sb-€42, Db-€55, Tb-€75, includes taxes, rooms facing the square have air-con and cost €3 extra, other rooms have fans, elevator, free Wi-Fi, first floor, tel. 915-326-812, fax 915-229-729, www.hostaltriana .com, triana@hostaltriana.com, Victor González).

$ Pension Arcos is tiny, granny-run, and old-fashioned— it's been in the Hernández family since 1936. You can reserve by phone—in Spanish, and you must pay in cash. But its five rooms are clean, quiet, and served by an elevator. You also have access to a tiny roof terrace and a nice little lounge. For cheap beds in a great locale, assuming you can communicate, this place is unbeatable (D-€36, Db-€40, fifth floor, air-con, closed Aug, tel. 915-324-994, Anuncia and Sabino).

More Cheap Sleeps at the Top of Calle de la Montera

These three places are a few minutes' walk from Puerta del Sol and a stone's throw from Gran Vía at the top of Calle de la Montera, which some dislike because of the young prostitutes that hang out here. They're legal, and the zone is otherwise safe and comfortable.

$ Hostal Aliste rents 11 decent rooms in a dreary-yet-secure building at a great price for readers of this book (Sb-€30, Db-€40, extra bed-€20, air-con, elevator, Internet access, Caballero de Gracia 6, third floor, tel. 915-215-979, h.aliste@teleline.es, Rachael and Edward speak English).

$ Hostal Residencia Luis XV is a big, plain, well-run, and clean place offering a good value. It's on a quiet eighth floor (there's an elevator). It can be smoky. They also run the 36-room **Hostal Jerez**—similar in every way—on the sixth floor (Sb-€45, Db-€59, Tb-€75, includes tax, air-con, elevator, free Wi-Fi with this book in 2010, Calle de la Montera 47, tel. 915-221-021, fax 915-221-350, www.hrluisxv.net, reservas@hrluisxv.net).

$ Hostal Metropol is a big, colorful, and very youthful youth hostel with 130 beds and an inviting pub and lounge (bed-€18, 4–6 beds per room, always co-ed, Sb-€35, Db-€60, includes a fitted sheet and breakfast, towel not included, free Internet access, Calle de la Montera 47, first floor, tel. 915-212-935, fax 915-212-934, www.metropolhostel.com, hotel-metropol@terra.es).

Other Budget Beds in the Center

$$ Ateneo Hotel, just steps off Puerta del Sol, lacks public spaces and character, but its 38 rooms are close to business-class (Db-€75–90, occasionally less or more, air-con, Internet access, Calle de la Montera 22, tel. 915-212-012, fax 915-233-136, www.hotel-ateneo.com, info@hotel-ateneo.com).

$ Hostal Mayrit rents 28 rooms with thoughtful touches on the newly pedestrianized Calle del Arenal (Sb-€50, Db-€65, air-con, near Metro: Ópera at Calle del Arenal 24, third floor, tel. 915-480-403). They also run **Hostal Ivor** downstairs (same comfort level and prices).

$ Hostal Santa Cruz, simple and well-located, has 16 rooms at a good price (Sb-€45, Db-€58, Tb-€85, air-con, a block off Plaza Mayor at Plaza de Santa Cruz 6, second floor, tel. 915-522-441, fax 915-237-088, www.hostalsantacruz.com, info@hostalsantacruz.com).

$ Madrid Municipal Youth Hostel (Albergue Juvenil Madrid) is the big new 132-bed hostel in town. It has four to six beds per room with lockers, modern bathrooms, and lots of extras such as bike rentals, billiards, and movies (dorm bed-about €22, co-ed rooms, Internet access, closed 11:00–15:00, Metro: Tribunal, then walk two minutes down Calle de Barceló to Calle de Mejia Lequerica 21, tel. 915-939-688, fax 915-939-684, www.ajmadrid.es, info@ajmadrid.es).

Near the Prado

To locate the following three places, please see "Madrid's Museum Neighborhood" map on page 343.

$$$ Hotel Lope de Vega offers good business-class hotel value near the Prado. It is a "cultural-themed" hotel inspired by the 17th-century writer Lope de Vega. With 60 rooms, it feels cozy and friendly for a formal hotel (Sb-€105, Db-€115–135, Tb-€180, one child sleeps free, prices about 20 percent lower Fri–Sun and during most of the summer, air-con, elevator, Internet access, parking-€23/day, Calle Lope de Vega 49, tel. 913-600-011, fax 914-292-391, www.hotellopedevega.com, lopedevega@hotellopedevega.com).

At Cervantes 34: Two fine budget *hostales* are at Cervantes 34 (Metro: Antón Martín—but not handy to Metro). Both are homey, with inviting lounge areas; neither serves breakfast. **$ Hostal Gonzalo** has 15 spotless, comfortable rooms on the third floor and is well-run by friendly and helpful Javier. It's deservedly in all the guidebooks, so reserve in advance (Sb-€45, Db-€55, Tb-€70, air-con, elevator, Wi-Fi, tel. 914-292-714, fax 914-202-007, www.hostalgonzalo.com, hostal@hostalgonzalo.com). Downstairs, the nearly as polished **$ Hostal Cervantes** also has 15 rooms (Sb-€50, Db-€60, Tb-€75, includes tax, cheaper when slow and for longer stays, some rooms with air-con, Internet access and Wi-Fi, tel. 914-298-365, fax 914-292-745, www.hostal-cervantes.com, correo @hostal-cervantes.com, Fabio).

Eating in Madrid

In Spain, only Barcelona rivals Madrid for taste-bud thrills. You have three dining choices: a memorable, atmospheric sit-down meal in a well-chosen restaurant; a forgettable, basic sit-down meal; or a stand-up meal of tapas in a bar...or four. Unless otherwise noted, these places start serving lunch at 13:00 or 13:30 and dinner from 20:30. You'll often find the places nearly empty with a few forlorn early-bird tourists and then thriving with locals after 14:00 and 22:00. Many restaurants close in August. Madrid has famously good tap water, and waiters willingly serve it free—just ask for *agua del grifo*.

I've grouped the recommended restaurants by neighborhood—near Plaza Mayor, Plaza Santa Ana, the Royal Palace, the Prado, and Puerta del Sol. I've listed a range of eateries, from splurges to cheap eats to fun pub crawls and churros with chocolate. Enjoy!

Near Plaza Mayor
Fine Dining
Restaurante Casa Paco is a Madrid tradition. Check out its old walls plastered with autographed photos of local celebrities who have enjoyed their signature dish—ox grilled over a coal fire. While popular with tourists, the place is authentic, confident, and uncompromising—let non-smokers be damned. It's a worthwhile splurge if you want to dine out well and carnivorously (€15–25 plates, ox sold by weight, 200 grams—which is almost half a pound—is a hearty steak, Plaza de la Puerta Cerrada 11, tel. 913-663-166).

Sobrino del Botín is a hit with many Americans because "Hemingway ate here." It's grotesquely touristy, pricey, and the last place Papa would go now...but still, people love it, and the food is excellent (roast suckling pig is the specialty). If phoning to make a reservation, choose the upstairs for a still-traditional, but airier style over the downstairs, which has a dark, medieval-cellar ambience (€30 meals, daily 13:00–16:00 & 20:00–24:00, a block downhill from Plaza Mayor at Cuchilleros 17, tel. 913-664-217).

Posada de la Villa serves Castilian cuisine in a 17th-century inn. This sprawling, multi-floor restaurant has open-beam ceilings, which give it a rustic flair. Peek into the big oven to see the baby pigs about to make some diner happy. If you're not going to Toledo or Sevilla, this is a good place to try roast lamb, the house specialty (€30 meals, closed Sun and Aug, Calle Cava Baja 9, tel. 913-661-860). Posada de la Villa's twin, **Taberna del Capitan Alatriste,** is

MADRID

Eating near Plaza Mayor

Legend:

1. Restaurante Casa Paco
2. Sobrino del Botín
3. Posada de la Villa
4. Taberna del Capitan Alatriste
5. Julian de Tolosa
6. Casa Lucio
7. Casa Rúa
8. Torre del Oro Bar Andalú
9. Sakura
10. Taberna Tempranillo
11. Txakolina Pintxoteca Madrileña
12. Taberna Los Lucio
13. El Madroño
14. Giangrossi Helado Artesanal Ice Cream
15. Las Carboneras (Flamenco)
16. Mesones ("Cave Bars")

MADRID

more fresh and modern, a half-block away, and run by the same owners. They serve classic cuisine with lots of game under open beams in a stylish medieval vault (€25 plates, closed Mon, Grafal 7, tel. 913-661-883).

Julian de Tolosa is chic, pricey, elegantly simple, and popular with natives who know good food. They offer a small, quality menu of Navarra's regional cuisine, from T-bone steak *(chuletón)* to red *tolosa* beans, in a spacious, sane setting with nothing touristic (€40 meals, closed Sun, Calle Cava Baja 18, tel. 913-658-210).

Casa Lucio is a favorite splurge among power-dressing Madrileños. The king and queen of Spain eat in this formal place, but it's accessible to commoners. This is a fine restaurant for a special night out and a full-blown meal, but you pay extra for this place's fame (€40 for dinner, nightly from 21:00, closed Aug, Calle Cava Baja 35; unless you're the king or queen, reserve several days in advance—and don't even bother on weekends; tel. 913-653-252).

Eating Cheaply

Madrileños enjoy a bite to eat on Plaza Mayor (without its high costs) by grabbing food to go from a nearby bar and just planting themselves somewhere on the square to eat (squid sandwiches are popular). But for many tourists, dinner at a sidewalk café right on Plaza Mayor is worth the premium price (consider Cervecería Pulpito, southwest corner of the square at #10).

Squid Sandwiches: Plaza Mayor is famous for its *bocadillos de calamares.* For a tasty €2.50 squid-ring sandwich, line up at **Casa Rúa** at Plaza Mayor's northwest corner, a few steps up Calle Ciudad Rodrigo (daily 9:00–23:00). Hanging up behind the bar is a photo-advertisement of Plaza Mayor from the 1950s, when the square contained a park.

Bullfighting Bar: The **Torre del Oro Bar Andalú** on Plaza Mayor has walls lined with grisly bullfight photos (read the gory description on page 708). While this place is good for drinks, you pay a premium for the tapas and food...the cost of munching amidst all that bullephenalia while enjoying their excellent Plaza Mayor outdoor seating (daily 8:00–15:00 & 18:00–24:00).

Japanese Restaurant: **Sakura** is nothing special but offers a welcome, ham-free oasis with air-conditioning and a hot face towel. Japanese-run, it serves a good €10 lunch special (daily from 12:00 and from 19:30, Calle de San Cristóbal 11, tel. 915-321-089).

Tapas on Calle Cava Baja, South of Plaza Mayor

Just three minutes south of Plaza Mayor, Calle Cava Baja fills each evening with mostly young, professional locals prowling for chic tapas and social fun. Tapas are the toothpick appetizers, salads, and deep-fried foods traditionally served in Spanish bars. Come at night only and treat the entire street as a destination. I've listed a few standards, but excellent new eateries are always opening up. For a good, authentic Madrid dinner experience, take time to survey the many options along this street and then choose your favorites. Remember, it's easier and touristy early, jammed with locals later. (If you want a formal dining experience on this street, try Posada de la Villa Julian de Tolosa, or Casa Lucio, recommended in "Fine Dining," earlier). These Calle Cava Baja tapas bars are worth special consideration:

Taberna Tempranillo, ideal for hungry wine-lovers, offers fancy tapas and fine wine by the glass (see listing on the board). While there are a few tables, the bar is just right for hanging out. With a phrasebook in hand or a spirit of adventure, use their fascinating menu to assemble your dream meal. It's packed and full of commotion—the crowds can be overwhelming. Arrive by 20:00 or plan to wait (closed Aug, Calle Cava Baja 38, tel. 913-641-532).

Txakolina Pintxoteca Madrileña is a thriving bar serving Basque-style *pinchos* (tiny fancy sandwiches—*pintxo* in Basque) to a young crowd (€3/*pincho*, Calle Cava Baja 26, tel. 913-664-877).

Taberna Los Lucio is a jam-packed bar serving good tapas, salads, *huevos estrellados* (scrambled eggs with fried potatoes), and wine. If you'd like to make it a sit-down meal, head to the tables in the back. Their basement is much less atmospheric (Calle Cava Baja 30, tel. 913-662-984).

El Madroño ("The Berry Tree," a symbol of Madrid) is more of a cowboy bar a block off the top of Calle Cava Baja. Preserving a bit of old Madrid, a tile copy of Velázquez's famous *Drinkers* grins from its facade. Inside, look above the stairs for photos of 1902 Madrid. Study the coats of arms of Madrid through the centuries as you try a *vermut* (vermouth) on tap and a €2 sandwich. Or ask to try the *licor de madroño;* a small glass *(chupito)* costs €1.50. While indoor seating is bright and colorful, the sidewalk tables come with great people-watching. Munch *raciones* at bar or front tables to be in the fun scene or have a quieter sit-down meal at the tables in the back (closed Mon, Plaza de la Puerta Cerrada 7, tel. 913-645-629).

Ice Cream Finale: **Giangrossi Helado Artesanal,** a popular chain, serves Argentinean-style ice cream, considered to be some of Madrid's best. With a plush white leather lounge and lots of great flavors, this hipster ice cream shop offers a sweet way to finish your dining experience in this area (at the end of Calle Cava Baja at #40, 50 yards from La Latina Metro stop, tel. 902-444-130).

Near Plaza Santa Ana

Fine Dining

El Caldero ("The Pot") is romantic and *the* place for paella and other rice dishes. A classy, in-the-know local crowd appreciates the subdued elegance and crisp service of this place. The house specialty is *arroz caldero* (a variation on paella). Served with panache from a cauldron hanging from a tripod, it serves two for €28. Most of the formal rice dishes come in pots for two—like the €30-per-couple paella (closed Sun–Mon, Calle de las Huertas 15—for location see map on page 378, tel. 914-295-044). Wash down your meal with the house sangria.

The Madrid Pub-Crawl Dinner (for Beginners)

For maximum fun, people, and atmosphere, go mobile for dinner: Do the "tapas tango," a local tradition of going from one bar to the next, munching, drinking, and socializing. While tiny €2 plates (tapas) are standard in Andalucía (and commonly served in Madrid's Calle Cava Baja area), these days most of Madrid's bars offer bigger €6 plates called *raciones*, ideal for a small group to share. The real action begins late (around 20:00). But for beginners, an earlier start, with less commotion, can be easier. The litter on the floor is normal; that's where people traditionally toss their trash and shells (it's unsanitary to put it back on the bar). Don't worry about paying until you're ready to go. Then ask for *la cuenta* (the bill).

If done properly, a pub crawl can be a highlight of your trip. Before embarking upon this culinary adventure, study and use the tapas tips on page 24. Your ability to speak a little Spanish will get you a much better (and less expensive) experience.

Prowl the area between Puerta del Sol and Plaza Santa Ana. There's no ideal route, but the little streets (in this book's map) between Puerta del Sol, San Jerónimo, and Plaza Santa Ana hold tasty surprises. Nearby, the street Jesús de Medinaceli is also lined with popular tapas bars. Below is a five-stop tapa crawl. These places are good, but don't be afraid to make some discoveries of your own. The more adventurous should read this crawl for ideas, and skip directly to the advanced zone (Lavapiés), described at the end of this section. For a more trendy pub crawl with designer tapas and finer wine, visit the bars on Calle Cava Baja (listed earlier).

• *From Puerta del Sol, walk east a block down Carrera de San Jerónimo to the corner of Calle Victoria.*

MADRID

Madrid Pub-Crawl Dinner

100 YARDS
100 METERS

TO Gran Via Ⓜ

CARMEN
MONTERA
BEAR TREE STATUE
Sol Ⓜ
PUERTA DEL SOL
KILO ZERO
SAN RICARDO
PAN
TO PLAZA MAYOR
CARRETAS
AHORROS
CALLE   ALCALA
Ⓜ Sevilla
SEVILLA
CEDACEROS
TÍO PEPE SIGN ❷
CARRERA
❶
ESPOZ Y
VICTORIA
MATHEU
POZO
❹
CADIZ
❸
❺
MINA
DE LA CRUZ
NUÑEZ DE ARCE
A. GATO
BOLSA
❶❸
CALLE
❶❹
PLAZA JACINTO BENAVENTE
CALLE
ATOCHA
SEB.
CAÑIZ.
❶❶
DE   SAN   JERÓNIMO
PRINCIPE
ECHEGARAY
VENTURA VEGA
TO PRADO + THYSSEN MUSEUMS
❶❷
C. MAN. FERN.
❼
PLAZA STA. ANA
PLAZA ANGEL
❿
❻
CALLE DE   PRADO
❽
INFANTE
LEON
CERVANTES
LOPE DE VEGA
❶❸
❾
CALLE   HUERTAS
TO ANTON MARTIN Ⓜ
+ LAVAPIÉS DISTRICT
TO PRADO
DCH

N

Ⓜ METRO STATION
PEDESTRIAN ZONES

Pub-Crawl Dinner

❶ Museo del Jamón & Lhardy Pastelería
❷ La Taurina Cervecería
❸ La Casa del Abuelo
❹ Oreja de Oro
❺ Casa Toni
❻ Cervecería de Santa Ana & Naturbier Microbrewery
❼ Vinoteca Barbechera
❽ Gonzalez Wine & Cheese Shop

Other

❾ El Caldero Restaurante
❿ Ginger Restaurante & Café Central Jazz Bar
❶❶ Taberna Casa Patas (Flamenco)
❶❷ Bar Viva Madrid
❶❸ Launderettes (2)
❶❹ Internet Café

Museo del Jamón (Museum of Ham): This frenetic, cheap, stand-up bar (with famously rude service) is an assembly line of fast and simple *bocadillos* and *raciones*. It's tastefully decorated— unless you're a pig (or a vegetarian). Take advantage of the easy photo-illustrated menus that show various dishes and their prices. The best ham is the pricey *jamón ibérico*—from pigs who led stress-free lives in acorn-strewn valleys. Just point and eat, but be specific: A plate of low-end *jamón blanco* costs only €2.50, while *jamón ibérico* costs €14. For a small sandwich, ask for a *chiquito* (€1, or €4 for *ibérico*). If on a budget, don't let them sell you the *ibérico* (daily 9:00–24:00, sit-down restaurant upstairs, air-con).

• *Nearby are two options. Across the street is the touristy and over-priced bull bar, La Taurina. (I wouldn't eat here but you're welcome to ponder the graphic photos that celebrate the gory art of bullfighting.) And next door, take a detour from your pub crawl with something better for grandmothers:*

Lhardy Pastelería: Offering a genteel taste of Old World charm in this district of rowdy pubs, this place has been a fixture since 1839 for Madrileños wanting to duck in for a cup of soup or a light snack. Step right in, and pretend you're an aristocrat back between the wars. Serve yourself. You'll pay as you leave (on the honor system). Help yourself to the silver water dispenser (free), a line of elegant bottles (each a different Iberian fortified wine: sherry, port, and so on, €2/glass), a revolving case of meaty little pastries (€1 each), and a fancy soup dispenser (chicken broth consommé–€2, or €2.50 with a splash of sherry...local style—bottles in the corner, help yourself; Mon–Sat 9:30–15:00 & 17:00–21:30, Sun 9:30–15:00 only, non-smoking, Carrera de San Jerónimo 8).

• *Next, forage halfway up Calle Victoria to the tiny...*

La Casa del Abuelo: This is where seafood-lovers savor sizzling plates of tasty little *gambas* (shrimp) and *langostinos* (prawns), with bread to sop up the delightful juices. As drinks are cheap and dishes are pricey, you might want

to just share a *ración*. Try *gambas a la plancha* (grilled shrimp, €7.60) or *gambas al ajillo* (ah-HEE-yoh, shrimp version of escargot, cooked in oil and garlic, €8.30) and a €2 glass of sweet red house wine (daily 12:00–24:00, Calle Victoria 12).

• *Across the street is...*

Oreja de Oro: The "Golden Ear" is named for what it sells— sautéed pigs' ears (*oreja*, €3). While pig ears are a Madrid specialty, this place is Galician, so people also come here for *pulpo* (octopus,

€12), *pimientos de padrón* (sautéed miniature green peppers—my favorite plate of the entire crawl, €3.50), and the distinctive *ribeiro* (ree-BAY-roh) wine, served Galician-style, in characteristic little ceramic bowls (to disguise its lack of clarity). Jaime is a frantic one-man show who somehow gets everything just right (closed Mon). Have fun here.

• *For a finale, continue uphill and around the corner to...*

Casa Toni: This memorable little spot, run by Toni, has a helpful English menu and several fun, classic dishes to try: *patatas bravas* (fried potatoes in a spicy sauce, €4), *berenjena* (deep-fried slices of eggplant, €5), *champiñones* (sautéed mushrooms, €5.50), and gazpacho—the cold tomato-and-garlic soup (€2.50) which is generally served only during the hot season, but available here year-round just for you (closed July, Calle Cruz 14).

More Options: If you're hungry for more, and want a trendy, up-to-date, pricier tapas scene, head for Plaza Santa Ana, with lively bars spilling out onto the square. Survey the entire scene. Consider **Cervecería de Santa Ana** (tasty tapas with two zones: rowdy, circa-1900 beer-hall and classier sit-down) or **Naturbier,** a local microbrewery. **Vinoteca Barbechera,** at the downhill end of the square, has an inviting menu of tapas and fine wines by the glass (indoor and outdoor seating).

Gonzalez, a venerable gourmet cheese and wine shop with a circa 1930s interior, offers a genteel opportunity to enjoy a plate of first-class cheese and a fine glass of wine with friendly service and a fun setting. Their €13 assortment of five Spanish cheeses—more than enough for two—is a cheese-lover's treat (€10 lunch buffet, nice wines by the glass, closed Sun–Mon, three blocks past Plaza Santa Ana at Calle de León 12, tel. 914-295-618, Francisco).

Near the Royal Palace

Casa Ciriaco is popular with Madrileños who appreciate good traditional cooking—stews and partridge—with no affectation (€35 meals, €20 fixed-price lunch and dinner, closed Wed and Aug, Calle Mayor 84, tel. 915-480-620). It was from this building in 1906 that an anarchist bombed the royal couple on their wedding day (for details, see page 335). Photos of the carnage are inside the front door.

La Bola Taberna, touristy but friendly and tastefully elegant, specializes in *cocido Madrileño*—Madrid stew. The €19 stew consists of various meats, carrots, and garbanzo beans in earthen jugs. This is a winter dish, prepared here for the tourists. The stew is served as two courses: First you enjoy the broth as a soup, then you dig into the meat and veggies (closed Sun, cash only, midway between Royal Palace and Gran Vía at Calle Bola 5, tel. 915-476-930).

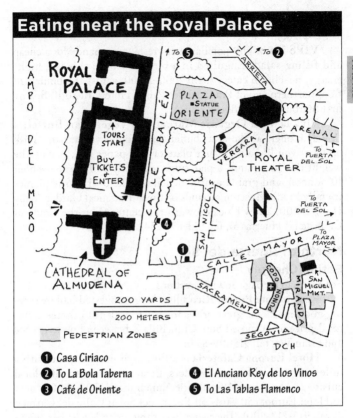

Eating near the Royal Palace

1. Casa Ciriaco
2. To La Bola Taberna
3. Café de Oriente
4. El Anciano Rey de los Vinos
5. To Las Tablas Flamenco

Café de Oriente serves a great three-course lunch special (€13, Mon–Fri, 13:00–16:00 only) in fin-de-siècle elegance immediately across the park from the Royal Palace. While its cafeteria area is reasonable, its restaurant is pricey (Plaza de Oriente 2, tel. 915-413-974).

El Anciano Rey de los Vinos is a venerable, circa 1909 wine bar famous for its vermouth on tap. It's expensive, but offers affordable tapas and drinks at its classic bar. A free small plate of tapas comes with each drink (closed Tue, across busy street from cathedral at Calle de Bailén 19, tel. 915-595-332).

Casual Dining near the Prado

Each of the three big art museums has a decent cafeteria. Or choose from these eateries, all within a block of the Prado (for locations, see "Madrid's Museum Neighborhood" map on page 343).

Taberna de Dolores, a winning formula since 1908, is a commotion of locals enjoying €2.50 *canapés* (open-face sandwiches), tasty *raciones* of seafood, and *cañas* (small beers) at the bar or at a few tables in the back (daily 11:00–24:00, Plaza de Jesús 4, tel. 914-292-243).

VIPS is a bright, popular chain restaurant, handy for a cheap and filling salad. Engulfed in a big bookstore, this is a high-energy, no-charm eatery (daily 9:00–24:00, across the boulevard from northern end of Prado, under Palace Hotel). In 2001, Spain's first Starbucks opened next door.

Viva la Vida Organic Market and Vegetarian Buffet, a tiny deli, offers a take-away buffet that delights vegetarians. Dish up what you like on a paper plate or in a paper box, pay by the weight (€2/100 grams, a plateful is generally 300 grams—about 10 ounces), and grab a nearby bench or hike over to the picnic-friendly Prado Museum grounds or Royal Botanical Garden (daily 11:00–24:00, a few blocks toward the center from the Prado at Calle de las Huertas 57, tel. 913-697-254).

North of Puerta del Sol
Eating Cheaply
See the map on page 369 for locations.

Restaurante Puerto Rico fills a long, congested hall by serving good meals for great prices to smart locals (€10 three-course fixed-price meal, closed Sun, Chinchilla 2, between Puerta del Sol and Gran Vía, tel. 915-219-834).

Hotel Europa Cafetería is a fun, high-energy scene with a mile-long bar, old-school waiters, great people-watching, local cuisine, and a fine €11 fixed-price lunch (daily 7:00–24:00, next to Hotel Europa, 50 yards off Puerta del Sol at Calle del Carmen 4, tel. 915-212-900). The menu lists three price levels: bar (inexpensive), table (generally pricey), or terrace (sky-high but with good people-watching). Your best value is to stick to the lunch menu if you're sitting inside, or order off the plastic *barra* menu if you sit at the bar (their €3 ham-and-egg toast makes a nice breakfast).

El Corte Inglés' seventh-floor cafeteria is fresh, modern, and—while not particularly cheap—popular with locals (Mon–Sat 10:00–22:00, closed Sun, non-smoking section, just off Puerta del Sol at intersection of Preciados and Tetuán).

Casa Labra Taberna Restaurante is famous as the birthplace of the Spanish Socialist Party in 1879...and as a spot for great cod. Packed with Madrileños, it manages to be both dainty and rustic. It's a wonderful scene with three distinct sections: the stand-up bar (cheapest, with two lines: one for munchies, the other for drinks), a peaceful little sit-down area in back (a little more expensive but still cheap; €6 salads), and a fancy restaurant (€20 lunches). Their tasty little €1.25 *tajada de bacalao* cod dishes put them on the map. The waiters are fun to joke around with

---

Breakfast in Madrid

As most hotels don't include breakfast (and many don't even serve it), you may be out on the streets first thing looking for a place. Non-touristy places only offer a hot drink and a pastry, with perhaps a potato omelet and sandwiches (toasted cheese, ham, or both). Touristy places will have a *desayuno* menu with various ham-and-eggs deals. Try *churros* once (see the listings for my favorite places). Starbucks, a temptation for many due to its familiarity, is always nearby. Get advice from your hotel staff for their favorite breakfast place.

(daily 11:00–15:30 & 18:00–23:00, a block off Puerta del Sol at Calle Tetuán 12, tel. 915-310-081).

La Gloria de Montera Restaurante, a hip Spanish bistro with white tablecloths and a minimalist-library ambience, serves mediocre food to locals at a cheap price (€8-10 fish and meat plates, daily, no reservations—arrive early or put your name on the list, a block from Gran Vía at Caballero de Gracia 10, tel. 915-234-407). **Ginger Restaurante,** a twin with the same menu and formula and a little more comfortable seating, is just off Plaza Santa Ana (on Calle de las Huertas at Plaza del Ángel 12—see map on page 378, tel. 913-691-059).

Fresc Co is the place for a cheap, modern, fast, and buffet-style meal. It's a chain with a winning plan: a long, appealing salad and buffet bar with one cheap price for all-you-can-eat, including dessert, a drink, and unlimited refills on everything (€9 lunch, €10 dinner, daily 12:30–24:00, air-con, Caballero de Gracia 8, tel. 915-216-052).

Vegetarian: **Artemisia II** is a hit with vegetarians who like good, healthy food in a smoke-free room without the typical hippie ambience that comes with most veggie places (great €11.25 three-course fixed-price lunch Mon–Fri only, open daily 13:30–16:00 & 21:00–24:00, 2 blocks north of Puerta del Sol at Tres Cruces 4, a few steps off Plaza del Carmen, tel. 915-218-721). **Artemisia I,** II's older sister, is located two blocks east of Plaza Santa Ana at Ventura de la Vega 4, off San Jerónimo (same hours, tel. 914-295-092).

Fast Food and Picnics

Fast Food: For an easy, light, cheap meal, try **Rodilla**—a popular sandwich and salad chain with a shop on the northeast corner of Puerta del Sol at #13 (daily 9:30–23:00). **Pans & Company,** with shops throughout Madrid and Spain, offers healthy, tasty sandwiches and pre-packaged salads (daily 9:00–24:00, locations at Puerta del Sol, on Plaza Callao, at Gran Vía 30, and many more).

Picnics: The department store **El Corte Inglés** has well-stocked meat and cheese counters downstairs (Mon–Sat 10:00–22:00, Sun 11:00–21:00, see "One-Stop Shopping" on page 321).

Churros con Chocolate

Those not watching their cholesterol will want to try the deep-fried doughy treats called *churros* (or the thicker *porras*), best enjoyed by dipping them in pudding-like hot chocolate. While many *chocolaterías* offer the dunkable fritters, *churros* are most delicious when consumed fresh out of the greasy cauldron at a place that actually fries them. See the map on page 369 for locations.

Chocolaterías Valor is a modern chain that does *churros* with pride and gusto. A few minutes' walk from nearly all my hotel recommendations, it's a fine place for breakfast. With a website like www.amigosdelchocolate.com, you know where their heart is (€4 *churros con chocolate,* daily 8:00–22:30, Fri–Sat until 24:00, a half-block below Plaza Callao and Gran Vía at Postigo de San Martín 7, tel. 915-229-288).

Chocolatería San Ginés is a classy institution, much beloved by Madrileños for its *churros con chocolate* (€4). Dunk your *churros* into the chocolate pudding, as locals have done here for more than 100 years. While quiet before midnight, it's packed with the disco crowd in the wee hours; the popular dance club Joy Eslava is next door (open 21 hours a day—it's only closed between 6:30–9:30; from Puerta del Sol, take Calle del Arenal 2 blocks west, turn left on bookstore-lined Pasadizo de San Ginés, and you'll see the café—it's at #5; tel. 913-656-546).

The Lavapiés District Tapas Crawl (for the Adventurous)

The neighborhood called Lavapiés is emerging as a colorful magnet for people-watching. This is where the multi-ethnic tapestry of Madrid society enjoys pithy, cheap, seedy-yet-fun-loving life on the streets. Neighborhoods like this typically experience an evolution: initially they're so cheap that only the immigrants, downtrodden, and counter-culture types live there. The diversity and color they bring attracts those with more money. Businesses erupt to cater to those bohemian/trendy tastes. Rents go up. Those who gave the area the colorful liveliness in the first place can no longer afford to live there. They move out...and here comes Starbucks. For now, Lavapiés is still edgy, yet comfortable enough for most.

This district has almost no tourists. (It's too scary.) Old ladies with their tired bodies and busy fans hang out on their tiny balconies as they have for 40 years, watching the scene. Shady types lurk on side streets (don't venture off the main drag, don't show your wallet or money, and don't linger on Plaza Lavapiés).

For food, you'll find all the various kinds of tapas bars described earlier in "The Madrid Pub-Crawl Dinner (for Beginners)," plus great Indian (almost all run by Bangladeshis) and Moroccan eateries. I've listed a couple of places that appealed to me...but explore your options. I'd recommend taking the entire walk once, then backtracking and eating at the place or places that appeal to you.

From the Antón Martín Metro stop (or Plaza Santa Ana), walk down Calle Ave María (on its way to becoming Calle Ave Allah) to Plaza Lavapiés (where old ladies hang out with the swarthy drunks and a mosaic of cultures treat this square as a communal living room; Metro station here), and then up Calle de Lavapiés to the newly remodeled square, Plaza Tirso de Molina (Metro stop). This square was once plagued by druggies. Now with flower kiosks and a playground, it's homey and inviting. This is a fine example of the new vision for Madrid's public spaces.

On Calle Ave María: **Bar Melos** is a thriving dive jammed with a hungry and nubile local crowd. It's famous for its giant patty melts called *zapatillas de lacón y queso* (because they're the size and shape of a *zapatilla* or slipper, €7, feeds at least two, Ave María 44, smoky tables in back). **Nuevo Café Barbieri,** one of a dying breed of smoky mirrored cafés with a circa-1940 ambience, offers classical music in the afternoon and jazz in the evening (Ave María 45).

On Calle de Lavapiés: At Calle de Lavapiés 44, consider an Indian place or drop into **Montes Wine Bar** (countless wines open and served by the glass, good tapas, crawl under the bar to get to the WC).

Connections

By Train

Remember that Madrid has two main train stations: Chamartín and Atocha. At the Atocha Station, AVE and other long-distance trains depart from a different area than local *cercanías* trains (for more details, see "Arrival in Madrid," page 317).

AVE Trains: Spain's AVE (AH-vay) bullet train opens up some good itinerary options. You can now get from Madrid's Atocha Station to **Barcelona** in three hours, with trains running almost hourly. The AVE train is generally faster (timed from downtown to downtown) and easier than flying, but not necessarily cheaper. Basic second-class tickets are €110 one-way for most departures and €130 for the fastest, peak-time departures. First-class tickets are €180. Advance purchase discounts (40–60 days ahead) are available through the national rail company (RENFE), but sell out quickly. Save by not traveling on holidays.

The AVE is also handy for visiting **Sevilla** (and, on the way, **Córdoba**). The basic Madrid–Sevilla second-class AVE fare is

€70–80, depending upon departure time; first-class AVE costs €140 and comes with a meal). Consider this exciting day trip to Sevilla from Madrid: 7:00–depart Madrid, 8:45–12:40-in Córdoba, 13:30–20:45-in Sevilla, 23:30–back in Madrid.

Other AVE destinations include **Toledo** (nearly hourly, 30 min, €10, from Atocha) and **Segovia** (8/day, 35 min, €10, from Chamartín Station, take train going toward Valladolid). For the latest, pick up the AVE brochure at the station, or check out www .renfe.es/ave. Prices vary with times and class. Eurailpass-holders get a big discount (e.g., Madrid to Sevilla is €9 second-class, but only at RENFE ticket windows—discount not available at ticket machines). Reserve each AVE segment ahead (tel. 902-240-202 for Atocha AVE info).

Below I've listed both non-AVE and (where available) AVE trains, to help you compare your options.

From Madrid by Train to: Toledo (AVE: nearly hourly, 30 min, from Atocha), **El Escorial** (1–2/hr, but bus is better—see page 391), **Segovia** (AVE: 8/day, 35 min plus 20-min shuttle bus into Segovia center, from Chamartín; slower *cercanías* trains: 9/day, 2 hrs, from both Chamartín and Atocha), **Ávila** (hourly until 21:30, 90 min, more departures from Chamartín than Atocha), **Salamanca** (7/day, 2.5 hrs, from Chamartín), **Santiago de Compostela** (2/day, 8–9.5 hrs, includes night train, from Chamartín), **Barcelona** (AVE: almost hourly, 3 hrs from Atocha; plus 1 night train from Chamartín, 9 hrs), **San Sebastián** (3/day, 5–6 hrs, from Atocha or Chamartín), **Pamplona** (4/day direct, 3 hrs, from Atocha), **Burgos** (7/day, 5 hrs, from Chamartín), **León** (11/day, 4 hrs, from Chamartín), **Granada** (2/day, 5 hrs, from Atocha), **Sevilla** (AVE: hourly, 2.5 hrs, departures from 16:00–19:00 can sell out far in advance, from Atocha), **Córdoba** (AVE: 28/day, 1.75 hrs; Altaria trains: 5/day, 2 hrs; all from Atocha), **Málaga** (AVE: 12/day, 2.5–3 hrs, from Atocha), **Algeciras** (Altaria trains: 2/day, 5.5 hrs, from Atocha), **Lisbon** (1/day departing at 22:45, 9 hrs, overnight Hotel Train from Chamartín), **Paris** (1/day, 13 hrs, direct overnight—a €185 Hotel Train, reserve more than 15 days in advance and hope there are seats left in the €89 *oferta mini* deals, from Chamartín). General train info: tel. 902-240-202, for international journeys: tel. 902-243-402, www.renfe.es.

By Bus

Madrid has several major bus stations, connected by Metro. If you take a taxi to any bus station, you'll be charged a legitimate €3 supplement. Buses to **Toledo** run from the bus station at Plaza Elíptica (2/hr, 1–1.5 hrs, €5 one-way, *directo* faster than *ruta*, Continental Auto bus company, tel. 915-272-961, Metro: Plaza Elíptica).

Estación Sur de Autobuses (South Bus Station): From here, you can catch buses to **Ávila** (8/day, 1.5 hrs, €13 round-trip), **Salamanca** (hourly express, 2.5 hrs, €20 one-way, tel. 902-020-052, www.avanzabus.com), **León** (10/day, 4 hrs, €21 one-way), **Santiago de Compostela** (5/day, 8 hrs, includes 24:30–9:00 night bus), and **Granada** (18/day, 5.25 hrs, €16 one-way, tel. 915-272-961). The station sits squarely on top of Metro: Méndez Álvaro (has TI, tel. 914-684-200, www.estacionautobusesmadrid.com).

Príncipe Pío Station: Príncipe Pío is the old North train station, which has now morphed into a trendy mall and a bus hub for local lines including **Segovia** (€7 one-way, €12 round-trip, 2/hr departing on half-hour from platforms 6 or 7, 1.25 hrs, Mon–Sat first departure at 6:30, last return at 21:30, Sun first 8:30 and last 22:30). From Metro: Príncipe Pío, follow signs to *terminal de autobuses* or follow pictures of a bus (tel. 915-598-955, www.la sepulvedana.es). Buy a ticket from the Sepulvedana window (platform 4). Reservations are rarely necessary.

Intercambiador de Moncloa Station: This station, in the Moncloa Metro station, serves **El Escorial** (4/hr, 45–55 min; for details, see page 391). To reach the **Valley of the Fallen,** you'll first go to El Escorial, then connect on the bus from there (1/day Tue–Sun only, 15 min from El Escorial; for details, see page 391).

Intercambiador de Avenida de América Station: Located at the Avenida de América Metro, buses go to **Burgos** (9/day, 3 hrs) and **Pamplona** (6/day, 5 hrs, Alsa, tel. 915-272-961, www .movelia.es).

Route Tips for Drivers

Avoid driving in Madrid. Rent your car when you depart. To leave Madrid from Gran Vía, simply follow signs for *A-6* (direction *Villalba* or *A Coruña*) for Segovia, El Escorial, or the Valley of the Fallen (see next chapter for details).

It's cheapest to make car-rental arrangements before you leave home. In Madrid, consider **Europcar** (central reservations tel. 902-105-030, San Leonardo 8 office tel. 915-418-892, Chamartín Station tel. 913-231-721, airport tel. 913-937-235), **Hertz** (central reservations tel. 902-402-405, Plaza de España 18 tel. 915-425-805, Chamartín Station tel. 917-330-400, airport tel. 913-937-228), **Avis** (central reservations tel. 902-200-162, Gran Vía 60 tel. 915-484-204, airport tel. 913-937-223), and **National Atesa** (central reservations tel. 902-100-515). Ask about free delivery to your hotel. At the airport, most rental cars are returned at Terminal 1.

Madrid's Barajas Airport

Ten miles east of downtown, Madrid's modern airport has four terminals. Terminals 1, 2, and 3 are connected by long indoor walkways (about an 8-min walk apart), and serve airlines including Continental, Delta, Northwest, United, US Airways, Air Canada, and Spanair. The newer Terminal 4 serves airlines including Iberia, Vueling, British, and American, and also has a separate satellite terminal called T4S. To transfer between Terminals 1–3 and Terminal 4, you can take a 10-minute shuttle bus (free, leaves every 10 min from departures level), or take the Metro (stops at Terminals 2 and 4). Make sure to allow enough time if you need to travel between terminals (and then for the long walk within Terminal 4 to the gates). For more information about navigating this massive airport, go to www.aena.es.

International flights typically use Terminals 1 and 4. At the Terminal 1 arrivals area, you'll find a helpful English-speaking **TI** (marked *Oficina de Información Turística*, Mon–Sat 8:00–20:00, Sun 9:00–14:00, tel. 913-058-656); **ATMs;** a **flight info office** (marked simply *Information* in airport lobby, open daily 24 hours, tel. 902-353-570); a **post-office** window; a **pharmacy;** lots of **phones** (buy a phone card from the nearby machine); a few scattered **Internet** terminals (small fee); **eateries;** a **RENFE office** (where you can get train info and buy long-distance train tickets, daily 8:00–21:00, tel. 902-240-202); and on-the-spot **car-rental agencies** (see previous page). The new super-modern Terminal 4 offers essentially the same services.

Iberia, Spanair, and Air Europa are Spain's airlines, connecting a reasonable number of cities in Spain, as well as international destinations (ask for best rates at travel agencies). Vueling is the most popular discount airline in Iberia (e.g., Madrid–Barcelona flight as cheap as €30 if booked in advance, tel. 902-333-933, www.vueling.com).

Getting Between the Airport and Downtown

By Public Bus: Bus #200 shuttles travelers between airport Terminals 1, 2, and 3 (departing from arrivals level every 10 minutes, runs 6:00–24:00) and the Metro stop Avenida de América (northeast of the historical center) in about 20 minutes. From that Metro stop, you can connect to your hotel by taking the Metro or hopping a taxi. Bus #204 serves Terminal 4 the same way. The trip costs only €1 (buy ticket from driver; or get a shareable 10-ride Metrobus ticket for €7.40 at a tobacco shop—for more info, see "Getting Around Madrid," page 323).

By Metro: The subway involves two transfers to reach the city center (€2; or add a €1 supplement to your €7.40 10-ride Metrobus ticket). The airport's futuristic "Aeropuerto T-1, T-2, T-3" Metro stop (notice the ATMs, subway info booth, and huge lighted map of Madrid) is in Terminal 2. Access the Metro at the check-in level; to reach the Metro from Terminal 1's arrivals level, stand with your back to the baggage claim, then go to your far right, up the stairs, and follow red-and-blue Metro diamond signs to the station (8-min walk). The Terminal 4 stop is the end of the line. To get to Puerta del Sol, take line 8 for 12 minutes to Nuevos Ministerios, then continue on line 10 to Tribunal, then line 1 to Puerta del Sol (30 min more total); or exit at Nuevos Ministerios and take a €5 taxi or bus #150 straight to Puerta del Sol.

By Minibus Shuttle: The AeroCity shuttle bus provides door-to-door transport in a seven-seat minibus with up to three hotel stops en route. It's promoted by hotels, but if you want door-to-door service, simply taking a taxi generally offers a better value.

By Taxi: Considering the speed, ease, and economy of riding the subway in from the airport, I'd opt for the Metro over taxis. If you take a taxi between the airport and downtown, allow about €25 during the day *(Tarifa 1)* or €35 at night and on Sundays *(Tarifa 2)*. For Terminal 4, add about €10. Insist on the meter. The €5 airport supplement is legal. There is no charge for luggage. Plan on getting stalled in traffic.

NORTHWEST OF MADRID

El Escorial • Valley of the Fallen • Segovia • Ávila

Before slipping out of Madrid, consider several fine side-trips northwest of Spain's capital city, all conveniently reached by car, bus, or train.

Spain's lavish, brutal, and complicated history is revealed throughout Old Castile. This region, where the Spanish language originated, is named for its many castles—battle scars from the long-fought Reconquista.

An hour from Madrid, tour the imposing and fascinating palace at El Escorial, headquarters of the Spanish Inquisition. Nearby at the awe-inspiring Valley of the Fallen, pay tribute to the countless victims of Spain's bloody civil war.

Segovia, with its remarkable Roman aqueduct (pictured above) and romantic castle, is another worthwhile side-trip. At Ávila, you can walk the perfectly preserved medieval walls.

Planning Your Time

See El Escorial and the Valley of the Fallen together in less than a day (but not on Monday, when both sights are closed). By car, do them en route to Segovia; by bus, make it a day trip from Madrid.

Segovia is worth a half-day of sightseeing and is a joy at night. Ávila, while it has its charm, merits only a quick stop (if you're driving and in the area, 1.5 hours from Madrid, also a logical stop on the way to Salamanca by train) to marvel at its medieval walls and, perhaps, check out St. Teresa's finger.

In total, these sights are worth two days if you're in Spain for less than a month. If you're a history buff in Spain for just a week, squeeze in a quick side-trip from Madrid to El Escorial and the Valley of the Fallen.

Northwest of Madrid

El Escorial

The Monasterio de San Lorenzo de El Escorial is a symbol of power rather than elegance. This 16th-century palace, 30 miles northwest of Madrid, gives us a better feel for the Counter-Reformation and the Inquisition than any other building.

Getting to El Escorial

Most people visit El Escorial from Madrid. By public transportation, the bus is most convenient (since it gets you closer to the palace). Remember that it makes sense to combine El Escorial with a visit to the nearby Valley of the Fallen (also described in this chapter).

Cheap Tricks

At El Escorial

Download and print out a free detailed English guide of three architectural and historic tours through San Lorenzo de El Escorial by clicking on the "Place for walks" link at www.san lorenzoturismo.org.

In Segovia

Segovia has plenty of little Romanesque churches that are free to enter, and many have architecturally interesting exteriors that are worth a look. On your way to the main sights, keep your eyes peeled for these hidden treasures: Coming from the bus station on Avenida de Fernández Ladreda toward the center of town, you can see the San Millán church; on Plazas San Martín and San Esteban are two churches sharing their squares' names; and on the way to the Alcázar on Plaza de la Merced is the San Andrés church.

In Ávila

As you're wandering the city and you see the arched gates leading out of the old center, pop out to the other side and take in the impressive wall. Exploring sections of it from the ground may be even better than walking along it, and saves you the admission fee.

By Bus: Buses leave from the Intercambiador de Moncloa, which is in the basement of Madrid's Moncloa Metro stop (4/ hr, fewer on weekends, 45–55 min, €3.40 one-way, buy ticket from driver; in Madrid take bus #664 or slower #661 from Intercambiador's platform 3, Herranz Bus, tel. 918-969-028). The bus drops you downtown in San Lorenzo de El Escorial, a pleasant 10-minute stroll from the palace (see map): Exit the bus station from the back ramp that leads over the parked buses, turn left, and follow the newly cobbled pedestrian lane, Calle San Juan. This street veers to the right and becomes Calle Juan de Leyra. In a few short blocks, it dead-ends at Duque de Medinaceli, where you'll turn left and see the palace. Stairs lead past several decent eateries, through a delightful park, past the TI (Mon–Fri 10:00–18:00, Sat–Sun 10:00–19:00, tel. 918-905-313), and directly to the tourist entry of the immense palace/monastery.

By Train: Local trains (*cercanías* line C-8A) run once or twice an hour from Madrid's Atocha and Chamartín Stations to El Escorial. From the station, walk 20 minutes uphill through Casita del Príncipe park, straight up from the station. Or you can take a shuttle bus (2/hr, €1) or a taxi (€5) to the San Lorenzo de El Escorial town center and the palace.

El Escorial Town

NORTHWEST OF MADRID

MARKET

TO VALLEY OF THE FALLEN, SEGOVIA & MADRID

BUS STATION

TO TRAIN STATION

PLAZA

PARK

GARDENS

EL ESCORIAL PALACE

TO AVILA & PHILIP'S SEAT

DCH

━━ 10-MINUTE WALK FROM BUS STATION TO PALACE

🅿 PARKING

❶ Entrance to Palace

❷ Plaza Jacinto Benavente

❸ Mercado Público (Market)

❹ La Clementina Restaurant

By Car: It's quite simple. Taxi to your car-rental office in Madrid (or ask if they'll deliver the car to your hotel). Pick up the car by 8:30 and ask for directions to highway A-6. From Gran Vía in central Madrid, follow signs to *A-6* (direction *Villalba* or *A Coruña*). The freeway leads directly out of town. Stay on A-6 past the first El Escorial exit. At kilometer 37, you'll see the cross marking the Valley of the Fallen ahead on the left. Exit 47 takes you to both the Valley of the Fallen (after a half-mile, a granite gate on right marks Valle de los Caídos turn-off) and El Escorial (follow *San Lorenzo del Escorial* signs).

The nearby **Silla de Felipe** (Philip's Seat) is a rocky viewpoint where the king would come to admire his palace as it was being built. From El Escorial, follow directions to Ávila, then M-505 to Valdemorillo; look for a sign on your right after about a mile.

When you leave El Escorial for Madrid, Toledo, or Segovia, follow signs to *A-6 Guadarrama*. After about six miles, you pass the Valley of the Fallen and hit the freeway.

Sights

▲▲▲Monasterio de San Lorenzo de El Escorial

Built at a time when Catholic Spain felt threatened by Protestant "heretics," the construction of this palace dominated the Spanish economy for a generation (1562–1584). Because of this bully in the national budget, Spain has almost nothing else to show from this most powerful period of her history.

Cost: The basic, unguided €8 *visita libre* **ticket** lets you tour the complex on your own (or with the help of a rentable audio-guide—see below; with this ticket the Royal Pantheon crypt is off-limits unless you rent an audioguide). The €10 *visita guiada* **ticket** includes a guided tour (ask for next tour in English; only sold until 90 min before closing time). If you're also going to the Valley of the Fallen, the **combo-ticket** sold here will save you some euros (€8.50 includes unguided El Escorial visit, €11 includes guided El Escorial visit, sold before 15:00 April–Sept or before 14:00 Oct–March).

Hours: April–Sept Tue–Sun 10:00–19:00, Oct–March until 18:00, always closed Mon, last entry one hour before closing, last English tour 90 min before closing.

Information: You'll find scant captions in English within the palace—if you want to visit on your own, you can take my self-guided tour (see below), which covers the basics. For more information, get the *Guide: Monastery of San Lorenzo El Real de El Escorial,* which follows the general route you'll take (€8, available at any of several shops in the palace). The audioguide rents for €2.30 (or pay €3 to get a voucher for an audioguide at the Valley of the Fallen as well). Tel. 918-905-904.

❷ Self-Guided Tour: The *monasterio* looks confusing at first, but the *visita* arrows and signs guide you clearly through one continuous path. This is the general order you'll follow.

Pass through the security scanner, buy your ticket, and then continue down the hall past the *consigna* baggage check (Sala 1) to the **Chamber of the Honor Guards.** This chamber is hung with 16th-century tapestries, including fascinating copies of Hieronymus Bosch's most famous and preachy paintings (which Philip II fancied). Don't miss El Greco's towering painting of the *Martyrdom of St. Maurice.* This was the artist's first commission after arriving in Spain from Venice. It was too subtle and complex for the king, so El Greco moved on to Toledo to find work.

Continue downstairs to the fascinating **Museum of Archi-**

El Escorial—Ground Floor

tecture (Museo de Arquitectura). It has long parallel corridors of fine models of the palace and some of the actual machinery and tools used to construct it. Huge stone-pinching winches, fat ropes, and rusty mortar spades help convey the immensity of this 21-year project involving 1,500 workers. At the big model, notice the complex is shaped like a grill, and recall how San Lorenzo—St. Lawrence, a Christian Spaniard martyred by pagan Romans (A.D. 258)—was burned to death on a grill. Throughout the palace, you'll see this symbol associated with the saint. The grill's "handle" was the palace, or residence of the royal family. The monastery and school gathered around the huge basilica.

Next, linger in the **Museum of Paintings** to consider the 15th- to 17th-century Flemish, Spanish, and Italian works. Contemplate Roger van der Weyden's *Calvary,* with mourning Mary and St. John at the feet of the crucified Christ. (It's interesting to compare it with van der Weyden's similar *Descent from the Cross,* which hangs in the Prado in Madrid.) Then pass through the peaceful and empty Courtyard of Masks to reach the **Hall of Battles** (Sala de Batallas). Its paintings celebrate Spain's great military victories—including the Battle of San Quentin over France (1557) on St. Lawrence's feast day, which inspired the construction of El Escorial. The sprawling series, painted in 1590, helped teach the

History of El Escorial

The giant, gloomy building made of gray-black stone looks more like a prison than a palace. About 650 feet long and 500 feet wide, it has 2,600 windows, 1,200 doors, more than 100 miles of passages, and 1,600 overwhelmed tourists.

Four hundred years ago, the enigmatic, introverted, and extremely Catholic King Philip II (1527–1598) ruled his bulky empire and directed the Inquisition from here. To Philip, the building embodied the wonders of Catholic learning, spirituality, and arts. To 16th-century followers of Martin Luther, it epitomized the evil of closed-minded Catholicism. To architects, the building—built on the cusp between styles— exudes both Counter-Reformation grandeur and understated Renaissance simplicity. Today, it's a time capsule of Spain's "Golden Age," packed with history, art, and Inquisition ghosts. (And at an elevation of nearly 3,500 feet, it can be friggin' cold.)

The building was conceived by Philip II to serve several purposes: as a grand mausoleum for Spain's royal family, starting with his father, Charles V (known as Carlos I in Spain); as a monastery to pray (a lot) for the royal souls; as a small palace to use as a Camp David of sorts for Spain's royalty; and as a school to embrace humanism in a way that promoted the Catholic faith.

new king all the elements of warfare. Stroll the length for a primer on army skills.

From here, a corridor lined with various family trees (some scrawny, others lush and fecund) leads into the royal living quarters (the building's grill handle). Immediately inside the first door, find the small portrait of Philip II flanked by two large portraits of his daughters. The palace was like Philip: austere. Notice the simple floors, plain white walls, and bare-bones chandelier. This was the bedroom of one of his daughters. Notice the sheet warmer beside her bed—often necessary during the winter. Bend down to see the view from her bed...of the high altar in the basilica next door. The entire complex of palace and monastery buildings was built around that altar.

In the next room, the **Guard's room,** notice the reclinable sedan chair that Philip II, thick with gout, was carried in (for seven days) on his last trip from Madrid to El Escorial. He wanted to be here when he died.

The **Audience Chamber** is now a portrait gallery filled with Habsburg royals painted by popular local artists. The portraits of unattractive people that line the walls provide an instructive peek at the consequences of mixing blue blood with more of the same blue blood (inbreeding among royals was a common problem throughout Europe in those days).

The Spanish emperor Charles V (1500–1558) is over the fireplace mantel. Charles, Philip II's dad, was the most powerful man in Europe, having inherited not only the Spanish crown, but also Germany, Austria, the Low Countries (Belgium and the Netherlands), and much of Italy. When he announced his abdication in 1555, his son Philip II inherited much of this territory... plus the responsibility of managing it. Philip's draining wars with France, Portugal, Holland, and England—including the disastrous defeat of Spain's navy, the Spanish Armada, by England's Queen Elizabeth I (1588)—knocked Spain from its peak of power and began centuries of decline.

The guy with the good-looking legs next to Charles was his illegitimate son, Don Juan de Austria—famous for his handsome looks, thanks to a little fresh blood. Other royal offspring weren't so lucky: When one king married his niece, the result was Charles II (1665–1700, opposite Charles V). His severe underbite (an inbred royal family trait) was the least of his problems. An epileptic before that disease was understood, poor "Charles the Mad" would be the last of the Spanish Habsburgs. He died without an heir in 1700, ushering in the continent-wide War of the Spanish Succession and the dismantling of Spain's empire.

In the **Walking Gallery,** the royals got their exercise privately, with no risk of darkening their high-class skins with a tan. Study the 16th-century maps that line the walls. The slate strip on the floor is a sundial from 1755. It lined up with a (now plugged) hole in the wall so that at noon a tiny beam hit the middle of the three lines. Palace clocks were set by this. Where the ray crossed the strip indicated the date and sign of the zodiac.

As you enter the **King's Antechamber,** look back to study the fine inlaid-wood door (a gift from the German emperor that celebrates the exciting humanism of the age).

Philip II's bedroom is austere, like his daughter's. Look at the king's humble bed...barely queen-size. He too could view Mass at the basilica's high altar without leaving his bed. The red box next to his pillow holds the royal bedpan. But don't laugh—the king's looking down from the wall behind you. At age 71, Philip II, the gout-ridden king of a dying empire, died in this bed (1598).

From here, his body was taken to the **Royal Pantheon** (Panteón Real), the gilded resting place of 26 kings and queens... four centuries' worth of Spanish monarchy (a detour on your route, and only accessible if you're on the guided visit or have the audioguide). All the kings are included—but only those queens who became mothers of kings.

There is a post-mortem filing system at work in the Pantheon.

From the entrance, kings are on the left, queens on the right. (The only exception is Isabel II, since she was a ruling queen and her husband was a consort.) The first and greatest, Charles V and his Queen Isabel, flank the altar on the top shelf. Her son, Philip II, rests below Charles and opposite (only) one of Philip's four wives, and so on. There is a waiting process, too. Before a royal corpse can rest in this room, it needs to decompose for several decades. The three empty niches are already booked. The bones of the current king Juan Carlos' grandmother, Victoria Eugenia (who died in 1964), are ready to be moved in, but the staff can't explain why they haven't been transferred yet. Juan Carlos' father, Don Juan (who died in 1993), is also on the waiting list...controversially. Technically, he was never crowned king of Spain—Franco took control of Spain before Don Juan could ascend to the throne, and he was passed over for the job when Franco reinstituted the monarchy. Juan Carlos' mother is the most recent guest in the rotting room. So where does that leave Juan Carlos and Sofía? This hotel is *todo completo*.

The next rooms are filled with the tombs of lesser royals: Each bears that person's name (in Latin), relationship to the king, and slogan or epitaph. From here, it's on to the wedding-cake **Pantheon of Royal Children** (Panteón de los Infantes, accessible with any kind of ticket), which holds the remains of various royal children who died before the age of seven (and their first Communion).

Head past the mini–gift shop and continue upstairs to the **Chapter Rooms** (Salas Capitulares). These rooms, where the monks met to do church business, are lined with big-name paintings by José Ribera, El Greco, Titian, and Velázquez. (More great

paintings are in the monastery's Museum of Painting.) Continue to the final room to see some atypical Bosch paintings and the intricate, portable altar of Charles V. The **cloister** glows with bright, newly restored paintings by Pellegrino Tibaldi. Off the cloister is the **Old Church** (Iglesia Vieja), which they used from 1571 to 1586, while finishing the basilica. During that time, the bodies of several kings, including Charles V, were interred here. Among the many paintings you'll see, look for the powerful *Martyrdom of St. Lawrence* by Tiziano (Titian) above the main altar.

Follow the signs to the **basilica,** which may be closed in 2010 for restoration. If it's open, find the flame-engulfed grill in the center of the altar wall that features San Lorenzo (the same St.

Lawrence from the painting) meeting his famous death—and taking "turn the other cheek" to new extremes. Lorenzo was so cool, he reportedly told his Roman executioners, "You can turn me over now—I'm done on this side." With your back to the altar, go to the right corner for the artistic highlight of the basilica: Benvenuto Cellini's marble sculpture *The Crucifixion*. Jesus' features are supposedly modeled after the Shroud of Turin. Cellini carved this from Carrara marble for his own tomb in 1562 (according to the letters under Christ's feet).

Last comes the immense **library** *(biblioteca)*—where it's clear that education was a priority for the Spanish royalty. Savor this

room. The ceiling (by Tibaldi, depicting various disciplines labeled in Latin, the lingua franca of the multinational Habsburg Empire) is a burst of color. At the far end of the room, the elaborate model of the solar system looks like a giant gyroscope, revolving unmistakably around the Earth, with a misshapen, under-explored North America. As you leave, look back above the wooden door. The plaque warns *"Excomunión..."*—you'll be excommunicated if you take a book without checking it out properly. Who needs late fees when you hold the keys to hell?

Eating in El Escorial

The **Mercado Público,** a four-minute walk from the palace, is the place to shop for a picnic (Mon–Fri 9:30–13:30 & 17:00–20:00, Sat 9:30–14:00, closed Thu and Sat afternoons and all day Sun, Calle del Rey 9).

La Clementina serves appealing tapas at their bar and full meals in the restaurant. In warm weather, their outdoor tables are a treat (daily 13:30–16:30 & 20:30–24:00, Plaza de la Constitución 9, tel. 918-901-192). Other restaurants sell *menú del día* (three-course fixed-price meals) options on nearby squares.

Valley of the Fallen

Six miles from El Escorial, high in the Guadarrama Mountains, is the Valley of the Fallen (Valle de los Caídos). A 500-foot-tall

granite cross marks this immense and powerful underground monument to the victims of Spain's 20th-century night-mare—its Civil War (1936–1939).

Cost: €5, or €8.30 to include the round-trip bus from El Escorial. But if you're also visiting El Escorial, buy the combo-ticket: €8.50 includes unguided El Escorial visit, €11 includes guided El Escorial visit (sold before 15:00 April–Sept or before 14:00 Oct–March).

Hours: April–Sept Tue–Sun 10:00–19:00, Oct–March until 18:00, closed Mon, last entry one hour before closing, basilica closes 30 min before site closes, tel. 918-905-611.

Getting There: Most visitors side-trip to the Valley of the Fallen from the nearby El Escorial. If you don't have your own wheels, the easiest way to get between these two sights is to nego-tiate a deal with a **taxi** (to take you from El Escorial to Valley of the Fallen, wait for you 30–60 min, and then bring you back to El Escorial, about €45 total). Otherwise, one **bus** a day (#660) con-nects El Escorial with the Valley of the Fallen (15 min, leaves El Escorial at 15:15, leaves Valley of the Fallen at 17:30, €8.30 round-trip includes admission to the site, or €4.30 round-trip for just the bus—if you've already bought the Escorial/Valley combo-ticket; no bus on Mon, when both sights are closed). Drivers can find tips under "Getting to El Escorial—By Car" on page 393.

Audioguide: The audioguide (€2, or included in €3 combo-ticket with El Escorial audioguide) is heavy on the theological message of the statues and tapestries, and it ignores Franco.

❸ Self-Guided Tour: Approaching by car or bus, you enter the sprawling park through a granite gate. The best views of the cross are from the bridge (but note that it's illegal for drivers to stop anywhere along this road). To the right, tiny chapels along the ridge mark the Stations of the Cross, where pilgrims stop on their hike to this memorial.

In 1940, prison workers dug 220,000 tons of granite out of the hill beneath the cross to form an underground basilica, then used the stones to erect the cross (built like a chimney, from the inside). Since it's built directly over the dome of the subterranean basilica, a seismologist keeps a careful eye on things.

The Spanish Civil War
(1936–1939)

Thirty-three months of warfare killed 200,000 Spaniards. Unlike America's Civil War, which split America roughly north and south, Spain's war was between classes and ideologies, dividing every city and village, and many families. It was especially cruel, with atrocities and reprisals on both sides.

The war began as a military coup to overthrow the democratically elected Republic, a government that the army and other conservative powers considered too liberal and disorganized. The rebel forces, called the Nationalists *(Nacionalistas),* consisted of the army, monarchy, Catholic Church, big business, and rural estates, with aid from Germany, Italy, and Portugal. Trying to preserve the liberal government were the Republicans *(Republicanos),* also called Loyalists: the government, urban areas, secularists, small business, and labor unions, with aid from the United States (minimal help) and the "International Brigades" of communists, socialists, and labor organizers.

In the summer of 1936, the army rebelled and took control of its own garrisons, rejecting the Republic and pledging allegiance to Generalísimo Francisco Franco (1892–1975). These Nationalists launched a three-year military offensive to take Spain region by region, town by town. The government ("Republicans") cobbled together an army of volunteers, local militias, and international fighters. The war pitted conservative Catholic priests against socialist factory workers, rich businessmen against radical students, sunburned farmers loyal to the old king against upwardly mobile small businessmen. People suffered. You'll notice that nearly every Spaniard in his or her 70s is very short—a product of growing up during these hungry and very difficult Civil War years.

Spain's Civil War attracted international attention. Adolf Hitler and Benito Mussolini sent troops and supplies to their fellow fascist, Franco. It was Hitler's Luftwaffe that helped Franco bomb the town of Guernica (April 1937), an event famously captured on canvas by Pablo Picasso (see pages 163 and 356). On the Republican side, hundreds of Americans (including Ernest Hemingway) steamed over to Spain, some to fight for democracy as part of the "Abraham Lincoln Brigade."

By 1938, only Barcelona and Madrid held out. But they were no match for Franco's army. On April 1, 1939, Madrid fell and the war ended, beginning 37 years of iron-fisted rule by Franco.

The stairs that lead to the imposing monument are grouped in sets of tens, meant to symbolize the Ten Commandments (including "Thou shalt not kill"—hmm). The emotional *pietà* draped over the basilica's entrance is huge—you could sit in the palm of Christ's hand. The statue was sculpted by Juan de Ávalos, the same artist who created the dramatic figures of the four Evangelists at the base of the cross. It must have had a powerful impact on mothers who came here to remember their fallen sons.

A solemn silence and a stony chill fill the basilica. At 300

yards long, the basilica was built to be longer than St. Peter's...but the Vatican had the final say when it blessed only 262 of those yards. Many Spaniards pass under the huge, foreboding angels of fascism to visit the grave of General Franco—an unusual place of pilgrimage, to say the least.

After walking through the two long vestibules, stop at the iron gates of the actual basilica. The line of torch-like lamps adds to the shrine ambience. Franco's prisoners, the enemies of the right, dug this memorial out of solid rock from 1940 to 1950. (Though it looks like bare rock still shows on the ceiling, it's just a clever design.) The sides of the monument are lined with copies of 16th-century Brussels tapestries of the Apocalypse, and side chapels contain alabaster copies of Spain's most famous statues of the Virgin Mary.

Interred behind the high altar and side chapels (marked "RIP, 1936–1939, died for God and country") are the remains of the approximately 50,000 people, both Franco's Nationalists and the anti-Franco Republicans, who lost their lives in the war. Regrettably, the urns are not visible, so it is Franco who takes center stage. His grave, strewn with flowers, lies behind the high altar. In front of the altar is the grave of José Antonio Primo de Rivera (1903–1936), the founder of Spanish fascism, who was killed by Republicans during the Civil War. Between these fascists' graves, the statue of a crucified Christ is lashed to a timber Franco himself is said to have felled. The seeping stones seem to weep for the victims. Today, families of the buried Republicans remain upset that their kin are lying with Franco and his Nationalists.

As you leave, stare into the eyes of those angels with swords and two right wings and think about all the "heroes" who keep dying "for God and country," at the request of the latter. A Mass closes off the entire front of the basilica (altar and tombs) to the public daily from 11:00 to 12:05. The resident boys' choir (the

"White Voices"—Spain's answer to the Vienna Boys' Choir) generally sings during the Mass (you can sit through the service, but not sightsee during this time).

The expansive view from the monument's terrace includes the peaceful, forested valley and sometimes snow-streaked mountains. For an even better view, consider taking a **funicular** trip—with a short commentary in English—to the base of the cross (€1.50 one-way, €2.50 round-trip, pay fare at machine, April–Sept Tue–Sun 11:00–18:30, 3/hr; Oct–March Tue–Sun 11:00–16:30, 2/hr; closed Mon, last ticket sold 30 min before closing; restaurant and public WC). You can hike back down in 25 minutes. If you have a car, you can drive up past the monastery and hike from the start of the trail marked *Sendero a la Cruz*.

Sleeping and Eating: Near the parking lot and bus stop at Valley of the Fallen are a small snack bar and picnic tables. Basic overnight lodging is available at the **Hospedería del Valle de los Caídos,** a 100-room monastery behind the cross (Sb-€46, Db-€91, includes meals, tax, and a pass to enter and leave the park after hours, tel. 918-905-494, fax 918-961-542, no English spoken). A meditative night here is good mostly for monks.

Segovia

Fifty miles from Madrid, this town of 55,000 boasts a thrilling Roman aqueduct, a grand cathedral, and a historic castle. Since the city is more than 3,000 feet above sea level and just northwest of a mountain range, the city is exposed to cool northern breezes, and people come here from Madrid for a break from the summer heat.

Day-Tripping from Madrid: Considering the easy train and bus connections (35 min one-way by AVE train, 2 hours by slower train, 1.5 hours by bus), Segovia makes a fine day trip from Madrid. The disadvantages of side-tripping are that you spend the coolest hours of the day (early and late) en route, you miss the charming evening scene in Segovia, and you'll pay more for a hotel in Madrid than in Segovia. If you have time, spend the night. But even if you just stay the day, Segovia still offers a rewarding and convenient break from the big-city intensity of Madrid.

Orientation to Segovia

Segovia is a medieval "ship" ready for your inspection. Start at the stern—the aqueduct—and stroll up Calle de Cervantes and Calle Juan Bravo to the prickly Gothic masts of the cathedral. Explore the tangle of narrow streets around playful Plaza Mayor and then descend to the Alcázar at the bow.

Tourist Information

Segovia has four TIs. The TI on Plaza Mayor covers both Segovia and the surrounding region (at #10, July–mid-Sept daily 9:00–20:00, mid-Sept–June 9:00–14:00 & 16:00–19:00, tel. 921-460-334). The TI at Plaza del Azoguejo at the base of the aqueduct specializes in Segovia and has lots of friendly staff, WCs, and a gift shop (daily 10:00–19:00, Sat until 20:00, see wooden model of Segovia, tel. 921-466-720, www.segovia.es). Two smaller TIs are at the bus station (behind a window, daily 10:00–14:00 & 15:30–17:00) and at the AVE train station (Mon–Fri 9:00–17:00, Sat–Sun 10:30–18:30, tel. 921-447-262).

Arrival in Segovia

Unfortunately, neither of the train stations nor the bus station has luggage storage. If day-tripping from Madrid, check the return schedule when you arrive here (or get one at the Segovia TI).

By Bus: It's a 10-minute walk from the bus station to the town center: Exit left out of the station, continue straight across the street, and follow Avenida Fernández Ladreda, passing San Millán church on the left, then San Clemente church on the right, before coming to the aqueduct.

By Train: From the **AVE train station** (called Guiomar), ride bus #11 for 20 minutes to the base of the aqueduct. To reach the center from the less-convenient *Cercanías* train station, you can catch bus #6 or #8; take a taxi; or walk 35 minutes (start at Paseo del Conde de Sepulvedana—which becomes Paseo Ezequiel González—to the bus station, then turn right and head down Avenida Fernández Ladreda to the aqueduct).

By Car: See "Route Tips for Drivers" on page 415.

Helpful Hints

Shopping: If you buy handicrafts such as tablecloths from street vendors, make sure the item you're buying is the one you actually get; some unscrupulous vendors substitute inferior goods at the last minute. A flea market is held on Plaza Mayor on Thursdays (roughly 8:00–15:00).

Local Guide: Elvira Valderrama Rascon, a hardworking young woman, is a good English-speaking guide (€100/half-day tour, mobile 636-227-949, elvisvalrras@yahoo.es).

Sightseeing Bus: Bus Turístico is a weak version of a hop-on, hop-off bus, but it does give you a nice chance to take great panoramic photos of Segovia's boat-like shape, with the mountains as a backdrop. Pick it up at the aqueduct, and stay on—it's not really worth using it as a means of getting around town; just stay on for the full loop (€5.60, buy ticket on bus; leaves at 11:00, 12:00, 13:00, 16:00, and 17:00; tel. 902-330-080).

Self-Guided Walk

Welcome to Historic Segovia

This 15-minute walk is all downhill from the city's main square along the pedestrian-only street to the Roman aqueduct. It's most enjoyable just before dinner, when it's cool and filled with strolling locals.

Start on Segovia's inviting **Plaza Mayor**—once the scene of executions, religious theater, and bullfights with spectators jamming the balconies. In the 19th century, the bullfights were stopped. When locals complained, they were given a more gentle form of entertainment—bands in the music kiosk. Today the very best entertainment here is simply enjoying a light meal, snack, or drink in your choice of the many restaurants and cafés lining the square. The Renaissance church opposite the City Hall and behind the TI was built to replace the church where Isabel was proclaimed Queen of Castile in 1474. The symbol of Segovia is the aqueduct—find it in the seals on the Theater Juan Bravo and atop the City Hall. Head down Calle de Isabel la Católica (downhill, to right of Hotel Infanta Isabel), and tempt yourself with the pastries in the window display of the corner bakery.

After 100 yards, at the first intersection, you'll see the Corpus Christi Convent on the right. For a donation, you can pop in to see the Franciscan church, which was once a synagogue, which was once a mosque. While sweet and peaceful, with lots of art featuring St. Francis, the church is skippable.

After another 100 yards, you come to the complicated Plaza de San Martín, a commotion of history surrounding a striking statue of Juan Bravo. When Charles V, a Habsburg who didn't even speak Spanish, took power, he imposed his rule over Castile. This threatened the local nobles, who—inspired and led by Juan

Segovia

1 Hotel Los Linajes
2 Hotel Infanta Isabel
3 Hostal Plaza & José María Rest.
4 Hostal Don Jaime
5 Hospedaje el Gato
6 Mesón de Candido Rest.
7 Rest. Casa Chapete
8 Café Jeyma
9 La Concepción Restaurante
10 Narizotas & Rest. Bar San Martín
11 Cueva de San Esteban
12 La Almuzara
13 Rodilla
14 Café La Colonial
15 Limon y Menta Pastry Shop
16 Museo de Arte Contemporáneo Esteban Vicente
17 Sightseeing Bus & Bus #11

Bravo—revolted in 1521. Although Juan Bravo lost the battle—and his head—he's still a symbol of Castilian pride. This statue was erected in 1921 on the 400th anniversary of his death.

On the same square, the 12th-century Church of St. Martín is Segovian Romanesque in style (a mix of Christian Romanesque and Moorish styles). The 14th-century Tower of Lozoya, behind the statue, is one of many fortified towers that marked the homes of feuding local noble families. Clashing loyalties led to mini–civil wars. In the 15th century, as Ferdinand and Isabel centralized authority in Spain, nobles were required to lop their towers. You'll see the once-tall, now-stubby towers of 15th-century noble mansions all over Segovia.

In front of the Juan Bravo statue (downhill end of square) stands the bold and bulky House of Siglo XV. Its fortified *Isabelino* style was typical of 15th-century Segovian houses. Later, in a more peaceful age, the boldness of these houses was softened with the decorative stucco work—Arabic-style floral and geometrical patterns—that you see today (for example, in the big house across the street). At Plaza del Platero Oquendo, 50 yards farther downhill on the right, you'll see a similar once-fortified, now-softened house with a cropped tower.

At the next corner, find the "house of a thousand beaks" with another truncated tower. This building, maintaining its original Moorish design, has a wall just past the door, which blocks your view from the street. This wall, the architectural equivalent of a veil, hid this home's fine courtyard—Moors didn't flaunt their wealth. Step inside; there may be art students at work and perhaps an exhibit on display.

From here, stroll 100 yards, and you'll see the Roman aqueduct, which marks the end of this walk (and is described next).

Sights

▲**Roman Aqueduct**—Segovia was a Roman military base and needed water. Emperor Trajan's engineers built a nine-mile aque-

duct to channel water from the Río Frío to the city, culminating at the Roman castle (which is the Alcázar today). The famous and exposed section of the 2,000-year-old *acueducto romano* is 2,500 feet long and 100 feet high, has 118 arches, was made from 20,000 granite blocks without any mortar, and can still carry a stream of water. It actually functioned until the late 19th century. On Plaza del Azoguejo, a grand stairway leads from the base of the aqueduct to the top—offering close-up looks at the imposing work.

▲**Cathedral**—Segovia's cathedral, built in Renaissance times

(1525–1768, the third on this site), was Spain's last major Gothic building. Embellished to the hilt with pinnacles and flying buttresses, the exterior is a great example of the final, overripe stage of Gothic, called Flamboyant. Yet the Renaissance arrived before it was finished—as evidenced by the fact that the cathedral is crowned by a dome, not a spire.

Cost and Hours: €3, free on Sun 9:30–13:15 but cathedral access only—no cloisters, open daily April–Oct 9:30–18:30, Nov–March 9:00–17:30, tel. 921-462-205.

◑ Self-Guided Tour: The spacious and elegantly simple interior provides a delightful contrast to the frilly exterior. The **choir** features finely carved wooden stalls from the previous church (1400s). The *catedra* (bishop's chair) is in the center rear of the choir. The many side chapels are mostly 16th-century, and come with big locking gates—a reminder that they were the private sacred domain of the rich families and guilds who "owned" them. They could enjoy private Masses here with their names actually spoken in the blessings, and a fine burial spot close to the altar. Find the **Capilla La Concepción** (a chapel in the rear that looks like a mini art gallery). Its many 17th-century paintings hang behind a mahogany wood gate imported from colonial America. The painting *Tree of Life*, by Ignacio Ries (left of the altar), shows hedonistic mortals dancing atop the Tree of Life. As a skeletal Grim Reaper prepares to receive them into hell (by literally chopping down the tree... timberrrr), Jesus rings a bell imploring them to wake up before it's too late. The center statue is Mary of the Apocalypse (as described in Revelations, standing on a devil and half moon, which looks like bull's horns). Mary's pregnant and the devil licks his evil chops, waiting to devour the baby Messiah.

Opposite from where you entered, a fine door (which leads into the cloister) is crowned by a painted Flamboyant Gothic *pietà* in its tympanum (the statue of Jesus with a skirt, on the left, is a reminder of how prudishness from the past looks silly in the present).

The **cloisters** hold a fine little one-room museum containing French tapestries, paintings, and silver reliquaries. Outside in the courtyard, a glass case holds keys to the 17th-century private-chapel gates. The gilded chapter room is draped with precious Flemish tapestries. Notice the gilded wagon. The Holy Communion wafer is placed in the top of this temple-like cart and paraded through town each year during the Corpus Christi festival. From the cloister courtyard, you can see the Renaissance dome rising above the otherwise Gothic rooftop.

▲**Alcázar**—In the Middle Ages, this fortified palace was one of the favorite residences of the monarchs of Castile, a key fortress for controlling the region. The Alcázar grew through the ages, and its function changed many times: After its stint as a palace, it was a prison for 200 years, and then a Royal Artillery School. It burned in 1862. Since the fire, it's basically been a museum.

Cost and Hours: €4 for palace, €2 for tower, daily April–Sept 10:00–19:00, Oct–March 10:00–18:00 (tower closed third Tue of month). Buy your tickets at Real Laboratorio de Chimia, facing the palace on your left. At the entrance, pass your ticket through the turnstiles on the right for the palace, or the turnstiles on the left for the tower. The 45-minute €3 audioguide describes each room. Pick up a free English leaflet. Tel. 921-460-759.

❺ **Self-Guided Tour:** You'll enjoy a one-way route through 11 rooms, including a fine view terrace. Visit the tower afterward (€2); its 152 steps up a tight spiral staircase reward you with the only 360-degree city view in town. What you see today in the Alcázar is rebuilt—a Disney-esque exaggeration of the original. Still, its fine Moorish decor and historic furnishings are fascinating. The sumptuous ceilings are accurately restored in Mudejar style, and the throne-room ceiling is the artistic highlight of the palace.

You'll see a big **mural** of Queen Isabel the Catholic being proclaimed Queen of Castile and León in Segovia's main square in 1474. The Hall of the Monarchs is lined with the busts of the 52 rulers of Castile and León who ruled during the long and ultimately successful Reconquista (711–1492): from Pelayo (the first), clockwise to Juana VII (the last). There were only seven queens during the period (the numbered ones). In this current age of Islamic extremists decapitating Christians, study the painting of St. James the Moor-Slayer—with Muslim heads literally rolling at his feet (poignantly...in the chapel). James is the patron saint of Spain. His name was the rallying cry in the centuries-long Christian crusade to push the Muslim Moors back into Africa.

Stepping onto the **terrace** (the site of the original Roman military camp, circa A.D. 100) with its vast views, marvel at the natural fortification provided by this promontory cut by the confluence of two rivers. The terrace is closed in the winter and sometimes on windy days. The Alcázar marks the end (and physical low point) of the gradual downhill course of the nine-mile-long Roman aqueduct. Can you find the mountain nicknamed *Mujer Muerta* ("dead woman")?

In the **armory** (just after the terrace), find the king's 16th-century ornately carved ivory crossbow, with the hunting scene shown in the adjacent painting. The final rooms are the Museum of Artillery, recalling the period (1764–1862) when this was the Royal Artillery School. It shows the evolution of explosive weaponry, with old photos and prints of the Alcázar.

Church of Santos Justo y Pastor—This simple yet stately old church has fascinating 12th- and 13th-century frescoes filled with Gothic symbolism, plus a stork's nest atop its tower. From the base of the aqueduct, it's a short climb uphill into the newer part of town (free, Tue–Sat 11:00–14:00 & 16:00–18:00; closed Sun–Mon and when the volunteer caretaker, Rafael, needs to run an errand; located a couple of blocks from Plaza del Azoguejo). Kind old Rafael probably won't let you risk climbing the dangerous, claustrophobic bell tower for a commanding Segovia view until they've finished cleaning the pigeon poop and renovating the tower, which may take a while, as they're having trouble gathering sufficient resources to finish the job.

Museo de Arte Contemporáneo Esteban Vicente—A collection of local artist Esteban Vicente's abstract art is housed in two rooms of the remodeled remains of Henry IV's 1455 palace. Wilder than Rothko but more restrained than Pollock, his vibrant work influenced post-WWII American art. The temporary exhibits can be more interesting than the permanent collection (€3, free on Thu, roughly Tue–Fri 11:00–14:00 & 16:00–19:00, Sat–Sun 11:00–20:00, closed Mon, tel. 921-426-010).

Near Segovia

Vera Cruz Church—This 12-sided, 13th-century Romanesque church, built by the Knights Templar, once housed a piece of the "true cross" (€2, Tue–Sun 10:30–13:30 & 15:30–19:00, closed Mon and Nov, closes at 18:00 in winter, outside town beyond the castle, a 25-min walk from main square, tel. 921-431-475). There's a postcard view of the city from here, and more views follow as you continue around Segovia on the small road below the castle, labeled *ruta turística panorámica*.

▲**La Granja Palace**—This "little Versailles," six miles south of Segovia, is much smaller and happier than nearby El Escorial. The palace and gardens were built by the homesick French-born King Philip V, grandson of Louis XIV. Today, it's restored to its original

18th-century splendor, with its royal collection of tapestries, clocks, and crystal (actually made at the palace's royal crystal factory). Plumbers and gardeners imported from France and Italy made Philip a garden that rivaled Versailles'. The fanciful fountains feature mythological stories (explained in the palace audioguide). The Bourbon Philip chose to be buried here rather than with his Habsburg predecessors at El Escorial. His tomb is in the adjacent church, included with your ticket (€5 with Spanish-speaking guide, €4.50 without guide, April–Sept Tue–Sun 10:00–18:00, closed Mon; Oct–March Tue–Sat 10:00–13:30 & 15:00–17:00, Sun 10:00–14:00, closed Mon; tel. 921-470-019, www.patrimonionacional .es). Fourteen buses a day (fewer on weekends) make the 25-minute trip from Segovia (catch at the bus station) to San Ildefonso–La Granja. The park is free (daily 10:00–20:00, until 19:00 in winter).

Sleeping in Segovia

The best places are on or near the central Plaza Mayor. This is where the city action is: the best bars, most touristic and *típico* eateries, and the TI. During busy times—on weekends and in July and August—arrive early or call ahead.

In the Old Center, near Plaza Mayor

$$$ Hotel Los Linajes is ultra-classy, with rusticity mixed into its newly poured concrete. This poor man's parador is a few blocks beyond Plaza Mayor, with territorial views and modern, air-conditioned niceties (Sb-€81, Db-€110, big Db-€142, Tb-€131, cheaper off-season, breakfast-€10, elevator, parking-€13, Dr. Velasco 9, tel. 921-460-475, fax 921-460-479, www.loslinajes.com, hotellos linajes@terra.es). From Plaza Mayor, take Escuderos downhill; at the five-way intersection, angle right on Dr. Velasco. Drivers, follow brown hotel signs from the aqueduct to its tight but handy garage.

$$$ Hotel Infanta Isabel, right on Plaza Mayor, is the ritziest hotel in the old town, with 38 elegant rooms, some with plaza views (Sb-€67–77, Db-€97–114 depending on room size, less in winter, breakfast on the square-€9, elevator, valet parking-€12, tel. 921-461-300, fax 921-462-217, www.hotelinfantaisabel.com, admin@hotelinfantaisabel.com).

$$ Hostal Plaza, just off Plaza Mayor, has extremely strict management, snaky corridors, and some tight squeezes. But its

---

Sleep Code

(€1 = about $1.40, country code: 34)
S = Single, **D** = Double/Twin, **T** = Triple, **Q** = Quad, **b** = bathroom, **s** = shower only. Unless otherwise noted, you can assume credit cards are accepted and English is spoken. Breakfast is generally not included.

To help you easily sort through these listings, I've divided the rooms into three categories, based on the price for a standard double room with bath during high season (breakfast not included):

$$$ Higher Priced—Most rooms €85 or more.
$$ Moderately Priced—Most rooms between €30-85.
$ Lower Priced—Most rooms €30 or less.

---

28 rooms are clean and cozy (Sb-€39, D-€35, Db-€48, Tb-€65, breakfast-€2.50, parking-€10, Cronista Lecea 11, tel. 921-460-303, fax 921-460-305, www.hostal-plaza.com, informacion@hostal-plaza.com).

Outside of the Old Town, near the Aqueduct

$$ Hostal Don Jaime, opposite the Church of San Justo, is a friendly family-run place with 38 basic, worn yet well-maintained rooms. Seven more rooms are in an annex across the street (S-€25, D-€32, Db-€50, Tb-€60, Qb-€70, show this book and get a free breakfast in 2010—otherwise €3.50, parking-€8, Ochoa Ondategui 8; from TI at Plaza del Azoguejo, cross under the aqueduct, go right, angle left, then snake uphill for 2 blocks; tel. & fax 921-444-787, hostaldonjaime@hotmail.com).

$$ Hospedaje el Gato, a family-run place on a quiet nondescript square just outside the old town, has 10 modern, comfortable rooms (Sb-€25, Db-€40, Tb-€55, air-con, smoky bar serves breakfast and good tapas, parking-€10, uphill from Hostal Don Jaime and aqueduct at Plaza del Salvador 10, tel. 921-423-244, mobile 678-405-079, fax 921-438-047, hbarelgato@yahoo.es but prefer phone or fax reservations).

Eating in Segovia

Look for Segovia's culinary claim to fame, roast suckling pig (*cochinillo asado:* 21 days of mother's milk, into the oven, and onto your plate—oh, Babe). It's worth a splurge here, or in Toledo or Salamanca.

For lighter fare, try *sopa castellana*—soup mixed with eggs, ham, garlic, and bread—or warm yourself up with the local *judiones de La Granja,* a popular soup made with flat white beans from the region.

Ponche segoviano, a dessert made with an almond-and-honey *mazapán* base, is heavenly after an earthy dinner or with a coffee in the afternoon (at the recommended Limon y Menta, described on the next page).

Roast Suckling Pig

Mesón de Cándido, one of the top restaurants in Castile, is famous for its memorable dinners. Even though it's filled with tourists, it's a grand experience. Take time to wander around and survey the photos of celebs—from King Juan Carlos to Antonio Banderas and Melanie Griffith—who've suckled here. Try to get a table in a room with an aqueduct view (figure on spending €35–40, daily 13:00–16:30 & 20:00–23:00, Plaza del Azogüejo 5, air-con, under aqueduct, call 921-428-103 for reservations, www.mesonde candido.es, candido@mesondecandido.es). Three gracious generations of the Cándido family still run the show.

José María is *the* place to pig out in the old town, a block off Plaza Mayor. While it doesn't have the history or fanfare of Cándido, locals claim this high-energy place serves the best roast suckling pig in town. It thrives with a hungry mix of tourists and locals—so reservations are usually necessary (€40 à la carte dinner, daily 13:00–16:00 & 20:30–23:30, air-con, Cronista Lecea 11, tel. 921-466-017, reservas@rtejosemaria.com).

Restaurante Casa Chapete, a homey little place filled with smoke, happy locals, and not a tourist in sight, serves traditional lamb and pig dishes—but only for lunch (€22 three-course meals including wine, €35 quarter *cochinillos* for 2–3 people, €9 simple three-course fixed-price meals on weekdays, daily 12:30–16:00, 2 blocks beyond aqueduct, across from recommended Hostal Don Jaime at Calle Ochoa Ondategui 7, tel. 921-421-096).

The Old Center (No Pig)

Plaza Mayor, the main square, provides a great backdrop for a light lunch, dinner, or drink. Prices at the cafés are generally reasonable, and many offer a good selection of tapas and *raciones.* Grab a table at the place of your choice and savor the scene. **Café Jeyma** has a fine setting and cathedral view. **La Concepción Restaurante** is also good (€35 meals, closer to the cathedral).

Narizotas serves more imaginative and non-Castilian alternatives to the gamey traditions. You'll dine outside on a delightful square or inside with modern art under medieval timbers. For a wonderful dining experience, try their chef's choice mystery samplers, either the "Right Hand" (€37, about 10 courses, with wine and dessert) or the "Left Hand" (€33, about six courses, with wine and dessert). They offer a less elaborate three-course €16 fixed-priced meal, and their à la carte menu is also a treat (daily 13:00–16:00 & 20:30–24:00, midway down Calle Juan Bravo at Plaza de Medina del Campo 1, tel. 921-462-679).

Restaurante Bar San Martín, a no-frills place popular with locals, has a lively tapas bar, great outdoor seating by a fountain on the same square as the recommended Narizotas, and a smoky restaurant in the back. I'd eat here only to enjoy the setting on the square (€10 three-course fixed-price meal on weekdays, tapas bar open Tue–Sun 9:00–24:00, restaurant open Tue–Sun 13:30–16:00 & 20:30–23:00, both closed Mon, Plaza de San Martín 3, tel. 921-462-466).

Cueva de San Esteban serves traditional home cooking with a stress-free photo menu at the door, and hearty, big-enough-to-split plates (daily 11:00–24:00, full meals 13:00–16:00, two blocks past Plaza Mayor on a quiet back street, Calle Valdelaguila 15, tel. 921-460-982).

La Almuzara is a garden of veggie and organic delights: whole-wheat pizzas, tofu, seitan, and even a few dishes with meat (€10 plates, Tue 20:00–24:00, Wed–Sun 13:00–16:00 & 20:00–24:00, closed Mon, between cathedral and Alcázar at Marques del Arco 3, tel. 921-460-622).

Rodilla, the popular chain, offers a tasty selection of sandwiches and salads (Mon–Fri 9:30–22:00, Sat–Sun 10:00–22:30, on Calle Juan Bravo, at intersection with Calle de la Herrería).

Breakfast: For breakfast, I like to sit on Plaza Mayor enjoying the cool air and the people scene (many choices). Or, 100 yards down the main drag toward the aqueduct, **Café La Colonial** serves good breakfasts (with seating on a tiny square or inside, Plaza del Corpus).

Nightlife: Inexpensive bars and eateries line Calle de Infanta Isabel, just off Plaza Mayor. For nightlife, the bars on Plaza Mayor, Calle de Infanta Isabel, and Calle Isabel la Católica are packed. There are a number of late-night dance clubs along the aqueduct.

Dessert: **Limon y Menta** offers a good, rich *ponche segoviano* (marzipan) cake by the slice for €3, or try the lighter honey-and-almond *crocantinos* (daily 9:30–21:30 but hours can vary, seating inside, Isabel La Católica 2, tel. 921-462-141).

Market: An outdoor produce market thrives on Plaza Mayor on Thursday (roughly 8:00–15:00). Nearby, a few stalls are open daily except Sunday on Calle del Cronista Ildefonso Rodríguez.

Connections

If you're side-tripping between Segovia and Madrid, note that the 35-minute AVE train takes less than half as long as the bus. However, you'll spend more time getting to the AVE Stations in Segovia and Madrid than to the bus stations, so the total time spent in transit is about the same. (In Madrid, the AVE goes to the Chamartín train station, while the bus goes to Príncipe Pío Metro station.) *Cercanías* commuter trains also run to Madrid, but take two hours and don't save you much money.

From Segovia by Bus to: La Granja Palace (14/day, fewer on weekends, 25 min), **Ávila** (5/day weekdays, 2/day weekends, 1 hr), **Madrid** (2/hr, departing on the half-hour, 1.25 hrs, €7; Mon–Sat first departure at 6:30, last return at 21:30; Sun first at 8:30, last at 22:30; many stop first at Madrid's Metro: Moncloa, where you can get off if convenient to your hotel, and the end of the line is the Príncipe Pío bus terminal and Metro stop, tel. 915-598-955, www.lasepulvedana.es), **Salamanca** (2/day, 3 hrs, transfer in Labajos; it's smart to call ahead to reserve a seat for the Labajos–Salamanca segment—call Madrid's La Sepulvedana office at tel. 915-598-955 to book your seat). Consider busing from Segovia to Ávila for a visit, then continuing to Salamanca by bus or train.

If you're riding the bus from Madrid to Segovia, about 30 minutes after leaving Madrid you'll see—breaking the horizon on the left—the dramatic concrete cross of the Valley of the Fallen. Its grand facade marks the entry to the mammoth underground memorial (described earlier in this chapter).

By Train to: Madrid (via high-speed AVE train: 8/day, 35 min, €10, leaves from Segovia's Guiomar Station, arrives at Madrid's Chamartín Station; via *cercanías* commuter train: 9/day, 2 hrs, €6, leaves from Segovia's inconvenient *Cercanías* Station, arrives in Madrid at both Chamartín and Atocha Stations). AVE trains leave from Segovia's Guiomar Station; to get there, take city bus #11 from the base of the aqueduct (20 min, buses usually timed to match arrivals). To reach the sleepy, dead-end *Cercanías* Station, walk 20 minutes past the bus station along Paseo de Ezequiel González (which turns into Paseo del Conde de Sepulvedana); catch bus #6 (leaves from the bus station) or #8 (leaves from the aqueduct); or take a taxi. Train info: tel. 902-240-202.

Route Tips for Drivers

From Madrid to Segovia: Leave Madrid on A-6. Exit 39 gets you to Segovia via a slow, winding route over the scenic mountain. Exit at 60 (after a long €3 toll tunnel) or get there quicker by staying on the toll road all the way to Segovia (add €2 weekdays or €3 on weekends). At the Segovia aqueduct, follow *casco histórico* signs to the old town (on the side where the aqueduct adjoins the crenellated fortress walls).

Parking in Segovia: Free parking is available in the Alcázar's lot, but you must move your car out by 19:00 (or by 18:00 Oct–March), when the gates close. Or try the lot northwest of the bus station by the statue of Cándido, along the street called Paseo de Ezequiel González. Outside the old city, there's an Acueducto Parking underground garage kitty-corner from the bus station. Although it can be a hard slog up the hill to the Alcázar on a hot day, it beats trying to maneuver uphill through tight bends. A huge garage is planned near the aqueduct (possibly completed in time for your visit).

While the city center has lots of parking spaces, they're not free. If you want to park in the old town, be legal or risk an expensive ticket. Buy a ticket from the nearby machine to park in areas marked by blue stripes, and place the ticket on your dashboard (€1.40/hr, pay meter every 2 hours 9:00–14:00 & 16:30–20:00; free parking 20:00–9:00, Sat afternoon, and all day Sun).

Segovia to Salamanca (100 miles): Leave Segovia by driving around the town's circular road, which offers good views from below the Alcázar. Then follow signs for *Ávila* (road N-110). Notice the fine Segovia view from the three crosses at the crest of the first hill. The Salamanca road leads around the famous Ávila walls to the right. The best wall view is from the signposted Cuatro Postes, a mile northwest of town. Salamanca (N-501) is clearly marked, about an hour's drive away.

About 20 miles before Salamanca, you might want to stop at the huge bull on the left side of the road. There's a little dirt lane leading right up to it. As you get closer, it becomes more and more obvious it isn't real. Bad boys climb it for a goofy photo. For a great photo op of Salamanca, complete with river reflection, stop at the edge of the city (at the light before the first bridge). In Salamanca, the only safe parking is in a garage; try the underground lot at Plaza Santa Eulalia, Plaza del Campillo, or Lemans (closer to recommended Petit Palace Las Torres), or even easier, try one of the hotels with valet parking for comparable fees. See the Salamanca chapter for more information.

Ávila

Yet another popular side-trip from Madrid, Ávila is famous for its perfectly preserved medieval walls, as the birthplace of St. Teresa, and for its yummy *yema* treats. For more than 300 years, Ávila was on the battlefront between the Muslims and Christians, changing hands several times. Today, perfectly peaceful Ávila has a charming old town. With several fine churches and monasteries, it makes for an enjoyable quick stop between Segovia and Salamanca (each about an hour away by car).

Orientation to Ávila

On a quick stop, everything in Ávila that matters is within a few blocks of the cathedral (actually part of the east end of the wall).

Tourist Information
The TI has fine, free maps and information on walking tours (daily 9:30–14:00 & 16:00–19:00, no afternoon closure July–mid-Sept, on Calle San Segundo, just outside the wall gate near the cathedral, tel. 920-211-387). Another TI, with a friendlier staff, is located outside the wall, opposite the Basilica of San Vicente (daily April–Oct 10:00–20:00, Nov–March 10:00–18:00, public WCs).

Sightseeing Train: A clunky tourist train departs from outside the wall by Puerta de San Vicente, heads into town, exits at the westernmost gate, loops by the Monasterio de la Encarnación (where St. Teresa lived), and then shudders along back to the north wall. Unfortunately, its daytime route doesn't stop at the worthwhile Cuatro Postes viewpoint (though it does stop there for a view of the illuminated wall at 22:00 on Fri–Sat in July–Aug). Check the *próxima salida* sign for departure times, which are usually twice an hour (€4 day, €7 night, daily 9:00–18:00, narration in Spanish unless you specify English, mobile 629-222-218).

Arrival in Ávila
Approaching by bus, train, or car, you'll need to make your way through the nondescript modern part of town to find the walled old town. From the cathedral and wall, the bus station is a 15-minute walk, while the train station is a 20-minute walk. City buses #4 and #1 run from the train station to the Basilica of San Vicente (to find the bus stop, exit the station to the right and walk one block). There are lockers at Ávila's bus station (use the newer-looking locks), but not at the train station. Drivers can use the public parking east of Puerta del Alcázar, just south of the cathedral, or at Parking Dornier (€1.25/hour).

Sights in Ávila

▲**The Wall**—Built from around 1100 on even more ancient remains, Ávila's fortified wall is the oldest, most complete, and best-preserved in Spain. It has four entrances, allowing visitors the chance to walk almost three-quarters of the wall: One entrance is just off Plaza de Santa Teresa (Puerta del Alcázar). The best one, which leads to a longer walk, starts at the gate closest to the cathedral (Puerta del Peso de la Harina) and takes you to the third, Puerta del Carmen (look for the door marked *subida a la muralla*). The fourth is at Puerta Puente Adaja, on the end farthest from the cathedral, and leads to only a small section of the wall (€4, April–mid-Oct Tue–Sun 10:00–20:00, mid-Oct–March 11:00–18:00, closed Mon except July–Aug, last entry 30 min before closing). A night visit gives you the same walk, with the wall beautifully lit (€4, mid-June–mid-Sept Sun–Wed 22:00–24:00). Your ticket has multiple stubs, which allow you to enter the wall at various points. You can use one stub to go up during the day, and save another to go up at night.

There's an interesting paseo scene along the wall each night—make your way along the southern wall (Paseo del Rastro) to Plaza de Santa Teresa for spectacular vistas across the plains. The best views of the wall itself are actually from street level (especially along the north side, which drivers will see as they circle to the right from Puerta de San Vicente to catch the highway to Salamanca). The finest overall view of the walled town is about a mile away on the Salamanca road (N-501), at a clearly marked turnout for the Cuatro Postes (four posts).

Cathedral—While it started as Romanesque, Ávila's cathedral, finished in the 16th century, is considered the first Gothic cathedral in Spain. Its position—with its granite apse actually part of the fortified wall—underlines the "medieval alliance between cross and sword." For €4, you can tour the cathedral, its sacristy, cloister, and museum—which includes an El Greco painting (Mon–Sat 10:00–19:30, Sun 12:00–17:00, off-season Mon–Sat 10:00–17:00, Sun 12:00–17:00—but hours often vary, Plaza de la Catedral).

Convent of St. Teresa—Built in the 17th century on the spot where the saint was born, this convent is a big hit with pilgrims (10-min walk from cathedral). A lavishly gilded side chapel marks the actual place of her birth (left of main altar, door may be closed). A separate room of relics (outside, facing the church on your right,

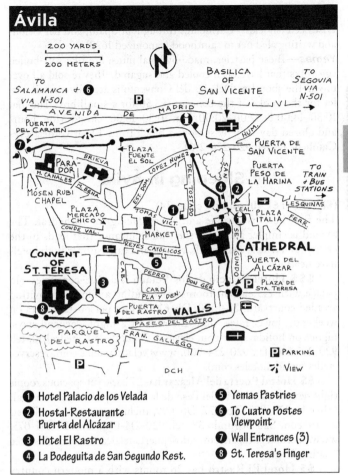

Ávila

200 YARDS
200 METERS

TO
SALAMANCA & **6**
VIA N-501

BASILICA
OF
SAN VICENTE

TO
SEGOVIA
VIA
N-501

AVENIDA DE MADRID

PUERTA
DEL CARMEN

7

PLAZA
FUENTE
EL SOL

BRIEVA

PARA-
DOR

M. CANALES

M. BENA

PUERTA DE
SAN VICENTE

PUERTA
PESO DE
LA HARINA

TO
TRAIN
& BUS
STATIONS

MÓSEN RUBÍ
CHAPEL

LÓPEZ NÚÑEZ

DEL TOSTADO

EST. DOM.

TOMÁS
VICT.

4 **2**

7

LESQUINAS

LEAL.

PLAZA
ITALIA

PLAZA
MERCADO
CHICO

1

CONDE VAL.

MARKET

REYES CATÓLICOS

CONVENT
OF
ST. TERESA

5

PEDRO

3

CARD.
C.A.B.

DON GER.

SE. SEGUNDO

CATHEDRAL

PUERTA DEL
ALCÁZAR

PLAZA DE
STA. TERESA

7

8

PLA Y DEN.
PUERTA
DEL RASTRO

WALLS

PASEO DEL RASTRO

PARQUE
DEL RASTRO

FRAN. GALLEGO

DCH

P PARKING

VIEW

1 Hotel Palacio de los Velada

2 Hostal-Restaurante
Puerta del Alcázar

3 Hotel El Rastro

4 La Bodeguita de San Segundo Rest.

5 Yemas Pastries

6 To Cuatro Postes
Viewpoint

7 Wall Entrances (3)

8 St. Teresa's Finger

Sala de Reliquias) houses a shop that shows off Teresa's finger, complete with a fancy emerald ring, along with one of her sandals and the bones of St. John of the Cross (free, no photos of finger allowed, daily 9:30–13:30 & 15:30–19:30, until 19:00 in winter). A museum in the crypt at the side entrance dedicated to the saint is worth a visit for devotees (€2, April–Oct Tue–Sun 10:00–14:00 & 16:00–19:00, Nov–March Tue–Sun 10:00–13:30 & 15:30–17:30, closed Mon, last entry 30 min before closing).

St. Teresa (1515–1582)—reforming nun, mystic, and writer—bought a house in Ávila and converted it into a convent with more stringent rules than the one she belonged to. She faced opposition in her hometown from rival nuns and those convinced her visions of heaven were the work of the devil. However, with her mentor and fellow mystic St. John of the Cross she established convents of Discalced (shoeless) Carmelites throughout Spain, and her visions and writings led her to sainthood (canonized 1622).

Yemas—These pastries, made by local nuns, are like soft-boiled egg yolks that have been cooled and sugared. They're sold all over town. The shop Las Delicias del Convento is actually a retail outlet for the cooks of the convent (€3.50 for a small box, Tue–Sat 10:30–14:00 & 17:00–20:00, Sun 10:30–18:00, closed Mon, hours and closed day vary by season, a block from TI, at Calle Reyes Católicos 12, tel. 920-220-293).

Sleeping in Ávila

(€1 = about $1.40, country code: 34)

The first hotel is antique and classy, facing the cathedral. The second is simpler and faces the wall's entrance that leads to the cathedral. Ávila is cold in fall, winter, and early spring; both hotels have heating.

$$$ Hotel Palacio de los Velada is a five-centuries-old palace with 145 elegant rooms surrounding a huge and inviting arcaded courtyard (Sb-€150, Db-€190, third person-€30 extra on weekends, lower rates Mon–Thu and for 2-night weekend stays, higher on holidays, air-con, elevator, Plaza de la Catedral 10, tel. 920-255-100, fax 920-254-900, www.veladahoteles.com, reserves .avila@veladahoteles.com).

$$ Hostal Puerta del Alcázar has 27 basic yet spacious rooms right next to the Puerta del Peso de la Harina just outside the wall (Sb-€43, Db-€55, Tb-€77, Qb-€99, includes tax and breakfast, no air-con, San Segundo 38, tel. 920-211-074, fax 920-211-075, www.puertadelalcazar.com, info@puertadelalcazar.com). Also see "Eating," next.

$$ Hotel El Rastro has 26 rooms with a modern country touch—but a stuffy staff—near Puerta del Rastro (Sb-€45, Db-€75, includes breakfast, Calle Cespedas s/n, tel. 920-352-225, fax 920-352-223, www.elrastroavila.com, info@elrastroavila.com, Pilar).

Eating in Ávila

La Bodeguita de San Segundo is a good bet for a classy light lunch. Owned by a locally famous wine connoisseur, it serves fine wine by the glass with gourmet tapas, including smoked-cod salad and wild-mushroom scrambled eggs (Thu–Tue 12:00–24:00, closed Wed, along the outside of wall near cathedral at San Segundo 19, tel. 920-257-309).

Hostal-Restaurante Puerta del Alcázar, filled with more locals than hotel guests, serves elaborate salads, fixed-price meals (for €13 and €21), and more. You can sit indoors, or even better, outdoors with cathedral views (Mon–Sat 13:30–16:00 & 21:00–23:30, Sun 13:30–16:00, San Segundo 38, tel. 920-211-074).

Café: For a pleasant break from sightseeing, pop in the courtyard of the recommended **Hotel Palacio de los Velada** for a drink (€3 coffee and hot chocolate).

Connections

The bus terminal is closed on Sundays, but you can purchase tickets when boarding the bus.

From Ávila to: Segovia (5 buses/day weekdays, 2 on weekends, 1.25 hrs), **Madrid** (1 train/hr until 21:55, 90 min, more frequent connections with Chamartín Station than Atocha; 8 buses/day, 4 on weekends, 1.5 hrs; Estación Sur de Autobuses in Madrid, tel. 914-684-200), **Salamanca** (6 trains/day, 1 hr; 4 buses/day, 2 on weekends, 1.5 hrs). Train info: tel. 902-240-202, www.renfe.es. Bus info: tel. 902-222-282, www.lasepulvedana.es.

TOLEDO

An hour south of Madrid, Toledo teems with tourists, souvenirs, and great art by day, and delicious dinners, echoes of El Greco, and medieval magic by night. Incredibly well-preserved and full of cultural wonder, the entire city has been declared a national monument.

Spain's former capital crowds 2,500 years of tangled history—Roman, Jewish, Visigothic, Moorish, and Christian—onto a high, rocky perch protected on three sides by the Tajo River. It's so well-preserved that the Spanish government has forbidden any modern exteriors. The rich mix of Jewish, Moorish, and Christian heritages makes it one of Europe's artistic highlights.

Today, Toledo thrives as a provincial capital and a busy tourist attraction. This decade has been an eventful one for Toledo. A new high-speed AVE train connection has made Toledo a quick, 30-minute ride from Madrid. While locals worried that this link would turn their town into a bedroom community for wealthy Madrileños, the already high real-estate prices minimized the impact. The city is also undergoing a major construction project: the building of a new convention center, the Palacio de Congresos Miradero (by Rafael Moneo, architect of the Los Angeles Cathedral). While the center itself remains under construction, its huge new underground parking garage and escalator into town are complete, making arrival by car much more efficient. The long-term vision is to make the old city center essentially traffic-free (except for residents' cars, public transit, and service vehicles).

Toledo remains the historic, artistic, and spiritual center of Spain. Despite tremendous tourist crowds, Toledo sits enthroned on its history, much as it was when Europe's most powerful king, Charles V, and its most famous resident artist, El Greco, called it home.

Planning Your Time

To properly see Toledo's sights—including its museums (great El Greco) and cathedral (best in Spain)—and to experience its medieval atmosphere (wonderful after dark), you'll need two nights and a day. Plan carefully for lunchtime closures and for Toledo's notorious midday heat in summer. Get an early start and stay out late... but take a rest during the unbearable summer afternoons.

Orientation to Toledo

Toledo sits atop a circular hill, with the cathedral roughly dead-center. Lassoed into a tight tangle of streets by the sharp bend of the Tajo River (called the Tejo in Portugal, where it hits the Atlantic at Lisbon), Toledo has Spain's most confusing medieval street plan. But it's a small town within its walls, with only 10,000 inhabitants (80,000 total live in greater Toledo, including its modern suburbs). The major sights are well-signposted, and most locals will politely point you in the right direction if you ask. (You are, after all, the town's bread and butter.)

The top sights stretch from the main square, Plaza de Zocodover (zoh-koh-doh-VEHR), southwest along Calle Comercio (a.k.a. Calle Ancha, "Wide Street") to the cathedral, and beyond that to Santo Tomé and more. The visitor's city lies basically along this small but central street, and most tourists never stray from this axis. Make a point to get lost. The town is small and bounded on three sides by the river. When it's time to return to someplace familiar, pull out the map or ask, *"¿Para Plaza de Zocodover?"* From the far end of town, handy bus #12 circles back to Plaza de Zocodover (see the "Bus #12 Self-Guided Tour" on page 443).

Keep in mind that sights appear closer on maps than they really are, because local maps don't factor into account the slope of the hill. In Toledo, they say everything's uphill—it certainly feels that way.

Tourist Information

Toledo has three TIs. There's one at **Bisagra Gate**, in a freestanding building in the park just outside the gate (Mon–Fri 9:00–18:00, Sat 9:00–19:00, Sun 9:00–15:00, longer hours in summer, tel. 925-220-843); another on Plaza del Ayuntamiento near the **cathedral** (Mon 10:30–14:30, Tue–Sun 10:30–14:30 & 16:30–19:00, WC, tel. 925-254-030), and a third on **Plaza de Zocodover** in Casa del

Toledo's History

Perched strategically in the center of Iberia, for centuries Toledo was a Roman transportation hub with a thriving Jewish population. After Rome fell, the city became a Visigothic capital (A.D. 554). In 711, the Moors (Muslims) made it a regional center. In 1085, the city was reconquered by Christians, but many Moors remained in Toledo, tolerated and respected as scholars and craftsmen.

While Jews were commonly persecuted elsewhere in Europe, Toledo's Jewish community—educated, wealthy, and cosmopolitan—thrived from the city's earliest times. Jews of Spanish origin are called Sephardic Jews. The American expression "Holy Toledo" likely originated from the Sephardic Jews who eventually immigrated to America. To them, Toledo was the holiest Jewish city in Europe...Holy Toledo!

During its medieval heyday (c. 1350), Toledo was a city of the humanities, where God was known by many names. In this haven of cultural diversity, people of different faiths lived together in harmony.

Toledo remained Spain's political capital until 1561, when Philip II moved to more-spacious Madrid. Historians fail to agree why the move was made; some say that Madrid was the logical place for a capital in the geographic center of newly formed *España*, while others say that Philip wanted to separate politics from religion. (Toledo remained Spain's religious capital.) Whatever the reason, when the king moved out, Toledo was mothballed, only to be rediscovered by 19th-century Romantic travelers. They wrote of it as a mystical place...which it remains today.

Mapa (daily 10:00–18:00). At any TI you can pick up the town map, a copy of the *Toledo Tourist and Cultural Guide*, and the monthly *Cultural Agenda*, which lists local events. The TIs share a website: www.toledo-turismo.com.

Arrival in Toledo

"Arriving" in Toledo means getting uphill to Plaza de Zocodover. As the bus and train stations are outside of town and parking can be a challenge, this involves a hike, taxi, or city bus ride.

By Train: Toledo's early-20th-century train station is Neo-Moorish and a national monument itself for its architecture and art, which celebrate the three cultures that coexisted here. From the train station, it's a 20-minute hike, a €4 taxi ride, or an easy ride on bus #5, #6, or #22 to Plaza de Zocodover (leaving the station you'll see the bus stop 30 yards to the right; €1, pay on bus, confirm by asking, "¿Para Plaza de Zocodover?"). Consider buying a city map at the kiosk; it's better than the free one at the TI. To walk, turn right leaving the station, cross the bridge with the mighty Alcázar on your left, pass the bus station (on right), go straight through the roundabout, continue uphill to Bisagra Gate, and head into the old town to Plaza de Zocodover.

By Bus: At the bus station, buses park downstairs. Luggage lockers and a small bus-information office are upstairs opposite the cafeteria. Before leaving the station, confirm your departure

Central Toledo

- View
- P Parking
- Ⓑ Bus Stop

200 YARDS
200 METERS

TO BULLRING + MADRID

BISAGRA GATE

BUS STATION

C. DE LA CARRERA

CITY WALLS

MEZQUITA

TO TRAIN STATION

TO RING ROAD + PARADOR

ESCALATORS

SUBIDA LA GRANJA

CUESTA

Ⓟ MIRA-DERO

SANTA CRUZ MUSEUM

CALLE REAL

S. LEO.

VISI-GOTHIC MUSEUM

POST

LA PLATA

CERVANTES

SAN JUAN DE LOS REYES

SANTO TOMÉ

ALFONSO XII

TRINIDAD

ALCÁZAR

MARKET

CATHEDRAL

SINAGOGA DE SANTA MARÍA LA BLANCA

MUSEO VICTORIO MACHO

EL GRECO'S HOUSE

PARK

CITY HALL (AYUNTAMIENTO)

RIO TAJO

SINAGOGA DEL TRÁNSITO

STREET WIDTH IS EXAGGERATED FOR CLARITY

DCH

❶ Plaza de Zocodover
❷ Mariano Zamorano Knife Workshop
❸ Mezquita del Cristo de la Luz (Mosque)
❹ Visigothic Museum
❺ Escalator to Miradero Garage

TOLEDO

time (probably 2/hr to Madrid). You can put off buying a return ticket until just minutes before you leave Toledo. Specify you'd like a *directo* bus, because the *ruta* trip takes longer (60 min vs. 90 min). If you miss the *directo* bus (or if it's sold out), the *ruta* option offers a peek of off-the-beaten-path Madrid suburbia; you'll arrive at the same time as taking the next *directo* bus. From the bus station, Plaza de Zocodover is a 15-minute hike, a €4 taxi ride, or a short bus ride (catch #5 or #12 downstairs; €1, pay on bus).

By Car: If you're arriving by car, you can enjoy a scenic big-picture orientation by following the *Ronda de Toledo* signs on a big circular drive around the city. You'll view the city from many angles along the Circunvalación road across the Tajo Gorge. Stop at a viewpoint or drive to Parador de Toledo, just south of town, for the view (from the balcony) that El Greco made famous in his portrait of Toledo. The best time for this trip is the magic hour before sunset, when the top viewpoints are busy with tired old folks and frisky young lovers.

The most convenient place to park is in the big new Miradero Garage at the convention center (€16/day; drive through Bisagra Gate, go uphill half a mile, look for sign on the left directing you to *Plaza del Miradero*). There is also parking farther into town at the Alcázar Garage (opposite the Alcázar—€2/hr, €18/day).

A car is useless within Toledo's city walls, where the narrow, twisting streets are no fun to navigate. Ideally, see the old town outside of car-rental time. Pick up or drop off your car on the outskirts of town; **Avis** is at the train station (Mon–Fri 9:30–13:30 & 16:30–19:30, Sat 9:30–13:30, closed Sun, handy early and late drop options, tel. 925-214-535).

By Escalator into Town: A series of escalators runs outdoors past Bisagra Gate, giving you a free ride up, up, up into town (until 22:00). You'll end up near San Ildefonso and far from Plaza de Zocodover, but it's worth it for the novelty. The other escalator, stretching from the new Miradero Garage up nearly to Plaza de Zocodover, is only helpful for people using the garage.

Helpful Hints

Local Guidebook: Consider the readable *Toledo: Its Art and Its History* (€6 big version, €5 small version, same text and photos in both, sold all over town). It explains all of the sights (which generally provide no on-site information) and gives you a photo to point at and say, *"¿Dónde está...?"*

Internet Access: You'll find **Internet Locutorio** shops with fast terminals and long hours throughout Toledo.

Tours in Toledo

▲**Tourist Train**—For a great city overview, hop on the cheesy Tren Imperial Tourist Tram. Crass as it feels, you get a 50-minute putt-putt through Toledo and around the Tajo River Gorge. It's a fine way for non-drivers to enjoy views of the city from across the Tajo Gorge (€4.50, buy ticket from convenience store at Calle de la Sillería 14, leaves Plaza de Zocodover daily on the hour from 11:00 into the evening, recorded English/Spanish commentary, tel. 925-220-300). There are no photo stops, but it goes slowly—for the best views of Toledo across the gorge, sit on the right side, not behind the driver.

For a cheap alternative to the tourist train, try the #7.1 **city**

Toledo at a Glance

▲▲▲**Cathedral** One of Europe's best, with a marvelously vast interior and great art. **Hours:** Mon–Sat 10:00–18:30, Sun 14:00–18:30. See page 429.

▲▲**Santa Cruz Museum** Renaissance building housing wonderful artwork, including 15 El Grecos. **Hours:** Mon–Sat 10:00–18:30, Sun 10:00–14:00. See page 435.

▲**Santo Tomé** Simple chapel with El Greco's masterpiece, *The Burial of the Count of Orgaz.* **Hours:** Daily 10:00–18:45, until 17:45 mid-Oct–March. See page 438.

▲**Museo Victorio Macho** Collection of 20th-century Toledo sculptor's works, with expansive river-gorge view. **Hours:** Mon–Sat 10:00–19:00, Sun 10:00–15:00. See page 440.

▲**San Juan de los Reyes Monasterio** Church/monastery intended as final resting place of Isabel and Ferdinand. **Hours:** Daily 10:00–18:45, until 17:45 in winter. See page 441.

▲**Tourist Train** Tacky but fun 50-minute trip through Toledo's highlights with great Tajo Gorge views. **Hours:** Daily on the hour from 11:00 until into the evening. See page 427.

Alcázar Imposing former imperial residence dominating Toledo's skyline. **Hours:** Interior closed for installation of new National Military Museum. See page 436.

Visigothic Museum Romanesque church housing the only Visigothic artifacts in town. **Hours:** Tue–Sat 10:00–14:00 & 16:00–18:30, Sun 10:00–14:00, closed Mon. See page 437.

El Greco's House Based on a lie, with no important originals by the artist who never lived there, and likely closed for renovation in 2010. See page 439.

Sinagoga del Tránsito Museum of Toledo's Jewish past. **Hours:** Tue–Sat 10:00–21:00, Sun 10:00–14:00, closed Mon. See page 439.

Sinagoga de Santa María la Blanca Synagogue that harmoniously combines Toledo's three religious influences: Jewish, Christian, and Moorish. **Hours:** Daily April–Sept 10:00–18:45, Oct–March 10:00–17:45. See page 441.

bus, which leaves Plaza de Zocodover hourly (7:50–21:50) and offers the same classic view across the gorge.

Local Guides—Two good guides who enjoy sharing their hometown in English are **Juan José Espadas** (a.k.a. Juanjo, tel. 667-780-475, juanjo@guiadetoledo.es) and **Almudena Cencerrado** (tel. 610-765-067, almuzen@hotmail.com). For a three-hour tour, they each charge about €140 (more on weekends).

Sights in Toledo

▲▲▲Cathedral

Holy Toledo! Spain's leading Catholic city has a magnificent cathedral. Shoehorned into the old center (on the spot where a

mosque once stood), its exterior is hard to appreciate. But the interior is so lofty, rich, and vast that it'll have you wandering around like a Pez dispenser stuck open, whispering "Wow."

Cost and Hours: Cathedral tickets are sold in the shop opposite the church entrance on Calle Cardenal (€7, Mon–Sat 10:00–18:30, Sun 14:00–18:30, open earlier for prayer only, last entry 30 min before closing, audioguide-€3, no photos, tel. 925-222-241). A modern WC is in the ticket center.

➋ Self-Guided Tour: Wander among the pillars, thick and sturdy as a redwood forest. Sit under one and imagine a time when the lightbulbs were candles and the tourists were pilgrims—before the *No Photo* signs, when every window provided spiritual as well as physical light. The cathedral is primarily Gothic. But since it took more than 250 years to build (1226–1495)—with continuous embellishments after that (every archbishop wanted to leave his imprint)—it's a mix of styles, including Gothic, Renaissance, Baroque, and Neoclassical. Enjoy the elaborate wrought-iron work, lavish wood carvings, and window after colorful window of 500-year-old stained glass. Circling the interior are ornate chapels, purchased by the town's most noble families. The sacristy has a collection of paintings that would put any museum on the map.

This confusing collage of great Spanish art deserves a close look. Hire a private guide, discreetly freeload on a tour (they come by every few minutes during peak season), rent an audioguide, or follow this quick tour. Here's a framework for your visit:

High Altar: First, walk to the high altar to marvel through the iron grille at one of the most stunning altars in Spain. Real

Cheap Tricks in Toledo

- Good news: Most of the city's sights charge less than €3 to enter. Or you can beat that price by going to the Sinagoga del Tránsito on Saturday afternoon or Sunday when it's free. El Greco fans can see his art for free at the Santa Cruz Museum.
- Use Toledo's public transportation for your tours. Take the bus #12 self-guided tour through town (see page 443). To get to El Greco's famous viewpoint, take bus #7.1, which leaves from Plaza de Zocodover at :50 hourly until 21:50. Its circular route loops around to the vista where you can hop off, snap some photos, and wait at the same stop for the next bus to take you back.
- Shop for picnics at the city market, Mercado Municipal, and choose an atmospheric square for your meal.

gold on wood, by Flemish, French, and local artists, it's one of the country's best pieces of Gothic art. Don't miss the finely worked gold-plated iron grille itself—considered to be the best from the 16th century in Spain. About-face to the...

Choir: Facing the high altar, the choir is famous for its fine and richly symbolic carving. It all seems to lead to the archbishop's throne in the rear center. First, look carefully at the fine alabaster relief above the throne: It shows a seventh-century Visigothic miracle, when Mary came down to give the local bishop the holy robe, legitimizing Toledo as the spiritual capital (and therefore political capital) of Spain.

Because of its primacy in Iberia, Toledo was the first city in the crosshairs of the Reconquista Christian forces. They recaptured the city in 1085 (over 400 years before they retook Granada). A local saying goes, "A carpet frays from the edges, but the carpet of Al-Andalus (Muslim Spain) frayed from the very center" (meaning Toledo). The fall of Toledo marked the beginning of the end of the Muslim domination of Iberia.

The lower wooden stalls are decorated with scenes showing the steady one-city-at-a-time finale of the Christian Reconquista, when Muslims were slowly pushed back into Africa. Set in the last decade of the Reconquista, these images celebrate the retaking of the towns around Granada: Each idealized castle has the reconquered town's name on it, culminating in the final victory at Granada in 1492 (the reliefs flank the archbishop's throne). While

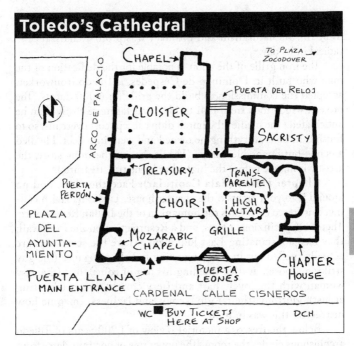

Toledo's Cathedral

- To Plaza Zocodover
- Chapel
- Arco de Palacio
- N
- Cloister
- Puerta del Reloj
- Sacristy
- Treasury
- Trans-parente
- Puerta Perdón
- Choir
- High Altar
- Plaza del Ayuntamiento
- Grille
- Mozarabic Chapel
- Puerta Llana — Main Entrance
- Puerta Leones
- Chapter House
- Cardenal Calle Cisneros
- WC ■ Buy Tickets Here at Shop
- DCH

TOLEDO

the castles are romanticized, the carvings of the clothing, armor, and weaponry are so detailed and accurate that historians have studied them to learn the evolution of weaponry.

The upper stalls feature Old Testament figures—an alabaster genealogy of the church—starting with Adam and Eve and working clockwise to Joseph and "S. M. Virgo Mater" (St. Mary the Virgin Mother). Notice how the statues on the Adam and Eve side are more lifelike; they were done by Alonso Berruguete, nicknamed "the Michelangelo of Spain" for his realistic figures. All this imagery is designed to remind viewers of the legitimacy of the bishop's claims to religious power. Check out the seat backs, made of carved walnut and featuring New Testament figures—with Peter (key) and Paul (sword)—alongside the archbishop himself.

And, as is typical of choir decoration, the carvings on the misericords (the tiny seats that allowed tired worshippers to lean while they "stand") represent various sins and feature the frisky, folksy, sexy, profane art of the day. Apparently, since you sat on it, it could never be sacred anyway.

Take a moment to absorb the marvelous complexity, harmony, and cohesiveness of the art around you. Look up. There are two fine pipe organs: one early 18th-century Baroque and the other late 18th-century Neoclassical. As you leave the choir, note the serene beauty of the 13th-century Madonna and child at the front (Virgin Blanca), thought to be a gift from the French king to Spain. Its naturalism and intimacy was proto-Renaissance—radical in its day.

The iron grille of the choir is notable for the dedication of the man who built it. Domingo de Céspedes, a Toledo ironworker, accepted the commission to build the grille for 6,000 ducats. The project, which took from 1541 to 1548, was far more costly than he anticipated. The medieval Church didn't accept cost overruns, so to finish it he sold everything he owned and went into debt. He died a poor—but honorable—man. (While that's a charming story, the artistic iron gate before the high altar is the true treasure.)

Chapter House (Sala Capitular): Face the altar, and go around it to your right to the chapter house. Under its lavish ceiling, this fresco celebrates the humanism of the Italian Renaissance. There's a Crucifixion, a *pietà*, and a Resurrection on the front wall; they face a fascinating Last Judgment, where the seven sins are actually spelled out in the gang going to hell: arrogance (the guy striking a pose), avarice (holding his bag of coins), lust (the easy woman with the lovely hair and fiery crotch), anger (shouting at lust), gluttony (the fat guy), envy, and laziness. Imagine how instructive this was in 1600.

Below the fresco, a pictorial review of 1,900 years of Toledo archbishops circles the room. The upper row of portraits dates from the 16th century. Except for the last two, these were not painted from life (the same face seems to be recycled over and over). The lower portraits were added one at a time from 1515 on and are of more historic than artistic interest. Imagine sitting down to church business surrounded by all this tradition and theology.

The current cardinal—whose portrait will some day grace the next empty panel—is the top religious official in Spain. He's as conservative as Pope Benedict XVI on issues unpopular with Spain's young: divorce, abortion, and contraception. When he speaks, it makes news all over Spain.

As you leave, notice the iron-pumping cupids carved into the pear-tree panels lining the walls.

Transparente: The *transparente*, behind the high altar, is a unique feature of the cathedral. In the 1700s, a hole was cut into the ceiling to let a sunbeam brighten Mass. Melding this big hole with the Gothic church presented a challenge, and the result was a Baroque masterpiece. Gape up at this riot of angels doing flip-flops, babies breathing thin air, bottoms of feet, and gilded sunbursts. Step back to study the altar, which looks chaotic, but is actually structured thoughtfully: The good news of salvation springs from Baby Jesus, up past the archangels (including one in the middle who knows how to hold a big fish correctly) to the Last Supper high above, and beyond into the light-filled dome. I like it, as did (I guess) the two long-dead cardinals whose faded red hats hang from the edge of the hole. (A perk that only a cardinal enjoys is to choose a burial place in the cathedral and hang his hat over that spot until the hat rots.)

Sacristy: The cathedral's sacristy is a mini-Prado, with 18 El Grecos and masterpieces by Francisco de Goya, Titian, Peter Paul Rubens, Diego Velázquez, Caravaggio, and Giovanni Bellini. First, notice the fine perspective work on the ceiling (fresco by Lucca Giordano from Naples, c. 1690). Then walk to the end of the room for the most important painting in the collection, El Greco's *The Spoliation* (a.k.a. *Christ Being Stripped of His Garments*).

Spain's original great painter was Greek, and this is his first masterpiece after arriving in Toledo. El Greco's painting from 1579 hangs exactly where he intended it to—in the room where priests prepared themselves for Mass. It shows Jesus surrounded by a sinister mob and suffering the humiliation of being stripped in public before his execution.

The scarlet robe is about to be yanked off, and the women (lower left) avert their eyes, turning to watch a carpenter at work (lower right) who bores the holes for nailing Jesus to the cross. While the carpenter bears down, Jesus—the other carpenter—looks up to heaven. The contrast between the motley crowd gambling for his clothes and Jesus' noble face underscores the quiet dignity with which he endures this ignoble treatment. Jesus' delicate white hand stands out from the flaming red tunic with an odd gesture that's common in El Greco's paintings. Some say this was the way Christians of the day swore they were true believers, not merely Christians-in-name-only, such as former Muslims or Jews who converted to survive.

On the right is a rare religious painting by Goya, the *Betrayal of Christ*, which shows Judas preparing to kiss Jesus, thus identifying him to the Roman soldiers. Enjoy the many other El Grecos. A small-but-lifelike 17th-century carving of St. Francis by Pedro de Mena is just to the right of the Goya.

The Cloister: The cloister is likely closed through 2010. If it's open, take a peaceful detour to a funerary chapel located at the far side of the cloister from the entrance. The ceiling over the marble tomb of a bishop is a fresco by a student of Giotto (a 14th-century Italian Renaissance master).

Treasury: The *tesoro* is tiny, but radiant with riches. The highlight is the 10-foot-high, 430-pound monstrance—the tower designed to hold the Holy Communion wafer (the host) during the

TOLEDO

festival of Corpus Christi ("body of Christ") as it parades through the city. Built in 1517 by Enrique de Arfe, it's made of 5,000 individual pieces held together by 12,500 screws. There are diamonds, emeralds, rubies, and 400 pounds of gold-plated silver. The inner part (which is a century older) is 35 pounds of solid gold. Yeow. The base is a later addition from the Baroque period.

To the right of the monstrance is a beautiful red-coral cross given by the Philippines. To the right of the cross is a facsimile of a 700-year-old Bible hand-copied and beautifully illustrated by French monks; it was a gift from St. Louis, the 13th-century king of France. Imagine looking on these lavish illustrations with medieval eyes—an exquisite experience. (The precious and fragile lambskin original is preserved out of public view.) The finely painted small crucifix on the opposite side in the corner—by the great Gothic Florentine painter Fra Angelico—depicts Jesus alive on the back and dead on the front, and was a gift from Mussolini to Franco. Underneath, you'll find Franco's rather plain sword. Hmmm. Near the door, find the gift (humble amid all this splendor) from Toledo's sister city, Toledo, Ohio.

Before 10:00, the cathedral is open only for prayer (from north entrance). If you're here to worship at 9:00, you can peek into the otherwise-locked **Mozarabic Chapel** (Capilla Mozárabe). The Visigothic Mass (in Latin), the oldest surviving Christian ritual in Western Europe, starts at 9:00 (Mon–Sat). You're welcome to partake in this stirring example of peaceful coexistence of faiths. Toledo's proud Mozarabic community of 1,500 people traces its roots to Visigothic times.

In Central Toledo

Plaza de Zocodover—The main square is Toledo's center and your gateway to the old town. The word Zocodover derives from the Arabic for horse market.

Because Toledo is the state capital of Castile–La Mancha, the regional government administration building overlooks Plaza de Zocodover. Look for the three flags: one for Europe, one for Spain, and one for Castile–La Mancha. And speaking of universal symbols—find the low-key McDonald's. A source of controversy, it was finally allowed...with only one small golden arch.

The square is a big local hangout and city hub. Once the scene of Inquisition executions and bullfights, today it's a lot more peaceful. Old people arrive in the morning, and young people come in the evening. The goofy white tourist train leaves from here, as do buses #5 and #6, which lumber to the train station. Just uphill is the stop for bus #12, which travels around the old town to Santo Tomé (and works as a good self-guided tour—described at the end of the "Sights" section) and for bus #7.1, which heads out to the panoramic viewpoint made famous by El Greco.

▲▲Santa Cruz Museum—For years, this museum has been in a confused state of renovation—not really open, not really closed. Officials hope to create a grand city museum by incorporating this fine building with the adjacent Santa Fe monastery. During renovation, the museum's cloister and a room full of its best art are open and free. If the core of the building is filled with a temporary exhibit, you can generally wander in for a free look (Mon–Sat 10:00–18:30, Sun 10:00–14:00; from Plaza de Zocodover, go through arch to Calle Miguel de Cervantes 3).

This stately Renaissance building was an orphanage and hospital, built from money left by the humanist and diplomat Cardinal Mendoza when he died in 1495. The cardinal, confirmed as Chancellor of Castile by Queen Isabel, was so influential that he was called "the third king."

Your visit has three parts: the main building (with temporary exhibit), the fine cloister, and the museum rooms off the cloister.

The building (especially its facade, cloister arches, and stairway leading to the upper cloister) is a fine example of the Plateresque style. This ornate strain of Spanish Renaissance is named for the fancy work of silversmiths of the 16th century. During this time (c. 1500–1550), the royal court moved from Toledo to Madrid—when Madrid was a village, and Toledo was a world power. (You'll see no Plateresque work in Madrid.) Note the Renaissance-era mathematics, ideal proportions, round arches, square squares, and classic columns.

The footprint of the main building makes a Greek cross. As 1500 was a time of transition, the fine ceiling is an impressive mix of two styles: indigenous Moorish and trendier Italian Renaissance. After renovation, the wings of the building will be filled with 16th-century art, tapestries, furniture, armor, and documents.

Enjoy the peaceful cloister. In the corner stands an ignored well (now capped), bearing an Arabic inscription and grooves made by generations of Muslims pulling their buckets up by rope. The well was once in the courtyard of an 11th-century mosque that stood where the cathedral does today.

The museum section features a collection of 15 El Grecos. The highlight: the impressive *Assumption of Mary,* a spiritual poem on canvas. This altarpiece, finished one year before El Greco's death in 1614, is the culmination of his unique style, combining all of his

---

Toledo's Muslim Legacy

You can see the Moorish influence in these sights:
- Mezquita del Cristo de la Luz, the last of the town's mosques
- Sinagoga del Tránsito's Mudejar plasterwork
- Sinagoga de Santa María la Blanca's mosque-like horseshoe arches and pinecone capitals
- Puerta del Sol (Gate of the Sun) and other surviving gates (with horseshoe arches) along the medieval wall
- The city's labyrinthine, medina-like streets

TOLEDO

techniques to express an otherworldly event.

Study the *Assumption* (which some believe is misnamed, and actually shows the Immaculate Conception). Bound to earth, the city of Toledo sleeps, but a vision is taking place overhead. An angel in a billowing robe spreads his wings and flies up, supporting Mary, the mother of Christ. She floats up through warped space, to be serenaded by angels and wrapped in the radiant light of the Holy Spirit. Mary flickers and ripples, charged from within by her spiritual ecstasy, caught up in a vision that takes her breath away. No painter before or since has captured the supernatural world better than El Greco.

Find the lavish but faded *Astrolabe Tapestry* (c. 1480, Belgian), which shows a new view of the cosmos at the dawn of the Renaissance and the Age of Discovery: God (far left) oversees all, as Atlas (with the help of two women and a crank handle) spins the universe, containing the circular earth. The wisdom gang (far right) heralds the wonders of the coming era. Rather than a map of earth, this is a chart showing the cosmic order of things as the constellations spin around the stationary North Star (center).

Upstairs is a wonderful exhibit for tile- and ceramic-lovers. The private collection of the Carranza family has been "on loan" to the museum for the past 20 years. They began collecting tile and assorted ceramics that date from the end of the Reconquista (1492). Each piece is categorized by the Spanish region where it was made and professionally displayed. In spite of the lack of English explanations, this is the only place in Spain where you can compare regional differences in tile work and pottery.

Alcázar—This huge former imperial residence—built on the site of Roman, Visigothic, and Moorish fortresses—dominates the Toledo skyline. It's been closed for years for renovation. When it finally reopens (perhaps in 2010), it will be a boring National Military Museum.

The Alcázar became a kind of right-wing Alamo during

Spain's Civil War, when Franco's Nationalists (and hundreds of hostages) were besieged for two months in 1936. Finally, after many fierce but futile Republican attacks that destroyed much of the Alcázar, Franco sent in an army that took Toledo. The place was rebuilt and glorified under Franco.

Unfortunately Spain's Civil War is still too hot a topic to address in any museum, even here at the Alcázar. While an exhibit on the major 20th-century event in Spain would be fascinating and teach valuable lessons, to this day Spain has no museum on its civil war.

Mezquita del Cristo de la Luz—Of Muslim Toledo's 10 mosques, this barren little building (dating from about 1000) is

the best survivor. Looking up, you'll notice the Moorish fascination with geometry—each of the domes is a unique design. The lovely keyhole arch faces Mecca. In 1187, after the Reconquista, the mosque was changed to a church, the Christian apse (with its crude Romanesque art) was added, and the former mosque got its current name. The fine garden with its fountains is a reminder of the Quranic image of heaven (€2.30, daily 10:00–18:45, until 17:45 in winter, Cuesta de las Carmelitas Descalzas 10).

Visigothic Museum in the Church of San Roman (Museo Visigoda Iglesia de San Roman)—This 13th-century Mudejar church (with its rare, strangely modernist 13th-century Romanesque frescoes) provides an exquisite space for a small but interesting collection of Visigothic artifacts. The Visigoths were the Christian barbarian tribe who ruled Spain between the fall of Rome and the rise of the Moors. The only thing Visigothic about the actual building are the few capitals topping its columns, recycled from a seventh-century Visigothic church. While the elaborate crowns are copies (the originals are in Madrid), other glass cases show off metal and stone artifacts from the age when Toledo was the capital of the Visigoths. The items, while featuring almost no human figures, are rich in symbolism. Their portability fits that society's nomadic heritage. Archaeologists have found almost no Visigothic artifacts within Toledo's fortified hill location. They lived in humble settlements along the river—apparently needing no defense system…until the Moors swept through in 711, ending two centuries of Visigothic rule in Iberia (free, Tue–Sat 10:00–14:00 & 16:00–18:30, Sun 10:00–14:00, closed Mon). Unfortunately the museum thinks the entire world speaks Spanish: The only English explains the cost of admission.

In Southwest Toledo

These sights cluster at the southwest end of town. For efficient sightseeing, visit them in this order, then zip back home on bus #12 (listed at the end of this section).

▲**Santo Tomé**—A simple chapel on the Plaza del Conde holds El Greco's most beloved painting. *The Burial of the Count of Orgaz*

couples heaven and earth in a way only The Greek could. It feels so right to see a painting left *in situ,* where the artist placed it 400 years ago (€2.30, daily 10:00–18:45, until 17:45 mid-Oct–March, tel. 925-256-098). Go early or late to avoid long lines of tour groups.

Take this slow. Stay a while—let it perform. The year is 1323. Count Don Gonzalo Ruiz has died. You're at his burial right here in this chapel. The good count was so holy, even saints Augustine and Stephen have come down from heaven to lower his body into the grave. (The painting's subtitle is "Such is the reward for those who serve God and his saints.")

More than 250 years later, in 1586, a local priest (depicted on the far right, reading the Bible) hired El Greco to make a painting of the burial to hang over the count's tomb. The funeral is attended by Toledo's most distinguished citizens. (El Greco used local nobles as models.) The painting is divided in two by a serene line of noble faces—heaven above and earth below. Above the faces, the count's soul, symbolized by a little baby, rises up through a mystical birth canal to be reborn in heaven, where he's greeted by Jesus, Mary, and all the saints. A spiritual wind blows through as colors change and shapes stretch. This is Counter-Reformation propaganda—notice Jesus pointing to St. Peter, the symbol of the pope in Rome, who controls the keys to the pearly gates. Each face is a detailed portrait. El Greco himself (eyeballing you, seventh figure in from the left) is the only one not involved in the burial. The boy in the foreground—pointing to the two saints as if to say, "One's from the first century, the other's from the fourth…it's a miracle!"—is El Greco's son. On the handkerchief in the boy's

El Greco
(1541–1614)

Born on Crete and trained in Venice, Doménikos Theotokópoulos (tongue-tied friends just called him "The Greek") came to Spain to get a job decorating El Escorial. He failed there, but succeeded in Toledo, where he spent the last 37 years of his life. He mixed all three regional influences into his palette. From his Greek homeland, he absorbed the solemn, abstract style of icons. In Italy, he learned the bold use of color, elongated figures, twisting poses, and dramatic style of the later Renaissance. These elements were then fused in the fires of fanatic Spanish-Catholic devotion.

Not bound by the realism so important to his fellow artists, El Greco painted dramatic visions of striking colors and figures—bodies unnatural and lengthened as though stretched between heaven and earth. He painted souls, not faces. His work is on display at nearly every sight in Toledo. Thoroughly modern in his disregard of realism, he didn't impress the austere Philip II. But his art still seems as fresh as contemporary art does today.

pocket is El Greco's signature, written in Greek.

Don Gonzalo Ruiz's actual granite tombstone is at your feet. The count's two wishes upon his death were to be buried here and for his village to make an annual charity donation to feed Toledo's poor. Finally, more than two centuries later, the people of Orgaz said, "Enough!" and stopped the payments. The last of the money was spent to pay El Greco for this painting.

El Greco's House (Museo El Greco)—This small art gallery in a house built upon the spot where El Greco lived cons countless tourists with its misleading name. For better El Greco, go to the Santa Cruz Museum (described above). El Greco's House will likely be closed for renovation in 2010 (Calle Samuel Leví).

Sinagoga del Tránsito (Museo Sefardí)—Built in 1361, this is the best surviving slice of Toledo's Jewish past. Serving as Spain's national Jewish museum, it displays Jewish artifacts, including costumes, menorahs, and books. The synagogue's interior decor looks more Muslim than Jewish. After Christians reconquered the city in 1085, many Moorish workmen stayed on, beautifying the city with their unique style called Mudejar. The synagogue's intricate, geometrical carving in stucco features leaves, vines, and flowers; there are no human shapes, which are forbidden by the

Torah—like the Quran—as being "graven images." In the frieze (running along the upper wall, just below the ceiling), the Arabic-looking script is actually Hebrew, quoting psalms (respected by all "people of the book"—Muslims, Jews, and Christians alike). The side-wall balcony is the traditional separate worship area for women. Scale models of the development of the Jewish quarter (on the ground floor) and video displays (upstairs) give a fuller picture of Jewish life in medieval Toledo.

This 14th-century synagogue was built at the peak of Toledo's enlightened tolerance—constructed for Jews with Christian approval by Muslim craftsmen. Nowhere else in the city does Toledo's three-culture legacy shine brighter than at this synagogue. But in 1391, just a few decades after it was built, the Church and the Spanish kings began a violent campaign to unite Spain as a Christian nation, forcing Jews and Muslims to convert or leave. In 1492, Ferdinand and Isabel exiled Spain's remaining Jews. It's estimated that, in the 15th century, a third of Spain's Jews were killed, a third survived by converting to Christianity, and a third moved elsewhere (€3, free Sat afternoon from 14:00 and all day Sun; open Tue–Sat 10:00–21:00, Sun 10:00–14:00, closed Mon; audioguide-€3, near El Greco's House on Calle de los Reyes Católicos).

▲**Museo Victorio Macho**—Overlooking the gorge and Tajo River, this small, attractive museum—once the home and workshop of the early-20th-century sculptor Victorio Macho—offers a delightful collection of his bold Art Deco–inspired work. Even if you skip the museum, enjoy the terrace view from its gate (€3, Mon–Sat 10:00–19:00, Sun 10:00–15:00, between the two *sinagogas* at Plaza de Victorio Macho 2, tel. 925-284-225).

The house itself is an oasis of calm in the city. Your visit comes in four stages: ticket room with theater, courtyard with view, crypt, and museum. The small theater in the ticket room shows a good nine-minute video (request the English-language version). Macho was Spain's first great modern sculptor. When his Republican politics made it dangerous for him to stay in Franco's Spain, he fled to Mexico and Peru, where he met his wife, Zoila. They later returned to Toledo, where they lived and worked until he died in 1966. Zoila eventually gave the house and Macho's art to the city.

Enjoy the peaceful and expansive view from the terrace. From here it's clear how the Tajo River served as a formidable moat protecting the city. Imagine trying to attack. The 14th-century bridge on the right, and the remains of a bridge on the left, connected the town with the region's *cigarrales*—mansions of wealthy families, whose orchards of figs and apricots dot the hillside even today.

The door marked *Crypta* leads to *My Brother Marcelo*—the touching tomb Macho made for his brother. Eventually he featured his entire family in his art. A dozen steps above the terrace you'll find a single room marked *Museo* filled with Macho's art.

A *pietà* is carved expressively in granite. Self-portraits show the artist's genius. Exquisite pencil on paper studies illustrate how a sculptor must understand the body (in this case, Zoila's body). Other statues show the strength of the peoples' spirit as Republicans stood up to Franco's fascist forces, and Spain endured its 20th-century bloodbath. The highlight is *La Madre* (from 1935), Macho's life-size sculpture of his mother sitting in a chair. It illustrates the sadness and simple wisdom of Spanish mothers who witnessed so much suffering. Upon a granite backdrop, her white marble hands and face speak volumes.

Sinagoga de Santa María la Blanca—This synagogue-turned-church has Moorish horseshoe arches and wall carvings. It's a vivid

reminder of the religious cultures that shared (and then didn't share) this city. While it looks like a mosque, it never was one. Built as a Jewish synagogue by Muslim workers around 1200, it became a church in 1492 when Toledo's Jews were required to convert or leave—hence the mix-and-match name. After being used as horse stables by Napoleonic troops, it was further ruined in the 19th century. Today, it's an evocative space, beautiful in its simplicity (€2.30, daily April–Sept 10:00–18:45, Oct–March 10:00–17:45, Calle de los Reyes Católicos 2).

Jewish Information Center—Casa de Jacob Librería & Judaica is a Jewish bookshop and cultural center on the street behind Santa María la Blanca. While there are books in English, most are in Spanish and Hebrew (Mon–Fri 10:00–20:00, Sun 11:00–14:00, closed Sat, Calle del Ángel 15, tel. 925-216-454, www.jewish toledo.com).

▲San Juan de los Reyes Monasterio—"St. John of the Monarchs" is a grand Franciscan monastery, impressive church, and delightful cloistered courtyard. The style is late Gothic, contemporaneous with Portugal's Manueline (c. 1500) and Flamboyant Gothic elsewhere in Europe. It was the intended burial site of the Catholic Monarchs, Isabel and Ferdinand. But after the Moors were expelled in 1492 from Granada, their royal bodies were planted there to show Spain's commitment to maintaining a Moor-free peninsula (€2.30, daily 10:00–18:45, until 17:45 in winter, San Juan de los Reyes 2, tel. 925-223-802).

The **facade** is famously festooned with 500-year-old chains. Moors used these to shackle Christians in Granada until 1492. It's said that the freed Christians brought these chains to the church, making them a symbol of their Catholic faith.

Even without the royal tombs that would have dominated the space, the glorious **chapel** gives you a sense of Spain when it was Europe's superpower. The monastery was built to celebrate the 1476 Battle of Toro, which made Isabel the queen of Castile. Since her husband, Ferdinand, was king of Aragon, this effectively created the Spain we know today. (You could say 1476 is to Spain what 1776 is to the US.) Now united, Spain was able to quickly finish the Reconquista, ridding Iberia of its Moors within the next decade and a half.

Sitting in the chapel, you're surrounded by propaganda proclaiming Spain's greatness. The coat of arms is repeated obsessively. The eagle with the halo disk represents St. John, protector of the royal family. The yoke and lions remind people of the power of the kingdoms yoked together under Ferdinand and Isabel. The coat of arms is complex because of Iberia's many kingdoms (e.g., a lion for Lyon, and a castle for Castile). Arrows represent the 10 or so kingdoms of Iberia—weak when single, yet mighty when bound together. This notion inspired fascists such as Franco and Mussolini (who used a similar image of sticks bound together for strength). All of this is carved in actual stone, not made of stucco—rare in Toledo.

As you leave, look up over the door to see the Franciscan coat of arms—with the five wounds of the crucifixion (the stigmata—which St. Francis earned through his great faith) flanked by angels with dramatic wings.

Enjoy a walk around the **cloister.** Notice details of the fine carvings. Everything had meaning in the 15th century. In the corner (opposite the entry), just above eye level,

find a monkey—an insulting symbol of Franciscans—on a toilet reading the Bible upside-down. Perhaps a stone carver snuck in a not-too-subtle comment on Franciscan pseudo-intellectualism, with their big libraries and small brains.

Napoleon's troops are mostly to blame for the destruction of the church, a result of Napoleon's view that monastic power in Europe was a menace. While Napoleon's biggest error was to invade Russia, his second dumbest move was to alienate the Catholic faithful by destroying monasteries such as this one. This strategic mistake eroded popular support from people who might have seen Napoleon as a welcome alternative to the tyranny of kings and the Church.

▲Bus #12 Self-Guided Tour (A Sweat-Free Return Trip from Santo Tomé to Plaza de Zocodover)—When you're finished with the sights at the Santo Tomé end of town, you can hike all the way back (not fun)—or simply catch bus #12 from Plaza del Conde in front of Santo Tomé (fun!). Santo Tomé is the end of the line, so buses wait to depart from here twice hourly (at :25 and :55, until 21:55, pay driver €1), heading to Plaza de Zocodover. Closer to the synagogues and monastery, you can also catch the same bus at Plaza del Barrio Nuevo. The bus offers tired sightseers a quick, interesting 15-minute look at the town walls. Here's what you'll see on your way from Santo Tomé:

Leaving Santo Tomé, you'll first ride through Toledo's Jewish section. On the right, you'll pass El Greco's House, Sinagoga del Tránsito, and Sinagoga de Santa María la Blanca, followed by—on your left—the ornate Flamboyant Gothic facade of San Juan de los Reyes Monasterio. After squeezing through the 16th-century city gate, the bus follows along the outside of the mighty 10th-century wall. (Toledo was never conquered by force...only by siege.)

Just past the big escalator (which brings people from parking lots up into the city), the wall gets fancier, as demonstrated by the

little old Bisagra Gate. Soon after, you see the big new Bisagra Gate, the main entry into the old town. While the city walls date from the 10th century, this gate was built as an arch of triumph in the 16th century. The massive coat of arms of Emperor Charles V, with the double eagle, reminded people that he ruled a unified Habsburg/Bourbon empire, and they were entering the capital of an empire that, in the 1500s, included most of Western Europe and much of America.

The TI is just outside the big gate, at the edge of a well-maintained and shaded park—a picnic-perfect spot and one of Toledo's few green areas. After a detour to the bus station basement to pick up people coming from Madrid, you swing back around Bisagra Gate. As you climb back into the old town, notice how the modern under-construction Palacio de Congresos Miradero convention center is being incorporated into the more historic cityscape. After passing the fine Moorish (14th-century) Sun Gate, within moments you pull into the main square, Plaza de Zocodover. You can do this tour in reverse by riding bus #12 from Plaza de Zocodover to Plaza del Conde (departing at :25 and :55, same price and hours).

Shopping in Toledo

Toledo probably sells more souvenirs than any city in Spain. This is *the* place to buy medieval-looking swords, armor, maces, three-legged stools, lethal-looking letter-openers, and other nouveau antiques. It's also Spain's damascene center, where, for centuries, craftspeople have inlaid black steel with gold, silver, and copper wire. Spain's top bullfighters wouldn't have their swords made anywhere else.

Knives: At the workshop of English-speaking **Mariano Zamorano,** you can see swords and knives being made. Judging by what's left of Mariano's hand, his knives are among the sharpest (Mon–Fri 10:00–14:00 & 16:00–19:00, Sat–Sun 10:00–14:00—although you may not see work done on weekends, 10 percent discount with this book, behind Ayuntamiento/City Hall at Calle Ciudad 19, tel. 925-222-634, www.marianozamorano.com).

Damascene: Shops selling the shiny inlaid plates and decorative wares are everywhere. The damascene is a real tourist racket, but it's fun to pop into a shop and see the intricate handwork in action.

Nun-Baked Sweet Treats: Convents all over town earn a little money by selling *Dulces Artesanos.*

El Martes: Toledo's colorful outdoor market is a lively local scene on Tuesdays at Paseo de Merchan, better known to locals as "La Vega" (9:00–14:00, outside Bisagra Gate near TI).

Sleeping in Toledo

Madrid day-trippers darken the sunlit cobbles, but few stay to see Toledo's medieval moonrise. Spend the night. Hotels often have a two-tiered price system, with prices 20 percent higher on Friday and Saturday. Spring and fall are high season; November through March and July and August are less busy.

Near Plaza de Zocodover

$$–$$$ Hotel Toledo Imperial sits efficiently above Plaza de Zocodover, and rents 29 business-class rooms. Because it has no public spaces and no restaurant, it's a super value (Db-€60 Sun–Thu, Db-€100 Fri–Sat, air-con, Wi-Fi, Calle Horno de los Bizcochos 5, tel. 925-280-034, fax 925-280-205, www.hoteltoledo imperial.com, hotel@hoteltoledoimperial.com).

Near Plaza de Zocodover

DOWN TO
BISAGRA GATE

CLOSED TO CARS

PLAZA DE ZOCODOVER

ARCH

TO SANTA CRUZ MUSEUM

ALFERECES

MAGDALENA CHURCH

TO CATHEDRAL + MOST SIGHTS

ALCAZAR

B BUS STOP

1. Hotel Toledo Imperial
2. Hotel Las Conchas
3. Hostal Centro
4. Hostal Nuevo Labrador
5. Pensión Castilla
6. Restaurante Ludeña
7. El Trébol & La Tabernita Tapas Bars
8. Supermarket Coviran
9. Santo Tomé Mazapán Shop
10. Tourist Train
11. Convention Center & Escalator to Miradero Garage

* NOT TO SCALE—
PLAZA ZOCODOVER TO
MAGDALENA CHURCH IS A
3 MIN. WALK
STREET WIDTH IS
EXAGGERATED FOR CLARITY

TOLEDO

$$ Hotel Las Conchas, a three-star hotel, gleams with marble. It's so sleek and slick it almost feels more like a hospital than a hotel. Its 35 rooms are plenty comfortable (Sb-€55; Db-€85, generally €15 less on weeknights and July–Aug; Db with terrace-€100, includes tax, 5 percent discount with this book in 2010, breakfast-€6, air-con, near the Alcázar at Juan Labrador 8, tel. 925-210-760, fax 925-224-271, www.lasconchas.com, lasconchas @ctv.es, Pablo and Yuki).

$ Hostal Centro rents 28 spacious rooms with sparse, well-worn furniture and a ramshackle feel. It's wonderfully central, with a third of its rooms overlooking the main square. Request a quiet room on the back side to minimize night noise (Sb-€35, Db-€50, Tb-€65, 10 percent discount with this book, inviting Astroturf roof terrace with sun lounge chairs, 50 yards off Plaza de Zocodover—take the first right off Calle Comercio to Calle Nueva 13, tel. 925-257-091, fax 925-257-848, www.hostalcentro.com, hostal centro@telefonica.net, warmly run by Asun and David).

$ Hostal Nuevo Labrador, with 12 simple and spacious rooms and no public spaces, is quiet, modern, and a good value (Sb-€30, Db-€50, bigger Db-€60, Tb-€65, Qb-€80, includes tax, no breakfast, air-con, elevator, Juan Labrador 10, tel. 925-222-620, fax 925-226-278, www.nuevolabrador.com, nuevolabrador @telefonica.net, César).

Sleep Code

(€1 = about $1.40, country code: 34)
S = Single, **D** = Double/Twin, **T** = Triple, **Q** = Quad, **b** = bathroom,
s = shower only. Unless otherwise noted, credit cards are
accepted and rooms have air-conditioning.
    To help you easily sort through these listings, I've divided
the rooms into three categories, based on the price for a
standard double room with bath during high season:

$$$ Higher Priced—Most rooms €90 or more.
 $$ Moderately Priced—Most rooms between €60–90.
  $ Lower Priced—Most rooms €60 or less.

$ Pensión Castilla, a dark family-run cheapie, is so humble
you can imagine lashing your burro out front. It rents seven basic
non-smoking rooms with ceiling fans (S-€18, Db-€30, cash only,
no air-con, Calle Recoletos 6, tel. 925-256-318, Teresa doesn't
speak English).

Near Bisagra Gate

$$$ Hostal del Cardenal, a 17th-century cardinal's palace built
into Toledo's wall, is quiet and elegant, with a cool garden and a
stuffy restaurant. This poor man's parador, at the dusty old gate of
Toledo, is closest to the station, but below all the old-town action
(Sb-€80, Db-€130, 20 percent cheaper mid-Dec–mid-March, 5
percent discount with this book, breakfast-€9, some free parking,
serioso staff, enter through town wall 100 yards below Bisagra Gate,
Paseo de Recaredo 24, tel. 925-224-900, fax 925-222-991, www
.hostaldelcardenal.com, cardenal@hostaldelcardenal.com).

$$ Hospedería de los Reyes has 15 colorful and thoughtfully appointed rooms in a new, attractive yellow building 100
yards downhill from Bisagra Gate, outside the wall (Sb-€40–50,
Db-€53–70, includes breakfast, air-con, Wi-Fi, free parking
nearby on the street, Calle Perala 37, tel. 925-283-667, fax 925-283-
668, www.hospederiadelosreyes.com, Alicia).

$ Hostal Puerta de Bisagra is in a sprawling old building that
is fresh and modern inside. Located just across from Bisagra Gate,
it's convenient for arrivals, but a long hike uphill to the action (hop
any bus). Its 33 comfortable rooms are rented at some of the best
prices in town (Db-€50 Sun–Thu, Db-€57 Fri–Sat and daily in
peak season, breakfast-€4, air-con, Wi-Fi, Calle del Potro 5, tel. &
fax 925-285-277, www.puertabisagra.com).

$ Hotel Sol, with 15 newly decorated pastel non-smoking
rooms, is a good value. It's on a quiet, ugly side street between

Bisagra Gate and Plaza de Zocodover (Sb-€44, Db-€59, Tb-€72, includes tax, 10 percent discount with this book, breakfast-€4, air-con, private parking-€10/day; leave the busy main drag at Hotel Real and head 50 yards down the lane to Azacanes 8; tel. 925-213-650, fax 925-216-159, www.hotelyhostalsol.com, info@hotely hostalsol.com, José Carlos). Their 11-room **$ Hostal Sol** annex across the street is just as comfortable, smoke-free, and a bit cheaper (Sb-€36, Db-€49, Tb-€59, Qb-€72, includes tax, 10 percent discount with this book, breakfast-€4).

Deep in Toledo

$$ La Posada de Manolo rents 14 thoughtfully furnished rooms across from the downhill corner of the cathedral. Manolo Junior recently opened this fine *hostal* according to his father's vision: a comfortable place with each of its three floors themed differ-ently—Moorish, Jewish, and Christian (Sb-€42, Db-€72, big Db-€84, includes buffet breakfast, 10 percent discount with this book when you reserve direct, air-con, Wi-Fi, no elevator, two nice view terraces, Calle Sixto Ramón Parro 8, tel. 925-282-250, fax 925-282-251, www.laposadademanolo.com, toledo@laposadade manolo.com).

$$ Hotel Eurico, fresh and new, cleverly fits 23 sleek rooms into a medieval building buried deep in the old town. The staff is friendly and the hotel offers a fine value (Sb-€55–60, Db-€70–80, Tb-€70–90, air-con, breakfast-€7, Calle Santa Isabel 3, tel. 925-284-178, fax 925-254-017, www.hoteleurico.com, reservas @hoteleurico.com).

$ Hotel Santa Isabel, in a 15th-century building two blocks from the cathedral, has 41 clean, modern, and comfortable rooms and squeaky tile hallways (Sb-€35, small old Db-€45, big new Db-€55, Tb-€70, includes tax, 5 percent discount with this book, breakfast-€5, air-con, elevator, scenic roof terrace, parking-€10/day, buried deep in old town—take a taxi instead of the bus, driv-ers enter from Calle Pozo Amargo, Calle Santa Isabel 24, tel. 925-253-120, fax 925-253-136, www.santa-isabel.com, santa-isabel @arrakis.es).

Outside of Town, near the Bullring

These places are on a modern street next to the bullring (Plaza de Toros, bullfights only on holidays), just beyond Bisagra Gate. In this area, parking is free on the street. The bus station is a five-minute walk away, and city buses lumber by every few minutes (all go directly to Plaza de Zocodover). There are many other similarly nondescript, comfy, and cheap places in this neighborhood.

$$$ Hotel María Cristina, a sprawling 74-room hotel, has all the comforts under a thin layer of prefab tradition (Sb-€68,

Toledo Hotels and Restaurants

STREET WIDTH IS
EXAGGERATED
FOR CLARITY

200 YARDS
200 METERS

🔭 VIEW

P PARKING

Ⓑ BUS STOP

N

TO MADRID & ⑦

TO ⓶

BUS STATION

L. DE LA CARRERA

BISAGRA GATE

CARD. TAV.

⓷ CITY WALLS

⓸

MIRA- DERO

TO TRAIN STATION & ⑧

⑨ TO

ESCALATORS

SUBIDA LA GRANJA

ALBIDES

MERCED

MEZQUITA

AZACANES

CUESTA

ARMAS

NUÑEZ

SILLERIA

⓭

SANTA CRUZ MUSEUM

CALLE REAL

LEO.

S. ILD.

POST

CADENAS

PL. ZOC.

CERVANTES

ALFERECES

SAN JUAN DE LOS REYES

NAV.

CABLO

⑮

PLATA

COMERCIO

Ⓑ

SANTO TOMÉ

VISI- GOTHIC MUSEUM

ALEX.

NUÑCIO

⑫

ALCMAN

DON.

⑭

ALFONSO

COMERCIO

⑯ ALCÁZAR

SINAGOGA DE SANTA MARÍA LA BLANCA

ANGEL

S. TOMÉ

TRINIDAD

⑩

MUSEO VICTORIO MACHO

Ⓑ

SAN JUAN DIO

S. ISABEL

⑪

⑤

CATHEDRAL

RIO TAJO

PARK

PASEO TRANS.

S. PEDRO

S. URSULA

SALV.

⑥

ℹ & CITY HALL (AYUNTAMIENTO)

EL GRECO'S HOUSE

SINAGOGA DEL TRÁNSITO

DCH

❶ Hostal del Cardenal

❷ To Hospedería de los Reyes

❸ Hostal Puerta de Bisagra

❹ Hotel Sol

❺ La Posada de Manolo & Madre Tierra Restaurante Vegetariano

❻ Hotel Eurico & Hotel Santa Isabel

❼ To Hotel María Cristina & Hostal Madrid

❽ To Albergue Juvenil San Servando (Hostel)

❾ To Parador de Toledo & Hotel La Almazara

❿ Los Cuatro Tiempos Rest.

⓫ Casa Aurelio I

⓬ Casa Aurelio II & III (on Sinagoga) & Pizzeria Pastucci

⓭ Rest./Cafeteria Casón López de Toledo & La Abadia Tapas Restaurante

⓮ Adolfo Vinoteca

⓯ Restaurante-Mesón Palacios

⓰ Mercado Municipal (Market)

TOLEDO

Db-€105, Tb-€142, suites-€140–170, tax not included, break-fast-€9, air-con, elevator, restaurant, parking-€12/day, Marqués de Mendigorría 1, tel. 925-213-202, fax 925-212-650, www.hotel mariacristina.com, informacion@hotelmariacristina.com).

$ Hostal Madrid has two locations on the same street with over 20 rooms and a café next door (Sb-€28, Db-€40, Tb-€54, includes tax, air-con, parking-€8/day, Marqués de Mendigorría 7 and 14, reception at #7, tel. 925-221-114, fax 925-228-113, www .hostal-madrid.net, info@hostal-madrid.net).

Hostel

The 96-bed **Albergue Juvenil San Servando** youth hostel is lavish but cheap, with small rooms for two, three, or four people (€14/ bed plus €12 obligatory *alberguista* membership, swimming pool, views, cafeteria, good management, located in 10th-century Arab castle of San Servando, 10-min walk from train station, 15-min hike from town center, over Puente Viejo outside town, tel. 925-224-554, reservations tel. 925-221-676, alberguesclm@jccm.es, no English spoken).

Outside of Town with the Grand Toledo View

$$$ Parador de Toledo, with 76 rooms, is one of Spain's best-known inns. Its guests enjoy the same Toledo view El Greco made famous from across the Tajo Gorge (Sb-€142, Db-€170, Db with view-€178, Tb-€230, Tb with view-€248, tax included, breakfast-€16, €31 fixed-price meals sans drinks in their fine restaurant overlooking Toledo, 2 windy miles from town at Cerro del Emperador, tel. 925-221-850, fax 925-225-166, www.parador.es, toledo@parador.es).

$ Hotel La Almazara was the summer residence of a 16th-century archbishop of Toledo. A hulking old place with cushy public rooms and 28 simple bedrooms (10 with views), it's truly in the country, but just 1.5 miles out of Toledo (Sb-€33, Db-€45, Db with view-€49, Tb-€62, tax not included, air-con, Carretera de Toledo Arges y Polan at kilometer 3.4, follow signs from circular Ronda de Toledo road, tel. 925-223-866, fax 925-250-562, www.hotel almazara.com, reservas@hotelalmazara.com). They serve breakfast, but not lunch or dinner (and there are no restaurants nearby).

Eating in Toledo

Dining in Traditional Elegance

A day full of El Greco and the romance of Toledo after dark puts me in the mood for game. Typical Toledo dishes include partridge *(perdiz)*, venison *(venado)*, wild boar *(jabalí)*, roast suckling pig *(cochinillo asado)*, or baby lamb *(cordero*—similarly roasted after a few weeks of mother's milk). After dinner, find a *mazapán* place (such as the Santo Tomé shops) for dessert. Restaurants generally serve lunch from 13:00 to 16:00 and dinner from 20:00 until very late (Spaniards don't start dinner until about 21:00).

Los Cuatro Tiempos Restaurante ("The Four Seasons") specializes in local game and roasts, proficiently served in a tasteful and elegant setting. They offer spacious dining with an extensive and inviting Spanish wine list. It's a good choice for a quiet, romantic dinner (€19 three-course lunches, €30 à la carte dinners, Mon–Sat 13:00–16:00 & 20:30–23:00, Sun 13:00–16:00 only, at downhill corner of cathedral, Sixto Ramón Parro 5, tel. 925-223-782).

The venerable **Casa Aurelio** has three branches, each offering traditional cooking (game, roast suckling pig, traditional soup, €40 dinners) in a classy atmosphere more memorable than the meals (generally 13:00–16:30 & 20:00–23:30, air-con). None have outdoor seating, and all are within three blocks of the cathedral: **Plaza del Ayuntamiento 4** is festive (closed Mon, tel. 925-227-716), **Sinagoga 6** is most *típico* (closed Wed, tel. 925-222-097), and **Sinagoga 1,** popular with Toledo's political class, is the newest and dressiest, with a wine cellar and more modern presentation (closed Mon, tel. 925-221-392).

Restaurante Casón López de Toledo, a fancy restaurant located upstairs in an old noble palace, specializes in Castilian food, particularly venison and partridge. As you tuck in your napkin, you'll feel like an 18th-century aristocrat (€40 fixed-price meals, €52 tasting *menu*, closed Sun, reservations smart, near Plaza de Zocodover at Calle de la Sillería 3, tel. 925-254-774).

Cafeteria Casón López de Toledo is the ground-floor version of the restaurant with the same name (previous listing). While called a "cafeteria," it's actually a quality restaurant in its own right, without the pretense you find upstairs and with a simpler and much less expensive menu (€8–10 plates, great €11 weekday lunch special; same days, address, and phone as restaurant). This is where the locals dine, enjoying the fancy restaurant's kitchen at half the price.

La Abadia Tapas Restaurante is a trendy scene, great for classy tapas and a young local crowd who want imaginative plates and quality ingredients. Their €14 "selection plate" feeds two. The front area is the bar scene. Beyond that is a labyrinth of isolated little dining rooms. I found its non-smoking room had the nicest atmosphere (daily, 20 yards downhill from Restaurante Casón López de Toledo at Plaza de San Nicolás 3, tel. 925-251-140).

Adolfo Vinoteca is the wine bar of the highly respected local chef Adolfo, who runs a famous gourmet restaurant across the street. His hope: to introduce the younger generation to the culture of fine food and wine. The bar offers up a pricey but always top-notch list of gourmet plates (€7–15 each) and fine local wines (€2–6 per glass—don't economize here). Adolfo's son, Javier, proved to me the importance of matching each plate with the right wine. I like to sit next to the kitchen to be near the creative action. If the Starship *Enterprise* had a Spanish wine-and-tapas bar on its holodeck, this would be it. Wine is sold at shop prices with a €3–6 cork fee (daily 12:00–24:00, across from cathedral at Calle Nuncio Viejo 1, tel. 925-224-244).

Eating Simply

For locations, see the maps on pages 445 and 448.

Restaurante-Mesón Palacios is a simple, sticky diner, serving good regional food at reasonable prices to families and tourists. Their bean soup with partridge *(judías con perdiz)* and roast suckling lamb and pig are good. They serve earlier than most restaurants—from noon and from 19:00 (€19 complete dinner with the local favorites, near Plaza de San Vicente at Alfonso X El Sabio 3, tel. 925-215-972, run by ladies' man Jesús).

Restaurante Ludeña is a classic eatery with a bar, a well-worn dining room in back, and four tables on a sunny courtyard. It's very central; locals duck in here to pretend there is no tourism in Toledo (Plaza de la Magdalena 13, tel. 925-223-384).

Madre Tierra Restaurante Vegetariano is Toledo's answer to a vegetarian's prayer. Bright, spacious, classy, air-conditioned, and tuned-in to the healthy eater's needs, its appetizing dishes are based on both international and traditional Spanish cuisine (€6–10 plates, good tea selection, great veggie pizzas, closed Mon–Tue, 20 yards below La Posada de Manolo at Bajada de le Tripería 2 near Plaza de San Justo, tel. 925-223-571).

Pizzeria Pastucci, while nondescript, is a local favorite for pizza and pasta (big €14 pizza feeds two, closed Mon, near cathedral at Calle de la Sinagoga 10).

Tapas Just Off Plaza de Zocodover: Plaza de Zocodover is busy with eateries serving edible food at affordable prices, and its people-watching scene is great. But to eat better with locals, drop by **El Trébol,** tucked peacefully away just a short block off Plaza de Zocodover. Señor Ventura seems to be the mastermind behind every new trendy bar in town, and at El Trébol he offers a menu elegant in its simplicity, a crisp interior, and an inviting outdoor terrace (daily 11:00–23:00, Calle de Santa Fe 1). The specialties are *pulgas* (fine little €2 sandwiches) and *rosea* (potato and meat with spicy sauce). **La Tabernita,** half a block away, is another good tapas bar (also a Ventura adventure) with more extensive and expensive tapas and a fun local scene. They serve a free tapa with each drink (Calle de Santa Fe 14).

Picnics: Picnics are best assembled at the city market, Mercado Municipal, on Plaza Mayor (on the Alcázar side of cathedral, with a supermarket inside open Mon–Sat 9:00–15:00 & 17:00–20:00 and stalls open mostly in the mornings until 14:00, closed Sun). This is a fun market to prowl, even if you don't need food. If you feel like munching a paper-plate-size Communion wafer, one of the stalls sells crispy bags of *obleas*—a great gift for your favorite pastor. For a picnic with people-watching, consider Plaza de Zocodover or Plaza del Ayuntamiento. The Supermarket Coviran on Plaza de la Magdalena has groceries at good prices (daily 9:30–22:00, just below Plaza de Zocodover).

And for Dessert: Mazapán

Toledo's famous almond-fruity-sweet *mazapán* is sold all over town. As you wander, keep a lookout for convents advertising their version, *Dulce Artesano*. The big *mazapán* producer is **Santo Tomé** (several outlets, including a handy one on Plaza de Zocodover, daily 9:00–22:00). Browse their tempting window displays. They sell *mazapán* goodies individually (two for about €1, *sin relleno*—without filling—is for purists, *de piñon* has pine nuts, *imperiales* is with almonds, others have fruit fillings). Boxes are good for gifts, but sampling is much cheaper when buying just a few pieces. Their *Toledana* is a nutty, crumbly, not-too-sweet cookie with a subtle thread of squash filling (€1.20 each).

For a sweet and romantic evening moment, pick up a few pastries and head down to the cathedral. Sit on the Plaza del Ayuntamiento's benches (or stretch out on the stone wall to the right of the TI). The fountain is on your right, Spain's best-looking City Hall is behind you, and there before you is her top cathedral, built back when Toledo was Spain's capital, shining brightly against the black night sky.

Connections

While the new AVE bullet train makes the trip to Madrid in half the time (nearly hourly, 30 min), buses depart twice as frequently. Either way, Madrid and Toledo are very easily connected.

From Toledo to Madrid: By bus (2/hr, 1–1.5 hrs, €5 one-way, *directo* is faster than *ruta,* bus drops you at Madrid's Plaza Elíptica Metro stop, Continental Auto bus company, tel. 925-223-641; you can almost always just drop in and buy a ticket minutes before departure), **by train** (AVE to Madrid's Atocha Station: nearly hourly, 30 min, €10, www.renfe.es/ave), **by car** (40 miles, 1 hr).

Toledo bus info: tel. 925-215-850; train info: tel. 902-240-202.

From Toledo to Other Points: To get to Granada and else-where in Spain from Toledo, assume you'll have to transfer in Madrid. See Madrid's "Connections" for information on reaching various destinations.

Route Tips for Drivers

Granada to Toledo (250 miles, 5 hours): The Granada–Toledo drive is long, hot, and boring. Start early to minimize the heat and make the best time you can. Follow signs for *Madrid/Jaén/N-323* into what some call "the Spanish Nebraska"—La Mancha (see next section). After Puerto Lapice, you'll see the Toledo exit.

Toledo to Madrid (40 miles, 1 hour): It's a speedy *autovía* north, past one last billboard to Madrid (on N-401). The highways converge into M-30, which encircles Madrid. Follow it to the left (*Nor* or *Oeste*) and take the Plaza de España exit to get back to Gran Vía. If you're airport-bound, keep heading into Madrid until you see the airplane symbol (N-II).

To drive to Atocha Station in Madrid, take the exit off M-30 for Plaza de Legazpi, then take Delicias (second on your right off the square). Parking for car return is on the north side of the train station.

TOLEDO

La Mancha

La Mancha, which is worth a visit if you're driving between Toledo and Granada, shows a side of Spain that you'll see nowhere else—

vast and flat. Named for the Arabic word for "parched earth," it makes you feel small—lost in rough seas of olive-green polka dots. Random buildings look like houses and hotels hurled off some heavenly Monopoly board.

This is the setting of Miguel de Cervantes' *Don Quixote*, pub-lished in the early 17th century, after England sank the Armada and the Spanish Empire began its decline. Cervantes' star character fights doggedly for good, for justice, and against the fall of Spain and its traditional old-regime ideals. Ignoring reality, Don Quixote is a hero fighting a hopeless battle. Stark La Mancha is the perfect stage.

The epitome of *Don Quixote* country, the town of **Consuegra** (TI tel. 925-475-731) must be the La Mancha Cervantes had in

mind. Drive up to the ruined 12th-century castle and joust with a windmill. It's hot and buggy here, but the powerful view overlooking the village, with its sun-bleached light-red roofs, modern concrete reality, and harsh, windy silence makes for a profound picnic (a one-hour drive south of Toledo). The castle belonged to the Knights of
St. John (12th and 13th centuries) and is associated with their trip to Jerusalem during the Crusades. Originally built from the ruins of a nearby Roman circus, it has been newly restored (€3). Sorry, the windmills are post-Cervantes, only 200 to 300 years old—but you can go inside the one that serves as the TI to see how it works (€1).

If you've seen windmills, the next castle north (above Almonacid, 8 miles from Toledo) is free and more interesting than the Consuegra castle. Follow the ruined lane past the ruined church up to the ruined castle. The jovial locals hike up with kids and kites.

GRANADA

For a time, Granada was the grandest city in Spain. But in the end, with the tumult that came with the change from Moorish to Christian rule, it eventually lost its power and settled into a long slumber. Today, Granada seems to specialize in evocative history and good living. We'll keep things fun and simple, settling down in the old center and exploring monuments of the Moorish civilization and its conquest. And we'll taste the treats of a North African–flavored culture that survives here today.

Granada's magnificent Alhambra fortress was the last stronghold of the Moorish kingdom in Spain. The city's exotically tangled Moorish quarter, the Albayzín, invites exploration. From its viewpoints, romantics can enjoy the sunset and evening views of the grand, floodlit Alhambra.

There is an old saying: "Give him a coin, woman, for there is nothing worse in this life than to be blind in Granada." This city has much to see, yet it reveals itself in unpredictable ways. It takes a poet to sort through and assemble the jumbled shards of Granada. Peer through the intricate lattice of a Moorish window. Hear water burbling unseen among the labyrinthine hedges of the Generalife Gardens. Listen to a flute trilling deep in the swirl of alleys around the cathedral. Don't be blind in Granada—open all your senses.

Planning Your Time

Granada is worth one day and two nights at a minimum. To use your time efficiently, reserve in advance for the Alhambra (see sidebar on page 466).

Here's the best intense one-day plan: In the morning, stroll the Pescadería market streets, follow my self-guided walk of the old town (or catch the 10:30 Cicerone walking tour), grab lunch, do the Alhambra in the afternoon (reservation essential), and tour the cathedral and Royal Chapel (both open roughly 16:00–19:30). Hike the hippie lane into the Albayzín Moorish quarter (or catch minibus #31 or #32) to the San Nicolás viewpoint for the magic hour, then find the right place for a suitably late dinner (taxi home for safety if in the Albayzín late).

When you're ready to move on, the Costa del Sol's best beach town, Nerja, is just a 1.5-hour drive or 2.5-hour bus ride away. You can also get to White Hill towns such as Ronda (by train) in that time; Sevilla is an easy three-hour train ride away. The Madrid–Granada train service is slow (5 hours), but passes through beautiful countryside.

Orientation to Granada

Modern Granada sprawls (300,000 people), but its sights are all within a 20-minute walk of Plaza Nueva, where dogs wag their

tails to the rhythm of modern hippies and street musicians. Most of my recommended hotels are within a few blocks of Plaza Nueva. Make this the hub of your Granada visit.

Plaza Nueva was a main square back when kings called Granada home. This historic center is in the Darro River Valley, which separates two hills (the river now flows under the square). On one hill is the great Moorish palace, the Alhambra, and on the other is the best-preserved Moorish quarter in Spain, the Albayzín. To the southeast are the cathedral, Royal Chapel, and Alcaicería (Moorish market), where the city's two main drags—Gran Vía de Colón (often just called "Gran Vía" by locals) and Calle Reyes Católicos—lead away into the modern city.

Tourist Information

The main TI is tucked away just above Plaza Nueva on Santa Ana (above the church, Mon–Fri 9:00–19:30, Sat–Sun 9:30–15:00, tel. 958-575-202). Another TI is at the entrance of the Alhambra (March–Oct Mon–Sat 8:00–20:00, Nov–Feb until 18:00, year-round Sun 8:00–13:30, tel. 958-544-003). Both cover Granada as well as all Andalucía. At either TI, get a free city map and the *Pocket Guía* magazine in easy Spanish (English magazines not always available), and verify your Alhambra plans. To save yourself

Greater Granada

TO BUS STN.
TO AIRPORT
TO CARTHUSIAN MONASTERY
¼ MILE
.5 KM
⌁ VIEW
AV. CONSTITUCIÓN
ANCHA DE CAPUCHINOS
REAL DE CARTUJA
TRAIN STATION
PLAZA TRIUNFO
MURCIA
PAGES
PLAZA LARGA
ALHACABA
PAN.
CUESTA DEL CHAPIZ
SACRO-MONTE
GRAN VÍA DE COLÓN
OLD WALL
SAN NICOLÁS
CAMINO DEL SACRO-MONTE
A L B A Y Z Í N
CALD. NUEVA SAN GREG.
PASEO DE LOS TRISTES
DARRO RIVER
CATHEDRAL + ROYAL CHAPEL
CALD. VIEJA
C. DEL DARRO
PALACIOS NAZARIES
PLAZA DE BIB-RAMBLA
GOMÉREZ
PLAZA NUEVA
ALHAMBRA
GENERA-LIFE
PLAZA DEL CARMEN
PLAZA ISABEL LA CATÓLICA
ENTRANCE ♁
RECOGIDAS
PUERTA REAL
TO FREEWAY
= HISTORIC CITY CENTER—SEE DETAIL MAPS
DCH

GRANADA

a trip to the train or bus stations, get schedule information (both TIs list all departures on the wall). During peak season (April–Oct), TI kiosks sometimes pop up in Plaza Nueva and Plaza de Bib-Rambla.

Arrival in Granada

By Train: Granada's train station is connected to the center by frequent buses, a €5 taxi ride, or a 30-minute walk down Avenida de la Constitución and Gran Vía. The train station does not have luggage storage. If your itinerary is set, reserve your train out upon arrival.

Exiting the train station, walk straight ahead down the tree-lined Avenida Andaluces. At the first major intersection (Avenida de la Constitución), you'll see a series of bus stops on your right. Buses #3 through #9 (and most other buses—check the easy-to-read map at the stop) go to the cathedral, the nearest stop to Plaza Nueva—confirm by asking the driver, "¿*Catedral?*"

(kah-tay-DRAHL). Buy a €1.20 ticket from the driver. Get off at the cathedral; cross the busy Gran Vía and walk three short blocks to Plaza Nueva.

By Bus: Located on the city outskirts, Granada's bus station, Estación de Autobuses, has a good and cheap cafeteria, ATMs, luggage storage, and an info office (tel. 958-185-480 for the Alsa company, which serves Barcelona and east-coast destinations). To get to the center, either take a 10-minute taxi ride (€6) or bus #3 or #33 (€1.20, pay driver). It's about a 20-minute bus ride; nearing the center, the bus goes up Gran Vía. For Plaza Nueva, get off at the cathedral (cathedral not visible from bus), a half-block before the grand square called Plaza Isabel La Católica (a three-block walk from Plaza Nueva).

By Car: Driving in Granada's historic center is restricted to buses, taxis, and (technically) tourists with hotel reservations. Signs are posted to this effect, and entrance is strictly controlled—but generally not by an officer. Hidden cameras snap a photo of your license plate as soon as you enter the restricted zone. Getting into the old center and finding your hotel or a parking garage is a major frustration because of these strict controls and the many one-way streets. Your hotelier can contact the local police department to register your car (and prevent a nasty surprise when you return your rental car). Some hoteliers have deals with nearby garages and can give you detailed directions to those spots.

The *autovía* (freeway) circles the city with a *circunvalación* road (Ronda Sur). If you're heading for a hotel near Plaza Nueva, take exit #129, direction Centro, Recogidas. Calle Recogidas becomes Calle Reyes Católicos where it enters the restricted zone, and leads directly into the heart of town. There might be a police block at Puerta Real (Victoria Hotel) because driving down Calle Reyes Católicos is now heavily controlled. Technically, you can pull into Plaza Nueva if you have a hotel reservation, but the road-side posts—which have a list of hotels with button buzzers to gain drivers entry—generally do not work.

Granada has several parking garages. Parking San Agustín—near the cathedral, just off Gran Vía—costs more than the others, but is the only lot that's an easy walk to my recommended hotels (€25/day; as you approach Plaza Isabel La Católica on Gran Vía, follow blue *Parking* sign).

By Plane: Granada's sleepy airport, which serves only a dozen or so planes a day, is about 10 miles west of the city center. To get between the airport and downtown, you can take a taxi (€25) or, much cheaper, the airport bus, timed to leave when flights arrive and depart (€3, 12/day, 40 min). Use the bus stop at Gran Vía del Colón, nearly across from the cathedral. Airport info: tel. 958-245-223 (press "9" for English).

Helpful Hints

Theft Alert: Gypsy (Roma) women, usually hanging out near the cathedral and Alcaicería, will accost you with sprigs of rosemary. The twig is free...and then they grab your hand and read your fortune for a tip. Coins are bad luck, so the minimum payment they'll accept is €5. Don't make eye contact, don't accept a sprig, and say firmly but politely, *"No, gracias."* While aggressive (especially in the morning), these Spanish Roma are harmless. Locals warn that Gypsies from Romania (new arrivals who tend to have gold teeth) are more likely to be pickpockets. In general, be on guard for pickpockets, especially late at night in the Albayzín (see "Safety in the Albayzín" sidebar on page 490). Your biggest threat is being conned while enjoying drinks and music in Sacromonte.

City Pass: The **Bono Turístico** city pass covers the Alhambra, cathedral, Royal Chapel, Carthusian Monastery, sightseeing bus, and city buses, plus minor sights and discounts on others (€30, valid for five days). When you buy your pass, the vendor schedules a time for your Alhambra visit. Passes are sold at a kiosk on Plaza Nueva by the minibus stop. Or you can buy a pass and book your Alhambra palace visit in advance online (http://caja.caja-granada.es; click "Bono Turístico Info y Compra"). Note that some of the fancier hotels provide one free pass per room for stays of two or more nights.

Festivals and Concerts: From late June to early July, the International Festival of Music and Dance offers classical music, ballet, flamenco, and zarzuela (light opera) nightly in the Alhambra at reasonable prices. The ticket office is located in the Corral de Carbón (open mid-April–Oct). Beginning in February, you can also book tickets online at www .granadafestival.org. This festival is one of the most respected and popular in Spain, and tickets for major performers typically sell out months in advance. During the festival, flamenco is free every night at midnight; ask the ticket office or TI for the venue.

From fall through spring, the City of Granada Orchestra offers popular weekly concerts that generally sell out quickly (€5–20, Sept–May only, Auditorio Manuel de Falla, ticket office in Corral de Carbón, Mon–Fri 12:00–14:00 & 17:00–19:00, Sat 12:00–14:00, closed Sun, www.orquesta ciudadgranada.es).

GRANADA

Granada at a Glance

▲▲▲**The Alhambra** The last and greatest Moorish palace, high-lighting the splendor of that civilization in the 13th and 14th centuries. Reservations are a must if you plan to visit during the day. **Hours:** The entire complex is open daily March–Oct 8:30–20:00, Nov–Feb 8:30–18:00. The Palacios Nazaries is open for nighttime visits March–Oct Tue–Sat 22:00–23:30, closed Sun–Mon; Nov–Feb Fri–Sat 20:00–21:30, closed Sun–Thu. See page 463.

▲▲**Royal Chapel** Lavish 16th-century Plateresque Gothic chapel with the tombs of Queen Isabel and King Ferdinand. **Hours:** March–Oct Mon–Sat 10:30–13:30 & 16:00–19:30, opens Sun at 11:00; Nov–Feb Mon–Sat 10:30–13:30 & 15:30–18:30, opens Sun at 11:00. See page 485.

▲▲**San Nicolás Viewpoint** Breathtaking vista over the Alhambra and the Albayzín. **Hours:** Always open; best at sunset. See page 490.

▲**Cathedral** The second-largest cathedral in Spain, unusual for its bright Renaissance interior. **Hours:** April–Oct Mon–Sat 10:45–13:30 & 16:00–20:00, Sun 16:00–20:00; Nov–March until 19:00. See page 487.

Alcaicería Tiny shopping lanes filled with tacky tourist shops. **Hours:** Always open, with shops open long hours. See page 479.

Corral del Carbón Granada's only surviving caravanserai (inn for traveling merchants), with impressive Moorish door. **Hours:** Always viewable. See page 479.

Paseo de los Tristes A prime strolling strip above the Darro River lined with eateries and peppered with Moorish history. **Hours:**

Internet Access: Many Internet points are scattered throughout Granada, often part of *locutorios* (call centers). A handy, friendly place is just across from Hotel Anacapri (on Calle Joaquín Costa).

Post Office: It's on Puerta Real (Mon–Fri 8:30–20:30, Sat 9:30–14:00, closed Sun, tel. 958-221-138).

Travel Agencies: All travel agencies book flights, and many also sell long-distance bus and train tickets. **Viajes Bonanza** sells it all at Calle Reyes Católicos 30 (Mon–Fri 9:00–13:00 & 17:00–20:00, Sat 10:00–13:30, closed Sun, tel. 958-223-578). Mega-chain **El Corte Inglés** sells plane and train tickets, but doesn't handle bus travel (Mon–Sat 10:00–21:00, closed Sun, Acera del Darro, floor 2, tel. 958-220-425).

Always open; best in the evenings. See page 483.

Hammam El Bañuelo 11-century ruins of Moorish baths. **Hours:** Unreliably Tue–Sat 10:00–14:00, closed Sun–Mon. See page 484.

Albayzín Spain's best old Moorish quarter. **Hours:** Always open but use caution after dark. See page 489.

Great Mosque of Granada Islamic house of worship featuring a minaret with a live call to prayer, an information center for the Muslim perspective on Granada history, and a courtyard with commanding views. **Hours:** Daily 11:00–14:00 & 18:00–21:00. See page 491.

Hammam Baños Árabes Tranquil spot for soaks and massages in Arab baths. **Hours:** Daily 10:00–24:00. See page 495.

Zambra Dance Touristy flamenco-like dance performance in Sacromonte district. **Hours:** Shows generally daily at 22:00. See page 493.

Center for the Interpretation of Sacromonte Digs into geology and cave building, as well as Roma (Gypsy) crafts, food, and music. **Hours:** April–Oct Tue–Sun 10:00–14:00 & 17:00–21:00; Nov–March Tue–Sun 10:00–14:00 & 16:00–19:00, closed Mon. See page 494.

Carthusian Monastery Lavish Baroque monastery on the outskirts of town. **Hours:** Daily April–Oct 10:00–13:00 & 16:00–20:00, Nov–March 10:00–13:00 & 15:00–18:00. See page 495.

Getting Around Granada

With cheap taxis, frisky minibuses, good city buses, and nearly all points of interest an easy walk from Plaza Nueva, you'll get around Granada easily.

Tickets for minibuses and city buses cost €1.20 per ride (buy from driver). Credibus magnetic cards save you money if you'll be riding often—or, since they're shareable, if you're part of a group (€5/7 trips, €10/16 trips, plus €2 for each card issued, buy from driver, valid on minibuses and city buses, no fee for connecting bus if you transfer within 45 min).

By Minibus: Handy little red minibuses, which cover the city center, depart every few minutes from Plaza Nueva and Plaza Isabel La Católica until late in the evening (about 22:30; some bus stops marked on map on page 468). Here are a few handy minibus routes to look for:

Bus #32 is the best for a trip up to the Alhambra, connecting the Alhambra and Albayzín (from the cathedral and Plaza Isabel La Católica, the bus goes up to the Alhambra, returns to Plaza Isabel La Católica, then loops through the Albayzín and back down Gran Vía).

Bus #31 does the Albayzín loop, departing from Plaza Nueva.

Bus #34 is the same as #31, with a side-trip into Sacromonte.

Bus #30 would normally be the most direct and quickest bet for getting up to the Alhambra, but its route—up Cuesta de Gomérez—is closed through 2010 while the Granada Gate is being restored. Although Cuesta de Gomérez is closed to vehicle traffic, eager pedestrians can still hike up to the Alhambra.

By City Bus: These are handy if you're visiting the Carthusian Monastery (bus #8) or going to the bus station (#3 or #33) or train station (#3–#9).

Tours in Granada

Walking Tours—Cicerone, run by María and Rosa, offers informative 2.5-hour tours (€12, show this book to save €2, kids under 14 free, March–Oct daily at 10:30, Nov–Feb Wed–Sun at 11:00; to book a tour, visit the kiosk labeled *Meeting Points* on Plaza de Bib-Rambla, or call mobile 607-691-676, 670-541-669, or 600-412-051; www.ciceronegranada.com, info@ciceronegranada.com). Cicerone's excellent guides describe the fitful and fascinating changes the city underwent as it morphed from a Moorish capital to a Christian one 500 years ago. While it doesn't enter any actual sights, the tour weaves together bits of the Moorish heritage that survive around the cathedral and the Albayzín. Tours start on Plaza de Bib-Rambla and finish on Plaza Nueva. Groups are small (may cancel if less than five show up, although you have the option of paying more for it to go). Visits are generally only in English, but may be in both English and Spanish on slow days.

Local Guides—Margarita Ortiz de Landázuri, an English-speaking guide, is a charming and effective teacher (tel. 958-221-406, www.alhambratours.com, info@alhambratours.com). If Margarita is busy, her partner, Miguel Ángel, and her cousin, Patricia Ortiz de Landazuri Quero (patlandazuri@yahoo.es, tel. 619-053-972), are also very good. Guide rates are standard (€130/2.5 hours, €260/day).

This is Granada Audio Tour—This service provides you with a pre-loaded MP3 player and map, and covers the entire city including the Alhambra with a fine audio tour. Two people get the system for up to five days for €15 (rent from kiosk on Plaza Nueva).

Olive Oil Tour—This company helps you explore Granada's countryside and taste some local olive oil. The morning tours include lunch; the afternoon tours don't (€55 with lunch, €38 without, both in English, tel. 958-559-643, mobile 651-147-504, www.olive oiltour.com, reservas@oliveoiltour.com).

Self-Guided Tour

▲▲▲The Alhambra

This last and greatest Moorish palace is one of Europe's top sights. Attracting up to 8,000 visitors a day, it's the reason most tourists

come to Granada. Nowhere else does the splendor of Moorish civilization shine so beautifully.

The last Moorish stronghold in Europe is, with all due respect, really a symbol of retreat. Granada was only a regional capital for centuries. Gradually the Christian Reconquista moved south, taking Córdoba (1237) and Sevilla (1248).

The Nazarids, one of the many diverse ethnic groups of Spanish Muslims, held together the last Moorish kingdom, which they ruled from Granada until 1492. As you tour their grand palace, remember that while Europe slumbered through the Dark Ages, Moorish magnificence blossomed—ornate stucco, plaster "stalactites," colors galore, scalloped windows framing Granada views, exuberant gardens, and water, water everywhere. Water—so rare and precious in most of the Islamic world—was the purest symbol of life to the Moors. The Alhambra is decorated with water: standing still, cascading, masking secret conversations, and dripdropping playfully.

Orientation: The Alhambra, not nearly as confusing as it might seem, consists of four sights clustered together atop a hill:

▲▲▲Palacios Nazaries—Exquisite Moorish palace, the one must-see sight.

▲Generalife Gardens—Fancy, manicured gardens with small summer palace.

▲Charles V's Palace—Christian Renaissance palace plopped on top of the Alhambra after the Reconquista, with a fine little Museo de la Alhambra (free entry).

Alcazaba—Empty old fort with tower and views.

These sights are described in more detail in "The Alhambra in Four Parts," below.

Cost: The Alcazaba fort, Palacios Nazaries, and Generalife

Gardens require a €12 combo-ticket. Reservations are essential if you want to see Palacios Nazaries during the day (see sidebar). If the Palacios Nazaries is booked up, consider getting the €6 ticket that covers only the Generalife Gardens and Alcazaba, so you can view the garden and fort during the day, and then visit the palace at night (see "The Alhambra by Moonlight," below). Only Charles V's Palace is free.

Hours: The Alhambra is open daily March–Oct 8:30–20:00, Nov–Feb 8:30–18:00 (ticket office opens at 8:00, last entry one hour before closing, tel. 902-441-221). The Palacios Nazaries is also open most evenings (see below).

The Alhambra by Moonlight: If you're frustrated by the reservation system, or just prefer doing things after dark, late-night visits to the Alhambra are easy (reservations are generally unnecessary—just buy your ticket upon arrival) and magical (less crowded and beautifully lit). The night visits only include the Palacios Nazaries (not the Alcazaba fort or the Generalife Gardens)—but, hey, the palace is 80 percent of the Alhambra's thrills anyway. For evening visits, it's open March–Oct Tue–Sat 22:00–23:30 (ticket office open 21:30–22:30), closed Sun–Mon; and Nov–Feb Fri–Sat 20:00–21:30 (ticket office open 19:30–20:30), closed Sun–Thu.

Getting to the Alhambra: There are three ways to get to the Alhambra:

1. From Plaza Nueva, hike 30 minutes up the street Cuesta de Gomérez. Keep going straight—you'll see the Alhambra high on your left. The ticket pavilion is on the far side of the Alhambra, near the Generalife Gardens.

2. From Plaza Isabel La Católica, catch a red #32 minibus, marked *Alhambra* (€1.20, runs every 15 min). There are three Alhambra stops: Justice Gate (below Palacios Nazaries and Charles V's Palace), Charles V, and Generalife (where you must pick up your tickets, closest to the gardens).

3. Take a taxi (€5, taxi stand on Plaza Nueva).

Don't drive. Though there's convenient parking near the entrance of the Alhambra (€1.50/hr), leaving via the one-way streets will send you into the traffic-clogged center of modern Granada.

Planning Your Visit: It's a 15-minute walk from the entry (at the top end) to Palacios Nazaries at the other end. Be sure to arrive at the Alhambra with enough time to make it to the palace before your allotted half-hour entry time slot ends. The ticket-checkers at Palacios Nazaries are strict. Remember that if you have an appointment for Palacios Nazaries after 14:00, you cannot get into the Alcazaba fort or the Generalife Gardens any earlier than 14:00. Once inside the Palacios Nazaries, you can stay as long as you want. Note that some rooms may be closed for renovation.

To minimize walking, see Charles V's Palace and the Alcazaba fort before your visit to Palacios Nazaries. When you finish touring the palace, you'll leave through the Partal Gardens near the Alhambra entrance, not far from the Generalife Gardens. Depending on the time, you can visit the Generalife Gardens before or after seeing Palacios Nazaries. If you have any time to kill before your palace appointment, do it luxuriously on the breezy view terrace of the parador bar (actually within the Alhambra walls). There are drinks, WCs, and guidebooks near the entrance of Palacios Nazaries, but none inside the actual palace.

If you're going to the Albayzín afterwards, catch minibus #32, which goes from the three Alhambra stops back through Plaza Isabel La Católica and then up into the Albayzín. Or, for a delightful escape, walk back into town along the Cuesta de los Chinos. (It starts near the ticket booth, by Restaurante La Mimbre and the minibus stop.) You'll walk on a desolate lane downhill along a stream, beneath the Alhambra ramparts, and past the sultan's cobbled horse lane leading up to Generalife Gardens. In 10 minutes you're back in town at Paseo de los Tristes. You can't get lost.

Audioguide: The €4 audioguide brings the palace to life, providing two hours of description for 48 stops (rent it at the entrance or at Charles V's Palace; you'll need to return it where you picked it up). Audioguides are not available for night visits.

Guidebooks: Consider getting a guidebook in town and reading it the night before to understand the layout and history of this remarkable sight before entering. The classic is *The Alhambra and the Generalife* (€10, includes great map, sold in town and throughout the Alhambra). I prefer the slick *Alhambra and Generalife in Focus*, which is more readable, has vibrant color photos, and costs less (€8, at bookstores). The "official guide" is not as good.

Eating: The only eateries within the Alhambra walls are the restaurant at the parador, the courtyard of the Hotel América (with pricey meals but affordable sandwiches and a great peaceful

Getting a Reservation for the Alhambra's Palacios Nazaries

Many tourists never get to see the Alhambra's Palacios Nazaries, because tickets sell out. Make a reservation as soon as you're ready to commit to a time (especially during Holy Week, on weekends, or on major holidays). During the off-season (July–Aug and winter), you might be able to walk right in. While things are improving, the crowds can still be unpredictable; luckily, getting a reservation is quite easy.

The Alhambra complex's top sight is the Moorish palace—Palacios Nazaries. Only 300 visitors are allowed to enter per half-hour (in 50-person spurts every five minutes). You must enter during the 30-minute time slot printed on your ticket. Once inside the palace, you can linger as long as you like. If your entry time to Palacios Nazaries is before 14:00, you can stroll the Alhambra grounds anytime in the morning, see the palace at your appointed time, and leave the Alhambra by 14:00 (although you can get away with staying longer in the fort, gardens, or palace, you won't be allowed to *enter* any of these sites after 14:00). If your ticket is stamped for 14:00 or later, you cannot go inside the Alhambra grounds any earlier than 14:00. For instance, if you have a reservation to visit Palacios Nazaries between 16:30 and 17:00, you can enter the Alhambra grounds starting at 14:00 and see the fort and Generalife Gardens before the palace. (Because of the time restriction on afternoon visits, morning tickets sell out the quickest. But for most travelers, an afternoon is ample time to see the site—the light is perfect, and there are fewer tour groups.)

Reserving in Advance: There are four options, each with a €1 surcharge.

• Order online at www.alhambra-tickets.es. This is easy and just takes a few minutes. You can reserve online up to three months in advance of your visit.

• Order by phone. Within Spain, dial 934-923-750 (cheaper), 902-888-001, or 902-505-061. To call internationally, dial the international access code first (00 from a European country, 011 from the US or Canada), then 34-934-923-750 (daily 8:00–24:00, can reserve between one day and a year in advance; while waiting for an operator, a recording tells you the date of the next available tickets). Pay with a credit card (Visa, MasterCard, or American Express).

• If you plan to stay at one of the fancier hotels, ask—when you book your hotel room—if the hotelier can make a reservation for you to visit the Alhambra the day after your arrival.

• If you buy a Bono Turístico city pass in advance, you can also book your Alhambra appointment then (explained earlier in "Helpful Hints" 459).

Picking Up Tickets: On the day of your tour, make sure you arrive at the Alhambra about an hour before your palace appointment, since the ticket line may require up to a 20-minute wait, and walking from the ticket office to the palace takes 15 minutes. Bring a photo ID and the same debit/credit card that you used to make the reservation. If you have a foreign card, you will need to wait in line at the windows marked *Retirada de Reservas* to pick up your tickets. Be prepared to enter your credit or debit card's PIN (this is the code required to withdraw cash, not your credit card's security code).

If You're in Granada Without a Palace Reservation: You have a number of options.

• Your hotel may able to book a reservation for you on short notice.

• Wake up early and stand in line. The Alhambra admits 7,800 visitors a day. Six thousand tickets are sold in advance. The remaining 1,800 are sold each day at the Alhambra ticket window labeled *Venta Directa*. The ticket office opens at 8:00, and on busy peak-season days, tickets can sell out quickly. (You'll hear periodic updates over the PA system about how many tickets are left for the day, which can help you judge whether it's worth waiting in line.) Generally, if you're in line by about 7:30, you'll get an entry time, probably for later that day. On a slow day, you'll get in right away. If the Palacios Nazaries is booked up during the day, you can get the €6 ticket that covers only the Generalife Gardens and the Alcazaba fort, then return to visit the palace at night (see "The Alhambra by Moonlight," 464).

• If you'll be staying in Granada at least two days, consider getting the Bono Turístico city pass, which comes with an entry time to the Alhambra.

• Take a tour of the Alhambra. The pricier hotels can book you on an expensive €49 GranaVisión tour that includes transportation to the Alhambra and a guided tour of the Palacios Nazaries (tel. 958-535-875, www.visitargranada.com).

• Easiest of all, simply go at night (Palacios Nazaries only; see "The Alhambra by Moonlight," 464).

The Alhambra

GRANADA

ⓑ Bus Stop ⟶ View ⊤ Taxi Stand
--- Footpath → One-Way Street
↓ 15-Min. Walk from Entrance to Palacios Nazaries

200 YARDS
200 METERS

N

DCH

GENERALIFE GARDENS

PALACE

THEATER

SHADE! ☺

WC

TICKETS

WC, BAR + ATM

P

P

ⓣ ⓑ
ⓞ

GENERALIFE STOP

ENTRANCE

CUESTA DE LOS CHINOS

PARADOR

To PASEO DE LOS TRISTES

SACROMONTE ←

← ALBAYZÍN

PALACIOS NAZARIES

DAMAS TOWER

PARTAL GARDENS

Charles V's Palace

Hotel América

CALLE REAL

CHARLES V STOP

To CITY

❸

❷

BAR

PLAZA ALJIBES

JUSTICE GATE

JUSTICE GATE STOP

ⓑ

TAXIS

ALCAZABA (FORT)

GRANADA GATE

CUESTA DE GOMÉREZ

To PLAZA NUEVA + MOST HOTELS ←

TORRES BERMEJAS

❶ Main Alhambra Entrance (Ticket Office)
❷ Wine Gate, WC & ATM
❸ Entrance to Palacios Nazaries
❹ Restaurante Jardines Alberto
❺ Hotel Guadalupe & Restaurante La Yedra Real

ambience), a small bar-café kiosk in front of the Alcazaba fort (near Palacios Nazaries entrance), and vending machines (at the WC) near Charles V's Palace. You're welcome to bring in a picnic as long as you eat it in a public area. There are plenty of better-value options around the parking lot and ticket booth at the top of the complex. **Restaurante La Yedra Real** is your best economic sit-down eatery, and is located over the Alhambra parking lot (Tue–Sun 9:30–17:00, closed Mon, €3 sandwiches, easy photo menu, air-con, efficient, Paseo de la Sabica 28, tel. 958-229-145). Across from the breezy Restaurante La Mimbre, the **Restaurante Jardines Alberto,** with a nice courtyard and a more formal menu, feels a little less touristy.

Photography: Photos are permitted.

The Alhambra in Four Parts

I've listed these sights in the order you're likely to visit them.

▲▲Charles V's Palace and the Museo de la Alhambra

It's only natural for a conquering king to build his own palace over his foe's palace, and that's exactly what the Christian king Charles

V did. The Palacios Nazaries wasn't good enough for Charles, so he built this new home, which was financed by a salt-in-the-wound tax on Granada's defeated Muslim population. With a unique circle-within-a-square design by Pedro Machuca, a devotee of Michelangelo and Raphael, this is Spain's most impressive Renaissance building. Stand in the circular court-yard surrounded by mottled marble columns, then climb the stairs. Perhaps Charles' palace was designed to have a dome, but it was never finished—his son, Philip II, abandoned it to build his own much more massive palace, El Escorial. Even without the dome, acoustics are perfect in the center—stand in the middle and sing your best aria. The palace doubles as one of the venues for the popular International Festival of Music and Dance.

The **Museo de la Alhambra** (ground floor of Charles V's Palace, free) shows off some of the Alhambra's best surviving Moorish art, along with one of the lions from Palacios Nazaries' fountain. While scant, the artifacts (with English descriptions) do help humanize the Alhambra visit. If you're early for your palace entry, spend your time in here (Tue–Sun 8:30–14:30, closed Mon). The Museo de Bellas Artes (upstairs, also free) is of little interest to most.

Alcazaba

This fort—the original "red castle" or "Alhambra"—is the oldest and most ruined part of the complex, offering exercise and fine

city views. What you see is from the mid-13th century, but there was probably a fort here in Roman times. Once upon a time, this tower defended a town (or medina) of 2,000 Muslims living within the Alhambra walls. From the top (looking north), find Plaza Nueva and the San Nicolás viewpoint (in the Albayzín). To the south are the Sierra Nevada mountains. Is anybody skiing today?

Think of that day in 1492 when the Christian cross and the flags of Aragon and Castile were raised on this tower, and the fleeing Moorish king Boabdil (Abu Abdullah in Arabic) looked back and wept. His mom chewed him out, saying, "You weep like a woman for what you couldn't defend like a man." With this defeat, more than seven centuries of Muslim rule in Spain came to an end. Much later, Napoleon stationed his troops at the Alhambra, contributing substantially to its ruin when he left.

▲▲▲Palacios Nazaries

During the 30-minute entry time slot stamped on your ticket, enter the jewel of the Alhambra: the Moorish royal palace. Once you're in, you can relax—there are no more time constraints.

You'll walk through three basic sections: royal offices, ceremonial rooms, and private quarters. Built mostly in the 14th century, this palace offers your best possible look at the refined, elegant Moorish civilization of Al-Andalus (Arabic for the Iberian Peninsula).

You'll visit rooms decorated from top to bottom with carved wood ceilings, stucco "stalactites," ceramic tiles, molded-plaster walls, and filigree windows. Open-air courtyards in the palace feature fountains with bubbling water like a desert oasis. A garden enlivened by lush vegetation and peaceful pools is the Quran's symbol of heaven. The palace is well-preserved, but the trick is to imagine it furnished and filled with Moorish life...sultans with hookah pipes lounging on pillows upon Persian carpets, heavy curtains on the windows, and ivory-studded

The Alhambra's Palacios Nazaries

wooden furniture. The whole place was painted with bright colors, many suggested by the Quran—red (blood), blue (heaven), green (oasis), and gold (wealth). And throughout the palace, walls, ceilings, vases, carpets, and tiles were covered with decorative patterns, mostly poems and verses of praise from the Quran written in calligraphy. Much of what is known about the Alhambra is known simply from reading the inscriptions that decorate its walls.

As you wander, keep the palace themes in mind: water, almost no figural images (forbidden by the Quran), "stalactite" ceilings—and few signs telling you where you are. As tempting as it might be to touch the stucco, don't—it is very susceptible to the oils from your hand. Use the map on this page to locate the essential stops listed below.

• *Begin by walking through a few administrative rooms (the* mexuar) *with a stunning Mecca-oriented prayer room (the* oratorio, *with a niche on the right facing Mecca) and a small courtyard with a round fountain, until you hit the big rectangular courtyard with a fish pond lined by a myrtle-bush hedge.*

❶ Court of Myrtles

Moors loved their patios—with a garden and water, under the sky. Women rarely went out, so they stayed in touch with nature in courtyards like the Court of Myrtles (Patio de los Arrayanes)—named for the two fragrant myrtle hedges that added to the courtyard's charm. One exotic theory about the function of this

GRANADA

The Alhambra Grounds

As you wander the grounds, remember that the Alhambra was once a city of 2,000 people fortified by a 1.5-mile rampart and 30 towers. The zone within the walls was the medina, a town with a general urban scene. As you stroll from the ticket booth down the garden-like Calle Real de la Alhambra to the palace, you're walking through the ruins of the medina (destroyed by the French in 1812).

The Palacios Nazaries, Alcazaba fort, and Generalife Gardens all have turnstiles. But the medina—with Charles V's Palace, a line of shops showing off traditional woodworking techniques, and the fancy Alhambra parador—is wide open to anyone with an Alhambra ticket.

It's especially fun to snoop around the historic **Parador de Granada San Francisco,** which—as a national monument—must technically be open to the public. Once a Moorish palace within the Alhambra, it was later converted into a Franciscan monastery, with a historic claim to fame: Its church is where the Catholic Monarchs (Ferdinand and Isabel) chose to be buried. For a peek, step in through the arch leading to a small garden area and reception. Enter to see the tomb, located in the open-air ruins of the church (just before the reception desk and the guests-only-beyond-this-point sign). The slab on the ground near the altar—a surviving bit from the mosque that was here before the church—marks the place where the greatest king and queen of Spain were buried until 1521 (when they were moved to the Royal Chapel—see page 485). The next room is a delightful former cloister. Now a hotel, the parador has a separate restaurant and café for non-guests.

The medina's main road dead-ended at the **Wine Gate** (Puerta del Vino), which protected the fortress. When you pass through the Wine Gate, you enter a courtyard that was originally a moat, then a reservoir (in Christian times). The well—now encased in a bar-kiosk—is still a place for cold drinks. If you're done with your Alhambra visit, you can exit down to the city from the Wine Gate.

complex is that the living quarters for the women (harem) were upstairs—the Quran let a man have four wives and an unlimited number of concubines—"all the women you can maintain with dignity." Notice the wooden screens (erected by jealous husbands) that allowed the cloistered women to look out without being clearly seen. The less interesting, but more likely, theory is that the upstairs was for winter use, and the cooler ground level was for the hotter summer.

• *Head left from the entry through gigantic wooden doors into the long narrow antechamber to the throne room, called the...*

❷ Boat Room

It's understandable that many think the Boat Room (Sala de la Barca) is named for the upside-down-hull shape of its fine cedar ceiling. But the name is actually derived from the Arab word *baraka,* meaning "divine blessing and luck" (which was corrupted to *barca,* the Spanish word for "boat"). As you passed through this room, blessings and luck are exactly what you'd need—because in the next room, you'd be face-to-face with the sultan.

• *Oh, it's your turn. Enter the ornate throne room.*

❸ Grand Hall of the Ambassadors

The palace's largest room, the Gran Salón de los Embajadores, functioned as the throne room. It was here that the sultan, seated on a throne opposite the entrance, received foreign emissaries. Ogle the room—a perfect cube—from top to bottom. The star-studded, domed wooden ceiling (8,017 inlaid pieces like a giant jigsaw puzzle) suggests the complexity of Allah's infinite universe. Wooden "stalactites" form the cornice, running around the entire base of the ceiling. The stucco walls, even without their original paint and gilding, are still glorious, decorated with ornamental flowers made by pressing a mold into the wet plaster. The filigree windows once held stained glass and had heavy drapes to block out the heat. Some precious 16th-century tiles survive in the center of the floor.

A visitor here would have stepped from the glaring Court of Myrtles into this dim, cool, incense-filled world, to meet the silhouetted sultan. Imagine the alcoves functioning busily as work stations, and the light at sunrise or sunset, rich and warm, filling the room.

Note the finely carved Arabic script. Muslims avoided making images of living creatures—that was God's work. But they could carve decorative religious messages. One phrase—"only Allah is victorious"—is repeated 9,000 times throughout the palace. Find the character for "Allah"—it looks like a cursive W with a nose on its left side. The swoopy toboggan blades underneath are a kind of artistic punctuation setting off one phrase.

In 1492, two historic events likely took place in this room. Culminating a 700-year-long battle, the Reconquista was completed here as the last Moorish king, Boabdil, signed the terms of his surrender before eventually leaving for Africa.

And it was here that Columbus made his pitch to Isabel and Ferdinand to finance a sea voyage to the Orient. Imagine the scene:

GRANADA

Islamic Art

Rather than making paintings and statues, Islamic artists expressed themselves with beautiful but functional objects. Ceramics (often blue and white, or green and white), carpets, glazed tile panels, stucco-work ceilings, and glass tableware are covered with complex patterns. The intricate interweaving, repetition, and unending lines suggest the complex, infinite nature of God, known to Muslims as Allah.

You'll see only a few pictures of humans or animals, since the Islamic religion was wary of any "graven images" or idols forbidden by God. However, secular art by Muslims for their homes and palaces was not bound by this restriction; you'll get an occasional glimpse of realistic art featuring men and women enjoying a garden paradise, a symbol of the Muslim heaven.

Look for floral patterns (twining vines, flowers, and arabesques) and geometric designs (stars and diamonds). The most common pattern is calligraphy—elaborate lettering of an inscription in Arabic, the language of the Quran. A quote from the Quran on a vase or lamp combines the power of the message with the beauty of the calligraphy.

The king, the queen, and the greatest minds from the University of Salamanca gathered here while Columbus produced maps and pie charts to make his case that he could sail west to reach the East. Ferdinand and the professors laughed and called Columbus mad—not because they thought the world was flat (most educated people knew otherwise), but because they thought Columbus had underestimated the size of the globe, and thus the length and cost of the journey.

But Isabel said *"Sí, señor."* Columbus fell to his knees (promising to pack light, wear a money belt, and use the most current guidebook available).

Opposite the Boat Room entrance, photographers pause for a picture-perfect view of the tower reflected in the Court of Myrtles pool. This was the original palace entrance (before Charles V's Palace was built).

• *Continue deeper into the palace, to a courtyard where, 600 years ago, only the royal family and their servants could enter. It's the much-photographed...*

❹ Courtyard of the Lions

The Patio de los Leones features a fountain that's usually ringed with 12 lions; however, they've been missing for the past two years

as they undergo restoration (they'll probably be back in place sometime in 2010). One of the lions is on display in the Museo de la Alhambra inside Charles V's Palace.

Why did the fountain have 12 lions? Since the fountain was a gift from a Jewish leader celebrating good relations with the sultan (Granada had a big Jewish community), the lions probably represent the 12 tribes of Israel. During Moorish times, the fountain functioned as a clock, with a different lion spouting water each hour. (Conquering Christians disassembled the fountain to see how it worked, and it's never worked since.) From the center, four streams went out—figuratively to the corners of the earth and literally to various apartments of the royal family. Notice how the court, with its 124 columns, resembles the cloister of a Catholic monastery. The craftsmanship is first-class. For example, the lead fittings between the pre-cut sections of the columns allow things to flex during an earthquake, preventing destruction during shakes.

Six hundred years ago, the Muslim Moors could read the Quranic poetry that ornaments this court, and they could understand the symbolism of this lush, enclosed garden, considered the embodiment of paradise or truth. ("How beautiful is this garden / where the flowers of Earth rival the stars of Heaven. / What can compare with this alabaster fountain, gushing crystal-clear water? / Nothing except the fullest moon, pouring light from an unclouded sky.") Imagine—they appreciated this part of the palace even more than we do today.

• *On the right, off the courtyard, is a square room called the...*

❺ Hall of the Abencerrajes

This was the sultan's living room, with an exquisite ceiling based on the eight-sided Muslim star. According to legend, the father of Boabdil took a new wife and wanted to disinherit the children of his first marriage—one of whom was Boabdil. In order to deny power to Boabdil and his siblings, the sultan killed nearly the entire pre-Boabdil Abencerraje family. He thought this would pave the way for the son of his new wife to be the next sultan. He happily stacked 36 Abencerraje heads in the pool under the sumptuous honeycombed stucco ceiling in this hall, called the Sala de los Abencerrajes. But his scheme failed, and Boabdil ultimately assumed the throne. Bloody power struggles like this were the norm here in the Alhambra.

• *At the end of the court opposite where you entered is the...*

❻ Hall of the Kings

Notice the ceilings of the three chambers branching off this gallery, the Hall of the Kings (Sala de los Reyes). Breaking from the tradition of imageless art, paintings on the goat-leather ceiling depict scenes of the sultan and his family. The center room's group portrait shows the first 10 of the Alhambra's 22 sultans. The scene is a fantasy, since these people lived over a span of many generations. The two end rooms display scenes of princely pastimes, such as hunting and shooting skeet. In a palace otherwise devoid of figures, these offer a rare look at royal life in the palace.

• *As you exit, you'll pass doors leading right and left to a 14th-century WC plumbed by running water and stairs up to the harem. Next is the...*

❼ Hall of Two Sisters

The Sala de Dos Hermanas—nicknamed for the giant twin slabs of white marble on the floor flanking the fountain—has another oh-wow stucco ceiling lit from below by clerestory windows. The room features geometric patterns and stylized Arabic script quoting verses from the Quran. If the inlaid color tiles look "Escher-esque," you've got it backwards: Escher is Alhambra-esque. M. C. Escher was inspired by these very patterns on his visit. Study the patterns—they remind us of the Moorish expertise in math. The sitting room (farthest from the entry) has low windows, because Moorish people sat on the floor. Some rare stained glass survives in the ceiling. From here the sultana enjoyed a grand view of medieval city (before the 16th-century wing was added that blocks the view today).

• *That's about it for the palace. From here, you wander past the domed roofs of the old baths down a hallway to a pair of rooms decorated with a mahogany ceiling. Marked with a large plaque is the...*

❽ Washington Irving Room

Washington Irving wrote *Tales of the Alhambra* in this room. While living in Spain in 1829, Irving stayed in the Alhambra. It was a romantic time, when the palace was home to Gypsies and donkeys. His "tales" kindled interest in the Alhambra, causing it to become recognized as a national treasure. A plaque on the wall thanks Irving, who later served as the US ambassador to Spain (1842–1846). Here's a quote from Irving's *The Alhambra by Moonlight:* "On such heavenly nights I would sit for hours at my window inhaling the sweetness of the garden, and musing on the

checkered fortunes of those whose history was dimly shadowed out in the elegant memorials around."
• *As you leave, stop at the open-air...*

❾ Hallway with a View

Here you'll enjoy the best-in-the-palace view of the labyrinthine Albayzín—the old Moorish town on the opposite hillside. Find the famous San Nicolás view-point (below where the white San Nicolás church tower breaks the horizon). Creeping into the mountains on the right are the Gypsy neighborhoods of Sacromonte. Still circling old Granada is the Moorish wall (built in the 1400s to protect the city's population, swollen by Muslim refugees

driven south by the Reconquista). For more on Albayzín sights, see page 489.

The Patio de Lindaraja (with its maze-like hedge pattern garden) marks the end of the palace visit. Before exiting, you can detour right into the adjacent "Secrets Room"—stark brick rooms of the former bath with fun acoustics. Whisper into a corner, and your friend—with an ear to the wall—can hear you in the opposite corner. Try talking in the exact center.

• *Leaving the palace, you enter the Partal Gardens (El Partal), where you can enjoy the reflecting pond of the Partal Palace. Climb a few stairs, continue through the gardens, and follow signs directing you left to the Generalife Gardens or right to the exit. If you're interested in poking around the Alhambra grounds, exit and do it now before entering the Generalife (because you can't easily backtrack into the Alhambra grounds after leaving the gardens).*

▲ Generalife Gardens

If you have a long wait before your entry to the Palacios Nazaries,

tour these gardens first, then the Alcazaba fort and Charles V's Palace.

The sultan's vegetable and fruit garden and summer palace, called the Generalife (hen-eh-raw-LEEF-ay), are a short hike uphill past the ticket office. The 2,000 residents of the Alhambra enjoyed the fresh fruit and veggies grown here. But most importantly, this little palace provided the sultan with a cool and quiet summer escape.

Follow the simple one-way path through the sprawling gardens (planted only in the 1930s—in Moorish times, there were no cypress trees here). The sleek, modern amphitheater was recently renovated and continues to be an important concert venue for Granada. It sees most activity during the International Festival of Music and Dance (see page 459). Many of the world's greatest artists have performed here, including Arthur Rubenstein, Rudolf Nureyev, and Margot Fonteyn. At the small palace, pass through the dismounting room (imagine dismounting onto the helpful stone ledge, and letting your horse drink in the trough here). Step past the guarded entry into the most perfect Arabian garden in Andalucía.

This summer home of the Moorish kings, the closest thing on earth to the Quran's description of heaven, was planted more than 600 years ago—remarkable longevity for a European garden. Five-hundred-year-old paintings show it looking essentially the same as it does today. The flowers, herbs, aromas, and water are exquisite... even for a sultan. Up the Darro River, the royal aqueduct diverted a life-giving stream of water into the Alhambra. It was channeled through this extra-long decorative fountain to irrigate the bigger garden outside, then along an aqueduct into the Alhambra for its 2,000 thirsty residents. While the splashing fountains are a delight, they are a 19th-century addition. The Moors liked a peaceful pond instead.

At the end of the pond, you enter the sultan's tiny three-room summer palace. From the end, climb 10 steps into the Christian Renaissance gardens. The ancient decrepit tree rising over the pond inspired Washington Irving, who wrote that this must be the "only surviving witness to the wonders of that age of Al-Andalus."

Exiting left to the top floor of the palace reveals a stunning view of the Albayzín. Don't climb the *Escalera del Agua* unless you need the exercise...it only goes up and then back down. Pass the turnstile (pausing for a view back down into the palace garden) and follow *salida* (exit) signs as you circle back to where you entered the Generalife.

Your visit to the Alhambra is complete, and you've earned your reward. "Surely Allah will make those who believe and do good deeds enter gardens beneath which rivers flow; they shall be adorned therein with bracelets of gold and pearls, and their garments therein shall be of silk" (Quran 22.23).

Sights in Granada

▲▲ Old Town Walk: The Transition from Moorish to Christian

This short walk orients you to the old town, and covers all the essential sights beyond the Alhambra. At the same time it helps you grasp the dramatic changes brought about as the Reconquista finished expelling Muslim culture and re-established Christian rule here.

• *Start at Corral del Carbón, near the Plaza de Carmen.*

❶ **Corral del Carbón:** A caravanserai (of Silk Road fame) was a protected place for merchants to rest their camels, spend the night, get a bite to eat, and spin yarns. This, the only surviving caravanserai of Granada's original 14, was just a block away from the silk market (Alcaicería; the next stop on this walk). Stepping through the caravanserai's fine Moorish door, you find a square with 14th-century Moorish brickwork surrounding a water fountain. This plain-yet-elegant structure evokes the times when traders would gather here with exotic goods and tales from across the Muslim world.

It's a common mistake to think of the Muslim Moors as somehow not Spanish. They lived here for seven centuries and were really just as "indigenous" as the Romans, Goths, and Celts. While the Moors were Muslim, they were no more connected to Arabia than they were to France.

After the Reconquista, this space was used as a coal storage facility (hence the name "Carbón"). These days it houses two offices where you can buy tickets for musical events.

• *From the caravanserai, walk down Puente del Carbón to the big street named Calle Reyes Católicos (for the "Catholic monarchs" Ferdinand and Isabel, who finally conquered the Moors). The street covers a river that once ran openly here, with a series of bridges (like the* carbón *bridge...Puente del Carbón) lacing together the two parts of town.*

Continue one block farther to the yellow gate marked "Alcaicería." The pedestrian street, Zacatín, was the main drag, which ran parallel to the river before it was covered. Today it's a favorite paseo destination, busy each evening with strollers. Pass through the Alcaicería gate and walk 20 yards into the old market to the first intersection.

❷ **Alcaicería:** Originally a Moorish silk market with 200 shops, the Alcaicería (al-kai-thay-REE-ah) was filled with precious salt, silver,

Granada's Old Town Walk

B BUS STOP W/#S
#32 To ALHAMBRA
#31 To ALBAYZÍN

P PARKING

T TAXI STAND

→ ENTRY POINT TO SIGHTS

TO TRAIN + BUS STATIONS

100 YARDS
100 METERS

ALBAYZÍN
MOORISH QUARTER

TO SAN NICOLÁS VIEWPOINT + PLAZA LARGA →

TO SACRO-MONTE

GRAN VIA DE COLÓN

CALLE VAL.

CALD. NUEVA   S. GREGORIO

CETTI.   ELVIRA   CALD. VIEJA   CÁRCEL ALTA   AIRE

MERCADO SAN AGUSTÍN   **P**

CATHEDRAL + ROYAL CHAPEL

PL. PESC.

3 PLAZA DE BIB-RAMBLA   **i**

ERMITA   ZACATÍN

OFICIOS

2

5

4

LA MADRAZA

ALMIR.

COSTA   ABEN.   SILL.   PAN.

DARRO   **8**

PLAZA NUEVA   PL. S. ANA

T   **7**   #31   **B**   S. ANA

CALLE REYES CATÓLICOS

6 PLAZA ISABEL LA CATÓLICA

1   START

CUCH.   ANIMAS

PAVANERAS

CUESTA GOMÉREZ

CUESTA S. ANA   **i**

TO ALHAMBRA →

CALLE NAVAS

PLAZA DEL CARMEN

← TO FREEWAY EXIT #129   PUERTA REAL

1 Corral del Carbón
2 Alcaicería
3 Plaza de Bib-Rambla
4 Cathedral
5 Royal Chapel Square
6 Plaza Isabel La Católica
7 Plaza Nueva
8 To Paseo de los Tristes & Moorish Baths

spices, and silk. It had 10 armed gates and its own guards. Silk was huge in Moorish times (silkworm-friendly mulberry trees flourished in the countryside), a product so important that the sultans controlled and guarded it by constructing this fine, fortified market. After the Reconquista, the Christians realized this market was good for business and didn't mess with it. Later, the more zealous Philip II had it shut down. A terrible fire in 1850 destroyed what was left. Today's Alcaicería was rebuilt in the late 1800s as a tourist souk (marketplace) to complement the romantic image of Granada popularized by the writings of Washington Irving.

Explore the mesh of tiny shopping lanes: overpriced trinkets, popcorn machines popping, men selling balloons, leather goods spread out on streets, kids playing soccer, barking dogs, dogged shoe-shine boys, and the whirring grind of bicycle-powered knife sharpeners. You'll invariably meet obnoxious and persistent Gypsy women pushing their sprigs on innocents in order to extort money. Be strong.

• *Turn left down Ermita lane. In 50 yards you leave the market via another fortified gate and enter a big square. The Neptune fountain marks the center of the...*

❸ **Plaza de Bib-Rambla:** This exuberant square, just two blocks behind the cathedral (from the fountain you can see its blocky spire peeking above the big red building) was once the center of Moorish Granada. While Moorish rule of Spain lasted 700 years, the last couple of centuries were a period of decline as Muslim culture split under weak leadership and Christian forces grew more determined. The last remnants of the Moorish kingdom united and ruled from Granada. As Muslims fled south from reconquered lands, Granada was flooded with refugees. By 1400 Granada had 120,000 people, huge for Europe. This was the main square, the focal point of market and festivals, but it was much smaller then than now, pushed in by the jam-packed city.

Under Christian rule, Moors and Jews were initially recognized as good for business and tolerated, and this area became the Moorish ghetto. Then, with the Inquisition (Philip II, c. 1550), ideology trumped pragmatism, and Jews and Muslims were evicted or forced to convert. The elegant square you see today was built, and built big. In-your-face Catholic processions started here. To assert Christian rule, all the trappings of Christian power were layered upon what had been the trappings of Moorish power. Between here and the cathedral were the Christian University (the big red building) and the adjacent archbishop's palace.

Today Plaza de Bib-Rambla is fine for coffee or a meal amid the color and fragrance of flower stalls and the burbling of its Neptune-topped fountain. It remains a multi-generational hangout where it seems everyone is enjoying a peaceful retirement. A block away (if Neptune turned 180 degrees and walked 100 yards), the Pescadería square is a smaller, similarly lively version of Bib-Rambla.

• *Leave the square toward the cathedral, heading down the lane between the big red building and Bar Manolo. In a block you come to a small square fronting a very big church.*

❹ **Cathedral:** Wow, the cathedral facade just screams triumph. In fact, its design is based on a triumphal arch and it was built over a destroyed mosque. Five hundred yards away, there was open space outside the city wall with good soil. But the Christian conquerors said, "No way." Instead, they destroyed the mosque and built their cathedral right here on difficult, sandy soil. This was the place where the people of Granada traditionally worshipped—and now they would worship as Christians.

The church has a Gothic foundation and was built mostly in the Renaissance style. Hometown artist Alonso Cano finished it, at the king's request, in Baroque. Accentuating the power of the Roman Catholic Church, the emphasis here is on Mary rather than Christ. The facade declares *Ave Maria*. (This was Counter-Reformation time and the Church was threatened by Protestant Christians. Mary was also more palatable to Muslim converts—she is revered in the Quran.)

• *The cathedral entrance is on the opposite side (and the interior is described in the self-guided cathedral tour, later in this chapter). Walk around to the right, popping into the Baroque chapel if open. Then circle around the cathedral until you reach the small square facing the Royal Chapel.*

❺ **Royal Chapel Square:** This square was once ringed by important Moorish buildings. A hammam (public bath), madrassa (school), caravanserai (Day's Inn), the silk market, and the leading mosque were all right here. With Christian rule, the madrassa (the building with the walls painted in 3-D Baroque style) because Granada's first City Hall. The royal coffins were moved from the Alhambra's parador to the oval Royal Chapel in 1521. (For a self-guided tour of the Royal Chapel, see next section.)

• *Continue up the cobbled, stepped lane to the big street, Gran Vía. With the arrival of cars and the modern age, the people of Granada wanted a Parisian-style boulevard. In the early 20th century they mercilessly cut through the old town and created the Gran Vía with its French-style buildings—in the process destroying everything in its path, including many historic convents.*

From here you could enter the cathedral, catch minibus #32 to the Alhambra, or go left two blocks, cross the street, and walk up Calle Cárcel Baja into the Albayzín. But for now, let's continue our orientation tour. Turn right and walk down Gran Vía to the big square ahead.

❻ **Plaza Isabel La Católica:** Granada's two grand boulevards, Gran Vía and Calle Reyes Católicos, meet a block off Plaza Nueva at Plaza Isabel La Católica. Above the fountain, a fine statue shows Columbus unfurling a long contract with Isabel. It lists the terms of Columbus' *mccclxxxxii* voyage: "Forasmuch as you, Columbus, are going by our command to discover and subdue some Islands and Continents in the ocean...." The two reliefs show the big events in Granada of 1492: Isabel and Ferdinand accepting Columbus' proposal and a stirring battle scene (which never happened) at the walls of the Alhambra.

Isabel was driven by her desire to spread Catholicism. Columbus was driven by his desire for money. As a reward for adding territory to Spain's Catholic empire, Isabel promised Columbus the ranks of Admiral of the Oceans and Governor of the New World. To sweeten the pie, she tossed in one-eighth of all the riches he brought home. Isabel died thinking that Columbus had found India or China. Columbus died poor and disillusioned.

Calle Reyes Católicos leads from this square to the busy intersection with Puerta Real. From there, Acera del Darro takes you through modern Granada to the river via the huge El Corte Inglés department store and lots of modern commerce. This area erupts with locals out strolling each night. For the best Granada paseo, wander the streets around here around 19:00.

• *Follow Calle Reyes Católicos a couple of blocks to the left where you'll find another square.*

❼ **Plaza Nueva:** Long a leading square in Granada, Plaza Nueva is dominated by the Palace of Justice (grand Baroque facade with green Andalusian flag). The fountain is capped by a stylized pomegranate—the symbol of the city, always open and fertile. The main action here is the comings and goings of the busy little shuttle buses serving the Alhambra and Albayzín. The local hippie community, nicknamed the *pies negros* (black feet) for obvious reasons, hangs out here and on Calle Elvira. They squat—with their dogs and guitars—in abandoned caves above those the Gypsies occupy in Sacromonte. Many are the children of rich Spanish families from the north, hell-bent on disappointing their high-achieving parents.

• *Our tour continues with a stroll up Paseo de los Tristes. Leave Plaza Nueva opposite where you entered and walk up the Darro River Valley. This is particularly enjoyable in the cool of the evening. If you're tired, note that minibuses #31 and #32 run from Plaza Nueva, up this lane, and then hook into and through the Albayzín quarter.*

❽ **Paseo de los Tristes:** This "Walk of the Sad Ones" was once the route of funeral processions to the cemetery at the edge of town. Leaving Plaza Nueva you pass the Church of Santa Ana. This was originally a mosque—the church tower replaced a minaret. Notice the ceramic brickwork. This is Mudejar art, a technique of Moorish craftsmen later employed by Christians. Inside you'll see a fine Alhambra-style cedar ceiling.

Follow Carrera del Darro high above the River Darro at the base of the Alhambra (look down by the river for a glimpse of feral cats). Six miles upstream, part of the Darro is diverted to provide water for the Alhambra's many fountains. Past the church on the left is Santa Catalina de Zafra, a convent of cloistered nuns (they worship behind a screen that divides the church's rich interior in half).

Farther ahead is the broken nub of a once-grand 11th-century bridge over the river, leading to the Alhambra. Notice two slits in the column: One held an iron portcullis to keep bad guys from entering the town via the river. The second held a solid door that was lowered to build up water, then released to flush out the river-bed and keep it clean.

• *Across from the remains of the bridge (and the stop for minibuses #31 and #34) is the brick facade of an evocative Moorish bath, the Hammam El Bañuelo.*

❾ **Hammam El Bañuelo (Moorish Baths):** In Moorish times, hammams (public baths) were a big part of the community (working-class homes didn't have bathrooms). Baths were strictly segregated (as they are today) and functioned as more than a place to wash: Business was done here, and it was a social meeting point. In Christian times, it was assumed that conspiracies brewed in these baths—therefore, only a few of them survive. This place gives you the chance to explore the stark but evocative ruins of an 11th-century Moorish public bath (free, unreliably Tue–Sat 10:00–14:00, closed Sun–Mon, borrow the English description at the door).

Entering the baths, you pass the house of the keeper and the foyer, then visit the cold room, the warm room (where services like massage were offered), and finally the hot or steam room. Beyond that, you can see the oven that generated the heat, which flowed under the hypocaust-style floor tiles (getting less hot with distance). The romantic little holes in the ceiling once had stained-glass louvers that attendants opened and closed with sticks to regulate the heat and steaminess. While Romans soaked in their pools, Muslims just doused. Rather than being totally immersed, people scooped and splashed water over themselves. Imagine attendants stoking the fires under the metal boiler...while people in towels and wooden slippers (to protect their feet from the heated floors) enjoyed all the spa services you can imagine as beams of light slashed through the mist. This was a great social mixer. As all were naked, class distinctions disappeared—elites learned the latest from commoners. Mothers found matches for their kids. The popular Muslim phrase summed up the attraction of the baths: "This is where anyone would spend their last coin."

• *Continuing straight ahead, you see the Church of San Pedro, the parish church of Sacromonte's Gypsy community (across from the Archaeological Museum). Within its rich interior is an ornate oxcart used to carry the host on the annual pilgrimage to Rocio near the Portuguese border. This walk ends at Paseo de los Tristes—with its restaurant tables spilling*

*out under the floodlit Alhambra. From here, the road arcs up into
Sacromonte.*

▲▲Royal Chapel (Capilla Real)

Without a doubt Granada's top Christian sight, this lavish
chapel holds the dreams—and bodies—of Queen Isabel and
King Ferdinand. The "Catholic Monarchs" were all about the
Reconquista. Their marriage united the Aragon and Castile kingdoms, allowing an acceleration of the Christian and Spanish push
south. In its last 10 years, the Reconquista snowballed. This last
Moorish capital—symbolic of their victory—was their chosen
burial place.

Cost, Hours, Location: €3.50; March–Oct Mon–Sat 10:30–
13:30 & 16:00–19:30, opens Sun at 11:00; Nov–Feb Mon–Sat
10:30–13:30 & 15:30–18:30, opens Sun at 11:00; no photos, entrance
on Calle Oficios, just off Gran Vía—go through iron gate, tel. 958-
227-848.

❷ Self-Guided Tour: In the lobby, before you show your
ticket and enter the chapel, notice the **painting of Boabdil** (on
the black horse) giving the key of Granada to the conquering King
Ferdinand. Boabdil wanted to fall to his knees, but the Spanish
king, who had great respect for his Moorish foe, embraced him
instead. They fought a long and noble war (for instance, respect-
fully returning the bodies of dead soldiers). Ferdinand is in red,
and Isabel is behind him wearing a crown. The painting is flanked
by two large portraits of Ferdinand and Isabel. Two small exhibits
celebrate the 500th anniversaries of the death of Isabel in 2004
and of Philip the Fair (her son-in-law) in 2006.

Isabel decided to make Granada the capital of Spain (and
burial place for Spanish royalty) for three reasons: 1) With the
conquest of this city, Christianity had finally overcome Islam in
Europe; 2) her marriage with Ferdinand, followed by the conquest
of Granada, had marked the beginning of a united Spain; and 3) in
Granada, she agreed to sponsor Columbus.

Show your ticket and step into the **chapel.** It's Plateresque
Gothic—light and lacy silver-filigree style, named for and inspired
by the fine silverwork of the Moors. The chapel's interior was originally austere, with fancy touches added later by Ferdinand and
Isabel's grandson Charles V. Five hundred years ago, this was the
most lavish interior money could buy. Ferdinand and Isabel spent
a quarter of their wealth on it. Because of its speedy completion
(1506–1521), the architecture is unusually harmonious.

The **four royal tombs** are Renaissance-style. Carved in Italy
in 1521 out of Carrara marble, they were sent by ship to Spain. The
faces—based on death masks—are considered accurate. If you're
looking at the altar, **Ferdinand** and **Isabel** are on the right. (Isabel

fans attribute the bigger dent she puts in the pillow to her larger brain.) Isabel's contemporaries described the queen as being of medium height, with auburn hair and blue eyes, and possessing a serious, modest, and gentle personality. (Compare Ferdinand and Isabel's tomb statues with the painted and gilded wood statues of them kneeling in prayer, flanking the altarpiece.)

Philip the Fair and **Juana the Mad** (who succeeded Ferdinand and Isabel) lie on the left. Philip was so "Fair" that it drove the insanely jealous Juana "Mad." Philip died young, and for two years Juana kept his casket at her bedside, kissing his embalmed body good night. Philip and Juana's son, Charles V (known as Carlos I in Spain), was a key figure in European history, as his coronation merged the Holy Roman Empire (Philip the Fair's Habsburg domain) with Juana's Spanish empire. Europe's top king, Charles V ruled a vast empire stretching from Holland to Sicily, from Bohemia to Bolivia (1519–1556, see sight listing for his palace within the Alhambra, page 469).

When Philip II, the son of Charles V, decided to build El Escorial and establish Madrid as the single capital of a single Spain, Granada lost power and importance. More importantly, Spain began to decline. After the reign of Charles V, Spain squandered her vast wealth trying to maintain this impossibly huge empire. The country's rulers did it not only for material riches, but to defend the romantic, quixotic dream of a Catholic empire—ruled by one divinely ordained Catholic monarch—against an irrepressible tide of nationalism and Protestantism that was sweeping across the vast Habsburg holdings in Central and Eastern Europe. Spain's relatively poor modern history can be blamed, in part, on its people's stubborn unwillingness to accept the end of this old-regime notion. Even Franco borrowed symbols from the Catholic Monarchs to legitimize his dictatorship and keep the 500-year-old legacy alive. Today's Spaniards reflect that the momentous marriage that created their country also sucked them into centuries of European squabbling, eventually leaving Spain impoverished.

Look at the fine carving on the tombs. It's a humanistic statement, with these healthy, organic, realistic figures rising out of the Gothic age.

From the feet of the marble tombs, step downstairs to see the actual **coffins.** They are plain. Ferdinand and Isabel were originally buried in the Franciscan monastery (in what is today the parador, up at the Alhambra). You're standing in front of the two people who created Spain. The fifth coffin (on right, marked *PM*) belongs to a young Prince Michael, who would have been king of a united Spain and Portugal. (A sad—but too long—story...)

The **high altar** is one of the finest Renaissance works in Spain. It's dedicated to two Johns: the Baptist and the Evangelist.

In the center, you can see the Baptist and the Evangelist chatting as if over tapas—an appropriately humanistic scene. Scenes from the Baptist's life are on the left: John beheaded after Salomé's fine dancing, and (below) John baptizing Jesus. Scenes from the Evangelist's life are on the right: John's martyrdom (a failed attempt to boil him alive in oil), and John on Patmos (where he wrote the last book of the Bible, Revelation). John is talking to the eagle that, according to tradition, flew him to heaven. A colorful series of reliefs at the bottom level recalls the Christian conquest of the Moors (left to right): Ferdinand, Boabdil with army and key to Alhambra, Moors expelled from Alhambra (right of altar table), conversion of Muslims by tonsured monks, and Ferdinand again.

A finely carved Plateresque arch, with the royal initials "F" and "Y," leads to a small glass pyramid in the **treasury**. This holds Queen Isabel's silver crown ringed with pomegranates (symbolizing Granada), her scepter, and King Ferdinand's sword. Beside the entry arch (on right) you'll see the devout Isabel's prayer book, in which she followed the Mass. The book and its sturdy box date from 1496. According to legend, the fancy box on the other side of the door is supposedly the one that Isabel (cash-poor because of her military expenses) filled with jewels and gave to Columbus. Columbus sold these to finance his journey. In the corner (and also behind glass) is the ornate silver-and-gold cross that Cardinal Mendoza, staunch supporter of Queen Isabel, carried into the Alhambra on that historic day in 1492. Next, the big silk, silver-and-gold tapestry is the altar banner for the mobile campaign chapel of Ferdinand and Isabel, who always traveled with their army. In the next case, you'll see the original Christian army flags raised over the Alhambra in 1492.

The room holds the first great art collection ever established by a woman. Queen Isabel amassed more than 200 important paintings. After Napoleon's visit, only 30 remained. Even so, this is a fine collection, all on wood, featuring works by Sandro Botticelli, Pietro Perugino, the Flemish master Hans Memling, and some less-famous Spanish masters.

Finally, at the end of the room, the two carved sculptures of Ferdinand and Isabel were the originals from the high altar. Charles V considered these primitive and replaced them with the ones you saw earlier.

To reach the cathedral (described next), exit behind Isabel, out through one iron gate and then immediately through the neighboring iron gate.

▲Cathedral

One of only two Renaissance churches in Spain (the other is in Córdoba), Granada's cathedral is the second-largest in Spain after

Sevilla's. While it was started as a Gothic church, it was built using Renaissance elements, and then decorated in Baroque style.

Cost, Hours, Location: €3.50; April–Oct Mon–Sat 10:45–13:30 & 16:00–20:00, Sun 16:00–20:00; Nov–March until 19:00; 45-min audioguide-€3, entrance off Gran Vía through iron gateway, tel. 958-222-959.

● **Self-Guided Tour:** You'll start your visit (after the ticket checker, step right) in the priests' wardrobe room. It's lush and wide-open; the gilded ceilings, mirrors, and wooden cabinets give this room a light, airy feel. Two grandfather clocks made in London (one with Asian motifs) ensured that everyone got dressed on time. The highlight of this room: the delicate painted wood statue of the *Immaculate Conception* by Granada's own Alonso Cano (1601–1667).

Wandering out, you'll be behind the main altar. A fine series of paintings by Cano, moved from under arches high above, now encircle the back of the altar. Their distortion was intentional, since the paintings were designed to look natural when viewed from floor level. As you walk around the pews and gigantic Baroque organs, you'll see the cathedral at its most beautiful.

Standing in front of the high altar, look up at the spread of vacant niches (with squares now filled with paintings). These were intended to hold the royal coffins. But Phillip II changed focus, abandoning Granada for El Escorial, and these sit empty to this day. Only four royals are buried in Granada (at the Royal Chapel). The cathedral's cool, spacious, bright interior is a refreshing break from the dark Gothic of so many Spanish churches. In a modern move back in the 18th century, the choir walls (the big heavy wooden box that dominates the center of most Spanish churches) were taken out so that people could be involved in the worship. At about the same time, a bishop ordered the interior painted with lime (for hygienic reasons, during a time of disease). The people liked it, and it stayed white. As you explore, remember that the abundance of Marys is all part of the Counter-Reformation. Most of the side chapels are decorated in Baroque style. To the right of the high altar is a politically incorrect version of St. James the Moor-Slayer, with his sword raised high and an armored Moor trampled under his horse's hooves.

Wander back through the pews toward the cathedral's main doors. A small sacristy museum is tucked away in the right corner (as you face the doors). There may be no detailed descriptions for any of the items, but a beautiful bust of St. Peter (with a flowing beard) by Cano is worth seeking out. Also on display is the confusing accounting book for the cathedral's construction. As you head out, look for the music sheets behind the main altar; they're mostly 16th-century Gregorian chants. Notice the sliding C clef. Rather than a fixed G or F clef, the monks knew that this clef—which could be located wherever worked best on the staff—marked middle C, and they chanted to notes relative to that. Go ahead—try singing a few verses of the Latin.

Immediately in front of the cathedral is the stop for minibus #32 to the Alhambra. And four blocks away (if you head left up the busy street, then turn right) is the Albayzín.

The Albayzín

Explore Spain's best old Moorish quarter, with countless colorful corners, flowery patios, and shady lanes. Climb high to the San Nicolás church for the best view of the Alhambra. Then wander through the mysterious backstreets. (I've listed these sights roughly in order from the San Nicolás viewpoint.)

Getting to the Albayzín: A handy city **minibus** threads its way around the Albayzín from Plaza Nueva (see "Albayzín Circular Bus Tour," next), getting you scenically and sweatlessly to the San Nicolás viewpoint. You can also **taxi** to the San Nicolás church and explore from there. Consider having your cabbie take you on a Sacromonte detour en route.

To **walk** up, leave the west end of Plaza Nueva on Calle Elvira. After about 200 yards, bear right on Calle Calderería Nueva. Follow this stepped street past Moroccan eateries and pastry shops, vendors of imported North African goods, *halal* butchers, and *teterías* (Moorish tea rooms). The lane bears right, then passes to the left of the church (becoming San Gregorio), and slants, winds, and zigzags uphill. San Gregorio eventually curves left and is regularly signposted. When you reach the Moorish-style house, La Media Luna, stop for a photo and a breather, then follow the wall, continuing uphill. At the next intersection, turn right on Aljibe del Gato. Farther on, this street takes a 90-degree turn to the left, becoming Calle Atarasana Vieja. It's confusing, but keep going up, up, up. At the crest, turn right on Camino Nuevo de San Nicolás, then walk 300 yards to the street that curves up left (look for a bus stop sign—this is where the minibus would have dropped you off). Continue up the curve and soon you'll see feet hanging from the plaza wall. Steps lead up to the church's viewpoint. Whew! You made it!

Albayzín Circular Bus Tour—The handy Albayzín minibus #31 gallops the 15-minute loop as if in a race, departing from Plaza Nueva about every 15 minutes (pay driver €1.20, minibus #32 does the same loop but—depending on where you catch it—goes to the

Safety in the Albayzín

With tough economic times, young ruffians are making the dark back lanes of the labyrinthine Albayzín quarter more dangerous. The big discussion in Granada is whether it's reckless to be out after dark in this charming Moorish district. While the area is certainly safe by day, it is questionable how safe it is after dark. There have been muggings, and they have been violent. I hate to hurt the business of the many fine little restaurants and hotels in this area. But if you want to play it safe—stay away after dark. And if you do venture in, leave your valuables at your hotel.

Alhambra first). While good for a lift to the top of the Albayzín (buzz when you want to get off), I'd stay on for an entire circle and return to the Albayzín later for dinner—either on foot or by bus again. (Note: Minibus #34 does same trip with a side-trip up into Sacromonte.)

Here's the route: You'll go along up above the Darro River, past the ruins of a bridge and gate and the Paseo de los Tristes square (see page 501). Turning uphill, you pass Sacromonte on the right (entrance to the neighborhood marked by a statue of a popular Gypsy guide). Then, turning left, you enter the actual Albayzín. After stopping at the church of San Salvador, you plunge into the thick of it, with stops below the San Nicolás church (famous viewpoint, and the jumping-off point for my suggested "Exploring the Albayzín" stroll—described later in this section) and at Plaza San Miguel Bajo (cute square with recommended eateries and another viewpoint). Then you descend, enjoying a commanding view of Granada on the left as you swing through the modern city. Hitting the city's main drag, Gran Vía, you make a U-turn at the Garden of the Triumph, celebrating the Immaculate Conception of the Virgin Mary (notice her statue atop a column). Behind Mary stands the old Royal Hospital—built in the 16th century for Granada's poor by the Catholic kings after the Reconquista, in hopes of winning the favor of the city's conquered residents. From here, you zip back into town, stopping at the cathedral, and back home to Plaza Nueva.

▲▲San Nicolás Viewpoint (Mirador de San Nicolás)— For one of Europe's most romantic viewpoints, be here at sunset, when the Alhambra glows red

Albayzín Neighborhood

STREET WIDTH IS EXAGGERATED FOR CLARITY

NOTE: NOT TO SCALE
➡ 20 MIN. UPHILL WALK FROM PLAZA NUEVA TO SAN NICOLÁS

✛ VIEW

MURCIA

PL. DE FATIMA

CALLE PAGES

ALHABACA

OLD WALL

PLAZA SAN MIGUEL EL BAJO

PUERTA NUEVA

ISABEL

ELVIRA

NUEVO SAN NIC.

PLAZA PANADEROS

PARDO

PLAZA LARGA

SAN NICOLÁS

ABAD

SALVADOR

CHORROHUMO STATUE

NUEVA

SAN GREGORIO

ALJIBE TRILLO

TOMASAS

VIEJA

SAN JUAN DE

MOORISH BATHS

LOS REYES

CHAPIN

CAMINO DEL SACROMONTE

PLAZA NUEVA

PL. S. ANA

C. DARRO

PASEO DE LOS TRISTES

RIO DARRO

TO CATHEDRAL

GOMEREZ

ARAB BATHS

ALHAMBRA

DCH

TO

GRANADA

❶ Hotel Santa Isabel la Real
❷ La Casa de Rafa (Apts.)
❸ Casa Torcuato (2 Locations)
❹ Restaurante El Ladrillo
❺ Bar Kiki
❻ Paseo de los Tristes Bars
❼ Carmen de las Tomasas & Carmen Mirador de Aixa
❽ Carmen Mirador de Morayma
❾ Carmen de Aben Humeya

❿ Arrayanes Restaurante
⓫ Calle Calderería Nueva Eateries
⓬ Great Mosque of Granada
⓭ Hammam El Bañuelo (Moorish Baths)
⓮ Hammam Baños Árabes (Arab Baths)
⓯ To Center for the Interpretation of Sacromonte, Roma Caves & Zambra Dance Clubs

and the Albayzín widows share the benches with local lovers, hippies, and tourists (free, always open). In 1997, President Clinton made a point to bring his family here—a favorite spot from a trip he made as a student. For a drink with the same view, step into the El Huerto de Juan Ranas Bar (just below and to the left, at Calle de Atarazana 8).

Great Mosque of Granada—Granada's Muslim population is on the rebound, and now numbers 8 percent of the city's residents.

A striking and inviting mosque is just next to the San Nicolás viewpoint (to your left as you face the Alhambra). Local Muslims write, "The Great Mosque of Granada signals, after a hiatus of 500 years, the restoration of a missing link with a rich and fecund Islamic contribution to all spheres of human enterprise and activity." Built in 2003 (with money from the local community and Islamic Arab nations), it has a peaceful view courtyard and a minaret that comes with a live call to prayer five times a day (printed schedule inside). It's stirring to see the muezzin holler "God is Great" from the minaret without amplification (locals didn't want it amplified). Visitors are welcome in the courtyard, which offers Alhambra views without the hedonistic ambience of the more famous San Nicolás viewpoint (free, daily 11:00–14:00 & 18:00–21:00).

While tourists come to Granada to learn about the expulsion of the Moors in 1492, local Muslims are frustrated by the "errors, nonsense, and lies local guides perpetuate without knowledge nor shame which flocks of passive tourists accept without questioning." A flier at the mosque tries to set the record straight, from the Muslim perspective: Muslims were as indigenous as any other group. After living here for seven centuries, the Muslims of Granada and Andalucía were as Iberian as the modern Spaniards of today. Islam is not a religion of immigrants. Islam is not a culture of the Orient and Arabs. Muslims and Arabs are different. The Muslims of Al-Andalus were not hedonistic. The Reconquista did not liberate Spain. Harems were not just full of sexy women. (For more on the Muslim perspective, visit the info desk at the mosque.)

The European Union sees Granada as a center for Muslim-Christian integration—or, at least, co-existence. To Muslims, the city is a symbol of the "holocaust" of the Reconquista, when 135,000 of their people were brutally expelled and many more suffered "forced conversion" in the 16th century. Today there are about 700,000 Muslims in Spain (and about 5 million in France).

Exploring the Albayzín—From the San Nicolás viewpoint and the Great Mosque, you're at the edge of a hilltop neighborhood even the people of Granada recognize as a world apart. Each of the district's 20 churches sits on a spot once occupied by a mosque. When the Reconquista arrived in Granada, the Christians attempted to coexist with the Muslims. But after seven years, this idealistic attempt ended in failure, and the Christians forced the Muslims to convert. In 1567, Muslims were expelled, leading to

200 years of economic depression for the city. Eventually, large walled noble manor houses with private gardens were built here in the depopulated Albayzín. These survive today in the form of the characteristic *carmen* restaurants so popular with visitors.

From the San Nicolás viewpoint, turn your back to the Alhambra and walk north (passing the church on your right and the Biblioteca Municipal on your left). A lane leads past a white stone arch (on your right)—now a chapel built into the old Moorish wall. You're walking past the scant remains of the pre-Alhambra fortress of Granada. At the end of the lane, step down to the right through the 11th-century "New Gate" (Puerta Nueva—older than the Alhambra) and into **Plaza Larga.** In medieval times, this tiny square (called "long," because back then it was) served as the local marketplace. It still is a busy market each morning. Casa Pasteles, at the near end of the square, serves good coffee and cakes.

Leave Plaza Larga on **Calle Agua de Albayzín** (as you face Casa Pasteles, it's to your right). The street, named for the public baths that used to line it, shows evidence of the Moorish plumbing system: gutters. Back when Europe's streets were filled with muck, Granada actually had Roman Empire–style gutters with drains leading to clay and lead pipes.

You're in the heart of the Albayzín. Explore. Poke into an old church. They're plain by design to go easy on the Muslim converts, who weren't used to being surrounded by images as they worshipped. You'll see lots of real Muslim culture living in the streets, including many recent Spanish converts.

Sacromonte

The Sacromonte district is home to Granada's thriving Roma community (see sidebar). Marking the entrance to Sacromonte is a statue of Chorrohumo (literally, "Exudes Smoke," and a play on the slang word for "thief"...*chorro*). He was a Roma from Granada, popular in the 1950s for guiding people around the city.

Sacromonte has one main street: Camino del Sacromonte is lined with caves primed for tourists and restaurants ready to fight over the bill. (Don't come here expecting to get a deal on anything.) Intriguing lanes run above and below this main drag.

Zambra Dance—A long flamenco tradition exists in Granada. Sacromonte is a good place to see *zambra,* a flamenco variation with a more Oriental feel in which the singer also dances. Two popular—or at least well-established—*zambra* venues are Zambra Cueva del Rocío (€25, includes a drink and a bus ride from hotel, €20 without transport, daily show at 22:00, 60 min, Camino del Sacromonte 70, tel. 958-227-129) and María la Canastera (€25, includes a drink and transportation from hotel, €17 without transport, daily

Granada's Roma (Gypsies)

Both the English word "Gypsy" and its Spanish counterpart, *gitano*, come from the word "Egypt"—where Europeans used to mistakenly believe these nomadic people originated. Today, the preferred term is "Roma," since the term "Gypsy" has acquired negative connotations (I've used both names throughout this book).

After migrating from India in the 14th century, the Roma people settled mostly in the Muslim-occupied lands in the south (such as the Balkan Peninsula, then controlled by the Ottoman Turks). Under the Muslims, the Roma enjoyed relative tolerance. They were traditionally good with crafts and animals.

The first Roma arrived in Granada in the 15th century—and they've remained tight-knit ever since. Today 50,000 Roma call Granada home, many of them in the district called Sacromonte. In most of Spain, Roma are more assimilated into the general population, but Sacromonte is a large, distinct Roma community. (After the difficult Civil War era, they were joined by many farmers who, like the Roma, appreciated Sacromonte's affordable, practical cave dwellings—warm in the winter and cool in the summer.)

Spaniards, who consider themselves accepting and not racist, claim that in maintaining such a tight community, the Roma segregate themselves. The Roma call Spaniards *payos* ("whites"). Recent mixing of Roma and *payos* has given birth to the term *gallipavo* (rooster-duck), although who's who depends upon whom you ask.

Are Roma thieves? Sure, some of them are. But others are honest citizens, trying to make their way in the world just like anyone else. It's wise to be cautious when dealing with a Roma person—but it's also important to keep an open mind.

show at 22:00, Camino del Sacromonte 89, tel. 958-121-183). I'd just go and explore late at night (with no wallet and €30 in my pocket) rather than booking an evening through my hotel (they'll likely offer to reserve for you).

Center for the Interpretation of Sacromonte (Centro de Interpretación del Sacromonte)—This facility is a kind of Roma open-air folk museum, offering an insight into Sacromonte's geology and environment, cave building, and Roma crafts, food, and musical traditions (with English explanations). There are also great views over Granada and the Alhambra. As you wander, imagine this in the 1950s, when it was still a bustling community of Roma cave-dwellers. Today, hippies squat in abandoned caves higher up. The center also features €12 flamenco shows and classical guitar concerts in its wonderfully scenic setting (details at TI), 300 yards up the steep hill from the Venta El Gallo restaurant on the main Sacromonte lane (€5; April–Oct Tue–Sun 10:00–14:00 & 17:00–21:00, Nov–March Tue–Sun 10:00–14:00 & 16:00–19:00, closed Mon; Barranco de los Negros, tel. 958-215-120, www.sacromontegranada.com). The closest a taxi can get you is the Venta El Gallo restaurant. From there, you climb on foot, following the signs.

Hammam Baños Árabes (Arab Baths)—For an intimate and subdued experience, consider some serious relaxation at the Arab Baths. A maximum of 16 people are allowed in the baths at one time. The 90-minute soak and a 15-minute massage cost €28; for a 90-minute bath only, it's €19 (daily 10:00–24:00, appointments scheduled every even-numbered hour, co-ed with mandatory swimsuits, quiet atmosphere encouraged, free lockers and towels available, just off Plaza Nueva at Santa Ana 16; from Plaza Nueva, it's the first right, over a bridge and past the church; 50 percent paid reservation required, tel. 958-229-978, www.hammamspain.com/granada).

Near Granada

Carthusian Monastery (La Cartuja)—A church with an interior that looks as if it squirted out of a can of whipped cream, La Cartuja is nicknamed the "Christian Alhambra" for its elaborate white Baroque stucco work. In the rooms just off the cloister, notice the gruesome paintings of martyrs placidly meeting their grisly fates (€3.50, daily April–Oct 10:00–13:00 & 16:00–20:00, Nov–March 10:00–13:00 & 15:00–18:00, tel. 958-161-932). It's a mile north of town on the way to Madrid. Drive north on Gran Vía de Colón and follow the signs, or take bus #8 from Gran Vía.

Sleeping in Granada

In July and August, when Granada's streets are littered with sunstroke victims, rooms are plentiful and prices soft. In the crowded months of April, May, September, and October, prices can spike up 20 percent. Except for the hotels in the Albayzín and near the Alhambra, most of my listings are within a five-minute walk of Plaza Nueva (see map on page 497).

Given all the restrictions, it is difficult to drive into Granada even when you know the system (see "Arrival in Granada," page 457). While few hotels have parking facilities, any of them can

Sleep Code

(€1 = about $1.40, country code: 34)
S = Single, **D** = Double/Twin, **T** = Triple, **Q** = Quad, **b** = bathroom, **s** = shower only. Unless otherwise noted, credit cards are accepted and English is spoken. Prices include the 7 percent tax. Breakfast may or may not be included.

To help you easily sort through these listings, I've divided the rooms into three categories based on the price for a standard double room with bath during high season:

$$$ Higher Priced—Most rooms €100 or more.
$$ Moderately Priced—Most rooms between €50–100.
$ Lower Priced—Most rooms €50 or less.

direct you to a garage (such as Parking San Agustín, just off Gran Vía, €25/day).

On or near Plaza Nueva

Each of these is big, professional, plenty comfortable, and perfectly located. Prices vary with demand.

$$$ Casa del Capitel Nazarí, just off the church end of Plaza Nueva, is a restored 16th-century Renaissance palace transformed into 17 small but tastefully decorated rooms facing a courtyard (Db-€115, extra bed-€38, breakfast-€8, includes afternoon tea/coffee and pastry, air-con, free Internet access, parking-€18.50/day, Cuesta Aceituneros 6, tel. 958-215-260, fax 958-215-806, www .hotelcasacapitel.com, info@hotelcasacapitel.com).

$$$ Hotel Maciá Plaza, right on the colorful Plaza Nueva, has 44 clean, modern, and classy rooms. Choose between an on-the-square view or a quieter interior room (Sb-€75, Db-€110, Tb-€123, 10 percent discount in 2010 when you show this book at check-in or reserve directly through their website, good buffet breakfast-€8, air-con, elevator, free Wi-Fi, Plaza Nueva 4, tel. 958-227-536, fax 958-227-533, www.maciahoteles.com, maciaplaza @maciahoteles.com).

$$ Hotel Inglaterra is a modern and peaceful chain hotel, with 36 rooms offering all the comforts (Db-€77–97, extra bed-€30, buffet breakfast-€12, air-con, elevator to third floor only, 20 parking spaces at €13/day, Cetti Merien 6, tel. 958-221-559, fax 958-227-100, www.nh-hotels.com, nhinglaterra@nh-hotels.com).

$$ Hotel Anacapri is a bright, cool marble oasis with 49 modern rooms and a quiet lounge (Sb-€55–65, Db-€75–97, Tb-€95–117, extra bed-€20, includes breakfast with direct bookings in 2010, air-con, elevator, 2 blocks toward Gran Vía from Plaza Nueva at Calle Joaquín Costa 7, just a block from cathedral bus stop,

Granada Hotels and Restaurants

P PARKING

100 YARDS
100 METERS

TO TRAIN & BUS STATIONS

ALBAYZÍN
MOORISH QUARTER

TO SAN NICOLÁS VIEWPOINT & PLAZA LARGA

MERCADO SAN AGUSTÍN **P**

CATHEDRAL
& ROYAL CHAPEL

CALD. NUEVA   S. GREGORIO

TO SACRA-MONTE

PL. PESC.

CETTI.

PLAZA DE BIB-RAMBLA

OFICIOS
LA MADRAZA
ZACATÍN

PLAZA ISABEL LA CATÓLICA

PLAZA NUEVA

PL. S. ANA

TO ARAB BATHS

ERMITA

CALLE REYES CATÓLICOS

ÁNIMAS

PAVANERAS

CUESTA GOMÉREZ

TO ALHAMBRA

PLAZA DEL CARMEN

CALLE NAVAS

PUERTA REAL

TO FREEWAY EXIT #129

DCH

GRANADA

❶ Casa del Capitel Nazarí	❾ To Hotel Reina Cristina & Zurita Pensión
❷ Hotel Maciá Plaza	❿ Hotel Los Tilos
❸ Hotel Inglaterra	⓫ Hotel Lisboa
❹ Hotel Anacapri	⓬ Bodegas Castañeda
❺ Pensión Landazuri	⓭ Restaurante Sevilla
❻ Hotel Puerta de las Granadas, Pensión Viena & Pensión Austria	⓮ La Cueva De 1900
❼ Hostal Residencia Britz	⓯ Los Italianos Ice Cream
❽ Hostal Navarro Ramos	⓰ To Paseo de los Tristes Eateries
	⓱ Market Scene

tel. 958-227-477, fax 958-228-909, www.hotelanacapri.com, reservas @hotelanacapri.com, helpful Kathy speaks Iowan).

Cheap Sleeps on Cuesta de Gomérez

These are inexpensive and ramshackle lodgings on the street leading from Plaza Nueva up to the Alhambra. A restoration project is currently blocking the end of the road, making it quieter and almost traffic-free. There are plans to make this a pedestrian-only street.

$$ Hotel Puerta de las Granadas is a basic value with 16 simple rooms, no-frills comforts, an inviting cafeteria courtyard, and a handy location (Db–€60–85, ask for 5 percent Rick Steves discount, air-con, free Internet access and Wi-Fi, free tea in cafeteria all day, Cuesta de Gomérez 14, tel. 958-216-230, fax 958-216-231, www.hotelpuertadelasgranadas.com, reservas@hotelpuertadelas granadas.com).

$ Pensión Landazuri is run by friendly English-speaking Matilde Landazuri and her son, Manolo. Some of their 18 rooms are well-worn, while others are renovated. It boasts hardworking, helpful management and a great roof garden with an Alhambra view (S–€24, Sb–€36, D–€34, Db–€45, Tb–€60, cheap eggs-and-bacon breakfast, cash only, parking–€10/day, Cuesta de Gomérez 24, tel. & fax 958-221-406). The Landazuris also run a good, cheap café.

$ Hostal Residencia Britz, overlooking Plaza Nueva, is simple and no-nonsense. All of its 22 basic rooms are streetside—bring earplugs (S–€25, D–€36, Db–€48, elevator, Plaza Nueva y Gomérez 1, tel. & fax 958-223-652).

$ Hostal Navarro Ramos is a little cash-only cheapie, renting seven stark rooms facing an interior airshaft with mostly shared bathrooms (S–€20, D–€27, Db–€36, Cuesta de Gomérez 21, tel. 958-250-555, Carmen).

$ Pensión Viena and **Pensión Austria,** run by English-speaking Austrian Irene (ee-RAY-nay), rent 32 basic backpacker-type rooms on a quiet side street (S–€26, Sb–€36, D–€36, Db–€46, T–€53, Tb–€62, family rooms, air-con, next-door bar noisy on weekends, 10 yards off Cuesta de Gomérez at Hospital de Santa Ana 2, tel. & fax 958-221-859, www.hostalviena.com, hostal viena@hostalviena.com, reception at Pensión Austria).

Near the Cathedral

$$$ Hotel Reina Cristina has 58 quiet, elegant rooms a few steps off Plaza Trinidad, a park-like square near the lively Pescadería and Bib-Rambla squares. Check out the great Mudejar ceiling and the painting at the entrance of this house, where the famous Spanish poet Federico García Lorca hid until he was captured and executed by the Guardia Civil (Sb–€53–78, Db–€75–114, Tb–€107–135, breakfast-€13, air-con, elevator, near Plaza de la Trinidad at Tablas 4, tel. 958-253-211, fax 958-255-728, www.hotelreinacristina.com, clientes@hotelreinacristina.com).

$$ Hotel Los Tilos offers 30 comfortable rooms (some with balconies) on the charming traffic-free Plaza de Bib-Rambla behind the cathedral. All clients are welcome to use the fourth-floor view terrace overlooking the great café, shopping, and people-watching neighborhood. The hall carpets are well-trafficked, but the in-room flooring has been renovated (Sb-€40–55, Db-€55–80, Tb-€77–100, prices may be cheaper if you reserve online, air-con, parking-€18/ day, Plaza de Bib-Rambla 4, tel. 958-266-712, fax 958-266-801, www.hotellostilos.com, clientes@hotellostilos.com, friendly José María).

$ Zurita Pensión is a well-run 14-room place facing a big and delightful square. Even with its double-paned windows it may come with night noise (S-€21, D-€34, Db-€42, Tb-€63, air-con, Plaza de la Trinidad 7, tel. 958-275-020, www.pensionzurita.com, pensionzurita@gmail.com, Francisco and Loli).

$ Hotel Lisboa, overlooking Plaza del Carmen and the start of the busy pedestrianized Calle Navas with its popular tapas bars, offers 28 simple but well-maintained rooms with friendly owners (S-€25, Sb-€36, D-€36, Db-€49, T-€44, Tb-€66, elevator, free Internet access, Plaza del Carmen 27, tel. 958-221-414, fax 958-221-487, www.lisboaweb.com, Mary).

In the Albayzín

Note that some consider this area unsafe after dark (see the "Safety in the Albayzín" sidebar, earlier).

$$ Hotel Santa Isabel la Real, an elegant medieval mansion, has 11 rooms ringing a noble courtyard. Buried deep in the Albayzín and furnished in a way that gives you the old Moorish Granada ambience, it offers a warm welcome and rich memories (Db-€85–105 with breakfast, air-con, free Internet access and Wi-Fi, midway between San Nicolás viewpoint and Plaza San Miguel Bajo on Calle Santa Isabel la Real, immediately at a bus stop, tel. 958-294-658, fax 958-294-645, www.hotelsantaisabella real.com, info@hotelsantaisabellareal.com).

$$ La Casa de Rafa is a traditional house in the heart of the Albayzín that's been converted into four small, funky kitchenette apartments with an eclectic, ever-evolving artistic feel (Chicago-raised owner Rafa lives on-site). You'll share two tiny patios and a rooftop terrace with a spectacular in-your-face view of the Alhambra (Sb-€35–45, Db-€45–60, extra person-€10–12.50, 2-night minimum, 5-min walk from Plaza Nueva at tiny Plaza Virgen del Carmen—see map page 491, tel. 958-220-682, mobile 610-322-216, www.elnumero8.com, casaocho@gmail.com). Call

Rafa to get (initially tricky) directions and set up a time to meet and check in.

In or near the Alhambra

If you want to stay on the Alhambra grounds, there are two popular options (famous, overpriced, and generally booked up long in advance) and one practical and economic place above the parking lot. All are a half-mile up the hill from Plaza Nueva.

$$$ Parador de Granada San Francisco offers 40 designer rooms in a former Moorish palace that was later transformed into a 15th-century Franciscan monastery. It's considered Spain's premier parador...and that's saying something (Db-€310, breakfast-€20, air-con, free parking, Calle Real de la Alhambra, tel. 958-221-440, fax 958-222-264, www.parador.es, granada@parador.es). You must book months ahead to spend the night in this lavishly located, stodgy, and historic palace. Any peasant, however, can drop in for a coffee, drink, snack, or meal. For details about the history of the building, see "The Alhambra Grounds" sidebar on page 472.

$$$ Hotel América is classy and cozy, with 17 rooms next to the parador (Sb-€70, Db-€115, breakfast-€8, closed Dec–Feb, Calle Real de la Alhambra 53, tel. 958-227-471, fax 958-227-470, www.hotelamericagranada.com, reservas@hotelamericagranada .com). Book well in advance.

$$ Hotel Guadalupe, big and modern with 57 rooms, is quietly and conveniently located overlooking the Alhambra parking lot. While a 20-minute hike above the town, many (especially drivers) find this to be a practical option (Sb-€50–60, Db-€60–80, Tb-€80–100, more during festivals, pricey "double superiors" aren't worth it, air-con, parking in Alhambra lot-€13, Paseo de la Sabica 30, tel. 958-225-730, www.hotelguadalupe.es, info@hotel guadalupe.es).

Eating in Granada

Many of Granada's bars still serve a small tapas plate free with any beer or wine—a tradition that's dying out in most of Spain.

Restaurants generally serve lunch from 13:00 to 16:00 and dinner from 20:00 until very late (Spaniards don't start dinner until about 21:00).

In search of an edible memory? A local specialty, *tortilla Sacromonte,* is a spicy omelet with pig's brain and other organs. *Berenjenas fritas* (fried eggplant)

GRANADA

and *habas con jamón* (small green fava beans cooked with cured ham) are worth seeking out. *Tinto de verano*—a red-wine spritzer with lemon and ice—is refreshing on a hot evening. For tips on eating near the Alhambra, see "Eating" on page 465.

In the Albayzín

The most interesting meals hide out deep in the Albayzín (Moorish quarter). The easy way to get there is by taking minibus #31 from Plaza Nueva or #32 from Plaza Isabel La Católica. To find a particular square, ask any local, or follow my directions and the map on page 491. If dining late, take the minibus or a taxi back to your hotel; Albayzín back streets can be dangerous because of pickpockets.

Part of the charm of the quarter is the lazy ambience on its squares: **Plaza Larga** is extremely characteristic, with tapas bar tables spilling out onto the square, a morning market, and a much-loved pastry shop. The farthest hike into the Albayzín, **Plaza San Miguel el Bajo** is a neighborhood square boasting my favorite funky, local scene—kids kicking soccer balls, old-timers warming benches, and women gossiping under the facade of a humble church. Its four square-side bars serve serious tapas and its good little restaurant offers a €10 fixed-price meal. This is a fine spot to end your Albayzín visit, as there's a viewpoint overlooking the modern city a block away. Minibuses #31 and #32 rumble by every few minutes, ready to zip you back to Plaza Nueva.

Casa Torcuato is a hardworking eatery serving straightforward yet creative food in a smart upstairs dining room. They serve a good €8 fixed-price meal. Plates of fresh fish run €8–12 and their tropical salad includes a Tahitian wonderland of fruits (closed Sun, 2 blocks beyond Plaza Larga at Calle Aqua 20, second location on nearby Calle Pagés, tel. 958-202-039).

Restaurante El Ladrillo, with outdoor tables on a peaceful square, is *the* place for piles of fish. Their popular €12 *barco* ("boat-load" of mixed fried fish) is a fishy feast that stuffs two to the gills. The smaller €8.50 half *barco* fills one person adequately, or, when combined with a salad, can feed two (daily, on Plaza Fátima, just off Calle Pages).

Near the San Nicolás Viewpoint: **Bar Kiki,** a laid-back and popular bar-restaurant on an unpretentious square, serves simple tapas. Try their tasty fried eggplant (long hours, closed Wed, just behind viewpoint at Plaza de San Nicolás 9).

Paseo de los Tristes: This is like a stage set of outdoor bars on a terrace over the river gorge. While there is no serious restaurant here and the food values are mediocre at best, the scene—cool along a stream under trees, with the floodlit Alhambra high above, and a happy crowd of locals enjoying a meal or drink out—is a winner. As this is at the base of the Albayzín, there is no issue of danger after dark here. You're a simple, level five-minute walk back to Plaza Nueva.

Carmens: For a more memorable but expensive experience, consider fine dining with Alhambra views in a *carmen,* a typical Albayzín house with a garden (buzz to get in). Following the Reconquista, the Albayzín became depopulated. Wealthy families took larger tracts of land and built fortified mansions with terraced gardens within their walls. Today, rather than growing produce, the gardens of many of these *carmens* host dining tables and romantic restaurants.

Carmen Mirador de Aixa, small and elegant, has the dreamiest Alhambra views among the *carmens.* You'll pay a little more, but the food is exquisitely presented and the view makes the splurge worthwhile (plan on €45 plus wine for dinner, next to Carmen de las Tomasas at Carril de San Agustín 2, tel. 958-223-616).

Carmen de las Tomasas serves gourmet traditional Andalusian cuisine with killer views in a dressy/stuffy atmosphere (€40 meals, Wed–Sun 21:00–24:00, generally closed Mon–Tue, call ahead as they sometimes close on Sun instead, reservations required, Carril de San Agustín, tel. 958-224-108, Cristina).

Carmen Mirador de Morayma boasts great atmosphere and fine rustic cuisine, but no commanding Alhambra views. This is where famous visitors dine to the sounds of classical guitar. For seating, choose between outdoor—on one of three garden terraces—or inside the noble mansion, where it's bright and nice, but not romantic (€30 tasting *menus,* closed Sun, Calle Pianista García Carrillo 2, tel. 958-228-290).

Carmen de Aben Humeya is the least expensive, least stuffy, and least romantic. Its outdoor-only seating lets you enjoy a meal or just a long cup of coffee while gazing at the Alhambra. This is a rare place enthusiastic about dinner salads (€10–15 plates, daily 13:00–24:00, food served 13:00–16:00 & 19:30–22:30—or until 24:00 in heat of summer, Cuesta de las Tomasas 12, tel. 958-226-665).

Near Plaza Nueva

For people-watching, consider the many restaurants on Plaza Nueva or Plaza de Bib-Rambla (south of cathedral). For a happening scene, check out the bars on and around Calle Elvira. It's best to wander and see where the biggest crowds are.

Bodegas Castañeda is the best mix of lively, central, untouristy, and cheap among the tapas bars I visited. Just a block off Plaza Nueva, it requires a bit of self-service: When crowded, you need to power your way to the bar to order; when quiet, you can order at the bar and grab a little table (same budget prices). Consider their *tablas combinadas*—variety plates of cheese, meat, and *ahumados* (four different varieties of smoked fish)—and tasty *croquetas* (breaded and fried mashed potatoes and ham). The big kegs tempt you with different local sherries. Tapas can be ordered from an easy menu and cost €2–3 apiece (daily 11:30–16:30 & 17:00–24:00, Calle Almireceros 1, tel. 958-215-464). Don't be confused by a different "Castaneda" restaurant nearby (unless you're hankering for stuffed potatoes).

Restaurante Sevilla, with its tight and charming little dining room behind a high-energy tapas bar, has been a favorite of well-dressed natives for 75 years. Specialties include paella, other rice dishes, soups, and salads. You'll eat surrounded by old photos of local big shots who've dined here. On hot nights, tables pour out onto the little square facing the Royal Chapel. It's a local-feeling, elegant, urban scene (€20 meals, summer closed Sun, rest of year closed Sun–Mon; across from Royal Chapel at Calle Oficios 12, tel. 958-221-223).

La Cueva de 1900 is a fresh family-friendly deli-like place on the main drag appreciated for its simple dishes and quality ingredients. It's proud of its homemade hams, sausages, and cheeses— sold in 100-gram lots and served with checkered-tablecloth style. If you've had enough meat, they have good €5 salads (Calle Reyes Católicos 42, tel. 958-229-327).

At **Arrayanes,** a good Moroccan restaurant, Mostafa will help you choose among the many salads, the *pastela* (a chicken-and-cinnamon pastry appetizer), the couscous, or *tajin* dishes. He treats you like an old friend...especially the ladies (Wed–Mon 13:30–16:30 & 19:30–23:30, closed Tue, Cuesta Marañas 4, where Calles Calderería Nueva and Vieja meet, tel. 958-228-401).

Hippie Options on Calle Calderería Nueva: From Plaza Nueva, walk two long blocks down Calle Elvira and turn right onto the wonderfully hip and Arabic-feeling Calle Calderería Nueva, which leads uphill into the Albayzín. The street is lined with trendy *teterías.* These small tea shops, open all day, are good places to linger, chat, and imagine you're in Morocco. Some are conservative and unmemorable, and others are achingly romantic, filled with incense, beaded cushions, live African music, and effervescent young hippies. They sell light meals such as crêpes, and a worldwide range of teas, all marinated in a candlelit snake charm.

Dessert: **Los Italianos,** Italian-run and teeming with locals, is popular for its ice cream, *horchata* (*chufa*-nut drink), and shakes (mid-March–mid-Oct daily 8:00–24:00, closed mid-Oct–mid-March, across the street from cathedral and Royal Chapel at Gran Vía 4, tel. 958-224-034).

Markets: Though heavy on meat, **Mercado San Agustín** also sells fruits and veggies. Throughout the EU, locals lament the loss

---

Cheap Tricks in Granada

- Buy some drinks and snacks near Plaza Nueva, and sling them up to the Albayzín. This makes for a great cheap date at the San Nicolás viewpoint or one of the scattered squares and lookout points.
- Have a drink at the Carmen de Aben Humeya—it's an inexpensive way to soak up great Alhambra views.
- Do a tapas crawl on Calle Navas right off Plaza del Carmen. Claim your "right" to a free tapa with every drink.

---

of the characteristic old market halls as they are replaced with new hygienic versions. If nothing else, it's as refreshingly cool as a meat locker (Mon–Sat 8:00–15:30, closed Sun, a block north of cathedral and a half-block off Gran Vía on Calle Cristo San Agustín). Tucked away in the back of the market is a very cheap and colorful little eatery: **Cafeteria San Agustín.** They make their own *churros* and give a small tapa free with each drink (menu on wall). If waiting for the cathedral or Royal Chapel to open, kill time in the market. The **Pescadería** square, downhill from the actual market and a block from Plaza de Bib-Rambla, is actually more popular with locals looking to buy produce.

Connections

From Granada by Train to: Barcelona (1/day Wed, Thu, and Sat only, 11.5 hrs; also 1/night daily, 12 hrs), **Madrid** (2/day, 5 hrs), **Toledo** (all service is via Madrid, nearly hourly AVE connections to Toledo), **Algeciras** (3/day, 4.25–5 hrs), **Ronda** (3/day, 2.5 hrs), **Sevilla** (4/day, 3 hrs), **Córdoba** (2/day, 2.5 hrs), **Málaga** (3/day, 2.5–3.25 hrs on AVE, transfer in Bobadilla or Antequera). Train info: tel. 902-240-202. Many of these connections have a more frequent (and sometimes much faster) bus option—see below.

 By Bus to: Nerja (5/day, 2.5 hrs, more with transfer in Motril), **Sevilla** (11/day, 3 hrs *directo*, 4 hrs *ruta*), **Córdoba** (8/day, 2.5–3 hrs), **Madrid** (18/day, 5.25 hrs), **Málaga** (hourly, 1.5–2 hrs), **Algeciras** (5/day, 4–5.5 hrs, some are *directo*, others are the slow *ruta*), **La Línea/Gibraltar** (2/day, 5 hrs), **Jerez** (1/day, 4.5 hrs). All of these buses are run by the Alsina Graells company (tel. 958-185-480, www.movelia.es).

By Car: To drive to Nerja (1.5 hours away), take the exit for the coastal town of Motril. You'll wind through 50 scenic miles south of Granada, then follow signs for Málaga. Note that you can also hop a taxi to Nerja (€125 fixed rate).

SEVILLA

Sevilla is the flamboyant city of Carmen and Don Juan, where bullfighting is still politically correct and little girls still dream of growing up to become flamenco dancers. While Granada has the great Alhambra and Córdoba has the remarkable Mezquita, Sevilla has a soul. (Soul—or *duende*—is fundamental to flamenco.) It's a wonderful-to-be-alive-in kind of place.

The gateway to the New World in the 16th century, Sevilla boomed when Spain did. The explorers Amerigo Vespucci and Ferdinand Magellan sailed from its great river harbor, discovering new routes and sources of gold, silver, cocoa, and tobacco. In the 17th century, Sevilla was Spain's largest and richest city. Local artists Diego Velázquez, Bartolomé Murillo, and Francisco de Zurbarán made it a cultural center. Sevilla's Golden Age—and its New World riches—ended when the harbor silted up and the Spanish empire crumbled.

In the 19th century, Sevilla was a big stop on the Romantic "Grand Tour" of Europe. To build on this tourism and promote trade among Spanish-speaking nations, Sevilla planned a grand exposition in 1929. Bad year. The expo crashed along with the stock market. In 1992, Sevilla got a second chance at a world's fair. This expo was a success, leaving the city with an impressive infrastructure: a new airport, train station, sleek bridges, and the super AVE bullet train (making Sevilla a 2.5-hour side-trip from Madrid). In 2007, the main boulevards—once thundering with noisy traffic and cutting the city mercilessly in two—were pedestrianized, giving Sevilla even more charm.

Today, Spain's fourth-largest city (pop. 700,000) is Andalucía's leading destination, buzzing with festivals, orange and jacaranda trees, sizzling summer heat, color, guitars, and castanets. James Michener wrote, "Sevilla doesn't *have* ambience, it *is* ambience." Sevilla has its share of impressive sights, but the real magic is the city itself, with its tangled Jewish Quarter, riveting flamenco shows, thriving bars, and teeming evening paseo.

Planning Your Time

If ever there was a big Spanish city to linger in, it's Sevilla. On a three-week trip, spend two nights and two days here. On even the

shortest Spanish trip, I'd zip here on the slick AVE train for a day trip from Madrid.

The major sights are few and simple for a city of this size; the cathedral and the Alcázar are worth about three hours, and a wander through the Santa Cruz district takes about an hour. You could spend half a day touring its other sights. Stroll along the bank of the Guadalquivir River and cross the Bridge of Triana (also known as the Isabel II Bridge) for a view of the cathedral and Golden Tower. An evening here is essential for the paseo and a flamenco show.

Bullfights take place on most Sundays in May and June, on Easter, and daily through the April Fair and in late September. Sevilla's Alcázar and Museo de Bellas Artes are closed on Monday, while the Museo Palacio de la Condesa de Lebrija is closed on Sunday. Tour groups clog the Alcázar and cathedral in the morning; go late in the day to avoid the lines.

Córdoba (see next chapter) is a convenient and worthwhile side-trip from Sevilla, or a handy stopover if you're taking the AVE to or from Madrid.

Orientation to Sevilla

For the tourist, this big city is small. Sevilla's major sights—including the lively Santa Cruz district and the Alcázar—surround the cathedral. The central north–south pedestrian boulevard, Avenida de la Constitución (with TIs, banks, and a post office), leads past the cathedral to Plaza Nueva (gateway to the shopping district). Nearly everything is within easy walking distance. The bullring is a few blocks west of the cathedral, and Plaza de España is a few blocks south. Triana, the area on the west bank of the Guadalquivir River, is working-class and colorful, but lacks tourist sights. With most sights walkable, and taxis so friendly, easy, and reasonable (€4 for a short ride), I rarely bother with the bus.

Tourist Information

Sevilla has tourist offices wherever you need them—at the **airport** (Mon–Fri 9:00–21:00, Sat–Sun 11:00–15:00, tel. 954-449-128), **train station** (overlooking track 6, Mon–Fri 9:00–19:30, Sat–Sun 9:30–15:00, tel. 954-782-003), and three along Avenida de la Constitución. These are located on the river side of the **Alcázar** (Mon–Fri 9:00–19:30, Sat–Sun 9:30–15:00, Avenida de la Constitución 21, tel. 954-787-578); across from the **cathedral** (Mon–Sat 10:30–14:30 & 15:30–19:30, Sun 10:30–14:30, Plaza del Triunfo, tel. 954-501-001); and at **Plaza Nueva** (Mon–Fri 9:00–19:30, Sat–Sun 10:00–14:00, on Plaza San Francisco, tel. 954-595-288, free Internet access for 1 hour).

At any TI, ask for the city map, the English-language magazines *Welcome Olé* and *The Tourist,* and a current listing of sights with opening times. The free monthly events guide—*El Giraldillo,* written in Spanish basic enough to be understood by travelers—covers cultural events throughout Andalucía, with a focus on Sevilla. As some of the TIs are regional as well as for Sevilla, think of any information you might need for elsewhere in Andalucía (for example, if heading south, ask for the free *Route of the White Towns* brochure and a Jerez map). Helpful websites are www.turismosevilla.org and www.andalucia.org.

The **Sevilla Card** (sold at the ICONOS shop next to the Alcázar TI, daily 10:00–19:00, or at the train station's hotel room–finding booth on track 11) covers admission to most of Sevilla's sights (cathedral, Alcázar, Flamenco Dance Museum, Museo Palacio de la Condesa de Lebrija, Basílica de la Macarena, Bullfight Museum, Itálica), and gives discounts at some hotels and restaurants. There are two types of Sevilla Cards—the pricier one includes the hop-on, hop-off bus and the boat cruise; the other one doesn't. Serious sightseers might get their money's worth with one of the cheaper multi-day cards (€28 or €50/1 day, €32 or €60/2 days, €36 or €65/3 days, www.sevillacard.es). Seniors (over 65) get into the Alcázar free and into the cathedral almost free.

Arrival in Sevilla

By Train: Trains arrive at the sublime Santa Justa Station (with banks, ATMs, TI, and *consigna*/baggage storage—€3/day, below track 1). If you don't have a hotel room reserved, the room-finding

Greater Sevilla

TO ITÁLICA & MÉRIDA

LA CORTA BRIDGE

ALAMILLO PARK

GUADALQUIVIR RIVER

ALAMILLO BRIDGE

TO A-4, AIRPORT & CÓRDOBA

FORMER EXPO SITE

BASÍLICA DE LA MACARENA

CARR. DE CARMONA

LA CARTUJA

MUSEO DE BELLAS ARTES

TO HUELVA

2

GIRALDA TOWER

SANTA JUSTA TRAIN STN.

MONTOTO

ANDALUCÍA

ISABEL II BRIDGE

TRIANA

ALCÁZAR

1

SAN TELMO BRIDGE

PLAZA DE ESPAÑA

APRIL FAIR FAIRGROUNDS

MARÍA LUISA PARK

AV. GARCIA MORATO

PASEO PALMERO

DCH

TO A-92 & MÁLAGA

TO A-376 & RONDA

1 MILE
1 KM

Bus Stations:
1 El Prado
2 Plaza de Armas

☐ = HISTORIC CITY CENTER-
SEE DETAIL MAP

booth above track 11 can help. You can also get maps and other tourist information here if the TI line is long (Mon–Sat 8:00–21:00, Sun 8:00–14:30). The plush little AVE Sala Club, designed for business travelers, welcomes those with a first-class AVE ticket and reservation (in front of track 1).

The town center is marked by the ornate Giralda Bell Tower, peeking above the apartment flats (visible from the front of the station—with your back to the tracks, using an imaginary clock for a compass, it's at 1 o'clock). To get into the center, it's a flat and boring 20-minute walk (longer if you get lost), a €5 taxi ride, or a short bus ride. Bus #C2 runs from 100 yards in front of the train station to Plaza de la Encarnación, but not to recommended hotels (€1.10, pay driver).

By Bus: Sevilla's two major bus stations both have information offices, cafeterias, and luggage storage. The **El Prado Station** covers most of Andalucía (daily 7:00–22:00, information tel. 954-417-111, no English spoken; luggage storage at back of station—€2/day, daily 9:00–21:00). To get downtown from the station, it's a 10-minute walk (use the color map in the front of this book). If your hotel is near Plaza Nueva, you could take the city's short tram from the station.

The **Plaza de Armas Station** (near the river, opposite the Expo '92 site) serves long-distance destinations such as Madrid, Barcelona, Lagos, and Lisbon. Luggage lockers are across from the ticket counters (€3/day). As you exit onto the main road (Calle Arjona), the bus stop is to the left, in front of the taxi stand (bus #C4 goes downtown, €1.10, pay driver, get off at Puerta de Jerez near main TI). Taxis to downtown cost around €5.

By Car: To drive into Sevilla, follow *centro ciudad* (city center) signs and stay along the river. For short-term parking on the street, the riverside Paseo de Cristóbal Colón has two-hour meters and hardworking thieves. Ignore the bogus traffic wardens who direct you to an illegal spot, take a tip, and disappear later when your car gets towed. For long-term parking, hotels charge as much as a normal garage. For simplicity, I'd just park at a central garage and catch a taxi to my hotel. Try the big one under the bus station at Plaza de Armas (€12/day), the Cristóbal Colón garage (by the bullring and river, €1.15/hr, €14/day), or the one at Avenida Roma/Puerta de Jerez (€14/24 hrs, cash only). For hotels in the Santa Cruz area, the handiest parking is the Cano y Cueto garage near the corner of Calle Santa María la Blanca and Menéndez Pelayo (€18/day, open 24/7, at edge of big park, unsigned and underground).

By Plane: The Especial Aeropuerto (EA) bus connects the airport with the train station and town center (€2.30, 2/hr, generally departs from airport at :15 and :45 past the hour, 30 min, buy ticket from driver). If going from downtown Sevilla to the airport, ask your hotelier or the TI where to catch it (the bus stop might change because of religious processions, construction, and other factors); in 2009, the stop was on Avenida del Cid by the Portugal Pavilion. You can also catch the bus at the Santa Justa train station. To taxi into town, go to one of the airport's taxi stands to ensure a fixed rate (€21–23, confirm price anyway); during Easter week the rate jumps to about €29, plus extra for luggage. For flight information, call 954-449-000.

Getting Around Sevilla

By Bus: On a hot day, buses in Sevilla can be a blessing. A single trip costs €1.10 (pay driver), or you can buy a Bonobus pass, which gives you 10 trips for €6 (shareable, sold at kiosks). The various #C buses make a circular loop that covers María Luisa Park and Basílica de la Macarena. The #C3 stops in Murillo Gardens, Triana (district on the west bank of the river), then Macarena. The #C4 goes the opposite direction without entering Triana. Spunky little #C5 is a minibus that winds through the old center of town, providing a fine and relaxing joyride (pick it up at Plaza Nueva). The #C5 can also be handy to get to the Museo de Bellas Artes.

By Taxi: Sevilla is a great taxi town. You can hail one anywhere (€3 drop, or €4 at night and on weekends, €21–23 to airport, extra for luggage and runs to/from the train and bus stations). While I'm quick to take advantage of a taxi, because of one-way streets and traffic congestion, you can often hoof it just as fast between central points.

Helpful Hints

Festivals: Sevilla's peak season is April and May, and it has two one-week festival periods when the city is packed: Holy Week and April Fair.

While **Holy Week** (Semana Santa) is big all over Spain, it's biggest in Sevilla. It's held the week between Palm Sunday and Easter Sunday (March 28–April 4 in 2010). Locals start preparing for the big event up to a year in advance. What would normally be a five-minute walk could take you an hour and a half if a procession crosses your path. But even these hassles seem irrelevant as you listen to the *saetas* (spontaneous devotional songs) and let the spirit of the festival take over.

Then, two weeks after Easter—after taking enough time off to catch its communal breath—Sevilla holds its **April Fair** (April 20–25 in 2010, described later in this chapter). This is a celebration of all things Andalusian, with plenty of eating, drinking, singing, and merrymaking (though most of the revelry takes place in private parties at a large fairground).

Book rooms well in advance for these festival times. Warning: Prices can go sky-high, food quality at touristy restaurants can plummet, and many hotels have four-night minimums.

Internet Access: Sevilla has plenty of places to get online. Near the recommended Santa Cruz hotels, head for **Internetia,** a thriving-with-students place that has a fine café and 30 terminals (€2.30/hr, Wi-Fi, disc-burning, daily 11:00–23:00, Avenida Menéndez Pelayo 43–45, tel. 954-534-003). Between the Alcázar and the river, try **Internet Workcenter** (daily

Cheap Tricks in Sevilla

- For an inexpensive lunch, many regular bar-cafeterias will make you a *bocadillo*. These are often simply ham and cheese or *tortilla española* (potato omelet) on a baguette, with no fixings. But at €3–4, they are perfect for a picnic in one of the many squares and parks. Plaza Doña Elvira is especially picturesque and shady.
- Instead of taking a guided tour, head to the Golden Tower and enjoy a walk along the Guadalquivir River. There's a bike path and plenty of sunbathers stretched out along the grassy sections. Spot the Giralda Bell Tower from a distance, look over at Triana, and watch rowers go down the river. You can also walk around a large sand-colored sculpture by the Basque artist Eduardo Chillida near the Isabel II Bridge.
- Need to get online? The Plaza Nueva TI on Plaza San Francisco offers free Internet access for up to one hour.

9:00–14:00 & 16:00–21:00, San Fernando 1, tel. 954-220-487). The **TI at Plaza Nueva** (on Plaza San Francisco) offers up to one hour of free Internet access from eight terminals, as well as free Wi-Fi (Internet available Mon–Fri 10:00–14:00 & 17:00–20:00, closed Sat–Sun).

Post Office: The post office is at Avenida de la Constitución 32, across from the cathedral (Mon–Fri 8:30–20:30, Sat 9:30–14:00, closed Sun).

Laundry: Lavandería Roma offers quick and economical drop-off service (€6/load wash and dry, Mon–Fri 9:30–14:00 & 17:30–20:30, Sat 9:00–15:00, closed Sun, 2 blocks inland from bull-ring at Castelar 2, tel. 954-210-535). Near the recommended Santa Cruz hotels, **La Segunda Vera Tintorería** has two machines for self-service (€10/load wash and dry, drop-off service also available, Mon–Fri 9:30–13:45 & 17:30–20:00, closed Sat–Sun, Avenida Menéndez Pelayo 11, tel. 954-534-219).

Train Tickets: The RENFE offices give out train schedules and sell train tickets. There's a RENFE Travel Center at the **train station** (daily 8:00–22:00, take a number and wait, tel. 902-240-202 for reservations and info) and one near **Plaza Nueva** in the center (Mon–Fri 9:30–14:00 & 17:30–20:00, Sat 10:00–13:30, closed Sun, Calle Zaragoza 29, tel. 954-211-455). Many travel agencies sell train tickets for the same price as the train station (look for a train sticker in agency windows). You can check schedules at www.renfe.es, but be warned that the English version of the site often freezes up during ticket purchases.

Tours in Sevilla

Guided City Walks by Concepción—Concepción Delgado, an enthusiastic teacher and a joy to listen to, takes small groups on English-language walks. Using me as her guinea pig, Concepción designed a fine two-hour **Sevilla Cultural Show & Tell**. This introduction to her hometown, sharing important insights the average visitor misses, is worthwhile, even on a one-day visit (€12/person, Sept–July Mon–Sat at 10:30; Aug Mon, Wed, and Fri at 10:30; starting from statue in Plaza Nueva).

For those wanting to really understand the city's two most important sights—which are tough to fully appreciate—Concepción also offers in-depth tours of the **cathedral** and the **Alcázar** (both tours last 1.25 hours, cost €6—not including entrance fees, and meet at 13:00 at the statue in Plaza del Triunfo; cathedral tours—Mon, Wed, and Fri; Alcázar tours—Tue, Thu, and Sat; no Alcázar tours in Aug).

While you can just show up for Concepción's tours, it's smart to confirm the departure times and reserve a spot (tel. 902-158-226, mobile 616-501-100, www.sevillawalkingtours.com, info @sevillawalkingtours.com). Concepción does no tours on Sundays or holidays.

Hop-on, Hop-off Bus Tours—Two competing city bus tours leave from the curb near the riverside Golden Tower. You'll see the buses parked with salespeople handing out fliers. Each does about an hour-long swing through the city with a recorded narration (€15, daily 10:00–21:00, green route has shorter option). The tours, which allow hopping on and off at four stops, are heavy on Expo '29 and Expo '92 neighborhoods—both zones of little interest in 2010. While the narration does its best, Sevilla is most interesting where buses can't go.

Horse and Buggy Tours—A carriage ride is a classic, popular way to survey the city and a relax- ing way to enjoy María Luisa Park (€50 for a 45-min clip-clop, find a likable English-speaking driver for better narration). Look for rigs at Plaza América, Plaza del Triunfo, Golden Tower, Alfonso XIII Hotel, and Avenida Isabel la Católica.

Sevilla at a Glance

▲▲▲**Flamenco** Flamboyant, riveting music-and-dance performances, offered at clubs throughout town. **Hours:** Shows start as early as 19:00. See page 543.

▲▲**Cathedral and Giralda Bell Tower** The world's largest Gothic church, with Columbus' tomb, a treasury, and climbable tower. **Hours:** July–Aug Mon–Sat 9:30–17:00, Sun 14:30–18:00; Sept–June Mon–Sat 11:00–18:00, Sun 14:30–19:00. See page 521.

▲▲**Alcázar** Palace built by the Moors in the 10th century, revamped in the 14th century, and still serving as royal digs. **Hours:** Peak season Tue–Sun 9:30–19:00, off-season Tue–Sun 9:30–17:00, closed Mon year-round. See page 529.

▲▲**Flamenco Dance Museum** High-tech museum explaining the history and art of Sevilla's favorite dance. **Hours:** Daily 9:00–19:00. See page 534.

▲▲**Basílica de la Macarena** Church and museum with the much-venerated Weeping Virgin statue and two significant floats from Sevilla's Holy Week celebrations. **Hours:** Daily 9:30–14:00 & 17:00–20:00. See page 538.

▲▲**Bullfight Museum** Guided tour of the bullring and its museum. **Hours:** Daily May–Oct 9:30–20:00, Nov–April 9:30–19:00, on fight days until 14:00. See page 540.

▲▲**Evening Paseo** Locals strolling in the cool of the evening, mainly along Avenida de la Constitución, Barrio Santa Cruz, the Calle Sierpes and Tetuán shopping pedestrian zone, and the Guadalquivir River. **Hours:** Spring through fall, until very late at night in summer. See page 543.

▲**Museo Palacio de la Condesa de Lebrija** A fascinating 18th-century aristocratic mansion. **Hours:** Mon–Fri 10:30–19:30, Sat 10:00–14:00, closed Sun. See page 535.

▲**Museo de Bellas Artes** Andalucía's top paintings, including works by Spanish masters Murillo and Zurbarán. **Hours:** Tue–Sat 9:00–20:30, Sun 9:00–14:30, closed Mon. See page 536.

▲**Bullfights** Some of Spain's best bullfighting, held at Sevilla's arena. **Hours:** Fights generally at 18:30 on most Sundays in May and June, on Easter, and daily through the April Fair and in late Sept. Rookies fight small bulls on Thursdays in July. See page 540.

Boat Cruises—Boring one-hour panoramic tours leave every 30 minutes from the dock behind Torre de Oro. The low-energy recorded narration is hard to follow, but there's little to see anyway (overpriced at €15, tel. 954-561-692).

Andalusian Minibus Tours—Aussie Paul McGrath, who's lived in Sevilla for 11 years, takes small groups on all-day tours in his nine-seat minivan. You'll head to the villages south of Sevilla, which are difficult to reach without a car. Paul provides some commentary en route. This is an efficient, economic way to explore the great whitewashed towns along the "Route of the Pueblos Blancos." You'll leave in the morning and visit Olvera, Zahara, Grazalema, and Setenil de las Bodegas; the tour also includes a stop at the Moorish castle Aguzaderas, an olive-oil mill, and a swimming-stop option in the summer (€53, leaves daily from Torre de Oro at 9:00, returns about 19:30, call or email to reserve, mobile 657-889-875, www.theotherspain.galeon.com, the-other-spain @hotmail.com).

More Tours—**Visitours**, a typical big-bus tour company, does €85 all-day trips to Córdoba Tuesday, Thursday, and Saturday (tel. 954-460-985, mobile 686-413-413, www.visitours.es/in, visitours@terra .es). For other guides, contact the **Guides Association of Sevilla** (tel. 954-210-037, www.apitsevilla.com, visitas@apitsevilla.com).

Self-Guided Walk

Barrio Santa Cruz

Of Sevilla's once-thriving Jewish Quarter, only the tangled street plan and a wistful Old World ambience survive. This classy maze of lanes (too narrow for cars), small plazas, tile-covered patios, and whitewashed houses with wrought-iron latticework draped in flowers is a great refuge from the summer heat and bustle of Sevilla. The narrow streets—some with buildings so close they're called "kissing lanes"—were actually designed to maximize shade. Even today, locals claim the Barrio Santa Cruz is three degrees cooler than the rest of the city.

Orange trees abound. Since they never lose their leaves, they provide constant shade. But forget about eating any of the oranges. They're bitter and used only to make vitamins, perfume, cat food, and that marmalade you can't avoid in British B&Bs.

The Barrio is made for wandering. Getting lost is easy, and I recommend doing just that. But to get started, here's a plaza-to-plaza walk that loops you through the *corazón* (heart) of the

Barrio Santa Cruz Self-Guided Walk

1. Plaza de la Virgen de los Reyes
2. Plaza del Triunfo
3. Patio de Banderas
4. Calle Agua
5. Plaza de la Santa Cruz
6. Plaza de Refinadores
7. Casa de Murillo
8. Convent of San José del Carmen
9. Plaza de los Venerables
10. Plaza de Doña Elvira
11. Plaza de la Alianza

50 YARDS
50 METERS

WALKING TOUR

SEVILLA

neighborhood and back out again. Ideally, don't do the walk in the morning, when the Barrio's charm is trampled by tour groups. Early evening (around 18:00) is ideal. Start in front of the cathedral.

❶ **Plaza de la Virgen de los Reyes:** This square is dedicated to the Virgin of the Kings. See her tile on the wall. She's big here because she was brought by the Spanish king when he retook the town from the Moors in 1248. The fountain dates from 1929. From this peaceful square, look up the street leading away from the cathedral and notice the characteristic (government-protected) 19th-century architecture. The iron work is typical of Andalucía, and the pride of Sevilla. You'll see it and these traditional colors all over the town center.

• *Walk with the cathedral on your right (passing the guard who allows only real worshippers into the royal chapel).*

❷ **Plaza del Triunfo:** The "Plaza of Triumph" is named for the 1755 earthquake that destroyed Lisbon, but didn't rock Sevilla or its tower. Notice the statue, thanking the Virgin.

• *Pass through an opening in the Alcázar wall under the arch. You'll emerge into a courtyard called...*

❸ **Patio de Banderas:** Named for "flags," not Antonio, the Banderas Courtyard was once a kind of military parade ground for the royal guard. The barracks surrounding the square once housed the king's bodyguards. Today it offers a postcard view of the Giralda Bell Tower.

• *Exit the courtyard at the far corner, through the Judería arch. Walking alongside the Alcázar wall, take the first left, then right, through a small square and follow the narrow alleyway called...*

❹ **Calle Agua:** This street is named for the water pipes in the wall that flowed into the Alcázar (you can see them at the end of the lane—they follow the wall of the Alcázar gardens). On the left, peek through iron gates for the occasional glimpse of the flower-smothered patios of exclusive private residences. The patio at #2 is a delight—ringed with columns, filled with flowers, and colored with glazed tiles. The tiles are not only decorative; they keep buildings cooler in the summer heat. At the end of the street (look back to see the old plumbing) is an entrance into the pleasant Murillo Gardens (to the right), formerly the fruit-and-vegetable gardens for the Alcázar.

• *Don't enter the gardens now, but instead cross the square and continue 20 yards down a lane to...*

❺ **Plaza de la Santa Cruz:** Arguably the heart of the Barrio, this was once the site of a synagogue (there were three, now there are none), which Christians destroyed. They replaced the synagogue with a church, which the French (under Napoleon) then demolished. It's a bit of history that locals remember when they see

Sevilla's Jews

In the summer of 1391, smoldering anti-Jewish sentiment flared up in Sevilla. On June 6, the city's Jewish Quarter (Judería) was ransacked by Christian mobs. Four thousand Jews were killed, 5,000 Jewish families were driven from their homes, synagogues were stripped and transformed into churches, the Star of David came down, and the former Judería eventually became the neighborhood of the Holy Cross—Barrio Santa Cruz. Sevilla's uprising spread through Spain (and Europe), the first of many nasty pogroms during the next century.

Before the pogrom, Jews had lived in Sevilla for centuries as the city's respected merchants, doctors, and bankers. They flourished under the Muslim Moors. When Sevilla was "liberated" by King Ferdinand (1248), Jews were given protection by Spain's kings and allowed a measure of self-government, though they were confined to the Jewish neighborhood.

But by the 14th century, Jews were increasingly accused of everything from poisoning wells to ritually sacrificing Christian babies. Mobs killed suspected Jews, some of Sevilla's most respected Jewish citizens had their fortunes confiscated, and Jewish kids were mocked and bullied on the playground.

After 1391, Jews faced a choice: Be persecuted (even killed), relocate, or convert to Christianity. Those who converted—called *conversos,* New Christians, or *marranos* ("swine")—were always under suspicion of practicing their old faith in private, undermining true Christianity. Fanning the suspicion was the fact that Old Christians were threatened by this new social class of converted Jews who now had equal status.

To root out the perceived problem of underground Judaism, the "Catholic Monarchs" Ferdinand and Isabel established the Inquisition in Spain (1478). Under the direction of Grand Inquisitor Tomás de Torquemada, these religious courts arrested and interrogated *conversos* suspected of practicing Judaism. Using long solitary confinement and torture, they extracted confessions.

On February 6, 1481, Sevilla hosted Spain's first auto-da-fé ("act of faith"), a public confession and punishment for heresy. Six accused *conversos* were paraded barefoot into the cathedral, made to publicly confess their sins, then burned at the stake. Over the next three decades, thousands of *conversos* (some historians say hundreds, some say tens of thousands) were tried and killed in Spain.

In 1492, the same year the last Moors were driven from Spain, Ferdinand and Isabel decreed that all remaining Jews convert or be expelled (to Portugal and ultimately to Holland). Spain emerged as a nation unified under the banner of Christianity.

Bartolomé Murillo
(1617–1682)

The son of a barber of Seville, Bartolomé Murillo got his start selling paintings meant for export to the frontier churches of the Americas. In his 20s, he became famous after he painted a series of saints for Sevilla's Franciscan monastery. By about 1650, Murillo's sugary, simple, and accessible religious style was spreading through Spain and beyond.

Murillo painted street kids with cute smiles and grimy faces, and radiant young Marías with Ivory-soap complexions and rapturous poses (Immaculate Conceptions). His paintings view the world through a soft-focus lens, wrapping everything in warm colors and soft light, with a touch (too much, for some) of sentimentality.

Murillo became rich, popular, a family man, and the toast of Sevilla's high society. In 1664, his wife died, leaving him heartbroken, but his last 20 years were his most prolific. At age 65, Murillo died painting, falling off a scaffold. His tomb is lost somewhere under the bricks of Plaza de la Santa Cruz.

the red, white, and blue French flag marking the French consulate, now overlooking this peaceful square. The painter Murillo, who was buried in the now-gone church, lies somewhere below you. On the square you'll find the recommended Los Gallos flamenco bar and Bar El Tamboríl, which combusts nightly after midnight with impromptu flamenco (described on pages 544 and 545).

• *Follow Calle Mezquita farther east to the nearby...*

❻ **Plaza de Refinadores:** Sevilla's most famous (if fictional) 17th-century citizen is honored here with a statue. Don Juan Tenorio—the original Don Juan—was a notorious sex addict and atheist who thumbed his nose at the stifling Church-driven morals of his day.

• *Backtrack to Plaza de la Santa Cruz and turn right (north) on Calle Santa Teresa. At #8 is...*

❼ **Casa de Murillo:** One of Sevilla's famous painters lived here, soaking in the ambience of street life and reproducing it in his paintings of cute beggar children (see sidebar).

• *Directly across from Casa de Murillo is the...*

❽ **Convent of San José del Carmen:** This is where St. Teresa stayed when she visited from her hometown of Ávila. The convent (closed to the public) keeps relics of the mystic nun, such as the manuscript of her treatise *Las Moradas* ("The Interior Castle," "where truth dwells").

Continue north on Calle Santa Teresa, then take the first left on Calle Lope de Rueda, then right on **Calle Reinoso.** This street—so narrow that the buildings almost touch—is one of the Barrio's "kissing lanes."

• *The street spills into...*

❾ **Plaza de los Venerables:** This square is another candidate for "heart of the Barrio." The streets branching off it ooze local ambience. The large harmonious Baroque-style Hospital de los Venerables (1675), once a priests' retirement home (the "venerables"), is now a museum (€4.75, includes audioguide). The highlight is the church and courtyard, featuring a round, sunken fountain. The museum also has a small Velázquez painting of Santa Rufina, one of two patron saints protecting Sevilla. The painting was acquired at a 2007 auction for more than €12 million.

• *Continuing west on Calle Gloria, you soon reach...*

❿ **Plaza de Doña Elvira:** This small square—with orange trees, tile benches, and a stone fountain—sums up our Barrio walk. Shops sell work by local artisans, such as ceramics, embroidery, and fans.

• *Cross the plaza and head north along Calle Rodrigo Caro into...*

⓫ **Plaza de la Alianza:** Ever consider a career change? Gain inspiration at the John Fulton Studio, a former art gallery featuring the work of the American who pursued two dreams. Though born in Philadelphia, Fulton got hooked on bullfighting. He trained in the tacky bullrings of Mexico, then in 1956 he moved to Sevilla, the world capital of the sport. His career as matador was not top-notch, and the Spaniards were slow to warm to the Yankee, but his courage and persistence earned their grudging respect. After retirement, he put down the cape and picked up a brush, making the colorful paintings in this studio.

• *From Plaza de la Alianza, you can return to the cathedral by turning left (west) on Calle Romero Murube (along the wall). Or head northeast on Callejón de Rodrigo Caro, which intersects with Calle Mateos Gago, a street lined with atmospheric tapas bars.*

Sights in Sevilla

▲▲Cathedral and Giralda Bell Tower

Sevilla's cathedral is the third-largest church in Europe (after St. Peter's at the Vatican and St. Paul's in London), and the largest Gothic church anywhere. When they ripped down a mosque of brick on this site in 1401, the Reconquista Christians bragged, "We'll build a cathedral so huge that anyone who sees it will take us for madmen." They built for 120 years. Even today, the descendants of those madmen proudly display an enlarged photocopy of their *Guinness Book of Records* letter certifying, "The cathedral with the largest area is: Santa María de la Sede in Sevilla, 126 meters long, 82 meters wide, and 30 meters high."

Cost and Hours: €8; July–Aug Mon–Sat 9:30–17:00, Sun 14:30–18:00; Sept–June Mon–Sat 11:00–18:00, Sun 14:30–19:00; last entry one hour before closing, WC and drinking fountain inside near entrance and in courtyard near exit, tel. 954-214-971.

Tours: My self-guided tour (next) covers the basics. The €3 audioguide explains each side chapel for anyone interested in all the old paintings and dry details. For €6, you can enjoy Concepción Delgado's tour instead (described on page 514).

◐ Self-Guided Tour: Enter the cathedral at the south end (closest to the Alcázar, with a full-size replica of the Giralda's weathervane statue in the patio).

• *First, head to the...*

Art Pavilion: Just past the turnstile, you step into a pavilion of paintings that once hung in the church, including works by Sevilla's two 17th-century masters—Bartolomé Murillo *(St. Ferdinand)* and Francisco de Zurbarán *(St. John the Baptist in the Desert)*. Also find a painting showing the two patron saints of Sevilla—Santa Justa and Santa Rufina. They are easy to identify by their pots and palm branches, and the bell tower symbolizing the town they protect. As you tour the cathedral, keep track of how many depictions of this dynamic and saintly duo you spot. They're everywhere.

• *Walking past a rack of church maps and a WC, enter the actual church.*

Restoration Braces: The first things you'll see are the restoration braces supporting huge pillars. These are intended to help keep the building from collapsing as people search for an answer to the problem of the pillars' cracking. (But I'd move right along.)

• *In the center of the church, sit down in front of the...*

High Altar: Look through the wrought-iron Renaissance grille at what's called the largest altarpiece *(retablo mayor)* ever made—65 feet tall, with 44 scenes from the life of Jesus carved out of walnut and chestnut, blanketed by a staggering amount of gold leaf (and dust). The work took three generations to complete (1481–1564). The story is told left to right, bottom (birth of Jesus) to top (Pentecost), with the Crucifixion at the dizzying summit.

Sevilla's Cathedral

AVENIDA DE LA

ALEMANES (STREET)

EXIT

18

CLOISTER

17

COURT OF THE ORANGE TREES

WC

20 YARDS
20 M

← GIRALDA TOWER

12

13

11

16

10

CHOIR
4

HIGH ALTAR
3

9

PLAZA VIRGEN DE LOS REYES

TO
19 ←
CONSTITUCIÓN

14

15

2

5

6

8

WC

1

7

← TREASURY

SHOP

DCH

ENTRY

PLAZA DEL TRIUNFO

SEVILLA

1 Art Pavilion
2 Pillar Restoration Braces
3 High Altar
4 Choir
5 Tomb of Columbus
6 Antigua Chapel
7 Sacristy
8 Treasury
9 Royal Chapel
10 Chapel of St. Peter

11 View of Plateresque Ceiling
12 Chapel of St. Anthony
13 Pennant of Fernando III
14 Back of the Nave
15 MURILLO – Guardian Angel
16 Giralda Tower Climb Entrance
17 Court of the Orange Trees
18 Moorish-Style Doorway
19 To Nun-Baked Goodies

• *Turn around and check out the...*

Choir: Facing the high altar, the choir features an organ of 7,000 pipes (played at the 10:00 Mass Mon–Fri, not in July–Aug, free for worshippers). A choir area like this one (an enclosure within the cathedral for more intimate services) is common in Spain and England, but rare in churches elsewhere. The big, spinnable book holder in the middle of the room held giant hymnals—large enough for all to chant from in a pre-Xerox age when there weren't enough books for everyone.

• *Now turn 90 degrees to the left and march to find the...*

Tomb of Columbus: In front of the cathedral's entrance for pilgrims are four kings who carry the tomb of Christopher Columbus. His pallbearers represent the regions of Castile, Aragon, León, and Navarre (identify them by their team shirts). Columbus even traveled a lot posthumously. He was buried first in Spain, then in Santo Domingo in the Dominican Republic, then Cuba, and finally—when Cuba gained independence from Spain, around 1900—he sailed home again to Sevilla. Are the remains actually his? Sevillans like to think so. (Columbus died in 1506. Five hundred years later, to help celebrate the anniversary of his death, DNA samples gave Sevillans the evidence they needed to substantiate their claim.) High above on the left is a mural of St. Christopher—patron saint of travelers—from 1584. The clock above has been ticking since 1788.

• *Head to the next chapel on the right to find the...*

Antigua Chapel: Within this chapel is the gilded fresco of the Virgin Antigua, the oldest art in the church. It was actually painted onto a horseshoe-shaped prayer niche of the former mosque on this site. After Sevilla was reconquered in 1248, the mosque served as a church for about 120 years—until it was torn down to make room for this huge cathedral. Builders, captivated by the beauty of the Virgin holding the rose and the Christ Child holding the bird (and knowing that she was considered the protector of sailors in this port city), decided to save the fresco.

• *Exiting the chapel, we'll tour the cathedral counterclockwise. As you explore, note that its many chapels are described in English, and many of the windows have their dates worked into the design. Just on the other side of Columbus, step into the...*

Sacristy: This space is used each morning before Mass. The Goya painting above the altar features Justa and Rufina—the two patron saints of Sevilla, who were martyred in ancient Roman times. In addition to the town bell tower, they're always shown with their trademark items. I say they're each holding a bowl of *gazpacho* (particularly refreshing on hot summer days) and sprigs of rosemary from local Gypsies (an annoyance even back then). Art historians claim that since they were pottery-makers, they are shown with earthenware, and the sprigs are palm leaves—symbolic of their martyrdom. Whatever.

• *A few rooms over is the...*

Treasury: The *tesoro* fills several rooms in the corner of the church. Start by marveling at the ornate, 16th-century Plateresque dome of the main room, a grand souvenir from Sevilla's Golden Age. The intricate masonry resembles lacy silverwork (it's named for *plata*—silver). God is way up in the cupola. The three layers of figures below him show the heavenly host; relatives in purgatory—hands folded—looking to heaven and hoping you do them well; and the wretched in hell, including a topless sinner engulfed in flames and teased cruelly by pitchfork-wielding monsters. Locals use the 110-pound silver monstrance, which dominates this room, to parade the holy host (communion bread) through town during Corpus Christi festivities.

Wander deeper into the treasury to find a unique oval dome. It's in the 16th-century chapter room *(sala capitular)*, where monthly meetings take place with the bishop (he gets the throne, while the others share the bench). The paintings here are by Murillo: a fine *Immaculate Conception* (1668, above the bishop's throne) and portraits of saints important to Sevillans.

The wood-paneled "room of ornaments" shows off gold and silver reliquaries, which hold hundreds of holy body parts, as well as Spain's most valuable crown. The Corona de la Virgen de los Reyes sparkles with 11,000 precious stones and the world's largest pearl—used as the torso of an angel. Opposite the crown is a reliquary featuring "a piece of the true cross."

• *Leave the treasury and cross through the church to see...*

More Church Sights: First you'll pass the closed-to-tourists **Royal Chapel,** the burial place of several of the kings of Castile (open for worship only—access from outside), then the **Chapel of St. Peter,** which is dark but filled with paintings by Francisco de Zurbarán (showing scenes from the life of St. Peter). At the far corner—past the glass case displaying the *Guinness* certificate declaring that this is indeed the world's largest church by area—is the entry to the Giralda Bell Tower. You'll finish your visit here. But for now, continue your counterclockwise circuit. Near the middle (and high) altar, crane your neck skyward to admire the **Plateresque tracery** on the ceiling.

The **Chapel of St. Anthony** (Capilla de San Antonio), the last chapel on the right, is used for baptisms. The Renaissance

Immaculate Conception

Throughout Sevilla and Spain, you'll see paintings titled *The Immaculate Conception,* all looking quite similar (see example on page 520). Young, lovely, and beaming radiantly, these virgins look pure, untainted...you might even say "immaculate." According to Catholic doctrine, Mary, the future mother of Jesus, entered the world free from the original sin that other mortals share. When she died, her purity allowed her to be taken up directly to heaven (the Assumption).

The doctrine of Immaculate Conception can be confusing, even to Catholics. It does not mean that the Virgin Mary herself was born of a virgin. Rather, Mary's mother and father conceived her in the natural way. But at the moment Mary's soul animated her flesh, God granted her a special exemption from original sin. The doctrine of Immaculate Conception had been popular since medieval times, though it was not codified until 1854. It was Sevilla's own Bartolomé Murillo (1617–1682) who painted the model of this goddess-like Mary, copied by so many lesser artists. In Counter-Reformation times (when Murillo lived), paintings of a fresh-faced, ecstatic Mary made abstract doctrines like the Immaculate Conception and the Assumption tangible and accessible to all.

An easy way to recognize an image of the Immaculate Conception is to look for the following clues: a radiant crown, a crescent moon at Mary's feet, and often a pose showing Mary stepping on cherubs' heads. Paintings by Murillo frequently portray Mary in a blue robe with long, wavy hair—young and innocent.

baptismal font has delightful carved angels dancing along its base. In Murillo's painting, *Vision of St. Anthony* (1656), the saint kneels in wonder as a baby Jesus comes down surrounded by a choir of angels. Anthony is one of Iberia's most popular saints. As he is the patron saint of lost things, people come here to pray for Anthony's help in finding jobs, car keys, and life partners. Above that is the *Baptism of Christ,* also by Murillo. You don't need to be an art historian to know that the stained glass dates from 1685. And by now, you must know who the women are...

Nearby, a glass case displays the **pennant of Fernando III,** which was raised over the minaret of the mosque on November 23, 1248, as Christian forces finally expelled the Moors from Sevilla. For centuries, it was paraded through the city on special days.

Continuing on, stand at the **back of the nave** (behind the choir) and appreciate the ornate immensity of the church. Can you see the angels trumpeting on their Cuban mahogany? Any birds?

Turn around. The massive candlestick holder dates from 1560. To the left is a niche with **Murillo's *Guardian Angel*** pointing to the light and showing an astonished child the way.

• *Backtrack the length of the church toward the Giralda Bell Tower, and notice the back of the choir's Baroque pipe organ. The* exit *sign leads to the Court of the Orange Trees and the exit. But first, some exercise.*

Giralda Tower Climb: Your church admission includes entry to the bell tower. Notice the beautiful Moorish simplicity as you climb to its top, 330 feet up, for a grand city view. The spiraling ramp was designed to accommodate riders on horseback, who galloped up five times a day to give the Muslim call to prayer.

• *Go back down the stairs and visit the...*

Court of the Orange Trees: Today's cloister was once the mosque's Court of the Orange Trees (Patio de los Naranjos).

Twelfth-century Muslims stopped at the fountain in the middle to wash their hands, face, and feet before praying. The ankle-breaking lanes between the bricks were once irrigation streams—a reminder that the Moors introduced irrigation to Iberia. The mosque was made of bricks; the church is built of stone. The only remnants of the mosque today are the Court of the Orange Trees, the Giralda Bell Tower, and the site itself.

• *You'll exit the cathedral through the Court of the Orange Trees (if you need to use the WCs, they're at the far end of the courtyard, downstairs). As you leave, notice the arch over the...*

Moorish-Style Doorway: As with much of the Moorish-looking art in town, it's actually Christian—the two coats of arms are a giveaway. The relief above the door (looking in from outside) shows the Bible story of Jesus ridding the temple of the merchants...a reminder to contemporary merchants that there will be no retail activity in the church. The plaque on the right is one of many scattered throughout town showing a place mentioned in the books of Miguel de Cervantes, the great 16th-century Spanish writer. (In this case, the topic was pickpockets.) The huge green doors predate the church. They are a bit of the surviving pre-1248 mosque—wood covered with bronze. Study the fine workmanship.

Giralda Tower Exterior: Step across the street from the exit gate and look at the bell tower. Formerly a Moorish minaret from

Christopher Columbus
(1451–1506)

This Italian wool-weaver ran off to sea, was shipwrecked in Portugal, married a captain's daughter, learned Portuguese and Spanish, and convinced Spain's monarchs to finance his bold scheme to trade with the East by sailing west. On August 3, 1492, Columbus set sail from Palos (near Huelva, 60 miles west of Sevilla) with three ships and 90 men, hoping to land in Asia, which Columbus estimated was 3,000 miles away. Three thousand miles later—with the superstitious crew ready to mutiny, having seen evil omens like a falling meteor and a jittery compass—Columbus landed on an island in the Bahamas (October 12, 1492), convinced he'd reached Asia. They traded with the "Indians" and returned home to Palos harbor, where they were received as heroes.

Columbus made three more voyages to the New World and became rich with gold. He gained a bad reputation among the colonists, was arrested, and returned to Spain in chains. Though pardoned, Columbus fell out of favor with the court. On May 20, 1506, he died in Valladolid. His son said he was felled by "gout and by grief at seeing himself fallen from his high estate," but historians speculate that diabetes or syphilis may have contributed. Columbus died thinking he'd visited Asia, unaware he'd opened up Europe to a New World.

which Muslims were called to prayer, it became the cathedral's bell tower after the Reconquista. A 4,500-pound bronze statue

symbolizing the Triumph of Faith (specifically, the Christian faith over the Muslim one) caps the tower and serves as a weather vane (*giraldillo* in Spanish). In 1356, the original top of the tower fell. You're looking at a 16th-century Christian-built top with a ribbon of letters proclaiming, "The strongest tower is the name of God" (you can see *Fortísima*—"strongest"—from this vantage point).

Now circle around for a close look at the corner of the tower at ground level. Needing more strength than their bricks could provide for the lowest section of the tower, the Moors used Roman-cut stones. You can actually read the Latin chiseled onto one of the stones 2,000 years ago. The tower offers a brief recap of the city's history—sitting on a Roman foundation, a long Moorish period capped by our Christian age. Today, by law, no building can be higher than the statue atop the tower.

• *If you've worked up an appetite, finish your cathedral tour with some...*

Nun-Baked Goodies: Stop by the El Torno Pasteleria de Conventos, a co-op where the various orders of cloistered nuns send their handicrafts (such as baby's baptismal dresses) and baked goods to be sold. "El Torno" is the lazy Susan that the cloistered nuns spin to sell their cakes and cookies without being seen. You'll have to go to a convent to see the *torno*, but this humble little hole-in-the-wall shop is still worth a peek (Sept–July Mon–Fri 10:00–13:30 & 17:00–19:30, Sat–Sun 10:30–14:00, closed Aug, across Avenida de la Constitución, immediately in front of the cathedral's biggest door, follow *dulces de convento* sign down a little covered lane to Plaza Cabildo 21, tel. 954-219-190).

Near the Cathedral

Avenida de la Constitución—Old Sevilla is bisected by its grand boulevard. It was named to celebrate the 1978 democratic constitution the Spanish people adopted as they moved quickly after the 1975 death of Franco to establish their freedom. Long a commercial street, it was made into a pedestrian boulevard in 2007. Overnight, the city's paseo route took on a new dimension. And suddenly cafés and shops here had an appeal. (Two Starbucks moved in, placed strategically like bookends on the boulevard, but they're having a tough time winning the loyalty of locals who like small coffees for €1 rather than mammoth ones for €4.) The tram line (which is infamous for being short—only three-quarters of a mile long) is controversial, as it violates what might have been a more purely people zone.

Alcázar and Nearby

▲▲**Alcázar**—Originally a 10th-century palace built for the governors of the local Moorish state, this building still functions as

a royal palace...the oldest in use in Europe. What you see today is an extensive 14th-century rebuild, done by Moorish (Mudejar) workmen for the Christian king, Pedro I. Pedro was nicknamed either "the Cruel" or "the Just," depending on which end of his sword you were on.

Cost and Hours: €7.50; peak season Tue–Sun 9:30–19:00, off-season Tue–Sun 9:30–17:00, closed Mon year-round; tel. 954-502-323. Tour groups clog the palace and rob it of any mystery in the morning (especially on Tue); come as late as possible.

Tours: The fast-moving, easy-to-use

€3 audioguide gives you an hour of information as you wander—
if you want that much (drop it off at the exit). Again, rather
then renting the audioguide, you could follow my self-guided
tour (next), or consider Concepción Delgado's €6 Alcázar tour
(described on page 514).

○ **Self-Guided Tour:** The Alcázar is a thought-provoking
glimpse of a graceful Al-Andalus (Moorish) world that might
have survived its Castilian conquerors...but didn't. The floor plan
is intentionally confusing, part of the style designed to make
experiencing the place more exciting and surprising. While
Granada's Alhambra was built by Moors for Moorish rulers,
what you see here is essentially a Christian ruler's palace, built in
the Moorish style.

Just past the turnstiles, walk through the **Patio of the Lions**
and stop under the arch of the wall to
orient yourself. Facing the **Patio de la
Montería**, you see the palace's three
wings. The wing on the right is the
16th-century Admiral's Apartments;
straight ahead is King Pedro the
Cruel's Palace; and on the left is the
13th-century Gothic wing. You'll tour
them in that order (entering the Gothic
wing from within Pedro's palace).

Before starting, notice the public WCs in the far-left corner,
and a staircase in the far-right corner leading up to the lived-in
Royal Apartments. (These are available by tour only. They're
similar to what you'll see downstairs, but with furniture. If interested, go there now to book a spot—€4 for a 25-min escorted walk
through 15 rooms with an audioguide, 15 people per tour, lockers
provided for your visit.)

• *Start by heading to the...*

Admiral's Apartments: When Queen Isabel debriefed
Columbus here after his New World discoveries, she realized this
could be big business. In 1503, she created this wing to administer
Spain's New World ventures. Step inside.

Straight ahead, through the main hall, you'll find the Admiral's
Lounge with a chapel featuring a **painting of Santa María de los
Buenos Aires Chapel** (St. Mary of the Fair Winds—or, as many
Spanish boys would say, "of the Good Farts"). The Virgin of the
Fair Winds was the patron saint of navigators and a favorite of
Columbus. Many historians believe that the fine Virgin of the
Navigators altarpiece (painted by Alejo Fernández in the 1530s)
has the only portrait of Ferdinand (on left, with gold cape) with
Columbus. Columbus is the blond guy on the right. Columbus'
son said of his dad: "In his youth his hair was blond, but when he

Alcázar

TO CATHEDRAL

PLAZA DEL TRIUNFO

BARRIO SANTA CRUZ

WALLS

ROM. MUR.

PATIO DE BANDERAS

ENTER

SHOP

EXIT

SHOP

TO ℹ️

C. MANARA

WALLS

CALLE DEAN MIRANDA

GATE

WC

PATIO DEL CRUCIERO

JUDERIA

VIDA

GARDENS

DCH

50 YARDS
50 METERS

SEVILLA

1 Patio of the Lions
2 Patio de la Montería
3 Stairs to Royal Apartments
4 Admiral's Apartments
5 Painting of Santa María de los Buenos Aires Chapel
6 Ornate Fans
7 Court of the Maidens

8 King Pedro the Cruel's Palace
9 Dolls' Court
10 Gothic Wing
11 Big Tapestries
12 Moorish Garden
13 Christian Garden
14 Elevated Walkway

reached 30, it all turned white." As it's likely the earliest known portrait of Columbus, it also might be the most accurate. Notice how the Virgin's cape seems to protect everyone under it—even the Native Americans in the dark background (the first time "Indians" were painted in Europe). Left of the painting is a model of Columbus' *Santa María,* his flagship and the only one of his three ships not to survive the 1492 voyage. Columbus complained that the *Santa María*—a big cargo ship, different from the sleek *Niña* and *Pinta* caravels—was too slow. On Christmas Day, it ran aground and tore a hole in its hull. The ship was dismantled to build the first permanent structure in America, a fort for 39 colonists. (After Columbus left, the natives burned the fort and killed the colonists.) Opposite the altarpiece (in the center of the back wall) is the family coat of arms of Columbus' descendants, who now live in Spain and Puerto Rico. Using Columbus' Spanish name, it reads: "To Castile and to León, Colón gave a new world."

Before leaving, return to the still-used reception room and pop into the room beyond the grand piano for a look at **ornate fans** (mostly foreign, described in English) and a long painting showing 17th-century Sevilla during Holy Week. Follow the procession, which is much like today's procession of traditional floats, carried by teams of 24 to 48 men and followed by a parade of KKK-looking penitents (who have worn these traditional costumes for centuries—long before such hoods became associated with racism in the American South).

• *Return to the main courtyard, enter the middle wing, and walk to the left through the vestibule until you hit the big courtyard called the* **Court of the Maidens** *(Patio de las Doncellas).*

King Pedro the Cruel's Palace: This is the 14th-century nucleus of the complex—the real Alcázar. Centered around the elegantly proportioned Court of the Maidens, the palace is decorated in 14th-century Moorish style below and a 16th-century Renaissance style above.

As you explore this wing, circulate counterclockwise through rooms branching off of this central courtyard and imagine day-to-day life in the palace (with VIP guests tripping on the tiny but jolting steps). King Pedro (1334–1369) cruelly abandoned his wife and moved into the Alcázar with his mistress. He hired Muslim workers from Granada to re-create the romance of that city's Alhambra in Sevilla's stark Alcázar. The designers created a microclimate engineered for coolness: water, plants, pottery, thick walls, and darkness. Even with the inevitable hodgepodge of style that comes with 600 years of renovation, this is considered Spain's best example of the Mudejar style. Notice the sumptuous ceilings; you'll see peacocks, castles, and kings that you wouldn't find in religious Muslim decor, which avoids images. The stylized Arabic script survives, creating a visual chant of verses from the Quran seen in Moorish buildings (including the Alhambra). The artisans added propaganda phrases such as, "Dedicated to the magnificent Sultan Pedro—thanks to God!"

The second courtyard, the smaller and more delicate **Dolls' Court** (Patio de las Muñecas), was for the king's private and family life. Originally, the center of the courtyard had a pool, cooling the residents and reflecting the decorative patterns once brightly painted on the walls.

• *Leave this wing from the big courtyard. Head to the staircase opposite from where you entered, and climb up into the...*

Gothic Wing: This wing of the palace shows fine tapestries from Brussels (1554). Find the second hall—with the **biggest tapestries**. These celebrate Emperor Charles V's 1535 victory in Tunis over the Turks (described both in Spanish along the top and in Latin along the bottom). The map tapestry comes with an unusual perspective—with Africa at the top (it's supposed to be from a Barcelona aerial perspective). Find the big fortified city in the middle (Barcelona, just above eye level), Santiago de Compostela, Lisboa (Lisbon), Gibraltar, the west edge of Italy, Rome, Sicily, and the Mediterranean islands. Don't try to navigate by this early map. Montserrat, which is just a few miles outside of Barcelona, is shown all the way over by Lisbon. The artist paints himself holding the legend—with a scale in both leagues and miles. This is an 18th-century copy of the original.

• *Head outside to...*

The Gardens: This space is full of tropical flowers, wild cats, cool fountains, and hot tourists. The intimate geometric zone nearest the palace is the Moorish garden. The far-flung garden beyond that was the backyard of the Christian ruler. The **elevated walkway** along the left side of the gardens (access at both ends) provides fine views. You can explore the gardens and return via this walkway, or vice versa.

Archivo de Indias—The Lonja Palace (across the street from Alcázar) was designed by the same person who designed El Escorial. Originally a market, it's the top building from Sevilla's 16th-century glory days. Today, it houses the archive of documents from the discovery and conquest of the New World. This could be fascinating, but little of importance is on display (old maps of Havana). The displays are in Spanish, but you can pick up English brochures describing both permanent and temporary exhibits (free, Mon–Sat 9:00–16:00, Sun 10:00–14:00, tel. 954-500-528).

Between the River and the Cathedral

Hospital de la Caridad—This Charity Hospital was founded by a nobleman in the 17th century. Peek into the fine courtyard. On the left, the chapel has some gruesome art (above both doors) illustrating that death is the great equalizer, and an altar so sweet only a Spaniard could enjoy it. The Dutch tiles depicting scenes of the Old and New Testament are a reminder of the time when the Netherlands was under Spanish rule in the mid-16th century (€5, slightly interesting audioguide for €2, erratic hours, but typically Mon–Sat 9:00–13:30 & 15:30–19:30, Sun 9:00–13:00, last entry 30 min before closing, tel. 954-223-232).

Golden Tower (Torre del Oro) and Naval Museum—Sevilla's historic riverside Golden Tower was the starting point and ending point for all shipping to the New World. It's named for the golden tiles that once covered it—not for all the New World booty that landed here. Since the Moors built it in the 13th century, it has been part of the city's fortifications, with a heavy chain draped across the river to protect the harbor. Today it houses a dreary little naval museum. Looking past the dried fish and charts of knots, find the mural showing the world-spanning journeys of Vasco da Gama, the model of Columbus' *Santa María* (the first ship to land in the New World), and an interesting mural of Sevilla in 1740. Enjoy the view from the balconies upstairs. The Guadalquivir River is now just a trickle of its former self, after canals built in the 1920s siphoned off most of its water to feed ports downstream (€2, includes audioguide, Sept–July Tue–Fri 10:00–14:00, Sat–Sun 11:00–14:00, closed Mon and Aug, tel. 954-222-419).

North of the Cathedral, near Plaza Nueva

▲▲**Flamenco Dance Museum (Museo del Baile Flamenco)**—If you want to understand more about the dance that embodies the spirit of southern Spain, this museum—while overpriced at €10—does the trick. The grande dame of flamenco, Cristina Hoyos, has collected a few artifacts and costumes and put together a series of videos explaining the art of flamenco. One particularly interesting film illustrates the key elements of the dance form: pain, joy, elegance, seduction, soul, and—I believe—love of ham (€10, daily 9:00–19:00, Calle Manuel Rojas Marcos 3, about three blocks east of Plaza Nueva, tel. 954-340-311, www.museo flamenco.com). Watch a dance class when visiting the museum, or participate in a one-hour lesson and take a little *olé* home with you (€60/person max, prices go down with more people, shoes provided). There are also dance shows on Friday and Saturday at

19:30 (€25, €30 combo-ticket includes museum and show, 10 percent discount off museum, show, or combo-ticket with this book in 2010).

▲**Museo Palacio de la Condesa de Lebrija**—This aristocratic mansion takes you back into the 18th century like no other place in town. The Countess of Lebrija was a passionate collector of antiquities. Her home's ground floor is paved with Roman mosaics (that you actually walk on) and lined with musty old cases of Phoenician, Greek, Roman, and Moorish artifacts—mostly pottery. To see a plush world from a time when the nobility had a private priest and their own chapel, take a quickie tour of the upstairs, which shows the palace as the countess left it when she died in 1938 (€4 for unescorted visit of ground floor, €8 includes tour of "lived-in" upstairs offered every 45 min, Mon–Fri 10:30–19:30, Sat 10:00–14:00, closed Sun, free and obligatory bag check, Calle Cuna 8, tel. 954-227-802).

South of the Cathedral, near Plaza de España

University—Today's university was yesterday's *fábrica de tabacos* (tobacco factory), which employed 10,000 young female *cigareras*—including the saucy femme fatale of Bizet's opera *Carmen*. In the 18th century, it was the second-largest building in Spain, after El Escorial. Wander through its halls as you walk to Plaza de España. The university's bustling café is a good place for cheap tapas, beer, wine, and conversation (Mon–Fri 8:00–21:00, Sat 9:00–13:00, closed Sun).

Plaza de España—This square, the surrounding buildings, and the nearby María Luisa Park are the remains of the 1929 international fair, where for a year the Spanish-speaking countries of the world enjoyed a mutual-admiration fiesta. When they finish the restoration work here (it's taking years), this delightful area—the epitome of

world's fair–style architecture—will once again be great for people-watching (especially during the 19:00–20:00 peak paseo hour). The park's highlight is the former Spanish Pavilion. Its tiles (a trademark of Sevilla) show historic scenes and maps from every province of Spain (arranged in alphabetical order, from Álava to Zaragoza). Climb to one of the balconies for a fine view. Beware: This is a classic haunt of thieves and con artists. Believe no one here. Thieves, posing as lost tourists, will come at you with a map unfolded to hide their speedy, greedy fingers.

Away from the Center
▲Museo de Bellas Artes

Sevilla's passion for religious art is preserved and displayed in its Museum of Fine Art. While most Americans go for El Greco, Goya, and Velázquez (not a forte of this collection), this museum gives a fine look at the other, less-appreciated Spanish masters: Zurbarán and Murillo. Rather than exhausting, the museum is pleasantly enjoyable.

Cost, Hours, Location: €1.50, Tue–Sat 9:00–20:30, Sun 9:00–14:30, closed Mon, last entry 15 min before closing, tel. 954-220-790. The museum is at Plaza Museo 9; it's a 15-minute walk from the cathedral, or a short ride on bus #C5 from Plaza Nueva. If coming from La Macarena (described next), take bus #C4 to the Torneo stop and walk inland four blocks. Pick up the English-language floor plan, which explains the theme of each room.

Background: Several of Spain's top artists—Zurbarán, Murillo, and Velázquez—lived in Sevilla. This was Spain's wealthy commercial capital, like New York City, while Madrid was a newly built center of government, like Washington, D.C. In the early 1800s, Spain's liberal government was disbanding convents and monasteries, and secular fanatics were looting churches. Thankfully, the region's religious art was rescued and hung safely here in this convent-turned-museum.

Spain's economic Golden Age (the 1500s) blossomed into the Golden Age of Spanish painting (the 1600s). Artists such as Zurbarán combined realism with mysticism. He painted balding saints and monks with wrinkled faces and sunburned hands. The style suited Spain's spiritual climate, as the Catholic Church used this art in its Counter-Reformation battle against the Protestant rebellion.

◆ Self-Guided Tour: The core of the collection is in Rooms 3 through 10. Most of the major works are displayed in Room 5, the convent's former chapel. It's difficult not to say "Wow!" when entering. Tour the collection starting upstairs in Room 10 (head into the cloister and climb the grand staircase). Then, after exploring the first floor according to your interests, finish in Room 5.

Francisco de Zurbarán (thoor-bar-AHN, 1598–1664) paints saints and monks, and the miraculous things they experience, presented with unblinking, crystal-clear, brightly lit, highly detailed realism. Monks and nuns could meditate upon Zurbarán's meticulous paintings (Room 10 and the room leading to 10) for hours, finding God in the details.

Zurbarán shines a harsh spotlight on his subject, creating strong shadows. Like the secluded monks themselves, Zurbarán's people stand starkly isolated against a dark single-color background. He was the ideal painter of the austere religion of 17th-century Spain.

In Zurbarán's **St. Hugo Visiting the Carthusian Monks at Supper** (Room 10), white-robed monks gather together for their simple meal in the communal dining hall. Above them hangs a painting of Mary, Baby Jesus, and John the Baptist. Zurbarán created paintings for monks' dining halls like this. His audience: celibate men and women who lived in isolation, as in this former convent, devoting their time to quiet meditation, prayer, and Bible study.

In *The Virgin of the Caves* (also in Room 10, just to the right), study the piety and faith in the monks' rustic faces. Zurbarán shows a protective Mary with her hands on the heads of the two top monks of that order. Note the loving detail on the cape embroidery, the brooch, and the flowers at her feet. But also note the angel babies holding the cape, with their painfully double-jointed arms. Zurbarán was no Leonardo.

The *Apotheosis of St. Thomas Aquinas* (ground level, Room 5) is considered Zurbarán's most important work. It was done at the height of his career, when stark realism was all the rage. Here again Zurbarán presents the miraculous moment (when the saint gets his spiritual awakening) in a believable, down-to-earth way.

Bartolomé Murillo (mur-EE-oh, 1617–1682) was another hometown boy (see page 520). In Room 5, his *Madonna and Child* (*La Servilletta*, 1665; at the end of the room in the center, where the church's altar would have been) shows the warmth and appeal of his work. By about 1650, Murillo's easy-to-appreciate style had replaced Zurbarán's harsh realism.

The Immaculate Conception (several versions in the museum, ground floor, Room 5) was Murillo's favorite subject. To many Spaniards, Mary is their main connection to heaven. They pray directly to her, asking her to intercede for them with God. Murillo's Marys are always receptive and ready to help.

▲▲Basílica de la Macarena

Sevilla's Holy Week (Semana Santa) celebrations are Spain's grandest. During the week leading up to Easter, the city is packed

with pilgrims witnessing 50 processions carrying about 100 religious floats. Get a feel for this event by visiting Basílica de la Macarena (built in 1947) to see the two most impressive floats and the darling of Holy Week, the Weeping Virgin (Virgen de la Macarena, a.k.a. La Esperanza). The church's museum has been closed for restoration, but should reopen in 2010—before making the trip, confirm at the TI that it's open and that you can see the *paso* (Mary's silver float, carried in the Holy Week procession).

Cost, Hours, Location: Church free, museum-€3.50, buy ticket at shop by entrance, daily 9:30–14:00 & 17:00–20:00, taxi to Puerta Macarena or bus #C3 or #C4 from Puerta de Jerez or Menéndez Pelayo, tel. 954-901-800.

◑ Self-Guided Tour: Grab a pew and study Mary, complete with crystal teardrops. She's like a 17th-century doll with human hair and articulated arms, and even dressed with underclothes. Her beautiful expression—halfway between smiling and crying—is moving, in a Baroque way. Her weeping can be contagious—look around you. Filling a side chapel (on the left) is the Christ of the Sentence (from 1654), showing Jesus the day he was condemned.

The two most important floats of the Holy Week parades—the floats that Jesus and Mary ride every Good Friday—are parked behind the altar (through the door left of the altar, museum ticket required).

The three-ton float that carries Jesus is slathered in gold leaf and shows a commotion of figures acting out the sentencing of Christ (whose statue—the one you saw in the church—is placed in the front of this crowd). Pontius Pilate is about to wash his hands. Pilate's wife cries as a man reads the death sentence. During the Holy Week procession, pious Sevillan women wail in the streets while relays of 48 men carry this float on the backs of their necks—only their feet showing under the drapes—as they shuffle through the streets from midnight until 14:00 in the afternoon every Good Friday. (The photo on the wall behind Pilate shows the float—with the bound Christ of the Sentence in place—pulling out of the church on Good Friday in 1986.) Shuffle upstairs for another perspective.

La Esperanza follows the Sentencing of Christ in the procession. Mary's smaller, 1.5-ton float, in the next room, seems all silver and candles—"strong enough to support the roof, but tender enough to quiver in the soft night breeze." Mary has a wardrobe of three huge mantles (each displayed here), worn in successive years. They are about 100 years old. Her six-pound gold crown/halo (in a glass case in the wall) is from 1913. This float has a mesmerizing effect on the local crowds. They line up for hours, clapping, weeping, and throwing roses as it slowly works its way through the city. My Sevillan friend explained, "She knows all the problems of Sevilla and its people. We've been confiding in her for centuries. To us, she is hope. That's her name—Esperanza."

Before leaving, find the case of matador garb (also upstairs) given to the church by bullfighters over the years. They are a token of thanks for the protection they feel they received from La Macarena. Considered the protector of bullfighters, she's big in bullring chapels. In 1912, the bullfighter José Ortega, hoping for protection, gave her the five emerald brooches she wears. It worked for eight years...until he was gored to death in the ring. (This was such a big deal that La Macarena was dressed in black—the only time that has happened.)

Outside, notice the best surviving bit of Sevilla's old walls. Originally Roman, what remains today is 12th-century Moorish, a reminder that off and on for centuries Sevilla was the capital of the Islamic kingdom in Iberia.

And yes, it's from this city that a local dance band (Los del Río) changed the world by giving us "The Macarena."

Near Sevilla

Itálica—One of Spain's most impressive Roman ruins is found outside the sleepy town of Santiponce, about six miles northwest of Sevilla. Founded in 206 B.C. for wounded soldiers recuperating from the Second Punic War, Itálica became a thriving town of great agricultural and military importance. It was the birthplace of famous Roman emperors Trajan and Hadrian. Today its best-preserved ruin is its amphitheater—one of the largest in the Roman Empire—with a capacity for 30,000 spectators. Other highlights include beautiful floor mosaics, such as the one in Casa de los Pájaros (House of the Birds) that shows more than 30 species of birds. To avoid the midday heat, plan your visit to arrive early or late, and definitely bring water (€1.50; April–Sept Tue–Sat 8:30–21:00, Sun 9:00–15:00; Oct–March Tue–Sat 9:00–18:00, Sun 10:00–16:00; closed Mon year-round; tel. 955-622-266).

Getting There: You can get to Itálica on bus #M172 (30-min trip, frequent departures from Sevilla's Plaza de Armas Station). If you're driving, head west out of Sevilla in the direction of Huelva; after you cross the second branch of the river, turn north on N-630, and after a few miles, get off at Santiponce. Drive past pottery warehouses and through the town to the ruins at the far (west) end.

Experiences in Sevilla

Bullfighting

▲**Bullfights**—Some of Spain's best bullfighting is done in Sevilla's 14,000-seat bullring, Plaza de Toros. Fights are held (generally at 18:30) on most Sundays in May and June; on Easter; and daily during the April Fair (April 20–25 in 2010) and at the end of September (during the Feria de San Miguel). These serious fights, with adult matadors, are called *corrida de toros* and often sell out in advance. On many Thursday evenings in July, there are *novil-* *lada* fights, with teenage novices doing the killing and smaller bulls doing the dying. *Corrida de toros* seats range from €25 for high seats looking into the sun to €150 for the first three rows in the shade under the royal box; *novillada* seats are half that—and easy to buy at the arena a few minutes before show time (ignore scalpers outside; get information at a TI, your hotel, by phone, or online; tel 954-210-315, www.lamaestranza.es).

▲▲**Bullfight Museum**—Follow a bilingual (Spanish and English) 25-minute guided tour through the bullring's strangely quiet and empty arena, its museum, and the chapel where the matador prays before the fight. (Thanks to readily available blood transfusions, there have been no deaths in nearly three decades.) The two most revered figures of Sevilla, the Virgin of Macarena and the Christ of Gran Poder (All Power), are represented in the chapel. In the museum, you'll see great classic scenes and the heads of a few bulls—awarded the bovine equivalent of an Oscar for a particularly good fight. The city was so appalled when the famous matador Manolete was killed in 1947 that even the mother of the bull that gored him was destroyed. Matadors—dressed to kill— are heartthrobs in their "suits of light." Many girls have their bedrooms wallpapered with posters of cute bullfighters. See page 708 for more on the "art" of bullfighting (€6, entrance with escorted tour only—no free time inside, 3/hr, daily May–Oct 9:30–20:00, Nov–April 9:30–19:00, until 14:00 on fight days, when chapel and horse room are closed). While they take groups of up to 50, it's still wise to call or drop by to reserve a spot in the busy season (tel. 954-210-315).

The April Fair

For seven days each April (April 20–25 in 2010), much of Sevilla is packed into its vast fairgrounds for a grand party. The fair, seem-ing to bring all that's Andalusian together, feels friendly, sponta-neous, and very real. The local passion for horses, flamenco, and sherry is clear—riders are ramrod straight, colorfully clad girls ride sidesaddle, and everyone's drink-ing sherry spritzers. Women sport outlandish dresses that would look clownish all alone but are somehow brilliant here en masse. Horses clog the streets in an endless parade until about 20:00, when they clear out and the streets fill with exuberant locals. The party goes for literally 24 hours a day for the entire week.

Countless private party tents, or *casetas,* line the lanes. Each tent is the private party zone of a family, club, or association. You need to know someone in the group—or make friends quickly—to get in. Because of the exclusivity, it has a real family-affair feeling. In each *caseta,* everyone knows everyone. It seems like a thousand wedding parties being celebrated at the same time.

Any tourist can have a fun and memorable evening by sim-ply crashing the party. The city's entire fleet of taxis (who'll try to charge double) and buses seems dedicated to shuttling people from downtown to the fairgrounds. With the traffic jams, you may be better off hiking: From the Golden Tower, cross the San Telmo Bridge to Plaza de Cuba and hike down Calle Asunción. You'll see the towering gate to the fairgrounds in the distance. Just follow the crowds (there's no admission charge). Arrive before 20:00 to see the horses, but stay later, as the ambience improves after they giddy-up on out. Some of the larger tents are sponsored by the city and open to the public, but the best action is in the streets, where party-goers from the livelier *casetas* spill out. Although private tents have bouncers, everyone is so happy that it's not tough to strike up an impromptu friendship, become a "special guest," and be invited in. The drink flows freely, and the food is fun and cheap.

Shopping in Sevilla

For the best local shopping experience, follow my shopping stroll (see next). The popular pedestrian streets Sierpes, Tetuán, and Velázquez—along with the surrounding lanes near Plaza Nueva—are packed with people and shops. Small shops close between 13:30 and 16:00 or 17:00 on weekdays, as well as on Saturday afternoons

and all day Sunday. But big ones
such as El Corte Inglés stay open
(and air-conditioned) right through
the siesta. El Corte Inglés also has a
supermarket downstairs and a good
but expensive restaurant (Mon–Sat
10:00–22:00, closed Sun). Popular
souvenir items include ladies' fans,
ceramics, and items related to flamenco (castanets, guitars, costumes)
and bullfighting posters).

Collectors' markets hop on Sunday: stamps and coins at
Plaza del Cabildo (near the cathedral) and art on Plaza del Museo
(by the Museo de Bellas Artes).

Mercado del Arenal, the covered fish-and-produce market,
is perfect for hungry photographers (Mon–Sat 9:00–14:30, closed
Sun, least lively on Mon, on Calle Pastor y Landero at Calle Arenal,
just beyond bullring). For suggestions on dining here (including a
small café-bar for breakfast and a fish restaurant inside), see page
557 in "Eating."

▲▲Shopping Paseo Tour

While many tourists never get beyond the cathedral and the Santa
Cruz neighborhood, it's important to wander west into the lively
pedestrian shopping center of town. These streets—Calle Tetuán
(which becomes Velázquez), Calle Sierpes, and Calle Cuna—also
happen to be part of the oldest section of Sevilla. A walk here is
a chance to join one of Spain's liveliest paseos—that bustling celebration of life that takes place before dinner each evening, when
everyone is out strolling. Locals stroll to show off their fancy shoes
and make the scene. This walk (if done between 18:00 and 20:00)
gives you a look at the paseo scene and the town's most popular
shops. You'll pass windows displaying the best in both traditional
and trendy fashion. The walk ends at a plush mansion of a local
countess (open to the public).

Start on the pedestrianized **Plaza Nueva,** a 19th-century
square facing the ornate city hall, which features a statue of
Ferdinand III, a local favorite because he freed Sevilla from the
Moors in 1248. From here, wander the length of **Calle Tetuán**
(notice the latest in outrageous shoes). Calle Tetuán becomes
Velázquez, and ends at La Campana (a big intersection and
popular meeting point, with the super department store, El Corte
Inglés, just beyond). At La Campana, tempt yourself with sweets
at the venerable Confitería La Campana.

Next, take two rights to get to **Calle Sierpes**, great for
shopping and strolling. Calle Sierpes is the main street of the

Holy Week processions—imagine it packed with celebrants and its balconies bulging with spectators. At the corner of Sierpes and Jovellanos/Sagasta, you're near several fine shops featuring Andalusian accessories. Drop in to see how serious local women are about their fans, combs, shawls, and *mantillas* (ornate head scarves). Andalusian women have various fans to match different dresses. The *mantilla* comes in black (worn only on Good Friday and by the mother of the groom at weddings) and white (worn at bullfights during the April Fair).

From here, turn left down **Calle Sagasta**. Notice that the street has two names—the modern version and a medieval one: Antigua Calle de Gallegos ("Ancient Street of the Galicians"). With the Christian victory in 1248, the Muslims were given one month to evacuate. To consolidate Christian control, settlers from the north were planted here. This street was home to the Galicians.

Finally, at the charming Plaza del Salvador, backtrack left along **Calle Cuna,** famous for its exuberant flamenco dresses and classic wedding dresses. (Flamenco miniskirts have been popular in recent years, but now hemlines are falling again.) If all this shopping makes you feel like a countess, Calle Cuna leads to the Museo Palacio de la Condesa de Lebrija (see listing on page 535).

Nightlife in Sevilla

▲▲**Evening Paseo**—Sevilla is meant for strolling. The paseo thrives every non-winter evening in these areas: along either side of

the river between the San Telmo and Isabel II bridges (Paseo de Cristóbal Colón and Triana district; see "Eating," page 552), up Avenida de la Constitución, around Plaza Nueva, at Plaza de España, and throughout the Barrio Santa Cruz. On hot summer nights, even families with toddlers are out and about past midnight. Spend some time rafting through this sea of humanity. Savor the view of floodlit Sevilla by night from the far side of the river—perhaps over dinner.

▲▲▲**Flamenco**—This music-and-dance art form has its roots in the Roma (Gypsy) and Moorish cultures. Even at a packaged "flamenco evening," sparks fly. The men do most of the flamboyant machine-gun footwork. The women concentrate on graceful turns and a smooth, shuffling step. Watch the musicians. Flamenco guitarists, with their lightning-fast finger-roll strums, are among the best in the world. The intricate rhythms are set by castanets or the hand-clapping (called *palmas*) of those who aren't dancing at the moment. In the raspy-voiced wails of the singers, you'll hear echoes of the Muslim call to prayer.

Like jazz, flamenco thrives on improvisation. Also like jazz, good flamenco is more than just technical proficiency. A singer or dancer with "soul" is said to have *duende*. Flamenco is a happening, with bystanders clapping along and egging on the dancers with whoops and shouts. Get into it. For a tourist-oriented flamenco show, your hotel can get you nightclub show tickets (happily, since they snare a hefty commission for each sale). But it's easy to book a place on your own.

Casa de la Memoria de Al-Andalus ("House of the Memory of Al-Andalus"), run by Andalusian-culture devotees Sebastián and Rosana, offers more of an intimate concert with a smaller cast and more classic solos. Other, touristy flamenco shows give you all the clichés, and they can feel crass; here, you'll enjoy an elegant and classy musical experience. In an alcohol-free atmosphere, 90 tourists sit on three rows of folding chairs circling a small stage for shows featuring flamenco and other Andalusian music performed by young professional local musicians. It's all acoustic, and the nightly musical mix varies according to the personalities of the performers. It's also a perfect place to practice your Spanish fan *(abanico)* skills on warm nights. Concerts are nightly all year at 21:00. With demand, shows are added at 22:30 in summer, or 19:30 during the rest of the year (€15, one-hour shows, reservations smart, box office open 10:00–14:00 and 18:00–22:00, same-day tickets generally available but better to buy tickets a day or more beforehand, arrive early for front-row seats, in Barrio Santa Cruz, adjacent to Hotel Alcántara at Ximénez de Enciso 28, tel. 954-560-670, memoria@terra.es).

Los Gallos presents nightly two-hour shows at 20:00 and 22:30 (€30 ticket includes a drink, €3/person discount with this book in 2010—but limited to two admissions, arrive 30 min early for best seats, noisy bar but no food served, Plaza de la Santa Cruz 11, tel. 954-216-981, managers José and Nuria promise goose bumps).

El Arenal has arguably more professional performers and a classier setting for its show—but dinner customers get the preferred seating, and waiters are working throughout the performance (€36 ticket includes a drink, €70 includes dinner, shows at 20:00 and

22:00, near bullring at Calle Rodó 7, tel. 954-216-492).

El Patio Sevillano is more of a variety show (€37 ticket includes a drink, 15 percent discount with Sevilla Card, shows at 19:00 and 21:30, next to bullring at Paseo de Cristóbal Colón, tel. 954-214-120).

The packaged shows described above can be a bit sterile, and an audience of tourists doesn't help. But I find both Los Gallos and El Arenal entertaining and riveting. While El Arenal may have a slight edge on talent, Los Gallos has a cozier setting, with cushy rather than hard chairs—and it's a bit cheaper.

Impromptu flamenco still erupts spontaneously in bars throughout the old town after midnight. Just follow your ears as you wander down Calle Betis, leading off Plaza de Cuba across the bridge. The **Lo Nuestro** and **Rejoneo** bars are local favorites (at Calle Betis 31A and 31B). Or find these:

Bar El Tamboríl is a funky local bar dedicated to the Virgin Mary—buried in the touristy Santa Cruz neighborhood, yet somehow still overlooked. It comes to life each midnight with a sung prayer. This kicks off the impromptu flamenco music (tourists welcome, no cover—just buy a drink, €4 wine, €7 cocktails, 50 yards in front of the Los Gallos flamenco show at Plaza de Santa Cruz, mobile 652-188-244).

La Carbonería Bar is the sangria equivalent of a beer garden. If the Beach Boys sang flamenco, they'd hang out here. It's a sprawling place with a variety of rooms leading to a big open tented area filled with young locals, casual guitar strummers, and nearly nightly flamenco music after midnight (no dancing). Located just a few blocks from most of my recommended hotels, this is worth finding if you're not quite ready to end the day (no cover, €2 sangria, daily 20:00–3:00 in the morning; near Plaza Santa María—find Hotel Fernando III, the side alley Céspedes dead-ends at Levies, head left to Levies 18, unsigned door; for location, see map on page 547).

Sleeping in Sevilla

All of my listings are centrally located, mostly within a five-minute walk of the cathedral. The first are near the charming but touristy Santa Cruz neighborhood. The last group is just as central but closer to the river, across the boulevard in a more workaday, less touristy zone.

Room rates as much as double during the two Sevilla fiestas (Holy Week—March 28–April 4 in 2010; and the weeklong April Fair, held two weeks after Easter—April 20–25 in 2010). In general, the busiest and most expensive months are April, May, September, and October. Hotels put rooms on the discounted push

Sleep Code

(€1 = about $1.40, country code: 34)

S = Single, **D** = Double/Twin, **T** = Triple, **Q** = Quad, **b** = bathroom, **s** = shower only. Unless otherwise noted, credit cards are accepted, hoteliers speak enough English, tax is usually included, and breakfast generally costs extra.

To help you easily sort through these listings, I've divided the rooms into three categories, based on the price for a standard double room with bath during high season:

$$$ Higher Priced—Most rooms €100 or more.
$$ Moderately Priced—Most rooms between €60–100.
$ Lower Priced—Most rooms €60 or less.

list in July and August—when people with any sense avoid this furnace—and from November through February. Prices generally include the 7 percent IVA tax. A price range indicates low- to high-season prices (but I have not listed festival prices). Ground-floor rooms come with more noise. Ask for upper floors *(piso alto)*. Always telephone to reconfirm what you think is a reservation.

If you do visit in July or August, the best values are central business-class places. They offer summer discounts and provide a necessary cool, air-conditioned refuge. But be warned that Spain's air-conditioning often isn't the icebox you're used to, especially in Sevilla. The best setup is an individual remote-controlled air-conditioner. If a hotel has central air-conditioning, owners often turn it off during the day—and even when it's on, they control the temperature.

Santa Cruz Neighborhood

These places are off Calle Santa María la Blanca and Plaza Santa María. The most convenient parking lot is the underground Cano y Cueto garage near the corner of Calle Santa María la Blanca and Menéndez Pelayo (€18/day, open 24/7, at edge of big park, unsigned). A fine Internet café and self-service launderette are a couple of blocks away up Menéndez Pelayo (see "Helpful Hints" on pages 511 and 512).

$$$ Hotel Las Casas de la Judería has quiet, elegant rooms and suites tastefully decorated with hardwood floors and a Spanish flair. The rooms, which surround a series of peaceful courtyards, are a romantic splurge (Sb-€112, Db-€140–200, extra bed-€45; low-season prices—July, Aug, and late-Nov–Feb—are discounted a further 10 percent to those with this book who ask in 2010, but check their website for even better rates; expensive but great buffet

Santa Cruz Hotels, Restaurants, and Flamenco

1 Hotel Las Casas de la Judería
2 Hotel Amadeus, La Música de Sevilla, Pensión Córdoba & Hostal Buen Dormir
3 Hotel Alcántara & Casa de la Memoria de Al-Andalus (Flamenco, Music)
4 YH Giralda
5 Pensión San Benito
6 Cervecería Giralda
7 Bodega Santa Cruz
8 Las Teresas Bar
9 Corral del Agua Restaurante
10 Restaurante Modesto (2)
11 Freiduría Puerta de la Carne
12 Bar Restaurante El 3 de Oro
13 Restaurante San Marco
14 Café Bar Carmela
15 Los Gallos Flamenco
16 Bar El Tamboril
17 To La Carbonería Bar
18 To Internet Café & Launderette

SEVILLA

breakfast-€19, air-con, elevator, valet parking-€19/day, Plaza Santa María 5, tel. 954-415-150, fax 954-422-170, www.casasypalacios .com, juderia@casasypalacios.com).

$$ Hotel Amadeus is a little gem that music-lovers will appreciate (it even has a couple of soundproof rooms with pianos—something I've never seen anywhere else in Europe). It's lovingly decorated with a music motif around a little courtyard and a modern glass elevator that takes you to a roof terrace. While small, this 14-room place is classy and comfortable, with welcoming public spaces and a very charming staff. The €8.50 breakfast comes on a trolley—enjoy it in your room, in the lounge, or in the delightful roof garden (Sb-€88, Db-€98, big Db-€115, 2 suites-€125 and €155, cheaper July–Aug, air-con, elevator, free Internet access, laundry-€15, Calle Farnesio 6, tel. 954-501-443, fax 954-500-019, www.hotelamadeussevilla.com, reservas@hotelamadeussevilla .com, wonderfully run by María Luisa and her staff—Zaida and Cristina). Their next-door annex is every bit as charming and a similarly good value: **$$$ La Música de Sevilla** offers six additional, beautifully appointed rooms; three rooms face the interior patio, and three are streetside with small balconies (patio Db-€115, exterior Db-€136, air-con, reserve and check in at Hotel Amadeus).

$$ Hotel Alcántara offers more no-nonsense comfort than character. Well-located but strangely out of place in the midst of the Santa Cruz jumble, it rents 21 slick rooms at a good price (Sb-€68, small Db-€79, bigger Db twin-€89, fancy Db-€112, 10 percent discount or a free breakfast—your choice—if you pay in cash and show this book in 2010, breakfast-€5, air-con, elevator, free Wi-Fi, rentable laptop, Ximénez de Enciso 28, tel. 954-500-595, fax 954-500-604, www.hotelalcantara.net, info@hotelalcantara .net). The hotel is adjacent to Casa de la Memoria de Al-Andalus, which offers concerts (described earlier under "Flamenco").

$$ YH Giralda, once an 18th-century abbots' house, is now a charming 14-room hotel tucked away on a little street right off Mateo Gagos, just a couple of blocks from the cathedral. The exterior rooms have windows onto a pedestrian street, and a few of the interior rooms have small windows that look into the inner courtyard (Sb-€54–80, Db-€62–90, Tb-€109–123, more on weekends, no breakfast, air-con, Calle Abades 30, tel. 954-228-324, fax 954-227-019, www.yh-hoteles.com, yhgiralda@yh-hoteles.com).

$ Pensión Córdoba, a homier and cheaper option, has 12 tidy, quiet rooms, solid modern furniture, and a showpiece tiled courtyard (S-€30, Sb-€40, D-€50, Db-€60, no breakfast, cash only, central air-con—on from evening to morning, on a tiny lane off Calle Santa María la Blanca at Farnesio 12, tel. 954-227-498, www.pensioncordoba.com, Ana and María).

Sevilla Hotels

- ① Hotel Husa Los Seises
- ② Hotel Alminar
- ③ Hotel San Francisco
- ④ Hotel Zurbarán
- ⑤ Hotel Vincci La Rábida & Laundry
- ⑥ Hotel Taberna del Alabardero
- ⑦ Hotel Maestranza
- ⑧ Hotel Europa
- ⑨ To Casa Sol y Luna & Oasis Backpackers Hostel
- ⑩ Internet Access

🔭 View

▨ Central Pedestrian Boulevard

200 YARDS
200 METERS

SEVILLA

$ Hostal Buen Dormir ("Good Sleep") is a quirky little family-run place with turtles and children in the blue-tinted courtyard. They rent 17 cheap, clean, basic rooms on a very quiet traffic-free lane. If there's a problem with your room, go to reception. Rene says if you don't tell him, he can't fix it (S-€20, D-€30, Ds-€35, Db-€40, Ts-€50, Tb-€55, air-con in all rooms except singles, Farnesio 8, tel. 954-217-492, Miriam and Rene).

$ Pensión San Benito, with eight humble rooms, faces a traditional Sevilla courtyard buried at the end of a dead-end lane just off Plaza Santa María. The rooms are dark, with windows that open onto an inner courtyard. The hardworking owners don't speak English, but offer some of the most conveniently located cheap rooms in town (S-€20, D-€36, Db-€42, Tb-€60, no breakfast, no air-con, parking-€12, on a tiny lane next to Cano y Cueto at Calle Canarios 4, tel. 954-415-255, www.hostalsanbenito.com, burlon 11@hotmail.com, the woman of the house—Charo—has that coo-chee-coo Charo attitude). They also rent two fully equipped apartments next door (about €35/person).

Near the Cathedral

$$$ Hotel Husa Los Seises is a modern 42-room business-class place spliced tastefully into the tangled old town. It offers a fresh and spacious reprieve for anyone ready for a mix of old and contemporary luxury. You'll eat breakfast amid Roman ruins. Its rooftop garden includes a pool and a great cathedral view (Db-€170–215, Tb for €30 more, lower prices in July–Aug and Dec–Feb, breakfast-€16, air-con, elevator, valet parking-€20/day, 2 blocks northwest of cathedral at Segovias 6, tel. 954-229-495, fax 954-224-334, www.hotellosseises.com, info@hotellosseises.com).

$$$ Hotel Alminar, opened in 2005, is a plush and elegant little place that rents 12 fresh, slick, minimalist rooms (Db-€95–125, superior Db-€115–155, extra bed-€25, breakfast-€6, air-con, just 100 yards from the cathedral at Álvarez Quintero 52, tel. 954-293-913, fax 954-212-197, www.hotelalminar.com, reservas@hotelalminar.com).

$$ Hotel San Francisco may have a classy facade, but inside it's sparse, clean, and quiet. It offers 17 rooms with metal doors and a central location (Sb-€40–55, Db-€50–68, Tb-€62–80, no breakfast, air-con, elevator, small rooftop terrace, located on quiet pedestrian street at Álvarez Quintero 38, tel. 954-501-541, www.sanfranciscoh.com, info@sanfranciscoh.com, Carlos).

$$ Hotel Zurbarán needs a fresh coat of blue paint, but its nine rooms are a decent deal, and the courtyard is pleasantly decorated with hanging plants and wicker furniture (Db-€55–90, Tb-€60–90, book direct for these rates, air-con, Mariana de Pineda 10, tel. 954-210-646, hostalzubaran@grupo-piramide.com).

West of Avenida de la Constitución

$$$ Hotel Vincci La Rábida, part of a big, impersonal hotel chain, offers four-star comfort with its 90 rooms, huge and inviting courtyard lounge, and powerful air-conditioning. Its pricing is dictated by a magical computer that has perfect price discrimination down to a science (see website for prices; on average it's Db-€132, spiking to €200 when possible and dipping to €80 during slow times, when that air-con is most welcome; Castelar 24, tel. 954-501-280, fax 954-216-600, www.vinccihoteles.com, larabida @vinccihoteles.com).

$$$ Hotel Taberna del Alabardero is a unique hotel with only seven rooms occupying the top floor of a poet's mansion (above a classy restaurant, Taberna del Alabardero, listed in "Eating," page 558). It's nicely located and a great value. The ambience is perfectly 1900 (Db-€130–160, Db suite-€150–190, 10 percent discount with this book in 2010, includes breakfast, air-con, elevator, closed in Aug, Zaragoza 20, tel. 954-502-721, fax 954-563-666, www.taberna delalabardero.es, hotel.alabardero@esh.es).

$$ Hotel Maestranza, sparkling with loving care and charm, has 18 small, clean, simple rooms well-located on a street just off Plaza Nueva. To escape the noise from the tapas bars below, ask for an interior room, especially on weekends (Sb-€53, Db-€87, extra bed-€20, 5 percent cash discount, check website for seasonal rates, family suite, no breakfast, air-con, elevator, free Wi-Fi, Gamazo 12, tel. 954-561-070, fax 954-214-404, www.hotelmaestranza.es, sevilla@hotelmaestranza.es, Antonio).

$$ Hotel Europa is a somber and sturdy place renting 23 rooms around an elegant wicker-furniture courtyard in what was a traditional old mansion (Db-€50–90, 40 percent more for Tb, 10 percent discount if you show this book and pay cash in 2010, no breakfast, air-con, elevator, parking-€16/day, 200 yards from cathedral and Plaza Nueva on a tranquil street, Calle Jimios 5, tel. 954-500-443, fax 954-210-016, www.hoteleuropasevilla.com, info@hoteleuropasevilla.com, Claudio).

North of Plaza Nueva, Between Plaza de la Encarnación and Plaza de la Alfalfa

$ Casa Sol y Luna is quaint, with a cordial staff. Run by an Englishman named Geno and his Spanish wife, Esther, it's inexpensive, but a bit farther (10-min walk) from the cathedral (S-€22, D-€38, Db-€45, cash only, Calle Pérez Galdós 1A, tel. 954-210-682, www.casasolyluna1.com, info@casasolyluna1.com).

$ Oasis Backpackers Hostel is the best new spot for cheap beds and a fine place to hang out and connect with young backpackers. Each room, with four double bunks, comes with a modern bathroom and individual lockers. The rooftop terrace—with lounge chairs, a small pool, and adjacent kitchen—is well-used (64 bunk beds in 8 rooms, €15–20/bed, includes breakfast, free Internet access, just off Plaza de la Encarnación behind the church at #29 1/2 on the tiny and quiet lane, tel. 954-293-777, www.hostelsoasis .com). They also have popular branches in Lisbon and Granada.

Eating in Sevilla

Local soups, such as *salmorejo* (Córdoba-style super-thick *gazpacho*) and *ajo blanco* (almond-based with garlic), are tasty. A popular Andalusian meal is fried fish, particularly marinated *adobo*. I like *taquitos de merluza* (hake fish), but for a mix of fish, ask for *frito variado*.

Restaurants generally serve lunch from 13:00 to 16:00 and dinner from 20:00 until very late (Spaniards don't start dinner until about 21:00). If you're hungry for dinner before the locals are, do the tapas tango, using the tapas tips on page 24. Wash down your tapas with *fino* (chilled dry sherry) or the more refreshing *tinto de verano* ("summer red wine"), an Andalusian red wine with soda, like a mild sangria. A good, light white wine is *barbadillo*. And for a heavy red, always go for the Rioja.

Eating in Triana, Across the River

The colorful Triana district—on the west bank of the river, between the San Telmo and Isabel II bridges—is filled with rustic and fun eateries. The riverside and traffic-free Calle Betis is lined with a variety of places to eat, from fine riverside restaurants to sloppy fish joints. It also comes with good picnic and take-out opportunities for romantic urchins.

Tapas in a Triana Neighborhood Joint

Bars along the river and the parallel street one block inland are good for tapas. Before sitting down, walk to the Santa Ana church (midway between the bridges, two blocks off the river), where tables spill into the square (Plazuela de Santa Ana) in the shadow of the floodlit church spire. It feels like the whole neighborhood is out celebrating.

Restaurante Bistec, with most of the square's tables, does grilled fish with gusto. They're enthusiastic about their cod cakes and calamari. Consider their indoor seating and the fun at the bar before sitting out on the square (€7 half-*raciones,* €13 full *raciones,* Thu–Tue 11:30–16:00 & 20:00–24:00, closed Wed, also closed Sun afternoons in winter, Plazuela de Santa Ana, tel. 954-274-759).

Taberna La Plazuela is self-service, doing simpler fare with enticing €12 *tostones* (giant fancy Andalusian bruschetta, good for 3–4 people) and €2 *montaditos* (little sandwiches). Get what

Sevilla Restaurants and Flamenco

1. Rest. Bistec & Taberna La Plazuela
2. Bar Santa Ana
3. Restaurante Río Grande
4. El Faro de Triana & La Taberna del Pescador
5. Bodega Restaurante La María
6. Los Chorritos
7. Horno San Buenaventura
8. Bodega Morales & Freiduría La Isla
9. Bodega Paco Góngora
10. Taberna Torre de la Plata
11. Cafetería Mesón Serranito
12. Marisquería Arenal Sevilla
13. Bar Restaurante Pepe Hillo
14. Restaurante Enrique Becerra
15. Taberna del Alabardero
16. El Arenal (Flamenco)
17. El Patio Sevillano (Flamenco)
18. Lo Nuestro & Rejoneo Bars

SEVILLA

you want and grab a table on the leafy square. Ignore the printed menu and read the daily specials board (same hours and owners as Restaurante Bistec, earlier).

Bar Santa Ana, just a block away on the side of the church, is a rustic neighborhood sports-and-bull bar with great seating on the street. Peruse the interior, draped in bullfighting and Weeping Virgin memorabilia. It's always busy with the neighborhood gang enjoying fun tapas like *delicia de solomillo* (tenderloin) and the bar's willingness to serve even cheap tapas at the outdoor tables (long hours, typically closed one day per week—closed Sun during April Fair, facing the side of the church at Pureza 82, tel. 954-272-102).

Riverside Dinners in Triana

Restaurante Río Grande is your stuffy, candlelit-fancy option— *the* place for a restaurant dinner with properly attired waiters and a full menu rather than tapas. Dining on the terrace is less expensive and more casual (€35 dinners, daily 13:00–16:00 & 20:00–24:00, air-con, paella and rice dishes are the house specialty, next to the San Telmo Bridge, tel. 954-273-956).

El Faro de Triana is actually the old yellow bridge tower overlooking the Isabel II Bridge. While professional, it's less formal and quirkier than Río Grande. They offer inexpensive tapas, €15 à la carte dishes, and grand views over the river from the top floor (the views are better than the food). Choose from four dining zones: rooftop, outdoor terrace just below the rooftop (perhaps the best), riverside metal tables on the sidewalk, and the bar. There's no cover charge, but they don't serve tapas on the roof or riverside (open daily, bar—8:00–24:00, restaurant—13:00–17:00 & 20:15–24:00, tel. 954-336-192).

La Taberna del Pescador, with tablecloths on its riverside tables, is fancier and more expensive (€12 and up *raciones* on the river, Wed–Mon 12:00–16:00 & 20:00–24:00, closed Tue, 50 yards from Puente de Isabel II on Calle Betis, tel. 954-330-069).

Bodega Restaurante La María also offers fine tablecloth-type restaurant seating on the riverside, but with a formal menu rather than tapas (€18 fish and meat plates, Wed–Mon 13:00–16:00 & 20:00–24:00, closed Tue, Calle Betis 12, tel. 954-338-461).

Los Chorritos is a carefree and sloppy riverside eatery—my choice for hearty seafood, great prices, and a fun atmosphere. They are enthusiastic about what the menu calls "roast" sardines— grilled rather than fried. Their banner reads, roughly, "Sardines rule. They don't bite. Can't eat just one. Go for it" (€6 half-*raciones*, €10 *raciones*, closed Mon and in winter, about midway between the two bridges on Calle Betis, tel. 954-331-499).

Near Recommended Hotels in Barrio Santa Cruz

These eateries—for tapas, dining, and cheap eats—are handy to my recommended Barrio Santa Cruz accommodations.

Tapas

For tapas, the Barrio Santa Cruz is trendy and *romántico*. Plenty of atmospheric-but-touristy restaurants fill the neighborhood near the cathedral and along Calle Santa María la Blanca. From the cathedral, walk up Mateos Gago, where several classic old bars—with the day's tapas scrawled on chalkboards—keep tourists and locals well-fed and watered. (Turn right at Mesón del Moro for several more.)

Cervecería Giralda is a long-established meeting place for locals. It's famous for its fine tapas (confirm prices, stick with straight items on menu rather than expensive trick specials proposed by waiters; open long hours daily, Mateos Gago 1).

A block farther, you'll find **Bodega Santa Cruz** (a.k.a. **Las Columnas**), a popular standby with good, cheap tapas and *montaditos* (little sandwiches). You can keep an eye on the busy kitchen from the bar, or hang out like a cowboy at the tiny stand-up tables out front. Separate chalkboards list €2 tapas and €2 *montaditos*.

Las Teresas is a characteristic small bar draped in fun photos. It serves good tapas from a tight little user-friendly menu. Prices at the bar and outside tables (for fun tourist-watching) are the same, but they serve tapas only at the bar. The hams (with little upside-down umbrellas to catch the dripping fat) are a reminder that they are enthusiastic about their cured-meat dishes (open daily but sometimes closed for the siesta, Calle Santa Teresa 2, tel. 954-213-069).

Dining

Corral del Agua Restaurante, a romantic pink-tablecloth place with a smart interior and charming courtyard seating, serves fine Andalusian cuisine deep in the Barrio Santa Cruz (€18 entrées, 3-course lunch special with wine for €20, Mon–Sat 12:00–16:00 & 20:00–24:00, closed Sun, arrive early or reserve ahead, Calle Agua 6, tel. 954-224-841).

Restaurante Modesto is a local favorite serving pricey but top-notch Andalusian fare—especially fish—with a comfortable dining room and atmospheric outdoor seating in the bright, bustling square just outside the Barrio Santa Cruz. They offer creative, fun meals—look around before ordering—and a good €20 fixed-price lunch or dinner served by energetic, occasionally pushy waiters. Their mixed salad is a meal, and their *fritura modesto* (fried seafood plate) is popular (€14.50, inside open daily 12:00–17:00 &

20:00–24:00, outside tables open daily 12:00–24:00, near Santa María la Blanca at Cano y Cueto 5, tel. 954-416-811). Note that they have indoor dining areas on both sides of the street (busy bar at one, non-smoking zone—in other words, tourists—at the other).

Eating Cheaply in Barrio Santa Cruz and Plaza Santa María la Blanca

Freiduría Puerta de la Carne and **Bar Restaurante El 3 de Oro** are a fried-fish-to-go place, with great outdoor seating, and a restaurant across the street serving fine wine or beer. You can order a cheap cone of tasty fried fish with a tomato salad, and sip a nice drink (served by a waiter from the restaurant), all while enjoying a great outdoor setting—almost dining for the cost of a picnic. Study the photos of the various kinds of seafood available—*un quarto* (250 grams for about €5) serves one (Mon–Sat until 24:00, Sun lunch only, Santa María la Blanca 34, tel. 954-426-820).

Restaurante San Marco offers cheap pizza and fun, basic Italian cuisine under the arches of what was a Moorish bath in the Middle Ages (and a disco in the 1990s). The air-conditioned atmosphere is easygoing and family-friendly, yet not cheesy (good salads, pizza, and pasta for €8, daily 13:00–16:15 & 20:00–24:00, Calle Mesón del Moro 6, tel. 954-564-390).

Breakfast on Plaza Santa María la Blanca: Several nondescript places seem to keep travelers happy at breakfast time on the sunny main square near most of my recommended hotels. I like **Café Bar Carmela.** For the cost of a continental breakfast at your hotel (€6), you can have a hearty American-style breakfast on the square (easy menus, metal tables, open from 9:30, Calle Santa María la Blanca 6, tel. 954-540-590).

Between the Cathedral and the River

I don't like the restaurants surrounding the cathedral, but many good places are just across Avenida de la Constitución. In the area between the cathedral and the river, you can find tapas, cheap eats, and fine dining.

Tapas

Calle García de Vinuesa leads past several colorful and cheap tapas places to a busy corner surrounded with happy eateries.

Horno San Buenaventura, across from the cathedral, is slick, chrome-filled, spacious, and handy for tapas, coffee, pastries, and ice cream. They are understandably happy to be booming now, thanks to the newly pedestrianized boulevard (open daily, light meals are posted by the door, avoid the frozen paella, good quiet seating upstairs).

Bodega Morales is farther up Calle García de Vinuesa, at #11. The front area is more of a drinking bar—go in the back section (around the corner) to munch tiny sandwiches *(montaditos)* and tapas, and sip wine among huge kegs. Everything is the same price (€2 *montaditos,* €2 tapas, €6 half-*raciones*—order at the bar), with the selections chalked onto giant adobe jugs (Mon–Sat 12:00–16:00 & 20:00–24:00, closed Sun, tel. 954-22-1242).

Freiduría La Isla, next door, has been frying fish since 1938 (they just renovated...and changed the oil). Along with *pescado frito,* they also sell wonderful homemade potato chips and fried almonds. It's family-friendly, with an easy English menu. Try their €5 *adobo* (marinated shark) or *frito variado* for a fish sampler. It's pretty much all fried fish, except for a tomato and pepper dish and their €1.20 *gazpacho,* offered only in the summer (Mon 20:00–23:00, Tue–Sat 13:00–15:30 & 20:00–23:00, closed Sun).

Bodega Paco Góngora is colorful and a bit classier than most tapas bars, with a tight dining area and delightful tapas dishes served at the bar. Its sit-down meals are well-presented and reasonably priced (daily 13:00–16:00 & 20:00–24:00, sometimes closed on Wed, ask for the English menu, off Plaza Nueva at Calle Padre Marchena 1, tel. 954-214-139).

Cheap Eats Between the Cathedral and the River

Taberna Torre de la Plata is a handy-to-the-Alcázar eatery close to the sights, but tucked away enough that it's mostly patronized by locals who appreciate its tasty dishes. Local guides take lunch here in the cool, quiet back courtyard (€10 plates, wine list, midway between the cathedral and the Torre del Oro at Calle Santander 1, tel. 954-228-761).

Cafetería Mesón Serranito is a family-friendly diner full of bull lore and happily munching locals (€9 *platos combinados,* Antonia Díaz 11, tel. 954-211-243).

Mercado del Arenal, the covered fish-and-produce market, is ideal for both snapping photos and grabbing a cheap lunch. As with most markets, you'll find characteristic little diners with prices designed to lure in savvy shoppers, not to mention a crispy fresh world of picnic goodies—and a riverside promenade with benches just a block away (Mon–Sat 9:00–14:30, closed Sun, sleepy on Mon, on Calle Pastor y Landero at Calle Arenal, just beyond bullring). There's also a fancier fish restaurant in the market with a great lunch deal (see Taberna del Alabardero, in next section).

Dining Between the Cathedral, Plaza Nueva, and the River

Marisquería Arenal Sevilla is a popular fish restaurant that thrives in the middle of the Arenal Market. When the market closes (daily at 14:30), this eatery stays open. You'll be eating in the empty Industrial Age market with workers dragging their crates around. It's a great family-friendly, finger-licking-good scene much appreciated by its enthusiastic local following. Fish is priced by weight, so be careful when ordering, and always double-check the bill (€8–20 fish plates, generally open 13:00–17:00 & 21:00–24:00, in summer closed Sat night and all day Sun, rest of year closed Mon, reservations smart for dinner, Mercado Arenal, enter on Calle Pastor y Landero 9, tel. 954-220-881).

Bar Restaurante Pepe Hillo serves upscale bar food with a bull motif, across from the bullring (and, therefore, riotous after fights). One side is a youthful tapas bar. But the other side is a delightful oasis serving big half-*raciones* from an inviting menu with creative house specialties and a good wine list (enter on Calle Pastor y Landero, Adriano 24, tel. 954-215-390).

Restaurante Enrique Becerra is a fancy little 10-table place popular with local foodies. It's well-known for its gourmet Andalusian cuisine and fine wine. Muscle past the well-dressed locals at their tapas bar for gourmet snacks and wine by the glass. While the restaurant satisfies its guests with quality food, given the tight seating and its popularity with tourists, it can feel like a trap (€40 dinners, Mon–Sat 13:00–16:30 & 20:00–24:00, closed Sun, reservations essentially required, Gamazo 2, tel. 954-213-049).

Taberna del Alabardero, one of Sevilla's finest restaurants, serves refined Spanish cuisine in chandeliered elegance just a couple of blocks from the cathedral. If you order à la carte it will add up to about €45 a meal, but for €60 you can have a fun seven-course fixed-price meal with lots of little surprises from the chef. Or consider their €18/person (no sharing) starter sampler, followed by an entrée. The service in the fancy upstairs dining rooms gets mixed reviews (carefully read and understand your bill)...but the setting is stunning (daily 13:00–16:30 & 20:00–24:00, closed Aug, air-con, reservations smart, Zaragoza 20, tel. 954-502-721).

Taberna del Alabardero Student-Served Lunch: Their ground-floor dining rooms (elegant but nothing like upstairs) are popular with local office workers for their great-value student-chef-prepared fixed-price sampler (€13 for three delightful courses Mon–Fri, €18 Sat–Sun, drink not included, open daily 13:00–16:30). To avoid a wait, arrive before 14:00 (no reservations possible).

Connections

Note that many destinations are well-served by both trains and buses.

From Sevilla by AVE Train to Madrid: The AVE express train is expensive (€78, €8 cheaper during off-peak times, €10 reservation fee with railpass) but fast (2.5 hrs to Madrid; departures 7:00–21:45, 22/day, see page 385 for more on the Sevilla–Madrid train route). Departures between 16:00 and 19:00 can book up far in advance, but surprise holidays and long weekends can totally jam up trains as well—reserve as far ahead as possible.

From Sevilla by Train to Córdoba: The fast 45-minute AVE train goes hourly, but it's pricey for such a short journey (€30, €47 round-trip—must reserve both ways when you book, with railpass you still must pay €10 reservation fee). The slower train to Córdoba takes 80 minutes, costs only €9 each way, and comes with no reservation headaches.

Other Trains from Sevilla to: Málaga (11/day, 2 hrs on AVE or AVANT, 2.5 hrs on other trains), **Ronda** (2/day, 4 hrs, transfer in Bobadilla), **Granada** (4/day, 3 hrs), **Jerez** (12/day, 1.25 hrs), **Barcelona** (3/day, 6–12 hrs), **Algeciras** (3/day, 5 hrs, transfer at Córdoba, Antequera, or Bobadilla). Trains run to **Lisbon, Portugal,** but they take a long time, since they go through Madrid; buses to Lisbon are far better (see below). Train info: tel. 902-240-202, www.renfe.es.

From Sevilla by Bus to: Madrid (departures generally on the hour, 6 hrs, €20, tel. 902-229-292), **Córdoba** (9/day, 2 hrs), **Málaga** (9/day, 7 direct, 2.5–3.5 hrs, connects to Nerja), **Ronda** (5/day, 2.5 hrs, fewer on weekends), **Tarifa** (4/day, 3 hrs), **La Línea/Gibraltar** (4/day, 4 hrs), **Granada** (11/day, 3 hrs *directo,* 4 hrs *ruta*), **Arcos** (2/day, 2 hrs, more departures with a transfer in Jerez), **Jerez** (7/day, 1.5 hrs), **Barcelona** (2/day), **Algeciras** (Linesur runs the most frequent direct buses—11/day, 2 direct, fewer on weekends, 2.25–2.5 hrs). Bus info: tel. 954-908-040 but rarely answered, go to TI for latest schedule info.

By Bus to Portugal: The best way to get to **Lisbon,** Portugal, is by bus (Alsa and Eurolines share a service offering 2/day, departures at 15:00 and 24:00, 7 hrs, €42 by way of Faro, departs Plaza de Armas Station, tel. 954-907-800 or 902-422-242, www.alsa.es). The midnight departure continues past Lisbon to **Coimbra** (arriving 9:45) and **Porto** (arriving 11:30). Sevilla also has a direct bus service to **Lagos,** Portugal, on the Algarve (4/day in summer, 2/day off-season, about 6 hrs, €20, buy ticket a day or two in advance May–Oct, tel. 954-907-737, www.damas-sa.es). The bus departs from Sevilla's Plaza de Armas bus station and arrives at the Lagos bus station. If you'd like to visit Tavira on the way to Lagos, purchase a bus ticket to Tavira, have lunch there, then take the train to Lagos.

CÓRDOBA

Straddling a sharp bend of the Guadalquivir River, Córdoba has a glorious Roman and Moorish past, once serving as a regional capital for both empires. It's home to Europe's best Islamic sight after Granada's Alhambra: the Mezquita, a splendid and remarkably well-preserved mosque that dates from A.D. 784. When you step inside the mosque, which is magical in its grandeur, you can imagine Córdoba as the center of a thriving and sophisticated culture. During the Dark Ages, when much of Europe was barbaric and illiterate, Córdoba was a haven of enlightened thought—famous for religious tolerance, artistic expression, and dedication to philosophy and the sciences.

Planning Your Time

Ideally, Córdoba is worth two nights and a day. Don't rush the magnificent Mezquita, but also stick around to experience the city's other pleasures: Wander the evocative Jewish Quarter, enjoy the tapas scene, and take the TI's guided town walk in the evening.

However, if you're tight on time, it's possible to do Córdoba more quickly—especially since it's conveniently located on the AVE bullet-train line (and because, frankly, Córdoba is less interesting than the other two big Andalusian cities, Sevilla and Granada). To see Córdoba as an efficient stopover between Madrid and Sevilla (or as a side-trip from Sevilla—hourly trains, 45-min trip), focus on the Mezquita: Taxi from the station, spend two hours there, explore the old town for an hour...and then scram.

Orientation to Córdoba

Córdoba's big draw is the mosque-turned-cathedral called the Mezquita (for pronunciation ease, think female mosquito). Most of the town's major sights are nearby, including the Alcázar, a former royal castle. While the town seems to ignore its river, there is a Renaissance triumphal arch on the riverbank next to a stout "Roman Bridge" which spans the marshy Guadalquivir River (a prime bird-watching area). The bridge leads to the town's old fortified gate (which now houses a fascinating museum on Moorish culture, the Museum of Al-Andalus Life). The Mezquita is buried in the characteristic medieval town. North of that stretches the Jewish Quarter, then the modern city—which feels much like any other in Spain, but with some striking Art Deco buildings at Plaza de las Tendillas and lots of Art Nouveau lining Avenida del Gran Capitán.

Tourist Information

Córdoba has three helpful TIs: at the train station, Mezquita, and Alcázar (all open daily 9:30–14:00 & 16:30–19:30, Alcázar TI open through midday break Fri–Sun, tel. 902-201-774, www.turismo decordoba.org). A small TI kiosk is on **Plaza de las Tendillas** (similar hours but until 21:30 in summer).

The TIs **Córdoba Card** is unlikely to be a good value for any short visit (€30–45, valid for one year).

Arrival in Córdoba

By Train or Bus: Córdoba's train station is located on Avenida de América. The bus station is across the street from the train station (on Avenida Vía Augusta, to the north). It's about a 25-minute walk from either station to the old town. There is no luggage storage at the train station, but you can stow your bag at the bus station for €3.20.

Built in 1991 to accommodate the high-speed AVE train line, the train station has ATMs, restaurants, a variety of shops, a TI booth, an information counter, and a small lounge for first-class AVE passengers. Taxis and local buses are just outside.

To get to the old town, hop a **taxi** (€6 to the Mezquita) or catch bus #3 or #4 (get off at San Fernando, ask driver for "Mezquita").

To **walk** the 25 minutes from the train station to the Mezquita, turn left onto Avenida de América, then right on Avenida del Gran Capitán, which becomes a pedestrian zone. At the end, ask someone, *"¿Dónde está la Mezquita?"* You'll be directed downhill, through the whitewashed old Jewish Quarter.

Córdoba

200 YARDS
200 METERS

BUS STN.

AV. DE LA LIBERTAD

AV. DE AMERICA

PLAZA COLÓN

PALACIO VIANA

STA. MARINA

ZARCO

AUGUSTA

TRAIN STATION

ARFE

AV. MOZARABES

JARDINES

DE

PASEO

AV. CERVANTES

AV. DE GRAN CAPITÁN

TEJARES

JOSÉ CRUZ

OSARIO

2

ALF. XII

SAN PABLO

JUAN RUFO

LOSA

AV. MEDINA AZAHARA

TO MADINAT AL-ZAHRA

CONC

CLAUDIO

P. LOPEZ

ANT. MAURA

AV. REP. ARGENTINA

LA VICTORIA

P

LOPE HOCES

AV. DE GRAN CAPITÁN

CONDE HERRERO

PLAZA TENDILLAS

J. VALERA

PL. CORRE-DERA

1

M. LUIS

SAN FERNANDO

ALF. XII

AV. AEROPUERTO

JEWISH QUARTER

CASA DE SEPARAD

BARROSO

CARD HERRERO

B

RIBERA

P.

SYNAGOGUE

OLD WALL

RUDIOS

MEZQUITA

ISASA

CONDE VALL.

SAN BASILIO

CAB.

RONDA

AV. CUSTODIOS

PATIOS AREA

ALCÁZAR

GUADAL QUIVIR

RIVER

ROMAN BRIDGE

M. PIDAL

CORR.

AV. ALCÁZAR

AV. DE FRA

ALBINO

MUSEUM OF AL-ANDALUS LIFE

TO MECCA

SEE CORDOBA CENTER DETAIL MAP

1 Taverna Salinas
2 Taberna San Miguel

P PARKING

B BUS STOPS FROM STATION

DCH

CÓRDOBA

Helpful Hints

Closed Days: The synagogue and Madinat Al-Zahra are closed on Monday, while the Palacio de Viana is closed Sunday. The Mezquita is open daily.

Festival: During the first half of May, Córdoba hosts the Concurso Popular de Patios Cordobeses—a patio contest (see "Patios" sidebar later in this chapter).

Cheap Tricks: Some minor sights, including the Baths of the Caliphate Alcázar and the Alcázar de los Reyes Cristianos, are free all day Wednesday. The Mezquita is free from Monday through Saturday, but only if you get there before 10:00.

Internet Access: Chat-is is a block down from Plaza de las Tendillas at Calle Claudio Marcelo 15 (Mon–Fri 9:30–13:30 & 17:00–20:30, closed Sat–Sun, tel. 957-475-500).

Laundry: The helpful staff at **Sol y Mar** will wash, dry, and fold your laundry (€12.50/load, usually same-day service, cheaper for self-service, Mon–Fri 9:00–13:30 & 17:00–20:30, Sat 9:30–13:30, closed Sun, Calle del Doctor Fleming 8, tel. 957-298-929).

Tours in Córdoba

Guided Walks—In summer, two-hour nighttime walks start at the TI on Plaza de las Tendillas and finish at a typical bar near the Mezquita (€15, includes a drink and tapa, April–Oct daily at 21:30, no tours Nov–March, prepay at TI, request English).

Local Guide—**Isabel Martinez Richter** is a charming archaeologist who loves to make the city come to life for curious Americans (mobile 669-369-645, isabmr@terra.es). **Angel Lucena** is also a good teacher and a joy to be with (€95/2.5 hours, mobile 607-898-079, aluc@eresmas.com).

Sights in Córdoba

▲▲▲The Mezquita

This massive former mosque—now with a 16th-century church rising up from the middle—was once the center of Western Islam and the heart of a cultural capital that rivaled Baghdad and Istanbul. A wonder of the medieval world, it's remarkably well-preserved, giving today's visitors a chance to soak up the ambience of Islamic Córdoba in its 10th-century prime.

Cost and Hours: €8, ticket kiosk inside the Patio de los Naranjos, free entry until 10:00 (because they don't want to charge a fee to attend Mass), dry €3.50 audioguide; open Mon–Sat 8:30–19:00, Sun 8:30–10:30 & 14:00–19:00, Christian altar accessible only after 10:30 unless you attend Mass, try to avoid midday

CÓRDOBA

The Mezquita

PUERTA DEL PERDÓN
ENTER

CALLE   HERRERO

50 YARDS
50 METERS

Tickets

PATIO DE LOS NARANJOS

Fountain

CALLE DE TORRIJOS

CALLE GONZÁLEZ FRANCES

CATHEDRAL

MIHRAB

WC

CÓRDOBA

CALLE CORR. LUIS DE LA CERDA

↓ TO RIVER ↓

DCH

1 Patio de los Naranjos
2 Bell Tower
3 Entrance
4 Visigothic Mosaic
5 Mihrab
6 Visigoth Ruins
7 Villaviciosa Chapel
8 Royal Chapel
9 Treasury
10 Stonemason Marks & Signatures
11 Cathedral
12 Choir

crowds (11:00–15:00) by coming early or late; tel. 957-470-512, www.mezquitadecordoba.org.

⊙ **Self-Guided Tour:** Before entering the patio, take in the exterior of the Mezquita. The mosque's massive footprint is clear when you survey its sprawling walls from outside. At 600 feet by 400 feet, it seems to dominate the higgledy-piggledy medieval town that surrounds it.

Patio de los Naranjos: The Mezquita's big and welcoming courtyard is free to enter. When this was a mosque, the Muslim faithful would gather in this courtyard to perform ablution—ritual washing before prayer, as directed by Muslim law. Historians believe this was the first such courtyard with trees for shade. The trees (probably olive, palm, or orange) were planted in rows that line up with the colonnades inside the mosque, symbolically extending the place of worship through the courtyard. The courtyard walls display many of the mosque's carved ceiling panels and beams, which date from the 10th century. Gaze up through the trees for views of the **bell tower** (c. 1600), built over the remains of the original Muslim minaret. For four centuries, five times a day, a cleric (called a muezzin) would climb the minaret that once stood here to call Muslims to face Mecca and pray.

• *Buy your ticket and enter the mosque, passing through the keyhole gate at the far right corner (pick up an English map-brochure as you enter).*

Interior: Entering the former mosque from the patio, you pass from an orchard of orange trees into a forest of delicate

columns dating from 786. The 850 red-and-blue columns are topped with double arches—a round Romanesque arch above a Visigothic horseshoe arch—made from alternating red brick and white stone. The columns and capitals (built of marble, granite, and alabaster) were recycled from ancient Roman ruins and conquered Visigothic churches. (Arabs excelled at absorbing both the technology and the building materials of the people they conquered.) The columns seem to recede to infinity, as if reflecting the immensity and complexity of Allah's creation. Supporting such a tall ceiling with thin columns required extra bracing with the double arches you see—a

Islamic Córdoba (756-1236): Medieval Europe's Cultural Capital

After his family was slaughtered by political rivals (A.D. 750), 20-year-old Prince Abd Al-Rahman fled the royal palace at Damascus, headed west across North Africa, and went undercover among the Berber tribesmen of Morocco. For six years, he avoided assassination while building a power base among his fellow Arab expatriates and the local Muslim Berbers. As an heir to the title of "caliph," or ruler of Islam, he sailed north and claimed Moorish Spain as his own, confirming his power by decapitating his enemies and sending their salted heads to the rival caliph in Baghdad. This split in Islam is much like the divide in Christianity between Protestants and Catholics.

Thus began an Islamic flowering in southern Spain under Abd Al-Rahman's family, the Umayyads. They dominated Sevilla and Granada, ruling the independent state of "Al-Andalus," with their capital at Córdoba.

By the year 950—when the rest of Europe was mired in poverty, ignorance, and superstition—Córdoba was Europe's greatest city, rivaling Constantinople and Baghdad. It had well over 100,000 people (Paris had a third that many), with hundreds of mosques, palaces, and public baths. The streets were paved and lighted at night with oil lamps, and running water was piped in from the outskirts of the city. Medieval visitors marveled at the size and luxury of the Mezquita mosque, a symbol that the Umayyads of Spain were the equal of the caliphs of Baghdad.

This Golden Age was marked by a remarkable spirit of tolerance and cooperation among the three great monotheistic religions: Islam, Judaism, and Christianity. Giving that society a positive spin, my guide explained, "Umayyad Al-Andalus was

beautiful solution to a practical problem.

Although it's a vast room, the low ceilings and dense columns create an intimate and worshipful atmosphere. The original mosque was brighter before Christians renovated the place for their use and closed in the arched entrances from the patio and street. The giant cathedral sits in the center of the mosque. For now, pretend it doesn't exist. We'll visit it after exploring the mosque.

The mosque sits on the site of an early-Christian church built during the Visigothic period (sixth century). Five columns in from the entrance, a wooden railing marks a hole where you can look down to see a Visigothic **mosaic** from that original church. This is important to the locals, proving there was a church here before the mosque and making it defensible for this newer church to have "violated" the great mosque. There's a little tension lately as some local Muslims are calling to have the Mezquita become a mosque again. The local bishop is responding by changing the tourist not one country with three cultures. It was one culture with three religions...its people shared the same food, dress, art, music, and language. Different religious rituals within the community were practiced in private. But clearly, Muslims ruled. No church spire could be taller than a minaret and while the call to prayer rang out five times daily, there was no ringing of church bells."

The university rang with voices in Arabic, Hebrew, and Latin, sharing their knowledge of *al-jibra* (algebra), medicine, law, and literature. The city fell under the enlightened spell of the ancient Greeks, and Córdoba's 70 libraries bulged with translated manuscripts of Plato and Aristotle, works that would later inspire medieval Christians.

Ruling over the Golden Age were two energetic leaders—Abd Al-Rahman III (912–961) and Al-Hakam II (961–976)—who conquered territory, expanded the Mezquita, and boldly proclaimed themselves caliphs.

Córdoba's Y1K crisis brought civil wars that toppled the caliph (1031), splintering Al-Andalus into several kingdoms. Córdoba came under the control of the Almoravids (Berbers from North Africa), who were less sophisticated than the Arab-based Umayyads. Then a wave of even stricter Islam swept through Spain, bringing the Almohads to power (1147) and driving Córdoba's best and brightest into exile. The city's glory days were over, and it was replaced by Sevilla and Granada as the centers of Spanish Islam. On June 29, 1236, Christians conquered the city. That morning Muslims said their last prayers in the great mosque. That afternoon, the Christians set up their portable road altar and celebrated the church's first Mass. Córdoba's days as a political and cultural superpower were over.

information to make it clear...this is a living church and will stay that way.

• *Walk to the center of the far wall (opposite the entrance), where you'll find the focal point of the mosque, the...*

Mihrab: The mosque equivalent of a church's high altar, this was the focus of the mosque and is the highlight of the Mezquita today. Picture the mosque at prayer time. Each floor stone is about the size of a prayer rug...more than 20,000 people could pray at once here. Imagine the multitude kneeling in prayer, facing the mihrab, rocking forward to touch their heads to the ground, and saying, *"Allahu Akbar, La illa a il Allah, Muhammad razul Allah"*— "Allah is great, there is no god but Allah, and Muhammad is his prophet."

The mihrab, a feature found in all mosques, is a decorated "niche"—in this case, more like a small room with a golden-arch entrance. During a service, the imam (prayer leader) would stand here to read scripture and give sermons. He spoke loudly into the niche, his back to the assembled crowd, and the architecture worked to amplify his voice so all could hear. Built in the mid-10th century by Al-Hakam II, the exquisite room reflects the wealth of Córdoba in its prime. Three thousand pounds of multicolored glass-and-enamel cubes panel the walls and domes in mosaics designed by Byzantine craftsmen, depicting flowers and quotes from the Quran. Gape up. Overhead rises a colorful, starry dome with skylights and interlocking lobe-shaped arches.

• *In the far-right corner, you'll find...*

Visigoth Ruins: On display in the corner to the right of the mihrab are bits of carved stone from the Visigothic Christian church of San Vicente that stood here in the sixth century. (The Christian symbolism was scratched off so the stones could be reused by Muslims.) Abd Al-Rahman I bought the church from his Christian subjects before leveling it to build the mosque. From here, pan 90 degrees to enjoy a view that reveals the vastness of the mosque. (Perhaps you might also appreciate a hidden WC and drinking fountain—in the corner.)

• *Immediately in front of the mihrab, in about the center of the mosque, is an open area that was the...*

Villaviciosa Chapel: In 1236, Saint-King Ferdinand III conquered the city and turned the mosque into a church. Still, the locals continued to call it "La Mezquita," and left the structure virtually unchanged (70 percent of the original mosque structure survives to this day). Sixteen columns were removed and replaced by Gothic arches to make this chapel. It feels as if the church architects appreciated the opportunity to incorporate the sublime architecture of the pre-existing mosque into their church. Notice how the floor was once almost entirely covered with the tombs of nobles and big shots eager to make this their final resting place.

• *Behind the wall, face the mihrab and look to the left to see the...*

Royal Chapel: The chapel—designed for the tombs of Christian kings—is completely closed off. While it was never open to the public, the tall, well-preserved Mudejar walls and dome are easily visible. The lavish Arabic-style decor dates from the 1370s, done by Muslim artisans after the Reconquista. The fact that a Christian king chose to be buried in a tomb so clearly Moorish in design indicates the mutual respect between the cultures (before the Inquisition changed all that).

• *Return to the mihrab. To your immediate left, enter the Baroque...*

Treasury (Tesoro): The treasury is filled with display cases of religious artifacts and the enormous monstrance that is paraded through the streets of Córdoba each Corpus Christi, 60 days after Easter (notice the handles). The monstrance was an attempt by 16th-century Christians to create something exquisite enough to merit being the holder of the Holy Communion wafer. As locals believed the wafer actually was the body of Christ, this trumped any relics. The monstrance is designed like a seven-scoop ice-cream cone, held together by gravity. While the bottom is silver-plated 18th-century Baroque, the top is late Gothic—solid silver with gold plating courtesy of 16th-century conquistadors.

The big canvas nearest the entrance shows Saint-King Ferdinand III, who conquered Córdoba in 1236, accepting the keys to the city's fortified gate from the vanquished Muslims. The victory ended a six-month siege and resulted in a negotiated settlement: The losers' lives were spared, providing they evacuated. Most went to Granada, which remained Muslim for another 250 years. The same day (exhibiting the same spirit of military glee enjoyed by American troops who set up camp in Saddam Hussein's palace), the Spaniards celebrated Mass in a makeshift chapel right here in the great mosque.

Among the other Catholic treasures, don't miss the ivory crucifix (next room, body carved from one tusk, arms carefully fitted on) from 1665. Get close to study Jesus' mouth—it's incredibly realistic. The artist? No one knows.

Just outside the treasury exit, a glass case shows off casts of the many **stonemason marks and signatures** found in this one building. Try to locate the actual ones on nearby columns. (I was five for six.) This part of the mosque has the best light for photography, thanks to skylights put in by 18th-century Christians.

The mosque grew over several centuries under a series of rulers. Remarkably, each ruler kept to the original vision—rows and rows of multicolored columns topped by double arches. Then came the Christians.

Cathedral: Rising up in the middle of the forest of columns is the bright and newly restored cathedral, oriented in the Christian tradition, with its altar at the east end. This doesn't jibe with the mihrab, which normally also faces east (but to Mecca not Jerusalem), because this mihrab actually faces south—as mosques in Syria do in order to face Mecca. (Syria was the ancestral home of Córdoba's jealous Umayyad branch of Islam.) Gazing up at the rich decoration, it's easy to forget that you were in a former mosque just seconds ago. While the mosque is about 30 feet high, the cathedral's ceiling soars 130 feet up. Look at the glorious ceiling.

In 1523, Córdoba's bishop proposed building this grand church in the Mezquita's center. The town council opposed it, but King Charles V ordered it done. According to a false but believable legend, when the king saw the final product, he declared that they'd destroyed something unique to build something ordinary. For a more positive take on this, acknowledge that it would have been quicker and less expensive for the Christian builders to destroy the mosque, but they respected its beauty and built their church into it.

It's interesting to ponder the aesthetics and psychology of the Catholic church versus Islam in the styles of these two great places of worship (horizontal, vertical, intimate, power, fear, love, guilt, dark, bright, simple, elaborate, feeling close to God, feeling small before God).

The basic structure is late Gothic with fancy Isabelline-style columns. The nave's towering Renaissance arches and dome emphasize the triumph of Christianity over Islam in Córdoba. The twin pulpits feature a marble bull, lion, angel, and eagle—symbols of the four evangelists. The cathedral's new Carrara marble throne is the seat of the bishop.

Choir: The Baroque-era choir stalls were added much later—made in 1750 of New World mahogany. While cluttering up a previously open Gothic space, the choir is considered one of the masterpieces of 18th-century Andalusian Baroque. Each of the 109 stalls (108 plus the throne—*catedra*—of the bishop) features a scene from the Bible: Mary's life on one side facing Jesus' life on the other. The lower chairs feature carved reliefs of the 49 martyrs of Córdoba (from Roman, Visigothic, and Moorish times), each with a palm frond symbolizing martyrdom and the scene of their death in the background. The medieval church strayed from the inclusiveness taught by Jesus. Choirs (which seem to consume otherwise-spacious church interiors throughout Spain) were only for canons, priests, and the bishop. Those days are long gone. In fact, a public Mass is now held right here (Mon–Sat at 9:30 in the morning).

Near the Mezquita

Just downhill from the mosque is the Guadalquivir River (which flows on to Sevilla and eventually out to the Atlantic). While silted up today, it was once navigable from here. The town seems to turn its back on the Guadalquivir, but the arch next to the Roman Bridge (with its ancient foundation surviving) and the fortified gate on the far bank (now a museum, described below) evoke a day when the river was key to the city's existence.

Triumphal Arch and Plague Monument—The unfinished Renaissance arch was designed to give King Philip II a royal welcome, but he arrived before its completion—so the job was canceled. The adjacent monument with the single column is an 18th-century plague monument dedicated to St. Raphael (he was in charge of protecting the population from the main scourges in this region at that time: plague, hunger, and floods).

Roman Bridge—The bridge sits on its first-century-A.D. foundations and retains its 16th-century arches, but was poorly restored in 2009. It feels like so much other modern work along this riverbank—done on the cheap. As it was the first bridge over this river, it established Córdoba as a strategic point. Walk across the bridge for a fine view of the city—especially the huge mosque with its cathedral busting through the center. You'll be steps away from the fascinating museum described next.

▲**Museum of Al-Andalus Life**—The Museo Vivo de Al-Andalus fills the fortified gate (built in the 14th century to protect the Christian city) at the far side of the Roman Bridge. It is a velvety, philosophical, almost evangelical attempt to humanize the Muslim Moorish culture funded by the Fundación Roger Garaudy (started by Garaudy, a former French politician and writer controversial for Holocaust revisionism). You don headsets and wander through simple displays with a clear, engrossing soundtrack letting you sit at the feet of the great poets and poke into Moorish living rooms. Garaudy's "How Man Became Human" 60-minute video is a flowery story taking you from prehistory to the formation of the great monotheistic religions...the greatest of which—in his opinion—is Islam (€4.50, daily May–Sept 10:00–14:00 & 16:30–20:30, Oct–April 10:00–18:00, "Multivision" is €1 extra, played in English, 6/day, generally on the hour—ask about next showing as you enter, Torre de la Calahorra, tel. 957-293-929, www.torrecalahorra.com).

Baths of the Caliphate Alcázar (Banos Califales)—The scant but evocative remains of these 10th-century royal baths are all that's left from the caliph's palace complex. They date from a time when the city had hundreds of baths and a population of several hundred thousand. The exhibit teaches about Arabic baths in general and the caliph's in particular. A 10-minute video (normally in Spanish, English on request) tells the story well (€2, May–June and Sept–mid-Oct Tue–Sat 10:00–14:00 & 17:30–19:30; July–Aug Tue–Sat 8:30–14:30; mid-Oct–April Tue–Sat 10:00–14:00 & 16:30–18:30; year-round: Sun 9:30–14:30, closed Mon; just outside the wall near the Alcázar).

Jewish Córdoba

Córdoba's Jewish Quarter dates from the late Middle Ages, after Muslim rule and during the Christian era. Now little remains. For a sense of it in its thriving heyday, visit the synagogue and the cultural center located a few steps away (both described in this section). For a pretty picture, find **Calle de las Flores** (a.k.a. "Blossom Lane"). This narrow flower-bedecked street frames the cathedral's bell tower as it hovers in the distance (the view is a favorite for local guidebook covers).

Synagogue (Sinagoga)—The small yet beautifully preserved synagogue was built in 1315, under Christian rule, but the Islamic decoration has roots way back to Abd Al-Rahman I (see "Islamic Córdoba" sidebar earlier in this chapter). During Muslim times,

Central Córdoba

CÓRDOBA

1. La Hospedería de El Churrasco & Rest. El Choto
2. Hotel Albucasis
3. Hotel González
4. Hotel Mezquita
5. Hotel Califa
6. Hotel Boston
7. Hostal Alcázar
8. To The Terrace Backpackers Hostel & Bodegas Campos
9. Bodegas Mezquita
10. Rest. San Basilio
11. Bodega Guzmán
12. Internet Café
13. Launderette
14. Café La Gloria
15. Baths of the Caliphate Alcázar
16. Calle de las Flores
17. Maimonides Statue & Puerta de Almodóvar Gate
18. Averroes Statue

Córdoba's sizable Jewish community was welcomed, though they paid substantial taxes to the city—money that enlarged the Mezquita and generated goodwill. That goodwill came in handy when Córdoba's era of prosperity and mutual respect ended with the arrival of the intolerant Almohad Berbers. Christians and Jews were repressed, and brilliant minds—such as the rabbi and philosopher Maimonides—fled for their own safety.

The Christian Reconquista of Córdoba (1236) brought another brief period of religious tolerance. That's when this synagogue was built—the result of a joint effort by Christians, Jews, and Muslim (Mudejar) craftsmen. By the end of the 14th century, however, Spain's Jews were again persecuted. They were finally expelled or forced to convert in 1492; this is one of only three surviving synagogues in Spain built before that year.

Rich Mudejar decorations of intertwined flowers, arabesques, and Stars of David plaster the walls. What appear to be quotes from the Quran in Arabic are actually quotes from the Bible in Hebrew. On the east wall (the symbolic direction of Jerusalem), find the niche for the Ark, which held the scrolls of the Torah (the Jewish scriptures). The upstairs gallery was reserved for women. This synagogue, the only one that survives in Córdoba, was left undisturbed because it was used as a church until the 19th century—in fact, you can see a cross painted into a niche (€0.30, Tue–Sat 9:30–14:00 & 15:30–17:30, Sun 9:30–13:30, closed Mon, Calle de los Judíos 20, tel. 957-202-928). To learn more about the synagogue and its community, head next to the Casa de Sefarad (described next), just 10 steps uphill.

Casa de Sefarad—Set inside a restored 14th-century home directly across from the synagogue, this interpretive museum brings to life Córdoba's rich Jewish past. Five rooms around a central patio are themed to help you understand different aspects of daily life for Spain's former Jewish community. The rooms focus on contributions from women in the community, Jewish holidays, musical traditions, and more. Upstairs is an interpretive center for the synagogue, along with rooms dedicated to Maimonides and to the synagogue. The Casa de Sefarad is a cultural center for Sephardic (the Hebrew word for "Spanish") Jewish heritage. Jaime and his staff stress that the center's purpose is not political or religious, but cultural. Along with running this small museum, they teach courses, offer a library, and promote an appreciation of Córdoba's Sephardic heritage (€4, Mon–Sat 11:00–19:00, Sun

11:00–14:00, 30-minute guided tours in English are available by request if a guide is available, next to the synagogue at the corner of Calle de los Judíos and Calle Averroes, tel. 957-421-404, www .casadesefarad.es). The Casa de Sefarad hosts weekly concerts—acoustic, Sephardic, and Andalusian, but no flamenco—on its patio (€10, most Saturdays in season at 20:00, reservations smart).

City Wall—Built upon the foundation of Roman Córdoba's wall, these fortifications date mostly from the 12th century. While the city stretched beyond the wall in Moorish times, this wall protected its political, religious, and commercial center. There were seven gates. Today the Puerta de Almodóvar (near the synagogue) is best preserved. Just outside the gate you'll find statues of Córdoba's great thinkers: Seneca (the Roman philosopher and adviser to Nero), Maimonides, and Averroes.

Statues of Maimonides and Averroes—Statues honor two of Córdoba's deepest-thinking homeboys—one Jewish, one Muslim, both driven out during the wave of Islamic intolerance after the fall of the Umayyad caliphate. (Maimonides is 30 yards downhill from the synagogue; Averroes is at the end of the old wall, where Cairuán and Doctor Fleming streets meet.)

Maimonides (1135–1204) was born in Córdoba and raised on both Jewish scripture and Aristotle's philosophy. Like many tolerant Córdobans, he saw no conflict between the two. Maimonides—sometimes called the "Jewish Aquinas"—wrote the *Guide of the Perplexed* (in Arabic), in which he asserted (as the Christian philosopher St. Thomas Aquinas later would) that secular knowledge and religious faith could go hand-in-hand.

Córdoba changed in 1147, when the fundamentalist Almohads assumed power. (Imagine Pat Robertson taking over the US.) Maimonides was driven out, eventually finding work in Cairo as the sultan's doctor. Today tourists, Jewish scholars, and fans of Aquinas rub the statue's foot in the hope that some of Maimonides' genius and wisdom will rub off on them.

The story of **Averroes** (1126–1198) is a near match of Maimonides', except that Averroes was a Muslim lawyer, not a Jewish doctor. He became the medieval world's number-one authority on Aristotle, influencing Aquinas. Averroes' biting tract *The Incoherence of the Incoherence* attacked narrow-mindedness, asserting that secular philosophy (for the elite) and religious faith (for the masses) both led to truth. The Almohads banished him from the city and burned his books, ending four centuries of Córdoban enlightenment.

Córdoba's Jewish Quarter: A Ten-Point Scavenger Hunt

While most of the area around the big mosque is commercial and touristy, the neighborhood to the east seems somehow almost untouched by tourism and the modern world (as you leave the Mezquita, turn right and exit the orange-grove patio). To catch a whiff of Córdoba before the onslaught of tourism and the affluence of the 21st century, explore this district. Just wander and observe. Here are a few characteristics to look for:

1. **Narrow streets.** Skinny streets make sense in hot climates, as they provide much-appreciated shade.

2. **Thick, whitewashed walls.** Both features serve as a kind of natural air-conditioning—and the chalk "bugs" bugs.

3. **Colorful doors and windows.** What little color there is in this famously white city helps counter the boring whitewash.

4. **Iron grilles.** Historically, these were more artistic, but modern ones are more practical. Their continued presence is a reminder of the persistent gap through the ages between rich and poor. The wooden latticework covering many windows is a holdover from days when women were extremely modest and wanted privacy.

5. **Stone bumpers on corners.** These protected buildings against reckless drivers. Scavenged second-hand ancient Roman pillars worked well.

6. **Scuff guards.** Made of harder materials, these guards sit at the base of the whitewashed walls—and, from the looks of it, are serving their purpose.

7. **Riverstone cobbles.** These stones were cheap and local, and provided drains down the middle of a lane. They were flanked by smooth stones that stayed dry for walking (and now aid the rolling suitcases of modern-day tourists).

8. **Pretty patios.** Córdobans are proud of their patios. Walk up to the inner iron gates of the wide-open front doors and peek in (see "Patios" sidebar later in this chapter).

9. **Remnants of old towers from minarets.** Muslim Córdoba peaked in the 10th century with an estimated 400,000 people, which meant lots of neighborhood mosques.

10. **A real neighborhood.** People really live here. There are no tacky shops, and just about the only tourist...is you.

More Sights in Córdoba

Alcázar de los Reyes Cristianos—Tourists line up to visit Córdoba's overrated fortress, the "Castle of the Christian Monarchs," which sits strategically next to the Guadalquivir River. Upon entering, look to the right to see a big, beautiful garden rich with flowers and fountains. To the left is a modern-feeling, unimpressive fort. While it was built along the Roman walls in Visigothic times, constant reuse and recycling has left it sparse and barren (with the exception of a few interesting Roman mosaics on the walls). Crowds squeeze up and down the congested spiral staircases of "Las Torres" for meager views. Ferdinand and Isabel donated the castle to the Inquisition in 1482, and it became central in the church's effort to discover "false converts to Christianity"—mostly Jews who had decided not to flee Spain in 1492 (€4, Tue–Fri 8:30–19:30, closes at 15:00 in summer, Sat–Sun 8:30–15:00, closed Mon). On Fridays and Saturdays you're likely to see civil wedding parties here.

Plaza de las Tendillas—While most tourists leave Córdoba having seen just the Mezquita and the cute medieval quarter that surrounds it, the modern city offers a good peek at urban Andalucía. Perhaps the best way to sample this is to browse Plaza de las Tendillas and the surrounding streets. The square, with an Art Deco charm, acts like there is no tourism in Córdoba. On the hour, a clock here chimes the guitar chords of Juan Serrano, a Córdoban classic.

Characteristic cafés and shops abound. For example, **Café La Gloria** provides an earthy Art Nouveau experience. Located just down the street from Plaza de las Tendillas, it has an unassuming entrance, but a sumptuous interior. Carved floral designs wind around the bar, mixing with *feria* posters and bullfighting memories. Pop in for a quick beer or coffee (daily from 8:30, quiet after lunch crowd clears out, Calle Claudio Marcelo 15, tel. 957-477-780).

Palacio de Viana—Decidedly off the beaten path, this former palatial estate is a 20-minute walk northeast from the cluster of sights near the Mezquita. A guided tour whisks you through each room of an exuberant 16th-century estate, while an English handout drudges through the dates and origin of each important piece. But the house is best enjoyed by ignoring the guide and gasping at the massive collection of—for lack of a better word—stuff. Decorative-art fans will have a field day. The sight is known as the "patio museum" for its 12

Patios

In Córdoba, patios are taken very seriously, as shown by the fiercely fought contest that takes place the first half of every May to pick the city's most picturesque. Patios, a common feature of houses throughout Andalucía, have a long history here. The Romans used them to cool off, and the Moors added lush, decorative touches. The patio functioned as a quiet outdoor living room, an oasis from the heat. Inside elaborate ironwork gates, roses, geraniums, and jasmine spill down whitewashed walls, while fountains play and caged birds sing. Some patios are owned by individuals, some are communal courtyards for several homes, and some grace public buildings like museums or convents.

Today, homeowners take pride in these mini-paradises, and have no problem sharing them with tourists. Keep an eye out for square metal signs that indicate historic homes. As you wander Córdoba's back streets, pop your head into any wooden door that's open. The proud owners (who keep inner gates locked) enjoy showing off their picture-perfect patios. A concentration of patio-contest award-winners runs along Calle de San Basilio and Calle Martín Roa, just across from the Alcázar gardens.

connecting patios, each with a different theme (house-€6, patios only-€3; June–Sept Mon–Sat 9:00–14:00, closed Sun; Oct–May Mon–Fri 10:00–13:00 & 16:00–18:00, Sat 10:00–13:00, closed Sun; no photos inside, Plaza Don Gome 2, tel. 957-496-741).

Away from the Center
Madinat Al-Zahra (Medina Azahara)—Five miles northwest of Córdoba, these ruins of a once-fabulous palace of the caliph were completely forgotten until excavations began in the early 20th century. Built in A.D. 929 as a power center to replace Córdoba, Madinat Al-Zahra was both a palace and an entirely new capital city—the "City of the Flower"—covering nearly half a square mile (only about 10 percent has been uncovered). Extensively planned

with an orderly design, Madinat Al-Zahra was meant to symbolize and project a new discipline on an increasingly unstable Moorish empire in Spain. It failed. Only 75 years later, the city was looted and destroyed.

The site is underwhelming—a jigsaw puzzle waiting to be reassembled by patient archaeologists. Upper terrace excavations have uncovered stables and servants' quarters. Farther downhill, the house of a high-ranking official has been partially reconstructed. At the lowest level, you'll come to the remains of the mosque— placed at a diagonal, facing true east. The highlight of the visit is an elaborate reconstruction of the caliph's throne room, capturing a moody world of horseshoe arches and delicate stucco. Legendary accounts say the palace featured waterfall walls, lions in cages, and—in the center of the throne room—a basin filled with mercury, reflecting the colorful walls. The effect likely humbled anyone fortunate enough to see the caliph.

Cost and Hours: €1.50, Tue–Sat 10:00–20:30, Sun 10:00– 14:00, closed Mon.

Getting There: Madinat Al-Zahra is located on a back road five miles from Córdoba. By **car,** head to Avenida de Medina Azahara (one block south of the train station), following signs for *A-431*; the site is well-signposted from the highway. Though the ruins aren't accessible via regular public transportation, the TI runs a **shuttle bus** that leaves each morning and returns two hours later (€6.50, buy ticket at Alcázar or Plaza Tendillas TIs, runs year-round Tue–Fri at 11:00, Sat–Sun at 10:00 and 11:00, informative English booklet provided). Catch the bus near the Mezquita at Avenida Alcázar, along the river.

Sleeping in Córdoba

The first four listings and Hostal Alcázar are within a five-minute stroll of the Mezquita (see map on page 572). The others are still central, but not buried in all that tangled medieval cuteness. If it's hot and you've got a lot of luggage, don't bother with the inconvenient city buses; just hop in a taxi.

$$$ La Hospedería de El Churrasco is a nine-room jewel box of an inn, featuring plush furniture, tasteful traditional decor, and hardwood floors. Quiet and romantic, it's tucked in the old quarter just far enough away from the tourist storm, yet still handy for sightseeing (Sb-€120, Db-€140, superior Db-€180, €20 more

---

Sleep Code

(€1 = about $1.40, country code: 34)
S = Single, **D** = Double/Twin, **T** = Triple, **Q** = Quad, **b** = bathroom,
s = shower only. Unless otherwise noted, credit cards are
accepted, English is spoken, and breakfast generally costs
extra.

To help you easily sort through these listings, I've divided
the rooms into three categories, based on the price for a
standard double room with bath during high season:

$$$ Higher Priced—Most rooms €100 or more.
$$ Moderately Priced—Most rooms between €60-100.
$ Lower Priced—Most rooms €60 or less.

---

per room in April–May and Oct, website shows off each distinct
room, no twin rooms, includes breakfast, air-con, Internet access,
parking-€20, midway between Puerta de Almodóvar and the
Mezquita at Calle Romero 38, tel. 957-294-808, fax 957-421-661,
www.elchurrasco.com, hospederia@elchurrasco.com).

$$ Hotel Albucasis, at the edge of the tourist zone, features
15 basic, clean rooms, all of which face quiet interior patios. The
friendly, accommodating staff and cozy setting make you feel right
at home (Sb-€55, Db-€85, breakfast-€6, air-con, parking-€12,
Calle del Buen Pastor 11, tel. 957-478-625, www.hotelalbucasis
.com, hotelalbucasis@hotmail.com).

$$ Hotel González, with many of its 17 basic rooms facing
its cool and peaceful patio, is sparse but sleepable. It's clean and
well-run, with a fine location and price (Sb-€43, Db-€78, Tb-€110,
includes breakfast, air-con, Wi-Fi, Manríquez 3, tel. 957-479-
819, fax 957-486-187, www.hotel-gonzalez.com, hotelgonzalez
@wanadoo.es).

$$ Hotel Mezquita, just across from the main entrance of
the Mezquita, rents 31 modern and comfortable rooms. The grand
entrance lobby elegantly recycles an upper-class mansion (Sb-€36,
Db-€74, Tb-€100, breakfast-€4, air-con, Plaza Santa Catalina
1, tel. 957-475-585, fax 957-476-219, www.hotelmezquita.com,
hotelmezquita@wanadoo.es).

$$ Hotel Califa, a modern business-class hotel from the
NH chain, sits on a quiet street a block off busy Paseo Victoria,
on the edge of the jumbled old quarter (65 rooms, vast price range
depending on demand but Db generally €80–90, around €70 in
heat of summer, air-con, parking-€15, Lope de Hoces 14, tel. 957-
299-400, www.nh-hotels.com, nhcalifa@nh-hotels.com).

$$ Hotel Boston, with 30 rooms, is a decent budget bet if you
want a reliable basic hotel away from the touristy Mezquita zone.

CÓRDOBA

It's a taste of workaday Córdoba (Db-€60–72, Málaga 2, just off Plaza de las Tendillas, tel. 957-474-176, www.hotel-boston.com).

$ Hostal Alcázar is your best cheapie. Run-down and budget-priced, without a real reception desk, this friendly place is just outside the old city wall on a quiet cobbled traffic-free street known for its prize-winning patios. Its 16 rooms are split between two homes on opposite sides of the lane, conveniently located 50 yards from a taxi and bus stop (Sb-€18, small Db-€30, bigger Db-€45, Tb-€45–54, two-room apartment-€60 for two or €80 for four, breakfast-€3, air-con, Wi-Fi, parking-€6, near Alcázar at Calle de San Basilio 2, tel. 957-202-561, www.hostalalcazar.com, hostalalcazar@hotmail.com, ladies' man Fernando and family, son Demitrio speaks English).

$ The Terrace Backpackers Hostel rents dorm beds and simple doubles in a great neighborhood (dorm beds-€15–19, D-€40–50, includes breakfast, air-con, Internet access, terrace, kitchen, lots of hostel-type info and help, at San Fernando bus stop—take #3 or #4 from station—at Calle Lucano 12, tel. 957-492-966, theterracebackpackershostel@yahoo.com).

Eating in Córdoba

Local specialties include *salmorejo*, Córdoba's version of *gazpacho*. It's creamier, with more bread and olive oil and generally served with pieces of ham and hard-boiled egg. Most places serve white wines from the nearby Montilla-Moriles region; these *finos* are slightly less dry but more aromatic than the sherry produced in Jerez de la Frontera.

Restaurants generally serve lunch from 13:00 to 16:00 and dinner from 20:00 until very late (Spaniards don't start dinner until about 21:00).

Many smaller places have "bar menus" with *raciones* and half-*(media) raciones* rather than typical first and second courses. Enjoy this as an opportunity to explore the regional cuisine. Ordering half-*raciones* may cost a bit more per ounce, but you'll broaden your tasting experience. Two people can fill up on four *media-raciones*. Don't be intimidated by the language barrier. Ask for the *lista de tapas* in English (there's usually one around somewhere). For a good value and truly local scene, explore the little characteristic bars in the lanes around Plaza de la Corredera.

Near the Mezquita

There are plenty of touristy options around the Mezquita, designed for out-of-towners and tour groups. By walking a couple blocks away along Calle del Cardenal González, you get into a district of cheap, accessible little places offering a better value. Listed here, in order, are a bright and efficient diner about 50 yards from the mosque, a colorful neighborhood restaurant, a down-and-dirty wine bar, a steak house, and (a 10-min walk away) my favorite place in town.

Bodegas Mezquita is a good bet for a bright, not-too-touristy, air-conditioned place a block from the mosque. They have a good *menu del dia,* or you can try the two-person special—eight tapas for €20—on weekdays (one block immediately in front of the Mezquita garden at Calle de Céspedes 12, tel. 957-498-117).

Restaurante San Basilio is the local hangout on Calle de San Basilio, just outside the wall. While there's no seating outside, the restaurant still offers great "patio ambience"—with a view of the kitchen action. No tourists, no pretense...it's understandably the neighborhood favorite (classic €18 fixed-priced meal, €8 lunch special weekdays, lots of €10 fish dishes, closed Sun, Calle de San Basilio 19, tel. 957-297-007). If this doesn't work for you, there's a fancier restaurant a block farther toward the church. And for something rougher—rustic meals, tapas, and crowds—go to the church and head a block left to Bodega San Basilio (Calle de Enmedio, tel. 957-297-832).

Bodega Guzmán, which proudly displays the heads of brave-but-unlucky bulls, serves cold, very basic tapas to locals who burst into song when they feel the flamenco groove. Arrive early to get a table. While it feels like a drinking place, they have rustic tapas and *raciones* (ask for the list in English). Choose a table or belly up to the bar and try a white wine: dry *(blanco seco)* or sweet *(blanco dulce)* for €1 a glass. For grape juice, ask for *mosto* (closed Thu; if entering the old town from Puerta de Almodóvar take the first right—it's 100 yards from the gate at Calle de los Judíos 7).

Restaurante El Choto is bright, formal, and dressy, with a small leafy patio, buried deep in the Jewish Quarter. It's touristy yet intimate, serving well-presented international dishes with an emphasis on grilled meat. The favorite is kid goat with garlic— *choto al ajillo* (€17 house menu, €33 tasting menu, closed Mon, Calle de Almanzor 10, tel. 957-760-115).

Bodegas Campos is a historic and venerable house of eating, attracting so many locals it comes with its own garage. They have a stuffy formal restaurant upstairs, but I'd eat in the more relaxed tavern on the ground floor. The service is great and the menu is inviting. In two visits I nearly ate my way through the offerings, half-*ración* at a time, and enjoyed each €5–8 dish. Experiment— you can't go wrong. House specialties are bull-tail stew (*rabo de toro*—rich, tasty, and a good splurge) and cod with tomato. Don't leave without exploring the sprawling complex. Behind the WC you'll discover a virtual museum of classic, original *feria* posters and great photos (closed Sun; from river end of Mezquita walk east along Cardenal González, continue 10 min straight to Calle de Lineros 32; tel. 957-497-500).

In the Modern City

Taverna Salinas feels like a movie set designed to give you the classic Córdoba scene. While all the seating is indoors, it's still pleasantly patio-esque, and popular with locals for its traditional cuisine and exuberant bustle. The fun menu features a slew of enticing €6 plates (spinach with chick peas is a house specialty). Study what locals are eating before ordering. There's no drink menu—just basic beer or inexpensive wine. If there's a line (as there often is later in the evening), leave your name and throw yourself into the adjacent tapas-bar mosh pit for a drink (closed Sun; from Plaza de las Tendillas walk 3 blocks to the Roman temple, then go 1 more block and turn right to Tendidores 3; tel. 957-480-135).

Taberna San Miguel is nicknamed Casa el Pisto for its famous *pisto,* the local ratatouille-like vegetable stew. Well-respected, it's packed with locals who appreciate regional cuisine, a good value, and a place with a long Córdoban history. Go to the bar to be seated (€8–10 plates, closed Sun–Mon and Aug, 2 blocks north of Plaza de las Tendillas at Plaza San Miguel 1, tel. 957-470-166). Walking here, you feel a world apart from the touristy scene.

Connections

From Córdoba by Train: Córdoba is on the slick AVE train line (reservations required), making it an easy stopover between **Madrid** (28/day, 1.75 hrs) and **Sevilla** (hourly, 45 min, €30 one-way, €47 round-trip—must reserve both ways when you book, with railpass you still must pay €10 reservation fee). The slow train to **Sevilla** doesn't require a reservation and is much cheaper (80 min, €9 one-way). Other trains go to **Granada** (2/day, 2.5 hrs), **Ronda** (2/day direct, 1.75 hrs; more with transfer in Bobadilla, 3.5 hrs), **Málaga** (15/day, 1 hr on fast AVE train; 2/day, 2.25–3 hrs on slower train), and **Algeciras** (2/day, 3.5 hrs). Train info: tel. 902-240-202.

By Bus to: Granada (8/day, 2.5–3 hrs), **Sevilla** (9/day, 2 hrs), **Madrid** (6/day, 5 hrs), **Málaga** (5/day, 3–3.5 hrs *directo*), **Barcelona** (2/day, 10 hrs). The efficient staff at the information desk prints bus schedules for you. Bus info: tel. 957-404-040.

ANDALUCÍA'S WHITE HILL TOWNS

Arcos de la Frontera • Ronda • Zahara •
Grazalema • Jerez

Just as the American image of Germany is Bavaria, the Yankee dream of Spain is Andalucía. This is the home of bullfights, flamenco, gazpacho, pristine whitewashed hill towns, and glamorous Mediterranean resorts. The big cities of Andalucía (Granada, Sevilla, and Córdoba) and the South Coast (Costa del Sol) are covered in separate chapters. This chapter explores its hill-town highlights.

The Route of the White Hill Towns (Ruta de los Pueblos Blancos), Andalucía's charm bracelet of cute towns perched in the sierras, gives you wonderfully untouched Spanish culture. Spend a night in the romantic queen of the white towns, Arcos de la Frontera. (Towns with "de la Frontera" in their names were established on the front line of the centuries-long fight to recapture Spain from the Muslims, who were slowly pushed back into Africa.) The hill towns—no longer strategic, no longer on any frontier—are now just passing time peacefully. Join them. Nearby, the city of Jerez, while teeming with traffic and lacking in charm, is worth a peek for its famous horses and a glass of sherry.

To study ahead, visit www.andalucia.com for information on hotels, festivals, museums, nightlife, and sports in the region.

Planning Your Time

On a three-week vacation in Spain, the region is worth two nights and up to two days sandwiched between visits to Sevilla and Tarifa. Arcos makes the best home base, as it's near Jerez, close to interesting smaller towns, and conveniently situated halfway between Sevilla and Tarifa. The towns can also be accessed from the Costa del Sol resorts via Ronda.

Southern Andalucía

20 MILES
50 KM

— AUTOPISTA (TOLL FREEWAY)
— OTHER ROADS
D.L.F = DE LA FRONTERA

SEE DETAIL MAP

TO CÓRDOBA

SANTIPONCE
ITÁLICA RUINS
A-49
TO HUELVA & PORTUGAL

GUADALQUIVIR RIVER
SEVILLA
A-4
A-364
A-92
AGUILAR
PUENTE GENIL
ESTEPA
A-92
TO GRANADA

AP-4
N-IV
SANLÚCAR
ARCOS D.L.F.
JEREZ D.L.F.
A-382
ROTA
CÁDIZ
A-381
A-4
A-1331
ZAHARA
A-384
OLVERA
TEBA
A-384
CHORRO GORGE
CARRA-TRACA
SETENIL
A-372
A-374
GRAZALEMA
UBRIQUE
A-343
A-373
PILETA CAVE
RONDA
A-397
TO MÁLAGA & NERJA
SAN PEDRO
AP-7

MEDINA SIDONIA
A-48
A-396
VEJER D.L.F.
N-340
A-2304
GAUCÍN
JIMENA
A-381
AP-7
ESTE-PONA
A-7
MARBELLA

COSTA DE LA LUZ
CAPE TRAFALGAR
ALGECIRAS
TARIFA
LA LÍNEA
GIBRALTAR (U.K.)
COSTA DEL SOL

ATLANTIC OCEAN
TANGIER
MOROCCO
CEUTA (SPAIN)
MEDITERRANEAN SEA

DCH

See Jerez on your way in or out, spend a day hopping from town to town in the more remote interior (Grazalema and Zahara, at a minimum), and enjoy Arcos early and late in the day. For more details on exploring this region by car, see "Route Tips for Drivers" at the end of this chapter.

Without a car, you might keep things simple and focus only on Arcos and Jerez (both well-served by public buses). Another option, if you're staying in Sevilla, is to use Andalusian Minibus Tours for an all-day excursion to Olvera, Zahara, Grazalema, and Setenil de las Bodegas (see page 516).

Spring and fall are high season throughout this area. In summer you'll find intense heat, but empty hotels and no crowds.

Arcos de la Frontera

Arcos smothers its long, narrow hilltop and tumbles down the back of the ridge like the train of a wedding dress. It's larger than most other Andalusian hill towns, but equally atmospheric. Arcos consists of two towns: the fairy-tale old town on top of the hill and the fun-loving lower, or new, town. The old center is a labyrinthine wonderland, a photographer's feast. Viewpoint-hop through town. Feel the wind funnel through the narrow streets as cars inch around tight corners. Join the kids' soccer game on the churchyard patio. Enjoy the moonlit view from the main square.

Though it tries, Arcos doesn't have much to offer other than its basic whitewashed self. The locally produced English guidebook on Arcos waxes poetic and at length about very little. You can arrive late and leave early and still see it all.

Orientation to Arcos

Tourist Information

The TI, on the main square across from the parador, is helpful and loaded with information, including bus schedules (summer Mon–Fri 10:00–14:30 & 17:00–20:00, Sat 10:00–13:30 & 17:00–19:00, Sun 10:30–13:30; rest of year Mon–Fri 10:00–14:30 & 16:00–19:00, Sat 10:00–14:30 & 16:00–18:00, Sun 10:30–13:30; Plaza del Cabildo, tel. 956-702-264, www.ayuntamientoarcos.org).

The TI organizes a one-hour **walking tour** of the old town, which describes the church and the town's history, lifestyles, and Moorish influences. You also get a peek at some private courtyard patios. Call or drop by the TI to make sure a tour is scheduled and to book in advance (€7, Mon–Fri at 11:00, leave from main square, in Spanish and/or English; for private tours call TI).

Arrival in Arcos

By Bus: The bus station is on Calle Corregidores, at the foot of the hill. To get up to the old town, catch the shuttle bus marked *Centro* (€1, pay driver, 2/hr, Mon–Fri 8:15–21:15, Sat 8:15–14:15, doesn't run on Sun), hop a taxi (€5 fixed rate), or hike 20 uphill minutes (see map).

By Car: The old town is a tight squeeze with a one-way traffic flow from west to east (coming from the east, circle south under town). The TI and my recommended hotels are in the west. If you miss your target, you must drive out the other end, double back, and try again. Driving in Arcos is like threading needles. Turns are tight, parking is frustrating, and congestion can lead to long jams.

Cheap Tricks in the White Hill Towns

Good news: In general, the south of Spain is cheaper than the north (especially in the small towns).

In Arcos de la Frontera
For an inexpensive (€1) and scenic loop around town, take the minibus joyride described in "Getting Around Arcos" (below).

In Ronda
Instead of going for the big meal with views, either grab a *bocadillo* (sandwich) from a bar or get picnic fixings at the supermarket, and eat your lunch in the Alameda del Tajo park. Then have a coffee at the Hotel Don Miguel terrace, where you feel like you're falling into the gorge.

In Jerez
Rather than attending the horse show, watch the cheaper training sessions. Afterwards, take the Sandeman sherry tour (without tapas), or just go to the Sandeman shop and buy a bottle to chill and drink at your hotel.

Small cars can park in the main square of the old town at the top of the hill (Plaza del Cabildo). Get a €3.50 all-day pass from your hotel or buy a ticket from the machine (€0.70/hr, 2-hr maximum, only necessary Mon–Fri 9:00–14:00 & 17:00–21:00 and Sat 9:00–14:00—confirm times on machine). If checking in, tell the uniformed parking attendant the name of your hotel. If there's no spot, wait until one opens up (he'll help...for a little tip). Once you grab a spot, tell him you'll be back from your hotel with a ticket.

It's less stressful (and better exercise) to park in the modern underground lot at Plaza de España in the new town. From this lot, catch a taxi or the shuttle bus up to the old town (2/hr; as you're looking uphill, the bus stop is to the right of the traffic circle), or hike 15 minutes.

Getting Around Arcos

The old town is easily walkable, but it's fun and relaxing to take a circular **minibus** joyride. The little shuttle bus constantly circles through the town's one-way system and around the valley (€1, 2/hr, Mon–Sat 8:15–21:15, may stop running after 14:00 on Sat, doesn't run on Sun). For a 30-minute tour, hop on. You can catch it just below the main church in the old town near the mystical stone circle (generally departs roughly at :20 and :50 past the hour). Sit in the front seat for the best view of the tight squeezes and the school kids hanging out in the plazas as you wind through the old town. After passing under a Moorish gate, you enter a modern

Arcos de la Frontera Overview

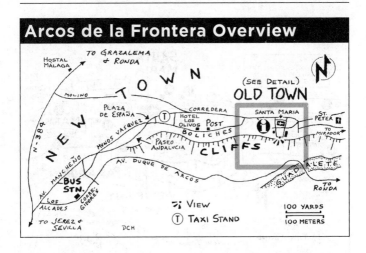

residential neighborhood, circle under the eroding cliff, and return to the old town by way of Plaza de España.

Helpful Hints

Internet Access: Try the single computer at the TI (€1/15 min).

Post Office: It's in the old town at Paseo de los Boliches 24, a few doors up from Hotel Los Olivos (Mon–Fri 8:30–14:30, Sat 9:30–13:00, closed Sun).

Viewpoint: For drivers, the best town overlook is from a tiny park just beyond the new bridge on the El Bosque road. In town, there are some fine viewpoints (for instance, from the main square), but the church towers are no longer open to the public.

Self-Guided Walk

Welcome to Arcos' Old Town

This walk will introduce you to virtually everything worth seeing in Arcos.

• *Start at the top of the hill, in the main square dominated by the church. (Avoid this walk during the hot midday siesta.)*

Plaza del Cabildo: Stand at the viewpoint opposite the church on the town's main square. Survey the square, which in the old days doubled as a bullring. On your right is the parador, a former palace of the governor. It flies three flags: Europe, Spain, and the

Arcos de la Frontera Center

NOT TO SCALE—
PLAZA CABILDO TO
MARKET IS ABOUT
A 3 MINUTE WALK

SANTA MARIA

TO ST. PETER

MAG. AMAYA

TO ⑨
CORREDERA BELÉN ⑦
GRADAS ⑬ ⑥
⑩
BOTICAS ④
⑤ MARKET
TO BOLICHES NUEVA ⑪ PLAZA CABILDO ⑫ ② MALDONADO
⑧, CASTLE (NOT OPEN) P ① ③
BUS STN. & NEW TOWN CLIFFS CLIFFS
PARADOR CLIFFS

N

VIEWPOINT

VIEW
ⓣ TAXI STAND

TO BUS STN. & NEW TOWN AV. DUQUE DE ARCOS RIO GUADALETE

TO RONDA

① Parador de Arcos de la Frontera
② Hotel El Convento
③ La Casa Grande
④ Rincón de las Nieves
⑤ Hostal & Rest. San Marcos
⑥ Hostal Callejón de las Monjas
⑦ Bar-Hostal Zindicato

⑧ Hotel Los Olivos
⑨ Hostal Málaga
⑩ Bar La Carcel
⑪ Alcaraván Restaurant
⑫ Plaza Boticas, Rest. Don Fernando & Cloistered Nuns
⑬ Mama Ttina
⑭ Las Doce Campañas Bakery

---

green Andalusian flag. On your left are the City Hall and the TI, below the 11th-century Moorish castle where Ferdinand and Isabel held Reconquista strategy meetings (castle privately owned and closed to the public).

Now belly up to the railing and look down. The people of Arcos boast that only they see the backs of the birds as they fly. Ponder the parador's erosion concerns (it lost part of its lounge in the 1990s—dropped right off), the orderly orange groves, and fine views toward Morocco. The city council considered building an underground parking lot to clear up the square, but nixed it because of the land's fragility. You're 330 feet above the Guadalete River. This is the town's suicide departure point for men (women jump from the other side).

• *Looming over the square is the...*

Church of Santa María: After Arcos was retaken from the Moors in the 13th century, this church was built atop a mosque. Notice the church's fine but chopped-off bell tower. The old one fell in the earthquake of 1755 (famous for destroying Lisbon). The replacement was intended to be the tallest in Andalucía after Sevilla's—but money ran out. It looks like someone lives on an upper floor. Someone does—the church guardian resides there in a room strewn with bell-ringing ropes.

The church may be closed for restoration through 2010; if it's open, buy a ticket and enter (€1.50, Mon–Fri 10:00–13:00 & 16:00–19:00, Sat 10:00–14:00, closed Sun and Jan–Feb). Once inside, step into the center, where you can see the finely carved choir. The organ was built in 1789 with that many pipes. The fine Renaissance high altar—carved in wood—covers up a Muslim prayer niche that survived from the older mosque. The altar shows God with a globe in his hand (on top), and scenes from the life of Jesus (on the right) and Mary (left). Circle the church counterclockwise and notice the elaborate chapels. While most of the architecture is Gothic, the chapels are decorated in Baroque and Rococo styles. The ornate statues are used in Holy Week processions. Sniff out the "incorruptible body" (miraculously never rotting) of St. Felix—a third-century martyr. Felix may be nicknamed "the incorruptible," but take a close look at his knee. He's no longer skin and bones...just bones and the fine silver mesh that once covered his skin. Rome sent his body here in 1764, after recognizing this church as the most important in Arcos. In the back of the church, under a huge fresco of St. Christopher (carrying his staff and baby Jesus), is a gnarly Easter candle from 1767.

• *Back outside, examine the...*

Church Exterior: Circle clockwise around the church, down four steps, to find the third-century Roman votive altar with a carving of the palm tree of life. Though the Romans didn't build this high in the mountains, they did have a town and temple at the foot of Arcos. This carved stone was discovered in the foundation of the original Moorish mosque, which stood here before the first church was built.

Head down a few more steps and come to the main entrance (west portal) of the church (closed until restoration is complete). This is a fine example of Plateresque Gothic—Spain's last and most ornate kind of Gothic.

In the pavement, notice the 15th-century magic circle with 12 red and 12 white stones—the white ones have various "constellations" marked (though they don't resemble any of today's star charts). When a child would come to the church to be baptized, the parents would stop here first for a good Christian exorcism. The exorcist would stand inside the protective circle and cleanse the baby of any evil spirits. While locals no longer do this (and a modern rain drain now marks the center), Sufis, members of a sect of Islam, still come here in a kind of pilgrimage every November. (Down a few more steps and 10 yards to the left, you can catch the public bus for a circular minibus joyride through Arcos; see "Getting Around Arcos," page 586.)

Continue around the church to the intersection below the flying buttresses. These buttresses were built to shore up the church when it was damaged by an earthquake in 1699. (Thanks to these supports, the church survived the bigger earthquake of 1755.) The spiky security grille (over the window above) protected cloistered nuns when this building was a convent. Look at the arches that prop up the houses downhill on the left; all over town, arches support earthquake-damaged structures.

At the corner, **Sr. González Oca's tiny barbershop** has some exciting posters of bulls running Pamplona-style through the streets of Arcos during Holy Week—an American from the nearby Navy base at Rota was killed here by a bull in 1994. (Sr. González Oca is now semi-retired, but if he's in, he's happy to show off his posters; drop in and say, "Hola." Need a haircut, guys? €9.) Downstairs in his son's bar, you can see a framed collection of euro coins from each of the 12 original participating nations (under the TV in the corner). Continuing along under the buttresses, notice the scratches of innumerable car mirrors on each wall (and be glad you're walking).

• *Now make your way...*

From the Church to the Market: Completing your circle around the church, turn left under more arches built to repair earthquake damage and walk east down the bright, white Calle Escribanos. From now to the end of this walk, you'll basically go straight until you come to the town's second big church (St. Peter's). After a block, you hit **Plaza Boticas.**

On your right is the last remaining **convent** in Arcos. Notice the no-nunsense window grilles high above, with tiny peepholes in the latticework for the cloistered nuns to see through. Step into the lobby under the fine portico to find their one-way mirror and a spinning cupboard that hides the nuns from view. Push the buzzer, and one of the eight sisters (several are from Kenya and speak English well) will spin out some €5 boxes of excellent, freshly baked pine-nut cookies for you to consider buying (open daily but not reliably 8:30–14:30 & 17:00–19:00; be careful—if you stand big and tall to block out the light, you can actually see the sister through the glass). If you ask for *magdalenas,* bags of cupcakes will swing around (€1.50). These are traditional goodies made from natural ingredients. Buy some cupcakes to support their church work, and give them to kids as you complete your walk.

The **covered market** *(mercado)* at the bottom of the plaza (down from the convent) resides in an unfinished church. At the entry, notice what is half of a church wall. The church was being built for the Jesuits, but construction stopped in 1767 when King Charles III, tired of the Jesuit appetite for politics, expelled the order from Spain. The market is closed on Sunday and Monday—since they rest on Sunday, there's no produce, fish, or meat ready for Monday. Poke inside. It's tiny but has everything you need. Pop into the *servicio público* (public WC)—no gender bias here.
• *Continue straight down Calle Boticas...*

From the Market to the Church of St. Peter: As you walk, peek discreetly into private patios. These wonderful, cool-tiled courtyards filled with plants, pools, furniture, and happy family activities are typical of Arcos. Except in the mansions, these patios are generally shared by several families. Originally, each courtyard served as a catchment system, funneling rainwater to a drain in the middle, which filled the well. You can still see tiny wells in wall niches with now-decorative pulleys for the bucket.

Look for **Las Doce Campañas bakery,** where Juan Miguel or Encarni sells traditional and delicious sultana cookies (€1.20 each). These big, dry macaroons (named for the wives of sultans) go back to Moorish times. At the next corner, squint back above the bakery to the corner of the tiled rooftop. The tiny stone—where the corner hits the sky—is a very eroded mask, placed here to scare evil spirits from the house. This is Arcos' last surviving mask from a tradition that lasted until the mid-19th century.

Also notice the ancient columns on each corner. All over town, these columns—many actually Roman, appropriated from their original ancient settlement at the foot of the hill—were put up to protect buildings from reckless donkey carts and tourists in rental cars.

As you continue straight, notice that the walls are scooped out on either side of the windows. These are a reminder of the days when women stayed inside but wanted the best possible view of any people action in the streets. These "window ears" also enabled boys in a more modest age to lean inconspicuously against the wall to chat up eligible young ladies.

Across from the old facade ahead, find the **Association of San Miguel.** Duck right, past a bar, into the oldest courtyards in town—you can still see the graceful Neo-Gothic lines of this noble home from 1850. The bar is a club for retired men—always busy when a bullfight's on TV or during card games. The guys are friendly, and drinks are cheap (a stiff Cuba Libre costs €1.50). You're welcome to flip on the light and explore the old-town photos in the back room.

Just beyond, facing the elegant front door of that noble house, is Arcos' second church, **St. Peter's** (€1 donation, Mon–Fri 10:30–14:00 & 17:00–19:00, Sat 10:30–14:00, closed Sun). You know it's St. Peter's because St. Peter, mother of God, is the centerpiece of the facade. Let me explain. It really is the second church, having had an extended battle with Santa María for papal recognition as the leading church in Arcos. When the pope finally favored Santa María, St. Peter's parishioners changed their prayers. Rather than honoring "María," they wouldn't even say her name. They prayed "St. Peter, mother of God." Like Santa María, it's a Gothic structure, filled with Baroque decor, many Holy Week procession statues, humble English descriptions, and relic skeletons in glass caskets (two from the third century A.D.).

In the cool of the evening, the tiny square in front of the church—about the only flat piece of pavement around—serves as the old-town soccer field for neighborhood kids. Until a few years ago, this church also had a resident bellman—notice the cozy balcony halfway up. He was a basket-maker and a colorful character, famous for bringing a donkey into his quarters, which grew too big to get back out. Finally, he had no choice but to kill and eat the donkey.

Twenty yards beyond the church, step into the fine **Galería de Arte San Pedro,** featuring artisans in action and their reasonably priced paintings and pottery. Walk inside. Find the water drain and the well.

Across the street, a sign directs you to **Mirador**—a tiny square 100 yards away that affords a commanding view of Arcos. The reservoir you see to the east of town is used for water sports in the summertime, and forms part of a power plant that local residents protested—to no avail—based on environmental issues.

From the Church of St. Peter, circle down and around back to the main square, wandering the tiny neighborhood lanes. Just below St. Peter's is a delightful little Andalusian garden (formal Arabic style, with aromatic plants such as jasmine, rose, and lavender, and water in the center). The lane, called Higinio Capote—below Santa María—is particularly picturesque with its many geraniums. Peek into patios, kick a few soccer balls, and savor the views.

Nightlife in Arcos

Evening Action in the New Town—The newer part of Arcos has a modern charm. In the cool of the evening, all generations enjoy life out around Plaza de España (10-min walk from the old town). Several fine tapas bars border the square or are nearby.

The big park (Recinto Ferial) below Plaza de España is the late-night fun zone in the summer (June–Aug) when *carpas* (restaurant tents) fill with merrymakers, especially on weekends. The scene includes open-air tapas bars, disco music, and dancing. Throughout the summer, there are free evening events here, including live concerts on Fridays and open-air cinema on Sundays.

Flamenco—The Flamenco en Escena festival takes place during June in Arcos (www.flamencoenescena.es). Flamenco action normally takes place around the old town especially on the Plaza de Cabildo (check with the TI).

Sleeping in Arcos

Hotels in Arcos consider April, May, August, September, and October to be high season. Note that some hotels double their rates during the motorbike races in nearby Jerez (usually April or May, varies yearly, call TI or ask your hotel) and during Holy Week (March 28–April 4 in 2010); these spikes are not reflected in the prices below. However, the IVA tax is included.

In the Old Town

$$$ Parador de Arcos de la Frontera is royally located, with 24 elegant, recently refurbished and reasonably priced rooms (8 have

balconies). If you're going to experience a parador, this is a good one (Sb-€115–124, Db-€144–155, Db with terrace-€173–186, cheaper rates are from Nov–Feb, breakfast-€15, air-con, elevator, minibar, free parking, Plaza del Cabildo, tel. 956-700-500, fax 956-701-116, www.parador.es, arcos@parador.es).

$$ Hotel El Convento, deep in the old town just beyond the parador, is the best value in town. Run by a hardworking family and their wonderful staff, this cozy hotel offers 13 fine rooms—all with great views, most with balconies. In 1998, I enjoyed a big party with most of Arcos' big shots as they dedicated a fine room with a grand-view balcony to "Rick Steves, Periodista Turístico." Guess where I sleep when in Arcos... (Sb with balcony-€55, Sb

Sleep Code

(€1 = about $1.40, country code: 34)

S = Single, **D** = Double/Twin, **T** = Triple, **Q** = Quad, **b** = bathroom, **s** = shower only. Unless otherwise noted, you can assume credit cards are accepted, English is spoken, and breakfast and the 7 percent IVA tax are not included.

To help you easily sort through these listings, I've divided the rooms into three categories, based on the price for a standard double room with bath during high season.

$$$ Higher Priced—Most rooms €100 or more.
$$ Moderately Priced—Most rooms between €50–100.
$ Lower Priced—Most rooms €50 or less.

with terrace-€68, Db with balcony-€70, Db with terrace-€85, extra person-€18; 10 percent discount in 2010 when you book direct, pay in cash, and show this year's book; cheaper Nov–Feb; parking on Plaza del Cabildo-€3.50, Maldonado 2, tel. 956-702-333, fax 956-704-128, www.hotelelconvento.es, reservas@hotelelconvento.es). Over an à la carte breakfast, bird-watch on their view terrace, with all of Andalucía spreading beyond your *café con leche*.

$$ La Casa Grande is a lovingly appointed *Better Homes and Moroccan Tiles* kind of place that rents eight rooms with big-view windows. Like in a lavish bed-and-breakfast, you're free to enjoy its fine view terrace, homey library, and classy courtyard, where you'll be served a traditional breakfast (Db-€70–84, Db suite-€82–118, Tb-€110–115, Qb suite-€122–138, breakfast-€9, air-con, free Internet access and Wi-Fi, Maldonado 10, tel. 956-703-930, fax 956-717-095, www.lacasagrande.net, info@lacasagrande.net, Elena).

$$ Rincón de las Nieves, with simple Andalusian style, has a cool inner courtyard and a handful of rooms. Some rooms have their own outdoor terraces with obstructed views, and all have access to the rooftop terrace. An apartment is also available for up to seven people (Db-€50–72, higher for Holy Week and Aug, apartment €20–24 per person, air-con, Boticas 10, tel. 956-701-528, mobile 656-886-256, rincondelasnieves@gmail.com).

$ Hostal San Marcos, run from a bar in the heart of the old town, offers four air-conditioned rooms and a great sun terrace with views of the reservoir above a neat little bar (Sb-€25, Db-€35, Tb-€45, includes tax, Marqués de Torresoto 6, tel. 956-700-721, mobile 615-375-077, sanmarcosarcos@mixmail.com). Loli speaks no English.

$ Hostal Callejón de las Monjas is open sporadically, but offers the best cheap beds in the old town. With a tangled floor plan and nine simple rooms, it's on a sometimes-noisy street behind the Church of Santa María (Sb-€20, D-€27, Db-€33, Db with terrace-€39, Tb-€44, Qb apartments-€66, includes tax, air-con, Calle Deán Espinosa 4, tel. & fax 956-702-302, padua @mesonelpatio.com, staff speak no English). Sr. González Oca, a ladies' man, runs a tiny barbershop in the foyer (see page 590) and a restaurant in the cellar.

$ At **Bar-Hostal Zindicato,** the bar comes first, but they also rent four tidy air-conditioned rooms really cheap out back on the ground floor (Db-€30, just below the old town gate at Calle Corredera 2, tel. 956-701-841, mobile 657-911-851).

In the New Town

$$ Hotel Los Olivos is a bright, cool, and airy place with 19 rooms, an impressive courtyard, roof garden, generous public spaces, bar, view, friendly folks, and easy parking. The seven view rooms can be a bit noisy in the afternoon, but—with double-paned windows— are usually fine at night (Sb-€40–45, Db-€60–75, Tb-€72–87, extra bed-€12, breakfast-€8, 10 percent discount with cash and this year's book, free Internet access and Wi-Fi, Paseo de los Boliches 30, tel. 956-700-811, fax 956-702-018, www.hotel-losolivos.es, reservas @hotel-losolivos.es, Raquel and Miguel Ángel).

$ **Hostal Málaga** is surprisingly nice, if for some reason you want to stay on the big, noisy road at the Jerez edge of town. Nestled on a quiet lane between truck stops on A-382, it offers 18 clean, attractive rooms and a breezy two-level roof garden (Sb-€20–25, Db-€35–38, Qb apartment-€50, air-con, easy parking, Ponce de León 5, tel. & fax 956-702-010, saturno1004@hotmal .com, Josefa speaks German if that helps).

Eating in Arcos

Restaurants generally serve lunch from 13:00 to 16:00 and dinner from 20:00 until very late (Spaniards don't start dinner until about 21:00).

Dining

The **Parador** (described earlier under "Sleeping") has an expensive restaurant with a cliff-edge setting. Its €36 11-course sampler menu is an interesting option. A costly drink on the million-dollar-view terrace can be worth the price (€25–30 fixed-price meal at lunch, open for lunch and dinner daily, on main square).

Tapas in Arcos' Old Town

There are four decent rustic bar-restaurants in the old town within a block or two of the main square and church. Most serve tapas at the bar and *raciones* at their tables. Prices are fairly consistent (€2 tapas, €5 *media-raciones*, €8 *raciones*).

Bar La Carcel ("The Prison") is run by a hardworking family that brags about its exquisite tapas and *montaditos* (small open-faced sandwiches). I agree. The menu is accessible; prices are the same at the bar or at the tables; and the place has a winning energy, giving the traveler a fun peek at this community (Tue–Sun 12:00–16:00 & 20:00–24:00, closed Mon; during July–Aug it's open Mon and closed Sun; Calle Deán Espinosa 18, tel. 956-700-410).

Alcaraván tries to be a bit trendier yet *típico*, with a hibachi hard at work out front. A flamenco ambience fills its medieval vault in the castle's former dungeon. This place attracts French and German tourists who give it a cool vibe. Francisco and his wife cook from 13:00 and from 21:00 (closed Mon, Calle Nueva 1).

Restaurante San Marcos is a tiny, homey bar with five tables, an easy-to-understand menu offering hearty, simple home-cooking, and cheap €5 plates and €7 fixed-price meals (14:00–16:00 & after 20:00, kitchen sometimes open during siesta hours, Marqués de Torresoto 6).

Restaurante Don Fernando gives rustic a feminine twist with an inviting bar, and both indoor and great outdoor seating on the square just across from the little market (13:30–16:00 & 20:15–23:00 for food, closed Mon, longer hours for drinks on the square, on Plaza Boticas).

Mama Ttina gives you a break from Andalucía, with its Italian pop music and international Italian/Andaluz/Moroccan/British staff. This Italian restaurant fires up the wood-burning oven, and serves up pizzas and pastas for around €9. On weekdays, they also offer a €9 three-course meal (daily 14:00–16:00 & 20:00–24:00, possibly closed Tue–Wed lunch hour, Dean Espinosa 10, tel. 956-703-937).

Tapas in the New Town

Plaza de España, in the lower new town, is lined with tapas bars and restaurants. There's even an Egyptian restaurant if you're in the mood for a change. For a great perch while enjoying the local family scene, consider the busy **Restaurante Bar Terraza** (€12 plates) at the end of Plaza de España. Just beyond that is **Casa Juan Bernal,** a little bar that's enthusiastic about its "prize-winning" tapas (the local gang injects energy after 21:00, Calle Munoz Vazquez 11).

Connections

By Bus

Leaving Arcos by bus can be frustrating (especially if you're going to Ronda)—buses generally leave late, the schedule information boards are often inaccurate, and the ticket window usually isn't open (luckily, you can buy your tickets on the bus). But local buses do give you a glimpse at *España profunda* ("deep Spain"), where everyone seems to know each other, no one's in a hurry, and despite any language barriers, people are quite helpful when approached.

Two bus companies (Los Amarillos and Comes) share the Arcos bus station. Call the Jerez offices for departure times, or ask your hotelier for help. If you want to find out about the Arcos–Jerez schedule, make it clear you're coming from Arcos (Los Amarillos tel. 956-341-063; Comes tel. 902-199-208, www.tgcomes.es). Also try the privately run www.movelia.es for bus schedules and routes.

From Arcos by Bus to: Jerez (hourly, 30 min), **Ronda** (2–3/ day, 2 hrs, 4 with transfer in Villamartín—when transferring, confirm with driver what the final destination is—bus could be headed to Ronda or Sevilla, and dashboard destination signs are often inaccurate), **Cádiz** (4–5/day, 1.25 hrs), **Sevilla** (2/day, 2 hrs, more departures with transfer in Jerez). Buses run less frequently on weekends. The closest train station to Arcos is Jerez.

Route Tips for Drivers

The trip to **Sevilla** takes just over an hour if you pay €5 for the toll road. To reach **southern Portugal,** follow the freeway to Sevilla, skirt the city by turning west on C-30 in the direction of Huelva, and it's a straight shot from there.

For more driving tips for the region, see the end of this chapter.

Ronda

With nearly 40,000 people, Ronda is one of the largest white hill towns. It's also one of the most spectacular, thanks to its gorge-

straddling setting. While day-trippers from the touristy Costa del Sol clog Ronda's streets during the day, locals retake the town in the early evening, making nights peaceful. If you liked Toledo at night, you'll love the local feeling of evenings in Ronda. Since it's served by train and bus, Ronda makes a relaxing break for non-drivers traveling between Granada, Sevilla, and Córdoba. Drivers can use Ronda as a convenient base from which to explore many of the other *pueblos blancos.*

Ronda's main attractions are its gorge-spanning bridges, the oldest bullring in

Spain, and an intriguing old town. The cliffside setting, dramatic today, was practical back in its day. For the Moors, it provided a tough bastion, taken by the Spaniards only in 1485, seven years before Granada fell. Spaniards know Ronda as the cradle of modern bullfighting and the romantic home of 19th-century *banditos*. The real joy of Ronda these days lies in exploring its back streets and taking in its beautiful balconies, exuberant flowerpots, and panoramic views. Walking the streets, you feel a strong local pride and a community where everyone seems to know everyone.

Orientation to Ronda

Ronda's breathtaking ravine divides the town's labyrinthine Moorish quarter and its new, noisier, and more sprawling Mercadillo quarter. A massive-yet-graceful 18th-century bridge connects these two neighborhoods. Most things of touristic importance (TI, post office, hotels, bullring) are clustered within a few blocks of the bridge. The paseo (early evening stroll) happens in the new town, on Ronda's major pedestrian and shopping street, Carrera Espinel.

Tourist Information

The central TI is on the main square, Plaza de España, opposite the bridge (Mon–Fri 9:00–19:30, Sat–Sun 10:00–14:00, longer hours in summer, tel. 952-871-272). Get the free Ronda map, the excellent Andalusian road map, and a listing of the latest museum hours. Consider picking up free maps of Granada, Sevilla, or the Route of the White Towns. Another TI is located opposite the bullring at Paseo Blas Infante (Mon–Fri 10:00–19:15, Sat–Sun 10:15–14:00 & 15:30–18:30, tel. 952-187-119, www.turismo deronda.es).

Local Guide: Energetic and knowledgeable **Antonio Jesús Naranjo** will take you on a two-hour walking tour of the city's sights (from €90 Mon–Fri, from €110 Sat–Sun and holidays, reserve early, tel. 952-879-215, mobile 639-073-763, guiajesus @yahoo.es). The TI has a list of other local guides.

Arrival in Ronda

By Train: The station is a 15-minute walk from the center: Turn right out of the station on Avenida de Andalucía, and go through the roundabout (you'll see the bus station on your right). Continue straight down the street (now called San José) until it dead-ends. Turn left and walk downhill past a church and the Alameda del Tajo park. Keep going down this street, passing the bullring, to get to the TI and the famous bridge. A **taxi** to the center costs about €5.

Ronda

TO PILETA CAVE, ARCOS, SEVILLA ⑬

BUS STATION

TO TRAIN STATION ⑪

ANDALUCÍA
MADRID
MONTE LIRIO
MONTE LAURIA
ALMENDRA
CRUZ VERDE
SOUBIRON
NARANJA
ESPINEL
CORTES
M. CABRERA
LOS REMEDIOS
CANTOS
REAL
PEÑAS
NUEVA
ROSARIO
TENORIO
S. DOMINGO
PASINAR
ARMIÑAN

CALLE JEREZ
SAN JOSÉ
POZO
SAN
VIRGEN DE LA
VIRGEN DE LA
SEC?

200 YARDS
200 METERS

PLAZA MERCED ⑨

WC
ALAMEDA
Post

PLAZA DEL SOCORRO

PLAZA C. ABELA

PLAZA DE ESPAÑA

PARADOR

GUADALEVÍN RIVER

PUENTE NUEVO

TRAIL TO PUERTA DE LOS MOLINOS

PLAZA DE MARÍA AUXILIADORA

MONDRAGÓN PALACE

SANTA MARÍA LA MAYOR

BULLRING

MERCADILLO
QUARTER

MOORISH
QUARTER

OLD BRIDGE

ARAB BRIDGE

ARAB BATHS MUSEUM

BANDOLERO MUSEUM

CITY WALL

TO COSTA DEL SOL, ⑬ & ㉒

Ⓣ **Taxi Stand**
✕ **View**
Ⓟ **Parking**

⑥ ⑫ ⑩ ⑳ ⑯ ⑭ ⑮ ⑰ ⑦ ⑲ ⑱ ⑤ ① ㉑ ② ㉓ ⑧ ㉔ ㉕ ③ ㉖ ④

❶ To Hotel Reina Victoria
❷ Hotel Don Miguel
❸ Hotel San Gabriel
❹ Hotel & Rest. Alavera de los Baños
❺ Hotel Enfrente Arte Ronda
❻ Hotel El Tajo & Spar Market
❼ Hotel San Francisco
❽ Hotel Ronda
❾ Hotel Royal
❿ Hostals Ronda Sol & Biarritz
⓫ To Hostal Andalucía
⓬ Hostal Doña Carmen
⓭ To Los Pastores
⓮ Confiteria Daver

⓯ Restaurante del Escudero
⓰ Restaurante Pedro Romero
⓱ Rest. Casa Santa Pola
⓲ Bar Lechuguita
⓳ Café & Bar Faustino
⓴ El Porton
㉑ Tragatapas
㉒ To Almocábar Gate, Casa Maria & Bodega Bar Rest. San Francisco
㉓ Casa del Rey Moro Garden
㉔ Palacio del Marqués de Salvatierra
㉕ Lara Museum
㉖ Museo Joaquín Peinado

By Bus: To get to the center from the bus station (lockers inside, buy token at kiosk by exit), leave the station walking to the right of the roundabout, then follow the directions for train travelers (above), heading down San José.

By Car: Street parking away from the center is often free. The handiest place to park in the center of Ronda is the underground lot at Plaza del Socorro (1 block from bullring, €18/24 hrs).

Sights in Ronda

Ronda's New Town

▲▲▲The Gorge and New Bridge (Puente Nuevo)—The ravine, called El Tajo—360 feet down and 200 feet wide—divides Ronda into the whitewashed old Moorish town (La Ciudad) and the new town (El Mercadillo) that was built after the Christian reconquest in 1485. The New Bridge mightily spans the gorge. A different bridge was built here in 1735, but fell after six years. This one was built from 1751 to 1793. Look down...carefully.

You can see the foundations of the original bridge (and a super view of the New Bridge) from the Jardines de Cuenca park (daily in summer 9:30–21:30, winter 9:30–18:30): From Plaza de España, walk down Calle Rosario, turn right on Calle Los Remedios, and then take another right at the sign for the park. There are good views from the parador, which overlooks the gorge and bridge from the new-town side.

▲▲▲Bullring—Ronda is the birthplace of modern bullfighting, and this was the first great Spanish bullring. Philip II initiated bullfighting as war training for knights in the 16th century. Back then, there were two kinds of bullfighting: the type with noble knights on horseback, and the coarser, man-versus-beast entertainment for the commoners (with no rules...much like when the WWF wrestlers bring out the folding chairs). Ronda practically worships Francisco Romero, who melded the noble and chaotic kinds of bullfighting with rules to establish modern bullfighting right here in the early 1700s. He introduced the scarlet cape, held unfurled with a stick. His son Juan further developed the ritual (or art—local aficionados would never call it a "sport"—you'll read newspaper coverage of fights not on the sports pages but in the culture section), and his grandson Pedro was one of the first great matadors (killing nearly 6,000 bulls in his career).

Ronda's bullring and museum are Spain's most interesting to

tour (even better than Sevilla's). To tour the ring, stables, chapel, and museum, buy a ticket at the back of the bullring, the farthest point from the main drag (€6, daily April–Sept 10:00–20:00, March and Oct 10:00–19:00, Nov–Feb 10:00–18:00, tel. 952-874-132). The excellent €2 audioguide describes everything and is essential to fully enjoy your visit. I'd visit in the order listed below:

Chapel: The bullfighters' **chapel** greets you at the entrance. Before going into the ring, every matador would stop here to pray to Mary for safety—and hope to see her again.

Museum: The museum is split in two separate sections (horse gear and weapons on the left; the story of bullfighting on the right, with English translations).

The **horse gear and guns exhibit,** a recent acquisition, makes the connection with bullfighting and the equestrian upper class. And, of course, nobles are into hunting and dueling, hence the fancy guns. Don't miss the well-described dueling section with gun cases for two, as charming as a picnic basket with matching wine glasses.

Backtrack past the chapel to see Spain's best **bullfighting exhibit.** With plenty of stuffed bull heads, photos, artwork (original Goya engravings celebrating the art of bullfighting), posters (all original except the Picasso), and costumes, it's a shrine to bullfighting and the historic Romero family. Displays cover dynasties of fighters, costumes, and capes (bulls are actually colorblind, but the traditional red cape was designed to disguise all the blood). Historically, there were only two arenas built solely as bull arenas: in Ronda and Sevilla. Elsewhere, bullfights were held in town squares—you'll see examples in the museum. (For this reason, to this day, arenas are generally called Plazas de Toros).

Arena: From the museum, take advantage of the opportunity to walk in the actual two-tiered arena, with plenty of time to play *toro*, surrounded by 5,000 empty seats. The arena was built in 1785—on the 300th anniversary of the defeat of the Moors in Ronda. Notice the 136 classy Tuscan columns, creating a kind of 18th-century Italian theater. Lovers of the "art" of bullfighting will explain that the event is much more than the actual killing of the bull. It celebrates the noble heritage and the Andalusian horse culture. With your back to the entry, look left to see the ornamental columns and painted doorway where the dignitaries sit (over the gate where the bull enters). On the right is the place for the band (marked "*música*"), which in the case of a small town like Ronda, is most likely a high school band.

Stables and Equestrian School: The bull thundered out into the arena directly under the dignitaries' box. Walk from the arena through the bulls' entry into the bullpen. There are six bulls per fight (and three matadors). Nine bulls were penned up here, and ropes and pulleys safely opened the right door at the right time. Climb upstairs and find the indoor arena (Picadero) and see Spanish thoroughbred horses training from the Equestrian School of the Real Maestranza (Mon–Fri).

Bullfights are scheduled only for the first weekend of September during the *feria* (fair) and occur rarely in the spring. While every other *feria* in Andalucía celebrates a patron saint, the Ronda fair glorifies legendary bullfighter Pedro Romero. For September bullfights, tickets go on sale the preceding July. (As these sell out immediately, Sevilla and Madrid are more practical places for a tourist to see a bullfight).

Alameda del Tajo—One block away from the bullring, the town's main park is a fine place for people-watching, a snooze in the shade, or practicing your Spanish with seniors from the old folks' home.

Ronda's Old Town

Santa María la Mayor Collegiate Church—This 15th-century church with a fine Mudejar bell tower shares a park-like square with orange trees and the City Hall. It was built on and around the remains of Moorish Ronda's main mosque (which was itself built on the site of a temple to Julius Caesar). In the room where you purchase your ticket, look for the only surviving mosque prayer niche (that's a mirror; look back at the actual mihrab, which faces not Mecca, but Gibraltar—where you'd travel to get to Mecca). Partially destroyed by an earthquake, the reconstruction of the church resulted in the Moorish/Gothic/Renaissance/Baroque fusion (or confusion) you see today.

The front of the church interior is dominated by a magnificent 18th-century Baroque high altar with the standard statue of the Immaculate Conception in the center. The even more ornate chapel to the right is a fine example of Churrigueresque architecture, a kind of Spanish Rococo in which decoration obliterates the architecture—notice that you can hardly make out the souped-up columns. This chapel's fancy decor provides a frame for an artistic highlight of the town, the "Virgin of the Ultimate Sorrow." The big fresco of St. Christopher with baby Jesus on his shoulders (on the left, where you entered) shows the patron saint both of Ronda and of travelers.

An elaborately carved choir with a wall of modern bronze reliefs depicting scenes from the life of the Virgin Mary faces the altar. Similar to the Via Crucis (Way of the Cross), this is the Via Lucis (Way of the Light) with 14 stations (such as #13—the Immaculate Conception, and #14—Mary's assumption into heaven) that serve as a worship aid to devout Catholics. The centerpiece is Mary as the light of the world (with the moon, stars, and sun around her). Don't miss the bright paintings around the choir by a French artist who gave sacred scenes a fresh twist—like the Last Supper attended by women or at least men with women's bodies). The treasury displays vestments that look curiously like matadors' brocaded outfits (€4, daily April–Sept 10:00–20:00, March and Oct 10:00–19:00, Nov–Feb 10:00–18:00, Plaza Duquesa de Parcent in old town).

Mondragón Palace (Palacio de Mondragón)—This beautiful Moorish building was erected in the 14th century, possibly as the residence of Moorish kings, and was carefully restored in the 16th century. Wander through its many rooms to find the kid-friendly prehistory museum, with exhibits on Neolithic toolmaking and early metallurgy (described in English). If you plan to visit the Pileta Cave (see page 605), find the panels that describe the cave's formation and shape. Even if you have no interest in your ancestors or speleology, the palace is worth a visit for the architecture alone. Don't miss the topographic model of Ronda at the entrance, which helps you envision the fortified old town apart from the grid-like new one (€3, May–Sept Mon–Fri 10:00–19:00, Sat–Sun 10:00–15:00, Oct–April closes an hour earlier, on Plaza Mondragón in old town, tel. 952-878-450). Linger in the two small gardens, especially the shady one.

Leaving the palace, wander left to the nearby Plaza de María Auxiliadora for more views and a look at the two rare *pinsapos* (resembling extra-large Christmas trees) in the middle of the park; this part of Andalucia is the only region in Europe where these ancient trees still grow. For an intense workout but a picture-perfect view, find the *Puerta de los Molinos* sign and head down, down, down. (Just remember you have to walk back up, up, up.) Not for the faint of heart or in the heat of the afternoon sun, this pathway leads down to the viewpoint where windmills once stood. Photographers go crazy reproducing the most famous postcard view of Ronda—the entirety of the New Bridge. Wait until just before sunset for the best light and cooler temperatures.

Lara Museum—This discombobulated collection of Ronda's history in dusty glass cases displays everything from sewing machines to fans to matador outfits (with decent English explanations). The highlight for many is the juvenile displays showing torture devices from the Inquisition and local witchcraft (€4, daily 11:00–20:00, until 19:00 in winter, Calle Arminan 29). The museum hosts flamenco shows three nights a week (€23 includes a drink, April–Nov Wed–Fri at 22:00, tel. 952-871-263).

Museo del Bandolero—This tiny museum, while not as intriguing as it sounds, is an interesting assembly of *bandito* photos, guns, clothing, and knickknacks. The Jesse Jameses and Billy el Niños of Andalucía called this remote area home, and brief but helpful English descriptions make this a fun detour. One brand of romantic bandits fought Napoleon's army—often more effectively than the regular Spanish troops (€3, daily May–Sept 10:00–20:00, Oct–April 10:00–18:00, across main street below Church of Santa María la Mayor at Calle Armiñan 65, tel. 952-877-785, www .museobandolero.com).

▲**Museo Joaquín Peinado**—Housed in an old palace, this fresh museum features a professional overview of the life's work of

Joaquín Peinado, a Ronda native and pal of Picasso. His style evolved through the big "isms" of the 20th century, ranging from Expressionist to Cubist, and even to erotic. Because Franco killed creativity in Spain for much of the last century, nearly all of Peinado's creative work was done in Paris. You'll have an interesting mod-ern-art experience here without the crowds of Madrid's museums (€4; summer Mon–Fri 10:00–19:00, Sat–Sun 10:00–15:00, closes an hour earlier in winter; Plaza del Gigante, tel. 952-871-585).

Walk Through Old Town to Bottom of Gorge—From the New Bridge, you can descend down Cuesta de Santo Domingo (take the first left at the former Dominican Church, once the head-quarters of the Inquisition in Ronda) into a world of whitewashed houses, tiny grilled balconies, and winding lanes—the old town.

The **Casa del Rey Moro** was never the home of any king (it was given its fictitious name by the grandson of President McKinley who once lived here). It offers visitors entry to the fine "Moorish-Hispanic" belle époque garden, designed in 1912 by a French landscape architect (the house interior is not open to visitors). Follow signs to "the Mine," an exhausting series of 280 slick, dark, and narrow stairs (like climbing down and then up a 20-story building) leading to the floor of the gorge. The Moors cut this zigzag staircase into the wall of the gorge in the 14th century to access water when under siege, then used Spanish slaves to haul water up to the thirsty town (€4, generally daily 10:00–19:00).

Fifty yards downhill from the garden is **Palacio del Marqués de Salvatierra** (closed to public). As part of the "distri-bution" following the Reconquista here in 1485, the Spanish king gave this fine house to the Salvatierra family (who live here to this day). The facade is rich in colonial symbolism from Spanish America—note the pre-Columbian-looking characters (four Peruvian Indians) flanking the balcony above the door and below the family coat of arms.

Just below the palace, stop to enjoy the view terrace. Look

below. A series of square vats are all that remains of the old tan-neries. There are two old bridges, with the Arab Baths just to the right, and at the edge of town is a rectangular horse-training area.

Twenty steps farther down, you'll pass through the Philip V gate, for centuries the main gate to the fortified city of Ronda. Continuing downhill, you come to the **Puente Viejo** (Old Bridge), rebuilt in 1616 upon the ruins of an Arabic bridge. Enjoy the views from the bridge (but don't cross it yet), then continue down the old stairs. From the base of the staircase, look back up to glimpse some of the surviving highly fortified Moorish city walls. You've now reached the oldest bridge in Ronda, the Arab Bridge (also called the San Miguel Bridge). Sometimes given the misnomer of Puente Romano (Roman Bridge), it was more likely built long after the Romans left. For centuries, this was the main gate to the fortified city. In Moorish times, you'd purify both your body and your soul here before entering the city, so just outside the gate was a little mosque (now the ruined chapel) and the Arab Baths.

The **Arab Baths**, worth ▲, are evocative ruins worth a quick look. They were located half underground to maintain the temper-ature and served by a horse-powered water tower. You can still see the top of the shaft (30 yards beyond the bath rooftops, near a cyprus tree, connected to the baths by an aqueduct). Water was hoisted from the river below to the aqueduct by ceramic containers that were attached to a belt powered by a horse walking in circles. Inside, two of the original eight columns scavenged from the Roman ruins still support brick vaulting. A delightful 10-minute video brings the entire complex to life—Spanish and English versions run alternately (€3, Mon–Fri 10:00–19:00, Sat–Sun 10:00–15:00, Nov–April closes Mon–Fri at 18:00).

From here, hike back to the new town along the other side of the gorge: Return to the bridge just uphill. Cross it and take the stairs immediately on the left, which lead scenically along the gorge up to the New Bridge.

Near Ronda: Pileta Cave

The Pileta Cave (Cueva de la Pileta) is the best and probably the most intimate look a tourist can get at prehistoric cave paintings in Spain. Because the famous caves at Altamira in northern Spain are closed (only a nearby replica cave is open), this is your only way to see real Neolithic and Paleolithic paintings that are up to 25,000 years old. Set in a dramatic, rocky limestone ridge at the eastern edge of Sierra de Grazalema Natural Park, Pileta Cave is 14 miles from Ronda, past the town of Benaoján, at the end of an access road.

Farmer José Bullón and his family live down the hill from the cave, and because they strictly limit the number of visitors, Pileta's rare paintings are among the best-preserved in the world. Sr. Bullón and his son lead up to 25 people at a time through the cave, which was discovered by Sr. Bullón's grandfather in 1905. Call the night before to make sure no groups are scheduled for the time you want to visit—otherwise you'll have to wait. Note that if the 13:00 tour is full, it'll be another three hours before the next one starts (€8, 60-min tours on the hour, daily 10:00–13:00 & 16:00–18:00, closes Nov–mid-April at 17:00, closing times indicate last tour, no reservations taken—just join the line, €10 guidebook, no photos, tel. 952-167-343, www.cuevadelapileta.org). Bring a flashlight, sweater, and good shoes. You need a good sense of balance to take the tour. The 10-minute hike, from the parking lot up a trail with stone steps to the cave entrance, is moderately steep. Inside the cave, there are no handrails, and it can be difficult to keep your footing on the slippery, uneven floor while being led single-file, with only a lantern light illuminating the way.

Sr. Bullón is a master at hurdling the language barrier. As you walk the cool half-mile, he'll spend an hour pointing out lots of black, ochre, and red drawings, which are five times as old as the Egyptian pyramids. Mostly it's just lines or patterns, but there are also horses, goats, cattle, and a rare giant fish, made from a mixture of clay and fat by finger-painting prehistoric *hombres*. The 200-foot main cavern is impressive, as are some weirdly recognizable natural formations such as the Michelin man and a Christmas tree.

Getting There: It's possible to get here without wheels, but I wouldn't bother (you'd have to take the Ronda–Benaoján bus—2/day, departs at 8:30 and 13:00, 30 min—and then it's a 2-hour, 3-mile uphill hike). You can get from Ronda to the cave by taxi —it's about a half-hour drive on twisty roads—and have the driver wait (€55 round-trip). If you're driving, it's easy: Leave Ronda through the new part of town, and take A-376. After a few miles, passing Cueva del Gato, exit left toward Benaoján on MA-555. Go through Benaoján and follow the numerous signs to the cave. Leave nothing of value in your car.

Eating near the Cave: Nearby Montejaque has a great outdoor restaurant, **La Casita** (tel. 952-167-120).

Sleeping near the Cave: A good base for visiting Ronda and the Pileta Cave (as well as Grazalema) is **$$ El Cortijo de las Piletas.** Nestled at the edge of Sierra de Grazalema Natural

Park, this spacious family-run country estate has opportunities for swimming, hiking, horseback riding, and exploring the surrounding area. Access is easy from the main highway (Sb-€68–74, Db-€84–90, extra bed-€15–18, includes breakfast, tel. 605-080-295, www.cortijolaspiletas.com, info@cortijolaspiletas.com, Pablo and Elisenda). Another countryside option is **$$ Finca La Guzmana,** run by expat Brits Peter and Claire. Five beautifully appointed pastel rooms surround an open patio at this renovated estate house. Bird-watching, swimming, and trekking are possible (Db-€80, includes tax and breakfast, dinner on request, tel. 600-006-305, www.laguzmana.com, info@laguzmana.com).

Sleeping in Ronda

(€1 = about $1.40, country code: 34)
Ronda has plenty of reasonably priced, decent-value accommodations. It's crowded only during Holy Week (the week leading up to Easter) and the first week of September. Most of my recommendations are in the new town, a short stroll from the New Bridge and about a 10-minute walk from the train station. In the cheaper places, ask for a room with a *ventana* (window) to avoid the few interior rooms. Breakfast is usually not included.

$$$ Hotel Reina Victoria, with its 89 rooms, hangs royally over the gorge at the edge of town and has a marvelous view—Hemingway loved it. I'd choose this, with all its romantic Old World elegance, over the more central parador (Sb-€97–117, Db-€112–156, breakfast-€13, air-con, elevator, pool, free parking, 10-min walk from city center; easy to miss—look for intersection of Avenida Victoria and Calle Jerez, Jerez 25; tel. 952-871-240, fax 952-871-075, www.hotelhusareinavictoriaronda.com, reinavictoria ronda@husa.es).

$$$ Hotel Don Miguel, facing the gorge, is just left of the bridge and has all the charm of a tour-group hotel. Of its 30 sparse but comfortable rooms, 20 have balconies and/or gorgeous views at no extra cost, but street rooms come with a little noise (Sb-€58–70, Db-€91–107, includes buffet breakfast, air-con, elevator, parking garage a block away-€10/day, Plaza de España 4, tel. 952-877-722, fax 952-878-377, www.dmiguel.com, reservas@dmiguel.com).

$$ Hotel San Gabriel has 21 pleasant rooms, a kind staff, public rooms filled with art books, a cozy wine cellar, and a fine garden terrace. If you're a cinephile, kick back in the charming TV room—with seats from Ronda's old theater and a collection of DVD classics—then head to the breakfast room to check out photos of big movie stars who have stayed here (Sb-€69, Db-€85–95, Db suite-€106, breakfast-€6.50, air-con, double-park in front and they'll direct you to a free parking place, follow signs on the main street of old town to Calle Marqués de Moctezuma 19, tel. 952-190-392, fax 952-190-117, www.hotelsangabriel.com, info@hotel sangabriel.com, family-run by José Manuel and Ana).

$$ Alavera de los Baños, located next to ancient Moorish baths at the bottom of the hill, has nine small rooms and big inviting public places, with an appropriately Moorish decor. This hotel offers a swimming pool, a peaceful Arabic garden, and a restaurant for guests. You're literally in the countryside, a 10-minute hike below town with sheep and horses outside near the garden (Sb-€60, Db-€80–95, Db with terrace-€90–105, includes tax and breakfast, closed Dec–Jan, free and easy parking, Calle San Miguel, tel. & fax 952-879-143, www.alaveradelosbanos.com, alavera@telefonica .net, personable Christian and Imma).

$$ Hotel Enfrente Arte Ronda is relaxed, funky, and friendly. The 14 rooms are spacious and exotically decorated, but dimly lit. There's also a peaceful bamboo garden, game room, small swimming pool, sauna, views, and terraces. Guests can enjoy themed dinners on certain nights (€15, confirm with reception). It's in all the guidebooks, so reserve in advance (Sb-€70, Db-€80–100, extra bed-€35, includes buffet breakfast and drinks from their bar, air-con, elevator, free Internet access, Real 40, tel. 952-879-088, fax 952-877-217, www.enfrentearte.com, reservations@enfrente arte.com).

$$ Hotel El Tajo has 33 decent, quiet rooms—once you get past the tacky faux-stone Moorish decoration in the foyer (Sb-€45, Db-€65, air-con, parking-€10/day, Calle Cruz Verde 7, a half-block off the pedestrian street, tel. 952-874-040, fax 952-875-099, www .hoteleltajo.com, reservas@hoteleltajo.com).

$$ Hotel San Francisco offers 27 small, nicely decorated rooms a block off the main pedestrian street in the town center (Sb-€40, Db-€60–70, Tb-€80, includes breakfast, air-con, 6 parking spaces-€15, María Cabrera 20, tel. 952-873-299, fax 952-874-688, hotelronda@terra.es).

$$ Hotel Ronda provides an interesting mix of minimalist and traditional Spanish decor, with five rooms located in the old town. Although there are no views, the refurbished mansion is quiet and homey (Sb-€50, Db-€65, additional bed-€20, includes tax, air-con, free Internet access, Ruedo Doña Elvira 12, tel. 952-872-232, www.hotelronda.net, laraln@telefonica.net, no English spoken).

$$ Hotel Royal has 29 clean, spacious, simple rooms—many on the main street that runs between the bullring and bridge. Thick glass keeps out most of the noise, while the tree-lined Alameda del Tajo park across the street is a treat (Sb-€38, Db-€57, Tb-€66, air-con, includes self-serve breakfast, Calle Virgen de la Paz 42, 3 blocks off Plaza de España, tel. 952-871-141, fax 952-878-132, www.ronda.net/usuar/hotelroyal, hroyal@ronda.net, some English spoken).

$ Hostal Ronda Sol has a homey atmosphere with 15 cheap but monkish rooms (S-€15, D-€25, cash only, parking-€10/day, Almendra 11, tel. 952-874-497, friendly María or Rafael). The same owner runs **Hostal Biarritz** next door, which offers 21 similar rooms, some with private bathrooms (S-€15, D-€25, Db-€35, cash only, parking-€10/day, Almendra 7, tel. 952-872-910, no English spoken).

$ Hostal Andalucía has 11 clean, comfortable, and recently renovated rooms immediately across the street from the train station (Sb-€25, Db-€40, includes tax, air-con, easy street parking, Martínez Astein 19, tel. 952-875-450, www.hostalandalucia.net, info@hostalandalucia.net).

$ Hostal Dona Carmen, another basic cheapie, rents 32 rooms in two sections. The rooms sharing a shower down the hall are especially reasonable (S-€15, Sb-€25, D-€25, Db-€45, air-con, Calle Naranja 28, tel. 952-871-994).

Near Ronda

$$ Los Pastores, 2.5 miles southwest of Ronda on A-369, is a pleasant renovated farmhouse in the countryside (Db-€60–75, four-person apartments-€60–95, one-night stay-€10 extra, breakfast-€6–10, four-course lunch or dinner-€15, Apartado de Correos 167, on A-369, tel. 952-798-305 or 952-114-464, www.fincalos pastores.com, info@lospastores.com, Martin).

Eating in Ronda

Plaza del Socorro, a block in front of the bullring, is an energetic scene, bustling with tourists and local families enjoying the square and its restaurants. The pedestrian-only Calle Nueva is lined with hardworking eateries. To enjoy a drink or a light meal with the best view in town, consider the terraces of Hotel Don Miguel just under the bridge. For coffee and pastries, locals like the elegant little **Confitería Daver** (daily until 20:30, Calle Los Remedios 6). Picnic shoppers find the **Spar** supermarket convenient, opposite Hotel El Tajo (Mon–Sat 9:00–21:30, closed Sun, Calle Cruz Verde 18). The Alameda del Tajo park (with WC) near the bullring is a good picnic spot.

In the City Center

Restaurante del Escudero serves tasty and lovingly presented Spanish food with a posh modern touch in a crystal- and cream-colored dining room or on a terrace overlooking the gorge (€14 fixed-price meals, €33 gourmet tasting meals, closed Sun, behind bullring at Paseo Blas Infante 1, tel. 952-871-367).

Restaurante Pedro Romero, while touristy and overpriced, is a venerable institution in Ronda. Assuming a shrine to bullfighting draped in *el toro* memorabilia doesn't ruin your appetite, it gets good reviews. Rub elbows with the local bullfighters or dine with the likes (well, photographic likenesses) of Orson Welles, Ernest Hemingway, and Francisco Franco (€17 fixed-price meals, or €30 à la carte, daily, air-con, across the street from bullring at Calle Virgen de la Paz 18, tel. 952-871-110).

Restaurante Casa Santa Pola offers gourmet versions of traditional food with friendly, professional service, with several small dining rooms and a delightful terrace perched on the side of the gorge (€17 fixed-price meal, €20 plates; good oxtail stew, roasted lamb, and honey-tempura eggplant; after crossing New Bridge from the bullring, take the first left downhill and you'll see the sign, Calle Santo Domingo 3; tel. 952-879-208).

Tapas in the City Center

Ronda has a fine tapas scene. You won't get a free tapa with your drink as in some other Spanish towns, but these bars have accessible tapas lists, and they serve bigger plates. While each of the following places could make a fine solo destination for a meal, I'd make a tapa pub crawl in the order listed.

Bar Lechuguita, a hit with older locals early and younger ones later, serves a long and tasty list of tapas for a good price. Rip off a tapas inventory sheet and mark which ones you want. Be adventurous and don't miss the bar's namesake, #14, *Lechuguita* (a wedge of lettuce with vinegar, garlic, and a secret ingredient). The order form routine makes it easy to communicate and get exactly what you like, plus you know the exact price (closed Sun, no chairs or tables, just a bar and tiny stand-up ledges, Calle los Remedios 35).

Café & Bar Faustino is a place Brueghel would paint—a festival of eating with a fun and accessible menu that works both at the bar and at tables (lots of €1 tapas). The atmosphere makes you want to stay and the selection makes you wish your appetite was even bigger (closed Mon, just off Plaza Carmen Abela at Santa Cecilia 4, tel. 952-190-307).

El Porton is a classy little bar with Ronda ambience a block in front of the bullring. Their €10 mixed plates (choose meat or fish, served at a table) makes a light meal for two. But I'd just belly up to the bar for a drink and their signature tapa—a tiny piece of oily toast with a slice of ham and a fried quail egg (€1, *huevo de codorniz*) that you eat in one delightful pop (Calle Pedro Romero 7, closed Sat–Sun, tel. 952-877-420).

Tragatapas, the accessible little brother of the acclaimed gourmet Restaurante Tragabuches, serves super-creative and always tasty tapas in a stainless-steel minimalist bar. There's just a handful of tall tiny tables and stools, and an enticing blackboard of the day's specials. If you want to sample Andalusian gourmet (e.g., a variety of €2 tapas such as asparagus on a stick sprinkled with manchego cheese grated coconut-style) without going broke, this is the place to do it (closed Mon, Calle Nueva 4, tel. 952-877-209).

Outside the Almocábar Gate

To entirely leave the quaint old town and bustling city center with all of its tourists and grand gorge views, hike 10 minutes out to the far end of the old town, past the Church of the Holy Ghost, to a big workaday square that goes about life as if the world didn't exist outside Andalucía. Among the numerous eateries here are two of special note: The tiny, quirky Casa Maria is the ultimate in an intimate home-cooking experience, and Bodega San Francisco is a cheap tapas bar and a more normal little restaurant.

Casa Maria is like eating in the home of Elias and Isabel and their daughter Maria. There's little English spoken and no menu, so this is the adventure—you trust Elias to cook up whatever's seasonal for a four-course rustic fiesta for €28 to €30, including drinks (Elias loves red meat). Show Elias this book and you'll get more than the standard glass of house wine, although wine-lovers will want to pay a bit more for a finer bottle (facing Plaza Ruedo Alameda at #27, tel. 952-876-212).

Bodega Bar Restaurante San Francisco is a rustic bar with tables upstairs and a homey restaurant across the street. The bar is your budget option with an accessible list of *raciones* and tapas; the restaurant, while also rustic, comes with serious plates and big splittable portions. This place is understandably a neighborhood favorite (closed Thu, Ruedo de Alameda 32, tel. 952-878-162).

Connections

Note that some destinations are linked with Ronda by both bus and train. Direct bus service to other hill towns can be sparse (as few as one per day), and train service usually involves a transfer in Bobadilla. It's worth spending a few minutes in the bus or train station on arrival to plan your departure. Your options improve from major transportation hubs such as Málaga.

From Ronda by Bus to: Algeciras (6/day, 2 hrs), **La Línea/ Gibraltar** (no direct bus, transfer in Algeciras; Algeciras to Gibraltar—2/hr, 45 min, can buy ticket on bus), **Arcos** (2–3/day, 2 hrs), **Benaoján** (2/day, 30 min), **Jerez** (4/day, 2.5–3 hrs), **Grazalema** (2/day, 45 min), **Zahara** (1/day, Mon–Fri only, 1 hr), **Sevilla** (5/day, 2.5 hrs, fewer on weekends; also see trains below), **Málaga** (10/ day, 1.75 hrs *directo*, 3 hrs *ruta*; access other Costa del Sol points

Route of the White Hill Towns

TO
SEVILLA
& FREEWAY

TO SEVILLA

TO SEVILLA

A-375

A-373

A-384

A-384

PUERTO
SERRANO

ALGODONALES

OLVERA

TO
GRANADA

A-384

N

BORNOS
RESERVOIR

ZAHARA

ZAHARA
RESERVOIR

SETENIL

A-384

A-372

ARCOS
RESERVOIR

❶

❸

❷

A-374

RONDA

TO
JEREZ

A-382

EL
BOSQUE

BENA.

PUERTO
BOYAR

MONTE-
SAQUE

GRAZALEMA

A-366

A-373

ARCOS
DE LA FRONTERA

BENAOJÁN

A-369

TO
MEDINA
SIDONIA,
VEJER,
& TARIFA

UBRIQUE

A-374

CORTES

A-375

PILETA
CAVE

TO
SAN
PEDRO
& MARBELLA

TO GIBRALTAR
& TARIFA

DCH

10 MILES

6 KM

SIERRA DE GRAZALEMA
NATURAL PARK

❶ Garganta Verde Hike

❷ El Torreón Hike

VIEW

❸ Pinsapar Hike

from Málaga), **Marbella** (6/day, 75 min), **Fuengirola** (5/day, 2 hrs), **Nerja** (4 hrs, transfer in Málaga; can take train or bus from Ronda to Málaga). If traveling to **Córdoba**, it's easiest to take the train since there are no direct buses (see below). There's no efficient way to call "the bus company" because four share the same station; one of them is at tel. 952-187-061. It's best to just drop by and compare schedules (on Plaza Concepción García Redondo, several blocks from train station).

By Train to: Algeciras (6/day, 1.5–2 hrs), **Bobadilla** (4/day, 1 hr), **Málaga** (2/day, 2 hrs—morning train direct, evening train with transfer in Bobadilla), **Sevilla** (2/day, 4 hrs, transfer in Bobadilla), **Granada** (3/day, 2.5 hrs), **Córdoba** (2/day direct, 1.75 hrs; more with transfer in Bobadilla, 3.5 hrs), **Madrid** (2/day, 4 hrs). Transfers are a snap and time-coordinated in Bobadilla; with four trains arriving and departing simultaneously, double-check that you're jumping on the right one. Train info: tel. 902-240-202.

More Hill Towns: Zahara and Grazalema

There are plenty of undiscovered and interesting hill towns to explore. About half of the towns I visited were memorable. Unfortunately, public transportation is frustrating, so I'd do these towns only by car. Or you could consider a tour—Andalusian Minibus Tours stops at Zahara and Grazalema on their all-day trip from Sevilla (see page 516). Useful information on the area is rare. Fortunately, a good map, the tourist brochure (pick it up in Sevilla or Ronda), and a spirit of adventure work fine. Along with Arcos, Zahara and Grazalema are my favorite white villages.

Zahara

This tiny town in a tingly setting under a Moorish castle (worth the climb) has a spectacular view. While the big church facing the town square is considered one of the richest in the area, the smaller church has the most-loved statue. The Virgin of Dolores is Zahara's answer to Sevilla's Virgin of Macarena (and is similarly paraded through town during Holy Week). While Grazalema is a better overnight stop, Zahara is a delight for those who want to hear only the sounds of the wind, birds, and elderly footsteps on ancient cobbles.

Orientation to Zahara

Tourist Information

The TI is located in the main plaza (daily 9:00–13:30, gift shop, Plaza del Rey 3, tel. 956-123-114). It has a single computer with Internet access (€1.50, one-hour limit). Upstairs from the TI are Spanish-only displays about the flora and fauna of nearby Sierra de Grazalema Natural Park. Drivers can park for free in the main plaza, or continue up the hill to the parking lot at the base of the castle, just past the cliffside Hotel Arco de la Villa, the town's only real hotel (16 small modern rooms, Db-€63, tel. 956-123-230, www.tugasa.com).

Sights in Zahara

▲**Zahara Castle**—During Moorish times, Zahara lay within the fortified castle walls above today's town. It was considered the gateway to Granada and a strategic stronghold for the Moors by the Christian forces of the Reconquista. Locals tell of the Spanish conquest of the Moors' castle (in 1482) as if it happened yesterday:

After the Spanish failed several times to seize the castle, a clever Spanish soldier noticed that the Moorish sentinel would check if any attackers were hiding behind a particular section of the wall by tossing a rock and setting the pigeons in flight. If they flew, the sentinel figured there was no danger. One night a Spaniard hid there with a bag of pigeons and let them fly when the sentinel tossed his rock. Upon seeing the birds, the guard assumed he was clear to enjoy a snooze. The clever Spaniard then scaled the wall and opened the door to let in his troops, who conquered the castle. Ten years later Granada fell, the Muslims were back in Africa, and the Reconquista was complete.

It's a fun climb up to the remains of the castle (free, tower always open). Start at the paved path across from the town's upper parking lot. It's a moderately easy 15-minute hike past newly discovered Roman ruins and along a cactus-rimmed ridge to the top, where you can enter the tower. Use your penlight or feel along the stairway to reach the roof, and enjoy spectacular views from this almost impossibly high perch far above the town. As you pretend you're defending the tower, realize that what you see is quite different from what the Moors saw: The huge lake dominating the valley is a reservoir—before 1991, the valley had only a tiny stream.

Molino El Vínculo—This family-run olive mill welcomes visitors for a look at its traditional factory, as well as a taste of some homemade sherry and olive oil, produced on this site for centuries by the Urruti family. Juan will treat you to a glass of sherry if you show this book (€6 for a formal tour and tasting, daily 9:30–14:00 & 16:00–18:00, on CA-531 a half-mile beyond the castle side of Zahara, tel. 956-123-002, mobile 696-404-368, www.molinoel vinculo.com, molinoelvinculo@telefonica.net). A short visit is often free—they hope you'll buy something.

Grazalema

A beautiful postcard-pretty hill town, Grazalema offers a royal balcony for a memorable picnic, a square where you can watch old-

timers playing cards, and plenty of quiet whitewashed streets and shops to explore. Grazalema, situated within Sierra de Grazalema Natural Park, is graced with lots of scenery and greenery. Driving here from Ronda on A-372, you pass through a beautiful park-like grove of cork trees. While the park is known as the rainiest place in Spain, the clouds seem to wring themselves out before they reach the town—I've only ever had blue skies. If you want to sleep in a small Andalusian hill town, this is a good choice.

The **TI** is located at the car park at the cliffside viewpoint, Plaza de los Asomaderos (tel. 956-132-073). Enjoy the view, then wander into the town. A tiny lane leads a block from the center rear of the plaza to Plaza de Andalucía (filled by the tables of a commotion of tapas bars). Shops sell the town's beautiful and famous handmade wool blankets and good-quality leather items from nearby Ubrique. A block farther uphill takes you to the main square with the church, Plaza de España. A coffee on the square here is a joy. Small lanes stretch from here into the rest of the town.

Popular with Spaniards, the town makes a good home base for exploring Sierra de Grazalema Natural Park—famous for its spectacularly rugged limestone landscape of cliffs, caves, and gorges (see sidebar). For outdoor gear and adventures, including hiking, caving, and canoeing, contact **Horizon** (summer Tue–Sat 9:00–14:00 & 17:00–19:00, rest of year Tue–Sat 9:00–14:00 & 16:00–19:00, closed Sun–Mon year-round, off Plaza de España at Corrales Terceros 29, tel. & fax 956-132-363, mobile 655-934-565, www.horizonaventura.com, grazalema@horizonaventura.com).

Sleeping in Grazalema

$$ La Mejorana Guest House is the best bet in town—if you can manage to get one of its six rooms. You won't want to leave this beautifully perched garden villa, with its royal public rooms overlooking the valley from the upper part of town. Helpful Ana and Andres will call to get you a hiking permit in the park (Db-€55, includes breakfast and tax, Wi-Fi, pool, located at top of town on tiny lane below Guardia Civil headquarters at Santa Clara 6,

Sierra de Grazalema Natural Park

Sierra de Grazalema Natural Park is unique for its rugged mountain landscape and its relatively rainy climate, which support a wide variety of animals and plant life.

One-third of Spain's flowers bloom here, wild ibex (mountain goats) climb the steep slopes, and Europe's largest colony of griffon vultures soars high above. The park's plant poster child is the *pinsapo,* a type of fir tree left over from the last Ice Age (the park is one of the few places in Europe where these trees still grow). About a fifth of the 200-square-mile park is a special reserve area, where access is limited, largely to protect these rare trees from forest fires. Hikers need to get (free) permits for most trails in the reserve.

Zahara, Grazalema, and the Pileta Cave all fall within the park boundaries. Drivers will get an eyeful of scenery just passing through the park on their way to these sights.

If you want to more fully experience the park—by hiking, caving, canoeing, kayaking, or horseback riding—the easiest way is to take a tour from Zahara Catur (in Zahara, www.zahara catur.com) or Horizon (in Grazalema, www.horizonaventura .com). They also handle the permit procedure for you.

If you want to hike in the park on your own, you'll need a park map, a permit for most hikes within the reserve area (see permit procedure on next page), and a car to get to the trailhead. And from July through September, you may have to go with a guided group anyway, if you want to hike in the reserve (about

tel. 956-132-327, mobile 649-613-272, www.lamejorana.net, info @lamejorana.net).

$$ Villa Turística de Grazalema is a big, popular national-park-lodge kind of place. It's good for kids, and has a huge lobby and fireplace. Its 38 apartments and 24 regular hotel rooms open onto either the swimming-pool garden from the ground floor, or balconies on the first floor (Sb-€37, Db-€60, extra person-€15, apartments-€70–123, extra bed-€23, includes breakfast, restaurant, turn right just before crossing the bridge into town, tel. 956-132-136, fax 956-132-213, www.tugasa.com).

$$ Hotel Peñón Grande, named for a nearby mountain, is just off the main square and rents 16 comfortable business-class rooms (Sb-€38, Db-€55, extra bed-€14, includes tax, air-con, Plaza Pequeña 7, tel. 956-132-434, fax 956-132-435, www.hotel grazalema.es, hotel@hotelgrazalema.es).

€12–16/person for a half-day hike, offered by Zahara Catur and Horizon).

Popular hikes in the reserve (all requiring permits) include:

Garganta Verde: Explore a canyon with a huge open cave near vulture breeding grounds (1.5 miles each way, initially gentle hike then very steep descent, allow 4–5 hours).

El Torreón: Climb the park's highest mountain, at 5,427 feet (1.75 miles each way, steep incline to summit, allow 4–5 hours).

Pinsapar: Hike on mountain slopes forested with *pinsapo* trees (8.5 miles each way, steep climb for first third of trail then downhill, allow 6 hours).

Information: The TIs in Grazalema and Zahara sell a Spanish-only park guide with descriptions and trail maps (€15).

Getting a Hiking Permit: A permit is free but required; a ranger will fine you if you don't have one. To get a permit, call or visit the park office in the town of El Bosque, a gateway to the park. You can request a permit for a specific hike up to 15 days in advance. Pick up the permit in El Bosque, or have them fax it to the TI in Grazalema or Zahara (El Bosque park office hours generally Mon–Sat 10:00–14:00 & 16:00–18:00, Sun 9:00–14:00, tel. 956-727-029, passport number required, Avenida de la Diputación, allow plenty of time for this process as it's hard to get through on the phone). If you're staying at the recommended La Mejorana Guest House in Grazalema, your host will call for you.

Hikes from Grazalema (No Permit Required): If you'd rather not hassle with getting a permit, or if you don't have a car to reach the trailheads, try one of several hikes that start from the town of Grazalema. You'll find descriptions in pamphlets available at the Grazalema TI or Horizon (€1).

$ Casa de Las Piedras, just a block from the main square, has 16 comfortable rooms with private baths and 14 super-cheap basic rooms with shared bathrooms. The beds feature the town's locally made wool blankets (Sb-€35, D-€25, Db-€48, 10 percent discount with this book and two-night minimum stay, buffet breakfast-€6, Calle Las Piedras 32, tel. & fax 956-132-014, www.casadelas piedras.org, info@casadelaspiedras.org, Katy and Rafi).

Eating in Grazalema

Grazalema offers many restaurants and bars. Tiny Plaza de Andalucía has several good bars for tapas with umbrella-flecked tables spilling across the square, including **Zulema** (big salads, tel. 956-132-402) and **La Posadilla** (tel. 956-132-051).

El Torreón specializes in local lamb and game dishes, and also has many vegetarian options (closed Wed, Calle Agua 44, tel. 956-132-313).

El Pinsapar, up the hill from the main plaza, is appreciated for its good prices and local specialties, including fresh trout (closed Wed, air-con, Dr. Mateos Gago 22, tel. 956-132-202).

Meson el Simancon serves well-presented cuisine typical of the region in a romantic setting. While a bit more expensive, it's considered the best restaurant in town (closed Tue, facing Plaza de los Asomaderos and the car park, tel. 956-132-421).

Connections

Bus service to Grazalema is provided by Los Amarillos (www .touristbus.es).

From Grazalema by Bus to: Ronda (2/day, 45 min), **El Bosque** (2/day, 45 min).

Jerez

With nearly 200,000 people, Jerez is your typical big-city mix of industry and dusty concrete suburbs, but it has a lively old center and two claims to touristic fame: horses and sherry.

Jerez is ideal for a noontime visit on a weekday. See the famous horses, sip some sherry, wander through the old quarter, and swagger out.

Orientation to Jerez

There is no easy way to feel oriented in Jerez due to the complicated, medieval street plan, so ask for directions liberally.

Tourist Information

The helpful TI, on Plaza Alameda Cristina, gives out free maps and info on the sights (June–mid-Sept Mon–Fri 9:00–15:00 & 17:00–19:00, Sat–Sun 9:30–14:30, mid-Sept–May Mon–Fri 8:00–15:00 & 16:30–18:30, Sat–Sun 9:30–14:30, tel. 956-338-874, www .turismojerez.com).

Arrival in Jerez

By Bus or Train: Both the bus and train stations are by the enormous headless statue at Glorieta del Minotauro. Unfortunately, you can't store luggage at either one. However, you can stow bags for free in the Royal Andalusian School's *guardaropa*, or coat room, if you attend their Horse Symphony show (see "Sights," page 620).

The center of town and the TI are a 20-minute walk from both stations. When exiting either station, keep the large parking lot on your left. You'll soon be greeted by the gigantic Glorieta del Minotauro statue at a traffic circle. Take the crosswalk straight over to Calle Medina and follow it faithfully. At the confusing five-way intersection, angle right on Honda, continue past a small roundabout decorated with empty sherry barrels, and go straight until you reach Plaza Alameda Cristina—the TI is tucked away on your right.

By Car from Arcos: Driving in Jerez can be frustrating. The outskirts are filled with an almost endless series of roundabouts. Continuing straight through each one will eventually bring a rail bridge into sight, with Bodegas Harvey on the right side. Continue to follow traffic and signs to *centro ciudad*. The route may seem circuitous (it is) but will eventually take you past the main TI on Plaza Alameda Cristina.

If you're going straight to see the horses, follow the directions in the listing on page 621; otherwise it's best to park in one of the many underground garages and catch a cab or walk. Plaza Arenal (€1.30/hr) is the most centrally located lot, or there's the handy underground parking lot at Plaza Alameda Cristina. For street parking, blue-line zones require prepaid parking tickets on your dashboard (Mon–Fri 9:00–13:30 & 17:00–20:00, Sat 9:00–14:00, Sun and July–Aug afternoons free).

Sights in Jerez

▲▲**Royal Andalusian School of Equestrian Art**—If you're into horses, this is a must. Even if you're not, this is art like you've never seen. The school does its Horse Symphony show Tuesday and Thursday at 12:00 during most of the year (also on Fri in Aug, Nov–Feb Thu only; €18 general seating, €24 "preference" seating, 90 min with 15-min intermission; no photos in show, stables, or museum; tel. 956-318-008, fax 956-318-015, tickets available online at www.realescuela .org). General seating is fine; some "preference" seats are too close for good overall views. The show explanations are in Spanish.

This is an equestrian ballet with choreography, purely Spanish music, and costumes from the 19th century. The stern riders and their talented, obedient steeds prance, jump, hop on their hind legs, and do-si-do in time to the music, all to the delight of an arena filled with mostly tourists and local horse aficionados.

The riders, trained in dressage (dreh-SAZH), cue the horses with the slightest of commands, whether verbal or with body movements. You'll see both purebred Spanish horses (of various colors, with long tails, calm personalities, and good jumping ability) and the larger mixed breeds (with short tails and a walking— not prancing—gait). The horses must be three years old before their three-year training begins, and most performing horses are male (stallions or geldings), since mixing the sexes brings problems.

The equestrian school is a university, open to all students in the EU, and with all coursework in Spanish. Although still a male-dominated activity, there have recently been a few female graduates. Tight-fitted mushroom hats are decorated with different stripes to show each rider's level. Professors often team with students and evaluate their performance during the show.

Training sessions on non-performance days offer the public a sneak preview (€10; Mon, Wed, and Fri—except no Fri in Aug,

Sherry

Spanish sherry is not the sweet dessert wine sold in the States as sherry. In Spain, sherry is (most commonly) a chilled white very dry fortified wine, often served with appetizers such as tapas, seafood, and cured meats.

British traders invented the sherry-making process as a way of transporting wines that wouldn't go bad on a long sea voyage. Some of the most popular brands (such as Sandeman and Osbourne) were begun by Brits, and for years it was a foreigners' drink. But today, sherry is typically Spanish.

Sherry is made by blending wines from different grapes and vintages, all aged together. Start with a strong, acidic wine (from grapes that grow well in the hot, chalky soil around Jerez). Mature it in large vats until a yeast crust *(flor)* forms on the surface, protecting the wine from the air. Then fortify it with distilled alcohol.

Next comes sherry-making's distinct *solera* process. Pour the young fortified wine into the top barrel of a unique contraption—a stack of oak barrels called a *criadera*. Every year, one-third of the oldest sherry (in the barrels on the ground level) is bottled. To replace it, one-third of the sherry in the barrel above is poured in, and so on. This continues until the top barrel is one-third empty, waiting to be filled with the new year's vintage.

Fino is the most popular type of sherry (and the most different from Americans' expectations)—white, dry, and chilled. The best-selling commercial brand of *fino* is Tío Pepe; *manzanilla* is a regional variation of *fino*—best from Córdoba. Darker-colored and sometimes sweeter varieties of sherry include *amontillado* and *oloroso.* And yes, Spain also produces the thick, sweet cream sherries served as dessert wines. A good raisin-y, syrupy-sweet variety is Pedro Ximénez, made from sun-dried grapes of the same name.

also on Tue in Nov–Feb; arrive anytime between 11:00–13:00). Big tour groups crowd in at 11:00 and schedules may vary, so it's wise to call ahead. Sessions can be exciting or dull, depending on what the trainers are working on. After the training session, you can take a 90-minute guided tour of the stables, horses, multimedia and carriage museums, tack room, gardens, and horse health center. Sip sherry in the arena's bar to complete this Jerez experience.

Getting There: After passing the TI on Plaza Alameda Cristina, follow pink signs with arrows pointing to the *Real Escuela* *de Arte Ecuestre.* Parking is located behind the horse school, and one-way streets mean there is only one way to arrive. Expect to make at least one wrong turn, so give yourself a little extra time.

From the bus or train stations to the horses, it's about a €5 taxi ride or a 40-minute walk.

▲▲**Sherry Bodega Tours**—Spain produces more than 10 million gallons per year of this fortified wine. The name "sherry" comes from English attempts to pronounce Jerez. While traditionally the drink of England's aristocracy, today it's more popular with Germans. Your tourist map of Jerez is speckled with *venencia* symbols, each representing a sherry bodega that offers tours and tasting. *Venencias* are specially designed ladles for dipping inside the sherry barrel, breaking through the yeast layer, and getting to the good stuff.

Sandeman Sherry: Just around the corner from the horse school is the venerable Sandeman winery, which has been pro-

ducing sherry since 1790 and is the longtime choice of English royalty. This tour is the aficionado's choice for its knowledgeable guides and their quality explanations of the process. Each stage is explained in detail, with visual examples of *flor* (the yeast crust) in backlit barrels, graphs of how different blends are made, and a quick walk-through of the bottling plant. The finale is a chance to taste three varieties (€6.50 for regular sherries, €10.50 for rare sherries, light tapas lunch with tour-€12.50, English tours on the half-hour Mon, Wed, and Fri 10:30–15:00, Sat 11:00–15:00, on the hour Tue and Thu 10:00–16:00, closed Sun, tour times adjust with the horse show, call to confirm, reservations not required, tel. 956-151-700, www.sandeman.com). It's efficient to see the Horse Symphony, which ends at 13:30, and then walk to Sandeman's for the next English tour.

Harveys Bodega: Their English-language tours aren't substantial, but they do include a 15-minute video, a visit to the winery, and all the sherry you like in the tasting room (€8.50, Mon–Fri at 12:00, 90-min tour, reservations recommended one day in advance, Calle Pintor Muñoz Cebrian, tel. 956-151-551, fax 956-349-427, www.bodegasharveys.es, bodegasharveys@beamglobal.com).

González Byass: The makers of the famous Tío Pepe offer a tourist-friendly tour, with more pretense and less actual sherry-making on display (it's done in a new, enormous plant outside of town). The tourist train through fake vineyards and a video presentation are forgettable, but the grand circle of sherry casks signed by a *Who's Who* of sherry-drinkers is worthwhile. Taste two sherries at the end of the 90-minute tour (€10, light tapas lunch with tour-€15, tours run hourly at :30 past the hour, Mon–Sat 11:30–17:30, extra tour at 14:00; July–Sept no tours at 14:00 and 15:30, extra tour at 18:30; Sun 11:30–14:00; Manuel María González 12, tel. 956-357-000, fax 956-357-046).

Alcázar—This gutted castle looks tempting, but don't bother. The €3 entry fee doesn't even include the Camera Obscura (€6.30 combo-ticket covers both, Mon–Sat 10:00–18:00, Sun 10:00–15:00). Its underground parking is convenient for those touring González Byass (€1.30/hr).

Connections

Jerez's bus station is shared by six bus companies, each with its own schedule. Some specialize in certain destinations, while others share popular destinations such as Sevilla and Algeciras. The big ones serving most southern Spain destinations are Los Amarillos (tel. 902-210-317, www.losamarillos.es), Comes (tel. 902-199-208, www.tgcomes.es), and Linesur (tel. 956-341-063, www.linesur .com). Shop around for the best departure time and most direct route. While here, clarify routes for any further bus travel you may be doing in Andalucía—especially if you're going through Arcos de la Frontera, where the ticket office is often closed. Also try the privately run www.movelia.es for bus schedules and routes.

From Jerez by Bus to: Tarifa (2/day on Algeciras route with Comes, 2 hrs, more frequent with transfer in Cádiz), **Algeciras** (2/day with Comes, 9/day with Linesur, 2.5 hrs), **Arcos** (hourly, 30 min), **Ronda** (4/day, 2.5–3 hrs), **La Línea/Gibraltar** (2/day, 3 hrs), **Sevilla** (7/day, 1.5 hrs), **Málaga** (3/day, 4.5–5 hrs), **Granada** (1/day, 4.5 hrs), **Madrid** (3/day, more service on weekends, 7 hrs).

By Train to: Sevilla (12/day, 1.25 hrs), **Madrid** (2/day, 4.5 hrs), **Barcelona** (one overnight, 12 hrs). Train info: tel. 902-240-202.

By Car: It's a zippy 30 minutes from Jerez to Arcos.

Stops for Drivers

If you're driving between Arcos and Tarifa, here are several sights to explore.

Yeguada de la Cartuja

This breeding farm, which raises Hispanic Arab horses according to traditions dating back to the 15th century, offers shows on Saturday at 11:00 (€18.50 for best seats in *tribuna* section, Finca Fuente del Suero, Carretera Medina–El Portal, km 6.5, Jerez de la Frontera, tel. 956-162-809, www.yeguadacartuja.com). From Jerez, take the road to Medina Sidonia, then turn right in the direction of El Portal—you'll see a cement factory on your right. Drive for five minutes until you see the farm. A taxi from Jerez will cost about €14 one-way.

Medina Sidonia

This town is as whitewashed as can be, surrounding its church and hill, which is topped with castle ruins. I never drive through here without a coffee break and a quick stroll. Signs to *centro urbano* route you through the middle to Plaza de España (lazy cafés, bakery, plenty of free parking just beyond the square out the gate). If it's lunchtime, consider buying a picnic, as all the necessary shops are nearby and the plaza benches afford a fine workaday view of a perfectly untouristy Andalusian town. According to its own TI, the town is "much appreciated for its vast gastronomy." Small lanes lead from the main square up to Plaza Iglesia Mayor (church and TI open in summer daily 10:00–14:00 & 17:00–19:00; in winter Tue–Sun 10:00–14:00 & 16:00–18:00, closed Mon; tel. 956-412-404). At the church, a man will show you around for a tip. Even without giving a tip, you can climb yet another belfry for yet another vast Andalusian view. The castle ruins just aren't worth the trouble.

Vejer de la Frontera

Vejer, south of Jerez and just 30 miles north of Tarifa, will lure all but the very jaded off the highway. Vejer's strong Moorish roots give it a distinct Moroccan (or Greek Island) flavor—you know, black-clad women whitewashing their homes, and lanes that can't decide if they're roads or stairways. Only a generation ago, women here wore veils. The town has no real sights—other than its women's faces—and very little tourism, making it a pleasant stop. The TI is at Marqués de Tamarón 10 (tel. 956-451-736).

The coast near Vejer has a lonely feel, but its fine, windswept beaches are popular with windsurfers and sand flies. The Battle of Trafalgar was fought just off Cabo de Trafalgar (a nondescript lighthouse today). I drove the circle so you don't have to.

Sleeping in Vejer: A newcomer on Andalucía's tourist map, the old town of Vejer has just a few hotels.

$$ Hotel La Botica, a boutique place high in the old town, provides 13 comfortable rooms in what was once a local apothecary. Homey decor and view patios—tailor-made for an afternoon beer—add to the charm (interior Db-€60, exterior Db-€70, €20 more in June–Aug, extra bed-€15–20, includes taxes and breakfast, mention this book to see if there are any deals, air-con, Wi-Fi, 200 yards above Plaza de España—go through the gate and left to Canalejas 13, tel. 956-450-225, mobile 617-477-636, www.labotica devejer.com, info@laboticadevejer.com). If Josip isn't home, call his mobile number and he will be.

$$ Convento de San Francisco is a poor man's parador in a refurbished convent with pristine, spacious rooms and elegant public lounges (Sb-€50, Db-€71, breakfast-€4, air-con, free Wi-Fi in lobby, La Plazuela, tel. 956-451-001, fax 956-451-004, convento -san-francisco@tugasa.com).

$$ Hotel Bandolero is for nature-lovers. Settle into the rustic rooms, go hiking and bird-watching, or take a dip in their pool (Sb-€45–50, standard Db-€64–101, superior Db-€73–111, Db suite-€90–128, restaurant, Avenida Havaral 43, tel. 952-183-660, www.hotelbandolero.com, reservas@hotelbandolero.com).

$ Hostal La Posada's 10 clean and charming rooms, in a modern apartment flat, are cheap and funky. This family-run place has no reception (S-€20, Db-€35–45, Los Remedios 21, tel. & fax 956-450-258, no English spoken).

Route Tips for Drivers

Sevilla to Arcos (55 miles): The remote hill towns of Andalucía are a joy to tour by car with Michelin map 578 or any other good map. Drivers can zip south on N-IV from Sevilla along the river, following signs to *Cádiz*. Take the fast toll expressway (blue signs, E-5, A-4); the toll-free N-IV is curvy and dangerous. About half-way to Jerez, at Las Cabezas, take CA-403 to Villamartín. From there, circle scenically (and clockwise) through the thick of the Pueblos Blancos—Zahara and Grazalema—to Arcos.

It's about two hours from Sevilla to Zahara. You'll find decent but winding roads and sparse traffic. It gets worse (but very scenic) if you take the tortuous series of switchbacks over the 4,500-foot summit of Puerto de Las Palomas (Pass of the Pigeons, climb to the viewpoint) on the direct but difficult road from Zahara to Grazalema (you'll see several hiking trailheads into Sierra de Grazalema Natural Park, though most require free permits—see sidebar on page 616).

Another scenic option through the park from Grazalema to

Arcos is the road that goes up over Puerto del Boyar (Pass of the Boyar), past the pretty little valley town of Benamahoma, and down to El Bosque. The road from Ronda to El Gastor, Setenil (cave houses and great olive oil), and Olvera is another picturesque alternative.

Arcos to Tarifa (80 miles): You can drive from Arcos to Jerez in 30 minutes. If you're going to Tarifa, take the tiny C-343 road at the Jerez edge of Arcos toward Paterna and Vejer. Later, you'll pick up signs to *Medina Sidonia,* and then to *Vejer* and *Tarifa.*

Costa del Sol to Ronda and Beyond: Drivers coming up from the coast catch A-397 at San Pedro de Alcántara and climb about 20 miles into the mountains. A-369 offers a much longer, winding, but scenic alternative that takes you through a series of whitewashed villages.

Beware if you have old maps. The road numbering system from the coast into Sevilla was changed a couple of years ago: From Marbella to Ronda, take A-397 (formerly A-376). From Ronda to Jerez, start on A-374 (formerly A-376) then get on A-384 (which at Arcos may still be labeled with its old number, A-382). To head to Seville, branch off from A-384 onto A-375.

SPAIN'S SOUTH COAST

Nerja • Gibraltar • Tarifa

Spain's famous Costa del Sol is so bad, it's interesting. To northern Europeans, the sun is a drug, and this is their needle. Anything resembling a quaint fishing village has been bikini-strangled and Nivea-creamed. Oblivious to the concrete, pollution, ridiculous prices, and traffic jams, tourists lie on the beach like game hens on skewers—cooking, rolling, and sweating under the sun.

Where Europe's most popular beach isn't crowded by high-rise hotels, most of it's in a freeway choke hold. Wonderfully undeveloped beaches between Tarifa and Cádiz, and east of Almería, are ignored, while human lemmings make the scene where the coastal waters are so polluted that hotels are required to provide swimming pools. It's a fascinating study in human nature.

Laugh with Ronald McDonald at the car-jammed resorts. But if you want a place to stay and play in the sun, unroll your beach

towel at **Nerja.** And don't forget that you're surprisingly close to jolly olde England: The land of tea and scones, fish-and-chips, pubs and bobbies awaits you— in **Gibraltar.** Beyond "The Rock," the whitewashed port of **Tarifa**—the least-developed piece of Spain's generally over-developed southern coast—provides an enjoyable springboard for a quick trip to Morocco (see next chapter). These three places alone—Nerja, Gibraltar, and Tarifa—make the Costa del Sol worth a trip.

Costa del Sol

Planning Your Time

My negative opinions on the "Costa del Turismo" are valid for peak season (mid-July–mid-Sept). If you're there during a quieter time and you like the ambience of a beach resort, it can be a pleasant stop. Off-season it can be neutron-bomb quiet.

The whole 150 miles of coastline takes six hours by bus or three hours to drive with no traffic jams. You can resort-hop by bus across the entire Costa del Sol and reach Nerja for dinner. If you want to party on the beach, it can take as much time as Mazatlán.

To day-trip to Tangier, Morocco, take a tour from Tarifa.

Nerja

While cashing in on the fun-in-the-sun culture, Nerja (NEHR-hah) has actually kept much of its quiet Old World charm. It has good beaches, a fun evening paseo (strolling scene) that culminates in the proud Balcony of Europe terrace, enough pastry shops and nightlife, and locals who get more excited about their many festivals than the tourists do.

Thanks to cheap airfares and the completion of the expressway, real estate boomed here in the last decade (property values doubled in six years). But when the recent financial crisis hit, the bubble collapsed. All along the Costa del Sol, real estate, construction, and tourism had powered the economy, and the effects of its decline are apparent. On the upside, restaurants have cut prices, and hotel rates are soft (but that could change by the time you're using this book). Meanwhile, however, crime and racial tension have risen, as many once-busy immigrants are now without work.

Because of "residential tourism," Nerja's population swells from about 22,000 in winter to about 90,000 in the summer. Most of the foreign visitors are British—you'll find beans on your breakfast plate and Tom Jones for Muzak. Spanish visitors complain that some restaurants have only English menus, and indeed, the typical expats here actually try *not* to integrate. I've heard locals say of the British, "If they could, they'd take the sun back home with them—but they can't, so they stay here." They enjoy English TV and radio, and many barely learn a word of Spanish. (Special school buses take British children to private English-language schools that connect with Britain's higher-education system.) For an insight into this British community, read the free local expat magazines.

There's a long tradition of Spanish people retiring and vacationing here as well. Pensioners from northern Spain retire here—enjoying long life spans, thanks in part to the low blood pressure that comes from a diet of fish and wine. While they could afford to travel elsewhere, an inertia remains from Franco's day, when people generally vacationed within the country. In summer, to escape the brutal heat of inland Spain and the exhaustion that comes with having kids at home from school all day, many Spanish moms take the kids to condos on the south coast, while dads stay home to work. This is a time when many husbands get to "be Rodriguez" (i.e., anonymous and free), and enjoy (at a minimum) a break from the rigors of family life.

Orientation to Nerja

The tourist center of Nerja is right along the water and crowds close to its famous bluff, the "Balcony of Europe" (Balcón de Europa). Two fine beaches flank the bluff. The old town is just inland from the Balcony, while the more modern section slopes up and away from the water.

Tourist Information

The helpful, English-speaking TI has bus schedules, tips on beaches and side-trips, and brochures for nearby destinations, such

Nerja

* NOT TO SCALE -
BUS INFO KIOSK TO
BALCON DE EUROPA
IS A 10 MIN. WALK

Ⓑ Bus Stop
View
Ⓟ Parking

BUS INFO KIOSK

TO CAVES OF NERJA
& GRANADA

N-340

TO MÁLAGA ← N-340 AV. DE PESCIA

PLAZA CANTARERO

PLAZA ERMITA

TO N-340 & FRIGILIANA

SAN MIGUEL

NUÑEZ

ALEJ.

BUENO

HERR. ORIA

CRISTO

RUPERTO

ANDEZ

TAPAS AREA

COLON

SAN JUAN

CARRETAS

PARRAS

LOS HUERTOS

FRIGILIANA

MENDEZ

PINTADA

ANGUSTIAS

BRONCE

NUEVA

CRUZ

ANIMAS

PEREZ

GRANADA

CASTILLA

DIPUTACIÓN

EL BARRIO

PLAZA CAVANA

DEL SALÓN BEACH

TO LA TORRECILLA BEACH

SAN SALV.

PASEO NUEVO

GLORIA

ALMIRANTE

FERRANDIZ

MUNICIPAL PARKING CARABEO (FREE)

POST

CARABEO

CALAHONDA BEACH

CARABEO BEACH

TO BURRIANA BEACH

BALCONY OF EUROPE

MEDITERRANEAN SEA

Ⓝ

❶ Hotel Balcón de Europa
❷ Hotel Plaza Cavana
❸ Hostal Marissal & Cochran's Terrace
❹ Hostal Don Peque
❺ Hostal Miguel
❻ Pensión Mena
❼ Hostal Lorca
❽ Papagayo Beach Rest.
❾ Casa Luque Restaurante
❿ Pepe Rico & El Pulguilla Rest.
⓫ Pinocchio Restaurante
⓬ Haveli Restaurante
⓭ El Chispa
⓮ La Puntilla Bar Restaurante
⓯ Los Cuñaos
⓰ To Ayo's Café
⓱ Bar El Molino
⓲ El Burro Blanco
⓳ Bodega Los Bilbainos
⓴ Mercadona Supermarket
㉑ To Internet Cafés (2)

as Málaga and Gibraltar (daily 10:00–14:00; 100 yards from the Balcony of Europe and half a block inland from the big church, tel. 952-521-531, www.nerja.org, turismo@nerja.org). Ask for a free city map and the *Leisure Guide*, which has a comprehensive listing of activities. Their *Hiking the Sierra of Nerja and Cliffs of Maro* booklet describes good local walks.

Arrival in Nerja

By Bus: The Nerja bus station is actually just a bus stop with an info booth on Avenida de Pescia (daily 6:00–20:15, schedules posted, tel. 952-521-504). To travel from Nerja, buy tickets at the info kiosk—don't assume they're available on the bus. Since many buses leave at the same times, arrive at least 15 minutes before departure to avoid having to elbow other tourists.

By Car: Follow *Balcón de Europa* signs, and then into the big €1/hr underground parking lot (which deposits you 200 yards from the Balcony of Europe). Or park for free at the circus grounds, which doubles as the enormous Municipal Parking Carabeo (except in October, when circus is in town; follow *parador* signs, at last roundabout follow signs to parking lot, entrance off Calle Frigiliana). While this is free and very handy, many fall prey to a bogus "parking attendant" (even in a yellow vest) soliciting a euro coin for his "service."

Helpful Hints

Internet Access: Nerja's scenically situated Internet café is on a square overlooking Playa Torrecilla, where Calle Castilla Pérez meets Calle Málaga: **Europ@Web** (daily 10:00–22:00, until 24:00 in summer, 24 computers, tel. 952-526-147).

Radio: For a taste of the British expat scene, pick up the monthly *Street Wise* magazine or tune in to Coastline Radio at 97.6 FM.

Local Guide: Carmen Fernandez is good, with knowledge of the entire region (standard rate €125/5-hour day, mobile 610-038-437, mfeyus@yahoo.es).

Massage: Tiny yet muscular Marie, who moved here from France, runs a massage parlor out of her apartment. She does an excellent one-hour massage for €40—just give her a call (**Amarilys Masaje,** Calle Castilla Perez 10, mobile 667-825-828).

Getting Around Nerja

You can easily walk anywhere you need to go. A goofy little **tourist train**—nicknamed the "Wally Trolley" by Brits here—does a half-hour loop through town every 45 minutes (€4, daily 10:30–22:30, until 24:00 July–Aug, until 18:30 or earlier in winter, departs from Plaza de Cavana). You can get on and off at will (use the same ticket to catch another train). Unfortunately, it doesn't go to the popular Burriana Beach (route is posted on door of train). Nerja's **taxis** charge set fees (e.g., €5 to Burriana Beach, tel. 952-524-519). To clip-clop in a **horse and buggy** through town, it's €30 for about 25 minutes (hop on at Balcony of Europe).

Sights in Nerja

In Nerja

▲▲Balcony of Europe (Balcón de Europa)—The bluff, jutting happily into the sea, is the center of Nerja's paseo and a magnet for street performers. The mimes, music, and puppets can draw bigger crowds than the Balcony itself, which overlooks the Mediterranean, miles of coastline, and little coves and caves below. A castle, and later a fort, occupied this spot from the ninth century until the earthquake of 1884. Now it's a people-friendly view terrace.

Built in the early 1800s to defend against Napoleon, the English-Spanish fort here protected the harbor with the help of seven cannons. When the 1884 earthquake destroyed the castle and fort, it sent the cannons into the sea. A century later, two were salvaged, cleaned up, and placed here. Study the beautifully aged metal work.

The cute statue of King Alfonso XII reminds locals of how this popular sovereign (the great-grandfather of today's King Juan Carlos) came here after the devastating earthquake (a huge number of locals had died). He mobilized the local rich to dig out the community and put things back together. Standing on this promontory amid the ruins of the earthquake-devastated castle, he marveled at the view and coined its now-famous name, "Balcón de Europa."

The Nerja castle was part of a 16th-century lookout system. After the Christian Reconquista in 1492 drove Muslim Moors into exile, pirate action from Muslim countries in North Africa picked up. Lookout towers were stationed within sight of each other all along the coast. Warnings were sent whenever pirates threatened (smoke by day, flames by night). Look to the east—you can see three towers crowning bluffs in the distance.

Also to the east you can just see the tip of Burriana Beach. Spaniards love their *chiringuitos*, as local beach restaurants are called. The *chiringuito* immediately below you, Papagayo, is understandably popular.

Scan the horizon. Until recently, this was a favored landing spot (just beyond the tighter security zone near Gibraltar) for ille-

Costa del Sol History

Many Costa del Sol towns come in pairs: the famous beach town with little history, and its smaller yet much more historic partner established a few miles inland—safely out of reach of the Barbary pirate raids that plagued this coastline for centuries. Nerja is a good example of this pattern. While it has almost no history and was just an insignificant fishing village until tourism hit, its more historic sister, Frigiliana, hides out in the nearby hills. The Barbary pirate raids were a constant threat. In fact, the Spanish slang for "the coast is clear" is *"no hay moros en la costa"* (there are no Moors on the coast).

Nerja was overlooked by the tourism scene until about 1980, when the phenomenal Spanish TV show *Verano Azul (Blue Summer)* was set here. This post-Franco program featured the until-then off-limits topics of sexual intimacy, marital problems, adolescence, and so on in a beach-town scene (imagine combining *All in the Family, Baywatch,* and *The Hills*). To this day when Spaniards hear the word "Nerja," they think of this TV hit.

Despite the fame, development didn't really hit until about 2000, when the expressway finally and conveniently connected Nerja with the rest of Spain. Thankfully, a building code prohibits any new buildings higher than three stories in the old town.

gal immigrants and drug runners coming in from Africa. Many Moroccan teens try to sneak into Europe here, as local laws prohibit turning away undocumented children (the police use DNA tests to determine the age of recent arrivals—if they're under 18, they stay). Laws also grant automatic EU citizenship to anyone born in Europe, so many pregnant women try to slip in (once the baby's born, the mother's legal, too). However, illegal immigration is down: With the help of a new high-tech satellite-scanning system, the Guardia Civil can now detect floating objects as small as makeshift rafts and intercept them before they reach land.

Walk below the Balcony for views of the scant remains (bricks and stones) of the ninth-century Moorish castle. Locals claim an underground passage connected the Moorish fortress with the mosque that stood where the San Sebastián church stands today.

Church of San Salvador—Just a block inland from the balcony, this church was likely built upon the ruins of a mosque (c. 1600). Its wooden ceiling is *mudéjar*—made by Moorish artisans working in Christian times. The woodworking technique is similar to that featured in the Alhambra in Granada. The modern fresco of the Annunciation (in the rear of the nave) is by Paco Hernandez, the top local artist of this generation. In front, on the right, is a niche featuring Jesus with San Isidoro (as a little boy). Isidoro is the patron saint of Madrid, Nerja, and farmers (sugar-cane farming was the leading industry here before tourism hit). From the porch of the church, look inland to see City Hall, marked by four flags (Andalucía's is green for olive trees and white for the color of the houses in this part of Spain).

Town Strolls—As Nerja was essentially destroyed after the 1884 earthquake—and at the time there was little more here beyond the castle anyway—there's not much to see in the town itself. However, a few of its main streets are worth a quick look. From the Balcony of Europe head inland, across the street from the horses. Consider first grabbing some ice cream at El Valenciano Helados, a local favorite run by a Valencia family (Spaniards think of Valencia as the city with the best ice cream). Try the refreshing tiger-nut specialty called *horchata*.

A block farther inland, the old town's three main streets come together. The oldest street, Calle Carabeo, heads off to your right (notice how buildings around here are wired on the outside). On the left, Calle Pintada heads inland. Its name means "the painted street," as it was spiffed up in 1885 for the king's visit. Today it's the town's best shopping street. And between those streets runs Calle Almirante Ferrandiz, Nerja's restaurant row, which is particularly lively in the evenings.

Seaside Promenades—Pleasant seaview promenades lead in opposite directions from the Balcony of Europe, going east to Burriana Beach and west to Torrecilla Beach. Start your day with an early-morning walk along the delightful Paseo de los Carabineros, which stretches from the Balcony of Europe to Burriana Beach past several coves (10-min walk, farther to get to Ayo's for breakfast—see "Eating in Nerja"). Spanish law requires that all beaches are open to the public (except the one in Rota, which is reserved for American soldiers). The Paseo de los Carabineros is technically closed for liability reasons, as a few places along the promenade are in disrepair, and high tide can make passing tricky. It still makes a nice hike, if you don't mind doing it at your own risk (you'll need to slip around two barriers and climb a six-foot brick wall).

Beaches (Playas)—Nerja has several good beaches. They are well-equipped, with bars and restaurants, free showers, and rentable lounges and umbrellas (about €4 per couple for chairs and umbrella, same cost for 10 min or all day). Nearby restaurants rent umbrellas, and you're welcome to take drinks and snacks out to your spot. During the summer, Spanish sun-worshippers pack the beach from about 11:00 until around 13:30, when they move into the beach restaurants for relief from the brutal sun. Watch out for red flags on the beach, which indicate when the seas are too rough for safe swimming (blue = safe, orange = caution, red = swimming prohibited). Don't take valuables to the beach, as thieves have fast fingers.

The pebbly **Calahonda Beach** (Playa Calahonda) is full of fun pathways, crags, and crannies (head down through the arch behind the horses). The humble Papagayo restaurant is open all day. Antonio can be seen each morning working with his nets and sorting through his fish. His little pre-tourism beach hut is wonderfully photogenic.

The sandiest—and most crowded—is **Del Salón Beach** (Playa del Salón), down the walkway to the right of Restaurante Marissal, just west of the Balcony of Europe. For great drinks-with-a-view, stop by either Cochran's Terrace or Casa Luque on the way down (see "Eating in Nerja"). Continuing farther west, you'll reach another sandy beach, **Playa La Torrecilla,** at the end of Calle Málaga.

El Playazo ("Big Beach") is a short hike west of Playa La Torrecilla. Locals prefer this beach, as it's less developed than the more central ones, offering a couple of miles of wide-open spaces that allow for fine walks and a chance to "breathe in the beach."

Burriana Beach (Playa de Burriana) is Nerja's leading beach (a 10-min walk east from the Balcony of Europe along the Paseo de los Carabineros—technically closed but easy to scale barriers if you like). It's fun for families, with paddleboats and entertainment options. It's also a destination for those visiting Ayo's paella-feast restaurant (see "Eating in Nerja").

Cantarriján Beach, a 15-minute drive east of Nerja (4.5 miles), is the nudists' choice (see next page).

Near Nerja

▲**Caves of Nerja (Cuevas de Nerja)**—These caves (2.5 miles east of Nerja, exit 295), with an impressive array of stalactites and stalagmites, are a classic roadside attraction. The huge caverns are filled with backlit formations and a big hit with cruise-ship groups and Spanish families. The visit involves a 30-minute unguided ramble deep into the mountain, up and down 400 dark stairs. At the end, you reach the Hall of the Cataclysm, where you'll circle the world's largest stalactite column (certified by *Guinness Book of World Records*). Someone figured out that it took one trillion drops to make the column (€8.50, daily 10:00–14:00 & 16:00–18:30, July–Aug until 19:30, easy parking-€1, tel. 952-529-520).

The free exhibit in the Centro de Interpretación explains the cave's history and geology (house next to bus parking; exhibit in Spanish, but includes free English brochure).

To get to the caves, catch a bus from the Nerja bus stop on Avenida de Pescia (€1, 13/day, 10 min). During the festival held here the third week of July, the caves provide a cool venue for hot flamenco and classical concerts (tickets sold out long in advance). The restaurant offers a view and three-course fixed-price meals for €8, and the picnic spot (behind the ticket office) offers pine trees, benches, and a kids' play area.

Frigiliana—This picture-perfect whitewashed village, only four miles inland from Nerja, is easy to reach by car or bus (€1, 9/day, 15 min, none on Sun). It's a worthwhile detour from the beach, particularly if you don't have time for the Pueblos Blancos hill towns. To bring the town to life, consider hiring David Riordan, an American who settled here nearly 20 years ago. He offers an entertaining 90-minute town walk for €7.50 per person, and will schedule a tour for as few as two people (reserve by phone or email, mobile 625-986-065, davidwriordan@gmail.com). He does Nerja and regional tours in his car as well.

Cantarriján Beach—If you're craving a more desolate beach—and have a car—drive 12 miles east (toward Herradura) to the Cerro Gordo exit, and follow *Playa Cantarriján* signs (paved road, just before the tunnel). Park at the viewpoint and hike 30 minutes down to the beach, where rocks and two restaurants separate two pristine beaches—one for people with bathing suits, the other for nudists. As this beach is in a natural park and requires a long hike, it provides a fine—and rare—chance to experience the Costa del Sol in some isolation.

Hiking—Europeans visiting the region for a longer stay generally use Nerja as a base from which to hike. The TI can describe a variety of hikes. One of the most popular includes a refreshing and delightful two- to three-hour walk up a river (up to your shins in water). Another, more demanding hike takes you to the 5,000-foot summit of El Cielo for the best memorable king-of-the-mountain feeling this region offers.

Nightlife in Nerja

Bar El Molino offers live Spanish folk singing nightly in a rustic cavern that's actually an old mill—the musicians perform where the mule once tread. It's touristy but fun (starts at 22:00 but pretty dead before 23:00, no cover—just buy a drink, Calle San José 4). The local sweet white wine, *vino del terreno*—made up the hill in Frigiliana—is popular here (€2.50 per glass).

El Burro Blanco is a touristy flamenco bar with shows nightly from 22:30. Keeping expectations pretty low, they advertise "The Best Flamenco Bar in Nerja" (no cover—just buy a drink, on corner of Calle Pintada and Calle de la Gloria).

Bodega Los Bilbainos is a classic old dreary dive—a favorite with local men and communists (tapas and drinks, Calle Alejandro Bueno 8).

For more trendy and noisy nightlife, check out the karaoke bar on Pintada (near El Burro Blanco) and the bars and dance clubs on Antonio Millón and Plaza Tutti Frutti.

Sleeping in Nerja

The entire Costa del Sol is crowded during August and Holy Week (March 28–April 4 in 2010), when prices are at their highest. Reserve in advance for peak season—basically mid-July through mid-September—which is prime time for Spanish workers to hit the beaches. Any other time of year, you'll find that Nerja has plenty of comfy, easy-going low-rise resort-type hotels and rooms. Room rates are generally three-tiered: low season (Nov–March), middle season (April–June and Oct), and high season (July–Sept).

Compared to the pricier hotels, the better *hostales* are an excellent value. Hostal Don Peque and Pensión Mena are each within three blocks of the Balcony of Europe.

Breakfast: Some hotels here overcharge for breakfast. Don't hesitate to go elsewhere, as many places serve breakfast for more reasonable prices. If you don't mind a short beach hike before

---

Sleep Code

(€1 = about $1.40, country code: 34)
S = Single, **D** = Double/Twin, **T** = Triple, **Q** = Quad, **b** = bathroom, **s** = shower only. Unless otherwise noted, credit cards are accepted and English is spoken. Breakfast is not included (unless noted).

To help you easily sort through these listings, I've divided the rooms into three categories, based on the price for a standard double room with bath during high season:

  $$$ **Higher Priced**—Most rooms €100 or more.
    $$ **Moderately Priced**—Most rooms between €50-100.
     $ **Lower Priced**—Most rooms €50 or less.

breakfast, consider **Ayo's** on Burriana Beach (see "Eating in Nerja"). For a cheap breakfast with a front-row view of the promenade action on the Balcony of Europe, head to **Hostal Marissal** and grab a wicker seat under the palm trees (€5 standard or English breakfasts). **Papagayo** serves breakfast on the beach, just below the Balcony of Europe, to those who like a little sand in their coffee (from 10:00).

Close to the Balcony of Europe

$$$ **Hotel Balcón de Europa** is the most central place in town. It's right on the water and the square, with the prestigious address Balcón de Europa 1. It has 110 rooms with all the modern comforts, including a pool and an elevator down to the beach. It's popular with groups. All the suites have seaview balconies, and most regular rooms also come with views (Sb-€71/82/107, standard Db-€98/115/148, about €40 extra for sea view and balcony, breakfast-€12, air-con, elevator, parking-€10/day, tel. 952-520-800, fax 952-524-490, www.hotelbalconeuropa.com, reservas@hotelbalcon europa.com).

$$$ **Hotel Plaza Cavana,** with 39 rooms, overlooks a plaza lily-padded with cafés. It feels institutional, but if you like a central location, marble floors, modern furnishings, an elevator, and a small rooftop swimming pool, dive in (Sb-€50–80, Db-€75–125, extra bed-€20, 10 percent discount and free breakfast for those booking direct with this guidebook in 2010, some view rooms, air-con, second small pool in basement, parking-€12/day, 2 blocks from Balcony of Europe at Plaza de Cavana 10, tel. 952-524-000, fax 952-524-008, www.hotelplazacavana.com, info@hotelplaza cavana.com).

$$ **Hostal Marissal** has an unbeatable location next door to the fancy Balcón de Europa hotel, and 23 modern, spacious rooms—some with small view balconies overlooking the action on the Balcony of Europe. Their cafeteria and bar, run by helpful staff, make the Marissal even more welcoming (Sb-€30/35/45, Db-€40/50/60, apartment for up to 4 people-€80–150, breakfast with beans-€5, double-paned windows, air-con, elevator, Internet access, Balcón de Europa 3, reception at Marissal café, tel. 952-520-199, fax 952-526-654, www.hostalmarissal.com, reserva @hostalmarissal.com, Carlos and María).

$$ **Hostal Don Peque** has 10 bright and cheery rooms, 8 with balconies. Owners Roberto and Clara moved here from France and have infused the place with their personality. They rent beach equipment at reasonable prices, but their bar-terrace with fantastic views may be more enticing (Sun–Thu: Db-€40/50/60, Tb-€55/75/90; Fri–Sat: Db-€50/60/75, Tb-€60/75/90; breakfast-€6, air-con, free Wi-Fi, Diputación 13, tel. 952-521-318,

www.hostaldonpeque.com, info@hostaldonpeque.com).

$ Hostal Miguel offers nine sunny and airy rooms in the heart of "Restaurant Row." Top-floor rooms have mountain views, and breakfast is served on the pretty green terrace. The owners—British expats Ian, Jane, and Hannah—are long-time Nerja devotees (Sb-€28–38, Db-€35–52, book direct for these prices, 4 percent more if paying with credit card, family suite, beach equipment available on request, Almirante Ferrándiz 31, tel. 952-521-523, mobile 696-799-218, www.hostalmiguel.com, hostalmiguel @gmail.com).

$ Pensión Mena rents 11 fine rooms—four with seaview terraces (€5 extra and worth it)—and offers a quiet, breezy garden (Sb-€18–25, Db-€27–40, some street noise, El Barrio 15, tel. & fax 952-520-541, hostalmena@hotmail.com, María). During the off-season, check–in is only available when reception is open (Nov–March daily 9:30–13:30 & 17:00–20:30).

In a Residential Neighborhood

$ Hostal Lorca is located in a quiet residential area five minutes from the center, three blocks from the bus stop, and close to a small, handy grocery store and free parking lot. Run by a friendly young Dutch couple, Femma and Rick, this *hostal* has nine modern, comfortable rooms and an inviting compact backyard with a terrace, palm tree, and small pool. You can use the microwave and take drinks (on the honor system) from the well-stocked fridge. This quiet, homey place is a winner (Sb-€25–33, Db-€29–50, extra bed-€12, cash only, look for yellow house at Mendez Nuñez 20, tel. 952-523-426, www.hostallorca.com, info@hostallorca.com).

Eating in Nerja

There are three Nerjas: the private domain of the giant beachside hotels; the central zone, packed with fun-loving (and often tipsy) expats and tourists eating and drinking from trilingual menus; and the back streets, where local life goes on as if there were no tourists. The whole old town (around the Balcony of Europe) is busy with lively restaurants. Wander around and see who's eating best.

To pick up picnic supplies, head to the **Mercadona** supermarket (Mon–Sat 9:15–21:15, closed Sun, inland from Plaza Ermita on Calle San Miguel).

Near the Balcony of Europe

Papagayo, a classic *chiringuito* (beach restaurant), lounges in the sand a few steps below the Balcony of Europe. While you'll pay for the location, it's quite a location. They serve drinks and snacks to those enjoying their beach umbrellas (open with demand, daily breakfast from 10:00, lunch 12:00–17:00, tel. 952-523-816, "moon beach parties" on summer evenings).

Cochran's Terrace serves mediocre meals in a wonderful seaview setting, overlooking Del Salón Beach (daily, open all day for drinks, 12:00–15:00 & 19:00–23:00 for meals, just behind Hostal Marissal).

Casa Luque, between the El Salvador Church and the cliff-side, is a worthwhile splurge, featuring a terrace in back with wicker furniture, sea views, and enough ambience to justify the price. Its dining room, despite its lack of view, is the most high-end and romantic I've seen in town (€22 for 7-tapas tasting meal, wines can be purchased by the glass, closed Sun lunch and all day Wed, tel. 952-521-004).

Along Restaurant Row

Strolling up Calle Almirante Ferrándiz (which changes its name farther uphill to "Cristo"), you'll find a good variety of eateries, albeit filled with Brits and possessing all the elegance of Blackpool. On the upside, the presence of expats means you'll find places serving food earlier in the evening than the Spanish norm. Here are my choices in four categories: Romantic, Italian, Indian, and Spanish seafood and tapas.

Pepe Rico is the most romantic along this street, with a big terrace and a cozy dining room (€25 4-course meals, closed Sun, Calle Almirante Ferrándiz 28).

Pinocchio seems to be the local favorite for Italian (€8 pizzas and pastas, daily, Calle Almirante Ferrándiz 51).

Haveli, run by Amit and his Swedish wife Eva, serves good Indian food. It's been a hit with Brits, who know their Indian food, for two decades (€10–12 plates, daily 19:00–24:00 in summer, closed Mon off-season, Cristo 42, tel. 952-524-297).

El Pulguilla is a great, high-energy place for Spanish cuisine, fish, and tapas. Its two distinct zones (tapas bar up front and more formal restaurant out back) are both jammed with enthusiastic locals and tourists. The lively no-nonsense stainless-steel tapas bar doubles as a local pick-up joint later in the evening. Drinks come with a free small plate of clams, mussels, shrimp, chorizo sausage, or seafood salad. For a sit-down meal, head back to the terrace. Though not listed on the menu, half-portions *(media-raciones)* are available for many items, allowing you to easily sample different dishes (€10–15 dinners, closed Mon, Almirante Ferrándiz 26, tel. 952-521-384).

Tapas Bars near Herrera Oria

A 10-minute uphill hike from the water takes you into the residential thick of things, where the sea views come thumbtacked to the walls, prices are lower, and locals fill the tables. These three eateries are within a block of each other. Each is a colorful local hangout with different energy levels on different nights. Survey all three before choosing one, or have a drink and tapa at each. These places are generally open all day for tapas and drinks, and serve table-service meals during normal dining hours. Remember—tapas are snack-size portions generally not for sale but free with each drink. To turn them into more of a meal, ask for the menu and order a full-size *ración,* or half-size *media-ración.* The half-portions are generally bigger than you'd expect.

El Chispa is big on seafood, which locals enjoy on an informal terrace. Their *tomate ajo* (garlic tomato) is tasty, and their *berenjenas* (fried and salted eggplant) comes piping hot and is also worth considering. They'll want you to try the molasses-like sugar-cane syrup on the eggplant. They serve huge portions—*media-raciones* are enough for two (closed Mon, San Pedro 12, tel. 952-523-697).

La Puntilla Bar Restaurante is a boisterous little place, with its rickety plastic furniture spilling out onto the cobbles on hot summer nights (generous splittable salads, daily 12:00–24:00, a block in front of Los Cuñaos at Calle Bolivia 1, tel. 952-528-951).

Los Cuñaos hangs the banners of the entire soccer league on the walls. Local women hang out to chat, and kids wander around like it's home. While it has the least interesting menu, it has the most interesting business card (closed Sat, Herrera Oria 19, tel. 650-359-226).

Paella Feast on Burriana Beach

Ayo's is famous for its character of an owner and its €6 beachside all-you-can-eat paella feast at lunchtime. For 30 years, Ayo—a lovable ponytailed bohemian who promises to be here until he dies—has been feeding locals. Ayo is a very big personality—one of the five kids who discovered the Caves of Nerja, formerly a well-known athlete, and now someone who makes it a point to hire hard-to-employ people as a community service.

The paella fires get stoked up at about noon. Grab one of a hundred tables under the canopy next to the rustic open-fire cooking zone, and enjoy the beach setting in the shade with a jug of sangria. Fill your plate as many times as you like for €6. It's a 20-minute walk from the Balcony of Europe to the east end of Burriana Beach—look for Ayo's orange rooftop pyramid (daily "sun to sun," breakfast from 9:00—see below, paella served only at lunch, Playa de Burriana, tel. 952-522-289).

Breakfast at Ayo's: Consider hiking the deserted beach early and arriving at Ayo's at 9:00 for breakfast. Locals order the *tostada con aceite de oliva* (toast with olive oil and salt-€0.50); Ayo also serves toasted ham-and-cheese sandwiches and good coffee.

Connections

Nerja

From Nerja by Bus to: Nerja Caves (13/day, 10 min), **Frigiliana** (9/day, 15 min, none on Sun), **Granada** (6/day, 2.5 hrs, more with transfer in Motril—but check the departure time from Motril to Granada to make sure you're really saving time; Nerja to Motril, 1 hr, Motril to Granada, 1.75 hrs), **Córdoba** (1/day, 4.5 hrs), **Sevilla** (3/day, 4 hrs). Remember to double-check the codes on bus schedule—for example, 12:00*S* means 12:00 daily except Saturday.

To the Málaga Airport (about 40 miles west): Catch the bus to Málaga (€4, 18/day, 1.25–1.5 hrs), then take a local bus to the airport (€1, about 2/hr, 30 min); or pay €55 for a taxi from Nerja (airport tel. 952-048-804).

Málaga

This seaside city's busy airport is the gateway to the Costa del Sol. The closest train station to Nerja is in Málaga.

Málaga's train and bus stations—a block apart—both have pickpockets and lockers (train station lockers are more modern; both cost €3/day). You can rent a car at the train station from Atesa or Europcar. If you have time to kill, the train station is connected to a modern shopping mall, and another mall is located across from the bus station roundabout. Both have decent food courts.

From Málaga by Train to: Ronda (1/day direct in evening, 2 hrs; 4/day with transfer in Bobadilla), **Algeciras** (3/day, 4 hrs, transfer in Bobadilla), **Madrid** (12/day, 2.25–3 hrs on AVE), **Córdoba** (15/day, 1 hr on fast AVE or AVANT trains; 2/day, 2.25–3 hrs on slower trains), **Granada** (3/day, 2.5–3.25 hrs on AVE, transfer in Bobadilla or Antequera), **Sevilla** (11/day, 2 hrs on AVE or AVANT, 2.5 hrs on other trains), **Barcelona** (3/day, fast AVE train leaves at 16:50, 5.5 hrs, 13 hrs on slow trains). Train info: tel. 902-240-202, www.renfe.es.

Buses: Málaga's bus station, a block from the train station, has a helpful information office with bus schedules (daily 7:00–22:00, tel. 952-350-061) and a TI (daily 11:00–19:00, Internet access, ATM, and lockers, on Paseo de los Tilos).

By Bus to: Algeciras (17/day, 1.75 hrs *directo*, 3 hrs *ruta*), **Nerja** (18/day, 1.25–1.5 hrs), **Ronda** (14/day, 1.75 hrs *directo*, 3 hrs *ruta*), **La Línea/Gibraltar** (4/day, 3 hrs), **Tarifa** (2/day, 3.5 hours), **Sevilla** (9/day, 7 direct, 2.5–3.5 hrs), **Jerez** (3/day, 4.5–5 hrs), **Granada** (hourly, 1.5–2 hrs), **Córdoba** (5/day, 3–3.5 hrs), **Madrid** (11/day, 6 hrs), **Marbella** (5/day, 50 min). Bus info: www.estabus.emtsam.es.

Between Nerja and Gibraltar

Buses take five hours to make the Nerja–Gibraltar trip, including a transfer in Málaga, where you may have to change bus companies (they leave nearly hourly from Nerja to Málaga). Along the way, buses stop at each of the following towns (see map on page 628).

Fuengirola and Torremolinos—
The most built-up part of the region, where those most determined to be envied settle down, is a bizarre world of Scandinavian package tours, flashing lights, pink flamenco, mul- tilingual menus, and all-night hap- piness. Fuengirola is like a Spanish Mazatlán with a few older, less-pre- tentious budget hotels between the main drag and the beach. The water here is clean and the nightlife fun and easy. James Michener's idyllic Torremolinos has been strip-malled and parking-metered.

Marbella—This is the most polished and posh town on the Costa del Sol. High-priced boutiques, immaculate streets set with intri- cate pebble designs, and beautifully landscaped squares testify to Marbella's arrival on the world-class-resort scene. Have a *café con leche* on the beautiful Plaza de Naranjos in the old city's pedes- trian section. Wander down to new Marbella and the high-rise beachfront apartment buildings to walk along the wide promenade lined with restaurants. Check out the beach scene. Marbella is an easy stop on the Algeciras–Málaga bus route (as you exit the bus station, take a left to reach the center of town). You can also catch a handy direct bus here from the Málaga airport (20/day, fewer off-season, 45 min, www.ctsa-portillo.com).

San Pedro de Alcántara—This town's relatively undeveloped sandy beach is popular with young travelers. San Pedro's neighbor, Puerto Banús, is "where the world casts anchor." This luxurious, Monaco-esque jet-set port, complete with casino, is a strange mix of Rolls-Royces, yuppies, boutiques, rich Arabs, and budget browsers.

Gibraltar

One of the last bits of the empire upon which the sun never set, Gibraltar is a quirky mix of Anglican propriety, "God Save the Queen" tattoos, English bookstores, military memories, and tourist shops. In 20 years the economy has gone from one dominated by the military to one based on tourism (as, it seems, happens to many empires). On summer days and weekends, the tiny colony is inundated by holiday-goers, primarily the Spanish (who come here for tax-free cigarettes and booze) and British (who want a change in weather but not in culture).

While it's hard to imagine a community of 30,000 that feels like its own nation, real Gibraltarians, as you'll learn when you visit, are a proud bunch. They were evacuated during World War II, and it's said that after their return, a national spirit was forged. If you doubt that, be here on Gibraltar's national holiday, September 10, when everyone's decked out in red and white, the national colors.

Gibraltarians have a mixed and interesting heritage. Spaniards call them Llanitos (yah-NEE-tohs), meaning "flat" in Spanish, though the residents live on a rock. The locals—a fun-loving and tolerant mix of British, Spanish, and Moroccan—call their place "Gib."

A passport is required to cross the border (you'll only get a stamp if you need a visa—otherwise, you'll just get a wave-through).

Planning Your Time

Make Gibraltar a day trip (or just one overnight); rooms are expensive compared to Spain.

For the best day trip to Gibraltar, consider this plan: Walk across the border, catch bus #3, and ride it to the end, following my self-guided tour (described later in this chapter). Ride bus #3 back to the cable-car station, then catch the cable car to the peak for Gibraltar's ultimate top-of-the-rock view. From there, either walk down or take the cable car back into town. From the cable-car station, follow my self-guided town walk all the way to Casemates Square. Spend your remaining free time in town before returning to Spain.

Tourists who stay overnight find Gibraltar a peaceful place in

Gibraltar

TO
ALGECIRAS
& TARIFA

S P A I N

LA LÍNEA
BUS STN.

FO CONA
PARKING

CUSTOMS

A I R S T R I P

FERRY TO
TANGIER

COACH
PARK

STADIUM

DEVIL'S
TOWER
ROAD

SIEGE
TUNNELS

CASEMATES
SQUARE

MAIN
ST.

MOORISH
CASTLE

QUEENSWAY

TOWN

CATALAN
BAY

COACH
PARK

MUSEUM

H A R B O R

CATCHMENT
BASIN

SEE
DETAIL
MAP

APE'S
DEN

O'HARA'S
BATTERY

CABLE
CAR

ST.
MICHAEL'S
ROAD

ST.
MICHAEL'S
CAVE

CITY
WALLS

PATH

N

EUROPA
ROAD

WIND-
MILL
HILL
RD.

300 YARDS

300 METERS

KING FAHD
MOSQUE

VIEW

TO AFRICA
15 MILES

EUROPA
POINT

DCH

the evening, when the town can just be itself. No one's in a hurry. Families stroll, kids play, seniors window-shop, and everyone chats...but the food is still pretty bad.

There's no reason to side-trip into Morocco from Gibraltar—for many reasons, it's better from Tarifa (specifics covered in next chapter).

Orientation to Gibraltar

(tel. code: 350-200)

Gibraltar is a narrow peninsula (three miles by one mile) jut-ting into the Mediterranean. Virtually the entire peninsula is dominated by the steep-faced Rock itself. The locals live down below in the long, skinny town at the western base of the mountain (much of it on reclaimed land).

For information on all the little differences between Gibraltar and Spain—from area codes to electricity—see "Helpful Hints," later in this chapter.

Tourist Information

Gibraltar's main TI is at Casemates Square, the grand square at the Spain end of town (Mon–Fri 9:00–17:30, Sat 10:00–15:00, Sun 10:00–13:00, tel. 74982, www.gibraltar.gi). Another TI is in the Duke of Kent House (off Cathedral Square in the town center, Mon–Fri 9:00–17:30, closed Sat–Sun, bus #3 stops here, tel. 74950).

Arrival in Gibraltar

By Bus: Spain's La Línea bus station is a five-minute walk from the Gibraltar border (baggage storage-€3/day, Mon–Fri 9:00–12:30 & 13:30–18:00, closed Sat–Sun, longer hours in summer, purchase token—*ficha*—from Portillo ticket counter). You'll need your passport to cross the border.

From the Border into Town: To get into town from the "fron-tier" (as the border is called), you can walk (30 min), take a taxi to the cable-car station (pricey at €9/£6), or hop on a bus (€1/£0.60, runs every 15 min). Catch either the #3 bus to the TI at Cathedral Square (you can also stay on to continue my self-guided tour, later) or the London-style double-decker bus to Casemates Square, which also has a TI. To get into town by foot, walk straight across the runway (look left, right, and up), then head down Winston Churchill Avenue, angling right at the Shell station on Smith Dorrien Avenue.

Spain vs. Gibraltar

Spain has been annoyed about Gibraltar ever since Great Britain snagged this prime 2.5-square-mile territory through the Treaty of Utrecht in 1713, at the end of the War of the Spanish Succession. Although Spain long ago abandoned efforts to reassert its sovereignty by force, it still tries to make Gibraltarians see the error of their British ways. Over the years, Spain has limited Gibraltar's air and sea connections, choked traffic at the three-quarter-mile border, and even messed with the local phone system in efforts to convince Britain to give back the Rock. Still, given the choice—which they got in referenda in 1967 and 2002—Gibraltar's residents steadfastly remain Queen Elizabeth's loyal subjects, voting overwhelmingly (99 percent in the last election) to continue as a self-governing British dependency. Gibraltar's governor, who is serving his third four-year term, is popular for dealing forcefully and effectively with Spain on these issues.

By Car: Customs checks at the border create a bit of a bottleneck for drivers getting in and out. But at worst, there's a 15-minute wait during the morning rush hour into Gibraltar and the evening rush hour back out. Parking is free and easy except for weekday working hours, when it's tight and frustrating. It's simpler to park in La Línea (explained below) and just walk across the border.

Freeway signs in Spain say *Algeciras* and *La Línea*, pretending that Gibraltar doesn't exist until you're very close. After taking the La Línea–Gibraltar exit off the main Costa del Sol road, continue as the road curves left (with the Rock to your right). Enter the left-hand lane at the traffic circle before the border and you'll end up in La Línea. The Fo Cona underground parking lot is handy (€1/hr, €6/day, on "20th of April" street). You'll also find blue-lined parking spots in this area (€1/hr from meter, 6-hr limit 9:00–20:00, free before and after that, bring coins, leave ticket on dashboard). From La Línea, it's a five-minute stroll to the border, where you can catch a bus or taxi into town (see "From the Border into Town," on previous page).

If driving into Gibraltar, drive along the sea side of the ramparts (on Queensway—but you'll see no street name). There are big parking lots here and at the cable-car terminal. Parking is generally free—if you can find a spot. By the way, while you'll still find the English-style roundabouts, cars here stopped driving on the British side of the road in the 1920s.

Helpful Hints

Gibraltar Isn't Spain: Gibraltar, a British colony, uses different coins, currency (see below), stamps, and phone cards than those used in Spain. Note that British holidays such as the Queen's (official) Birthday (June 15 in 2010) and Bank Holidays (May 3, May 31, and Aug 30 in 2010) are observed, along with local holidays such as Gibraltar's National Day (Sept 10).

Use Pounds, not Euros: Gibraltar uses the British pound sterling (£1 = about $1.60). They also accept euros...but for about a 20 percent extra cost to you. Gibraltar is expensive even at fair pound sterling rates. You'll save money by hitting up an ATM and taking out what you'll need. But before you leave, stop at an exchange desk and change back what you don't spend (at about a 5 percent loss), since Gibraltar currency is hard to change in Spain. (If you'll be making only a few purchases, you can try to avoid this problem by skipping the ATM and buying things with your credit card.) Be aware that if you pay for anything in euros, you may get pounds back in change.

Hours: This may be the United Kingdom, but Gibraltar follows a siesta schedule, with some businesses closing 13:00–15:00 on weekdays, and shutting down at 14:00 on Saturdays until Monday morning.

Electricity: If you have electrical gadgets, note that Gibraltar uses the British three-pronged plugs (not the European two-pronged ones). Your hotel may be able to loan you an adapter.

Telephone: To telephone Gibraltar from anywhere in Europe, dial 00-350-200 and the five-digit local number. To call Gibraltar from the US or Canada, dial 011-350-200-local number.

Internet Access: Café Cyberworld has pricey Internet access (daily 12:00–24:00, Queensway 14, in Ocean Heights Gallery, an arcade 100 yards toward the water from Casemates Square, tel. 51416). **Western Union** has an Internet center on Main Street (£0.75/hr; at #269, right before Convent Square). Another cheap place for Internet access is the cultural center listed next.

John Mackintosh Cultural Centre: This is your classic British effort to provide a cozy community center. The upstairs library, without a hint of tourism, welcomes drop-ins to enjoy all the local newspapers and publications, and to check their email cheaply and easily (£0.85/30 min, Mon–Fri 9:30–19:30, closed Sat–Sun).

Side-Trip to Tangier, Morocco: Travel agencies in Gibraltar sell trips to Tangier. Ferries cross the strait only a few days a week, leaving Gibraltar at 23:00 and departing Tangier at 19:00 Morocco time (£32 one-way, £57 round-trip). Because Gibraltar is expensive compared to Spain, it makes sense to use your time here to see the Rock, but to day-trip to Morocco from Tarifa instead (see page 662).

Self-Guided Bus Tour

Gibraltar Town Bus #3 Orientation Tour

Upon arrival at the "frontier," pick up a map at the TI window. Then walk straight ahead for 200 yards to the bus stop on the right. Catch bus #3 and enjoy this three-mile orientation ride that takes you from one end of the colony to the other (Mon–Fri 4/hr, Sat–Sun 2–3/hr, buy ticket from driver, ride 20 min to the end of the line: Europa Point). A single ticket gives you on-and-off privileges for an hour (€1/£0.60). To save money, ask the driver for an all-day ticket (€1.90/£1).

Here's the tour. It goes quickly. Read fast...

Airstrip: You enter Gibraltar by crossing an airstrip. Three or four times a day, the entry road into Gibraltar is closed to allow planes to land or take off. Originally a horse-racing stadium, this area was later filled in with stones excavated from the 30 miles of military tunnels carved into the Rock. This airstrip was a vital lifeline in the days when Spain and Britain were quarreling over Gibraltar (especially 1970–1985) and the border was closed. If you look at the face of the Rock, you can see the tiny windows that were once perches from where big cannons could fire. Behind them lie siege tunnels, open as a tourist attraction (described later in this chapter).

Moorish Castle: Just after the airstrip, at the first round-about, the bus passes a road leading left (which heads clockwise around the Rock to the town of Catalan Bay, peaceful beaches, and the huge mountainside rainwater-catchment wall). The Moorish Castle above dates back over a thousand years. On the right is land reclaimed in 1989, filled mostly with government-subsidized apartments.

Ramparts: You'll cross the bridge and drive onto the ramparts. Water once came all the way up to the ramparts—50 percent of the city is on reclaimed land. Gibraltar's heritage shows in the architecture: tiles (Portuguese), shutters (Genoese Italian), and wrought iron (Georgian English).

On the right after the next stop, you'll see World War memorials. The first is the American War Memorial (the building-like structure with a gold plaque and arch), built in 1932 to commemorate American sailors based here in World War I. Farther along you'll see 18th-century cannons and a memorial to Gibraltarians who died in World War II.

Downtown: The following sights come up quickly: Passing the NatWest House office tower on the left, you'll immediately see a **synagogue** (only the top peeks out above a wall; the wooden doors in the wall bear the Star of David). In the 19th century, half of Gibraltar was Jewish. The Jewish community now numbers 600. Just after the synagogue is little **Cathedral Square,** with a playground, TI, and the Moorish-looking Anglican cathedral (behind the playground). Gibraltar is the European headquarters of the Anglican Church. Now you'll pass a long wall; most of it is the back of the Governor's Residence (a.k.a. The Convent).

Charles V Wall: The next bus stop is at the old Charles V wall, built in response to a 1552 raid in which the pirate Barbarossa captured 70 Gibraltarians into slavery. Immediately after you pass under the wall, you'll see a green park on your left that contains the **Trafalgar cemetery.** Buried here are some British sailors who died defeating the French off the coast of Spain's Cape Trafalgar in 1805.

Botanical Gardens: The next stop is at the big parking lot for the **cable car** to the top of the Rock, as well as for the **botanical gardens** (free, daily 8:00–sunset), located at the base of the lift. You can get off to do this now—or finish the tour and come back here later, on the way back into town.

Out of Town: Heading uphill out of town, your best views are on the right. It's believed that the body of Admiral Nelson was pickled in a barrel of spirits in a harbor just below you after his victorious (yet fatal) Battle of Trafalgar. You pass the big former naval hospital and barracks. Reaching the end of the Rock, you pass modern apartments and the mosque.

King Fahd Mosque: This $20 million gift from the Saudi sultan was completed in 1997, and Gibraltar's 900 Muslims worship here each Friday. Five times a day—as across the strait in Morocco—an imam sings the call to prayer.

Europa Point: The lighthouse marks windy Europa Point—the end of the line. Buses retrace the route you just traveled, departing about every 15 minutes (every 20–30 min on weekends). Europa Point, up the mound from the bus stop and tourist shop (on right), is an observation post. A plaque here identifies the mountains of Morocco 15 miles across the strait. The glow of the lighthouse (150 feet tall, from 1841, closed to visitors) can be seen from Morocco.

Your tour is finished. Enjoy the views before catching a bus back into town. Get off at the cable-car station to ride to the top of the Rock, tour the botanical gardens, or begin the town walk described next.

Self-Guided Walk

Welcome to Gibraltar

Gibraltar town is long and skinny, with one main street (called Main Street). Stroll the length of it from the cable-car station to Casemates Square, following this little tour. A good British pub and a room-temperature pint of beer await you at the end.

Just past the cable-car terminal is the **Trafalgar cemetery,** a reminder of the colony's English military heritage. Next you come to the **Charles V wall**—a reminder of its Spanish military heritage—built in 1552 by the Spanish to defend against marauding pirates. Gibraltar was controlled by Moors (711–1462), Spain (1462–1704), and then the British (since 1704). Passing through the Southport Gates, you'll see one of the many red history plaques posted about town.

Heading into town, you pass the tax office, then the **John Mackintosh Cultural Centre,** which has cheap Internet access and a copy of today's *Gibraltar Chronicle* upstairs in its library. The *Chronicle* comes out Monday through Friday and has covered the local news since 1801. The Methodist church sponsors the cheap and cheery **Carpenter's Arms** tearoom just above one of several fish-and-chips joints (rare in Iberia).

The pedestrian portion of Main Street begins near the **Governor's Residence.** The British governor of Gibraltar took over a Franciscan convent, hence the name of the local white house: The Convent. The **Convent Guard Room,** facing the Governor's Residence, is good for photos.

Gibraltar's courthouse stands behind a **small tropical garden,** where John and Yoko got married back in 1969 (as the ballad goes, they "got married in Gibraltar near Spain"). Sean Connery did, too. Actually, many Brits like to get married here because weddings are cheap, fast (only 48 hours' notice required), and legally recognized as British.

Main Street now becomes a **shopping drag.** You'll notice lots of colorful price tags advertising tax-free booze, cigarettes, and sugar (highly taxed in Spain). Lladró porcelain, while made in Valencia, is popular here (because it's sold without the 16 percent Spanish VAT—Value-Added Tax). The big **Marks & Spencer department store** helps vacationing Brits feel at home, while the Catholic cathedral retains a whiff of Arabia (as it was built upon the remains of a mosque).

The town (and this walk) ends at **Casemates Square.** While a lowbrow food circus today, it originated as a barracks and place for ammunition storage. When Franco closed the border with Spain in 1969, Gibraltar suffered a labor shortage, as Spanish guest workers could no longer commute into Gibraltar. The colony countered by inviting Moroccan workers to take their place—ending a nearly 500-year Moroccan absence, which began when the Moors fled in 1462. As a result, today's Moroccan community dates only from the 1970s. While the previous Spanish labor force had simply commuted into work, the Moroccans needed apartments, so Gibraltar converted the Casemates barracks for that purpose. Cheap Spanish labor has crept back in, causing many locals to resent store clerks who can't speak proper English.

On Casemates Square, there's a crystal shop that makes its own crystal right there (you can watch). They claim it's the only thing actually "made in Gibraltar." But just upstairs, on the upper floor of the barracks, you'll find a string of local crafts shops. Beyond the square (behind the TI) is the covered **produce market.**

Sights in Gibraltar

In Gibraltar Town

▲**Gibraltar Museum**—Built atop a Moorish bath, this museum tells the story of a chunk of land that has been fought over for centuries. Start with the fine 15-minute video overview of the story of the Rock—a worthwhile prep for the artifacts (such as ancient Roman anchors made of lead) you'll see in the museum. Then, wander through the scant remains of the 14th-century Moorish baths. Upstairs you'll see military memorabilia, a 15-foot-long model of the Rock, wonderful century-old photos of old Gibraltar, paintings by local artists, and, in a cave-like room off the art gallery, a collection of prehistoric remains and artifacts. The famous skull of a Neanderthal woman found in Forbes' Quarry is a copy (the original is in the British Museum in London). Found in Gibraltar in 1848, this was the first Neanderthal skull ever discovered. No one realized its significance until a similar skull found years later in Germany's Neanderthal Valley was correctly identified—stealing the name, claim, and fame from Gibraltar (£2, Mon–Fri 10:00–18:00, Sat 10:00–14:00, last entry 30 min before closing, closed Sun, no photos, on Bomb House Lane near the cathedral).

Up on the Rock

The actual Rock of Gibraltar is the colony's best sight. Its attractions: the stupendous view from the very top, quirky apes, a hokey cave (St. Michael's), and the impressive Siege Tunnels drilled through the rock face for military purposes. The Rock, which is technically called the "Upper Rock Nature Reserve," is open daily 9:30–19:00.

You have two £8 options for touring the Rock: Ride the cable car or take a 90-minute taxi tour. The taxi tour includes a couple of extra stops and the running commentary of your licensed cabbie/guide. Hikers can ride the lift up and walk down, connecting the various sights (you'll walk on paved military lanes, not trails).

In either case, to tour St. Michael's Cave or the Siege Tunnels, you'll need to pay £8 extra for a combo-ticket. Because the cable car doesn't get you very close to the cave and tunnels, take the taxi tour if you'll be visiting these sights. On the other hand, the cable car takes you to the very top of the Rock (which the taxi tours don't). Frankly, the sights are not much; the Rock's best attractions—enjoying views from the top and playing with the monkeys—are free.

There's certainly no reason to take a big bus tour (advertised and sold all over town) considering how fun, cheap, and easy the taxi tours are. Private cars are not allowed high on the Rock.

Taxi Tours: Minibuses driven by cabbies trained and licensed to lead these little trips are standing by at the border and on Cathedral Square in town. They charge £32 per carload

or £8 per person, whichever is more. (Remember, you'll pay an additional £8 for admission to the cave and the tunnels; if you opt out, you'll have to sit in the car while the other passengers make these little visits.) Taxi tours and big buses do the same 90-minute loop tour with four stops: a Mediterranean viewpoint (called the Pillar of Hercules), St. Michael's Cave (15-min visit), a viewpoint near the top of the Rock where you can get up close to the monkeys, and the Siege Tunnels (20-min visit). Buddy up with other travelers and share the cost.

Cable Car to the Summit: The ride costs £8 (6/hr, daily 9:30–17:15, last ride down at 17:45, closed Sun in winter and when windy or rainy—ask at TI if cable car is running when weather is questionable, pick up map with ticket). Your cable-car ride includes a multimedia device that explains what you're seeing from the spectacular viewpoints (pick it up at the well-marked booth when you disembark at the top). The cable car stops halfway down for those who want to get out, see the monkeys, and take a later car down. From there, many hike to St. Michael's Cave (skippable and described below).

To see all the sights, you'll end up hiking down, rather than taking the cable car back. Approximate hiking times: from the top of the cable car to St. Michael's Cave—25 minutes; from the cave to the Apes' Den—20 minutes; from the Apes' Den to the Siege Tunnels—30 minutes; from the tunnels back into town, passing the Moorish Castle—20 minutes. Total from top to bottom: about 90 minutes (on paved roads with almost no traffic), not including sightseeing.

▲▲▲The Summit of the Rock—The cable car takes you to the real highlight of Gibraltar: the summit of the spectacular Rock

itself. (Taxi tours do not go here— they stop on a ridge below the summit, where you enjoy a commanding view—but one that's nowhere near as good.) The limestone massif, or large rock mass, is nearly a mile long, rising 1,400 feet high with very sheer faces. According to legend, this was one of the Pillars of Hercules (paired with Djebel Musa, another mountain across the strait in Morocco), marking the edge of the known world in ancient times. Local guides say that these pillars are the only places on the planet where you can see two seas and two continents at the same time.

In A.D. 711, the Muslim chieftain Tarik ibn Ziyad crossed over from Africa and landed on the Rock, beginning the Moorish conquest of Spain and naming the Rock after himself—Djebel-Tarik ("Rock of Tarik"), which became "Gibraltar."

At the top of the Rock (the cable-car terminal) there's a view terrace and a restaurant. From here, you can explore old ramparts and drool at the 360-degree view of Morocco (including the Rif Mountains and Djebel Musa), the Strait of Gibraltar, the bay stretching west toward Algeciras, and the twinkling Costa del Sol arcing eastward. The views are especially crisp on brisk off-season days. Below you (to the east) stretches the giant catchment system that the British built to collect rainwater in the not-so-distant past, when Spain allowed neither water nor tourists to cross its disputed border. Broad sheets catch the rain, sending it through channels to reservoirs located inside the rock.

O'Hara's Battery—While it's closed to visitors, some travelers still hike up here (20 min from the top of the cable-car lift). At 1,400 feet, this is the actual highest point on the Rock. A 100-ton nine-inch gun sits on the summit where a Moorish lookout post once stood. It was built after World War I, and the last test shot was fired in 1974. Locals are glad it's been mothballed—during test firings, they had to open their windows, which might otherwise have shattered from the pressurized air blasted from this gun.

The iron rings you see every 30 yards or so along the military lanes around the Rock once anchored pulleys used to haul up guns like the huge one at O'Hara's Battery.

▲**St. Michael's Cave**—Studded with stalagmites and stalactites, eerily lit, and echoing with classical music, this cave is dramatic, corny, and slippery when wet. Considered a one-star sight since Neolithic times, these caves were alluded to in ancient Greek legends—when the caves were believed to be the Gates of Hades (or the entrance of a tunnel to Africa). All taxi tours stop here. This sight requires a long walk for cable-car riders.

▲**Apes of Gibraltar**—The Rock is home to about 200 "apes" (actually, tailless Barbary macaques—a type of monkey). Taxi tours come with great monkey fun.

Those riding the cable car can get off halfway down to photograph the apes. The males are bigger, females have beards, and newborns are black. They live about 15–20 years. Legend has it that as long as the apes remain here, so will the Brits. Keep your distance from the apes. (Guides say that for safety reasons, "They can touch you, but you can't touch them.") Beware of their kleptomaniac tendencies; they'll ignore the peanut in your hand and claw after the full bag in your pocket. If there's no ape action, wait for a banana-toting taxi tour to stop by and stir some up.

▲**Siege Tunnels**—Also called the Upper Galleries, these chilly tunnels were blasted out of the rock by the Brits during the Spanish

and French siege (1779–1783). The clever British, safe inside the Rock, used hammers and gunpowder to carve these tunnels in order to plant four big guns on the north face and drive off the French. During World War II, 30 more miles of tunnels were blasted out. Hokey but fun dioramas help recapture a time when Brits were known more for conquests than for crumpets.

Moorish Castle—Actually more a tower than a castle, this building offers a tiny museum of Moorish remnants and carpets. (In the interest of political correctness, the tourist board is trying to change the name to "Medieval Castle"...but it is Moorish.) It was constructed on top of the original castle built in A.D. 711 by the

Moor Tarik ibn Ziyad, who gave his name to Gibraltar. The tower marks the end of the Upper Rock Nature Reserve. A short hike downhill drops you back in town.

Nightlife in Gibraltar

Gibraltar is quiet at night. You can sip a drink on the waterfront at the Queensway Quay Marina (see page 659). Other than that, it's music in the pubs and lounges. O'Callaghan Eliott Hotel hosts free live jazz on Monday and Thursday evenings, and Casemates Square is everyone's choice for live music in the pubs. The Queen's Cinema (by the cable car) is the colony's only movie theater.

Sleeping in Gibraltar

Gibraltar is not a good value for hotels. Except at the hostel, the beds are either bad or overpriced. Remember, you'll pay a 20 percent premium if paying with euros—pay with local cash or your credit card.

$$$ O'Callaghan Eliott Hotel, with four stars, boasts a rooftop pool with a view, a fine restaurant, bar, terrace, inviting sit-a-bit public spaces, and 120 modern if sterile rooms (sky-high rack rates of Db-£240–270, but often around Db-£100 with Web booking during non-peak days, breakfast-£13, non-smoking floors, air-con, elevator, free parking, centrally located at Governor's Parade up Library Street from main drag, tel. 70500, fax 70243, www.ocallaghanhotels.com, reservations@ocallaghanhotels.com).

$$$ Bristol Hotel offers basic English rooms in the heart of Gibraltar (Sb-£63–68, Db-£81–87, Tb-£93–99, higher prices for exterior rooms, breakfast-£5, air-con, elevator, swimming pool, free parking, Cathedral Square 10, tel. 76800, fax 77613, www.bristolhotel.gi, reservations@bristolhotel.gi).

Gibraltar Town

1. O'Callaghan Eliott Hotel
2. Bristol Hotel
3. Queen's Hotel
4. Continental Hotel
5. Cannon Hotel
6. Emile Hostel
7. The Clipper Pub
8. The Star Bar
9. Carpenter's Arms
10. Queensway Quay Marina & Eateries
11. All's Well Pub
12. Market Place & Produce Market

13. Marks & Spencer
14. Cathedral Square
15. John Mackintosh Cultural Centre
16. Governor's Residence
17. Convent Guard Room
18. John & Yoko's Wedding Site
19. Café Cyberworld

$$ Queen's Hotel, near the cable-car lift, has 62 comfortable remodeled rooms in a noisy location (Sb-£60, Db-£70, seaview Db-£85–95, Tb-£90, Qb-£110, includes English breakfast, 20 percent discount for students with ISIC cards and paying cash, elevator, free parking, at #3 bus stop, Boyd Street 1, tel. 74000, fax 40030, www.queenshotel.gi, queenshotel@gibtelecom.net).

$$ Continental Hotel isn't fancy, but it has a friendly feel. Its 17 high-ceilinged, air-conditioned rooms border an unusual elliptical atrium (Sb-£52, Db-£70, Tb-£85, Qb-£95, includes continental breakfast, elevator, a couple of blocks south of Casemates TI in Main Street pedestrian area, Engineer Lane, tel. 76900, fax 41702, contiho@gibtelecom.net).

$$ Cannon Hotel is a run-down dive. But it's also well-located and friendly and has the only cheap hotel rooms in town. Its 18 rooms (most with wobbly cots and no private bathrooms) look treacherously down on a little patio (S-£29, D-£40, Db-£50, T-£50, Tb-£66, includes full English breakfast, behind cathedral at Cannon Lane 9, tel. 51711, fax 51789, www.cannonhotel.gi, cannon@gibnet.gi).

$ Emile Hostel, charming and the cheapest place in town, welcomes people of any age (42 beds, dorm bed-£15, S-£20, D-£35, includes breakfast, on Montagu Bastion diagonally across the street from a petrol station, ramped entrance on Line Wall Road, tel. & fax 51106, www.emilehostel.com, emilehostel@yahoo.co.uk).

Eating in Gibraltar

Take a break from *jamón* and sample some English pub grub: fish-and-chips, meat pies, jacket potatoes (baked potatoes with fillings), or a good old greasy English breakfast. English-style beers include chilled lagers and room-temperature ales, bitters, and stouts. In general, the farther you venture away from Main Street, the cheaper and more local the places become.

The Clipper, my favorite pub for dinner, is friendly and offers filling £6 meals and Murphy's stout on tap (English breakfast-£5, Mon–Sat 9:30–22:00, Sun 10:00–22:00, on Irish Town Lane).

The Star Bar, which brags that it's "Gibraltar's Oldest Bar," is on a quiet street with a pubby interior and good £7 plates (daily 7:00–24:00, food served till 22:00, on Parliament Lane off Main Street, across from Corner House Restaurant).

Carpenter's Arms is a fast, cheap-and-cheery café run by the

Methodist church, serving £3 meals with a missionary's smile. It's upstairs in the Methodist church on Main Street (Mon–Fri 9:00–14:00, closed Sat–Sun and Aug, volunteer-run, 100 yards past the Governor's Residence at 297 Main Street).

Queensway Quay Marina: To dine in yacht-club ambience, stroll the marina and choose from a string of restaurants serving the boat-owning crowd. When the sun sets, the quay-side tables at each of these places are prime dining real estate. **Waterfront Restaurant** has a lounge-lizard interior and great marina-side tables outside (£15 plates with daily specials, Indian, and classic British; daily 9:00–24:00, last orders 22:45, tel. 45666). **Claus on the Rock Bistro** has a colorful menu with dishes from around the world (£15 plates, closed Sun, tel. 48686). The marina promenade also has Italian and Indian restaurants.

Casemates Square Food Circus: The big square at the entrance of Gibraltar contains a variety of restaurants, ranging from fast food (fish-and-chips joint, Burger King, and Pizza Hut) to inviting pubs spilling out into the square. The **All's Well** pub serves £8 meals (Moroccan *tajine,* salads, burgers, fish-and-chips, and more) and offers pleasant tables with umbrellas under leafy trees (daily 9:30–19:00). Fruit stands and cheap take-out food stalls bustle just outside the entry to the square at the **Market Place** (Mon–Sat 9:00–15:00, closed Sun).

Groceries: An **In & Out** minimarket is on Main Street, off Cathedral Square (Mon–Fri 8:30–20:00, Sat 8:30–18:00, closed Sun). Nearby, **Marks & Spencer** has an inside take-out window that serves roast chicken and fresh-baked cookies (Mon–Sat 8:30–19:00, Sun 10:00–15:00).

Connections

Gibraltar is expanding its flight schedule. Currently there are daily Iberia Airlines flights to Madrid and about four British Air flights a day between London/Gatwick and Madrid. The discount airline Monarch flies to London's Luton Airport.

Bus travelers walk five minutes from Gibraltar's border into Spain to reach La Línea, the nearest bus station (tel. 902-199-208 or 956-172-396). The nearest train station is at Algeciras, which is the region's main transportation hub (for Algeciras connections, see "Connections" near the end of this chapter).

From La Línea by Bus to: Algeciras (2/hr, 45 min, can buy ticket on bus), **Tarifa** (7–8/day direct, 1 hr; 10/day with change in Algeciras, 1.5 hrs), **Málaga** (4/day, 3 hrs), **Ronda** (no direct bus, transfer in Algeciras; Algeciras to Ronda: 6/day, 2 hrs), **Granada** (2/day, 5 hrs), **Sevilla** (4/day, 4 hrs), **Jerez** (2/day, 3 hrs), **Huelva** (1/day, 6 hrs), **Madrid** (2/day, 8 hrs).

Tarifa

Europe's southernmost town is whitewashed and Arab-looking, with a lovely beach, an old castle, restaurants swimming in fresh seafood, inexpensive places to sleep, enough windsurfers to sink a ship, and best of all, hassle-free boats to Morocco.

As I stood on Tarifa's town promenade under the castle, looking out at almost-touchable Morocco across the Strait of Gibraltar, I regretted only that I didn't have this book to steer me clear of gritty Algeciras on earlier trips. Tarifa, with daily 35-minute boat transfers to Tangier, is the best jumping-off point for a Moroccan side-trip.

Tarifa has no blockbuster sights (and can be quiet off-season), but it's a town where you just feel good to be on vacation. Given its lofty status as a breezy mecca among windsurfers, it's mobbed with young German and French adventure-seekers in July and August.

Orientation to Tarifa

The old town, surrounded by a wall, slopes gently up from the water's edge. The modern section stretches farther inland from Tarifa's fortified gate.

Tourist Information

The TI is on Paseo de la Alameda (June–Sept daily 10:00–13:30 & 18:00–20:00; Oct–May Mon–Fri 10:00–14:00 & 16:00–18:00, Sat–Sun 10:00–14:00; hours may vary slightly on slow or bad-weather days, tel. 956-680-993, turismo@aytotarifa.com).

Arrival in Tarifa

By Bus: The bus station (actually a couple of portable buildings with an outdoor sitting area) is on Batalla del Salado, about a five-minute walk from the old town. (The more-central TI also has bus schedules.) Buy tickets directly from the driver if the ticket booth is closed (Mon–Fri 7:30–9:30 & 10:00–11:00 & 14:30–18:30, Sat–Sun 15:00–19:30, hours vary slightly depending on season, tel. 956-684-038, 902-199-208). To reach the old town, walk away from the wind generators perched on the mountain ridge.

By Car: If you're staying in the center of town, follow signs for *Alameda* or *Puerto,* and continue along Avenida de Andalucía.

Tarifa

1. Hostal Alborada
2. Hotel La Mirada
3. La Sacristía
4. Casa Blan+co
5. Hotel Misiana
6. La Casa Amarilla
7. Hostal La Calzada
8. Hostal Alameda
9. Hostal Africa
10. Pensión Correo
11. Hostal Villanueva
12. Restaurante Morilla
13. Rest. La Pescadería
14. Pizzeria La Capricciosa
15. Ristorante La Trattoria
16. To Restaurante Souk
17. Café Central & FIRMM
18. Bar El Francés
19. Café Bar Los Mellis & Bar El Pasillo
20. Casino Tarifeño
21. Confitería LaTarifeña
22. Churrería La Palmera
23. Supermarket
24. Mercado (Market)
25. Internet Café
26. Girasol Adventure
27. Whale Watch España & Marruecotur
28. Speedlines Tours

P PARKING

⌇ VIEW

TO **16**
BOS

TO BEACH

TO BUS STATION,
WIND SURFING BEACH
PLAYA PUNTA PALOMA
+ SEVILLA

BULLRING

GEN. RIVERA

CALLAO CAN.

SEBASTIAN SAN JOSE BATALLA CAN.

NAVAS TOLOSA CANA.

AREPILES PIO XII

DEL

NUMANCIA ANT.

SAN ISIDRO SAN JOSE SALADO

200 YARDS
200 METERS

P PARKING
⌇ VIEW

OLD GATE

TO ALGECIRAS VIA N-340

AVENIDA DE ANDALUCÍA AMADOR DE LOS RIOS

TO BEACH

PESO

SILOS

JEREZ

NUESTRA SEÑORA

SAN ROS

PARRAS

CALZADILLA TELLEZ

TO HUERTA DEL REY (1 block)

J.T. ARTIGAS

S. JULIAN

SAN FRANCISCO

CARN.

CASTELAR

LEÑA

EL BRAVO

GEN COPONS

SAN MATEO

JUAN NÚÑEZ

TO BEACH

PASEO ALAMEDA

AV. DE LA CONSTITUCIÓN

SAN TRINIDAD

GUZMAN

SANTO DOMINGO

MELO

PLAZA SAN MATEO

DOUBLE ARCH

CASTLE

AMARGURA

OLD CITY WALLS

BOAT TO MOROCCO

CUSTOMS TERMINAL

P

HARBOR

BOAT TO MOROCCO

DCH

Side-Tripping to Morocco

Tangier, worth ▲▲▲, is the main reason to go to Tarifa. The fast, modern catamaran ride (a huge car ferry that zips over every two hours all year long) takes less than an hour. You walk from the Tangier port into a remarkable city—the fifth-largest in Morocco—which is no longer the Tijuana of Africa, but a booming town enjoying the enthusiastic support and can-do vision of a new and activist king.

Most tourists do the mindless belly-dancing-and-shopping excursion (which costs about €65 including the ferry ride—essentially the same as the round-trip ferry ride sans tour). They're met by a guide, taken on a bus tour and a walk through the old town market, offered a couple of crass Kodak moments with snake charmers and desert dancers, and given lunch with live music and belly-dancing. Then they visit a big shop and are hustled back down to their boat where—five hours after they landed—they return to the First World thankful they don't have diarrhea.

The alternative is to simply take the ferry on your own and leave the tourist track. Things are cheap and relatively safe. Since more than 90 percent of visitors choose the comfort of a tour, independent adventurers rarely see another tourist and avoid all the kitsch. You can catch the first boat (9:00) and spend the entire day, returning that evening; extend with an overnight in Tangier; or even head deeper into Morocco.

If you're planning a day trip or an overnight stay, see the Tangier chapter for all the details. If you're going to stay longer in Morocco, you'll need the help of another guidebook.

Follow signs to make an obligatory loop to the port entrance, and park at Calle Juan Núñez (on the harbor, at the base of the castle, reasonable cost, generally a place available). Note that Avenida de la Constitución is one-way (going away from the port). There's plenty of free parking just outside Tarifa's old town walls. Blue lines indicate paid parking.

Helpful Hints

Internet Access: Pandor@, in the heart of the old town, is across from Café Central and near the church (generally in summer daily 10:00–24:00, in winter daily 10:00–14:30 & 16:30–18:00, 15 computers).

Excursions: Girasol Adventure offers a variety of outdoor excursions, including mountain-bike rentals (€18/day with helmet), guided bike tours, hikes in the national park, beginners' rock-climbing classes, and, when you're all done...a massage (€45/hr). The various activities generally last a half-day and cost around €25. Ask Sabine or Chris for details (Mon–Fri

10:15–14:00 & 18:30–20:30, Sat 11:00–14:00, closed Sun, Calle Colón 12, tel. 956-627-037, www.girasol-adventure.com).

Sights in Tarifa

Church of St. Matthew (Iglesia de San Mateo)—Tarifa's most important church, facing its main drag, is richly decorated for being in such a small town. Most nights, it seems life squirts from the church out the front door and into the fun-loving Calle El Bravo. Wander inside (daily 9:00–13:00 & 17:30–20:30; there may be English-language leaflets inside on the right).

Find the fragment of an ancient tombstone—a tiny square (eye-level, about the size of this book) in the wall just before the transept on the right side. Probably the most important historical item in town, this stone fragment proves there was a functioning church here during Visigothic times, before the Moorish conquest. The tombstone reads, in a kind of Latin Spanish (try reading it), "Flaviano lived as a Christian for 50 years, a little more or less. In death he received forgiveness as a servant of God on March 30, 674. May he rest in peace." If that gets you in the mood to light a candle, switch on an electric "candle" by dropping in a coin. (It works.)

Step into the side chapel around the corner in the right transept. The centerpiece of the **altar** is a boy Jesus. By Andalusian tradition, he used to be naked, but these days he's clothed with outfits that vary with the Church calendar. Cherubs dance around on the pink-and-purple interior above an exquisite chandelier.

A statue of **St. James the Moor-Slayer** (missing his sword) is on the right wall of the main central altar. Since the days of the Reconquista, James has been Spain's patron saint. For more on this important figure—and why he's fighting invaders that came to Spain centuries after his death—see page 265.

The left side of the nave harbors several **statues**—showing typically over-the-top Baroque emotion—that are paraded through town during Holy Week. The **Captive Christ** (with hands bound, on left wall) evokes a time when Christians were held captive by Moors. The door on the left side of the nave is the **"door of pardons."** For a long time, Tarifa was a dangerous place—on the edge of the Reconquista. To encourage people to live here, the Church offered a second helping of forgiveness to anyone who lived in Tarifa for a year. One year and one day after moving to Tarifa, they would have the privilege of passing through this special "door of pardons," and a Mass of thanksgiving would be held in that person's honor.

Castle of Guzmán el Bueno—This castle is a concrete hulk in a vacant lot, interesting only for the harbor views from its ramparts (closed indefinitely for restoration). It was named after a 13th-century Christian general who gained fame in a sad show of courage while fighting the Moors. Holding Guzmán's son hostage, the Moors demanded he surrender the castle or they'd kill the boy. Guzmán refused, even

throwing his own knife down from the ramparts. It was used on his son's throat. Ultimately, the Moors withdrew to Africa, and Guzmán was a hero. *Bueno* (when open: €2, Tue–Sat 11:00–14:00 & 18:00–20:00, Sun 11:00–14:00, closed Mon).

If you can't get into the castle, you'll get equally good views from the plaza just left of the town hall. Follow *ayto* signs to the ceramic frog fountain in front of the Casa Consistorial and continue left.

Bullfighting—Tarifa has a third-rate bullring where novices botch fights on occasional Saturdays through the summer. Professional bullfights take place the first week of September. The ring is a short walk from town. You'll see posters everywhere.

▲Whale-Watching—Daily whale- and dolphin-watching excursions are offered by several companies in Tarifa. In little more than 40 years, people in this area went from eating whales to protecting them and sharing them with 20,000 visitors a year. Talks are under way between Morocco and Spain to protect the Strait of Gibraltar by declaring it a national park.

For any of the tours, it's wise (but not always necessary) to reserve one to three days in advance. You'll get a multilingual tour and a two-hour boat trip (usually no WC on board). Sightings occur more than 90 percent of the time. Dolphins and pilot whales frolic here any time of year (they like the food), sperm whales visit May through July, and orcas pass through in July and August. In bad weather, boats may leave instead from Algeciras—drivers follow in a convoy, people without cars usually get rides from staff, and you'll stand a lesser chance of seeing whales.

The best company is the Swiss nonprofit **FIRMM** (Foundation for Information and Research on Marine Mammals), which gives a 25-minute educational talk before departure (€30/person, 1–5 trips/day April–Oct, sometimes also Nov, also offers courses, around the corner from Café Central—one door inland at Pedro Cortés 4, tel. 956-627-008, mobile 619-459-441, www.firmm.org, firmm98 @aol.com). If you don't see any whales or dolphins on your tour, you can join another trip for free.

Whale Watch España is another good option (Avenida de la Constitución 6, tel. 956-627-013, mobile 639-476-544, www.whalewatchtarifa.net, run by Lourdes and Flor).

▲▲**Windsurfing**—Tarifa's vast, sandy beach stretches west for about five miles. You can walk the beach from Tarifa or those with a car can explore farther (following Cadiz

Road). On windy summer days, the sea is littered with sprinting windsurfers, while kitesurfers flutter in the sky. It's a fascinating scene: A long string of funky beach resorts is packed with vans and fun-mobiles from northern Europe under mountain ridges lined with modern energy-generating windmills. The various resorts each have a sandy access road, parking, a cabana-type hamlet with rental gear, beachwear shops, a bar, and a hip, healthy restaurant. I like Valdevaqueros beach (five miles from Tarifa), with a wonderful thatched restaurant serving hearty salads, paella, and burgers. Camping Torre de la Peña also has some fun beach eateries.

Camping—In July and August, inexpensive buses do a circuit of nearby campgrounds, all on the waterfront (€2, departures about every 2 hours, confirm times with TI). Trying to get a parking spot in August can take the joy out of this experience.

Sleeping in Tarifa

Room rates vary with the season. For many hotels, I've listed the three seasonal tiers (highest prices—mid-June–Sept; medium prices—spring and fall; and lowest prices—winter).

Outside the City Wall

These hotels are about five blocks from the old town, right off the main drag, Batalla del Salado, in the plain, modern part of town. They are close to the beach and the bus station with free and easy street parking.

$$ Hostal Alborada is a squeaky-clean, family-run 37-room place with two attractive courtyards and modern conveniences. Carlos, Quino, and family offer to help make your Morocco tour or ferry reservation. If they're not too busy, they'll even give you a free lift to the port (Sb-€35/50/60, Db-€46/65/80, Tb-€70/80/99, pay for first night when reserving, upon arrival show this book for a 10 percent discount in 2010—*except* during high season, strict 15-day cancellation policy, breakfast-€2.50–5, air-con, pay Internet access, free Wi-Fi, laundry-€12, Calle San José 40, tel. 956-681-140, fax 956-681-935, www.hotelalborada.com, alborada@cherry tel.com).

Sleep Code

(€1 = about $1.40, country code: 34)
S = Single, **D** = Double/Twin, **T** = Triple, **Q** = Quad, **b** = bathroom, **s** = shower only. Unless otherwise noted, credit cards are accepted and English is spoken. Breakfast is not included (unless noted).

To help you easily sort through these listings, I've divided the rooms into three categories, based on the price for a standard double room with bath during high season:

$$$ Higher Priced—Most rooms €100 or more.
$$ Moderately Priced—Most rooms between €50–100.
$ Lower Priced—Most rooms €50 or less.

$$ Hotel La Mirada has 25 mod and renovated rooms, most with sea views at no extra cost (Sb-€45/50/60, Db-€60/75/90, breakfast-€5, elevator, free Wi-Fi, expansive sea views from large roof terrace with inviting lounge chairs, Calle San Sebastián 41, tel. 956-684-427, fax 956-681-162, www.hotel-lamirada.com, reservas@hotel-lamirada.com, Antonio and Salvador).

On or Inside the City Wall

$$$ La Sacristía, formerly a Moorish stable, now houses travelers who want stylish surroundings. It offers 10 fine rooms, each decorated differently: chic Spanish on the first floor, Asian-style on the second floor. They offer spa treatments, custom tours of the area, and occasional special events—partake in the party since you won't sleep (Db-€115, superior Db-€135, extra bed-€35, same prices all year, includes breakfast, fans, massage room, roof terrace, very central at San Donato 8, tel. 956-681-759, fax 956-685-182, www .lasacristia.net, tarifa@lasacristia.net, helpful Teresa).

$$$ Casa Blan+co, where minimalist meets Moroccan, is the newest reasonably priced designer hotel on the block. Each of its seven rooms (with double beds only—no twins) is decorated (and priced) differently. The place is decked out with practical amenities (mini-fridge and stovetop) as well as romantic touches—loft beds, walk-in showers, and subtle lighting (Db-€52–70 in low season, Db-€91–134 in high season, breakfast, small roof terrace, off main square at Calle Nuestra Señora de la Luz 2, tel. & fax 956-681-515, www.casablan-co.com, info@casablan-co.com).

$$$ Hotel Misiana has 13 comfortable, newly remodeled, spacious rooms. Their designer gave the place a mod, pastel boutique-ish ambience. To avoid street noise, request a room on a higher floor (Sb-€50/60/115, Db-€70/85/135, fancy top-floor Db suite-€110/140/250, low and mid-season rates are €10–20 more on weekends, includes breakfast, double-paned windows, elevator, 100 yards directly in front of the church at Calle Sancho IV El Bravo 18, tel. 956-627-083, fax 956-627-055, www.misiana.com, reservas@misiana.com).

$$ La Casa Amarilla ("The Yellow House") offers 10 posh apartments plus three regular rooms with modern decor and tiny kitchens (three Db-€43/63/80, larger apartment Db-€55/77/102, secure reservation with credit card, across street from Café Central, Calle Sancho IV El Bravo 9, tel. 956-681-993, fax 956-684-029, www.lacasaamarilla.net, info@lacasaamarilla.net).

$$ Hostal La Calzada has eight airy, well-appointed rooms right in the lively old-town thick of things (Db-€50–80, extra bed-€15, closed Nov–March, air-con, 20 yards from church at Calle Justino Pertinez 7, tel. 956-681-492, fax 956-680-366, www.hostallacalzada.com, Diego).

$$ Hostal Alameda, overlooking a square where the local children play, glistens with pristine marble floors and dark red decor. The main building has 11 bright rooms and the annex has 16 more-modern rooms; both face the same delightful square (Db-€60/70/90, extra bed-€20–30, can gouge in Aug, includes tax, air-con, Paseo de la Alameda 4, tel. 956-681-181, fax 956-680-264, www.hostalalameda.com, reservas@hostalalameda.com, Antonio).

$$ Hostal Africa, with 13 bright rooms and an inviting roof garden, is buried on a very quiet street in the center of town. Its dreamy blue-and-white color scheme and stripped-down feel give it a Moorish ambience (S-€20/25/35, Sb-€25/35/50, D-€30/40/50, Db-€35/50/65, Tb-€50/75/100, laundry-€10 (€20 in high season), storage for boards and bikes, Calle María Antonia Toledo 12, tel. 956-680-220, mobile 606-914-294, hostal_africa@hotmail.com, Miguel and Eva keep the reception desk open only from 9:00–24:00).

$$ Pensión Correo rents 12 simple rooms at a fair value— especially Room 8, with its private roof terrace (S-€20–35, D-€35–60, Db-€45–80, extra bed-€15–20, reservations accepted within 24 hours of arrival, roof garden, Coronel Moscardo 8, tel. 956-680-206, www.pensioncorreo.com, welcome@pensioncorreo.com, María José and Luca).

$ Hostal Villanueva offers 12 remodeled rooms at budget prices. It's simple, clean, and friendly, and includes an inviting terrace that overlooks the old town. On a busy street, it's dominated by its restaurant, with no lounge or public area. Pepe asks that you reconfirm your reservation by phone the day before you arrive (Sb-€25–30, Db-€35–45, higher rates in July–Aug, just west of the old-town gate at Avenida de Andalucía 11, access from outside the wall, tel. & fax 956-684-149).

Eating in Tarifa

I've grouped my recommendations below into two categories: Sit down to a real restaurant meal, or enjoy a couple of the many characteristic tapas bars in the old town.

Restaurant Dining

Restaurante Morilla, facing the church and on the town's prime piece of people-watching real estate, serves tasty local-style fish—grilled or baked. This is a real restaurant (no tapas) with good indoor and outdoor seating. A list of the day's available fish is scribbled on a piece of paper that the waiter reviews with you; it's sold by weight, so confirm the price carefully (€12 fish plates, daily 12:00–24:00, Calle Sancho IV El Bravo, tel. 956-681-757).

Restaurant La Pescaderia is a thriving fish place with an inviting menu and great seating, both inside and on delightful Paseo de la Alameda. Their specialty is a paella-style rice and fish stew (€10–15 fish plates, daily 13:00–16:30 & 20:00–23:00, in summer till 23:30, no reservations, tel. 956-627-078).

Pizzeria La Capricciosa, cozy and fun, is one of the numerous pizza-and-pasta joints supported by the large expat Italian community. It serves creative, hearty dinner salads and €8 pizzas and pastas under a wall full of Sergio's bike trophies (daily 20:00–24:00, July–Aug also open 13:00–16:00, at the beginning of Calle San Francisco 6, tel. 956-685-040).

Ristorante La Trattoria, on the Alameda, is another good Italian option, with cloth-napkin class and a friendly staff (€9–12 pizzas and pastas, Thu–Tue 19:30–24:00, closed Wed, Paseo de la Alameda, tel. 956-682-225).

Outside of Town

Restaurante Souk serves a tasty fusion of Moroccan, Indian, and Thai cuisine in a dark, exotic, and romantic ambience. This is a fine place to spend €20—if you don't mind a 10-minute walk out of town. Head up Calle San Sebastian until you see a big staircase on the right, which you'll take to Mar Tirreno 46 (daily 18:00–24:00, closed Tue in Sept–June, also closed Feb–March, good wine list, tel. 956-627-065, friendly Patricia).

Tapas

Café Central is *the* happening place nearly any time of day—it's the perch for all the cool tourists. The tapas are priced at €1.30; just go to the bar and point. They also offer breakfast with eggs; great ingenious €6 salads (study the menu); and impressively therapeutic healthy fruit drinks (daily 9:00–24:00, off Plaza San Mateo, near church, tel. 956-680-560).

Bar El Francés is a thriving hole-in-the-wall where "Frenchies" (as the bar's name implies) Marcial and Alexandra serve tasty little plates of tapas. From Café Central, follow the cars 100 yards to the first corner on the left to reach this simple, untouristy standing-and-stools-only eatery. This spot is popular for its fine *raciones* (€5–9) and tapas (generally €1.30)—especially oxtail *(rabo del toro)*, pork with tomato sauce *(carne con tomate)*, and pork with spice *(chicharrones)*. The outdoor terrace with restaurant-type tables (no tapas served here) is an understandably popular spot to enjoy a casual meal (Mon–Fri open long hours, especially April–Sept; closed Sat–Sun and Jan except open some summer weekends; show this book and Marcial will be happy to bring you a free sherry, Calle Sancho IV El Bravo 21A).

Café Bar Los Mellis is a local favorite for feasts on rickety tables set on cobbles. This family-friendly place offers a good chorizo sandwich and *patatas bravas*—potatoes with a hot tomato sauce served on a wooden board (Thu–Tue 13:00–16:00 & 20:00–24:00, closed Wed, run by brothers José and Ramón; from Bar El Francés, cross parking lot and take Calle del Legionario Ríos Moya up 1 block). **Bar El Pasillo,** next to Los Mellis, also serves tapas (closed Mon).

Casino Tarifeno is just to the sea side of the church. It's an old-boys' social club "for members only," but it offers a musty Andalusian welcome to visiting tourists, including women. Wander through. There's a low-key bar with tapas, a TV room, a card room, and a lounge. There's no menu, but prices are standard. Just point and say the size you want: tapa, *media-ración*, or *ración*.

Pastries, Beach Bars, and Picnics

Breakfast or Dessert: **Confitería La Tarifeña** serves super pastries and flan (closed Mon, at the top of Calle Nuestra Señora de la Luz, near the main old-town gate).

Churrería La Palmera serves breakfast before most hotels and cafés have even turned on the lights—early enough for you to get your coffee fix, and/or bulk up on *churros* and chocolate, before hopping the first ferry to Tangier (Sanchez IV El Bravo 34, across from Bar El Francés).

Windsurfer Bars: If you have a car, head to the string of beaches. Many have bars and thatched fun-loving restaurants that keep the wet-suited gang fed and watered (see "Windsurfing," earlier in the chapter).

Picnics: Stop by the *mercado municipal* (farmers market, Mon–Sat 8:00–14:00, closed Sun, in old town, inside gate nearest TI), any grocery, or the **Eroski Center supermarket** (Mon–Sat 9:15–21:15, closed Sun, has simple cafeteria, near the hotels in the new town at Callao and San José).

Connections

Tarifa

From Tarifa by Bus to: La Línea/Gibraltar (6/day direct, 1 hr, starting around 12:00; 10/day with transfer in Algeciras, 1.5 hrs), **Algeciras** (10/day, 30 min, first departure from Tarifa weekdays at 6:30, on Sat 8:00, on Sun 10:00; return from Algeciras as late as 21:00), **Jerez** (2/day, 2 hrs, more frequent with transfer in Cádiz), **Sevilla** (4/day, 3 hrs), **Huelva** (for those Portugal-bound, 1/day, 5 hrs), and **Málaga** (2/day, 3.5 hrs). All bus service from Tarifa is by Comes (tel. 902-199-208, www.tgcomes.es).

Algeciras

Algeciras is only worth leaving. It's useful to the traveler mainly as a transportation hub, offering ferries to Tangier and trains and buses to destinations in southern and central Spain. The **TI** is on Juan de la Cierva, a block inland from the port. It's on the same street as both the train and bus station, which runs frequent service to Tarifa and La Línea.

Trains: The train station is four blocks inland, opposite Hotel Octavio (tel. 956-630-202). If arriving by train, head down San Bernardo toward the sea to Juan de la Cierva for the TI and port. As an alternative, you can also purchase ferry tickets at the train station branch of Viajes Algemar Travel (open daily, follows train schedules, tel. 956-657-311).

From Algeciras by Train to: Madrid (2/day, 5.5 hrs, arrives at Atocha), **Ronda** (6/day, 1.5–2 hrs), **Granada** (3/day, 4.25–5 hrs), **Sevilla** (3/day, 5 hrs, transfer at either Córdoba, Antequera, or Bobadilla), **Córdoba** (2/day, 3.5 hrs), **Málaga** (4/day, 4 hrs, transfer in Bobadilla). With the exception of the route to Madrid, these are particularly scenic trips; the best is the mountainous journey to Málaga via Bobadilla.

Buses: Algeciras is served by three different bus companies (Comes, Portillo, and Linesur), all located in the same terminal next to Hotel Octavio and directly across from the train station. The companies generally serve different destinations, but there is some overlap. Compare schedules and rates to find the most convenient bus for you. By the ticket counter you'll find an easy red letter board listing departures. Lockers are by the platforms—purchase a token at the machines.

Comes (tel. 902-199-208, www.tgcomes.es) runs buses to **La Línea** (2/hr, 45 min, 7:00–22:30), **Tarifa** (10/day, 30 min), **Sevilla** (4/day, 3.5 hrs), **Jerez** (2/day, 2.5 hrs), **Huelva** (1/day, 6 hrs), and **Madrid** (4/day, 8 hrs).

Portillo (tel. 956-654-304, www.ctsa-portillo.com) offers buses to **Málaga** (17/day, 1.75 hrs *directo*, 3 hrs *ruta*, some buses run by Alsina Graells) and **Granada** (5/day, 4–5.5 hrs).

Linesur (tel. 956-667-649, www.linesur.com) runs the most frequent direct buses to **Sevilla** (11/day, 2 direct, fewer on weekends, 2.25–2.5 hrs) and **Jerez** (9/day, 2.5 hrs).

Ferries from Algeciras to Tangier, Morocco: If you plan to sail from Algeciras, buy your ticket at the port instead of one of the many divey-looking travel agencies littering the town. To find the ticket office, go to the farthest building at the port, which is labeled in large letters: *Estación Marítima Terminal de Pasajeros* (luggage storage available here, easy parking at port–€6). The official offices of the seven boat companies are inside this main port building, directly behind the helpful little English-speaking info kiosk (8–22 ferries/day, port open daily 6:45–21:45, tel. 956-585-463).

Route Tips for Drivers

Tarifa to Gibraltar (45 min): This short drive takes you past a silvery-white forest of windmills, from peaceful Tarifa past Algeciras to La Línea (the Spanish town bordering Gibraltar). Passing Algeciras, continue in the direction of Estepona. At San Roque, take the La Línea–Gibraltar exit.

Gibraltar to Nerja (130 miles): Barring traffic problems, the trip along the Costa del Sol is smooth and easy by car—much of it on a new highway. Just follow the coastal highway east. After Málaga, follow signs to *Almería* and *Motril*.

Nerja to Granada (80 miles, 1.5 hrs, 100 views): Drive along the coast to Motril, catching N-323 north for about 40 miles to Granada. While scenic side-trips may beckon, don't arrive late in Granada without a confirmed hotel reservation.

MOROCCO

MOROCCO

Al-Maghreb

 A young country with an old history, Morocco is a photographer's delight and a budget traveler's dream. It's cheap, exotic, and easier and more appealing than ever. Along with a rich culture, Morocco offers plenty of contrast—from beach resorts to bustling desert markets, from jagged mountains to sleepy, mud-brick oasis towns. And there's a distinct new energy as its popular activist king asserts his vision.

Morocco (*Marruecos* in Spanish; *Al-Maghreb* in Arabic) also provides a good dose of culture shock—both bad and good. It makes Spain and Portugal look meek and mild. You'll encounter oppressive friendliness, brutal heat, the Arabic language, the Islamic faith, ancient cities, and aggressive beggars.

While Morocco is clearly a place apart from Mediterranean Europe, it doesn't really seem like Africa either. It's a mix, reflecting its strategic position between the two continents. Situated on the Strait of Gibraltar, Morocco has been flooded by waves of invasions over the centuries. The Berbers, the native population, have had to contend with the Phoenicians, Carthaginians, Romans, Vandals, and more.

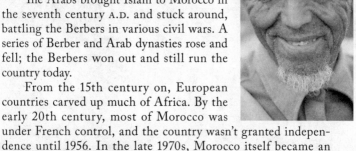

The Arabs brought Islam to Morocco in the seventh century A.D. and stuck around, battling the Berbers in various civil wars. A series of Berber and Arab dynasties rose and fell; the Berbers won out and still run the country today.

From the 15th century on, European countries carved up much of Africa. By the early 20th century, most of Morocco was under French control, and the country wasn't granted independence until 1956. In the late 1970s, Morocco itself became an invading country, grabbing Spain's Western Sahara territory and causing the relatively few inhabitants to clamor for independence. Western Sahara's claim still has not been settled by the United Nations.

Unfortunately, most of the English-speaking Moroccans whom the typical tourist meets are hustlers. Most visitors develop some intestinal problems by the end of their visit. Most women are harassed on the streets by horny but generally harmless men. Things don't work smoothly. In fact, compared to Morocco, Spain resembles Sweden in terms of efficiency.

When you cruise south across the Strait of Gibraltar, leave your busy itineraries and split-second timing behind. Morocco must be taken on its own terms. In Morocco things go smoothly only *"Inshallah"*—if God so wills.

Helpful Hints

Politics: Americans pondering a visit understandably wonder how they'll be received in this Muslim nation. Al Jazeera blares from televisions in all the bars. Regardless, I saw no angry graffiti or posters and felt no animosity toward American individuals there. Western visitors feel a warm welcome in post-9/11 Morocco. And it's culturally enriching for Westerners to experience Morocco—a Muslim monarchy with women still in traditional dress and roles, succeeding on its own terms without embracing modern "norms."

Hustler Alert: While Moroccans are some of Africa's wealthiest people, you are still incredibly rich to them. This imbalance causes predictable problems. Wear your money belt. Assume con artists are more clever than you. Haggle when appropriate (prices skyrocket for tourists). You'll attract hustlers like flies at every famous tourist sight. In the worst-case scenario, they'll lie to you, get you lost, blackmail you, and pester the heck out of you. Never leave your car

or baggage where you can't get back to it without someone else's "help." Anything you buy in a guide's company gets him a 20 percent commission. Normally locals, shopkeepers, and police will come to your rescue if the hustlers' heat becomes unbearable. Consider hiring a guide, since it's helpful to have a translator, and once you're "taken," the rest seem to leave you alone.

Marijuana Alert: In Morocco, marijuana *(kif)* is as illegal as it is popular, a fact that many Westerners in local jails would love to remind you of. As a general rule, just walk right by those hand-carved pipes in the marketplace. Some dealers who sell it cheap make their profit after you get arrested. Cars and buses are stopped and checked by police routinely throughout Morocco—especially in the north and in the Chefchaouen region, which is Morocco's *kif* capital.

Health: Morocco is much more hazardous to your health than Spain or Portugal. Eat in clean—not cheap—places. Peel fruit, eat only cooked vegetables, and drink reliably bottled water (Sidi Harazem or Sidi Ali). When you do get diarrhea—and you should plan on it—adjust your diet (small and bland meals, no milk or grease) or fast for a day, but make sure you replenish lost fluids. Relax: Most diarrhea is not serious, just an adjustment that will run its course.

Closed Days: Friday is the Muslim day of rest, when most of the country (except Tangier) closes down.

Ramadan: During this major month-long religious holiday (Aug 11–Sept 10 in 2010), Muslims focus on prayer and reflection. Following Islamic doctrine, they refrain during daylight hours from eating, drinking (including water), smoking, and having sex. On the final day of Ramadan, Muslims celebrate *Eid* (an all-day feast and gift-giving party, similar to Christmas) and travelers may find some less-touristy stores and restaurants closed.

Money: Euros work here (as do dollars and pounds). If you're on a five-hour tour, bring along lots of €1 and €0.50 coins for tips, small purchases, and camel rides. But if you plan to do anything independently, change some money into Moroccan dirhams upon arrival (8 Moroccan dirhams = about $1). Banks and ATMs have uniform rates. If you use an exchange desk, just be sure you can see the buying and selling rates; they should be within 10 percent of each other with no extra fees. Don't leave the country with Moroccan money unless you want a souvenir, since few places in Spain are willing to change dirhams to euros or dollars.

Information: Travel information, English or otherwise, is rare here. For an extended trip, bring guidebooks from home or Spain. Lonely Planet and Rough Guide both publish good ones, and the green Michelin *Morocco* guidebook is worthwhile (if you read French). Buy the best map you can find locally—names are always changing, and it's helpful to have towns, roads, and place names written in Arabic.

Language: It's unusual to be in a country where a trilingual sign or menu doesn't include English. English ranks fourth here after Arabic, French, and Spanish. The Arabic squiggle-script, its many difficult sounds, and the fact that French is Morocco's second language combine to make communication tricky for English-speaking travelers. A little French goes a long way, but learn a few words in Arabic. Have your first local friend help you with the pronunciation:

English	Arabic	Pronounced
Hello. ("Peace be with you")	*Salaam alaikum.*	sah-LAHM ah-LAY-koom
Hello. (response: "Peace also be with you")	*Wa alaikum salaam.*	wah ah-LAY-koom sah-LAHM
Please.	*Min fadlik.*	meen FAHD-leek
Thank you.	*Shokran.*	SHOH-kron (like "sugar on")
Excuse me.	*Ismahli.*	ees-SMAH-lee
Yes.	*Yeh.*	EE-yeh
No.	*Lah.*	lah
Give me five. (kids enjoy this...not above but straight ahead)	*Ham sah.*	hahm sah
OK.	*Wah hah.*	wah hah
Very good.	*Miz yen biz ef.*	meez EE-yehn beez ehf
Goodbye.	*Maa salama.*	mah sah-LEM-ah

Moroccans are more touchy-feely than their Spanish neighbors. Expect lots of hugs if you make an effort to communicate. When greeting someone, a handshake is customary, followed by a fist over your heart. Listen carefully and write new words phonetically. Bring an Arabic phrase book. In markets, I sing, "la la la la la" to my opponents. *Lah shokran* means, "No, thank you."

Getting Around Morocco: Moroccan trains are quite good. Second class is cheap and comfortable. Buses connect all smaller towns quite well. By car, Morocco is easy, but drive defensively and never rely on the oncoming driver's skill. Night driving is dangerous. Pay a guard to watch your car overnight.

Keeping Your Bearings: Navigate the labyrinthine *medinas* (old towns) by altitude, gates, and famous mosques or buildings. Write down what gate you came in, so you can enjoy being lost—temporarily. *Souk* is Arabic for a particular market (such as leather, yarn, or metalwork).

TANGIER

Go to Africa. As you step off the boat, you realize that the crossing (less than an hour) has taken you further culturally than did the trip from the US to Spain. Morocco needs no museums; its sights are living in the streets. For decades, its coastal city of Tangier deserved its reputation as the "Tijuana of Africa." But that has changed. The new king is enthusiastic about Tangier, and there's a fresh can-do spirit in the air. The town is as Moroccan as ever...yet more enjoyable and less stressful.

Morocco in a Day?

While Morocco certainly deserves more than a day, many visitors touring Spain see it in a quick side-trip. And, though such a short sprint through Tangier is only a tease, it's far more interesting than another day in Spain. A day in Tangier gives you a good introduction to Morocco, a legitimate taste of North Africa, and a non-threatening slice of Islam. All you need is a passport (no visa or shots required) and €66 for the round-trip ferry crossing. Your big decisions: where to sail from; whether to go on your own or buy a ferry/guided tour day-trip package; and whether to make it a day trip or spend the night.

Time Difference: Morocco is on Greenwich Mean Time (like Great Britain), and does not observe Daylight Saving Time. This means it's two hours behind Spain in summer, and one hour behind in winter.

Terminology: Note that the Spanish refer to Morocco as "Marruecos" (mar-WAY-kohs) and Tangier as "Tanger" (pronounced with a guttural "g" at the back of the throat, sounding like TAHN-hair).

Going on Your Own, by Ferry from Tarifa

While the trip from Spain to Tangier can be made from three different ports (Tarifa, Algeciras, or Gibraltar), it's easiest, fastest, and cheapest from Tarifa. I'll describe the trip assuming you're sailing from Tarifa, which is most logical for the typical traveler.

Ferry Crossing: Just buy a ferry ticket (at the port, through your Tarifa hotel, or from a local travel agency). There is only one ferry company (FRS), and prices should be the same everywhere (€37 one-way, €66 round-trip). In summer, the ferry departs daily from Tarifa to Tangier at 9:00, 11:00, 13:00, 15:00,

17:00, 19:00, 21:00, and 23:00; and from Tangier to Tarifa at 7:00, 9:00, 11:00, 13:00, 15:00, 17:00, 19:00, and 21:00. In winter, boats leave Tangier on the even hours—the first at 8:00, and the last at 22:00 (the winter schedule starts when Daylight Saving Time ends in Spain). Because of its popularity with tours, the 9:00 ferry in July and August is sometimes too full for walk-ons. Boats are most crowded in July (when Moroccans in Spain go home for holiday), and in August (when the Costa del Sol groups come en masse). A few crossings a year are canceled because of storms or wind, mostly in winter.

Procedure: The ferry from Tarifa is a fast Nordic hydrofoil that theoretically takes 35 minutes to cross. It often leaves late. You'll go through Spanish customs at the port and Moroccan customs on the ferry. Whether taking a tour or traveling on your own, you *must* get a stamp (available on board) from the Moroccan immigration officer. After you leave Spain, find the customs desk on the boat, line up, and get your passport and entry paper stamped. If you're coming back the same day and know your return time, the immigration official will also give you an exit stamp (for your return from Morocco)—this prevents delays at the port at departure time. (If your return is open, you will have to go through a passport check and get your exit stamp on the way back to Spain.) The ferry is equipped with WCs, a shop, and a snack bar. Tarifa's modern little terminal has a cafeteria and WCs.

Hiring a Guide: Even if you're visiting Morocco independently, I recommend hiring a local guide to show you around Tangier (for tips, see "Guides," later in this chapter).

Taking a Tour

Taking a tour is easier but less rewarding than doing it on your own. A typical day-trip tour includes a round-trip crossing and a guide who meets you at a prearranged point in Tangier, then hustles you through the hustlers and onto your tour bus. Several guides await the arrival of each ferry in Tangier and assemble their groups. (Tourists wear stickers identifying which tour they're with.) All offer essentially the same five-hour Tangier experience: a city bus tour, possibly a trip to the desolate Atlantic Coast for some rugged African scenery, the famous ride-a-camel stop (five-minute camel ride for a couple of euros), a drive through the ritzy palace neighborhood, a walk through the medina (old town), and a too-thorough look at a sales-starved carpet shop (where prices include a 20 percent commission for your guide and tour company). The tour wraps up with lunch in a palatial Moroccan setting with live music (and non-Moroccan belly dancing), topped off by a final walk back to your boat through a gauntlet of desperate merchants.

Sound cheesy? It is. But no amount of packaging can gloss over this exotic and different culture. This kind of cultural voyeurism is almost embarrassing, but it's nonstop action. The shopping is...Moroccan. Bargain hard!

The day trip is so tightly organized that tourists have hardly any time alone in Tangier. For many people, that's just fine. But frankly, seeing a line of day-trippers clutching their bags nervously like paranoid kangaroos reminded me of the Tehran hostage crisis—the big difference being this one is self-imposed. It was pathetic.

You rarely need to book a tour more than a day in advance, even during peak season. Tours generally cost about €65, roughly the same price as a ferry ticket alone—the tour company makes its money off commissions if you shop, and gets a group rate on the ferry tickets. Prices are roughly the same at the various travel agencies. I wouldn't worry about which tour company you select. (They're all equally bad.)

Tours generally leave Tarifa on the 9:00 ferry and return at 13:00 (15:00 Spanish time), or they depart on the 13:00 ferry and return at 17:00 (19:00 Spanish time).

Those taking the tour have an option to spend the night at a fancy Tangier hotel (about €35 extra, includes dinner). If you stay overnight, the first day is the same as the one-day tour, but rather than catching the boat that afternoon, you take the same boat—on your own—24 hours later.

Independent types can also take the one-day tour (you'll need to stay with your group until you return to the ferry dock) and then just slip back into town thinking, "Freedom!" You're welcome to use your return ferry ticket on any later boat (departures every two hours).

Travel Agencies Offering Tours: Travel agencies throughout southern Spain sell Tangier ferry and ferry/tour tickets. Here are two in Tarifa: Marruecotur (daily in summer 7:40–21:00, across from the TI at Avenida de la Constitución 5, tel. 956-681-242) and Speedlines Tours (Batalla del Salado 10, tel. 956-627-048). Many hotels are happy to book a tour for you (ask when you reserve). If they offer this service and you want a tour, go for it.

You can also just drop by the port in Tarifa and buy your ferry/tour ticket directly from the ferry company (FRS Maroc at Tarifa's dock, tel. 956-684-847, www.frs.es). FRS also offers a **"VIP tour"** for up to four people. For an additional €15 per person (after buying individual ferry tickets), your group receives a private guide and vehicle, plus lunch. This is actually quite economical if you're traveling as a foursome.

Tangier

Artists, writers, and musicians have always loved Tangier. Matisse was drawn to the evocative light. The Beat generation, led by William S. Burroughs and Jack Kerouac, sought the city's multicultural, otherworldly feel. Paul Bowles found his sheltering sky here. From the 1920s through the 1950s, Tangier was an "international city," too strategic to give to any one nation, and jointly governed by France, Spain, Britain, and Italy. It attracted playboy millionaires, bon vivants, globetrotting scoundrels, con artists, and expat romantics.

Tangier is always defying expectations. Ruled by Spain in the 19th century and France in the 20th, it's a rare place, where signs are in three languages...and English doesn't make the cut. In this Muslim city, you'll find a synagogue, Catholic and Anglican churches, and the town's largest mosque within close proximity.

Because of its "international zone" status, Morocco's previous king neglected the city, denying it national funds for improvements. Neglected Tangier became the armpit of Morocco. But when the new king—Mohammed VI—was crowned in 1999, the first city he visited was Tangier. His vision is to restore Tangier to its former glory.

Thanks to King Mohammed VI, Tangier (with a population of 700,000 and growing) is experiencing a rebirth. Restorations are taking place on a grand scale: The beach has been painstakingly cleaned, pedestrian promenades are popping up everywhere, and gardens bloom with lush new greenery. In the works are a new soccer stadium and a project to move the shipping port beyond the bay where the ferry docks are (which will clear current traffic congestion and make Tangier's ferry terminal much more welcoming). However, the economic downturn has slowed much of the development in the city. Many once-active construction sites are now either empty or at least lethargic, with just a handful of workers and machines in action.

Nevertheless, I'm uplifted by the new Tangier—it's affluent and modern without having abandoned its roots and embraced Western values. A visit here lets a Westerner marinated in anti-Muslim propaganda see what Islam aspires to be, and can be—and realize it is not a threat to the West.

TANGIER

Planning Your Time

If you're on your own, either hire a guide upon arrival (see "Guides," later in this chapter), or stop by the TI first thing to get oriented (you can walk or catch a Petit Taxi from the port to the TI). Exit the TI to the right and continue up to Place de Faro, with its cannons and views back to Spain. Beyond that, at Place de France (at Café du Paris), turn right on Rue de la Liberté, which leads directly into Grand Socco square, the hub of old Tangier. Orient from here with the map on page 690. For the quickest visit, first cover the old town (Museum of the Kasbah, Dar el-Makhzen palace, Old American Legation Museum, and Petit Socco). Then catch a taxi to the beach (Plage de Corniche), and sightsee along the beach and then along Avenue Mohammed VI back to the port. You'll rarely see other tourists outside the tour-group circuit.

After Dark: Nighttime is great in Tangier. If spending the night, don't relax in a fancy hotel restaurant. Get out and about in the old town after dark. It's an entirely different experience and a highlight of any visit. (But remember, this isn't Spain—things die down by around 22:00.)

Orientation to Tangier

Like almost every city in Morocco, Tangier is split in two. From the ferry dock, you'll see the old town (medina)—encircled by its

medieval wall—on your right, behind Hotel Continental. The old town has the markets, the Kasbah (with its palace and the mosque of the Kasbah—marked by the higher of the two minarets you see), cheap hotels, homes both decrepit and recently renovated, and 2,000 wannabe guides. The twisty, hilly streets of the old town are caged within a wall accessible by keyhole gates. The larger minaret (on the left) belongs to the modern Mohammed V mosque—the biggest one in town.

The new town, where the TI and fancy hotels reside, sprawls past the industrial port zone to your left. The big square, Grand Socco, is the link between the old and new parts of town.

Because Tangier is the fifth-largest city in Morocco, many assume they'll get lost here. Although the city could use more street signs, it's laid out simply. Nothing listed under "Sights in Tangier" is more than a 15-minute walk from the port. Petit Taxis (described under "Getting Around Tangier," below) are a godsend for the hot and tired tourist. Use them liberally.

Tourist Information

Get a free map and advice at the TI. A little bit of French goes a long way here (Mon–Fri 8:30–16:30, closed Sat–Sun, in new town at Boulevard Pasteur 29, tel. 0539-94-80-50). They try to have a few guides standing by in the morning when boats arrive.

Arrival in Tangier

By Ferry

If you're taking a tour, just follow the leader.

Independent travelers will walk five minutes from the ferry past trucks and warehouses (follow signs to *sortie*), and through the gate at the end of the port. Change money at any little exchange desk (those at the gate are good—they have a straight and fair buy-and-sell rate and are open long hours).

The big Port de Tanger gateway (a few hundred yards from the ferry dock) defines the end of the port area and the start of the city. Leave mental breadcrumbs, so you can find your way back to your boat. Your first glimpse of the city will be a line of decent fish restaurants; restored French colonial buildings; and a fancy palm tree–lined pedestrian boulevard arcing along the beach into the new town. From this delightful square, stairs (on the right) lead up into the old town and the market.

A Petit Taxi is your easiest way into town (described under "Getting Around Tangier"); unfortunately, prices are not regulated from the port. An honest cabbie will charge you 10 dirhams (about $1.25) for a ride from the ferry into town, while less scrupulous drivers will try to charge closer to 100 dirhams. Set your price before hopping in.

By Plane

The Tangier Airport has expanded recently, but it's still quite small. Iberia, Royal Air Maroc, and easyJet fly from here to Madrid (easyJet may also open a route to London as well). To get

Tangier

STRAIT OF GIBRALTAR

BOATS TO SPAIN & GIBRALTAR

TO CAPE SPARTEL

GUIDES, HUSTLERS & WAITING TOUR BUSES

FERRY TERMINAL & CUSTOMS

PETIT & GRAND TAXIS

KASBAH

OLD TOWN

PORT

RUE DE LA KASBAH

RUE D'ITALIE

PETIT SOCCO

PORT DE TANGER GATEWAY

AVE HASSAN I

RUE AS-SIAGHIN

JEMAA KABIR

GRAND SOCCO

RUE BOUARRAQUIA

SEE OLD TOWN DETAIL MAP

RUE SIDI BOUABIB

RUE DE PORTUGAL

TO MOHAMMAD V MOSQUE

MARKET

FACTORY AREA

AVE D'ESPAGNE

RUE DE LA PLAGE

RUE D'ANGLETERRE

RUE DE LA LIBERTE

NEW CITY

STAIRS

BEACH "PLAGE DE CORNICHE"

KING MOHAMMAD VI

PLACE DE FRANCE

BLVD PASTEUR

RUE DE PRINCE

R. MARCO POLO

RUE DE MEXIQUE

MOULAY ABDALLAH

BLVD MOH AMMED V

RUE AL-ANTAKI

TO & TRAIN STN.

RUE ALLAL

VIEW

100 YARDS
100 METERS

1. Hotel Rembrandt
2. To Rif & Spa Hotel
3. Hotel El Djenina
4. Hotel d'Anjou
5. Hotel Andalucía
6. Le Saveur du Poisson
7. El Minzah Hotel & Rest.
8. Café du Paris
9. Place de Faro Viewpoint

into town, taxis should run you about 150 dirhams and take 30–45 minutes.

Getting Around Tangier

There are two types of taxis: Avoid the big, beige Mercedes "Grand Taxis," which are most aggressive and don't use their meters. Look instead for Petit Taxis—blue with a yellow stripe (they fit up to three people). These generally use their meters, are very cheap, and only circulate within the city. However, at the port, Petit Taxis are allowed to charge whatever you'll pay without using the meter, so it's essential to agree on a price up front (see "Arrival in Tangier," earlier).

Helpful Hints

Money: The exchange rate is 8 dirhams = about $1; 12 dirhams = about €1. The most convenient banks with ATMs are opposite the TI along Boulevard Pasteur. There are also several in the Grand Socco. While most businesses happily take euros or dollars, it's classier to use the local currency—and you'll save money. If you're on a tour, they'll rip you off anyway, so just stick with euros. If you're on your own, it's fun to get a pocket full of dirhams. ATMs work as you expect them to. Exchange desks are quick, easy, and fair. (Just understand the buy and sell rates—there should be no other fee. If you change €50 into dirhams and immediately change the dirhams back, you should have about €45.) Look for the official *Bureaux de Change* offices, where you'll get better rates than at the banks. There are some on Rue Pasteur, and a handful between the Grand and Petit Soccos. The first in a row is across from the Mamounia Palace restaurant on Rue As-Siaghin. The official change offices all offer the same rates, so there's no need to shop around.

Convert your dirhams back to euros before catching the ferry—it's cheap and easy to do here (change desks at the port keep long hours), but very difficult once you're back in Spain.

Telephone: To call Tangier from Spain, dial 00 (Europe's international access code), 212 (Morocco's country code), then the local number (dropping the initial zero). To dial Tangier from elsewhere in Morocco, dial the local number in full (keeping the initial zero).

In 2009, Moroccan phone numbers all added a new second digit—either a 5 (for land-line numbers) or a 6 (for mobile numbers). We've listed full numbers here, but in case you see older phone numbers listed elsewhere (on billboards, etc.), keep in mind that all Tangier phone numbers will start with either 0539 (land-line) or 0639 (mobile).

Navigation: Tangier's maps and street signs are frustrating. I ask in French for the landmark: *"oo ay Medina?"*, *"oo ay Kasbah?"*, and so on. It's fun to meet people this way. But to avoid getting unwanted company, ask for directions from people who can't leave what they're doing (such as the only clerk in a shop) or from women who aren't near men. There are fewer hustlers in the new (but less interesting) part of town. Be aware that most people don't know the names of the smaller streets (which don't usually have signs), and they tend to navigate by landmarks. In case you get the wrong directions, ask three

Women in Morocco

Most visitors to Tangier expect to see the women completely covered head-to-toe by their kaftan. In fact, only about one-quarter of Moroccan women still adhere strictly to this religious code. Some just cover their head (allowing their face to be seen), while others eliminate the head scarf altogether. Some women wear only Western-style clothing. This change in dress visibly reflects deeper, more fundamental shifts in Moroccan attitudes about women's rights.

Morocco happens to be one of the most progressive Muslim countries around. As in any border country, contact with other cultures fosters the growth of new ideas. Bombarded with Spanish television and visitors like you, change is inevitable. Another proponent of change is King Mohammed VI, who was only 35 years old when he rose to the throne in 1999. For the first time in the country's history, the king personally selected a female adviser to demonstrate his commitment to change. The king also married a commoner for...get this...*love*. And even more shocking, she's seen in public. (It's a first—locals don't even know what King Mohammed VI's mother looks like, as she is never in the public view.)

Recent times have brought even more sweeping transformations to Moroccan society. In order to raise literacy levels and understanding between the sexes, schools are now co-ed—something taken for granted in the West for decades. In 2004 the Mudawana, or judiciary family code, was shockingly overhauled. The legal age for women to marry is now 18 (just like men) instead of 15. Other changes make it more difficult to have a second wife. Verbal divorce and abandonment are no longer legal—disgruntled husbands must now take their complaints to court before divorce is granted. And for the first time, women can divorce their husbands. If children are involved, whoever takes care of the kids gets the house. Of course, not everyone has been happy with the changes, and Islamic fundamentalists were blamed for a series of bombings in Casablanca in 2003. But the reforms became law, and Morocco became a trendsetter for women's equality in the Islamic world.

times and go with the consensus. If there's no consensus, it's time to hop into a Petit Taxi.

Mosques: Mosques are not open to non-Muslim visitors in Tangier (unlike mosques in some other Muslim cities).

Guides

If you're on your own, you'll be to street guides what a horse's tail is to flies...all day. In order to have your own translator and a shield from less scrupulous touts who hit up tourists constantly throughout the old town, I recommend hiring a guide. Stress your interest in the people and culture rather than shopping. Guides, hoping to get a huge commission from your purchases, can cleverly turn your Tangier day into the Moroccan

equivalent of the Shopping Channel. Truth be told, some of these guides would work for free, considering all the money they make on commissions when you buy stuff.

That said, I've had good luck with the private guides who meet the boat. If you are a decent judge of character, interview guides when you get off the ferry, find one you click with, and negotiate a good price. These hardworking, English-speaking, and licensed guides offer their services for the day for €15.

To avoid the stress of being mobbed by potential guides at the port, book one before you arrive, and arrange for the guide to meet you at the port (through FRS in Tarifa, or through the guides' association—tel. 0539-931-372, dttanger@menara.com). Once in town, the TI (tel. 0539-948-050) can often set you up with a guide.

Aziz Begdouri is a great local guide who will show you the very best of his hometown. He enjoys teaching about Moroccan

society and culture. Aziz can also arrange ferry tickets from Tarifa in advance. He meets you at the boat. If you don't want to do any shopping, make it clear to him (5-hour walking tour—€15 per person, groups limited to 4–5 people; 8-hour grand tour with minibus ride to resorts, the Caves of Hercules, and Cape Spartel—€35 per person; easier to reach him from Spain on his Spanish mobile—tel. 607-897-967—than his Moroccan mobile, tel. 00-212-6-6163-9332 from Spain, aziztour@hotmail.com). Aziz is a friend. Even if you're not hiring him, give him a call if you're in a jam.

Sights in Tangier

▲▲**Grand Socco**—This big, noisy square is a transportation hub, market, and gateway to the medina (old town). Five years ago, it was a pedestrian nightmare and a perpetual traffic jam. Use the map to orient yourself from here, as this is the center of the visitor's Tangier. On the downhill side, a fancy gate leads into the medina. An incredible market is opposite the mosque.

Anglican Church—St. Andres Anglican Church was built in a Moorish style, but is still Christian. The Lord's Prayer rings the arch in Arabic, as verses of the Quran would in a mosque. The land on which the church sits was a gift from the sultan to the British community in 1881, during Queen Victoria's era. The church was built shortly thereafter. Knock on the door—Mustapha will greet you and give you a "thank you very munch" tour. Leave a donation in the church's alms box.

The Medina and Petit Socco—A maze of winding lanes and tiny alleys weave through the old-town market area. The Petit Socco,

a little square (souk) in the old town, is lined with tea shops. A casual first-time visitor cannot stay oriented. I just wander, knowing that uphill will eventually get me to the Kasbah and downhill will eventually lead me to the port. Expect to get a little lost...going around in circles is part of the fun. Pop in to see artisans working in their shops: mosaic tile-makers, thread spinners, tailors. Many people can't afford private ovens, phones, or running water, so there are economical communal options: phone desks, baths, and bakeries. Notice locals dropping off their ready-to-cook dough at bakeries. Ornate "keyhole" doors lead to neighborhood mosques. Green doors are the color of Islam and symbolize peace. The Petit Socco is a people- (and now tourist-) friendly little square, great for a mint tea and some casual people-watching.

The **Market,** just off the Grand Socco, is a highlight. Wander past piles of fruit, veggies, and olives, countless varieties of bread, and fresh goat cheese wrapped in palm leaves. Phew! Venturing right, you'll eventually come to less perishable (and less aromatic) items—clothing, recordable CDs, and lots of electronics. You'll find everything but pork. The chickens are plucked and hung to show they have been killed according to Islamic guidelines (Halal): Animals are slaughtered with a sharp knife in the name of Allah, head to Mecca, and drained of their blood.

• *When you've soaked in enough old-town atmosphere, make your way*

Tangier's Old Town

NOTE:
TANGIER'S OLD TOWN (MEDINA) IS
A MAZE OF TINY STREETS.
ONLY MAJOR STREETS ARE SHOWN.

TO
CAPE
SPARTEL

KASBAH
GATE

PLACE
DU
TABOR

R. RIAD SULTAN

TOWN

STRAIT
OF
GIBRALTAR

100 YARDS

100 METERS

WALLS

RUE TABOR

RUE DE LA KASBAH

KASBAH

PLACE
DE
LA KASBAH

TO
PORT

VIEW

R. JEN. CAPTAN RAISOUL

DAR EL BAROUD

BAB EL-
MARSA
(GATE)

RUE D'ITALIE

RUE AL MANZOR

OLD

ALMOHADES

TORRES

COMM.

JEMAA
EL-KEBIR
Mosque

MENDOUBIA
GARDENS

GATE

R. BOUARRAQUIA

RUE AS-SIAGHIN

MOKHTAR
AHARDAN

PORT DE
TANGER
GATEWAY

SIDI BOUABIB
Mosque

GRAND SOCCO

TOUAHINE

PETIT
SOCCO

TOWN

RUE DE LA PLAGE

RUE D'ANGLETERRE

RUE DE LA LIBERTE

RUE DE PORTUGAL

DCH

JEWISH
CEMETERY

NEW   TOWN

TO BEACH
PROMENADE

1 Hotel Continental
2 Hamadi Restaurant
3 Mamounia Palace Rest.
4 Maison Communitaire
   des Femmes (Café)

5 Tangier American Legation Mus.
6 Rif Cinema
7 Anglican Church
8 Market
9 Bureau de Change

*to the Kasbah (see map). Within the medina, head uphill, or exit the
medina gate and go right on Rue de la Kasbah, which follows the old
wall uphill to Porte de la Kasbah, a gateway into the Kasbah.*

Kasbah—This is the fortress (now a residential area) atop old
Tangier. On Place de la Kasbah, you'll find the Dar el-Makhzen,
a former sultan's palace that now houses a history museum (10
dirhams, Wed–Mon 9:00–16:00, closed Tue, tel. 0539-932-097,
no English, building more interesting than exhibit). You'll also
encounter a vivid gauntlet of amusements waiting to ambush

parading tour groups: snake charmers, squawky dance troupes, and colorful water vendors. Before descending out of the Kasbah, don't miss the ocean viewpoint. The artist Matisse, who traveled here in 1912, was inspired by his wanderings through this area, picking up themes that show up in much of his art.

Leaving the Kasbah, on your way downhill you'll pass the colorful Kodak-moment hustlers who make their living off the many tour groups passing by daily. (As you're cajoled, remember that the daily minimum wage here for men as skilled as these beggars is $10. That's what the gardeners you'll pass in your walk earn each day. In other words, a €1 tip is an hour's wage for these people.) A few steps past the lowest corner, you come to a musical ambush. If you draft behind a tour group, you won't be the focus of the hustlers. If you take a photo, you must pay.

Tangier American Legation Museum—Morocco was one of the first countries to recognize the newly formed United States as an independent country (in 1777). The original building, given to the United States by the sultan of Morocco, became the fledgling government's first foreign acquisition. This was the US embassy (or consulate) in Morocco from 1821 to 1956, and it's still American property—our only National Historic Landmark overseas. Today this nonprofit museum and research center, housed in a 19th-century mansion, is a strangely peaceful oasis within Tangier's intense old town. It offers a warm welcome and lots of interesting artifacts: a 19th-century safe, a letter with the news of Lincoln's assassination, photos of kings with presidents, and paintings—all well described in English in an evocative building. A visit here is a fun reminder of how long the US and Morocco have had good relations (guided English tour free but donations appreciated, Mon–Thu 10:00–13:00 & 15:00–17:00, Fri 10:00–12:00 & 15:00–17:00, during Ramadan holiday 10:00–15:00, closed Sat–Sun, ring bell, Rue d'Amérique 8, tel. 0539-935-317, www.maroc.net/museums).

Tangier Beach (Plage de Corniche)—Lined with lots of entertaining and fishy eateries, this fine, wide white-sand crescent beach stretches eastward from the port. It's packed with locals doing what people around the world do at the beach—with a few variations. Traditionally clad moms let their kids run wild. Along with lazy camels, you'll see people—young and old—covered in hot sand to combat rheumatism. Early, late, and off-season, the beach becomes a popular venue for soccer teams. The palm-lined pedestrian street along the waterfront was renamed for King Mohammed VI, in appreciation for recent restorations.

Just past the beach on the port side is a zone of nondescript factories. Here local women sew clothing for big, mostly European companies that pay $8 a day. Each morning and evening rush hour, the street is filled with these women commuters...on foot.

Evenings in Tangier—Most important: Be out in the **medina** around 21:00. In the cool of the evening, the atmospheric squares and lanes become even more evocative. Then at about 22:00 things get dark, lonely, and foreboding.

El Minzah Hotel hosts **traditional music** most nights (see "Eating in Tangier"; 85 Rue de la Liberté, tel. 0539-935-885).

The **Rif Cinema** shows movies in French—which the younger generation must learn—and Arabic. The cinema is worth popping into, if only to see the Art Deco interior. As movies cost only 15 dirhams, consider dropping by to see a bit of whatever's on...in Arabic (on the Grand Socco, tel. 0539-934-683).

Sleeping in Tangier

These hotels are centrally located, near the TI, and within walking distance of the market. The first two are three-star hotels and take credit cards; the others are cash-only. To reserve from Europe, dial 00 (Europe's international access code), 212 (Morocco's country code), 539 (Tangier's city code), then the local number. July through mid-September is high season, when rooms may be a bit more expensive and reservations are wise. Most hotels charge an extra tax of 10 dirhams per person per night (included in the prices I've listed here).

$$$ Hotel Rembrandt just feels like the 1940s, with a restaurant, bar, and swimming pool surrounded by a great grassy garden. Its 75 rooms are clean and comfortable, and some come with views (Sb-530–630 dirhams, Db-710–780 dirhams, higher prices are for June–Aug, sea view-100 dirhams extra, includes tax, breakfast-80 dirhams, air-con, elevator, Boulevard Mohammed VI 1, tel. 0539-937-870, fax 0539-930-443, www.hotel-rembrandt .com, hotelrembrandt@menara.ma).

Sleep Code

(8 dirhams = about $1, country code: 212, area code: 539)

S = Single, **D** = Double/Twin, **T** = Triple, **Q** = Quad, **b** = bathroom, **s** = shower only. Unless otherwise noted, credit cards are accepted, English is spoken, and breakfast is included.

To help you easily sort through these listings, I've divided the rooms into three categories, based on the price for a standard double room with bath (during high season):

$$$ Higher Priced—Most rooms 500 dirhams or more.

$$ Moderately Priced—Most rooms between 300-600 dirhams.

$ Lower Priced—Most rooms 300 dirhams or less.

$$$ Rif & Spa Hotel, recently restored to its 1970s glamour, is a worthy splurge. Offering 130 plush, modern rooms, sprawling public spaces, a garden, a pool, and grand views, it feels like an oversized boutique hotel. The great Arabic lounge with harbor view is a momentum-buster (Sb-1,060–1,150 dirhams, Db-1,220–1,460 dirhams, includes tax, see website for specials, breakfast-100 dirhams, air-con, elevator, 3 restaurants, Avenue Mohammed VI 152, tel. 0539-349-300, fax 0539-321-904, www.hotelsatlas.com, riftanger@menara.ma).

$$ Hotel Continental is the Humphrey Bogart option, a grand old place sprawling along the old town. It overlooks the port, with lavish atmospheric and recently renovated public spaces, a chandeliered breakfast room, and 70 spacious bedrooms with rough hardwood floors and new bathrooms. Jimmy, who's always around and runs the shop adjacent to the lobby, says he offers everything but Viagra. When I said, "I'm from Seattle," he said, "206." Test him—he knows your area code (Sb-422 dirhams, Db-552 dirhams, about 100 dirhams more July–Sept, includes tax and breakfast, cash only, Dar Baroud 36, tel. 0539-931-024, fax 0539-931-143, hcontinental@iam.net.ma).

$$ Hotel El Djenina is a local-style business-class hotel—extremely plain, reliable, safe, and well-located. Its 30 rooms are a block off the harbor, midway between the port and the TI. Request a room on the back side to escape the street noise (Sb-292–356 dirhams, Db-356–464 dirhams, higher prices are for mid-May–Aug, cash only, tel. 0539-942-244, fax 0539-942-246, Rue al-Antaki 8, eldjenina@menara.ma).

$ Hotel d'Anjou is a sleepable dive—the best dirt-cheap option I could find—renting 20 safe-feeling rooms on a quiet street two blocks off the harbor (Sb-140–215 dirhams, Db-160–270 dirhams, Tb-220–320 dirhams, higher prices are for summer, breakfast included only in summer, cash only, just off Rue al-Antaki at Rue Ibn Albanna 3, tel. & fax 0539-942-784, Hakim speaks English).

$ Hotel Andalucía is solid, clean, and minimal. It's in the new town, about a 20-minute walk from the Grand Socco. It has 19 rooms, a small reception, and a peaceful lobby (Sb-195–230 dirhams, Db-230–260 dirhams, higher prices are for mid-June–mid-Sept, cash only, Rue Ibn Hazim 14, tel. 0539-941-334, Azdeen speaks a little English).

Eating in Tangier

For the local equivalent of a yacht club restaurant, survey the places along the beach. The first two places I list below are buried in the medina and are disgustingly touristy. As they're designed for groups, the only locals you'll see here are the waiters. Still, they offer travelers a safe, comfortable break. The last three include a seafood paradise hole-in-the-wall; a big, fancy hotel restaurant with live traditional music; and a charity-run refuge that provides a quality, low-stress, and safe lunch.

Tourist Traps: Hamadi is as luxurious a restaurant as a tourist can find in Morocco, with good food at reasonable prices (Rue Kasbah 2, tel. 0539-934-514). **Mamounia Palace** is right on the Petit Socco and more in the middle of the action. A meal here will cost you about 100 dirhams for three courses—less if you order from the menu. Both of these places are tour-group hell and make you thankful to be free.

Le Saveur du Poisson is an excellent choice for the more adventurous, featuring one Tiki Hut–type room with a busy kitchen. There are no choices here. Just sit down and let owner Muhammad or his son, Hassan, take care of the rest. You get a rough one-use spoon and fork carved just for you...a fine souvenir. Surrounded by lots of locals and unforgettable food, you'll be treated to a multi-course menu. Savor the delicious fish dishes—Tangier is one of the few spots in Morocco where seafood is a major part of the diet. The fruit punch—a mix of seasonal fruits brewed overnight in a vat—simmers in the back room. Ask for an explanation, or even a look. After trying their dessert, Nuts 'n' Honey will never be the same. The big sink in the room is for locals who prefer to eat with their fingers (150-dirham fixed-price meal, Sat–Thu 12:00–16:00 & 19:00–22:00, closed Fri and during Ramadan; walk down Rue de la Liberté—roughly a block past El Minzah Hotel, take the stairs on the right and go down until you see fish on the grill, Escalier Waller 2, tel. 0539-336-326).

El Minzah Hotel offers a fancier yet still authentic experience. The atmosphere is classy but low-stress. It's where unadventurous tourists and local elites dine. Dress up and choose between a continental (French) dining area or the Moroccan lounge, where you'll be serenaded by live traditional music (music nightly 20:00–23:00, belly-dance show at 21:30 and 22:30, no extra charge for music). Entrées (including *tajines* and couscous) in either restaurant average 180 dirhams. There's also a cozy wine bar here—a rarity in a Muslim country. Light meals and salads are served poolside (daily 13:00–16:00 & 20:00–22:00, Rue de la Liberté 85, tel. 0539-935-885, www.elminzah.com).

Maison Communitaire des Femmes, a community center for women, hides an inexpensive, hearty lunch spot that's open to everyone. A tasty three-course lunch is only 50 dirhams. Profits support the work of the center (Mon–Sat 12:00–16:00, last order at 15:30, also open 9:30–11:30 & 15:30–18:00 for cakes and tea, closed Sun, near slipper market just outside Grand Socco, Place du 9 Avril).

Connections

In Tangier, all train traffic comes and goes from the suburban Gare Tanger Ville train station, one mile from the city center and a short Petit Taxi ride away (10–20 dirhams). If you're traveling inland, check the information booth at the entrance of the train station for schedules (www.oncf.ma).

From Tangier by Train to: Rabat (5/day, 5 hrs), **Casablanca** (station also called **Casa Voyageurs**, 6/day, 5 hrs), **Marrakech** (4/day, 12 hrs), **Fès** (4/day, 4.5 hrs).

From Tangier by Bus to: Ceuta and **Tétouan** (hourly, 1 hr).

From Fès to: Casablanca (9/day, 4.5 hrs), **Marrakech** (7/day, 7 hrs), **Rabat** (9/day, 4 hrs), **Meknès** (10/day, 45 min), **Tangier** (5/day, 5.5 hrs).

From Rabat to: Casablanca (2/hr, 45 min), **Fès** (9/day, 3.5 hrs), **Tétouan** (2 buses/day, 4.5 hrs, 3 trains/day, 6 hrs).

From Casablanca to: Marrakech (9/day, 3.5 hrs).

From Marrakech to: Meknès (7/day, 7 hrs), **Ouarzazate** (4 buses/day, 4 hrs).

By Plane: Flights within Morocco are convenient and reasonable (about $150 one-way from Tangier to Casablanca).

Extended Tour of Morocco

Morocco gets much better as you go deeper into the interior. The country is incredibly rich in cultural thrills, though you'll pay a

price in hassles and headaches—it's a package deal. But if adventure is your business, Morocco is a great option. Invest in a good Morocco guidebook to make this trip. Below are a few tips and insights to get you started.

To get a fair look at Morocco, you must get past the hustlers and con artists of the north coast (Tangier, Tétouan). It takes a minimum of four or five days to make a worthwhile visit—ideally seven or eight. Plan at least two nights in either Fès or Marrakech. A trip over the Atlas Mountains gives you an exciting look at Saharan Morocco. If you need a vacation from your vacation, check into one of the idyllic Atlantic beach resorts on the south coast. Above all, get past the northern day-trip-from-Spain, take-a-snapshot-on-a-camel fringe. (Oops, that's us. Oh, well.)

If you're relying on public transportation for your extended tour, sail to Tangier, blast your way through customs, ignore any hustler who tells you there's no way out until tomorrow, and hop into a Petit Taxi for the Tanger Ville train station one mile away. From there, set your sights on Rabat, a dignified, European-type town with fewer hustlers, and make it your get-acquainted stop in Morocco. Trains go farther south from Rabat.

If you're driving a car, crossing the border can be a bit unnerving, since you'll be forced to jump through several bureaucratic hoops. You'll go through customs at both borders, buy Moroccan insurance for your car (cheap and easy), and feel at the mercy of a bristly bunch of shady-looking people you'd rather not be at the mercy of. Don't pay anyone on the Spanish side. Consider tipping a guy on the Moroccan side if you feel he'll shepherd you through. Relax and let him grease those customs wheels. He's worth it. As soon as possible, hit the road and drive to Chefchaouen, the best first stop for those with their own wheels.

Moroccan Towns

▲▲**Chefchaouen**—Just two hours by bus or car from Tétouan, this is the first pleasant town beyond the north coast. Monday and Thursday are colorful market days. Stay in the classy old Hotel Chaouen on Place el-Makhzen. The Hotel Parador (historic inn, but not the same as the Spanish government–run chain) faces the old town and offers fine meals and a refuge from hustlers. Wander deep into the whitewashed old town from here.

▲▲**Rabat**—Morocco's capital and most European city, Rabat is the most comfortable and least stressful place to start your North African trip. You'll find a colorful market (in the old neighboring town of Salé), bits of Islamic architecture (Mausoleum of Mohammed V), the king's palace, mellow hustlers, and fine hotels.

▲▲▲**Fès**—More than just a funny hat that tipsy Shriners wear, Fès is Morocco's religious and artistic center, bustling with craftspeople, pilgrims, shoppers, and shops. Like most large Moroccan cities, it has a distinct new town from the French colonial period, as well as an exotic (and stressful) old, walled Arabic town (the medina), where you'll find the market.

For 12 centuries, traders have gathered in Fès, founded on a river at the crossroads of two trade routes. Soon there was an irrigation system, a university, resident craftsmen from Spain, and a diverse population of Muslims, Christians, and Jews. When France claimed Morocco in 1912, they made their capital in Rabat, and Fès fizzled. But the Fès marketplace is still Morocco's best.

▲▲▲**Marrakech**—Morocco's gateway to the south, Marrakech is where the desert, mountain, and coastal regions merge. This market city is a constant folk festival, bustling with Berber tribespeople and a colorful center. The new city has the train station, and the main boulevard (Mohammed V) is lined with banks, airline offices, a post office, a tourist office, and comfortable hotels. The old city features the maze-like market and the huge Djemaa el-Fna, a square seething with people—a 43-ring Moroccan circus.

▲▲▲**Over the Atlas Mountains**—Extend your Moroccan trip several days by heading south over the Atlas Mountains. Take a bus from Marrakech to Ouarzazate (short stop), and then to Tinerhir (great oasis town, comfy hotel, overnight stop). The next day go to Er Rachidia and take the overnight bus to Fès.

By car, drive from Fès south, staying in the small mountain town of Ifrane, and then continue deep into the desert country past Er Rachidia and on to Rissani (market days: Sun, Tue, and Thu). Explore nearby mud-brick towns still living in the Middle Ages. Hire a guide to drive you past where the road stops, and head cross-country to an oasis village (Merzouga), where you can climb a sand dune and watch the sun rise over the vastness of Africa. Only a sea of sand separates you from Timbuktu.

SPAIN: PAST AND PRESENT

The distinctive Spanish culture has been shaped by the country's history. Roman emperors, Muslim sultans, hard-core Christians, conquistadors, French dandies, and Fascist dictators have all left their mark on Spain's art, architecture, and customs. Start by understanding the country's long history of invasions and religious wars, and you'll better appreciate the churches, museums, and monuments you'll visit today.

History

In 1492, Columbus sailed the ocean blue—and Spain became a nation, too. Iberia's sunny weather, fertile soil, and Mediterranean ports made it a popular place to call home. The original "Iberians" were a Celtic people, who crossed the Pyrenees around 800 B.C. The Phoenicians established the city of Cádiz around 1100 B.C., and Carthaginians settled around 250 B.C.

Romans (c. 200 B.C.–A.D. 400)

The future Roman Emperor Augustus finally quelled the last Iberian resistance (19 B.C.), making the province of "Hispania" an agricultural breadbasket (olives, wine) to feed the vast Roman Empire. The Romans brought the Latin language, a connection to the wider world, and (in the fourth century) Christianity. When the empire crumbled around A.D. 400, Spain made a peaceful transition, ruled by Christian Visigoths from Germany who had strong Roman ties. Roman influence remained for centuries after, in the Latin-based Spanish language, irrigation, and building materials and techniques. The Romans' large farming estates would change hands over the years, passing from Roman senators to Visigoth kings to Islamic caliphs to Christian nobles. And, of course, the Romans left wine.

Moors (711–1492)

In A.D. 711, 12,000 zealous members of the world's newest religion—Islam—landed on the Rock of Gibraltar and, in three short years, conquered the Iberian Peninsula. These North African Muslims—generically called "Moors"—dominated Spain for the next 700 years. Though powerful, they were surprisingly tolerant of the people they ruled, allowing native Jews and Christians to practice their faiths, so long as the infidels paid extra taxes.

The Moors were themselves an ethnically diverse culture, including both crude Berber tribesmen from Morocco and sophisticated rulers from old Arab families. From their capital in Córdoba, various rulers of the united Islamic state of "Al-Andalus" pledged allegiance to foreign caliphs in Syria, Baghdad, or Morocco.

With cultural ties that stretched from Spain to Africa to Arabia to Persia and beyond, the Moorish culture in Spain (especially around A.D. 800–1000) was perhaps Europe's most advanced, a beacon of learning in Europe's so-called "Dark" Ages. Mathematics, astronomy, literature, and architecture flourished. Even winemaking was encouraged, though for religious reasons Muslims weren't allowed to drink alcohol. The Moorish legacy lives on today in architecture (horseshoe arches, ceramic tiles, fountains, and gardens), language (e.g., Spanish *el* comes from Arabic *al*)...and wine.

SPAIN: PAST & PRESENT

Reconquista (711–1492)

The Moors ruled for more than 700 years, but throughout that time they were a minority ruling a largely Christian populace. Pockets of independent Christians remained, particularly in the mountains in the peninsula's north. Local Christian kings fought against the Moors whenever they could, whittling away at the Muslim empire, "reconquering" more and more land in what's known as the "Reconquista." The last Moorish stronghold, Granada, fell to the Christians in 1492.

The slow, piecemeal process of the Reconquista split the peninsula into many independent kingdoms and dukedoms, some Christian, some Moorish.

The Reconquista picked up steam after A.D. 1000, when Al-Andalus splintered into smaller regional states—Granada, Sevilla,

Spaniards Throughout History

Hadrian (A.D. 76–138)—Roman Emperor, one of three born in Latin-speaking "Hispania" (along with Trajan, reigned 98–117, and Marcus Aurelius, reigned 161–180), who ruled Rome at its peak of power.

El Cid (1040?–1099)—A real soldier-for-hire who inspired fictional stories and Spain's oldest poem, El Cid (literally, "The Lord") fought for both Christians and Muslims during the wars of the Reconquista. He's best known for liberating Valencia from the Moors.

St. Teresa of Ávila (1515–1582)—Mystic nun whose holiness and writings led to convent reform and to her sainthood. Religiously intense Spain produced other saints, too, including **Dominic** (1170–1221), who founded an order of wandering monks, and **Ignatius of Loyola** (1491–1556), who founded the Jesuits, an order of "intellectual warriors."

Ferdinand (1452–1516) and Isabel (1451–1504)—Their marriage united most of Spain, ushering in its Golden Age. The "Catholic Monarchs" drove out Moors and Jews, and financed Columbus' lucrative voyages to the New World.

Hernán Cortés (1485–1547)—Conquered Mexico in 1521. Along with Vasco Núñez de Balboa, who discovered the Pacific, and Francisco Pizarro, who conquered Peru, Cortés and other Spaniards explored and exploited the New World.

El Greco (1541–1614)—The artist is known for his ethereal paintings of "flickering" saints.

Diego Velázquez (1599–1660)—Velázquez painted camera-eye realistic portraits of the royal court.

Valencia—ruled by local caliphs. Toledo fell to the Christians in 1085. By 1200, the neighboring Christian state of Portugal had the borders it does today, making it the oldest unchanged state in Europe. The rest of the peninsula was a battleground, a loosely knit collection of small kingdoms, some Christian, some Muslim. Heavy stone "castles" dotted the interior region of "Castile," as lords and barons duked it out. Along the Mediterranean coast (from the Pyrenees to Barcelona to Valencia), three Christian states united into a sea-trading power, the kingdom of Aragon.

In 1469, Isabel of Castile married Ferdinand II of Aragon, uniting the peninsula's two largest kingdoms, and instantly making united Spain a European power. In 1492, while Columbus explored the seas under Ferdinand and Isabel's flag, the Catholic Monarchs (Ferdinand and Isabel) drove the Moors out of Granada and expelled the country's Jews, creating a unified, Christian, militaristic nation-state, fueled by the religious zeal of the Reconquista.

Francisco de Goya (1746–1828)—The artist is best known for his expressionistic nightmares (see page 345 for more).

Francisco Franco (1892–1975)—General who led the military uprising against the elected Republic, sparking Spain's Civil War (1936–1939). After victory, he ruled Spain for more than three decades as an absolute dictator, maintaining its Catholic, aristocratic heritage while slowly modernizing the country.

Salvador Dalí (1904–1989)—A flamboyant, waxed-mustachioed Surrealist painter, Dalí and a fellow Spaniard, filmmaker Luis Buñuel, made one of the first art films, *An Andalusian Dog* (see sidebar on page 114).

Pablo Picasso (1881–1973)—Though he lived most of his adult life in France, the 20th century's greatest artist explored Spanish themes, particularly in his famous work *Guernica,* which depicts Civil War destruction (see sidebar on page 356).

Placido Domingo (b. 1941)—The son of zarzuela singers in Madrid (but raised in Mexico), this operatic tenor is just one of many classical musicians from Spain, including fellow "Three Tenors" singer José Carreras, composer Manuel de Falla, cellist Pablo Casals, and guitarist Andrés Segovia.

Spaniards in the News Today—King Juan Carlos I and his Greek-born wife, Queen Sofía; their son Felipe and his wife, Letizia; left-of-center prime minister José Luis Rodríguez Zapatero; bicyclists Oscar Pereiro, Igor Astarloa, and Tour de France cyclist Alberto Contador; soccer star Raúl; golfer Sergio Garcia; tennis player Rafael Nadal; pop singer Julio Iglesias (father of pop singer Enrique Iglesias); and Oscar Award–winning actor Javier Bardem and movie directors Pedro Almodóvar and Pedro Amenábar.

The Golden Age (1500–1600)

Spain's bold sea explorers changed the economics of Europe, opening up a New World of riches and colonies. The Spanish flag

soon flew over most of South and Central America. Gold, silver, and agricultural products (grown on large estates with cheap labor) poured into Spain. In return, the stoked Spaniards exported Christianity, converting the American natives with kind Jesuit priests and cruel conquistadors.

Ferdinand and Isabel's daughter (Juana the Mad) wed a German prince (Philip the Fair), and their son inherited both crowns. Charles V (1500–1558, called Carlos I in Spain) was the most powerful man in the world, ruling an empire that stretched

SPAIN: PAST & PRESENT

Six Dates that Changed Spain

711   Muslims from North Africa invade and occupy Iberia.

1492   Columbus sails Spain into a century of wealth and power.

1588   Spain's Armada is routed by the British, and the country's slow decline begins.

1898   Thrashed by the US in the Spanish-American War, Spain reaches a low ebb.

1936   The Civil War begins, killing hundreds of thousands during its three-year span, and brings on more than three decades of Franco's fascist rule.

1975   King Juan Carlos I leads the nation to democracy and the European Union.

from Holland to Sicily, and from Bohemia to Bolivia. The aristocracy and the clergy were swimming in money. Art and courtly life flourished during this Golden Age, with Spain hosting the painter El Greco and the writer Miguel de Cervantes.

But Charles V's Holy Roman Empire was torn by different languages and ethnic groups, and by protesting Protestants. He spent much of the nation's energies at war with Protestants, encroaching Muslim Turks, and Europe's rising powers. When an exhausted Charles announced his abdication (1555) and retired to a monastery, his sprawling empire was divvied up among family members, with Spain and its possessions going to his son, Philip II (1527–1598).

Philip II conquered Portugal (1580, his only successful war), moved Spain's capital to Madrid, built El Escorial, and continued fighting losing battles across Europe (the Netherlands, France) that drained the treasury of its New World gold. In the summer of 1588, Spain's seemingly unbeatable royal fleet of 125 ships—the Invincible Armada—sailed off to conquer England, only to be unexpectedly routed in battle by bad weather and Sir Francis Drake's cunning. Just like that, Britannia ruled the waves, and Spain spiraled downward, becoming a debt-ridden, overextended, flabby nation.

Slow Decline (1600–1900)

The fast money from the colonies kept Spain from seeing the dangers at home. They stopped growing their own wheat and neglected their fields. Great Britain and the Netherlands were the rising sea-trading powers in the new global economy. During the centuries when science and technology developed as never before in other European countries, Spain was preoccupied by its failed colonial politics. (Still, Spain in the 1600s produced the remarkable painter Diego Velázquez.)

By 1700, once-mighty Spain lay helpless while rising powers France, England, and Austria fought over the right to pick Spain's next king in the War of the Spanish Succession (1701–1714), which was fought partly on Spanish soil (e.g., Britain holding out against the French in the Siege of Gibraltar). The rightful next-in-line was Louis XIV's son, who was set to inherit both France and Spain. The rest of Europe didn't want powerful France to become even stronger. The war ended in compromise, preventing Louis XIV from controlling both countries, but allowing his grandson to become King of Spain (Spain lost several possessions). The French-born, French-speaking Bourbon King Philip V (1683–1746) ruled Spain for 40 years. He and his heirs made themselves at home building the Versailles-like Royal Palace in Madrid and La Granja near Segovia.

The French Revolution spilled over into Spain, bringing French rule under Napoleon. In 1808, the Spaniards rose up (chronicled by Goya's paintings of the second and third of May, 1808), sparking the Peninsular War—called the War of Independence by Spaniards—that finally won Spain's independence from French rule.

Nineteenth-century Spain was a backward nation, with internal wars over which noble family should rule (the Carlist Wars), liberal revolutions put down brutally, and political assassinations. Spain gradually lost its global possessions to other European powers and to South American revolutionaries. Spain hit rock bottom in 1898, when the upstart United States picked a fight and thrashed them in the Spanish-American War, taking away Spain's last major possessions: Cuba, Puerto Rico, and the Philippines.

The 20th Century

A drained and disillusioned Spain was ill-prepared for modern technology and democratic government.

The old ruling class (the monarchy, church, and landowners) fought new economic powers (cities, businessmen, labor unions) in a series of coups, strikes, and sham elections. In the 1920s, a military dictatorship under Miguel Primo de Rivera kept the old guard in power. In 1930, he was ousted and an open election brought a modern democratic Republic to power. But the right wing regrouped under the Falange (fascist) party, fomenting unrest and sparking a military coup against the Republic in 1936, supported by General Francisco Franco (1892–1975).

For three years (1936–1939), Spain fought a bloody Civil War between Franco's Nationalists (also called Falangists) and the Republic (also called Loyalists). Some 600,000 Spaniards died (due to all causes), and Franco won. (For more on the Civil War, see "Valley of the Fallen," page 400.) For nearly the next four decades, Spain was ruled by Franco, an authoritarian, church-blessed dictator who tried to modernize the backward country while shielding it from corrupting modern influences. Spain was neutral in World War II, and the country spent much of the postwar era as a world apart. (On my first visit to Spain in 1973, I came face-to-face with fellow teenagers—me in backpack and shorts, the Spaniards in military uniforms, brandishing automatic weapons.)

Before Franco died, he handpicked his protégé, King Juan Carlos I, to succeed him. But to everyone's surprise, the young, conservative, mild-mannered king stepped aside, settled for a figurehead title, and guided the country quickly and peacefully toward democratic elections (1977).

Spain had a lot of catching up to do. Culturally, the once-conservative nation exploded and embraced new ideas, even plunging to wild extremes. In the 1980s, Spain flowered under the left-leaning Prime Minister Felipe González. Spain showed the world its new modern face in 1992, hosting both a World Exhibition at Sevilla and the Summer Olympics at Barcelona.

Spain Today

From 1996 to 2004, Spain was led by the centrist Prime Minister José María Aznar. He adopted moderate policies to minimize the stress on the country's young democracy, fighting problems such as unemployment and foreign debt with reasonable success. However, his support of George W. Bush's pre-emptive war in Iraq was extremely unpopular with the vast majority of Spaniards. In spring of 2004, the retiring Aznar supported a similarly centrist successor, Mariano Rajoy, who seemed poised to win the election. On the eve of the election, on March 11, three Madrid train stations were bombed at the height of rush hour, killing 200 people. The terrorist group claiming responsibility denounced Spain's Iraq policy, and three days later, Aznar's party lost the election. The new prime minister, left-of-center José Luis Rodríguez Zapatero, quickly began pulling Spain's troops out of Iraq, as well as enacting sweeping social changes in Spain.

Until recently, Spain enjoyed a strong economy, thanks in part to a thriving tourism industry and a real-estate boom. But the country was hit hard by the global economic downturn, resulting in a high unemployment rate. Because it's such a tourist draw, Spain is in a good position to rebound.

Artists

El Greco (1541–1614) exemplifies the spiritual fervor of much Spanish art. The drama, the surreal colors, and the intentionally unnatural distortion have the intensity of a religious vision. (For more on El Greco, see page 351.)

Diego Velázquez (1599–1660) went to the opposite extreme. His masterful court portraits are studies in camera-eye realism and cool detachment from his subjects. Velázquez was unmatched in using a few strokes of paint to suggest details.

Francisco de Goya (1746–1828) lacked Velázquez's detachment. He let his liberal tendencies shine through in unflattering portraits of royalty, and in emotional scenes of abuse of power. He unleashed his inner passions in the eerie, nightmarish canvases of his last, "dark" stage. (For more on Goya, see page 345.)

Bartolomé Murillo (1617–1682) painted a dreamy world of religious visions. His pastel, soft-focus works of cute baby Jesuses and radiant Virgin Marys helped make Catholic doctrine palatable to the common folk at a time when many were defecting to Protestantism. (For more on Murillo, see page 520.)

You'll also find plenty of foreign art in Spain's museums. During its Golden Age, Spain's wealthy aristocrats bought wagonloads of the most popular art of the time—Italian Renaissance and Baroque works by Titian, Tintoretto, and others. They also loaded up on paintings by Peter Paul Rubens, Hieronymus Bosch, and Pieter Brueghel from the Low Countries, which were then under Spanish rule.

In the 20th century, **Pablo Picasso** (see his inspirational antiwar *Guernica* mural in Madrid, described on page 356), **Joan Miró**, and Surrealist **Salvador Dalí** (see sidebar on page 114) made their marks. Great museums featuring all three are in or near Barcelona.

Architecture
Spanish History Set in Stone

The two most fertile periods of architectural innovation in Spain were during the Moorish occupation and in the Golden Age. Otherwise, Spanish architects marched obediently behind the rest of Europe. Modern architects have finally brought Spain back to the forefront of construction and design.

Spain's history is dominated by 700 years of pushing the

Church Architecture

Knowing a few simple terms will make your church visit a lot richer. Note that not every church will have every feature, and that a "cathedral" isn't a type of architecture, but rather a governing center for a local bishop.

Aisles: The long, generally low-ceilinged arcades that flank the nave.

Altar: The raised area with a ceremonial table (often adorned with candles or a crucifix), where the priest prepares and serves the bread and wine for Communion.

Apse: The space beyond the altar, generally bordered with small chapels.

Choir: A cozy area, often screened off, located within the church nave and near the high altar where services are sung in a more intimate setting.

Cloister: A square-shaped series of hallways surrounding an open-air courtyard, traditionally where monks and nuns got fresh air.

Facade: The outer wall of the church's main (west) entrance, viewable from outside and generally highly decorated.

Groin Vault: An arched ceiling formed where two equal barrel vaults meet at right angles. Less common usage: term for a medieval jock strap.

Nave: The long, central section of the church (running west to east, from the entrance to the altar) where a medieval congregation stood through the service.

Transept: The northsouth part of the church, which crosses (perpendicularly) the eastwest nave. In a traditional Latin cross-shaped floor plan, the transept forms the "arms" of the cross.

West Portal: The main entry to the church (on the west end, opposite the main altar).

Muslim Moors back into Africa (711–1492). Throughout Spain, it seems every old church was built upon a mosque (Sevilla's immense cathedral, for one). Granada's Alhambra is the best example of the secular Moorish style. It's an *Arabian Nights* fairy tale: finely etched domes, lacey arcades, keyhole arches, and lush gardens. At its heart lies an elegantly proportioned courtyard, where the designers created an ingenious microclimate: water, plants, pottery, thick walls, and darkness...all to be cool. The stuccoed walls are ornamented with a stylized Arabic script, creating a visual chant of verses from the Quran.

As the Christians slowly reconquered Iberian turf, they turned their fervor into stone, building churches in the lighter, heaven-reaching, stained-glass Gothic style (Toledo and Sevilla). Gothic was an import from France, trickling into conservative Spain long after it had swept through Europe.

As Christians moved in, many Muslim artists and architects stayed, giving the new society the Mudejar style. (Mudejar means "those who stayed.") In Sevilla's Alcázar, the Arabic script on the walls relates not the Quran, but New Testament verses and Christian propaganda, such as "Dedicated to the magnificent Sultan, King Pedro—thanks to God!" (The style of Christians living under Moorish rule is called Mozarabic.)

The money reaped and raped from Spain's colonies in the Golden Age spurred new construction. Churches and palaces borrowed from the Italian Renaissance and the more elaborate Baroque. Ornamentation reached unprecedented heights in Spain, culminating in the Plateresque style of stonework, so called because it resembles intricate silver *(plata)* filigree work (see, for example, the facade of the University of Salamanca).

The 1500s was also the era of religious wars. The monastery/palace of El Escorial, built in sober geometric style, symbolizes the austerity of a newly reformed Catholic Church ready to strike back. King Philip II ruled his empire and directed the Inquisition from here, surrounded by plain white walls, well-scrubbed floors, and simple furnishings. Built at a time when Catholic Spain felt threatened by Protestant heretics, its construction dominated the Spanish economy for a generation (1563–1584). Because of this bully in the national budget, Spain has almost nothing else to show from this most powerful period of her history.

For the next three centuries (1600–1900), backward-looking Spain recycled old art styles.

As Europe leapt from the 19th century into the 20th, it celebrated a rising standard of living and nearly a century without a major war. Art Nouveau architects forced hard steel and concrete into softer organic shapes. Barcelona's answer to Art Nouveau was Modernisme, and its genius was Antoni Gaudí, with his asymmetrical "cake-in-the-rain" buildings like Casa Milà and Sagrada Família.

Much of Spain's 20th-century architecture follows patterns seen elsewhere in Europe—the minimal fascist style of the Valley of the Fallen and ugly concrete apartments. But Spain today produces some of Europe's most interesting structures. Santiago Calatrava (from Valencia, born 1951) uses soaring arches and glass to create bridges (such as the new one in Venice), airports, and performance halls (including Valencia's Opera House). One of the world's most striking buildings in recent years—Frank Gehry's Guggenheim Museum—is in Bilbao, and similarly innovative structures are popping up everywhere.

Bullfighting

A Legitimate Slice of Spain, or a Cruel Spectacle?

The Spanish bullfight is as much a ritual as it is a sport. Not to acknowledge the importance of the bullfight is to censor a venerable part of Spanish culture. But it also makes a spectacle out of the cruel killing of an animal. Should tourists boycott bullfights? I don't know.

Today bullfighting is less popular among locals. If this trend continues, bullfighting may survive more and more as a tourist event. When the day comes that bullfighting is kept alive by our tourist dollars rather than by the local culture, then I'll agree with those who say bullfighting is immoral and that tourists shouldn't encourage it by buying tickets. Consider the morality of supporting this gruesome aspect of Spanish culture before buying a ticket. If you do decide to attend a bullfight, here is what you'll see.

While no two bullfights are the same, they unfold along a strict pattern. The ceremony begins punctually with a parade of participants across the ring. Then the trumpet sounds, the "Gate of Fear" opens, and the leading player—*el toro*—thunders in. A ton of angry animal is an awesome sight, even from the cheap seats (with the sun in your eyes).

The fight is divided into three acts. Act I is designed to size up the bull and wear him down. With help from his assistants, the matador ("killer") attracts the bull with the shake of the cape, then directs the animal past his body, as close as his bravery allows. The bull sees only things in motion and (some think) in red. After a few passes, the *picadores* enter, mounted on horseback, to spear the swollen lump of muscle at the back of the bull's neck. This tests the bull, while the matador watches studiously. It also lowers the bull's head and weakens the thrust of his horns. (Until 1927, the horses had no protective pads, and were often killed.)

In Act II, the matador's assistants *(banderilleros)* continue to enrage and weaken the bull. They charge the charging bull and—leaping acrobatically across its path—plunge brightly colored barbed sticks into the bull's vital neck muscle.

After a short intermission, during which the matador may, according to tradition, ask permission to kill the bull and dedicate the kill to someone in the crowd, the final and lethal Act III begins.

The matador tries to dominate and tire the bull with hypnotic cape work. A good pass is when the matador stands completely

still while the bull charges past. Then the matador thrusts a sword between the animal's shoulder blades for the kill. A quick kill is not always easy, and the matador may have to make several bloody thrusts before the sword stays in and the bull finally dies. Mules drag the dead bull out, and his meat is in the market *mañana* (barring "mad cow" concerns—and if ever there was a mad cow...). *Rabo del toro* (bull-tail stew) is a delicacy.

Throughout the fight, the crowd shows its approval or impatience. Shouts of *"¡Olé!"* or *"¡Torero!"* mean they like what they see. Whistling or rhythmic hand-clapping greets cowardice and incompetence.

You're not likely to see much human blood spilled. In 200 years of bullfighting in Sevilla, only 30 fighters have died (and only three were actually matadors). If a bull does kill a fighter, the next matador comes in to kill him. Historically, even the bull's mother is killed, since the evil qualities are assumed to have come from the mother.

After an exceptional fight, the crowd may wave white handkerchiefs to ask that the matador be awarded the bull's ear or tail. A brave bull, though dead, gets a victory lap from the mule team on his way to the slaughterhouse. Then the trumpet sounds, and a new bull charges in to face a fresh matador.

Fights are held on most Sundays Easter through September (at 18:30 or 19:30). Serious fights with adult matadors are called *corrida de toros*. These are often sold out in advance. Summer fights are often *novillada*, with teenage novices doing the killing. *Corrida de toros* seats range from €20 for nosebleed seats in the sun to €140 for front-row seats in the shade. *Novillada* seats are half that, and generally easy to get at the arena a few minutes before showtime. Many Spanish women consider bullfighting sexy. They swoon at the dashing matadors who are sure to wear tight pants (with their *partas nobles*—noble parts—in view, generally organized to one side, farthest from the bull).

A typical bullfight lasts about two hours and consists of six separate fights—three matadors (each with his own team of *picadores* and *banderilleros*) fighting two bulls each. For a closer look at bullfighting by an American aficionado, read Ernest Hemingway's classic, *Death in the Afternoon*.

APPENDIX

Contents

Tourist Information

Spain has a national tourist office in the **US:** tel. 212/265-8822, www.spain.info. Before you go, scan its website or call to briefly describe your trip and request information. They'll mail you a general-interest brochure, and you can download many other brochures free of charge at the website.

In **Spain,** your best first stop in a new city is the *Turismo*, the tourist information office (abbreviated in this book as **TI**). Try to arrive, or at least telephone, before it closes. Get a city map and advice on public transportation (including bus and train schedules), special events, and recommendations for nightlife. Some TIs have information on the entire country or at least the region, so try to pick up maps for towns you'll be visiting later in your trip.

While TIs are eager to book you a room, use their room-finding service only as a last resort (bloated prices, fees, no opinions, and they take a cut from your host). You'll get a far better value by using the listings in this book and booking direct.

Websites for Spain: In addition to the Spanish Tourist Board site listed above, consider visiting www.mcu.es (museums and historic sites in Spain) and www.renfe.com (train info and schedules).

For Gibraltar: Try the Gibraltar Information Bureau (from the US, dial 011-350-74950; www.gibraltar.gov.uk).

For Morocco: Contact the Moroccan National Tourist Office (from the US, dial 011-212-537-674-013; www.visitmorocco.com).

Communicating

The Spanish Language Barrier

Spain presents the English-speaking traveler with one of the most formidable language barriers in Western Europe. Many Spanish people—especially those in the tourist trade and in big cities—speak English. Still, many people don't. Locals visibly brighten when you know and use some key Spanish words (see "Spanish Survival Phrases" later in this chapter). Learn the key phrases. Travel with a phrase book, particularly if you want to interact with local people. You'll find that doors open quicker and with more smiles when you can speak a few words of the language.

Telephones

Smart travelers use the telephone to reserve or reconfirm rooms, get tourist information, reserve restaurants, confirm tour times, or phone home. Generally the easiest, cheapest way to call home is to use an international phone card purchased in Spain. This section covers dialing instructions, phone cards, and types of phones.

How to Dial

Calling from the US to Europe, or vice versa, is simple—once you break the code. The European calling chart (later in this chapter) will walk you through it.

Dialing Within Spain

About half of all European countries use area codes; the other half use a direct-dial system without area codes.

All phone numbers in Spain are nine digits (no area codes) that can be dialed direct throughout the country. For example, to call a recommended Madrid hotel, you'd dial the same number (tel. 915-212-941) whether you're calling from the Madrid train station or from Barcelona.

Dialing Internationally to or from Spain

If you want to make an international call, follow these steps:

1. Dial the international access code (00 if you're calling from Europe, 011 from the US or Canada).

2. Dial the country code of the country you're calling (34 for Spain, or 1 for the US or Canada).

3. Dial the entire phone number, keeping in mind that calling many countries requires dropping the initial zero of the phone number (see chart above for specifics per country).

Calling from the US to Spain: To call the Madrid hotel from the US, dial 011 (the US international access code), 34 (Spain's country code), then 915-212-941.

Calling from Spain to the US: To call my office in Edmonds, Washington, from Spain, I dial 00 (Europe's international access code), 1 (the US country code), 425 (Edmonds' area code), and 771-8303.

Note: You might see a + in front of a European number. When dialing the number, replace the + with the international access code of the country you're calling from (00 from Europe, 011 from the US or Canada).

Public Phones and Hotel-Room Phones

To make calls from public phones, you'll need a prepaid phone card. There are two different kinds of phone cards: international and insertable. Both types of phone cards work only in Spain. If you have a live card at the end of your trip, give it to another traveler to use up.

International Phone Cards: These prepaid cards, called *tarjetas telefónicas con código*, are the cheapest way to make international calls from Europe—with the best cards, it costs literally pennies a minute. To use the card, you'll dial a toll-free access number, then type in your scratch-to-reveal PIN number. You can use international phone cards from any type of phone, even your hotel-room phone (but ask at the front desk if there are any fees for toll-free calls). Cards are marked as national (for Spain) or international. All cards work for domestic or international calls, but you get better rates if you use the card for the purpose it was intended—so if you plan to use your card mostly for calls home, ask for an international card.

You can buy an international phone card at most kiosks and newsstands, but the best selection is usually at hole-in-the-wall shops catering to immigrants, who are the leading experts on calling home cheaply. You can also find them at call centers (*locutorios*). These cards, made by numerous (sometimes fly-by-night) companies, offer good rates but don't consistently work well. Try to confirm that the card can be used for calls to America (the salesclerk may not know), and buy a lower-denomination card in case the card is a dud.

Insertable Phone Cards: These cards, called *tarjetas telefónicas*, can only be used at pay phones for domestic or international

European Calling Chart

Just smile and dial, using this key:
AC = Area Code, LN = Local Number.

European Country	Calling long distance within ...	Calling from the US or Canada to ...	Calling from a European country to ...
Austria	AC + LN	011 + 43 + AC (without the initial zero) + LN	00 + 43 + AC (without the initial zero) + LN
Belgium	LN	011 + 32 + LN (without initial zero)	00 + 32 + LN (without initial zero)
Bosnia-Herzegovina	AC + LN	011 + 387 + AC (without initial zero) + LN	00 + 387 + AC (without initial zero) + LN
Britain	AC + LN	011 + 44 + AC (without initial zero) + LN	00 + 44 + AC (without initial zero) + LN
Croatia	AC + LN	011 + 385 + AC (without initial zero) + LN	00 + 385 + AC (without initial zero) + LN
Czech Republic	LN	011 + 420 + LN	00 + 420 + LN
Denmark	LN	011 + 45 + LN	00 + 45 + LN
Estonia	LN	011 + 372 + LN	00 + 372 + LN
Finland	AC + LN	011 + 358 + AC (without initial zero) + LN	999 + 358 + AC (without initial zero) + LN
France	LN	011 + 33 + LN (without initial zero)	00 + 33 + LN (without initial zero)
Germany	AC + LN	011 + 49 + AC (without initial zero) + LN	00 + 49 + AC (without initial zero) + LN
Gibraltar	LN	011 + 350 + LN	00 + 350 + LN
Greece	LN	011 + 30 + LN	00 + 30 + LN
Hungary	06 + AC + LN	011 + 36 + AC + LN	00 + 36 + AC + LN
Ireland	AC + LN	011 + 353 + AC (without initial zero) + LN	00 + 353 + AC (without initial zero) + LN
Italy	LN	011 + 39 + LN	00 + 39 + LN

European Country	Calling long distance within ...	Calling from the US or Canada to ...	Calling from a European country to ...
Montenegro	AC + LN	011 + 382 + AC (without initial zero) + LN	00 + 382 + AC (without initial zero) + LN
Morocco	LN	011 + 212 + LN (without initial zero)	00 + 212 + LN (without initial zero)
Netherlands	AC + LN	011 + 31 + AC (without initial zero) + LN	00 + 31 + AC (without initial zero) + LN
Norway	LN	011 + 47 + LN	00 + 47 + LN
Poland	LN	011 + 48 + LN (without initial zero)	00 + 48 + LN (without initial zero)
Portugal	LN	011 + 351 + LN	00 + 351 + LN
Slovakia	AC + LN	011 + 421 + AC (without initial zero) + LN	00 + 421 + AC (without initial zero) + LN
Slovenia	AC + LN	011 + 386 + AC (without initial zero) + LN	00 + 386 + AC (without initial zero) + LN
Spain	LN	011 + 34 + LN	00 + 34 + LN
Sweden	AC + LN	011 + 46 + AC (without initial zero) + LN	00 + 46 + AC (without initial zero) + LN
Switzerland	LN	011 + 41 + LN (without initial zero)	00 + 41 + LN (without initial zero)
Turkey	AC (if no initial zero is included, add one) + LN	011 + 90 + AC (without initial zero) + LN	00 + 90 + AC (without initial zero) + LN

APPENDIX

- The instructions above apply whether you're calling a land line or mobile phone.
- The international access codes (the first numbers you dial when making an international call) are 011 if you're calling from the US or Canada, or 00 if you're calling from virtually anywhere in Europe (except Finland, where it's 999).
- To call the US or Canada from Europe, dial 00, then 1 (the country code for the US and Canada), then the area code and number. In short, 00 + 1 + AC + LN = Hi, Mom!

calls. They're sold at post offices and many newsstand kiosks. Spanish pay phones are easy to find but refuse to be rushed. After you *"inserta"* your *"tarjeta"* into the phone, wait until the digital display says *"Marque número"* and then dial. Dial slowly and deliberately. Push the square R button to get a dial tone for a new call. The phone doesn't beep to remind you that you've left the card in, so don't forget to remove it when you're done. The cost of the call is automatically deducted from your card.

Coin-Operated Phones: The original kind of pay phone is becoming increasingly rare, and requires you to have enough change to complete your call.

Hotel-Room Phones: Calling from your room can be cheap for local calls (ask for the rates at the front desk first), but is often a rip-off for long-distance calls (unless you use an international phone card, explained earlier). Incoming calls are free, making this a cheap way for friends and family to stay in touch (provided they have a good long-distance plan for calls to Europe—and a list of your hotels' phone numbers).

US Calling Cards: These cards, such as the ones offered by AT&T, Verizon, or Sprint, are the worst option. You'll nearly always save a lot of money by using a local phone card instead.

Metered Phones: In Spain, phones with meters are sometimes available in telephone centers *(locutorios)* and bigger post offices. You can talk all you want, then pay the bill when you leave—but be sure you know the rates before you have a lengthy conversation.

Mobile Phones

Many travelers enjoy the convenience of traveling with a mobile phone. Here are the basics you'll need to know (for more in-depth information, see www.ricksteves.com/phones).

Using Your Mobile Phone: Your US mobile phone works in Europe if it's GSM-enabled, tri-band or quad-band, and on a calling plan that includes international calls. For example, with a T-Mobile phone, you'll pay $1 per minute to make or receive a call, and about $0.35 apiece for text messages.

You can save money if your phone is electronically "unlocked"—then you can simply buy a **SIM card** (a fingernail-sized chip that stores the phone's information) in Europe. SIM cards, which give you a European phone number and some prepaid calling time, are sold at mobile-phone stores and some newsstand kiosks for about €4–8. You may need to show ID, such as your passport, when you buy a SIM card. Simply insert the SIM card in your phone (usually in a slot behind the battery), and it'll work like a European mobile phone. When buying a SIM card, always ask about fees for domestic and international calls, roaming charges, and how to check your credit balance and buy more time.

Many **smartphones**, such as the iPhone or BlackBerry, work in Europe—but beware of sky-high fees, especially for data downloading (checking email, browsing the Internet, watching videos, and so on). Ask your provider in advance how to avoid unwittingly "roaming" your way to a huge bill. Some applications allow for cheap or free smartphone calls over a Wi-Fi connection (see "Calling over the Internet," below).

Using a European Mobile Phone: Local mobile-phone shops all over Europe sell basic phones for around €35–75. If you don't speak Spanish and buy your phone in Spain, you might find it hard to figure out the basics, but any young Spaniard can bail you out in a snap. You'll need to buy a SIM card (explained above) and prepaid credit for making calls. If you remain in the phone's home country, domestic calls are reasonable, and incoming calls are free. You'll pay more if you're "roaming" in another country. If your phone is "unlocked," you can swap out its SIM card for a new one in other countries.

Calling over the Internet

Some things that seem too good to be true...actually are true. If you're traveling with a laptop, make calls using VoIP (Voice over Internet Protocol). With VoIP, two computers act as the phones, and the Internet-based calls are free (or you can pay a few cents to call from your computer to a telephone). The major providers are Skype (www.skype.com) and Google Talk (www.google.com /talk).

Useful Phone Numbers

In Spain, numbers that start with 900 are toll-free; numbers that start with 901 and 902 can be expensive to call. Note that you can't call Spain's toll-free numbers from America, nor can you count on reaching America's toll-free numbers from Spain.

Embassies and Consulates

US Embassy in Madrid, Spain: tel. 915-872-240, after-hours emergency tel. 915-872-200 (Calle Serrano 75, www.embusa.es /cons/services.html)

US Embassy in Gibraltar: Call US Embassy in Madrid.

US Consulate General in Casablanca, Morocco: tel. 0522-264-550 or 0522-267-151, after-hours emergency tel. 0661-172-367 (Boulevard Moulay Youssef 8, www.usembassy.ma)

Canadian Embassy in Madrid, Spain: tel. 914-233-250 (Núñez de Balboa 35, www.espana.gc.ca)

Canadian Embassy in Rabat, Morocco: tel. 0537-687-400, (13, bis rue Jaâfa-as-Sadik, www.morocco.gc.ca)

APPENDIX

Emergency Needs
Police: Spain—tel. 091, Morocco—tel. 19
Ambulance: Spain—tel. 112, Morocco—tel. 15

Travel Advisories
US Department of State: tel. 202/647-5225, www.travel.state.gov
Canadian Department of Foreign Affairs: Canadian tel. 800-267-6788, www.dfait-maeci.gc.ca
US Centers for Disease Control and Prevention: tel. 800-CDC-INFO (800-232-4636), www.cdc.gov/travel

Directory Assistance
In Spain, dial 11811 (€0.40/min) or 11818 (€0.55/call from private numbers, free from phone booths).

Trains
Train (RENFE) Reservation and Information: tel. 902-240-202, www.renfe.es

Airports
The following airports share a customer assistance line, tel. 902-404-704, and a website, www.aena.es.
    Barcelona: El Prat de Llobregat Airport
    Madrid: Barajas Airport
    Sevilla: San Pablo Airport

Internet Access

Many hotels offer a computer in the lobby with Internet access for guests. Smaller places may sometimes let you sit at their desk for a few minutes just to check your email, if you ask politely. If you're traveling with a laptop, see if your hotel has Wi-Fi (wireless Internet access) or a port in your room for plugging in a cable to get online. Some hotels offer Wi-Fi for free; others charge by the minute. If your hotel doesn't have access, ask your hotelier to direct you to the nearest place to get online. Telefónica, the Spanish telecom, offers Wi-Fi hot spots at some hotels, restaurants, and cafés (www.telefonicaonline.com/on/es/wifi).

Mail

While you can arrange for mail delivery to your hotel (allow 10 days for a letter to arrive), phoning and emailing are so easy that I've dispensed with mail stops altogether.

Transportation

By Car or Train?

Cars are best for three or more traveling together (especially families with small kids), those packing heavy, and those scouring the countryside; but are an expensive headache in bigger cities. Trains and buses are best for solo travelers, blitz tourists, and city-to-city travelers.

Overview of Trains and Buses

Public transportation in Spain is becoming slick, modern, and efficient. The best option is to mix bus and train travel. Always verify schedules before your departure. Don't leave a station without your next day's schedule options in hand. To ask for a schedule at an information window, say, *"Horario para* (fill in names of cities), *por favor."* (The local TI will sometimes have schedules available for you to take or copy.) To study train schedules in advance, visit Germany's excellent all-Europe website, http://bahn.hafas.de/bin /query.exe/en, or Spain's site, www.renfe.es. For Comes buses in southern Spain, check www.tgcomes.es. Or try www.movelia.es, a private site listing several bus companies.

Trains

You can buy a Spain "flexi" railpass that allows travel for a given number of days over a longer period of time, but you'll pay separately ($15–35) for seat reservations on all trains. Buying individual train tickets in advance or as you go in Spain can be less expensive, and gives you better access to seat reservations (which are limited for railpass-holders). Some individual ticket prices already include seat reservations when required (i.e., for fast trains).

If your trip also includes a neighboring country, consider the France-Spain, Portugal-Spain, or Italy-Spain passes (see chart in this chapter). A Eurail Selectpass lets you travel even farther. Spain also offers a rail-and-drive pass, which gives you the ease of big-city train hops and the flexibility of a car for rural areas such as the Andalusian hill towns. These passes are sold only outside of Europe. For specifics, check the railpass chart, contact your travel agent, or see my *Guide to Railpasses* at www.ricksteves.com/rail. Even if you have a railpass, use buses when they're more convenient and direct than the trains. Remember to reserve ahead for the fast AVE trains and overnight journeys.

RENFE (the acronym for the Spanish national train system) used to mean "Really Exasperating, and Not For Everyone," but it has moved into the 21st century. For information and reservations, dial RENFE's national number (tel. 902-157-507) from anywhere

Buying Train Tickets

As trains can sell out, it's smart to buy your tickets a day in advance even for short rides. You generally have three options for buying train tickets: at the station, at a travel agency, or online. Since station ticket offices can get very crowded, most travelers will find it easiest to go to a travel agency.

At the Station: You will likely have to wait in a line to buy your ticket. First find the correct line—at bigger stations, there might be separate windows for short-distance, long-distance, advance, and "today" *(para hoy)* tickets. To avoid wasting time in the wrong line, read the signs carefully, and ask a local (or a clerk at an information window) which line you need. You might have to take a number—watch locals and follow their lead. To avoid waiting, you can sometimes use your credit card at an automated machine (which looks like an ATM)—but only for trains between major destinations. Some travelers report problems using these automated machines; if one of your credit cards doesn't work, try an alternate card.

As another option, you could buy tickets or reservations at the RENFE offices located in more than 100 city centers. These are more central and multilingual—also less crowded and confusing—than the train station.

Travel Agency: The best choice for most travelers is to buy tickets at an English-speaking travel agency. The El Corte Inglés department stores (with locations in most Spanish cities) often have handy travel agencies inside. I've recommended these and other travel agencies throughout this book.

Online: You can buy tickets online for any type of train except local commuter trains *(cercanías)*. Use the RENFE site at www.renfe.es (choose "English" in the drop-down box labeled *Seleccione su idioma*). Long-distance trains require reservations, which are automatic when you buy online. Some discounts are available if you book early, starting 60 days in advance of travel (see "The Fine Print," below). First-time users must pick up tickets in person at the station and show ID. Repeat users can print tickets at home. When the online form asks for your Spanish national ID number, enter your passport number. The only drawback for buying tickets online is that if your plans change, you can only change your ticket at one of the automated machines at the station (which you might not find at some small-town stations).

The Fine Print: First-class tickets cost 50 percent more than second class—often as much as a domestic flight (see "Cheap Flights," later in this chapter). Some advance-purchase discounts are available when you purchase point-to-point tickets through RENFE. Discounted tickets come with restrictions, such as being nonrefundable and nonchangeable. Be sure to read all the details carefully at time of purchase.

Railpasses

Prices listed are for 2009 and are subject to change. For the latest prices, details, and train schedules (and easy online ordering), see my comprehensive *Guide to Eurail Passes* at www.ricksteves.com/rail.

"Saver" prices are per person for two or more people traveling together. "Youth" means under age 26. The fare for children 4–11 is half the adult individual fare or Saver fare. Kids under age 4 travel free.

SPAIN RAIL & DRIVE PASS

Any 3 rail days and 2 car days in 2 months.

Car Category	1st Class	2nd Class	Extra car day
Economy car	$333	$275	$46
Compact car	340	282	54
Intermediate car	366	308	80
Intermediate auto. car	401	343	114
Full size	427	370	140

Prices are per person, two traveling together. Solo travelers pay about $100 extra. Third and fourth people sharing car buy only the railpass. Extra rail days (max 7) cost $35–$42 per day. To order Rail & Drive passes, call your travel agent or Rail Europe at 800-438-7245. *This pass is not sold by Europe Through the Back Door.*

SPAIN PASS

	1st Class	2nd Class
3 days in 2 months	$261	$208
Extra rail days (max 7)	$38-40	$30-32

SPAIN-PORTUGAL PASS

	Individual 1st Class	Saver 1st Class
3 days in 2 months	$299	$254
Extra rail days (max 7)	40	$35

Map key:
Approximate point-to-point one-way second-class rail fares in US dollars. First class costs 50 percent more. Add up fares for your itinerary to see whether a railpass will save you money. Dashed lines are buses.

SELECTPASS

This pass covers travel in three adjacent countries. Please visit **www.ricksteves.com/rail** for four- and five-country options.

	Individual 1st Class	Saver 1st Class	Youth 2nd Class
5 days in 2 months	$442	$375	$288
6 days in 2 months	488	416	320
8 days in 2 months	578	494	375
10 days in 2 months	670	567	434

FRANCE–SPAIN PASS

	Individual 1st Class	Individual 2nd Class	Saver 1st Class	Saver 2nd Class	Youth 2nd Class
4 days in 2 months	$356	$312	$312	$275	$235
Extra rail days (max 6)	42	35	35	30	27

in Spain. For tips on buying tickets, see the "Buying Train Tickets" sidebar.

Spain categorizes trains this way:

The high-speed train called the **AVE** (AH-vay, stands for *Alta Velocidad Española*) whisks travelers between Madrid and Toledo in 30 minutes, Madrid and Sevilla or Madrid and Barcelona in less than three hours, and Madrid and Málaga in three hours. Franco left Spain a train system that didn't fit Europe's gauge, and AVE trains run on European-gauge tracks. AVE trains can be priced differently according to their time of departure. Peak hours *(punta)* are most expensive, followed by *llano* and *valle* (quietest and cheapest times).

AVE is almost entirely covered by the Eurailpass (book ahead, a seat reservation fee from Madrid to Sevilla costs Eurailers about $23 in second class; $38 for first class, includes meal). High-speed lines are currently under construction to the Basque Country and French border.

The **TALGO** is fast, air-conditioned, and expensive, and runs on AVE rails. **Intercity** and **Electro** trains fall just behind TALGO in speed, comfort, and expense. **Rápido, Tranvía, Semidirecto,** and **Expreso** trains are generally slower. **Cercanías** are commuter trains for big-city workers and small-town tourists. **Regional** and **Correo** trains are slow, small-town milk runs. Trains get more expensive as they pick up speed, but all are cheaper per mile than their northern European counterparts. Spain loves to name trains, so you may encounter types of trains not listed here. The names Euromed, Alaris, Altaria, and Arco all indicate faster trains that require reservations.

Salidas means "departures" and *llegadas* is "arrivals." On train schedules, "LMXJVSD" stands for the days of the week in Spanish, starting with Monday. A train that runs "LMXJV-D" doesn't run on Saturdays. *Laborables* can mean Monday through Friday or Monday through Saturday.

Overnight Trains: For long trips, I go overnight on the train or I fly (domestic shuttle flights are generally less than $100). Overnight trains (and buses) are usually less expensive and slower than the daytime rides. Most overnight trains have berths and beds that you can rent (not included in the cost of your train ticket or railpass). A sleeping berth *(litera)* costs extra, with the price depending on the route and type of compartment. Night trains are popular, so it's smart to reserve in advance, even from home. Travelers with first-class reservations are entitled to use comfortable "Intercity"

Public Transportation Routes in Iberia

lounges in train stations in Spain's major cities.

Hotel Trains: The term "Hotel Train" *(Trenhotel)* usually means fancy and expensive. The pricey overnight Hotel Train between Madrid and Lisbon is called the "Lusitania" (first class-$225, including a bed in a double compartment; second class-$124 in a quad; pay $54 or more for a sleeper if you have a railpass, additional cost for singles or a shower in your compartment). Unfortunately, no cheaper rail option exists between these two capital cities. You can save money by taking a bus, or save time by taking a plane. Hotel Train prices are at least as high between other major cities, such as Barcelona–Valencia or Barcelona–Madrid.

Pricey international Hotel Trains connect France, Italy, and Switzerland with Spain. All of these spendy overnight trains (known collectively as Elipsos) have names: Francisco de Goya (Madrid–Paris), Joan Miró (Barcelona–Paris), Pau Casals (Barcelona–Zürich), and Salvador Dalí (Barcelona–Milan). Full fares range from $270 in a quad to $749 for a Gran Clase single compartment. Travelers with any railpass that covers at least one country on the route of travel (including Swiss Passes but not Swiss Cards) can use a railpass travel day and pay about half the full fare. For more information on international Hotel Trains, see www.elipsos.com. If you can easily afford to take a Hotel Train, consider flying instead to save time (see "Cheap Flights," later in this chapter).

To avoid the expensive luxury of an international Hotel Train, you can take a cheaper train trip that involves a transfer at the Spanish border (at Irún on Madrid–Paris runs, at Cerbère on the eastern side). You'll connect to a normal night train with $35 *literas* *(couchette* berths) on one leg of the trip. This plan is more time-consuming, and may take two days of a flexipass.

Buses

Spain's bus system is confusing. There are a number of different bus companies (though usually clustered within one building), sometimes running buses to the same destinations and using the same transfer points. If you have to transfer, make sure to look for a bus with the same name/logo as the company you bought the ticket from. The larger stations have an information desk with all of the schedules. In smaller stations, check the destinations and schedules posted on each office window. Bus service on holidays, Saturdays, and especially Sundays can be less frequent.

If you arrive in a city by bus and plan to leave by bus, upon your arrival at the bus station check your departure options and buy a ticket in advance if necessary (and possible). If you're downtown, need a ticket, and the bus station isn't central, save time by asking at the tourist office about travel agencies that sell bus tickets.

Smoking is no longer allowed on buses, and most people respect this new law. This is the best evidence that Spain isn't stuck in the past—even though people are complaining all the way into the future. You can (and most likely will be required to) stow your luggage under the bus. For longer rides, give some thought to which side of the bus will get the most sun, and sit on the opposite side, even if the bus is air-conditioned and has curtains. Your ride will likely come with a soundtrack: taped Spanish pop music, a radio, or sometimes videos. If you prefer silence, bring earplugs.

Drivers and station personnel rarely speak English. Buses generally lack WCs, but they stop every two hours or so for a break (usually 15 min, but can be up to 30). Drivers announce how long the stop will be, but if in doubt, ask the driver, "How many minutes here?" *("¿Cuántos minutos aquí?")* so you know if you have time to get out. Listen for the bus horn as a final call before departure. Bus stations have WCs (rarely with toilet paper) and cafés that offer quick and slightly overpriced food.

Taxis

Most taxis are reliable and cheap. Drivers generally respond kindly to the request, "How much is it to _____, more or less?" *("¿Cuánto cuesta a _____, más o menos?")*.

Spanish taxis have extra supplements (for luggage, nighttime, Sundays, train-station or airport pickup, and so on). Rounding the fare up to the nearest large coin (maximum of 10 percent) is adequate for a tip. City rides cost $4 to $6. Keep a map in your hand so the cabbie knows (or thinks) you know where you're going. Big cities have plenty of taxis. In many cases, couples travel by cab for little more than two bus or subway tickets.

Cars

Car Rental

To drive in Spain, you need to have your US driver's license along. If you'll be driving outside of Spain, look into getting an International Driving Permit (IDP), required by some countries (sold at your local AAA office for $15, plus two passport photos; www.aaa.com).

To rent a car in Spain, you must be at least 21 years old and have held your license for one year. Drivers under the age of 25 may incur a young-driver surcharge, and some rental companies do not rent to anyone 75 and over. If you're considered too young or old, look into leasing, which has less-stringent age restrictions (see

"Leasing," on the next page).

Research car rentals before you go. It's cheaper to arrange most car rentals from the US. Call several companies and look online to compare rates, or arrange a rental through your hometown travel agent. Two reputable companies among many are Auto Europe (www.autoeurope.com) and Europe by Car (www.ebctravel.com). For the best rental deal, rent by the week with unlimited mileage. I normally rent the smallest, least-expensive model with a stick-shift (cheaper than an automatic). If you want an automatic, reserve the car at least a month in advance and specifically request an automatic. Cars with automatic transmissions are generally larger, making them less than ideal for narrow, winding roads (such as in Andalucía's hill towns).

For a three-week rental, allow $875 per person (based on two people sharing a car), including insurance, tolls, gas, and parking. But for trips of this length, consider leasing; you'll save money on insurance and taxes. Compare pick-up costs (downtown can be cheaper than the airport) and explore drop-off options.

When you pick up the car, check it thoroughly and make sure any damage is noted on your rental agreement. Find out how your car's lights, turn signals, wipers, and gas cap function.

Returning a car at a big-city train station can be tricky; get precise details on the car drop-off location and hours. Note that rental offices usually close from midday Saturday until Monday. When you return the car, make sure the agent verifies its condition with you.

Car Insurance Options

Accidents can happen anywhere, but when you're on vacation, the last thing you need is stress over car insurance. Limit your financial risk by choosing one of these three options: buy Collision Damage Waiver (CDW) coverage from the car-rental company, get coverage through your credit card (free, but more complicated), or buy coverage through Travel Guard.

While each rental company has its own variation, the basic **CDW** costs $15–25 a day and reduces your liability, but does not eliminate it. When you pick up the car, you'll be offered the chance to "buy down" the basic deductible to zero (for an additional $10–30/day; sometimes called "super CDW").

If you opt for **credit-card coverage,** there's a catch. You'll technically have to decline all coverage offered by the car-rental company, which means they can place a hold on your card (which can be up to the full value of the car). In case of damage, it can be time-consuming to resolve the charges with your credit-card company. Before you decide on this option, quiz your credit-card company about how it works.

Driving in Spain: Distance and Time

Santiago de Compostela
Comillas
Santillana del Mar 20m•.75h
St. Jean-de-Luz
Bilbao
San Sebastián
FRANCE
285m•6h
200m•4.5h
10m•.25h
Potes
95m 2.5h
50m 1.5h
125m 2.5h
80m•1.5h
60m 1.25h
25m•1.5h
Barcelona to Cerbère (French border) 110m•2h
León
150m 3h
120m•2h
135m 2.5h
Pamplona
270m•5.5h
140m•2.5h
210m•3.5h
Porto
Salamanca
Burgos
150m•2.5h
125m 3.5h (via Logroño)
220m•4h
60m 1.5h
55m 1h
3h
Coimbra
75m•1.25h
185m•4h
Segovia
60m 1.25h
Zaragoza
115m•2h
80m 1.25h
Ávila
70m•1.5h
Madrid
205m 3.5h
Barcelona
Nazaré
PORTUGAL
8h
520m•8h
45m 1h
225m•4h
220m•3.5h
80m•1.5h
125m•2h
315m•5.5h
Toledo
SPAIN
Lisbon
85m•1.5h
Évora
220m•4h
Valencia
190m•3.5h
200m•3h
Córdoba
225m•4h
330m•5.5h
200m•3.5h
180m•3h
90m•2h
100m•2h
Salema
Sevilla
155m•3h
Granada
55m•1.5h
Arcos
80m•2h
Ronda
120m•2h
65m•1.25h
70m•2h
Nerja
50m•1.25h
70m•1.5h
Tarifa
60m•1.75h
.5h Ferry
Tangier
Gibraltar

m = miles
h = hours
···· = ferry

Note: Your times may vary based on traffic, construction, and road conditions.

Finally, you can buy car-rental insurance from **Travel Guard** ($9/day plus a one-time $3 service fee covers you up to $35,000, $250 deductible, tel. 800-826-4919, www.travelguard.com). It's valid everywhere in Europe but the Republic of Ireland, and some Italian car-rental companies refuse to honor it. Residents of Washington State aren't eligible for this coverage.

For more fine print about car-rental insurance, see www.rick steves.com/cdw.

Leasing

For trips of three weeks or more, consider leasing (which automatically includes zero-deductible collision and theft insurance). By technically buying and then selling back the car, you save lots of money on tax and insurance. Leasing provides you a brand-new car with unlimited mileage and a 24-hour emergency assistance program. You can lease for as little as 17 days to as long as 6 months. Car leases must be arranged from the US. One of many reliable companies offering affordable lease packages is Europe by Car (US tel. 800-223-1516, www.ebctravel.com).

Driving

Driving in Spain is great—sparse traffic and generally good roads—but a pain in big cities such as Madrid. Good maps are available and inexpensive throughout Spain. Freeways come with tolls (about $4/hr) but save huge amounts of time. Always pick up a ticket as you enter a toll freeway. On freeways, navigate by direction *(norte, oeste, sur, este)*. Also, since road numbers can be puzzling and inconsistent, navigate by city names. Mileage signs are in kilometers (see page 737 for conversion formula into miles). In smaller towns, following signs to *centro ciudad* will get you to the heart of things.

Drive defensively. If you're involved in an accident, you will be blamed and will be in for a monumental headache. Seatbelts are required by law. Children under 12 must ride in the back seat, and children up to age 3 must have a child seat. You must put on a reflective safety vest any time you get out of your car on the side of a highway or unlit road (most rental-car companies provide one—but check when you pick up the car). Those who use eyeglasses are required by law to have a spare pair in the car.

Watch for traffic radars and expect to be stopped for a routine check by the police (be sure your car-insurance form is up-to-date). Small towns come with speed traps and corruption. Tickets, especially for foreigners, are issued and paid for on the spot. Insist on a receipt, so the money is less likely to end up in the cop's pocket.

Gas and diesel prices are controlled and the same everywhere—about $6 a gallon for gas, less for diesel. Unleaded gas *(gasolina sin plomo)* is either *normal* or *super*. Note that diesel is called *diesel* or *gasóleo*—pay attention when filling your tank.

Choose parking places carefully. Leave valuables in the trunk during the day and leave nothing worth stealing in the car overnight. While you should avoid parking lots with twinkly asphalt, thieves break car windows anywhere, even at stoplights. If your car's a hatchback, take the trunk cover off at night so thieves can look in without breaking in. Try to make your car look locally owned by hiding the "tourist-owned" rental-company decals and putting a local newspaper in your front or back window. Parking attendants all over Spain holler, *"Nada en el coche"* ("Nothing in the car"). And they mean it. Ask your hotelier for advice on parking. In cities you can park safely but expensively in guarded lots.

Cheap Flights

If you're visiting one or more cities on a longer European trip, you might want to look into the affordable intra-European airlines. While trains are still the best way to connect places that are close together, a flight can save both time and money on long journeys.

One of the best websites for comparing inexpensive flights is www.skyscanner.net. Other comparison search engines include www.mobissimo.com and www.wegolo.com.

For flights within Spain, try www.vueling.com, www.iberia.com, or www.spanair.com. Other well-known cheapo airlines include easyJet (www.easyjet.com) and RyanAir (www.ryanair.com). Be aware of the potential drawbacks of flying on the cheap: nonrefundable and nonchangeable tickets, rigid baggage restrictions (and fees if you have more than what's officially allowed), use of airports far outside town, tight schedules that can mean more delays, little in the way of customer assistance if problems arise, and, of course, no frills. To avoid unpleasant surprises, read the small print—especially baggage policies—before you book.

Resources

Resources from Rick Steves

Rick Steves' Spain 2010 is one of more than 30 titles in a series of **books** on European travel, which includes country guidebooks, city guidebooks (Venice, Florence, Rome, Paris, London, etc.),

and my budget-travel skills handbook, *Rick Steves' Europe Through the Back Door*. My phrase books—for Spanish, Italian, French, German, and Portuguese—are practical and budget-oriented. My other books are *Europe 101* (a crash course on art and history in full color), *Travel as a Political Act* (a travelogue sprinkled with advice for bringing home a global perspective), *European Christmas* (on traditional and modern-day celebrations), and *Postcards from Europe* (a fun memoir of my travels over 25 years). For a complete list of my books, see the inside

Begin Your Trip at www.ricksteves.com

At our travel website, you'll find a wealth of free information on European destinations, including fresh monthly news and helpful tips from thousands of fellow travelers. You'll also find my latest guidebook updates (www.ricksteves.com/update) and my travel blog.

Our **online Travel Store** offers travel bags and accessories specially designed by me and my staff to help you travel smarter and lighter. These include my popular carry-on bags (roll-aboard and rucksack versions), money belts, totes, toiletries kits, adapters, other accessories, and a wide selection of guidebooks, planning maps, and DVDs.

Choosing the right **railpass** for your trip—amidst hundreds of options—can drive you nutty. We'll help you choose the best pass for your needs, plus give you a bunch of free extras.

Rick Steves' Europe Through the Back Door travel company offers **tours** with more than three dozen itineraries and about 300 departures reaching the best destinations in this book...and beyond. Our 16-day Best of Spain + Morocco tour includes the big-city thrills of Barcelona, Madrid, Sevilla, and Tangier, as well the small-town gems of Ronda and the whitewashed village of Arcos. The eight-day Best of Barcelona & Madrid tour explores Spain's top two cities, while the seven-day Best of San Sebastián & the Basque Countryside tour takes you to an often overlooked, idyllic corner of Europe. You'll enjoy great guides, a fun bunch of travel partners (with small groups of generally around 28), and plenty of room to spread out in a big, comfy bus. You'll find European adventures to fit every vacation length. For all the details, and to get our Tour Catalog and a free Rick Steves Tour Experience DVD (filmed on location during an actual tour), visit www.ricksteves.com or call us at 425/608-4217.

of the last page of this book.

My **TV series**, *Rick Steves' Europe*, covers European destinations in 100 shows, with five episodes on Spain. My weekly **public radio** show, *Travel with Rick Steves*, features interviews with travel experts from around the world, including several hours on Spain and Spanish culture. All the TV scripts and radio shows (which are easy and free to download to an iPod or other MP3 player) are at www .ricksteves.com.

If you're traveling beyond Spain to England, France, or Italy, take advantage of my free self-guided **audio tours** of the major sights in Paris, Florence, Rome, Venice, and London. Simply download them from www.ricksteves .com or iTunes (search for "Rick Steves' tours" in the iTunes Store), then transfer them to your iPod or other MP3 player.

Maps

The black-and-white maps in this book, designed by David Hoerlein, are concise and simple. The maps are intended to help you locate recommended places and reach TIs, where you'll find more in-depth (and often free) maps of cities or regions. Better maps are sold at newsstands—take a look before you buy to be sure the map has the level of detail you want.

Michelin maps are available—and cheaper than in the US—throughout Spain at bookstores, newsstands, and gas stations. Train travelers can do fine with a simple rail map (such as the one that comes with a train pass) and city maps from the tourist information offices. For drivers, I'd recommend a 1:200,000- or 1:300,000-scale map.

Other Guidebooks

If you're like most travelers, this book has more than enough information. But if you're heading beyond my recommended destinations, $30 for extra maps and books can be money well-spent.

The following books are worth considering, but are not updated annually; check the publication date before you buy. Lonely Planet's guide to Spain is well-researched, with good maps and hotel recommendations for low- to moderate-budget travelers. The similar *Rough Guide to Spain* is hip and insightful, written by British researchers. Students and vagabonds like the highly opinionated *Let's Go: Spain & Portugal*, updated by Harvard students. Let's Go is best for backpackers who stay at hostels, use railpasses, and dive into the youth and nightlife scene.

The Eyewitness series has about a dozen editions covering

Visiting Valencia?

This guidebook is designed to be selective, covering the best Spanish destinations in depth. But plenty of visit-worthy places didn't make it in the book, including sunny Valencia.

Valencia—famous for paella and home to El Cid—is Spain's third-largest city and throws its biggest street party, Las Fallas. The thriving city is a cultural center with a popular Mediterranean promenade. It's a leader in Spanish avant-garde architecture—thanks to works by Sir Norman Foster and native son Santiago Calatrava. Equidistant (220 miles) from both Madrid and Barcelona, and located on Spain's east coast, Valencia can be a handy stop with a good day's worth of sightseeing within its characteristic Old Town.

My friend Tooraj Fooladi, who lives in Valencia (and guides tours of Spain for my company), loves his town and has written a fine chapter on Valencia that is available for free at www.ricksteves.com/valencia. If you're visiting Valencia, I hope you can download this chapter, pack it along, and take advantage of Tooraj's hard work. Happy Valencian travels!

Spain, including Barcelona, Madrid, and Sevilla/Andalucía. They're extremely popular for great, easy-to-grasp graphics and photos, but the written content in Eyewitness is relatively skimpy, and the books weigh a ton. I simply borrow them for a minute from other travelers at certain sights to make sure I'm aware of that place's highlights. Time Out travel guides provide good, detailed coverage of Madrid, Barcelona, and Andalucía, particularly on arts and entertainment.

The popular, skinny Michelin Green Guides to Spain are excellent, especially if you're driving. They're known for their city and sightseeing maps, dry but concise and helpful information on major sights, and good cultural and historical background. English editions, covering most of the regions you'll want to visit, are sold in Spain.

I like Cadogan guides for their well-presented background information and coverage of cultural issues. Their recommendations suit upscale travelers. Older travelers enjoy Frommer's Spain guides even though those, like the Fodor's guides, ignore alternatives that enable travelers to save money by dirtying their fingers in the local culture. The encyclopedic Blue Guides to Spain are dry as the plains in Spain, but just right for scholarly types.

If you'll be traveling to neighboring countries, consider *Rick Steves' Portugal* and *Rick Steves' France*.

Recommended Books and Movies

Spain is overwhelmingly rich in history, art, and culture. For information on Spain past and present, check out a few of these books or films.

Non-Fiction

Spain has undergone incredible changes since the death of Franco in 1975. *The New Spaniards* (Hooper) is a survey of all aspects of modern Spain, including its politics, economy, demographics, education, religion, and popular culture.

For a sympathetic cultural history of the Basque people, their language, and contributions from Roman times to the present, read *The Basque History of the World* (Kurlansky).

George Orwell traded his press pass for a uniform, fought against Franco's Fascists in the Spanish Civil War of 1936–1939, and then wrote an account of his experiences in his gripping *Homage to Catalonia. The Battle for Spain* (Beevor) re-creates the political climate during the Civil War.

James Michener traveled to Spain for several decades, and his tribute, *Iberia*, describes how Spain's dark history created a contradictory and passionately beautiful land.

Hemingway shows his journalistic side in two books on bullfighting: *Death in the Afternoon* and *The Dangerous Summer.*

Travelers' Tales: Spain (McCauley) offers dozens of essays about Spain and its people from numerous authors.

Penelope Casas has written many popular books on the food of Spain, including tapas, paella, and regional cooking. Her *Discovering Spain: An Uncommon Guide* blends references to history, culture, and food with travel information. For deciphering menus in restaurants, foodies like *The Marling Menu-Master for Spain.*

The nature of pilgrimage is explored along the famous Camino de Santiago trail in northern Spain in *Following the Milky Way* (Aviva) and *On Pilgrimage* (Lash).

The eccentricities of village life in the mountains south of Granada are lovingly detailed in a British expat's 1920s experiences in *South from Granada* (Brenan). A contemporary family's adjustments to living in the same region are described in *Driving Over Lemons: An Optimist in Spain* (Stewart) and his later books.

Fiction

Fans of classic literature will want to read Cervantes' *Don Quixote.* Another classic, Irving's *Tales of the Alhambra*, weaves fact, mythical tales, and descriptions of Granada and its beautiful Moorish castle complex—the Alhambra—during his 19th-century visit.

Hemingway fans will enjoy *The Sun Also Rises*; this story of expats living in post-WWI France and Spain introduced many readers to bullfighting. Hemingway's *For Whom the Bell Tolls*, a tale of idealism and harsh reality, is set against the complexity of the Spanish Civil War.

The brutality and intolerance of the dark years of the Spanish Inquisition are illuminated in Winstein's *The Heretic*, with Sevilla as the backdrop. *The Last Jew* (Gordon) is one man's story of survival in Inquisition-era Spain. *Stories from Spain* (Barlow and Stivers) relates well-known Spanish legends that chronicle nearly 1,000 years of Spanish history.

The 2005 bestselling thriller *The Shadow of the Wind* (Zafón) takes place in 1950s Barcelona. Robert Wilson's popular police thrillers, including *The Blind Man of Seville*, are set in Spain and Portugal.

Films

In *The Mystery of Picasso* (1956), Picasso is filmed painting from behind a transparent canvas, allowing a unique look at his creative process.

Peter O'Toole and Sophia Loren star in the musical version of Don Quixote, *Man of La Mancha* (1972).

In the first of Carlos Saura's flamenco dance trilogy, *Blood Wedding* (1981), he adapts Federico García Lorca's play about a wedding imposed on a bride in love with another man. *Carmen* (1983) shows a Spanish cast rehearsing the well-known French novel and opera. *El Amor Brujo* (1986) is a ghostly love story.

L'auberge Espagnole (2002) tells the story of the loves and lives of European students sharing an apartment in Barcelona.

In *Barcelona* (1994), two Americans in Spain try to navigate the Spanish singles scene and the ensuing culture clash.

The Spanish film *Open Your Eyes* (1997) inspired the 2001 Tom Cruise thriller *Vanilla Sky*, where a car accident sets off an intricate series of events.

Woody Allen's *Vicky Cristina Barcelona* (2008) stars Javier Bardem as a macho Spanish artist romancing two American women, when suddenly his stormy ex-wife (Penelope Cruz, in an Oscar-winning role) re-enters his life.

Pedro Almodóvar's piquant films about relationships in the post-Franco era have garnered piles of international awards. Spanish actors Bardem, Cruz, and Antonio Banderas have starred in his films. Almodóvar's best-known films include *Women on the Verge of a Nervous Breakdown* (1988), *All About My Mother* (1999), *Talk to Her* (2002), and *Volver* (2007).

2010

JANUARY						
S	M	T	W	T	F	S
					1	2
3	4	5	6	7	8	9
10	11	12	13	14	15	16
17	18	19	20	21	22	23
24/31	25	26	27	28	29	30

FEBRUARY						
S	M	T	W	T	F	S
	1	2	3	4	5	6
7	8	9	10	11	12	13
14	15	16	17	18	19	20
21	22	23	24	25	26	27
28						

MARCH						
S	M	T	W	T	F	S
	1	2	3	4	5	6
7	8	9	10	11	12	13
14	15	16	17	18	19	20
21	22	23	24	25	26	27
28	29	30	31			

APRIL						
S	M	T	W	T	F	S
				1	2	3
4	5	6	7	8	9	10
11	12	13	14	15	16	17
18	19	20	21	22	23	24
25	26	27	28	29	30	

MAY						
S	M	T	W	T	F	S
						1
2	3	4	5	6	7	8
9	10	11	12	13	14	15
16	17	18	19	20	21	22
23/30	24/31	25	26	27	28	29

JUNE						
S	M	T	W	T	F	S
		1	2	3	4	5
6	7	8	9	10	11	12
13	14	15	16	17	18	19
20	21	22	23	24	25	26
27	28	29	30			

JULY						
S	M	T	W	T	F	S
				1	2	3
4	5	6	7	8	9	10
11	12	13	14	15	16	17
18	19	20	21	22	23	24
25	26	27	28	29	30	31

AUGUST						
S	M	T	W	T	F	S
1	2	3	4	5	6	7
8	9	10	11	12	13	14
15	16	17	18	19	20	21
22	23	24	25	26	27	28
29	30	31				

SEPTEMBER						
S	M	T	W	T	F	S
			1	2	3	4
5	6	7	8	9	10	11
12	13	14	15	16	17	18
19	20	21	22	23	24	25
26	27	28	29	30		

OCTOBER						
S	M	T	W	T	F	S
					1	2
3	4	5	6	7	8	9
10	11	12	13	14	15	16
17	18	19	20	21	22	23
24/31	25	26	27	28	29	30

NOVEMBER						
S	M	T	W	T	F	S
	1	2	3	4	5	6
7	8	9	10	11	12	13
14	15	16	17	18	19	20
21	22	23	24	25	26	27
28	29	30				

DECEMBER						
S	M	T	W	T	F	S
		1	2	3	4	
5	6	7	8	9	10	11
12	13	14	15	16	17	18
19	20	21	22	23	24	25
26	27	28	29	30	31	

APPENDIX

Holidays and Festivals

Spain erupts with fiestas and celebrations throughout the year. Semana Santa (Holy Week) fills the week before Easter with processions and festivities all over Iberia, but especially in Sevilla. To run with the bulls, be in Pamplona—with medical insurance—July 6–14.

This is a partial list of holidays and festivals. For more information, contact the Spanish Tourist Office (www.spain.info, US tel. 212/265-8822).

Jan 1	New Year's Day
Jan 6	Epiphany
Early Feb	La Candelaria (religious festival), Madrid
Feb 28	Day of Andalucía (some closures), Andalucía
March 28–April 4	Holy Week

April 5	Easter Monday
April 20–25	April Fair, Sevilla
May 1	Labor Day (closures)
May 2	Day of the Autonomous Community, Madrid
May 2–9	Feria del Caballo (horse pageantry), Jerez
Throughout May	San Isidro (religious festival on May 15; also bullfights and zarzuelas all month long), Madrid
June	La Patum (Moorish battles), Barcelona
June 3	Corpus Christi
June 24	St. John the Baptist's Day
Late June–Early July	International Festival of Music and Dance, Granada
July 6–14	Running of the Bulls (Fiesta de San Fermín), Pamplona
Aug	Gràcia Festival, Barcelona
Mid-Aug	Verbena de la Paloma (folk festival), Madrid
Aug 15	Assumption of Mary (religious festival)
Sept	Autumn Festival (flamenco, bullfights), Jerez
Late Sept	La Mercé (parade), Barcelona
Oct 12	Spanish National Day
Late Oct–Nov	International Jazz Festival, Madrid
Nov 1	All Saints' Day
Nov 9	Virgen de la Almudena, Madrid
Dec 6	Constitution Day
Dec 8	Feast of the Immaculate Conception
Dec 13	Feast of Santa Lucía
Dec 25	Christmas
Dec 31	New Year's Eve

Conversions and Climate

Numbers and Stumblers

- Europeans write a few of their numbers differently than we do. 1 = 1, 4 = 4, 7 = 7.
- In Europe, dates appear as day/month/year, so Christmas is 25/12/10.
- Commas are decimal points and decimals commas. A dollar and a half is 1,50, and there are 5.280 feet in a mile.
- When pointing, use your whole hand, palm down.
- When counting with fingers, start with your thumb. If you hold up your first finger to request one item, you'll probably get two.

- What Americans call the second floor of a building is the first floor in Europe.
- On escalators and moving sidewalks, Europeans keep the left "lane" open for passing. Keep to the right.

Metric Conversions (approximate)

A kilogram is 2.2 pounds, and 1 liter is about a quart, or almost four to a gallon. A kilometer is six-tenths of a mile. I figure kilometers to miles by cutting them in half and adding back 10 percent of the original (120 km: 60 + 12 = 72 miles, 300 km: 150 + 30 = 180 miles).

1 foot = 0.3 meter	1 square yard = 0.8 square meter
1 yard = 0.9 meter	1 square mile = 2.6 square kilometers
1 mile = 1.6 kilometers	1 ounce = 28 grams
1 centimeter = 0.4 inch	1 quart = 0.95 liter
1 meter = 39.4 inches	1 kilogram = 2.2 pounds
1 kilometer = 0.62 mile	32°F = 0°C

Clothing Sizes

When shopping for clothing, use these US-to-European comparisons as general guidelines (but note that no conversion is perfect).

- Women's dresses and blouses: Add 30 (US size 10 = European size 40)
- Men's suits and jackets: Add 10 (US size 40 regular = European size 50)
- Men's shirts: Multiply by 2 and add about 8 (US size 15 collar = European size 38)
- Women's shoes: Add about 30 (US size 8 = European size 38½)
- Men's shoes: Add 32–34 (US size 9 = European size 41; US size 11 = European size 45)

Climate

First line, average daily high; second line, average daily low; third line, days of no rain. For more detailed weather statistics for destinations in this book (as well as the rest of the world), check www.worldclimate.com.

J	F	M	A	M	J	J	A	S	O	N	D
SPAIN											
Madrid											
47°	52°	59°	65°	70°	80°	87°	85°	77°	65°	55°	48°
35°	36°	41°	45°	50°	58°	63°	63°	57°	49°	42°	36°
23	21	21	21	21	25	29	28	24	23	21	21

APPENDIX

J	F	M	A	M	J	J	A	S	O	N	D

Barcelona

55°	57°	60°	65°	71°	78°	82°	82°	77°	69°	62°	56°
43°	45°	48°	52°	57°	65°	69°	69°	66°	58°	51°	46°
26	23	23	21	23	24	27	25	23	22	24	25

Almería (Costa del Sol)

60°	61°	64°	68°	72°	78°	83°	84°	81°	73°	67°	62°
46°	47°	51°	55°	59°	65°	70°	71°	68°	60°	54°	49°
25	24	26	25	28	29	31	30	27	26	26	26

MOROCCO
Marrakech

65°	68°	74°	79°	84°	92°	101°	100°	92°	83°	73°	66°
40°	43°	48°	52°	57°	62°	67°	68°	63°	57°	49°	42°
24	23	25	24	29	29	30	30	27	27	27	24

Temperature Conversion:
Fahrenheit and Celsius

FOR WEATHER   FOR HEALTH

Europe takes its temperature using the Celsius scale, while we opt for Fahrenheit. For a rough conversion from Celsius to Fahrenheit, double the number and add 30. For weather, remember that 28°C is 82°F—perfect. For health, 37°C is just right.

Essential Packing Checklist

Whether you're traveling for five days or five weeks, here's what you'll need to bring. Remember to pack light to enjoy the sweet freedom of true mobility. Happy travels!

- ❑ 5 shirts
- ❑ 1 sweater or lightweight fleece jacket
- ❑ 2 pairs pants
- ❑ 1 pair shorts
- ❑ 1 swimsuit (women only—men can use shorts)
- ❑ 5 pairs underwear and socks
- ❑ 1 pair shoes
- ❑ 1 rainproof jacket
- ❑ Tie or scarf
- ❑ Money belt
- ❑ Money—your mix of:
    - ❑ Debit card for ATM withdrawals
    - ❑ Credit card
    - ❑ Hard cash in US dollars ($20 bills)
- ❑ Documents (and back-up photocopies)
- ❑ Passport
- ❑ Printout of airline e-ticket
- ❑ Driver's license
- ❑ Student ID and hostel card
- ❑ Railpass/car rental voucher
- ❑ Insurance details
- ❑ Daypack
- ❑ Sealable plastic baggies
- ❑ Camera and related gear
- ❑ Empty water bottle
- ❑ Wristwatch and alarm clock
- ❑ Earplugs
- ❑ First-aid kit
- ❑ Medicine (labeled)
- ❑ Extra glasses/contacts and prescriptions
- ❑ Sunscreen and sunglasses
- ❑ Toiletries kit
- ❑ Soap
- ❑ Laundry soap
- ❑ Clothesline
- ❑ Small towel
- ❑ Sewing kit
- ❑ Travel information
- ❑ Necessary map(s)
- ❑ Address list (email and mailing addresses)
- ❑ Postcards and photos from home
- ❑ Notepad and pen
- ❑ Journal

If you plan to carry on your luggage, note that all liquids must be in three-ounce or smaller containers and fit within a single quart-size baggie. For details, see www.tsa.gov/travelers.

Hotel Reservation

To: _____   _____
         hotel   **email or fax**

From: _____   _____
              name   **email or fax**

Today's date: _____ /_____ /_____
                    day   month   year

Dear Hotel _____ ,
Please make this reservation for me:

Name: _____

Total # of people: _____   # of rooms: _____   # of nights: _____

Arriving: _____ /_____ /_____   My time of arrival (24-hr clock): _____
                day   month   year   (I will telephone if I will be late)

Departing: ____ /____ /____
                 day   month   year

Room(s): Single____   Double ____   Twin____   Triple ____   Quad____

With: Toilet ____   Shower____   Bath ____   Sink only____

Special needs: View____   Quiet____   Cheapest ____   Ground Floor____

Please email or fax confirmation of my reservation, along with the type of room reserved and the price. Please also inform me of your cancellation policy. After I hear from you, I will quickly send my credit-card information as a deposit to hold the room. Thank you.

_____
Name

_____
Address

_____
City   **State**   **Zip Code**   **Country**

Before hoteliers can make your reservation, they want to know the information listed above. You can use this form as the basis for your email, or you can photocopy this page, fill in the information, and send it as a fax (also available online at www.ricksteves.com/reservation).

Spanish Survival Phrases

Spanish has a guttural sound similar to the J in Baja California. In the phonetics, the symbol for this clearing-your-throat sound is the italicized *h*.

English	Spanish	Phonetics
Good day.	Buenos días.	**bway**-nohs **dee**-ahs
Do you speak English?	¿Habla usted inglés?	ah-blah oo-**stehd** een-**glays**
Yes. / No.	Sí. / No.	see / noh
I (don't) understand.	(No) comprendo.	(noh) kohm-**prehn**-doh
Please.	Por favor.	por fah-**bor**
Thank you.	Gracias.	**grah**-thee-ahs
I'm sorry.	Lo siento.	loh see-**ehn**-toh
Excuse me.	Perdóneme.	pehr-**doh**-nay-may
(No) problem.	(No) problema.	(noh) proh-**blay**-mah
Good.	Bueno.	**bway**-noh
Goodbye.	Adiós.	ah-dee-**ohs**
one / two	uno / dos	**oo**-noh / dohs
three / four	tres / cuatro	trays / **kwah**-troh
five / six	cinco / seis	**theen**-koh / says
seven / eight	siete / ocho	see-**eh**-tay / **oh**-choh
nine / ten	nueve / diez	**nway**-bay / dee-**ayth**
How much is it?	¿Cuánto cuesta?	**kwahn**-toh **kway**-stah
Write it?	¿Me lo escribe?	may loh ay-**skree**-bay
Is it free?	¿Es gratis?	ays **grah**-tees
Is it included?	¿Está incluido?	ay-**stah** een-kloo-ee-doh
Where can I buy / find...?	¿Dónde puedo comprar / encontrar...?	**dohn**-day **pway**-doh kohm-**prar** / ayn-kohn-**trar**
I'd like / We'd like...	Quiero / Queremos...	kee-**ehr**-oh / kehr-**ay**-mohs
...a room.	...una habitación.	**oo**-nah ah-bee-tah-thee-**ohn**
...a ticket to ___.	...un billete para ___.	oon bee-**yeh**-tay **pah**-rah
Is it possible?	¿Es posible?	ays poh-**see**-blay
Where is...?	¿Dónde está...?	**dohn**-day ay-**stah**
...the train station	...la estación de trenes	lah ay-stah-thee-**ohn** day **tray**-nays
...the bus station	...la estación de autobuses	lah ay-stah-thee-**ohn** day ow-toh-**boo**-says
...the tourist information office	...la oficina de turismo	lah oh-fee-**thee**-nah day too-**rees**-moh
Where are the toilets?	¿Dónde están los servicios?	**dohn**-day ay-**stahn** lohs sehr-**bee**-thee-ohs
men	hombres, caballeros	**ohm**-brays, kah-bah-**yay**-rohs
women	mujeres, damas	moo-*heh*-rays, **dah**-mahs
left / right	izquierda / derecha	eeth-kee-**ehr**-dah / day-**ray**-chah
straight	derecho	day-**ray**-choh
When do you open / close?	¿A qué hora abren / cierran?	ah kay **oh**-rah **ah**-brehn / thee-**ay**-rahn
At what time?	¿A qué hora?	ah kay **oh**-rah
Just a moment.	Un momento.	oon moh-**mehn**-toh
now / soon / later	ahora / pronto / más tarde	ah-**oh**-rah / **prohn**-toh / mahs **tar**-day
today / tomorrow	hoy / mañana	oy / mahn-**yah**-nah

In the Restaurant

I'd like / We'd like...	**Quiero / Queremos...**	kee-**ehr**-oh / kehr-**ay**-mohs
...to reserve...	**...reservar...**	ray-sehr-**bar**
...a table for one / two.	**...una mesa para uno / dos.**	oo-nah **may**-sah **pah**-rah oo-noh / dohs
Non-smoking.	**No fumadores.**	noh foo-mah-**doh**-rays
Is this table free?	**¿Está esta mesa libre?**	ay-**stah** ay-stah **may**-sah lee-bray
The menu (in English), please.	**La carta (en inglés), por favor.**	lah **kar**-tah (ayn een-**glays**) por fah-**bor**
service (not) included	**servicio (no) incluido**	sehr-**bee**-thee-oh (noh) een-kloo-**ee**-doh
cover charge	**precio de entrada**	**pray**-thee-oh day ayn-**trah**-dah
to go	**para llevar**	**pah**-rah yay-**bar**
with / without	**con / sin**	kohn / seen
and / or	**y / o**	ee / oh
menu (of the day)	**menú (del día)**	may-**noo** (dayl **dee**-ah)
specialty of the house	**especialidad de la casa**	ay-spay-thee-ah-lee-**dahd** day lah **kah**-sah
tourist menu	**menú de turista**	meh-**noo** day too-**ree**-stah
combination plate	**plato combinado**	**plah**-toh kohm-bee-**nah**-doh
appetizers	**tapas**	**tah**-pahs
bread	**pan**	pahn
cheese	**queso**	**kay**-soh
sandwich	**bocadillo**	boh-kah-**dee**-yoh
soup	**sopa**	**soh**-pah
salad	**ensalada**	ayn-sah-**lah**-dah
meat	**carne**	**kar**-nay
poultry	**aves**	**ah**-bays
fish	**pescado**	pay-**skah**-doh
seafood	**marisco**	mah-**ree**-skoh
fruit	**fruta**	**froo**-tah
vegetables	**verduras**	behr-**doo**-rahs
dessert	**postres**	**poh**-strays
tap water	**agua del grifo**	**ah**-gwah dayl **gree**-foh
mineral water	**agua mineral**	**ah**-gwah mee-nay-**rahl**
milk	**leche**	**lay**-chay
(orange) juice	**zumo (de naranja)**	**thoo**-moh (day nah-**rahn**-hah)
coffee	**café**	kah-**feh**
tea	**té**	tay
wine	**vino**	**bee**-noh
red / white	**tinto / blanco**	**teen**-toh / **blahn**-koh
glass / bottle	**vaso / botella**	**bah**-soh / boh-**tay**-yah
beer	**cerveza**	thehr-**bay**-thah
Cheers!	**¡Salud!**	sah-**lood**
More. / Another.	**Más. / Otro.**	mahs / **oh**-troh
The same.	**El mismo.**	ehl **mees**-moh
The bill, please.	**La cuenta, por favor.**	lah **kwayn**-tah por fah-**bor**
tip	**propina**	proh-**pee**-nah
Delicious!	**¡Delicioso!**	day-lee-thee-**oh**-soh

For hundreds more pages of survival phrases for your trip to Spain, check out *Rick Steves' Spanish Phrase Book*.

APPENDIX

INDEX

INDEX

INDEX

MAP INDEX

Free information and great gear to

▸ Plan Your Trip

Browse thousands of articles and a wealth of money-saving tips for planning your dream trip. You'll find up-to-date information on Europe's best destinations, packing smart, getting around, finding rooms, staying healthy, avoiding scams and more.

▸ Eurail Passes

Find out, step-by-step, if a rail pass makes sense for your trip—and how to avoid buying more than you need. Get a bunch of free extras!

▸ Graffiti Wall & Travelers' Helpline

Learn, ask, share—our online community of savvy travelers is a great resource for first-time travelers to Europe, as well as seasoned pros.

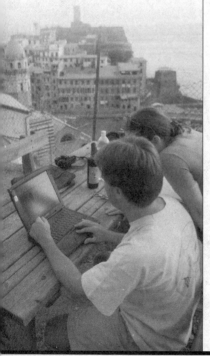

Rick Steves' Europe Through the Back Door, Inc.

Rick Steves

www.ricksteves.com

TRAVEL SKILLS
Europe Through the Back Door

EUROPE GUIDES
Best of Europe
Eastern Europe
Europe 101
European Christmas
Postcards from Europe

COUNTRY GUIDES
Croatia & Slovenia
England
France
Germany
Great Britain
Ireland
Italy
Portugal
Scandinavia
Spain
Switzerland

CITY & REGIONAL GUIDES
Amsterdam, Bruges & Brussels
Athens & The Peloponnese
Budapest
Florence & Tuscany
Istanbul
London
Paris
Prague & The Czech Republic
Provence & The French Riviera
Rome
Venice
Vienna, Salzburg & Tirol

PHRASE BOOKS & DICTIONARIES
French
French, Italian & German
German
Italian
Portuguese
Spanish

RICK STEVES' EUROPE DVDs
Austria & The Alps
Eastern Europe
England
Europe
France & Benelux
Germany & Scandinavia
Greece, Turkey, Israel & Egypt
Ireland & Scotland
Italy's Cities
Italy's Countryside
Rick Steves' European Christmas
Spain & Portugal
Travel Skills & "The Making Of"

PLANNING MAPS
Britain, Ireland & London
Europe
France & Paris
Germany, Austria & Switzerland
Ireland
Italy
Spain & Portugal

JOURNALS
Rick Steves' Pocket Travel Journal
Rick Steves' Travel Journal

NOW AVAILABLE

RICK STEVES APPS FOR THE iPHONE OR iPOD TOUCH

With these apps you can:

▸ Spin the compass icon to switch views between sights, hotels, and restaurant selections—and get details on cost, hours, address, and phone number.

▸ Tap any point on the screen to read Rick's detailed information, including history and suggested viewpoints.

▸ Get a deeper view into Rick's tours with audio and video segments.

Go to iTunes to download the following apps:

Rick Steves' Louvre Tour

Rick Steves' Historic Paris Walk

Rick Steves' Orsay Museum Tour

Rick Steves' Versailles

Rick Steves' Ancient Rome Tour

Rick Steves' St. Peter's Basilica Tour

Once downloaded, these apps are completely self-contained on your iPhone or iPod Touch, so you will not incur pricey roaming charges during use overseas.

Rick Steves books and DVDs are available at bookstores and through online booksellers.

Rick Steves guidebooks are published by Avalon Travel, a member of the Perseus Books Group.

Rick Steves apps are produced by Übermind, a boutique Seattle-based software consultancy firm.

Credits

Researcher
To help update this book, Rick relied on...

Amanda Buttinger

Amanda moved to Madrid in 1998 thinking she'd be there a year. Since then she's found many reasons to stay, from learning more Spanish to guiding and travel writing to the best of all—sunny city walks with her dog and her man.

Contributors
Cameron Hewitt

Cameron wrote this book's original chapters on the Camino de Santiago, Santiago de Compostela, and Cantabria—driving 500 miles from the French hillsides across the desolate Castilian plains, then up into lush Galicia. Cameron lives in Seattle with his wife Shawna.

Gene Openshaw

Gene is the co-author of seven Rick Steves guidebooks. For this book, he wrote material on the Prado, Picasso's *Guernica,* and other topics. When not traveling, Gene enjoys composing music, recovering from his 1973 trip to Europe with Rick, and living everyday life with his daughter.

Images

Location	Photographer
Spain	
Full page image: Moorish Arches	David C. Hoerlein
Barcelona: Barcelona's Montjuïc	David C. Hoerlein
Near Barcelona: Cadaqués	Rick Steves
Basque Region: Guggenheim Bilbao	Rick Steves
Cantabria: Picos de Europa	Cameron Hewitt
The Camino de Santiago:	
Puente de la Reina	Cameron Hewitt
Santiago de Compostela:	
Santiago's Cathedral	Cameron Hewitt
Salamanca:	
Salamanca's Plaza Mayor	Rick Steves
Madrid: Madrid's Retiro Park	David C. Hoerlein
Northwest of Madrid:	
Segovia's Aqueduct	Rick Steves
Toledo: Toledo Overview	Rick Steves
Granada: The Alhambra	Robert Wright
Sevilla: Sevilla Skyline	Rick Steves
Córdoba: Córdoba's Mezquita	Robert Wright
Andalucía's White Hill Towns: Arcos	David C. Hoerlein
Spain's South Coast: Nerja	Rick Steves
Morocco	
Full page image:	
Moroccan Woman, Tangier	Rick Steves
Tangier: Market Vendor	Rick Steves

Rick Steves' Guidebook Series

Country Guides

Rick Steves' Best of Europe
Rick Steves' Croatia & Slovenia
Rick Steves' Eastern Europe
Rick Steves' England
Rick Steves' France
Rick Steves' Germany
Rick Steves' Great Britain
Rick Steves' Ireland
Rick Steves' Italy
Rick Steves' Portugal
Rick Steves' Scandinavia
Rick Steves' Spain
Rick Steves' Switzerland

City and Regional Guides

Rick Steves' Amsterdam, Bruges & Brussels
Rick Steves' Athens & the Peloponnese
Rick Steves' Budapest
Rick Steves' Florence & Tuscany
Rick Steves' Istanbul
Rick Steves' London
Rick Steves' Paris
Rick Steves' Prague & the Czech Republic
Rick Steves' Provence & the French Riviera
Rick Steves' Rome
Rick Steves' Venice
Rick Steves' Vienna, Salzburg & Tirol

Rick Steves' Phrase Books

French
French/Italian/German
German
Italian
Portuguese
Spanish

Other Books

Rick Steves' Europe 101: History and Art for the Traveler
Rick Steves' Europe Through the Back Door
Rick Steves' European Christmas
Rick Steves' Postcards from Europe
Rick Steves' Travel as a Political Act

Avalon Travel
a member of the Perseus Books Group
1700 Fourth Street
Berkeley, CA 94710

Text © 2009 by Rick Steves
Maps © 2009 Europe Through the Back Door. All rights reserved.
Printed in the US by Worzalla. First printing September 2009.

For the latest on Rick Steves' lectures, guidebooks, tours, public television series, and public radio show, contact Europe Through the Back Door, Box 2009, Edmonds, WA 98020, tel. 425/771-8303, fax 425/771-0833, www.ricksteves.com, rick@ricksteves.com.

ISBN (13) 978-59880-295-5
ISSN 1551-8388

Europe Through the Back Door Managing Editor: Risa Laib
ETBD Editors: Tom Griffin, Gretchen Strauch, Jennifer Madison Davis, Cathy Lu, Cathy McDonald, Sarah McCormic
Research Assistance: Amanda Buttinger
Avalon Travel Senior Editor and Series Manager: Madhu Prasher
Avalon Travel Project Editor: Kelly Lydick
Copy Editor: Amy Scott
Proofreader: Jean Butterfield
Indexer: Stephen Callahan
Production and Typesetting: McGuire Barber Design
Cover Design: Kimberly Glyder Design
Graphic Content Director: Laura VanDeventer
Maps and Graphics: David C. Hoerlein, Lauren Mills, Laura VanDeventer, Barb Geisler, Mike Morgenfeld
Front Matter Color Photos: p. i, Córdoba © Rick Steves; p. xxiv, Arcos Street © David Hoerlein
Cover Photo: Plaza de España, Sevilla © David C. Hoerlein
Photography: David C. Hoerlein, Rick Steves, Cameron Hewitt, Robert Wright, Steve Smith, Dominic Bonuccelli, and Cathy McDonald

Foldout Color Map ▶

The foldout map on the opposite page includes:
- **A map of Spain on one side**
- **City maps, including Madrid, Barcelona, Sevilla, Granada, Toledo, and Lisbon on the other side**